THE ULTIMATE LOVE SIGN BOOK
Accurate...Detailed...Easy to Use

What are you looking for in a lover or potential mate? If it's money, set your sights on a Pisces/Taurus. Is exercise and health food your passion? Then a Virgo/Cancer will share it with you. Have you recently fallen for a Taurus/Gemini? Brace yourself— you may be in for heartbreak and broken promises!

You don't need to know a thing about astrology to use this book!

Where do you find these people? They're all here, in *The Book of Lovers*. Astrologer Carolyn Reynolds introduces a new and accurate way to determine romantic compatibility through the use of Sun *and* Moon sign combinations. And the beautiful thing is that *you don't need to know a thing about astrology* to benefit from her highly accurate system. All you need to know is the birthdate of the person in question.

It's like your personal "little black book"!

Here you will find descriptions of every man and woman born between the years 1900 and 2000. To see whether that certain someone could be "the one," simply locate his or her birthdata in the chart at the back of the book. Then flip to the relevant pages and read all about that person's sex appeal, personality and compatibility with you.

Gain more in-depth information than with Sun Sign books!

Astrologically, the Moon is said to rule emotions. When you analyze the Sun sign with the Moon sign, you tap into the deeper side of people. You learn what they look for in a relationship, what kind of lover they will be and if they are right for you. Ordinary Sun Sign horoscope books just don't provide that kind of depth.

PLUS, you also get a section on Ascendants (rising signs) that provides *even more* indications of potentially exciting romance!

Become your own matchmaker today with *The Book of Lovers*!

About the Author

Carolyn Reynolds has been a professional astrologer for more than 20 years. She has taught astrology, and scripted and voiced "Las Vegas Dial Astrology" which received over 100,000 calls each month. She has written a teaching manual for students and now the book for everyone: *The Book of Lovers*. She is also a social worker, a painter, and raises Old English Sheepdogs. She resides in Las Vegas, Nevada.

To Write to the Author

We cannot guarantee that every letter written to the author can be answered, but all will be forwarded. Both the author and the publisher appreciate hearing from readers, learning of your enjoyment and benefit from this book. Llewellyn also publishes a bi-monthly news magazine with news and reviews of practical esoteric studies and articles helpful to the student, and some readers' questions and comments to the author may be answered through this magazine's columns if permission to do so is included in the original letter. The author sometimes participates in seminars and workshops, and dates and places are announced in *The Llewellyn New Times*. To write to the author, or to ask a question, write to:

Carolyn Reynolds
c/o THE LLEWELLYN NEW TIMES
P.O. Box 64383-289, St. Paul, MN 55164-0383, U.S.A.
Please enclose a self-addressed, stamped envelope for reply, or $1.00 to cover costs.

Llewellyn's Popular Astrology Series

The Book of Lovers

Men Who Excite Women
Women Who Excite Men

A Personal Guide to
Astrological Relationships

Carolyn Reynolds

1992
Llewellyn Publications
St. Paul, Minnesota, U.S.A. 55164-0383

FIRST EDITION
Second Printing, 1992

Cover Photo by Michael Yencho
Cover Design by Terry Buske and Christopher Wells

Library of Congress Cataloging-in-Publication Data

The book of lovers: men who excite women, women who excite men /
    by Carolyn Reynolds.
      p.   cm. -- (Llewellyn's popular astrology series)
    ISBN 0-87542-289-6
    1. Astrology and sex.   I. Title.   II. Series.
BF1729.S4R49   1992
133.5'83067—dc20   91-46568
                                                CIP

Llewellyn Publications
A Division of Llewellyn Worldwide, Ltd.
P.O. Box 64383, St. Paul, MN 55164-0383

About Llewellyn's Popular Astrology Series

Astrology has been called "the oldest science," for it has evolved from Man's first sense of wonder at the Universe around him, and from his earliest efforts at finding meaning to his place in the Universe.

Astrology sees the Universe as organic—alive and inter-related at every level and place. Astrology sees Man as a miniature of the Universe—the Microcosm to the Macrocosm—and ascribes to the Hermetic axiom: As Above, So Below. Based on that concept, astrology may be used to gain better understanding of those events on Earth and in the lives of Men, and to forecast trends based on the cyclical movements of the planets.

Llewellyn is the oldest publisher of astrology books in the Western Hemisphere, and has always sought to bring to the public the practical benefits of applied astrology. In this series of Popular Astrology books, we bring to the lay-person texts without involvement in complex calculations or difficult terminology, intended to give the reader the opportunity to—in some sense—take command over his or her life by understanding the Planetary Factors at work.

We can shape our destiny. We can live our lives better, and we can and must assume more responsibility for the greater community in which we live. It is only with awareness of the trends in current events that we can take responsible action to resolve the man challenges of the next few years. Astrology, and this book in particular, brings this awareness to everyone.

Popular Astrology gives Man insight into human nature and into Nature itself. With Vision, there is the power to take action. To act with awareness of trends is to assume responsibility. And to act responsibly is the mark of an awakened Human Being.

—Carl Llewellyn Weschcke

DEDICATION

This book is dedicated to my mother who told me I could be anything I wanted to be (except a prima ballerina), and to Leonard Franklin, my Old English Sheepdog, who sat with me during the long hours of writing, listening to the sound of the typewriter keys (Gemini Moon), hoping I would make some money (Taurus Sun).

ACKNOWLEDGEMENTS

Upon completion of this book I met a stranger with whom I developed immediate trust and rapport. He promised me he would hand deliver my manuscript to Llewellyn Publications. Against all logic, I gave him the manuscript and he delivered it. I have never again heard from him. So, special thanks to you, Craig Michael, wherever you are. Thank you also to Tom Bridges, my wonderful first editor, and Emily, my second editor, and to the Llewellyn family; to my friends, especially Chris, Suzanne, and Louise who gave me inspiration during the long process from writing to publication, and, of course, to the men in my life who know, without seeing their names in print, that they are the names after which I sign the words, I love you.

Contents

Preface

This book is about men and women, what they're like and who they're attracted to. It will give you instant insight into the personalities that have been determined by the position of the Sun and Moon on a person's day of birth. *The Book of Lovers* will reveal for you the Good, the Bad, and the Ugly of the Zodiac.

Let me explain. There are many planetary configurations that determines a person's personality, but the two most important are the position of the Sun and the position of the Moon on the day of birth. The Sun's position explains a person's character, and the Moon's position explains their emotional needs and predisposition. These two illuminaries team up to incline a person to behave in a particular way.

The importance of the Sun/Moon combination was revealed by psychology's great Dr. Carl Jung in 1930. His research uncovered definite parallels and connections between the Sun/Moon configurations of married couples. The startling conclusion was that certain Sun/Moon aspects between birthdates and marriages were found to be three times higher than chance would predict.

The strongest connections were:

A. the Moon in the same sign as another person's Sun sign;
B. the Moon in compatibility with another person's Sun sign;
C. the Moon in the other person's Ascendant (determined by time of birth).

To find the correct Sun/Moon combination for the person you're interested in, turn to the tables in the back. If their birthday falls on a day when the Moon changes, look also to the preceding day and read both profiles. You should be able to tell right away which one is correct.

While I emphasize the various Sun and Moon combinations in this book, and give a description of the personalities represented by the Sun-Moon combinations for each Sun sign, I have also included a brief description of the Ascendant personality and a table for determining one's Ascendant or Rising sign. My reason for doing so is that, in Dr. Jung's findings, he went so far as to say that when the Moon was in the same sign as the other person's Ascendant, there was a greater possibility of marriage. Therefore, he assumed that the Ascendant was important to the psychological makeup of lovers.

Introduction
How to Use This Book

Let me explain how this book works. There are many planetary configurations in a person's chart. The two most important, however, are the Sun and Moon combinations.

The Sun position on the day of "his" or "her" birth you probably already know: that is the very popular Sun sign astrology. However, the Moon was also positioned in an astrological sign on the day she/he was born. The Sun position explains the character traits of the person (e.g. values, ethics, objectives, approaches to situations), while the Moon explains emotional needs and predisposition or temperament. This *Book of Lovers* is essentially a reference book to all possible combinations of Sun-Moon placements from 1900 to 2000. In addition, it includes a separate table for Rising signs (based on time of birth), which represents the outer personality of the person, or the persona—the self people most often show to the world.

However, in intimate relationships, it is the Sun and Moon which team up to incline a people to behave the way they do. If you want to get to know someone better, or find out who's a good match for you, look at the tables for Moon and Sun Ingresses in the back of the book. You'll only need to know the day, the month and the year of his/her birth. Once you have used this table to determine the correct Sun/Moon configuration, you may then use the Guide to Men or Guide to Women to obtain an instant personality sketch.

How To Determine Compatibility

The Moon has been overshadowed by the Sun for far too long. There are times when, no matter how pretty you are, how nice, how talented and sweet you are, someone else has a corner on the Moon. To you men: If your Moon's not where her emotional needs are, changing your wardrobe or your bone structure will probably not work out. You cannot change your Moon, and you'll probably be glad you can't when Mr. or Mrs. Right comes along.

The single most significant indication of compatibility is the Sun in your chart being in the same sign, or a harmonious sign, as the Moon in your partner's chart. The next most important indicator is having the Moon in his chart in harmony with yours. Harmony is created when your "planets" (Sun and Moon) are in the same element (see chart 1), or when your Moon is two signs in front of or behind his Moon (see chart 2). These are the basic rules, and all you need to remember for using this book. Rather than putting these rules in every profile, I will remind you only when I feel it is especially important for a particular male or female.

Chart 1. The Moon's Elements or the Four Temperaments

The elements of the Moon are Fire, Earth, Water and Air. People get along best with matching elements.

FIRE	EARTH	AIR	WATER
Aries	Taurus	Gemini	Cancer
Leo	Virgo	Libra	Scorpio
Sagittarius	Capricorn	Aquarius	Pisces

Chart 2. The Oppositions of the Moon

Aries is opposite Libra	Cancer is opposite Capricorn
Taurus is opposite Scorpio	Leo is opposite Aquarius
Gemini is opposite Sagittarius	Virgo is opposite Pisces

These Moons are 180 degrees apart. They are in stressful relationships to one another. They cause the "we live in two different worlds" feeling between people.

Chart 3. Sign Combinations

Harmonious	Disharmonious
Aries, Leo, Sagittarius	Aries, Cancer, Libra, Capricorn
Taurus, Virgo, Capricorn	Gemini, Virgo, Sagittarius, Libra
Gemini, Libra, Aquarius	Taurus, Leo, Scorpio, Aquarius
Cancer, Scorpio, Pisces	

Simply put, if you have a Sun in Sagittarius, and your Moon is in Scorpio, look to the mate who has his/her Sun in Scorpio and/or a Moon in Sagittarius. For further possible combinations, look for those who have the same Moon as yours, or Sun or Moon in the same sign, or in a harmonious element as your Sun and Moon (i.e., Fire likes Fire, Air likes Air, and so forth). Whether in love or in friendship, the most compatible relationships are the ones in which the Moon is in the same element. The reason for this is that there is an easy emotional understanding, a harmonious adjustment to each other's habits and feelings. Psychologically, you feel in touch with one another. If your Moon is in the same element as the one you are interested in, you will have an easy understanding of him or her.

When your Moon is in the same sign as the Moon of a particular person, whether a friend or lover, co-worker, parent or child, there is very little division between needs. You feel better, emotionally, by their very presence. You are able to communicate emotional patterns and your reactions to life easily. So easily, in fact, that you often need little discussion about your actions. This may make for a lazy relationship where neither one of you has to reach, grow, or work very hard at developing common ground.

In most cases, the profiles presented in this book will apply. There are exceptions to every rule, however, and in addition to the hour and place of birth on a given day, a preponderance of other aspects (including malefic degrees or fixed stars) can have some effect on some of the birth configuration. These degrees are unusual and so individual that they are not taken into consideration in this book. My personality outlines can give insight into the assets and liabilities of a vast number of people, but not to the rare exceptions. To know more about a particular individual, you would have to take a person's complete birth data (includes place of birth) to a professional astrologer and have a complete astrological profile done on the person.

Introduction to the Guide to Men

This part of the book is about men and whatever roles they play in your life. "The Guide to Men" can provide you with instant insights into the men you deal with, and will reveal the Good, Bad and Ugly of the Zodiac.

Men make up about 50% of the people we meet. With the increasing presence of women in the workplace, and more demanding professional and social interaction with men, women need a reference source from which to gain quick personality insights into the men in their lives. Whether the men in question are neighbors, coworkers, lawyers, doctors, friends, or, yes, even the ones who spark romantic interest, "The Guide to Men" will help you understand them.

Now, men have a funny habit of responding to the gravitation of the Moon just like oysters. Let me tell you a story. I have a dear friend who was so infatuated with a man that she became nearly babbling when he called long distance. He picked odd hours and days, and she was spending her life waiting for the phone to ring. So we devised a plan where she went back over the days he'd called her in the past, and guess what? Every time the Moon was in Cancer, he called. He called because it fell in his House of Clandestine Affairs (we knew his exact birth time, but you don't have to know this). She was, as she already knew, one of his girls in every city. After the discovery of his pattern in response to the Moon, we could predict the days he would be calling. We were right. Now she could expect to babble only on the Cancer Moon days. It probably saved her career. You can do the same thing by keeping track of where the Moon is when he calls. (If he calls every day, you don't need my help.)

As I stated in the introduction to this book, it is best to have the Moon in the same sign as the other person's Sun or Moon—these are the relationships that encourage marriage and that last the longest (like 'til death do us part). Admittedly, there may be a few separations and divorces along the way, but these people are truly fated.

Famous Lovers

Here are a few examples of Sun/Moon connections:

Richard Burton had his Sun in Scorpio and his Moon in Virgo. **Elizabeth Taylor** had her Sun in Pisces and her Moon in Scorpio. While their Moons were opposite each other (see chart 2), which always creates a lot of tension, they were irresistibly drawn to each other over and over again, because of their Sun and Moon in Scorpio.

Robert Wagner had the Aquarius Sun and the Cancer Moon combination. **Natalie Wood** had the Cancer Sun and the Aries Moon. Now, the Aquarius and the Aries may not get along the best, but their Cancer Sun and Moon were made in heaven.

Clark Gable had his Sun in Aquarius and his Moon in Cancer. **Carol Lombard** had her Sun in Libra and her Moon in Aquarius. They had the fated Sun/Moon combinations that hold a relationship together through thick and thin.

In the case of **Paul Newman** and **Joanne Woodward**, who have both matching Suns to Moons (his Aquarius Sun/Pisces Moon, her Pisces Sun/Aquarius Moon), they became a special couple indeed.

Now, as in the case of the famous lovers whose Sun was in the same sign as his lover's Moon, you often get matches that are inharmonious or stressful. In the case of the Burtons, their Suns and Moons made two aspects. One was called an opposition. This is just as it sounds. People who have this aspect can be at almost constant odds emotionally.

This is not necessarily bad, even when it will bring out a more combative nature among couples with this configuration. While this is not a harmonious work combination, sometimes the Sun/ Moon opposition (see chart 2) creates an atmosphere of tremendous potential for growth within a relationship. It may encourage you to get things out in the open, teach you to communicate better or give you a chance to grow in other areas of your life.

The emotions within the relationships of the people with opposite Moons run high. Energies do not flow easily and they have to work hard to develop harmony and overcome difficulties. These matches can be the best in spite of themselves because each helps the other to gain strength, see the other side of an issue, or gain new confidence. These opposite Moons are powerful for instant, and lasting, physical attraction.

When You've Got Him And You're Not Sure You Want Him

I do not believe in the perfect marriage or relationship, nor do I believe that marriages made in heaven are effortless happenings that occur in one lifetime. People who say they have been married for fifty years and never had a fight must have had a few other lifetimes in which to have ironed out the wrinkles; or else they have a very poor memory in this lifetime. At any rate, Sun/Moon combinations that are less than perfect oftentimes come to us in the form of a parent or other relative, a co-worker or authority figure. The result is mismatched emotional needs and character traits. If you are in a relationship with someone who causes constant stress, one of you is going to have to make some concessions. Who can compromise the easiest? Sagittarius, Virgo, Gemini or Pisces. Who will have the most difficulty? Leo, Taurus, Aquarius, and Scorpio.

If, regardless of the harmony of a relationship, you have an attraction for a particular Moon, you will be drawn to that person time and time again. Maybe, if you are married, you need to opt for more space in your union, instead of marrying and remarrying after every quarrel. (Refer to Oppositions of the Moon, chart 2.)

The General Types of Sun Sign Fathers

When your father is a difficult man for you and you can't throw him out of the house, there is a reason. Perhaps he was thrown into your astrological path to teach you independence. Perhaps he will be the impetus for you to determine young to be a better parent yourself, or to be wise enough to know when motherhood is not for you. My father was so lax and easy going about everything, that he taught me early on to get organized. His children have to this day a look of terror in their eyes at the prospect of a temporary loss of job, or a shortage of canned goods in the pantry. His inability to endure taught me to be a top notch survivor. Whatever the case with your parent, you can be sure you are gaining knowledge. Unfortunately, some of us have to learn more from the negative than from the positive. But again, it helps us to complete our personalities.

The **Aries Sun father** has a tendency to dictate. He will relate better to his children away from the dining room table and at the baseball diamond, or on the camping weekend.

The **Taurus Sun father** is patient, he handles his children with a firm hand. He provides a stable environment and takes fatherhood seriously.

The **Gemini Sun father** wants to be a friend to his children, above all. He will promote the love of adventure and freedom, and encourage resourceful and adventurous behavior. He is often inconsistent in his child rearing endeavors.

The **Cancer Sun father** is one of the best of the Zodiac. He is gentle, caring, receptive and genuinely understanding. He doesn't dote so much as he adores his children.

The **Leo Sun father** is another of the best of the Zodiac. He loves hard. He worships his children. He is generous to a fault. Openly affectionate, he is often lax in the discipline department. His children compensate for this with their respect for him.

The **Virgo Sun father** is the most dutiful of the Zodiac. He is a taskmaster and trains his children in work ethics and service to others. He will help with the homework. He is often detached in his behavior with the children. He is not openly affectionate.

The **Libra Sun father** rarely dreams of having children but can be touched by a sad story and end up adopting a few extras to go with his natural children. He is a fair man in all matters involving his children and is normally sweet tempered and gentle. He will treat them as adults early on.

The **Scorpio Sun father** is stern. He is no-nonsense, and wants to be respected and yes, obeyed. He rarely see the humor in a child's misdeeds. Nonetheless, he is devoted to the raising of his children, and his love is deep. It will not be the gushy look at my photographs-of-the-baby kind of fatherhood.

The **Sagittarius Sun father** is often lukewarm with his affections towards his children; since he has not fully grown up yet, he does not like it when fatherhood interferes with his own childhood. He likes children best as they grow older. He encourages them to learn, to excel and to aspire.

The **Capricorn Sun father** is very serious about the duties of fatherhood. He wants to provide for them and their futures. He will demand they learn to respect law and order around the house and other people's property. He is busy raising little adults and is not into open adoration. He loves hard, nonetheless.

The **Aquarius Sun father** has enough adventure in him to fascinate every child on the block. He will teach his children to explore the universe, and often forget they need food, a bath or his attention when he has his own adventures on his mind. He is another of the fathers of the Zodiac who is a pal to his children first.

The **Pisces Sun father** is fun because his imagination can get right down to the child's level. He can plan fun games that eventually inspire creativity in his children. He can also get down in the dumps and ask the children to father him. His love will be deep, but not always stable.

Aries

March 21–April 20

ARIES-ARIES

The impetuous double Aries man will find that he cannot resist two things: flattery and a fascinating challenge. He is impatient, headstrong, daring, dynamic and he resents sharing his innermost thoughts. He does not want a conventional partner; he is looking for someone to stir his inner fire and help him climb the ladder of success. He is gallant and romantic in a dashing sort of way. He will always remain the boss, no matter how infatuated he may be with you. He is a troubling husband, a fearless co-worker, and an unconventional father. He is nearly impossible to resist at his peak. This man is Marlon Brando in *A Streetcar Named Desire*. Ask him to clear the table for you and you'll be sorry. He does have a nasty temper. You can expect numerous interruptions from his multiple and varied business ventures. This is as vital as romance for him. In fact, work can excite him almost to the point of arousal. As long as you understand this. His approach in all matters is confident, direct and very blunt. If you are up to all that, you can expect him to take you to some very exciting and unusual places. He loves to travel to exotic places, especially the great outdoors—though his idea of the great outdoors may include a trip around the world. Don't get your heart set on a luxury cruise; you may end up navigating the boat—he prefers to do things the hard way. Another thing about him is that he likes to be the first. If he isn't the first big love of your life, at least pretend. You can also tell him you find him the most exciting man you have ever been with. He will be sure of this in his own way

7

anyhow. He is not especially intuitive or tuned in to your feelings so you can tell him what he wants to hear and he will be happy. The Aries man is always a playboy at heart, so don't take him too seriously, unless you are perhaps a lovely Libra, a spirited Sagittarius, or you have your own Moon in the sign of Aries. If you are faint hearted, don't even bother to pursue this man. If you are provocative and independent, repeat after me: "There are two things the double Aries cannot resist: flattery and a fascinating challenge." And remember, the color red excites him.

His illumination: Passion for life.

His dark side: Quick temper.

ARIES-TAURUS

Here the fiery Ram meets the stubborn Bull. My dear, why are you even looking this one up? Oh, I know. . . he is so charming. And yes, he is exciting. He is also a fabulous money maker. So, okay. The absolute first thing that you must do is get some Flamenco music and yes, I mean it! This man wants to indulge and to go to extremes. He wants to be led on a merry chase. He may drive you almost to drink by his careless spending when it comes to luxury or sports and gambling. He has a roving eye, but it is nothing to worry about. He really is just looking. He likes to think that he dates only the best and the prettiest. He will not be at all offended by a girl that pumps iron. The Taurean influence wants something in the way of a chest, so pull yourself together and be the best you can be. He, however, can be a bit overweight and is, in fact, beginning to gain weight by his thirties. You, however, the girl of his ardent dreams, are going to sit, once settled, on a very high pedestal. Once he places you there, he will find you sexy in thermals. He can become that devoted. He is smart and very capable, so don't be vacuous. Be accessible, but not too available until he demands that you take the relationship more seriously. Then, of course, obey. He probably won't want to get married until the mortgage is paid off (he doesn't even have one yet), so you might have to settle for moving in for six or seven years and serving lots of beer to his Monday night football friends. But he does offer two things: sweet excitement and well planned futures. He is eventually a good husband and father. Co-workers respect him. An Aries girl who never says rude and nasty things, except in bed, or a beautifully souled Taurus has the best chance. Capricorns make him nervous—they like to be on time; he doesn't find that a plus.

His illumination: Ability to seize opportunities.

His dark side: Tendency to be selfish.

ARIES-GEMINI

We might as well get it over with, I have a prejudice. A Gemini Moon. I try, I really do, but they are such buggers. There are a couple of age groups that produced some Gemini Moon combinations that are not real easy to live with. In fact, there are a lot of fortyish men running around now that are always going to be looking for another lover, another wife, etc. Maybe both. They sorta can't help it. You just have to not take it personally, so as a husband he's a handful. As a father, he's often detached. Of course, if you are a Gemini Sun or Moon yourself, you can feel yourself getting sucked into the vortex almost at first sight. Destiny sets in, you know. Anyway, they always want more. And they aren't too happy about it when they get it. These guys are glib. Your only recourse is to be a little more slick. To make a hit with this one, you must be funny, ambitious, slender, and footloose. He is often more apt to talk a good game than to actually do it, whatever "it" is. This man will usually be found hanging around press clubs, and radio stations, and he will be fun. You need to be a companion first, and full of surprises second. But don't be caught dead with lists, schedules or routines. Tell him you take alternate routes to work (never mind you had to get up an hour early to do it), just so that you didn't feel like you were getting caught in a rut. Make him think he is a touch too dependable. Be capricious, outgoing, social. He may decide, in a lightning quick moment, that he needs to settle you down, for your own good, of course. Why bother? Because Executive is written all over him. Co-workers fear him. He will succeed, and will show you a dazzling good time. But if you want depth. . . read on about someone else. If this is still the one for you, pray that you are a fire sign, have some Virgo in your chart, and that he hasn't met his Gemini yet. If you are a Pisces and absolutely cannot control yourself, go directly to the courthouse and get your birthday changed. Or inject steel into your sweet little veins.

His illumination: Executive material.

His dark side: Restless.

ARIES-CANCER

Now we are getting somewhere. This man is so personable. He has a flaw, but it is not a big deal. He acts a lot more selfless than he is. He can be pretty self-centered, but you'll show no ill effects from it. This one can capture your heart in a flash. He can sense your every desire, and make them his own. His top layer is very confident, and very assured. But, he can be bruised easily as he is impressionable. Be gentle with him. If you are not, he will quite simply never see you again, and he will replace you instantly. This man, for all he has to offer, does not come by relationships that work well easily. The result, perhaps, of earlier tensions with his mother. This may have left him defensive and emotionally insecure. Just enough for you to watch your p's and q's. One slight and he broods forever. He wants a cozy home, and in fact, he can usually be found in real estate or real estate related fields. Learn to be a good cook. Meat and potatoes will not cut it. He needs the exotic in food. I'll tell you what would make you perfect for this man. Imagine this day. . . he comes home from the office and you whisk him off to a seminar on real estate money-making schemes, or to an acting class (he is a born actor), or any sort of surprise. Now while you're gone, you set the timer to bake some Chinese dish, and the VCR to record some boxing event. Upon your return let him talk until he's sleepy, then unbutton his clothes (he'll usually wear buttons on things as much as possible), and tuck him in. That ought to wake him enough to get his kinky little dramas going. And then you can co-star. Or star, depending on how well the rest of the evening went. And, no, I do not know how you can possibly set all those timers. He's a capable co-worker, a sensitive husband and parent. So if you are a Cancer or Pisces, or have that Moon position you are off to a good start. If you are a Leo with some bucks, and can have some fool doing the chores while you're out for the evening, you double your chances.

His illumination: Ability to emphasize.

His dark side: Tension with mother.

ARIES-LEO

This guy is popular with everyone. . . men, women, co-workers, children. Speaking of children, he'll want to have several, if only for his own basketball team. Further, he will want a lovely home, domestic harmony, and family gatherings. He impresses people of influence and is absolutely smoldering hot in the rack. Since he pretty much has it all, and good luck to boot, he will want whoever is hard to catch. It is just good common sense. He wants an active, professional, upscale life and a good family to come home to nights. He has a tendency to go after everything in a near frenzy. He is busy and seems to always be rushing about from one appointment to another. He likes to pan for gold, sky dive, gamble his paycheck, and "invest" in lotteries. He is lucky though, so his flash in the pan schemes may not be so impractical after all. He is attracted to qualities in a woman like pride, loyalty, and sincerity. He'll be looking for someone to help him with his social climbing. He also wants someone who can add to his sense of drama. He needs a daring co-partner. He needs someone who can add spice to his sex life. He may want more power and control in a relationship than most women are ready to give. He may have fantasies of moving and altering his entire lifestyle. This will pass. He has a lot to offer and perhaps you should hang in there for a while. He is such a lover that he could bring new meaning to the word. Once he settles down, he doesn't look seriously for anyone else. While most men stray at one time or another, try to remember he is only human if he falters. What he looks for in a woman is quality. He wants her to have flair, but how his loved one dresses is of no other importance to him so long as it is not drab. The one lucky enough to catch this one will probably be a Sagittarian with an Aries Moon. After all, he can afford to get really picky. A Virgo will probably bore him to tears, and Scorpios will bore him everywhere except in bed. . . after the first night. Another match could be a Leo with lots of Cancer in her chart.

His illumination: General popularity and good fortune.

His dark side: Excessive need for attention.

ARIES-VIRGO

This man is a cool one. He is analytical, critical, and often suspicious. He loves routine and controlling others' routines. If he could set up a time clock for his family to punch at home he would really be delighted. He needs to get into time management, science, or be a lawyer or judge. He behaves like all the above in social situations anyway. He has a strict code of living, and is excellent in sitting in judgement of his friends and family. As a boss, he wants to know why you wrote that letter, why you made that appointment. He does not delegate. He has the air of one in authority. He looks the part of the executive. But, you check out his briefcase. Underneath the computer printouts, there it is—the medicines. All over-the-counter medicines. He does not trust his doctors' judgments, and will diagnose his own stomach disorders and headaches. He is not usually into illegal drugs. He just has this inclination for being his own doctor. The exactness carries over into debates, or arguments as they are known at home. As a husband, he will split hairs with you over how long it took you to prepare breakfast. He enjoys making you explain. He doesn't really give a damn as to why (like the oven caught fire); having you explain yourself to him gives him a strange little feeling of control. If he sounds like the one for you, you can find him fidgeting at a party, his face calm and serene, his hands twisting and turning. He doesn't want to be there. He has a routine and he has just had it broken tonight. He may also have a slight limp to his walk. Probably got it one day when he let the daring Aries side of his nature take over and he hiked a bit too far into the wilderness. He then twisted his ankle running from a swarm of bees. Two good things about him, you won't spend your life picking up his socks, and he won't forget your birthday. He is a loner basically, but a Virgo, A Gemini, or a Capricorn could steal his pacemaker.

His illumination: Ability to survive.

His dark side: Hypochondria.

ARIES-LIBRA

Here is a man who goes from one infatuation to another. Unless you can handle his inconsistencies, and understand that something happened to him as a child that he can't recover from easily, you are going to have your hands full. Maybe his parents were separative, combative or lukewarm in their affections. Regardless, this left scars, and for him it is easier to fall in and out of love than to work on making a relationship last. He has a lot of charm once you understand what makes him tick. He is probably very talented in the arts, but severely lacking in direction. This is where you come into the picture. He needs your direction. He tends to build his castles in the sand, but with a little solid structure could end up with a wonderful career as a teacher or mentor; maybe an inventor. His co-workers admire him. He needs a real steamroller behind him to spur him on. The early 1980's were brutal to this man and he is just now fully recovering. He likes to have full support and approval for his actions and plans from those closest to him. If he does not have this, and goes ahead with his plans, then he has terrible bouts with guilt. He also has the emotional problem of letting go of the past. He is not as quick to act as the average Arian. This is a good thing as he does not have the physical stamina of most of the other Aries configurations. Since the right choice of a partner is so vital to him, I will suggest all that I can because he's a decent husband and father. He needs an earth/fire sign combination to get him rolling. A Leo or Sagittarius with a Taurus Moon would be just what the astrologer ordered. A Libra who has her Moon in Leo, or an Aries would do well with him also. The Libra Moon always attracts people, so the girls should be pretty well lined up for this one. Ms. Right must be a caretaker and wonderfully lovely to look at to sustain his affection.

His illumination: Artistic talents.

His dark side: Infatuation junkie.

ARIES-SCORPIO

I have to say it, but no one will really care. Mars and Pluto meet here. Mars is the planet of energy, and Pluto is the mysterious planet of regeneration. That is a lot to contend with in one body. This man reeks of self-respect. He is imposing in a quiet way. His co-workers know it. He is energetic, sky high and rock bottom. You are dealing with a man of depth here. He draws people to him like a magnet. You will never guess what is going on inside this man the entire time he is attracting people. He worries. He gets headaches. He will never tell you about this, unless it is to ask for an aspirin. He is not trying to be macho, he just prefers to keep it to himself. And, while he will patiently listen to your worries and his children problems, he will keep his to himself. When he loves someone, it is with a white hot fire. Nothing would be too difficult to do to prove his love and devotion. He cannot give too much to his love, as long as she does not ask for his independence, or too much of his savings. You can give this man lots of rope, he will not hang himself with it; he won't cheat while his lover is out of town. What he wants in return is devotion and loyalty. He is a faithful husband. Sleep around on him and it is all over. Nothing frivolous attracts him for long. Oh, dark magenta colors, mysterious glances, black garters will get his attention; but his belief that you find him irresistible, nearly flawless, and beautifully sexual keeps him by your side. He thinks of sex a lot more often than anyone could ever guess. He doesn't want to make a lot of changes in his life, but his Moon keeps him busy reorganizing the way he lives from time to time. He lives strictly by rules, I know of one who actually has one alcoholic drink a day. It consists of a tablespoon of alcohol swirled in a glass before bedtime. He says it is the right amount to relax the blood vessels. He also does his back exercises on the floor while conversing with company. It all goes back to that mysterious energy. Another Aries, a Leo or a Pisces can be swept away by him. He needs a Scorpio. Don't bother working on this one. He will find you.

His illumination: Enormous self-respect.

His dark side: Peculiar habits.

ARIES-SAGITTARIUS

Mundanity bores him. This man aspires to greater things, and does not want to get bogged down with petty emotions. If you go tracking this one down, look to a public relations firm for him first, or try the head of your local political party, or the host of the best social events of the season. He is progressive, idealistic, and outgoing. You had better be too. He is always on the move for something better. His co-workers fear this—it could be their jobs. He will also move on to other women, so you'd best be fully able to take care of yourself financially and emotionally. This future lawyer, actor, doctor will be first and foremost aroused by your mind and your crusades, not your dress size. This one is not romantic. The most you can hope for as a gift is a pack of cigarettes, and a bunch of bananas picked up hastily on the way to your house. It's that bad. I know one who came to this country with twelve dollars, made millions, and ended up giving much of his monies away to charities. He is not stingy. He just is not romantic. He figures if you don't see the romance in flying across country in his little plane, or taking pictures of your camp sight, that this is your problem. He is full of adventure, so you don't have to worry about becoming a bored housewife with him. Even his mistress is kept too busy to shop and get her nails done. His children don't get a lot of his time. I tell you he is a handful. He soaks up each and every moment of life. He doesn't want to miss a single thing. Even though he is far too blunt, he means to be honest and kind. He has a nice oval face, shiny and handsome, and is so sincere, how can you resist? Yet resist you must, to some degree, otherwise you won't be enough of a challenge to hold his attention for very long. A Sagittarius, Aries or Leo Sun is needed here. A Scorpio will fascinate in mid life. A Pisces may offer a sweet tranquility for a year or so after a breakup with a more compatible sign, but this one isn't very steady. He is almost literally following a new skirt. He is a leg man, by the way.

His illumination: Full of adventure.

His dark side: Tendency to womanize.

ARIES-CAPRICORN

This one knows timing. He craves recognition and will plow his way to the top—his employees are treated well, though. He is a wonderful host, and is sweet and charming, but no one will get the better of him for all his charm. If you do you will wish you hadn't. He is determined. Actually, he has a rather rigid personality that only a few know well. Full of vitality, his dream girl is energetic, outdoorsy on the weekends, and executive material weekdays. He'll need to be mothered on occasion. When he does you'd better give it 100 percent. Remember, he gives 100 percent to his goals, and will want the same from you. Oh, while you're being perfect, don't forget he wants a clean, well organized home that has lots of office space, possibly a mini gym, and lots of room to entertain. Picture yourself keeping it all in order as you jog with him, briefcase in hand. He's got a lot to offer, and marriage will just happen with the right girl. Like the common law statutes are up and you have a very unromantic service between business appointments. Marriage is not what he dreams of. It is an incident that just sort of sneaks up on him, like the children he has by accident. He doesn't mind really, as long as he is proceeding with other goals. You can't be too sentimental, he'll break your heart. He looks for a practical girl, organized, and yes, pretty, too. Of course, you need a Capricorn girl here, or another Aries. Someone strong. One weekend with him leaves the Pisces girl shattered. An Aquarian will find him a colossal bore, and a Leo will not want the ego competition. Make him number one and he's all yours.

His illumination: Commitment to goals.

His dark side: Need to be mothered.

ARIES-AQUARIUS

This one offers romance, and all the "right" things. He comes from a good background, education, social circle, etc. He smoked a pipe at an early age. He was the liberal at school. He has a secret invention in the works. He keeps everyone spellbound, if he so desires, including his co-workers. He needs to sell, promote, design, and control. He'd be a perfect citizen astronaut. He likes to laugh a lot and to party. Just make sure the surroundings aren't tacky. This one must associate with class. He'll get some strange ideas from time to time, some little group sex experiments (he will not think this tacky). But surprise, he won't expect you to go along. He actually wants you to have a mind of your own. He likes the soft and cuddly type, as long as she is a real person underneath it all. He can tell about people better than most any man. He builds his life on people and dealing with groups. He won't be fooled. Be the genuine article and he'll see lots of you. Keep your metallics for the bedroom, and wear the lace and velvets in public. He's got an old fashioned streak about his woman. He wants an ideal mate (he's pretty ideal himself). Someone "well bred." He will probably meet the woman of his dreams at the local planetarium, or in a computer class. He will stare ahead absentmindedly pretending not to notice you. He was just taking inventory. If you did not meet all his physical specifications, he really will ignore you. The physical specifications he was taking stock of were: good teeth, clear eyes, good posture, general alertness, etc. He has his own standards of beauty. Long term relationships are best for him with an Aquarius with some Leo in her chart. Or a Leo with some Pisces. Or, well, gee, he loves them all.

His illumination: A spellbinder.

His dark side: Snobbish.

ARIES-PISCES

He's creative. He's dreamy and starry-eyed. He broods a lot. He reminds me of an artist who is always a brush stroke away from his masterpiece. A lot happens with a Pisces Moon. They drink too much, get involved in drugs too often, get tangled up with the wrong circle of friends, fall in love with someone who is all wrong for them. That sort of thing. Then he retreats to solitude, and more brooding. I hope you are a Pisces yourself (not Moon, though, you'd drown each other in sorrow), and want nothing more than to look after him for the rest of your lives. There is a wonderful side to this man. He's sensitive, caring, romantic. He has an uncanny knack of knowing what your emotional needs are. He'll remember anniversaries, and bring flowers to all of you. Sorry about that, but he has tons of women in his life. Marriage and children usually aren't on his mind. He's got the combination of sporty good looks (muscular and athletic), and watery eyes that drive the ladies crazy. He'll usually be found sculpting the latest art form, studying the latest research, or trying to advance in some sort of social work or creative endeavor for the betterment of mankind. He is a caring supervisor, but he will not be what you call a well rounded personality. His interests are very specific. If you want to make one of them you, have outlets for your time away from him. He will spend lots of his time in solitude. He'll need his space. It is enough to know that you are there. And above all, respect his privacy. He'll have lots of secrets. Don't try to find them out. He'll never forgive you. He needs a Pisces, another Aries, or a lovely Taurus.

His illumination: Concern for mankind.

His dark side: Falling in love with the wrong woman.

Taurus

April 20–May 21

TAURUS-ARIES

Taurus is steady and slow. Aries is not. That is the basic conflict here. So he can surprise you; poke along, and then be lightning quick to a decision, action, or adventure. This man likes to please people, and he gets along well at work. If he falls in love with you, you can be sure he'll keep you, and your happiness, in his thoughts. He will try to be a good husband. Another batch of good news about this one, you'll never have to guess how he is feeling or what he is thinking; nor will your children. He'll tell you. Rather bluntly, in fact. He is that way about sex, too. Earthy, and no pretenses. A natural born money maker, he has plenty of drive. A business deal will energize him into a near frenzy romantically. Remember I said he lets all his feelings show, so you won't have to wonder why he's so excitable, even in bed. He wants and needs the same genuine responses from you. Insipid creatures will not attract him. The Aries Moon has a tendency to bring out a quickly angered personality, and the Taurus Sun can be really stubborn! This is a combination he will learn to overcome in time, in order to survive this world, because the Taurus wants peace and tranquility above all. He is also a creature of comfort. So, even if he hasn't quite learned to control his temper yet, he is quick to forgive and basically very loving. Venus ruled sun and Mars ruled emotions leave no doubt about his masculine traits. He'll be steady and faithful (once he settles in), and spend lots of time trying to make you one of the boys. But he'll want you to be ultra feminine; dainty, curvy, perfumed and dressed to kill. A Capri-

19

corn, another Taurus and an Aries with plenty of earthy planets in her chart stands the best astrological chance of snagging this one.

His illumination: Genuine responsibilities.

His dark side: Stubbornness.

TAURUS-TAURUS

Whenever you see a man with the Sun and the Moon in the same sign, think of double trouble and strong struggles for power. There is nothing half way about this man. He knows what he wants and will not change his mind. There is an intensity here that few men have. This man wants a home, a family, and a wife that can handle money and cook. He wants money and luxuries for the both of you. But you'd better let him be the one to make the money for the household. He is a very loving person and will have lots of women to choose from. He pays no attention really, and rather shrugs it off with a, "What, hon, you think she still has feelings for me?" and he means it. He is unaware of his charms. There is very little conceit with this combination. He never wants to hurt anyone. Even in a fit of stubbornness he wants his way to work out peacefully and to everyone's benefit. This is a nice man, a conventional man, and excellent husband and father material. He does not understand infidelities. He does not understand anyone who does not want the best out of life: travel, good food, bank accounts, and beautiful surroundings. Although he starts out slowly, he climbs the ladder of success beautifully. By mid-life, when everyone else is having their crises, he is reaping the harvest of plodding, slow labor. He has arrived but he will not be boastful about it. Instead, he will feel, bashfully, that he has simply earned it. His co-workers will like him. It can work out if you have a full time career, but you'd better prepare for the 80 hour work week, where he gets his full forty hours of wife. And don't forget to learn to be the best cook in the neighborhood. Best bet: Another Taurus Sun or Moon, a Cancer, or a Libra who does not try to manipulate him.

His illumination: Strong values.

His dark side: Overindulgence.

TAURUS-GEMINI

Just when you begin to think that the Taurus male is something of a saint, with all his loyalty and devotion, here comes that old Gemini Moon again. Remember, I told you about it already. Well, even a nice, steady, usually faithful Taurus cannot stand up to his restless, fickle Moon. He will wander. And leave lots of broken, unsuspecting hearts in the wake. Lots. And with it, many broken promises. He didn't mean any harm, really, but he simply found you irresistible at first, and then a little less exciting, and so on, until you actually bored him. On the other hand, so and so is looking better and more exciting every day. Can you stay in the background for a long time providing the strong home ties and very little constraints? Perhaps you are a very stable person with a career such as advertising, that causes you to announce unexpectedly that you have to catch the next plane for wherever, and leave. Just like that. Just like he would. He, unlike most other Taureans, won't care in the least about good home cooking and a dependable family life. He'll be relieved. You were beginning to burden him. He was feeling guilty about all the late night outings with "the boys" and getting plenty bored with the demands of a relationship. (He will never quite measure up to a commitment.) His positive traits depend on how he diffuses his Moon energies. He needs to be busy to the point of exhaustion. Lots of variety in work and avocation. Pray he is a traveling salesman, who has to study like mad to keep up with the competition. He'll be popular with clients and co-workers. A Libra with a Gemini Moon can understand and cope with it all. Other earth signs will bore him. A Gemini or an Aquarian will attract him the most and for the longest.

His illumination: Lots of potential.

His dark side: Values subject to change.

TAURUS-CANCER

This is a difficult Moon and Sun position. It indicates a series of difficulties with women, beginning early on in life. Success with the opposite sex comes later, at almost 35 years of age. Maybe he should wait until then for a wife and children. Success in love affairs begins in first grade, but it is all so fleeting. He goes around trying to make everyone comfortable and happy, hiding very well his own feelings. But they are there, and they run deep. In fact, he loves or hates with quiet intensity. And, since he is given to long periods of silence, you may never even know about it. He imagines things that may not be so. That someone is against him, for example, perhaps at work. And he can hold grudges until the day he dies. Don't even think of crossing him. He is very sensitive, and always reading things between the lines as a result. He's a gentle soul, and needs careful handling. He likes a lot of variety in women, and is a rather quiet, gentlemanly type of Don Juan. He seems much more of a pushover than he is. Because he has a very definite mind of his own, he just wants you to think that you are pulling one over on him. He can lead just about anyone into thinking that he needs their care, attention, and often money. You will end up giving him the shirt off your back, if that is what he wants. And he will be ever so loving and appreciative. But, if he wants more, and you don't produce, you're out of the game. When he has money, he'll gladly give you whatever he wants to give you (not necessarily what you were needing or hoping for, and how dare you be ungrateful). This one is touchy. He will be sweet, and when he is good, well, you know the old expression. This inconsistency is part of his charm. Just be careful here. A Cancer, a Scorpio, or a Pisces who has some earth in her chart is the best bet for a successful relationship.

His illumination: Gentle soul.

His dark side: Holds grudges.

TAURUS-LEO

This one could be a real prize, if he likes you enough to let you enter into his inner circle; perhaps he may even confide in you about himself if you get lucky. He will want to know all about you if he is interested in you, but will rarely reveal that much about himself. He's quite proud and aloof, so he doesn't share feelings all that well. He has nothing to hide as a rule, for he is a genuine, caring, and very pleasant fellow. He can out sell, out build, out promote, out design just about anyone. His accomplishments are legion. His main claim to fame, however, is his ability to sense things about people. He zooms right in on people's fatal flaws. If he doesn't like yours, you'll know right up front. This may explain his treatment of you at work.

He's the opposite of the Moon position that precedes his. He is never at a loss for words, imagination, or conviction. He doesn't have a lot of crises in his life like the Cancer Moon, but he does have a series of readjustments. Since he is not fond of change and likes to map life out himself, these adjustments, however minor, do not come easy for him. That is where you come in. He needs to be reassured in this one area only. But this area is a big one to him. He draws people of importance to him, those who can help him on his way to the top; but he can alienate them just as fast with his snap, usually correct, judgements. He'll be blunt and to the point. Regardless, almost everyone likes him. He is very popular, usually good looking, and romantic to boot. The object of his affections is usually regal, and somehow dazzling. It may be her career, her background, or her presence, but she will be special. And he will adore her and his children. A Leo is perfect for him. A Sagittarius stands for a wonderful, but not lengthy relationship as a rule. A Capricorn entices.

His illumination: One of the catches!

His dark side: Excessive pride.

TAURUS-VIRGO

Life brings a lot of good things to this position, one of which is a good woman to spur him on to his highest success. Virgo is a mental sign and therefore this Taurus will intellectualize most situations subconsciously. He is looking for lots of adventure in life; safaris, expeditions, and exciting, earthy women. There is a sort of dashing demeanor about him that really appeals to women. He's naturally masculine and therein lies his appeal. He won't get overly sentimental or romantic but he does have tons of animal magnetism, in spite of himself. You must earn his respect, as co- workers find out fast. He wants a woman who can stand up for herself. A career oriented woman usually wins his admiration. Independent himself, he is turned on by it in a woman. If you were the head of your class, or are the head of the corporation, can wear something red and slinky, and will let him know you'd love to look after him in your spare time, he'll give you his immediate attention. Fawn all over him and you are sunk. The out of sync relationship will appeal to him for a strong beginning. Deep down he wants to be married, and once he makes the commitment he'll back you up all the way and be a fine husband. Unless, of course, you do something really tacky like fool around with his best friend. He's too smart for any maneuvering, so try really hard to be the best you are. He really won't settle for less. And he'll teach you new dimensions in earthy sexuality. Vital, carrying Scarlet O'Hara up the staircase, sex is his forte. Let him conquer you and he is yours. If there is a delay in the courtship due to your own problems, like your having to finish law school, or terminate a prior relationship, he will wait. He will wait for his children too—he'll be a great dad. Another Taurus, a Gemini or Virgo could fill the bill. The Scorpio could lose out to a Capricorn with vitality.

His illumination: Vitality.

His dark side: Fussy with possesssions.

TAURUS-LIBRA

There are about a dozen of the most loveable, popular men of the Zodiac (whether or not you happen to be in love with one), and this double Venus combination is one. How can anyone resist? They usually place people, and personal things, above material things, and therefore appear to be slow in the business world. They are not. They just have different priorities—home life, wife and children are first. Natural born negotiators, they are the fence menders in other people's lives and at work. No matter how heavy their own burdens are, they will not inflict their troubles on the ones they love. They are too kind to ever do things like that. If they have problems to bear, they usually will be of the health variety. People seem to want nothing more than to fulfill their every desire. One of the few ideal husbands or sweethearts of the Zodiac, this one can, unfortunately, choose the wrong first love. Whenever they are in disharmonious surroundings, they are miserable. They need a happy environment. That is why it is such a shame to see this one married or involved with the wrong lady. A crafty Libra (and no one can top them in the female configurations for being manipulative) has a strong chance, sad as it may be. He will definitely look for beauty. His eye is trained for this. And for intelligence. There is usually something very vibrant about the girl of his choice. She will not be a quiet, introverted person regardless of her appearance. The Air (Gemini, Aquarius, Libra) signs have a good chance as can everyone, until he meets the right, or the wrong one, as the case may be. He needs someone he can count on. If you are lucky enough to catch this one, don't (promise me) take advantage. If he is of the more poetic variety, a Pisces Sun-Libra Moon combination stands an excellent chance.

His illumination: Everybody loves 'em.

His dark side: His first love damages.

TAURUS-SCORPIO

Parents that were in conflict, lukewarm family ties, and a tendency to self destruction all rear their ugly heads with this configuration. You'll hardly notice though, because he is the epitome of charm. He catches your imagination right a way. He can be almost irresistible until one of his little weaknesses shows up. One of which may be laziness. He is a wonderful short term relationship, fun, passionate, and considerate. Heaven help you though, if he is not ready to move on (as he usually is) to the next relationship. He is possessive. He will want to know where you are every moment. He begins a relationship telling you how much he needs his freedom, and warns you that he hasn't even fallen in love before, nor does he want to. Usually he is right. Occasionally, he is mistaken, and he will want a very long term relationship with you. It is almost irresistible at first. He is so devoted. If you are a working woman, he will find it sweet. And after patronizing you and flattering you, he will gradually try talking you out of the whole thing. He really does not want his woman running around for everyone to see. He invented jealousy, and he does have a nasty temper about it. If you can handle that, he will ask only for your devotion. You can be sure, if you are the one he wants, he wouldn't even consider looking at another woman. Even drunk. Which is a lot to say about a man or future husband. Help him break away from his bad habits, and he may surprise you by being very successful. His success will not come at a job that is conventional or secure, and co-workers find him unreliable. He may win a lottery or large inheritance, for example. And he will want to offer you everything imaginable, including a few babies. A Capricorn could snag this one, a Scorpio, or Cancer also has a good chance.

His illumination: Devoted.

His dark side: Has some bad habits.

TAURUS-SAGITTARIUS

There he is, the investment counselor, or rising young corporate star, walking hurriedly along the corridors. Pleasant and sunny, he has a nice hello for everyone. You'd never know underneath it all he has snide thoughts about breeding, morals, and social status. Anyone who does not possess a fair degree of heritage will be considered a lesser being. He is, quite simply, a snob. And absolutely no one could ever guess. He is a steamroller combination, who can get things done. He is full of energy, a sports enthusiast, and one who uses the golf course to further his career. He does think things through, but he is given to impulsive spells, and he often makes a rash decision after much deliberating, only to regret it later. He does this with women, too. He can impulsively decide to marry, and spend a few years regretting it. He can be a difficult husband and parent as a result. Then he'll treat his wife like such a peon that she will fulfill his desires and leave—he'd hate to do the leaving. It's almost against his principles, or his version of morality. These are his deep dark secrets, though, and hardly anyone would find him anything but dazzling, pleasant, and sociable. He is a real go-getter. Co-workers find him brilliant. Just pretend you don't know all this about him and hitch your wagon to his star. Here's what he'll want from you: everything. Good background, family, education, intelligence, aspirations, morality and wondrous good looks. Oh yes, I hope you make good money and are very playful and adventurous in bed. He really does believe in your having it all. A Sagittarius or an Aires would do wonders for him. He'll break a Cancer's heart. And a Scorpio won't put up with any of it. A Libra could manage nicely to meet most all his considerable needs. A Capricorn can make the match on paper, but the chemistry may be a bit off.

His illumination: A go-getter.

His dark side: Tendency to marry in haste.

TAURUS-CAPRICORN

This one is a love. He's even fun at work. He's practical, stable, down to earth, very sensual, and devoted to home and heart. He knows what he wants and is determined to arrive at a very elevated standard of living for you and his children. In spite of all his nice guy traits, he is not boring. He is, in fact, terribly funny once you get the gist of his sense of humor. He loves to go places and do things. Good perfume on you and good wines in him will turn him on. You can forget being frivolous with this man. That really would be a faux-pas. Even when you have a good deal of money, he will want you to get the best deal on your purchase. That includes your clothes from Neiman-Marcus. It will be okay, if you examine and find a mark-down, to spend lots of money. But don't ever let him see you dashing about having a wonderful time in the process of acquiring (his sense of humor is not that good). He works hard, and does not arrive at the top quickly. You will have to weather some hard times before you get to the good. Can you endure? Are you steady and dependable yourself? Are you a good listener for his depressive moods? Or for the stories of his excessive worries? If so, you may have found your match. He can be a truly wonderful man. Don't push it by being messy, disorganized, or leaving traces of your makeup lying on pillow cases or towels. He likes to believe that you were born with black eyelashes. After all, you belong up there on that pedestal for him, and glimpses of a mere human being are unsettling. Crackers in bed are unforgivable, feeding him caviar is okay though, even in bed. A nice Capricorn would be perfect. A terrific health nut Virgo, or a lovely plodding Taurus are also first choices. A sensitive little Cancer may also fill the bill.

His illumination: Sense of humor.

His dark side: Depressive moods.

TAURUS-AQUARIUS

Genuine. That's him. He is sincere to the core, loves everyone, and vice versa. He couldn't resist a damsel in distress, or a lonely hitch-hiker. He is the humanitarian of the Zodiac. A very nice person, with no deep dark secrets, or ulterior motives. He would be a wonderful counsellor or leader of a charity or social cause. He has ambitions, but unlike most of his Taurean brothers, they are not altogether for money. His goals are more basic. Humanitarian and yes, even spiritual. He thinks about universal love, not personal stuff. This is not to say that he cannot be romantic or in fact, in love with love. He just externalizes a lot of his needs. He has emotions on a larger scale than most of us, so you cannot be possessive, jealous, or confining. He does things in his odd little way and in his own fashion. After a while you will find his quirks not only acceptable, but loveable, and actually join in. He should have a wonderful combination of masculine good looks, strong and muscular, with a light, airy, ethereal quality about him that charms you to the nth degree. You simply won't be able to resist, unless, of course, you want more financial goals out of life. In that case, he is simply not the one for you. A leftover flower child, or a new generation spiritualist, he is a person all to his own. He needs another much like himself. Someone who is a pixie sort, running around trying to save the whales. How could he resist? You'd have a delightful life, if unusual marriage. If you're slick and sophisticated, or found in the social register, I'd suggest that you plan on a few memorable nights and move on. If you could get that far. Chances are he'd much more likely turn out strictly platonic with you. He needs an Aquarian. A Gemini. Maybe a Pisces. Forget Leo and Aries. He's not up to that, bless his heart.

His illumination: Loveable.

His dark side: Often detatched.

TAURUS-PISCES

Here is a very basic equation: Neptune = Deception, and Venus = Love, Therefore Taurus-Pisces = Deception in Love. He'll be deceived many times. He really does have a tendency to have his head in the clouds. He is so romantic that his life all depends on the girl that captures his heart. Hopefully it will be someone who will appreciate his good qualities. He isn't exactly ambitious, that would be too mundane for him. But he is loving and sincere. A rare find, wouldn't you say? Depends though on what you are looking for. If you want passion, fire, adventure, ambition, look elsewhere. If you want someone with a good heart and a strong sense of romance, then he is yours; but not without a snag. He can be blunt. He will say the wrong things to the wrong people. He really won't care either. In fact, he may even find it humorous; his co-workers won't. But he'll be a faithful husband. Unless you have too many problems, then he'll back off. He doesn't like that sort of thing. He'll have enough of his own from a previous bad relationship, over indulgence in food, drink, drugs, or all of the above. To add your problems to his would be insurmountable. You have to be pretty independent for this one.

Pretty and "evolved." Or at least trying to get your karma together. He won't demand that you are a wifey. But he will demand that you at least share his enthusiasm for research, humanity, hospitals, or the occult. He is looking for a soul mate, and if she comes in some odd, assorted package of weights and heights, or ways and means, then that is okay. To be expected, actually. He needs an exotic inno-cent (is there such a thing?) to fulfill his fantasies. And he has lots of fantasies. Offer to move near the beach or at least a lake, and you up your chances considerably. Plan to take the kiddies along on your adventures—he needs his family nearby. He needs a Pisces, a Virgo, maybe a Libra. Keep away if you're a Sagittarian—he wants to dream of far away places, not actually go there.

His illumination: Sincere.

His dark side: Head in the clouds.

Gemini

May 22–June 22

GEMINI-ARIES

Let's sing a verse of the song "Urgent." "You play tricks on my mind, you're everywhere, but you're so hard to find." Got it? He is a little selfish, glib, on-the-go, fast talking, fickle. This is one of the guys you could send to the store for a loaf of bread, and not see again for several years. But he'll leave you with the impression that he really thought you were wonderful. And, there are many of you who will anxiously await his return. It was after all, exciting, was it not? He is, after all, fun, witty, and has a rhythm sexually that is all his own. He is a lot of different things, to a lot of people. Whatever his profession, he approaches it haphazardly, yet finishes with a brilliant flash. I'm never quite sure how, except that he will deliver a marvelous speech. Often he will not know much about what he is talking, but he is so sincere. Eventually his co-workers find him deceptive. Or so it seems. He can be a real con. He is also unpredictable. You will definitely have your hands full with this one. You can find him in fields that are involved with travel, sports, politics, communications. A freelance sports writer would be, no doubt, his dream profession. His dream girl is another matter. She is the one that wins out by sheer, unwavering patience, as he can be a roving husband. She will stand by him through all his moods, adventures, infidelities, and lost dreams. She will need an abundance of energy and humor. She will also, no doubt, be petite and graceful. She will know instinctively when to let him dangle and when to reel him back in. She will be able to subtly impress him with her appeal to the opposite sex. She will be someone he feels he has to protect, in his

31

own fashion. He will be protective as a father because of this trait. Look for girls with the Moon in Aries, Leo, or the other Fire sign, Sagittarius, or even a Gemini Moon. Look for the Sun in the Air signs, Libra or Aquarius. Best bet, a Leo with a Gemini Moon.

His illumination: Flashes of brilliance.

His dark side: All that glitters is not gold.

GEMINI-TAURUS

This is one of the more stable and lovable Gemini positions. With Gemini you always get the twins (or in some cases triplets) and they can be very unpredictable and erratic. The emotional needs found in the Moon indicate, in this combination, that love and steadfastness are important. This, for some other signs, could create a real conflict, but here the emotional needs are stronger. He wants love, friendship, popularity, his feet firmly planted on the ground, and someone decent in his life. This is why he excels as a father—he instills solid values in his children. And he will have so many friends that he can easily make this a reality. He is the life of the party, and is an excellent judge of character. He will gather business cards of the guests, invite a few over and promote himself unselfconsciously along the way. He does best in artistic professional fields where he can utilize his ability to communicate. His co-workers find him a strong shoulder to lean on. He could sell investment services, banking products, design business interiors, the list is unlimited. Naturally a little bit laid back, the Taurus influence is overruled by the Gemini vitality. Energy will abound. He is most attracted to a girl with a marvelous social life, lots of flair and a sense of drama. If she is a little lacking in stability, he will romanticize her situation, and want nothing more than to come to her rescue. If there is something a little off the wall or odd about her, he will be immediately attracted. Once Cupid's arrow hits, he'll be a pretty steady fellow. He will provide a nice home base, but be prepared to take off on spur of the moment excursions, and he'll be delighted. A Virgo Sun or Moon, stands the best chance here. A Taurus or Aquarian can be very appealing. If the competition is heavy, you might want to throw in your culinary skills. Or maybe you can sing and play the guitar. Do something. He needs attention, and to be entertained.

His illumination: Life of the party.

His dark side: Attracted to the peculiar.

GEMINI-GEMINI

Here we go with another double sign. Only this is double the sign of twins. What you get as a result is a lot of personalities within one person. Getting to know the many hims, and keeping up with his mood changes takes a lot of doing because he can't keep up with himself. He can be sweet, or he can be nasty. But he is always busy. Restless. I think of him as the restless wind. He is witty, and smart, and interesting, and bright on the good side. He is not looking for commitment, or housing, or cooking, or much of anything in the way of female companionship. He can even pass up sex for another activity. Relationships mean very little to him (sorry, I hope you were just curious and didn't have your heart set on this one). Marriage usually doesn't appeal to him. He is very much his own person, and likes to be everywhere and surrounded with a lot of buddies. He has difficulty in obtaining what he wants out of life except adventure. He usually marries but doesn't put much stock in his relationships, and his several marriages don't quite ever work out. His children may feel almost abandoned. His career pursuits never quite jelled. He will frequently let his co-workers down with his inconsistencies. He is a nervous wreck because he has far too much energy and is stimulated far too easily for any one body. He can't help it really. It's hard on him too, you know. So, if you just have to have this one, be prepared to serve as a sort of nurse for his frequent health disorders. He will have a lot of them, headaches, tense muscles, lung disorders (you can bet he smokes), nervous fits, nightmares, etc. Get relaxing environmental disks for the sounds and smells of relaxation. Soothe him. Quiet him. Take the phone off the hook. He needs it every so often, although he'll fight it. You'd better be a triplet yourself. Light and airy. Double Aquarian, a Libra, a Virgo, or a Gemini with lots of Earth signs in your chart can handle this one.

His illumination: Curious.

His dark side: Babbles.

GEMINI-CANCER

This man is a nervous worrier who has a tendency to sulk. He is a grown child who has to sleep with the light on, and with someone in his arms. He needs lots of mothering. Something was not quite right with his own mother, chances are. He also wants to be entertained. He'll appreciate a girl who is full of surprises yet who is emotionally stable. He couldn't handle any more problems than he has already. He is highly intuitive and receptive to situations. You start moving in on him and he's gone. One of the reasons that he succeeds in work is that he has such excellent insight into things. He's a good co-worker to ask for input into your work assignments. No one can really deceive him for long. He seems to be born with experience and good judgement. That will take him a long way in life, in spite of himself. He, like the previous Sun/Moon combination, is a bundle of nerves. He may imagine things from time to time that are not quite so. He is fearful. He is easily hurt. His relationships with women need work, especially if he is in his early thirties. There will be lots of upsets with his attachments. How not to be one of them? You could be committed to someone else, and he'll stick with you longer. A lot of times he will feel more secure if he thinks he is not your main man. He likes to think you are not "after him." Let him do the chasing. That will really attract his attention. Also, he may be attracted to an older woman who seems to have arrived. You can curse around this one, he will actually find your four letter words rather amusing. You can sleep around a little. Well, as long as you tell him, that is. Should he find out that it was nothing compared to him, he will forgive you. When he marries he will try to be a loving husband and father. A Cancer who regrets her shortcomings, another Gemini, a Virgo, or even a Pisces could cope. A Scorpio could intrigue for quite a while, but their fights are usually too nasty for him to survive.

His illumination: Receptive.

His dark side: Emotionally needy.

GEMINI-LEO

He spends his life communicating with those in authority, or power, or politics, or superstardom, so you'll have to fit in with his image. He will be very image conscious. You'd better look good, be tons of fun, have a lot on the ball, and his same footloose attitude. While he has one affair after the other, he gets really picky about "the one." She needs to be extraordinary, and very loyal, although he may slip every now and then. (Who said life was fair?) He really believes in the double standard. If you don't, pretend you do and cover your tracks. Let's pretend that he started out as an engineer. He meets all the right people, and advances accordingly. He is now in some sort of public relations and his whole manner is different. Don't remind him of his more humble roots. He can't forgive you for that either. He loves all sorts of recreation, just so long as it is active, not passive. He even loves children, though not especially his own. He is bound to have a few of his own though. If you can fit into all of this, you have for yourself a man who is clever, shrewd, curious, capable, vibrant, and usually good looking in a regal sort of way. Bonus of all, he improves with age. He will be one of the ones who can settle into a good profession, a good social life, and a stable and lasting family life. He is no fool. He will spend lots of time looking for Ms. Right, chase her relentlessly, and adore her ever after. He will be generous, and want to lavish her and his children with praise, affection and gifts. He can be unusually romantic for a Gemini. Sentimental, too. He's definitely worth the wait, which he is famous for. For all his romance and quick action, choosing his mate is one area where he will take his time. Prepare to take yours. Leo girls are best. A Capricorn with a Gemini Moon, an Aquarian or Libra are next best.

His illumination: Tremendous power and talent.

His dark side: Elusive in love.

GEMINI-VIRGO

Mercury is the ruler of both of these signs. That means he is very mental. Catch his attention between the ears. I know it is unusual, but not all men have the same erotic appendages. He is also nervous (as are most of the Gemini's, as you have probably noted by now) and discontented. He has the classic artistic temperament, and craves all the artsy things in life. This means he's a tough co-worker when it comes to temperament. He wants the proper circle of friends, the most dramatic love life, lots of impassioned ideas, and even nourishes the desire to be a famous writer or orator. Think of John Kennedy. Wasn't he the epitome of the impassioned intellectual, with the ability to speak to the heart of all of us? He captures the imagination. He captures our social conscience. And he captures lots of women along the way. More, in fact, than he desires to. A little fling, and he goes on about his business. The lovely little blonde, had better be a scholar, or at least have social standing or status to get beyond the one night stand. He can be shallow about sex. Sex carries little or no sentiment with it for him, you can be sure. A fiery woman, however, with tons of ideas, and an artistic ability, or one who can match his independence can enter into the realms of his higher sexual consciousness. It is in his makeup to be very exacting and indeed, calculating. This includes friendships and love affairs. He has always thought everything over first and is looking out for himself. If you can adapt to that philosophy (and it is not all that bad once you understand it), then your chances of happiness in an independent sort of way are excellent because he'll make a nice home for you and the children. A Capricorn, Virgo, or any of the Fire signs can best understand his mentality. Pisces would be downright insulted by any of his suggested arrangements. Another Gemini will attract and repel at the same time. Mirror images would annoy him; he hates to be reminded of his shortcomings.

His illumination: Intellectual superiority.

His dark side: Calculating.

GEMINI-LIBRA

Libra is the artistic judge of the Zodiac. And the two things the Libra Moon has in common with the Gemini Sun, are its intellectual nature, and its ability to fall in love with love. It often is not any deeper than that. Here's a charmer. He has a hearty laugh, a lighthearted approach and a gift of gab. All these traits are delightful. They are also superficial and glossy characteristics. Don't look too deep here. You won't find much. Expect a very good time and a delightful companion. This can be more than enough depending on where you are coming from or who you just left. He looks for gaiety, vibrancy, good times and he wants it packaged in wondrous beauty. You won't be able to talk him out of it. He sees with an artist's eye and he knows what he wants. If you are not his version of beautiful, it won't get too serious. He appreciates other qualities, but he gets infatuated with shape and form. That means he is not the best husband and father when it comes to consistency. His feet, traveling ones at that, are not planted firmly on the ground. I tell you all this to warn you, but you won't listen. He's just too appealing. He can make you feel like you've just won a million dollars, that you are the only one in the very crowded room, and on and on. It is powerful stuff, this Libra Moon. You will forget that he may not be actually good looking when you stop to analyze it. But you will find women carrying torches for him lining the streets. He knows it, too. But you'll never hear him admit it. He is too romantic to face such an ugly reality as this: he breaks hearts. Life plays tricks, and chances are he gets his heart smashed up once, too. Probably by a Libra. These Libra women are famous for their beauty and advantage taking nature. It won't deter him in his other pursuits, but he never fully recovers either. An Aquarius, another Gemini, and every Libra in sight will catch his eye first.

His illumination: Charming, delightful.

His dark side: "Once burned. . ."

GEMINI-SCORPIO

Up front, before you get too attached to his qualities and personality: he won't care who you are, what you have, what you look like—if you don't continue to live up to all his expectations, he will leave you at the drop of a hat. You won't know what hit you. He won't look back; he will probably have replaced you before he left. He believes he will find much better (usually in serial relationships), and he usually does find better in one fashion or another. Intense, he will go through periods of total devotion, and like the hot summer wind, change direction and be gone. No one quite knows why. Perhaps another opportunity arose elsewhere. Perhaps, he needed more attention, devotion or return for his investment. Either way, you are out. This one will rarely settle down. This does not provide for good husband and father material, though he usually loves his children very much. How he turns out in mid life usually depends on his peer group and surroundings. Self indulgent, he can give in to his cravings of over-indulgence in food, luxury, drugs, etc. There is no middle ground for him until he is in a solid, peaceful surrounding. Then of course, it depends on how long he wants to stay there. Passion, and there are all sorts of passions in his life, is the key word here. He needs amour, intense sexuality and white hot romance. Tie him up, not down, and you have a chance. He figures a little kink never hurt anyone. Travel everywhere, be seen everywhere, keep busy and he will definitely notice you. Allow him to experience everything, excess everything, and he will keep you around a little longer than usual. A Scorpio, Virgo, Capricorn Sun, or Water sign Moon has the best chance for a little extra happiness in this relationship.

His illumination: Tremendous will to improve.

His dark side: Blows hot and cold.

GEMINI-SAGITTARIUS

Except for variety, he does not know what he really wants. He dreams different dreams from time to time. You can find him working in the personnel office, in the courthouse or traveling from one adventure to another. He makes a lot of promises and then bows out because of some make believe mishap that prevents him from finishing the assignment, the job, or the relationship. When he is ready to move on, usually quite literally (he changes addresses a lot) he will tell you out of the blue that he has a disease and won't burden you with it. But he always leaves an out, like if they ever find a cure, and I should be so lucky that you will still want me, I'll be back. He sees no harm in a few broken promises, broken hearts, or some out and out lies. It solved his problem, did it not? If you have any questions about his recent erratic behavior, "cherchez les femmes." He will have a new one up his sleeve. He's very bright and is supposed to be a lot of fun. I, however, have seen a lot of depression in these charts. It is based on that (sorry to nag about this) old Gemini Moon who always wants something else. A lot of romances, a lot of marriages here. Do you really want to be one of the girls? He isn't all that capable of real love and devotion, and yes, he will use you. He is his most kind, by the way, as he is about to exit; and pretty nasty prior to that in his decision making days. You have to catch him on the good days for the both of you to have fun. Once he is in a slump, he is there to stay. Underneath it all he is a romantic at heart; that is why he is still searching. Too impossible to live with for long stretches, you will likely tire of him and vice versa. Look out. Leo, Sagittarius, Gemini girls, and often Scorpio girls get to be some of his ex-wives.

His illumination: Multi-talented.

His dark side: Broken promises.

GEMINI-CAPRICORN

Sorry, but the Capricorn Moon is cold. They crave money, status, and all the finer things in life. The Gemini Sun is happy and popular, so this one will often confuse you as to what he is after. Never think for one moment, even with his mood swings, that he does not know what he wants. He does. He will use you, or anyone else he has to get what he wants. He is usually very successful in business and shrewd in his business ventures, as well as his personal ventures. Naturally, he may be a schemer at work. He will not get carried away with you. He will analyze you and decide, in the most calculating manner, how you could fit into his plans for advancement. How can you further his ambitions? He will have his own standards, and you had better live up to them. His purpose and ambition will be hard to imagine underneath that friendly and most pleasant manner. Trust me, it is there. As long as you never jeopardize his status, can further his aims, meet his standards of practicability, dependability and devotion, you will have won him over. A flashy dresser, an airhead, a heavy drinker, will simply never get to first base. The rules are strict here. He's usually attractive, lean, agile, with great bone structure, and an aura of dash and flash, that is unusually appealing. When he has chosen his wife, he will expect, on top of everything else, for her to be able to stand on her own two feet, because he won't want to hang out at home much, leave alone dote on the children. He would prefer a good company party, or better yet, closing some extra business deals long after other offices have shut down. He may also bring you a bit of the old mother-in-law problems, because he'll be very close to her. You must accept this, too. Boy, you are thinking to yourself, this sure doesn't sound like him. Well then, you don't know him very well yet. You just wait. A Capricorn or Virgo, or a bright little Aquarius is the best bet for this one.

His illumination: Steadfast in aims.

His dark side: Cold streak.

GEMINI-AQUARIUS

See him? He's really the life of the party. People love him, and vice versa. He can argue and debate and make the other fellow glad he shared his thoughts. He has a great wit and charm, and his laugh is delightful. His ever changing philosophy is enchanting. You will have to trip over both men and other women to get near him. He's often the subject of adoration at work, except for his lack of punctuality. If you dress romantically, frilly and with imagination (would your looking positively ethereal be too much to ask?) he will notice you; he will pursue you; he will wine and dine you. He will forget his business appointments for you, as he doesn't get too involved in business anyway. He will charm you, and soon you are in love. So is he. Sounds simple, huh? It is not. He loves everyone. He wants romance, not commitments, which is fine for some of us. He is not at all conventional as the fellow before him with the Capricorn Moon was. You'll probably do your fair share of tossing and turning nights trying to figure him out. He is a mental sign and thinks in other terms and realms than you or I might. He was probably a whiz kid in school, and never bothered to crack open a book. The universe just hands this knowledge to him. He will further confuse you because he will not always bother to put all his intellect to full use. He is an airy sort of person, and really does not have his feet on the ground. If the $1,500 suit and a bulging portfolio turns you off, chances are you will love this one. He will be making some drastic changes during the next few years, so don't get static on him, and set your hopes on a white picket fence. Home life isn't usually all that stable for him. Libras will fascinate him, an Aquarius could lead him to the altar, and anyone with a Gemini Moon can relate to his innermost thoughts. Some of these thoughts he hasn't quite figured out for himself yet. A little mind reading ability here couldn't hurt your chances. A strong Leo can take this one in tow.

His illumination: Mr. Popularity.

His dark side: Doesn't know where Wall Street is.

GEMINI-PISCES

You've got your hands full here. He is ruled by two dual signs and a lot of imagination, with a sixth or seventh sense. While this man is kind, he is remote, easily hurt and usually in some state of crisis or turmoil. He'll take you dancing or to nice theaters, and yet seem a little inaccessible. He will also fall in love at first sight. You may not know that though as there is more reserve than usual here for a Gemini; he is more introspective, and less able to bounce back than most men. His hands move and wave as he talks, his feet are tender, his mind fluid. He says first one thing and then another. His goals fluctuate. He will nearly drive his office staff nuts. He is fickle. He daydreams. He often finds attachments most appealing when they are the worst for him, like a woman who has another date in twenty minutes. If that is you, don't contribute to his downfall. Guide him, don't cater to him. Comfort him, don't smother him. Let him dream his dreams, but don't get caught up in them. He's looking for a wife he can idolize. He'll love gadgets, and want to invent a few. The world of television, or illusion, or electronics, will fascinate him. He will be another child with his children. In fact, you will have to probably accompany him on his jaunts to wherever he can satisfy his curiosity for the technological age. A pretty harmless habit, wouldn't you say? If he doesn't find some good constructive outlets for his nervous energy and imagination, you will find yourself picking him up from all night parties where he over indulged (again) in the liquid bubbly. He will no doubt have a face that you want to study as his expressions change like liquid mercury. In fact, I think that liquid mercury runs through his veins, pumping intrigue, mystery, and sex appeal. You will have to have some mystery on your own in turn to attract this one. Best chances are with a Pisces or Virgo girl. Most Earth signs won't even bother with this man. Cancer and Scorpio girls might be the soul mate of which his dreams are made.

His illumination: Seventh sense.

His dark side: Needs day to day guidance.

Cancer

June 22–July 23

CANCER-ARIES

Cancers usually aren't given credit for their money making abilities often enough. They do a fine job financially. If you read about the Cancer men, you often get the impression that he likes to sit home and wait for his next meal to be served, while brooding and being crabby. Erase all that and start all over with this: Here is a man who adds daring to intuition and receptivity. He pursues activity, loves a good social life, has a series of hot flashes of temper, and then forgets and goes on to happier things: Things like sports, adventure, following the stock market, collecting, accumulating, going to every social event. In fact, you could find him at one of the small gathering of his friends in the center of the action. He'll have definite ideas and goals and you will know him right off. He won't be shy, or wishy washy, and thinks of himself as quite a lover. Women are usually very attracted to him. He'll have a nice round sort of face with an expression of a decided sense of purpose. He's also got a lot of common sense and a whole list of positive traits. He's a soft touch for anyone with a problem, and often acts in haste to try and resolve it for them. His co-workers love him for this. His little flaws are his instant reaction to things. His jumping to conclusions, his black and white attitude about right and wrong are his most annoying traits. The fact that he is attached to his mother's apron strings is an unpleasant truth. (Hey! No one is perfect!) He'll take his time about getting married, but he has every intention of being a good, solid, devoted husband and father. If, however, the girl of his dreams does not live up to his expectations, he'll be tempted to look elsewhere. Be outgoing, warm, loving, and have fire in your veins. Never tease him, he's got a sensitive side. Pisces, Scorpio and Aries girls stand the best chance of a finish is this race. And believe me, he travels in some pretty fast circles.

His illumination: Solid husband material.

His dark side: Jumps to conclusions.

CANCER-TAURUS

He's pure charm. This hunk is sweet, thoughtful, and basically honest. If, however, there's something he can get from you, or talk you out of, he'll have no qualms about doing so. Sometimes, if he feels that life has given him a bad deal and he's a little short of luxuries which are essential to him, he'll become something of a miser. And then he can get really selfish. Otherwise, he'll shower you with love, admiration and gifts. He's sentimental. He'll match the flowers on the front of your mushy card, to the flowers from the florist. When he loves you, there's not much he won't do to make you happy. If you've lost favor with him, or he has settled down you can brace yourself for some pretty icy indifference. You'll even wonder if his original love and affection was for real. Usually it was the genuine article, but occasionally, it will have been an act to please you or those around you, or to gain some sort of favor. He'll be handsome, very masculine looking and possess a strong sturdy physique. He won't brag about his conquests, he's too gentle for that. But you can be sure he could attract just about anyone that he wanted. It usually takes him a bit longer than his male friends to settle down. A home life is important to him only after he has one. He'll want children to adore, a wife to keep the fires burning, and some property, stocks and bonds to fall back on. Sounds pretty wonderful, huh? Well, it is. Except for his nasty days when he'll be feeling crabby and can act like an old man. It would probably be a good time for you to get out of the house to visit friends, and let him aggravate his co-workers on these days. Sexually, he'll want your heart and soul, and a lot of earthy imagination thrown in. The Scorpio, Pisces, or Taurus girls are the best bets. A Taurus or Capricorn Moon will be the perfect match.

His illumination: Usually a hunk.

His dark side: Icy indifference.

CANCER-GEMINI

He probably has had his share of misfortunes, like a troubled child-hood, love affairs gone wrong due to poor timing, people who have taken advantage of him, misunderstood emotions, and so on. These guys all have a tale of woe underneath their air of self assurance. Mess with him, though, and he can be a foe forever. His eyes will get watery as he plots it all, but he will have a plan for revenge. Even when he knows that it was not your fault, but his, as it often is. You see, he misinterprets things. His messages get scrambled. His impressions are not at all reliable. He will still blame you. Except for these situations, he will be pretty adaptable, sensitive, and pleasant to be around. He will be a mass of contradictions (his Moon, you know) and over stimulated emotions. I have noticed that a lot of strong Cancer influences are easily taken in in the romance department and get hurt. They have a lot of rough times until around 35 when they seem to wise up and get a grip on reality. That is where you hope to come in (why enter before his crisis are over, for the most part?). He wants money but is not fond of planning to make it. Maybe you could help. He needs lots of affection and a warm, cozy type of woman to snap him out of his low moods. These moods occur often. He is basically a nice guy, husband, father, and co-worker who needs a lot of attention and support. Here is your chance to be Wendy. The Gemini Moon will attract a lot of women, because it is so intellectually versatile. This guy can talk about anything, and conversation is where he is attracted first. A bright, almost studious girl from the signs of Gemini, Virgo, or Aquarius can stand the best chance. An Aquarian Sun and Cancer Moon would do just fine for this attractive Peter Pan and all his wants and needs.

His illumination: Great conversationalist.

His dark side: He gets even.

CANCER-CANCER

I hope you don't have a lot of other interests, because this man is a full time job. And, if you have a strong background in psychology or inherent nurturing instincts, then perhaps you can deal with the ultra-sensitive and moody double Cancer. He's got a lot of wonderful qualities if you are able to pry him out of his shell and relate to you. Qualities, like being unusually successful in business, being a caring, loving, romantic, and sweet gentle man, husband, and father. He can't stand ugliness or too much reality. He will need to be protected from this. Like the crab, he will withdraw into his shell if things aren't going just right. He wants someone like, well, like Melanie in *Gone with the Wind*. He needs a good cook and a motherly sort. Many men with strong Cancer in their chart will marry an older woman. They don't know quite how to handle the inconsistencies of youth, because they are rather inflexible. The woman of this man's dreams must be very feminine. Lots of lacy, fluttery clothes will bring out the romantic in him. He won't demand that you are model slim, or cover pretty; but he will demand that you are delicate, always there for him, and cuddly. He can be the victim of illusions away from the work force, so make your home a safe harbor. Where to meet this one? Probably through his mother or sister. Or through a real estate venture. He excels in real estate or stock speculations, and is a nurturing, honest co-worker. He will be active in making your home a castle. You don't have to worry that he'll be at the top of the ski slopes, or out hunting when you need him. He will be there for you. In fact, once he has found the girl, he never even wants to hear about that ugly word, divorce. Best bets for this one, obviously another Cancer, a gentle version of a Capricorn, a sweet little Pisces, or an evolved Scorpio. Coarse or earthy types need not apply.

His illumination: Doesn't think IRA's are for old bald men.

His dark side: Ultra sensitive.

CANCER-LEO

The receptive Cancer, who feels every little thing so deeply, and the daring, social climbing Leo Moon combine to make a delightful combination. This one craves attention. He wants to be reassured that he is wonderful (not in the boastful way of the Aries). He is, simply put, very loving and caring for his family. If you are in his circle of loves, you will be amazed at how loyal and attentive this man can be. He'll hold your hand and take long walks with you for important talks. Because he's romantic, he can put drama back into your life. He will want the girl of his dreams to have exceptional social grace and poise. He wants a girl who can handle authority. If you are in the dramatic, artsy fields, instant attraction is likely. He will not only understand your overindulgence on clothing and jewelry, but in all probability encourage it. You will be his showpiece. Never be caught dead with curlers in your hair (yes, hot rollers count) or anything less than a knockout outfit on. Generous, almost to a fault, he will not understand any pettiness in his sweetheart. No black hearted girls for him. Sexually, he can be narcissistic, but even that he does well. This narcissistic streak can be played out with videos and mirrors. He will aspire to many things, but his aspirations are quite stable, and while a terrible flirt (he needs constant reassurance of his charm), once he finds someone queenly enough for him he is actually quite devoted. He needs to be pampered and waited on. But he'll be so appreciative, how can you resist? He will be brilliant in his field, and his co-workers will be awed. Sagittarius, Leo or Aries Moon girls do best with this one. Scorpios are great sexually, but this one needs the more gentle sorts of sexual expression on a regular basis.

His illumination: One of the sweetest.

His dark side: Fixation with mirrors.

CANCER-VIRGO

You've probably already met this man. He is the one you asked to babysit your house and water your plants last vacation. And didn't he do a good job? Made you feel a little guilty he was so competent. You remember him, the nice guy . . . conventional, unassuming, unpretentious, and pleasant. You should have looked closer. This one lacks the instant chemistry that drives most women mad, but is he ever a catch! Better go back and take a look again. He'll probably be working late at the office, and though he is much too modest to tell you, he is very successful. He has never been in the unemployment line. And, as his partner, neither will you. He is very practical and efficient. He comes across as Steady Eddy. He isn't really all that predictable though, so watch it. He can cook for large crowds, nurture dying animals back to health, bring out the best in children, decorate the office and get wild and crazy at parties. He's probably got a ton of platonic relationships and plays big brother to some pretty glamorous sorts. The one who will catch his eye is very intelligent and romantic. He needs to be awakened. And when he is awakened, he gets pretty nearly kinky. He'll surprise you. If you break a vow or commitment, you can kiss this one goodbye. He really can't handle it. He will always let his head rule his heart. He doesn't want to make many mistakes, and if you are one, he can get you out of his life early in the game. He would be most attracted to a Virgo girl, a Pisces (who could help him with his bouts of hypochondria) or a steady, sensuous Taurus girl. Whatever you are, have a big heart. To match his. It's only fair.

His illumination: All around good catch.

His dark side: Holds grudges.

CANCER-LIBRA

Here is a man of contradictions. He comes across strong and independent. A go-getter. He usually initiates the parties, or enterprises; but all the while he is looking for someone he can rely on to do it for him. He will get his way, no doubt about it. But he will make you believe that it was what you wanted. Yes, he is manipulative. We all are to some degree, but this is the combination of a real pro. Watch your step. The Libra Moon is very charming, persuasive, and irresistible. And, you could be the one dominated. Tyranny of the weak, according to F. Scott Fitzgerald. Secretly he worries and frets a lot. He may even bite his nails, or worse, yours. He can be the most generous or arrogant of co-workers because he is a near perfectionist. He may look like any other participant at any social gathering, amiable, well-dressed, pleasant; but, in reality, he is an observer. He is sitting back and analyzing everyone. If he observes you as a sociable, sensitive, intelligent person, he will ask you out. You will be one of the many girls he will approach. He is a womanizer, and he takes his time in choosing a more singular relationship. If you must pursue this one, take it easy. Be subtle. His world is fragile, in that he doesn't like rash, impulsive actions. He spends a lot of time in his head. He turns out best with proper career direction; like counseling, psychology, or writing. Personnel work, where he has to hire and fire, can make him physically sick. He can, like his female counterpart, make some sudden turns in life. Like coming home and saying that he has found someone else. He will still visit the children, though. Best to catch him after he turns 30-35. Librans, Sagittarius or Capricorn girls fare best. Having a Libra or Taurus Moon is a definite plus.

His illumination: Gets his way!

His dark side: Gets his way!

CANCER-SCORPIO

Here is a boiling pot of emotion. This man is explosive in temperament and he knows the razor's edge of love and hate. You will never have to wonder what he thinks about you. His emotions are very much on the surface. I hate to say it, but he can get real nasty, at home and at work. The Scorpio Moon is prone to some pretty intense anger. If he thinks that his lady fair has crossed him, he is pretty volatile. Unfortunately, if you have already seen him, you won't listen to a word of warning. He is fascinating, magnetic (as is the Scorpio-Cancer configuration), and irresistible to most women. He is fully aware of his appeal to women and uses it to his advantage. He may come on like a school boy, bearing gifts and flowers. It isn't to win your heart, it is to prepare you for the stormy days ahead when his behavior will be nothing short of rotten. If you really can't control yourself and must get involved, then at least act like you are not totally gone, yet. Let him pursue you, or you lose already. If you should get really involved, you are in for a life of extremes. You will have crisis in temperament, in lifestyle, in finances, and adventures. You yourself must have an impetuous side to survive this relationship. There will most probably not be nice get togethers with your family, your life with him may be too chaotic. The wrong word and he explodes with his inlaws. If you crave stability, look elsewhere, especially if you want your children to have good roots. If it is lust, passion and fire and ice you want, hope that you are a steamy little Scorpio, all feminine and frilly with a deep, throaty voice. Or at least a Scorpio Moon. An Aries can handle this man. A Libra may even get him to behave a tad. A Capricorn (who he is very much attracted to) will simply go over the edge eventually.

His illumination: Bears gifts.

His dark side: Volatile.

CANCER-SAGITTARIUS

This man needs to find his security blanket. He looks for it in another person. He doesn't want to get used to you and then have you change on him. No fad styles, no moving the furniture around; things like that. He is pleasant and easygoing. Not prone to volatile episodes, or temperamental outbursts, he is easy to mix and mingle with. He will have high expectations and will expect some ambition and fire from you. People who haven't discovered themselves yet will get a sympathetic ear and lots of advice and counseling from him; but he falls in love with a girl who can pull herself together, the girl who is into an honest relationship. Nothing less will do. And, don't try to con him. It won't work. Perceptive, he can see through any facade. He may not confess to that ability, but he has it. Deceit in any form disappoints him and turns him off. He is exceedingly honest with friends and co-workers. You will find him charming, but not really very interested, if you hurt him with dishonesty. He wants things. The Sagittarius Moon always does. They aspire to great heights. They dream of leaving the world a better place, of having made some sort of mark on the world, and of being visibly successful, as in making money, obtaining the PhD, or arriving at a particular station in life. You, too, must possess those qualities. His religious beliefs may be unorthodox. But he is committed to them. He is active. He may move about often, or change jobs quite a bit. He is an outdoorsman, and a bit of a wanderer (unusual for the Cancer). He can be very blunt, and if you're thick-skinned or shallow, don't even consider this one. Otherwise he can be considered good husband material. Best bet for romance that lasts is a Sagittarian (perfect), or a Leo. A Capricorn with wanderlust in her chart would also be a good bet.

His illumination: Aspires to great things.

His dark side: Frequent job changes.

CANCER-CAPRICORN

The full Moon person often looks to another to solve his problems, or to provide him with the answers for his life. While the Cancer-Capricorn personality is contradictory, there are basic needs here to be met that are quite simple to understand. The need to acquire, to nurture (or be nurtured) the desire for a strong sense of family, and to a secure, not too off-the-wall life. This is the combination of a strong administrator, organizer and executive, and a capable, energetic co-worker. He does not dream vague dreams. He builds from his dreams. Surprisingly, for all his need for the practical and stable in his life, he needs to be creative. Maybe even invent something. There are a few disappointments in love along the way, and some emotional turmoil before he settles into the right relationship. But, he wants to settle, and like his other dreams, this too will come true. He may appear on the surface to be rather cold, or aloof. Don't let this fool you. He is very deep and romantic, and, yes, sexy, once he lets go. He is earthy, in fact. The sensitive nature, the touch of aloofness, the gentle manner of this man, all add up to someone women generally find a favorite. His charm can invade even the steeliest of hearts. His personal and private success generally comes late in life; so if this is the one for you, you need to be prepared to wait. His timing is uncanny, trust him. A very ladylike, mannered, well-bred lady with the ability to run a home or office is just right for him. Don't insult his family, pick your teeth in public, or wear mini-skirts (even when in fashion) and you stand a good chance of attracting his attention. Plan on children, he'll adore them. A Capricorn understands his emotional needs, a Scorpio, his passions, a Pisces, his dreams. Aries scare the wits out of him. And, God bless her, a Leo is much too dramatic and fashionable for him.

His illumination: Capable.

His dark side: Victim of the full Moon.

CANCER-AQUARIUS

Two words describe him best: intuitive and imaginative. An educator, social worker, fund raiser, a member of various organizations, this charming little man will capture your attention. His nice Moon face, and electric blue eyes keep the girls intrigued. He probably bought this, and many similar books, for you. Astrology fascinates him. He is one of the few men who will admit to it. Looking into the future does not scare him in the least. He lives in the future. Even the most timid of the Cancer types (and they can be quite timid) want to venture out into the world with the eccentric Aquarian Moon. What he looks for in a woman is devotion (not necessarily to match his own) individuality, intelligence, and a wonderful sense of humor. This man needs to laugh. He needs to talk. You won't mind, because he can talk for hours about things, ideas, theories, and other people. He can listen just as well as talk. He will not be an egomaniac, or a macho man. An outer space man, maybe, but none of the usual manly things. He can fix your VCR in the dark. Your computer will be on a first name basis with him. He will love your friends, and miracle of all, enjoy your best friend. Other values are more important to him than money, and while he may be a workaholic, it will be to create, not to acquire. Your life can be erratic from time to time. Mundanity will not entice him. But, you should never find him boring. He will help you with the housework, and surprise you by being your most trustworthy and faithful friend. I hope he finds his Aquarian, or Gemini. A Libra can mold him for a few years. Virgos put him to sleep. And Tauruses are just too attached to earthly things for him to fully appreciate.

His illumination: Visionary.

His dark side: Needs to learn to laugh.

CANCER-PISCES

Is he in time management, speculation, or some sort of an efficiency expert? Does he bewilder his staff? Is he pleasant, side stepping on all issues, and has he been reading your mind? Well, you can be pretty sure this one is a crabby fish. His Moon in a dual sign, he may have more than one profession, and both water combinations make him practically a genius at guessing the market, or everyone's real motives. He probably knows more about you than you'd care to know. He has an excellent insight into people. On the other hand, he will be quite secretive about his feelings and emotions. You won't know where he stands on much of anything. He plans to keep it that way, so don't push. Don't pry. He probably has a few deep, dark secrets and it's for both your best interests to stay clear of discovery. This Moon's murky waters can lead him into some pretty deep pits of over-indulgence in food, drink, and yes, love affairs. He has to have fantasy and one logical way to accomplish this is to go from lover to lover. Unless, of course, you are very good at spinning a few fantasies in the bedroom. Stay pretty clear of reality around him. Don't tell him the washer broke. Instead, call a repairman and hide the bill. Get the chicken soup ready when he has his bout with the blues, because the world can't understand him (this is what he wants, though). The truth is hard for him to come by occasionally, so try not to be gullible. Otherwise, you won't survive it as well as he'd hope you would. Oddly enough, for all his insight and understanding, he won't lavish it on you or his children. He needs tender loving care. He doesn't necessarily give it. Pisces, and Scorpio are wonderful for him. A Virgo nurse is excellent. An inquisitive Aries will simply drive him to drink.

His illumination: Great judge of character.

His dark side: A few dark secrets.

Leo

July 23–August 23

LEO-ARIES

He talks fast, walks fast and thinks fast. He is impulsive, rash, daring, exciting, and he reacts to everything with a fierce intensity. He is outdoorsy, hyperactive, a real handful. Short on sentiment and long on ego, he needs your constant assurance that you and everyone else likes him. His need for approval is just about the strongest of any in the male Zodiac, but don't fawn over him. Sigh in appreciation every now and then, and then waltz off with someone else. You need to be a fiery sort yourself. Independent, passionate and even sassy. He's not interested in lesser stuff. He's a loyal friend, once you get his attention and respect. He will fight to the finish to defend your honor or his as a husband and father. He picks up quite a few enemies along the way in life. He does have a sharp tongue, and a nasty, nasty temper. He is a real hot head, to be honest. Fearless, he reminds me of a little boy unaware of the danger as he climbs to the top of everything from mountains, to social status, to career goals. That he might make a few bitter enemies in his work environment does not concern him one bit. It should. The Aries Moon is not usually that appealing to most people, especially sensitive folks who can't handle blunt individuals or who take everything personally. For sheer vitality and adventure, this combination can't be beat. If you are trying to attract his attention, best to ignore him. Not freeze him out, but reek of the word challenge. He needs it. His romantic dream is to take all the fire out of the girl of his dreams. Let that remain his fantasy. Turn docile and he walks. He needs a Sagittarian, Leo or Aries girl. A spirited Gemini can also captivate him.

His illumination: Pure excitement.

His dark side: Hot head.

LEO-TAURUS

Think elegance, luxury, security, acquisition, and beauty. This is what this man is really looking for, and the girl who can provide it in her packaging fares the best in capturing this good husband and father material. He will be there for his friends, and even yours. Call him late at night and bear your soul. He'll listen. What's more, he'll care about your problems. He will even try to help. He will not be afraid to loan you a few bucks, or let you live at his place for awhile 'til you pull yourself together. But don't ask to borrow one thing. Like a lot of earth people, the Taurus Moon begs to hold on to his things. Material possessions are like one big giant security blanket for him. It shows tangible proof that he is accomplishing something, and that his dreams of material comfort are coming true. He wants to amount to something not only for himself but to validate his importance to others, especially his co-workers. He'll teach the Joneses they need to keep up. He will have the extra toothbrush for overnight guests. He is not only considerate, he is practical. God forbid, you would use his toothbrush, however! Food is important too. He will notice what you put on the table. Meat and potato stuff. And, he'll notice how you look. He is attracted to beauty. A few extra pounds on your frame won't deter him. He won't care what your background is, as long as you have some good common sense. The disheveled, sexy, giggly sort is not for him. He wants substance. He is a dominant sort of man, and that includes in the bedroom, where he is apt to have gold framed mirrors all over the place. He is very physical, and sensual. He will leave you weak. Which is exactly what he wants. A Taurus, a Capricorn, another Leo does well with this one. Pisces protect yourself, stay away.

His illumination: Good listener.

His dark side: Food on his tie.

LEO-GEMINI

This guy has gotta be a salesman. He is in, perhaps, radio sales. Whatever his profession, he uses words to trade. I don't know for sure, but I bet he talks in his sleep. Quick-witted, restless, intelligent, light hearted—these men are ever so enchanting. You can usually find them in some sort of a class or another. The Moon position creates a perpetual student. While physically active, and sports minded, he finds a good book fascinating, too. He won't read a book, though, unless he is learning something or doing it for the children. He has friends all over the place, and of every type. He hates schedules and is on them only for appointments he considers important. The restless nature of the Moon demands variety in life: job changes, residence changes, and often changes in the woman in his life. It takes a bit of a whirlwind to keep up with him, at any rate. Leo wants a family life, Gemini doesn't, so there will always be some conflict over his domestic needs. Maybe just a nice place and a wife he can drop in on from time to time. He's going to be hard to figure because he is restless and honestly isn't sure what he wants. Maybe, if you don't try to tie him down, you can keep him around. There is a brief, curious fascination with almost every woman he meets. The longer infatuations come with someone he can relate to, the lifelong infatuations are a rare combination of a number of things like the ability to let him play, be a child, to express his ego, to flirt, for you to be intelligent, and beautiful (Leo knows beauty). This is the sort of stuff that calls for superwoman. I really can't say who does the very best with this one. Perhaps an Aquarian, for sure a Gemini, or a girl with a nice childlike Leo Moon. Don't enable him to be a child. Be one with him.

His illumination: Quick-wit.

His dark side: Child-like.

LEO-CANCER

The Sun is the ruler of Leo, and the Moon is the ruler of Cancer. Here we find the planets in their dignity, or simply put, where they belong. Dignity is a word that describes this man well. He is a perfect gentleman, and charmer. He has a soft way of presenting himself that commands everyone's attention. He can do exceptionally well in the boardroom, or the bedroom. He can be a real heartbreaker, and whose gets broken the most often? Mr. Leo-Cancer. Part of the reason, is that he sometimes slips on his code of ethics (he couldn't resist her advances), or inadvertently lets someone down. When he settles down, he wants to provide the best and most lavish for his wife and family. If he fails to be able to do so (and this usually won't happen) he is devastated. Think of him as a young, idealistic Gregory Peck type in *To Kill A Mockingbird*. He is genuine, sincere, and loyal, whether at work or at home. Imagine how he would hate to not be the best friend, or best lover that you have ever known. Handle him with care, as he is sensitive, and oh, so adorable. Okay, so you want to know his flaw. Well, he does have a quick and nasty temper. He is prone to depression when he gets emotionally hurt. Often, this manifests in backaches and stomachaches. He receives impressions much like a mold. A lot of his happiness depends on you. He needs to be babied, but he'll be worth it. He will love your children as much as his. He will smile as he helps you with the household or cooking chores. Just keep in mind, he is still the King as he helps you wash the dishes. Don't demand anything, and he will do his best to give you everything. He is a sucker for pretty girls; dainty and curvy, feminine and fragile. A Cancer Sun and Leo Moon is, of course, perfect. A Sagittarian or Pisces is a good match also.

His illumination: Gentleman.

His dark side: Needs to be babied.

LEO-LEO

This man must have the center stage at all times. That includes the center of the bed. Sharing is not a thing they come by easily—ego is. Remember this as he goes about the business of breaking your heart. He has a one track mind—his goals. Should you become one of his desires, even if for only a little while, he will not rest until he has you body and soul. There are no gray areas to this man. It is black or white and that is that. He will go to any lengths to accomplish what he wants. He can be ruthless at work. He is driven to achieve and to acquire. He wants the very best and most that life has to offer. He has to leave his mark on the world in everything that he touches. He wants his children to excel too. Magnetic and commanding, he will not be found in a low rent section, nor will he pick you up in one, for very long. He may try to elevate you, educate you, and enslave you. If he cannot (and that would be rare) he will move on to someone else and pity you for the error of your ways. If you should resist his domination, and damage his ego in the process, better stay clear of him. He will never, ever forgive you. His boss usually favors him, and an ambitious wife would be a tremendous asset. Ambitious for him, naturally. Aquarian women sometimes make this mistake with him, and I can't think of anything scarier than a Scorpio with this man. A Capricorn can help him climb to the top of the ladder, which is the only place either of them want to be. He can teach a Pisces new meaning for pain. An Aries can teach him a few tricks about domination, and a Sagittarius can take it all in stride. He must find the one, to be the most dazzling creature under the Sun. And that is where he will want her to stay.

His illumination: Attracts power and favor.

His dark side: Wants to enslave.

LEO-VIRGO

Here is a complex fellow. Uninhibited one minute and guilt ridden the next. Spontaneous and fun . . . critical and analyzing. You don't even want to hear about how long he can take to make some decisions, and how precise he wants everything to be. That, unfortunately, includes you. He can pick you apart and wonder what in the world you are pouting about. He probably will spend long hours telling you his every little worry. Worries, like the germs on the doorknob, why his back is really aching, and if he will get that next promotion. The Moon takes about two and one half days to move from one sign to the next, but oh, what a difference it makes here. His is so very different from the Leos with Leo or Libra Moons. He can be the most stubborn man, who is positive of only one thing: that he is always right. You had better be fastidious (disorder drives him crazy), punctual (your being late is nearly a sin), and organized. Routines are vital. Your children will also have to meet high standards. He will no doubt be easy to spot, should you want to meet him. Perfectly groomed, preening discreetly, worry lines in place, sipping a Perrier (he has a queasy stomach tonight ... do you think it could be the flu? And with all his appointments next week, well, you can guess the rest). He will need your constant flattery and attention. He will demand that your hairbrush never ends up in the drawer with his. Needless to say, he often has trouble finding just the right girl, or landing just the right job. He lacks the ability to be a really good administrator, so you Capricorns could handle him, but probably won't because of that flaw. A Virgo woman would be heaven. You could both get crazy over a dust ball. An Aries can often adapt. A Gemini could drive him over the edge.

His illumination: High standards.

His dark side: Compulsive.

LEO-LIBRA

Sweet. This one is lovely. And so handsome you could faint. He is the hero of the romantic novel come to life. You will have to stand in line for this man. Of all the Leos he has the least vanity (except maybe the Cancer Moon), and that in itself is enchanting. He's also the least aggressive of the Leos. He is, in fact, aloof and often tends to be a loner. Especially if born from 1945 to 1952. He knows that everyone is besotted with his charms, he is fully aware that he is unusually good looking, but he does have other interests. You'd better also. He is not superficial. He is really quite complex and is trying very hard to develop some inner qualities, and values. He looks for the finest and most beautiful in everything and everyone, including his wife and children. He absolutely must have harmony in everything, especially his work and home environment. He will feel ill with discordant surroundings. He spends a lot of time just thinking of grand ideas and life on the cosmic scale. He is not altogether practical. Leo is lavish and loves to spend money. This guy has that quality plus he isn't all that practical. In business, however, he can paradoxically handle someone else's finances fabulously. Or he can organize complex plans for others and forget to buy food for his own party. This wouldn't matter as he is such a great host, hardly anyone would notice. You will have to be careful not to be stampeded in your search for this one. Count on one thing, he will be hard to pin down. He knows he is hot property. Libras stand the best chance. Aquarians could run a close race. An Aries can offer an irresistible force.

His illumination: Strong inner qualities.

His dark side: Unharmonious surroundings make him ill.

LEO-SCORPIO

I didn't even want the Leo and Scorpio to meet, let alone inhabit the same body. Talk about volatile. This man is on low boiling all the time. And there is something so compelling about him, that hardly anyone can resist the magnetism of his presence. Like a double Scorpio, he can really get bogged down in too much sex. He is so excessive, in fact, that it can become a top priority in his life. A string of affairs can lead to a string of broken marriages, especially for those men who were born around noon. Oftentimes, there is a tendency to an almost ruthless animal nature. If these intense energies are channeled properly through creative endeavors, he can be very successful. Maybe he needs a little help from you to work things out in the bedroom. Create a lot of fantasies. Be every girl and a few men, too. This guy can be real kinky. Once you get over his sexuality, you will find a man set on the best life has to offer. You will also have a man that once he settles down, is so protective and possessive of you, you can hardly imagine his more untamed days. He will actually learn to lean on you in a mutually supportive atmosphere. No one could be more courageous in life's battles with you than he. He is a pleasant co-worker, and would be a wonderful policeman, or surgeon, or something along these lines. If not, he may try to police you, or cut you to ribbons verbally. He needs help to find himself, and then turn all his negatives into positives. Until then, you might want to wait out his growth period. The Scorpio Moon is always the most difficult for any spouse or child to deal with. When things don't work out, he'll injure the other person's emotions. Pisces, Aries, Sagittarius, and yes, another Scorpio, are best.

His illumination: Courageous.

His dark side: "Me Tarzan, you Jane."

LEO-SAGITTARIUS

The personal magnetism of this double Fire sign is bright and exciting. This is one of the more aspiring configurations of the Zodiac. This man wants it all, and, chances are, if he can work on one thing at a time, he will have it all. Usually, though, there is a scattering of energies. Like little brush fires all over the place, instead of one big blaze. He is always looking for another opportunity, another fortune, another lively companion. Attracted to a wide range of interests, whether sporting or intellectual, this man can be found shining brightly just about anywhere. He is basically happy and outgoing in nature and has a wide variety of friends, especially from work. He will usually be found clowning around (this combination is a perpetual child by nature) and smiling. Hardly anyone can resist this man. His madcap sense of humor is never at the expense of anyone else. He is usually very, very bright. He would be a good politician because he is naturally charismatic and persuasive. He often doesn't get into that line of work because the goals are too long in coming. However, he tires of things rather quickly, whether in business or in love. He will paradoxically dog an idea or project to death in order to conquer or win. Once the project has been obtained, he loses interest. That includes you, no matter how enticing you are, and how independent. If you were to allow him total freedom (a Sagittarius Moon must always have this) he may stick around awhile longer . . . he does have aspirations of roots and family. But for all his razzle dazzle, that is a bitter pill for most women to swallow. Aries, Leo, Sagittarius girls give him the best chase, he chews up Cancer, infuriates Scorpio, and Gemini is about as non-committal as he is.

His illumination: Varied interests.

His dark side: Scatters energies.

LEO-CAPRICORN

This is a steamroller combination. Remember the song, "I'm a steamroller, baby, I'm gonna roll all over you"? Well, this man means it. Warnings fair, only the best, and most capable need to even consider a match with this one. He is always working on his own P.R. (very subtly, though), and since you are part of the package, you had better fill the bill. He must be able to count on you to never embarrass him publicly. You will have to walk that careful line of being glittering but not gaudy, sweet but not insipid, loving but not clinging. You'd better be pretty tailor made to his public image. You can have a number of faults, as long as they are not public. Only you will get to know the fearful interior of this man. He hides his insecurities well, and you will be called upon to encourage him in his nearly impossible goals. Nearly impossible, I say, because these fellows can pull off just about anything. That is part of their immense charm. This position often creates an immediate love-hate relationship with people (more so with the female with this combination). People tend to react instantly to his purpose and drive, his excessive ambition and his total capabilities. Some people can handle the jealousy over his accomplishments, some cannot. It is that simple. His intense nature extends to his sex life. He is passionate, but not necessarily romantic. He hides his sentiment well, especially from his children whom he finds enchanting. He is forthright, not gushy or sniveling, and he hopes for the same from you. Anything insincere or shallow turns him off. Try to develop his better side, because this is a cold, cold Moon. A Capricorn woman understands, as will an Aries, or Scorpio. Other signs must be prepared to bounce back, and make a speedy recovery.

His illumination: One of the most ambitious.

His dark side: Hidden fears.

LEO-AQUARIUS

Idealistic, romantic and somewhat flighty, this man has a lot of women in his life. He usually pursues ideas, not women, and since women usually have to come to him, you can be sure he has a few tales to tell. This one will kiss and tell, by the way. Traits like loyalty and devotion are often strangers to him. He loves on an abstract basis, to be sure. He is eccentric, inventive and almost (he'll never admit it) poetic. He can envision, rationalize, and philosophize better than almost anyone. His lightning quick change of moods is fun. His unpredictability is exciting, except at work, where it borders on erratic. If you can hang in there and accept him for what he is, he is a perfect date. He is a Full Moon baby with all the implications, but he has more of a chance of projecting his insecurities into creative channels, and to utilize his talents for public affairs or dramatics more than other Full Moonies. He's friendly and will love your parties, your friends, and your dreams. He won't, however, get all wrapped up in you. Nor will he be possessive. His relationships are platonic even in the height of passion. He has a fondness for children and can play with them on their level. He does well with the raising of children when he does not have to carry the entire financial load. Too much responsibility makes him bolt. A people watcher, he wants to be fascinated by the complexities of mankind. You will need to offer him a head full of ideas. Maybe your inventions are better than his and your ideas more far out. Appeal to him between the ears. This is his most erogenous zone. He looks for his companionship along the signs of Aquarius, Gemini, Sagittarius, and Leo.

His illumination: Great with children.

His dark side: Kisses and tells.

LEO-PISCES

He's not flashy and glittery, but he'll steal the show, and your heart, regardless. He's a kindly fellow, found either wandering around hospitals, or fund-raising for one. He's a sporting man, found relaxing around a large body of water. He's an elegant man, found at the best social events, looking cool and casual, and irresistible. He's usually quite handsome, and has a quiet sex appeal that will drive you nuts. He's a steady fellow with some pretty fixed ideas that he will believe in with all his heart until he has a change of mind. This change of heart will be with good reason, and everyone will understand. There is nothing not to like about him. He is an idealist, a humanitarian, a soft touch for a sob story and a loan. He is friendly and has a way a reaching out to touch people that melts their hearts. And he has it all together professionally and financially. Perfect? Well, not quite. But you won't care. He is subject to the depressions of the truly sensitive. He is inconsistent in love, and will rather abruptly end a relationship if disillusioned. You will pick up your broken heart and feel sorry that he is taking the loss so badly. For each and every relationship does mean something very special to him. You will regret the heartache you caused him for not being everything that he wanted. Not many men can pull that off. He is generous and will probably give you a spectacular parting gift. He gives away too much of himself really. He tries to be all things to all people, co-workers, lovers, and children. It's hard on a fellow. That's what his Pisces Moon does to him. He'll be worth the experience, especially in bed. He needs you Pisces, and you too, Cancer. Another Leo would be helpful. Even a Sagittarius girl has a good chance with this man.

His illumination: Quiet sex appeal.

His dark side: Fixed ideas.

Virgo

August 23–September 23

VIRGO-ARIES

Virgo lacks originality and Aries lacks attention to details. This combination blends these deficiencies. Both signs tend to be combative and super critical, selfish and cold. You will not have to wonder for long why he has few co-worker friends. He will not be the most popular man you've ever been with. He will pick you apart and notify you of every shortcoming that is in your character, even suspected ones. For those of you who can handle all that, you will get a rare kind of devotion. It won't be the gushy, romantic, head over heels kind of love. It will be a cold, analytical Mr. Spock kind of loyalty. He will take much more than he will give. Yet, in his complexity, he will defend you to the death, if he feels anyone has been unjust with you (except him). He will be the ultimate egomaniac with everyone, but not in a way that demands attention. It will be instead an odd sort of way. He takes everything personally. He can stand anything except the thought that someone does not like or approve of him. His need for approval is second to none. He has a hair trigger temper, and is often moody and uncommunicative. He is intelligent, conscientious, ambitious, energetic, and witty. As a husband and father he is quarrelsome. He wants an honest and decent (squeaky clean) relationship. He wants this relationship with a daring, independent and fiery sort of girl. His sexuality is meticulous and deliberate. Oftentimes Virgos are unusually kinky. Maybe yours will have a spark of originality and put some life into the relationship. You'll need it somewhere, God knows. Best bets for happiness are a Leo with a lot of Virgo planets, an Aries, Virgo and even a Gemini. You sensitive signs better move out fast.

His illumination: Strong sense of loyalty.

His dark side: Excessive need for approval.

VIRGO-TAURUS

Just when you think Virgos don't know how to have a good time, here comes the Taurean influence. Emotionally, he needs comfort, luxury, peace and harmony. This will help him to lighten up and get sensual and romantic. He is enduring, steady, stable and has a nice blend of conservative qualities and yet, is not boring or stifling. This is not a nervous, restless, flighty type of man. His qualities are truly sterling and rock solid. This is a very nice combination of character-istics. His business sense is extraordinary . . . he can envision and at-tend to details. He can live the work ethic and the Golden Rule. A Taurus Moon does very well financially no matter what the early environment. He may notice your flaws, but be gentle enough to mention only your assets. He will not dash off in a romantic whirl with someone else. He understands commitment. He will expect you to do the same. Although a near whiz in business, he is not boastful; although this is an unusually attractive configuration, he does not stand out in a crowd. He moves slowly, cautiously and de-liberately. A moderate man, his only excess is usually lavish sur-roundings and good food. He will excel in the banking or nutrition fields, or anything service related. He won't gamble away your money. Speculation on a few blue chip stocks will be his greatest risk-taking adventure. He will have a wide circle of sensible friends and work associates. He won't quit when the going gets rough. He won't abandon you when you're old and gray. He will do every-thing possible to help you look after the children. He will snort like a bull if you are messy, disorganized and impractical. He will get practically mushy over a well-cooked meal served in candlelight, or a nice warm bubble bath and massage. A Taurus, or Capricorn girl would be great. A Libra woman excellent. A Scorpio would be an exciting little fling.

His illumination: Very top notch.

His dark side: Needs to hang loose.

VIRGO-GEMINI

There he is...the photographer for the television documentary, or the announcer for the radio remote. They like the communication fields. They love talking, writing, reading, and documenting. He's quick, he's reasoning, he's usually precise. He is also interesting, and can talk your ear off. Especially nights when he has one of his frequent bouts with insomnia. He's a very nervous fellow, and so energetic that he wears himself out, literally. He is fun and less morose than some Virgo combinations. He has more health problems than most men, and less tendency to discuss them with you. He is a perpetual student, especially if he was born about 1954. He is often inclined to start a great many projects and not finish a one (a trait that drives his mate fairly nuts). He has a definite green thumb and will actually enjoy puttering around the house. He will be quite handy at home, as a matter of fact. He may even invent a few labor-saving devices along the way. Since he is not especially openly affectionate, you and the children may wonder if he really cares. He does. He just has odd and peculiar ways of showing it. Like making the children study, bringing you vitamins and raw nuts. This display of concern is about the extent of his sentimentality. But he means well. His trying to get you to change is another way of expressing his love and affection for you. This goes for his co-workers as well. He likes you in a constant state of self-improvement. The obvious matches here are the Virgo and Gemini (Mercury ruled people understand them best), but they could use some Aquarian balance, or the Sagittarian fire. A Capricorn/Gemini would be heaven-sent.

His illumination: Great communicator.

His dark side: Insomniac.

VIRGO-CANCER

We all are resistant to change, but it really scares the wits out of this man. He needs immense order and routine in his life. He'll mother and even try to smother you. Then it will be your turn to baby him (chances are his mamma didn't do such a hot job of it), and you'd better do your mothering well or he'll get really sick. His stomach will ache. He'd be a good candidate for ulcerative colitis. He is super sensitive, and often very crabby. Unlike the Fire signs, he will not stand out in a crowd, he will not seek the limelight, and won't sweep you off your feet. He will be reserved and bashful. He will work in a quiet little office, at a quiet little job. He doesn't make waves with his co-workers. He is not stellar quality. He is more dependable though, because once he has made a commitment to a job, or lifestyle, or you, he has no intentions of breaking those vows. He's a sensitive, caring parent. Security is so vital to this man, he will at least obtain enough money to hold on to. He saves old string, so how could you not expect him to hang on to money? No spendthrift, he. He stabilizes in his early thirties, and finds himself the mate he plans to persevere with. It may not be a bed of roses, but he will hang in there. Tradition is important to this man, one shortcoming he won't be able to deal with is a woman who flaunts unconventionality in his face. If you've got a few other flaws he'll forgive you, and be the most understanding, sympathetic ear and best friend you can have. A nice Pisces, a Cancer, or a hot ticket Scorpio offer exciting matches. A Capricorn is probably the one that will appeal to him the most, though.

His illumination: Keeps promises.

His dark side: Passion for orderliness.

VIRGO-LEO

This man would be one I would not consider a well-rounded personality. He will tend to have a rather narrow scope of interests, and while very capable, he tends to hold himself back. If only the Virgo would let the Lion roar! There would be so much less conflict and confusion for this poor man if he'd relax. He wants to play and to party. But he's trapped inside his conservative Virgo shell. You will catch glimpses of this man courting attention. While he is not exactly a Don Juan, he is popular. He has the best of intentions. He will be a trusted, reliable and generous friend. He won't cut you off in the middle of a story, unless it is a tawdry one. He has a rather rigid moral code. He is impressed with detail, quality and the best. A cute little tart will never do for this man. And, please, don't ever try to borrow his toothbrush. It could send him right into analysis. While not totally exciting as an individual, in business he is one of the most tireless workers. This earth and fire combination is dynamic when it comes to getting the task done. Especially the tasks everyone else refuses. He is not a quitter and has strong work ethics. This willingness to work long and hard inspires others. He will want to provide you with an ordered, clean, decent, lifestyle and if in the process he provides in the "queenly" manner he decides you deserve, he will be all the happier. He will fawn over his children. This one should be given a second look. Remember some of the best of the Zodiac require a good second look. Love at first sight often shouldn't have been. Libras are very appealing to him. Taurus understands the need for comfort, and a Leo would be divine.

His illumination: Decent.

His dark side: Rigid.

VIRGO-VIRGO

Obsessed by routine. These three little words describe him to a tee. So don't go messing with any of his details, like how all the cans of peas are after the cans of corn. Don't be messy. Don't be late. Don't change appointment times. Help him recover from his bouts with mysterious bugs. Help him with all his rituals, and chants. Show your fascination with his social work, his greenhouse, his dietary and nutritional studies. Your life with him is a page out of Mother Earth. He is austere, unpretentious, discriminating, and smart as a whip. I bet anything you met him through a video dating service, or his aunt. He has the strange habit of marrying someone with a problem with drugs, illness, neurosis, or something he can't tolerate in himself or others. He likes to play savior. Just keep your problems consistent and in order. He can't stand confusion. Don't mix phobias into your three o'clock martinis. His bosses just love him, as do his co-workers. He will happily slave over every assignment and never expect to be advanced. He likes to play second fiddle. He is not a masochist. That is just the order of things the way he prefers it. If he gets involved in religion, he will do best with one with a lot of rituals. I hate to keep stressing this, but he is compulsive. If you don't like a lot of change and surprises scare you, grab him up. He'll be a concerned, active father who is involved in his children's lives. Plan to live a quiet life. No champagne or bubbles. Just plain tap water. Go for it. Be a Virgo. Or be a Pisces or Pisces Moon girl. A Cancer under 35 has a good chance. Or you could be a Taurus who mistakes all this for stability.

His illumination: Father Earth.

His dark side: Playing Savior.

VIRGO-LIBRA

Here is the most charming of the Virgo combinations. The Libra Moon adds harmony, beauty, and oodles of charms to this man. He is always thinking, and is rather dispassionate about many things. You can be sure, whatever your relationship with him, however, that he will manipulate you. It will be subtle, but you will find yourself adapting or even changing to suit him. This goes for the children too, though he means well. He is not a live wire, and you will either stay at home a lot, or go out only with those people who meet his approval (He can be a snob). And sex? Well, unless he has Mars in Scorpio, he can be very lukewarm about that. He can be exceptionally talented in the commercial arts, and yet have very little interest in this, or many other, professions. This is not a big brute of a man. He is apt to be somewhat thin, or asthenic in his build. He is not the dashing young man with broad shoulders and smoldering passion who dreams only of sweeping you off your feet. If that is what you're looking for, get with one of the Scorpios. But, if you are looking for an Ashley Wilkes sort of grace and detachment, this guy is for you. Ashley wasn't real ambitious either, remember. But he will compliment you, flatter you, entertain you, and show you the feminine side of his nature that will delight you. He knows where he is going and what he wants. What he wants will be eccentric. You will understand. And you will let him move in for awhile, borrow your car, and you'll think it is pretty terrific stuff all this assistance he will allow you to do for him. Not just everyone gets the honor. Another Libra, maybe. A Pisces girl, a Taurus, can put up with all this. A Cancer is a good match. A Gemini is good too, but only until the first manipulation.

His illumination: Sense of grace.

His dark side: Not especially ambitious.

VIRGO-SCORPIO

If ever a Virgo thinks passionately, it is this one. The intensity of this Moon position lends an entirely different quality to this personality. He will be deep, intense, and dogmatic. You will need to be very persuasive to get him to even consider your viewpoint. And then you'd better have good reason, or he will have the uncanny knack of seeing right through it. He can get into some pretty obsessive, dogmatic behavior. Other factors in his chart can lighten him up, but if he has Mars in Scorpio, his rigid way of thinking can really channel into sexual excesses. He needs drama, and he hungers for adventures on the darker side of life. He is not a man to be taken lightly. His emotional nature is secretive, deep. He may get into overindulgence in drugs, sex, or other not so hot vices. Is he a reformer, a policeman, an insurance salesman? Whatever he is, he will be the keeper of a great many secrets. His co-workers can confide in him and never worry about betrayal. He can spend a lot of time in muck, and wake up to the realization that he is destroying himself and stop his self-destruction. He can do it because he has the natural instincts of a fighter. He has more raw courage than any ten men put together. For all his emotional intensity, he is hard to get close to. He will fight the one thing they want the most—a close, intimate relationship. As a husband and father he's not easy to live with. He wants someone to worship at his feet. He will remain aloof for years and then suddenly lighten up and start participating in life and in all types of friendships. He is mysterious. His moods will run so deep it may take you years to figure him out. Remember, the Scorpio Moon leaves its mark. A hang tough sign is best. Capricorn, Scorpio, or Pisces women who can delve into his deep wells of reserve do best with this man. And don't expect to change him. He will decide if and when he needs changing. Until then, you're out of luck.

His illumination: Raw courage.

His dark side: Hard to figure.

VIRGO-SAGITTARIUS

Jupiter is the planet of travel and expansion, meets the sign of Mercury, which is also the sign of travel. The outcome is someone who is on the go. This particular Virgo is up and moving. He will have almost unlimited energy. Much of his energy is restless. Looking for a teacher for channeling? This man would be great. He loves to moralize, to teach, to preach, and to act. In short, anything that involves moving, learning, talking, and expressing himself appeals to him. He aspires to a great many things. He commits to a few plans for a while, and then is gone again in another direction. Naturally, this is hard on the more reliable of his co-workers. Life with him will not be dull. He will have many job and residence changes. He absorbs knowledge like a sponge. He can analyze you on the first date and know you better than your best friend, while not even seeming to pay attention to you at all. He loves women, and they will not escape his single-minded pursuit once his interest is peaked. The woman who appeals to him knows a little about a lot of things. He will not be offended by superficial knowledge, if it is broad in scope. He will ask the girl of his dreams to be versatile, adventurous, vibrant, and bright. Her appearance and sexuality is of secondary importance to him. He will be difficult for his mate and his children to reach on an emotional level. This man, while ardent in pursuit, may be hesitant to show it, and therefore, cover it elaborately. If yours is a commuter romance, have no fears. He will travel an ocean or two to get to you. He will be a considerate lover for the girl who finally captures his heart. He may be a little down in the cups by the time he finally finds you and decides to settle down, however. After all, his first priority was to be footloose and fancy free. Obviously, he needs a Gemini, Virgo, or Sagittarius. A Taurus can be fascinating. But, for the walk down the aisle, I'll bet on the Sagittarius.

His illumination: Your spiritual guide.

His dark side: Emotionally masked.

VIRGO-CAPRICORN

Shy, aloof, nervous, serious, often morose and solid, this man will still win his way into a lot of hearts. There is something very magical about him. He may start off as your counselor or dear friend, and suddenly you feel the earthiness and the caring that makes him nearly irresistible. He won't exactly sweep you off your feet, but when the fire ignites, you will be totally overwhelmed. His is such a subtle combination of good traits. His integrity, his sweet consideration for others, will leave you breathless. Oh, you won't really notice him at first, he will be like a deer in the meadow; beautiful and moving with utmost caution, as if afraid to mingle. At the rare parties he will attend (company functions, no doubt), he will be the one who is helping the host to serve. Brazen overtures will embarrass him. Be a little coy and frightened or vulnerable, and you've got yourself a good start. In any aspect of life, he will be an expert in timing. He will build slowly to any endeavor. He will know when the time is right to advance, ask for a raise, and even you. He will never push situations, or step on another person's back to get to the top. But, he will get there. Once at the top, he can keep every detail in his head from the annual reports of twenty years ago to the latest competitive patents by the rival companies. He will eat, sleep, and shower in the office if he has the facilities. This man was born to work. His energy for service and work is boundless. He epitomizes the tortoise. He has barriers to overcome from his childhood, and a long hard climb to the top. Don't let that fool you. He will arrive. He will win whatever he sets his mind to. He will want the best for his children. Another Virgo or Capricorn is the best bet. Sometimes a beautiful little Pisces runs off with this prize.

His illumination: Magical.

His dark side: Workaholic.

VIRGO-AQUARIUS

This is the most innovative, and imaginative of the Virgo combinations. He can often turn into quite the eccentric. You have met this friendly little fellow, with the electric blue eyes and the funny little space between his front teeth at a club or organization he holds so dear, no doubt. He will be the most unpredictable Virgo that you have ever met, changing his mind about many things. His lightning fast insights to people and situations are often unnerving ("How did he know that?"). Most often this Moon position lends a dash of excitement to this otherwise rock solid Earth sign. He communicates well with his computer. Has probably taught it the fine arts, and has it turning out some pretty unusual printouts. If you are a bit odd yourself, a bit preoccupied and detached, he'll take instant notice. If you are a bit on the masculine side, he will snap to attention. Male-female traditional roles are not at all important to him. He expects you to work on his car with him, just as he takes it for granted that he will do dishes with you. He is not impressed with time and tradition. He will be searching for some universal truth, some innovative way to better mankind. He may, as a result, get lost from time to time on his way to work. Be prepared to expect the unexpected with him. You've got to be a little like this to live with it and not go over the edge. But there is a certain charm to life with him. His Woody Allen approach to life is such fun. His children will have a father unlike any other—sound in the center, eccentric on the edges. It'll certainly break the monotony of your work week. An Aquarius, Gemini, or Libra girl can get in touch with his emotional needs. A Pisces could work out here also.

His illumination: Friendly.

His dark side: Doesn't do mundanity very well.

VIRGO-PISCES

This full Moon configuration produces an interesting combination. Two things are different about him. One, he may not look to you to help him solve his problems, he may let you look to him to solve yours. Two, he finds a good balance with logic and intuition that is very valuable to him. He is shy, sweet-natured, intelligent, and charming. What's he got to worry about? Plenty. He is a natural worrier. He has anxiety attacks. He bites his nails. He worries not only about himself, but everyone who has confided their tale of woe to him. He really does care. He wants to know where the justice of it all is. Why does so and so have to suffer? That is why, for all his health consciousness, he may overindulge in alcohol or drugs (usually prescription). This man smokes. He doesn't mean to do that either. But, to tell you the truth, he's such a nervous sort that he needs a calming influence. He needs lots of leisure activities like song writing, the theatre or the arts, to balance his life. His work will usually be found serving people in an emotional or physical way (prisons, hospitals, institutions, etc.) and leaves him emotionally drained. This caring extends to his adopted family and to his co-workers. He can achieve a great many things. Whatever his accomplishments, like helping others, studying new fields of endeavor, his work will be more rewarding than any monetary gains. Actually, as long as he has a roof over his head and three meals a day, he is content. He doesn't need a whole lot more. If he was born in the early morning about 6 or 8, chances are he will have several marriages. Look for the best matches with a Pisces or Libra. A Scorpio is also appealing to him.

His illumination: Caring for others.

His dark side: A worry junkie.

Libra

September 23–October 23

LIBRA-ARIES

When the light and airy Libra teams up with the combative, fiery Aries Moon, you can expect a personality full of surprises. He wants peace and harmony, fun and games. He needs a few battles along the way. This is a volatile combination. He can fascinate and charm one minute, but heaven help you the next, if he gets angry. Highly individual, he is one of the most difficult men in the Zodiac to pin down. This is the one Libra who is not seeking a partnership. Serial relationships are preferred. This full moon position brings out the aggressive nature of the normally harmonious Libra. Many disputes, some legal, result from this configuration. In career matters, as in love, this person prefers to go it alone. He will do some one-of-a-kind craftsmanship or entrepreneuring of top caliber. He will be handsome in a fine-boned, arrogant manner. He will use every trick he can imagine to lure the woman of the moment, and only the visually impaired could resist such persuasion. He can flash the famous dimpled smile (especially those born between 6-8 a.m.) and simply melt your resolve to never see him again after he thoughtlessly forgets that important date. Or you. It really did slip his mind. You can forget all your hard and fast rules about what you will and won't put up with in a relationship. He will decide the course of your relationship. If he wants to keep you waiting for several years while he decides your place in his life . . . well, you will wait. He is romantic in an odd sort of way. He is cuddly, and cozy and all the sweet things

77

you can conjure up. He is also rather a drifter, who really just wants to explore the world on his own. Husband and father material he is not. A Sagittarius, yes. Another Libra, Aries, or even Aquarius are also good matches.

His illumination: Cuddly.

His dark side: Tendency to drift.

LIBRA-TAURUS

This guy is in love with love, and work will not take precedence over his love relationships. He's affectionate, sentimental, romantic, tactful, and he is easy to snag. He is not so easy to hang on to, though, with his constant quest for the romantic ideal. This makes it rough on the wife and kids. Besides that, a guy can't help it he is so popular. Like a puff of air, he is all over. You can find him at the house of a friend, the theatre, shopping (this one shops) looking for something to beautify his residence, or at the jewelry store where he is about to engrave your jewelry. He is usually more comfortable and successful in the arts and crafts fields. He'll be the first in his group to purchase his dream house, and wouldn't consider asking a woman to move in without having something of substance to offer. He may even want to wait until he's got his house in order before any trips down the altar. He is a dreamer. He wants a woman who can be part of these dreams. Crude language, harsh makeup, hard lines in clothing will turn him off. Delicacy is the name of the game with him. You must be as gentle as a summer's breeze when you creep into his life. He does judge a book by the cover. If you are not exceptionally pretty, don't get all worked up over this one. You must appeal to his physical senses first. Your mind comes last. Not that he doesn't want that too. These men with a strong Libra influence are scary. They know beauty. As the rose fades, disenchantment often sets in. This is one of his little flaws. Can you bear the scrutiny? He will probably get a bit pudgy, but he won't count that. Pisces, Libra, Taurus girls can cast a spell. A fine-boned Capricorn could have a chance.

His illumination: Eveyone's favorite.

His dark side: A beauty junkie.

LIBRA-GEMINI

This is a real type B personality. A little prone to procrastination and laziness. The teaming up of two air signs leaves a personality that is easygoing, intelligent and that spends most of his life caught up in his ideas. He is light and airy, and like the restless wind, prefers to wander. He travels, not necessarily abroad, extensively. He is always on the go. He hasn't any hard and fast goals. He is much more a spur-of-the-moment person. If, however, he is lucky enough to land in the fields of promotion, public speaking, teaching or travel-related areas, he will take on more stability. He is persuasive and has a good sense of what is and is not marketable. How to cope with this man? Change your interest every few weeks, change your topic of conversation every few minutes, your hair color and your state of emotions. Then talk like crazy the few moments he is quiet. Do you look like the lady in red? Good for you. It'll drive him crazy. He loves a beautiful woman. Wear lots of jewelry. Dress with drama. Put *Woman's Wear Daily* to shame. Praise him. Flatter him. Talk softly and carry a big boa. He may even give some thought to wandering back to you from time to time. Why bother? Because he is so charming, and usually quite appealing, to boot. And think of the challenge. Chances are, he will not make tons of money. But, he will want to spend what he can to beautify his home and you. He'll help you shop for the children's clothes, and he'll read them bedtime stories. He isn't usually a drunk (well, maybe if he was born during the 1940s or in the early morning hours) nor is he typically a wife-beater or a compulsive gambler. He is sweetness and light, and he will be intellectually romantic. What does that mean, you ask? Get to know him better. It'll knock you off your satin slippers. Best bet: Libra, Aquarius, Gemini or Taurus.

His illumination: Social poise.

His dark side: Wanders.

LIBRA-CANCER

Do you like bondage? What about being controlled, and manipulated to the max? Do you want your children to toe the mark? This guy is for you. Thing is, you have no idea that he is doing any of this to you, and in fact, won't believe me. It will dawn on you one day when you figure out why you changed your major, gave up your previous social circle, your hobbies, your family, and even let all the community property end up in his name. Where were you? In his capable hands. Being brought to your fullest potential. He is charming, commanding, hardworking, a money maker, a love devotee. He doesn't mean to break you heart and soul. But, then again, he will say it is your fault for not looking out for yourself a little better. He is usually a teacher or counselor, or both. He is very easy-going most of the time. He figures getting along with everyone is a sure way to the top. He won't have to scramble up on the backs of others, he finds people willingly lay down for him to walk over, such is the magnitude of his charm. Often, just when you have arrived at your fullest potential (have changed totally for him) he finds another love. He did not mean to let you down, or to be unfaithful. But, then again, he will say you should have been more independent, more self-assured. The men of this configuration are very good-looking, with sweet little dimpled faces. He was so pleasant and helpful, you could have sworn you were helping him chart his course in life. Beware, the sailboat was in his name too. To be forewarned is to be forearmed. It can work if you understand the game plan and never lose your course. A Libra can match him. A Cancer can reach the depths of his soul. A Pisces could get creamed, and so could the Aquarian.

His illumination: Easy going.

His dark side: Likes to mold his women.

LIBRA-LEO

This man is in my top ten of appeal. Not that he will have the best qualities, necessarily, but that he has an especially appealing personality. He fairly oozes charm. He is the sort of man who makes other men's attempts at romance seem somewhat lackluster. He will do everything to make your life easier and more pleasant. His own, however, can be plagued by turmoil. This moon position gives him the ability to wing it, and he will therefore, have a greater potential to impress employers and co-workers. His life will never be dull; especially if he was born about 1-2 a.m. There will be, in fact, a lot of changes in his life. Impressionable and infatuated with love, he is drawn to inconsistency against his better judgement. This energy can be channeled positively with a job that requires travel and creative endeavors. He will use his idealism, his single red rose, his travel tickets for the weekend to capture your hearts. He is traditional in the way he treats his women, with respect and tenderness. The modest way he presents himself leaves you nearly spellbound. Chances are, he has had an early marriage. He can endure most anything in his efforts to make the union survive. He won't be big on shouting matches. Even when he is angry, his voice will be soft spoken, and mild. He is great with the children too. He is no fool, and you can't pull one over on him unless he wants you to. He moves at his own mysterious pace, which alternates from frenzied to near lazy. When he doesn't want to be pushed, he won't be. That includes making a commitment. I hope you are a Leo, Libra, Aquarius or a long-legged Sagittarius. He will notice the most beautiful girls first, by the way.

His illumination: Top ten in appeal.

His dark side: Fear of intimacy.

LIBRA-VIRGO

Oh boy! How much time do you have? This man can ponder and debate and analyze with the best of them. He can also take seemingly forever to arrive at one simple decision. Don't plan on spontaneous, impulsive adventures. Plan instead to be used as a sounding board for the pros and cons for a very long time. In exchange for this you get an honest man, usually frank and open. He won't get into the macho thing, of keeping his feelings to himself. He will expect the same thing from you. Order, cleanliness, and partnership are his goals. He doesn't want to do things alone, and that includes lunch. This is one reason he is a good parent—he'll spend time with the children. You won't find him sitting in the park taking a break. Left to his own devices, he will wander about bookstores or health food stores. That in fact would be a nice place to meet him. He will be cool and unemotional upon your first meeting, no matter what inner fires you may have stirred. He may respond to your invitation to cook up a batch of bran muffins. It won't be romantic. He means well, in fact, he may even consider doing something rash like bringing you a cookbook—but, alas, the decisions and the implications that may be involved! It's enough to make him reach for the old protein powder. Another way to make an approach is to invite him to help you critique (he is a natural at this) any art or literary event. Some men are the hunters, others, the hunted. Don't expect him to come on to you first. Meeting him at work is a good bet, but his concentration will be so focused he may not even remember your name after the introduction. He will not want to go out for a wild night of dancing or partying. This is one Libra fellow who wants his socializing nice and sensible. A Capricorn girl would be wonderful. Capricorns can be very patient with this sort of man, as long as he is making some bucks. Gemini is wonderful with him, and a Taurus divine.

His illumination: Mr. Sensible.

His dark side: Too focused.

LIBRA-LIBRA

By now you surely will remember what I have said about the double Sun and Moon combinations. It emphasizes every single thing over again about the sun sign. He is a dreamer, and unfortunately a bit of a schemer. And although I am not saying that he is unusually feminine, he does have a lot of feminine characteristics. He will understand your "mall-aholic" tendencies, and enjoy shopping. He will appreciate why you over-spent on redecorating your apartment and have to eat rice for the next several months. He will laugh and get silly with you over some crazy incident. He will cry at the movies with you. You will love it. He will also have a lot of buddies, and he will not confine the boys' night out to special occasions. If he gets lost on the way home from work, you can probably find him out with the gang. His co-workers are his closest friends. Don't, however, let him know you were looking. He wants your companionship and partnership on his own terms. This man should be a talent scout for a modeling agency. He can see real beauty at 300 feet. He knows instinctively the difference between natural hair and weaved color. He will be the first to notice the beginnings of crows feet in your twenties. He will proceed to tell you. He may even buy you the latest cream. If he is madly in love he will offer to save with you for your eventual plastic surgery. Inner beauty counts, but outer beauty is what he prizes above all. There can be no ugly, tawdry side to you. Four letter words from you will leave him absolutely queasy. Don't,

for heaven's sake, pick your teeth after meals. It will upset his delicate balance. Live near a junkyard and he will lose it altogether. Set
the stage properly and he comes alive. He is the essence of charm, a
real Cary Grant type. He is sweet and romantic. He can earn his way
out of poverty, and wants to better your life as well. He never wants
his children to know poverty. He is magnetic. You can't really resist.
A Pisces, a Taurus girl, any of the Air signs, or one of the beautiful
Libras stand the best chance.

His illumination: Everybody's buddy.

His dark side: Spots a beauty at 300 feet.

LIBRA-SCORPIO

This configuration often lends itself to a set of planets pretty lop-
sided, especially in the area of love and sex. They may almost become one dimensional about it all. Extraordinarily passionate about
everything, this man is sexually magnetic. A little spice and vice
make him more vital than a lot of the other Libra configurations. He
is also more independent and ambitious than his co-Sun-signers. He
is not above deceiving his co-workers to get ahead. His ambitions
run along the lines of medical research, insurance sales, anything as-
sociated with taxes, inheritances, or detective work. The combative
Scorpio Moon coupled with the peace-seeking Sun makes for an
odd combination. This man will be a lover and a fighter. He will
fight for the principle, the underdog, the downtrodden and oppressed. His children get less severe treatment because his love for
them is very strong. His jealousy will know no bounds. He will spy
on you on the one hand, and leave you alone and ignored on the
other. This contrasting nature can leave you confused and bewildered. This very complex configuration gives you a macho man
who needs love and affection more than anything. He covers this
need that he considers to be a flaw, with sarcasm and nasty snide remarks about love and romance. He is subject to dark and morbid
moods and thoughts. If your reaction to a quarrel with him is to
leave him, he will put you out of his life forever. If he walks out on
you, however, you can expect him to return contrite, with bouquet
in hand. It takes a lot of strength to live with this explosive nature. If
this is the one for you, please remember to keep your independence.
He will despise you for allowing him to possess and dominate you.

Which is what he thinks he wants to do. It is not. He admires strength and substance. A sensual woman is just his cup of tea, especially if she is a Scorpio, Pisces, Sagittarius. Sometimes a Capricorn can intrigue him.

His illumination: Vital and yummy.

His dark side: Jealous.

LIBRA-SAGITTARIUS

The lucky Sagittarius Moon finds a nice home with the charming, but not so lucky Libra. This is a combination of an aspiring, lecturing, philosophizing, preaching individual. He does well at work, and is trustworthy. His sights are often set so high, and on such perfection that he is too hard on himself when he falls short of all his loftier aims. He is energetic, enthusiastic, adventurous. He is constantly seeking to learn more, to broaden his horizons, and improve and expand his life perimeter. He is constantly on the move, so you cannot be a dud. You will need high levels of energy, at least intellectually, to keep up with him. He may be very inconsistent. He likes changes. Don't remind him that he has altered his original position on a subject 180 degrees. He will defend his new stance. Don't remind the middle aged of these species that he is not as beautiful as he once was. You will provoke him. Don't try to tie him down, for his nature is like a hot little puff of air. Let him get out and about or you will find he has traded the cozy little dinner for two for a safari to the wilds of Africa, and you will not be invited. He dreams like no other man—big, expansive, childlike fantasies of adventure, and fame. He thinks he is here on this earth to bring sunshine and light, not to sit at home with you and the kids. He deals best with children on a part-time basis. His dreams are impressive, and he usually has a fair degree of success in accomplishing them. These men born around 8 and 9 a.m. will have a tendency to marry several times ... those dreams again. Who can live up to them? You Sagittarian ladies understand his emotional needs, Libra and Cancer can cope with him and Aries and Leos truly fascinate him. His little black book may not be so little. You keep your heart out of danger here.

His illumination: Adventure seeking.

His dark side: Forgets to take you along.

LIBRA-CAPRICORN

Strong motivation and concern for self mark this man. His needs come first and if that doesn't suit you, well ... that is just tough. He usually has to make big compromises and sacrifices to gain whatever it is he wants from life. This goes against his grain, and that is enough of a cross to bear. He doesn't need your head trips, too, he figures. He is the least charming of the Libra configurations with the cold, wintry moon emotions of the Capricorn. His chances for success are better if he was born around noon, but his combativeness at home is heightened. His children will not be strangers to conflict. He usually has some sort of lifelong enemy that brings him a lot of grief. He eventually triumphs over this person, however. Like the rest of his eventual positive outcome, it takes some time and effort to surmount. He will accomplish, and accumulate. It just takes most of his energies to do it. He is going to expect a superwoman. He is highly impressed by hardworking, beautiful, domesticated women. Life, after all, is a marketplace. He is trading his charm (yes, he still has it) and his considerable earning power for a mate. He will be romantic in the traditional ways. He will offer loyalty, security and a safe harbor from the rest of the world. He won't leave you destitute in order to run off with your best friend. His sense of decency would never permit it. He wants romance and mush. He wants it to come from you. He has no plans to give it to you. That would embarrass him to no end. He believes in good old fashioned things like hard work and tradition. It is vital for you to believe in these same things also. He'll break a Pisces heart. An Aries might punch him out the first date. Cancer, Capricorn, and Virgo ladies are the best matches.

His illumination: Offers a safe harbor.

His dark side: Can be aloof.

LIBRA-AQUARIUS

This man is interesting, friendly, and original. The Uranus ruled Moon makes him exciting and he loves variety and change. He also loves falling in love. His strong good looks should be enhanced by an unusual feature (Are his eyes oddly spaced?), or dark blue eyes. While his moods can change lightning fast, adding excitement to your relationship, his idealistic approach to love leaves him a top flight romantic. His departures into the world of fantasy may leave you less than content, but his dreamy little face leaves you enchanted. There is something so childlike and naive about this man, that he brings out all the maternal feelings in women, and near adoration in children. His talents run from science, computers, innovation, the arts, or drama. The problem is getting him to settle down to any one of them. He needs a strong manager to help him tow the line at work. If successful, this direction can produce a top notch executive, with improved working environments. His ability to succeed should never be underestimated because of his calming and charming manner. Speaking of calming, while he does this for others, he is prone to all sorts of nervous energies himself. You will need to calm him down. He is interested in many things, the occult or astrology, for one. If you were to have his chart done to help understand him or better your relationship, he will be appreciative. He may take a couple of years to determine if it has any meaning for him, but he is nonetheless intrigued, and will probably follow your resulting suggestions. Intelligent, discriminating, eccentric, unusual girls like himself he finds the most desirable. His flaws are his inconsistencies, and oddities...his vague way of having out of body experiences in the middle of dinner. Most women can handle that, but an Aquarian, Gemini, or Sagittarian copes the best. Another Libra is also a good match.

His illumination: Child-like charm.

His dark side: Needs grounding.

LIBRA-PISCES

Sensitive and overly emotional, this man puts each and every woman he likes on a pedestal. As soon as he finds the flaws, she begins to topple from her stand. Each affair, and there will be many, is deep and meaningful while it lasts. It is just that he feels very let down that the perfect woman of his dreams was just human after all. His common sense will never tell him that the flawless woman does not exist. It is simply too harsh a reality. He will therefore, be inclined to periods of depression, overindulgence, intemperance. He weaves drama into everything. His day takes on colors and feelings unknown to the rest of the world. He has, with the exception of romance, an almost sixth sense into people. He belongs working in or around hospitals, institutions, the sick and the poor. His love of humanity extends to his over-protected children. Oddly enough, he can handle the disharmony of these surroundings, because he feels he is almost on a mission to better their lives. However, your hanging around the house in an old bathrobe, or heaven forbid, allowing him to see you with rollers in your hair, will leave him devastated. The vision of you in that condition will haunt him as he sees his coworkers in their nice business clothes, fully made up. Then the need to flee to comfort of a prettier set of arms arises, right there by the water cooler. Multiple relationships are not unusual for this man. He possesses a quiet, sweet charm, and a just and fair way of handling people that lures many a woman into his bed. He is sensitive to drugs and to sugar. It is important for his mental health to have a diet free of sugar, and a lifestyle free of drugs. Another beautiful Libra, a sensitive Pisces, Cancer, or a devoted Taurus are his best matches.

His illumination: Love of humanity.

His dark side: Multiple relationships.

Scorpio

October 23–November 23

SCORPIO-ARIES

Two combative signs make for a man with a white hot intensity and a predisposition for angry temper tantrums. What will interest him the most (it may be the only thing that interests him) is himself. His aims, his ambitions, his recreation, his feelings, are the only thing that counts...and don't ever for one minute think otherwise. His world can be very small and restricted because of his one track mind. Since he spends most of his time alienating people, offending people, and brutalizing them, his lack of friendships becomes his eventual downfall, especially those men born about seven in the morning. As a parent, you may surmise that he is stern and often cold. If he has a lot of the sunnier planets in Sagittarius, he lightens up to the point where some people can have fun with him sometimes. If you are the rare duck who falls in love with this man, expect to live where he wants, to put up your money to have the property in his name, eat the foods he wants, when he wants, etc. I am sorry to be so brutal, but I do want you to get the picture. He comes across as merely intense upon trying to make a good first impression. Serious, and even conscientious. Do not be misled. He is looking you over for spare parts. He is black and white. He is the least magnetic of the Scorpios, and I fear his sexuality is entwined with leather and whips. I fortunately would not know first hand. Only another Scorpio, an Aries, or a cold Capricorn Moon can do battle with this one.

His illumination: Conscientious.

His dark side: Looks you over for spare parts.

89

SCORPIO-TAURUS

Like the preceding man, this one has an intensity and sense of purpose. While he is materialistic, he is not necessarily selfish, or cruel. He will be rather earthy, passionate, and loaded with sex appeal. He has a fabulous ability to make money, and is so resourceful when low on funds that you could hardly ever tell. He knows what he wants and goes after it with single-minded determination. As a co-worker you needn't worry that he will want your job—he just wants to create his own niche in the company. As for the object of his affection, whether wife or child, he can be very devoted. He will chase you. If he is not interested, you can forget it. No feminine wiles work here. This is the Rhett Butler of the Zodiac. He can be a very bad boy and still manage to maintain a fair degree of social status. Lucky in love, he has a wide choice of companions. A business whiz, he could be a fine doctor as well. He dominates the social situations with his quiet, strong sensuality and masculine presence. He will never blend into the woodwork and he doesn't want a woman who can. Although he is strongly dominant, he wants a woman who can stand on her own two feet and offers him an exciting challenge. While attracted to beauty and intelligence in a woman, the fiery, passionate sort holds his attention. Unusually handsome, he has a strong, solid and very muscular build. He can handle the outdoors, and is interested in football, boxing, and fishing. If you are not, you don't have to worry about it mattering to this man. He expects you to have other interests. He is not looking for a companion, or a mother, for that matter. He wants a lover. Stay home and keep the incense burning. He likes feminine women, and can tell the difference between the unconstructed look, the silhouette fashion, and the layered or blunt cut. He's nobody's fool when it comes to money, women, and what he wants. A Leo catches his eye, as does a Taurus, Capricorn, Pisces, or another Scorpio.

His illumination: Oozes sex appeal.

His dark side: Spooked by changes.

SCORPIO-GEMINI

This man fights the Leo for center stage. He is the chain smoker who just can't sit still. He fidgets, gets restless, and likes to be continually on the go. He will be this way when he is 80. He knows all his neighbors, and shares in their parties, moves, and job changes. He doesn't miss much at all, and yet, he is not a gossip. He is, rather, really interested in his fellow man. Being somewhat secretive himself, his friends are not usually invited to his house. They will also (if they stop to think about it), have little knowledge about him. If he takes you to his place, it will be for a specified period of time, with the drapes drawn. He is not trying to hide you, he is merely protecting his space. It is a fine line, but he will teach you the difference between friendliness and openness. For all his love of his mole hole (dwelling to you), for his dark colors and mystery, he is a witty, exciting, and fun sort of man. He is complex. He can look for a mate for years, and then when he finds the one he wants he will propose within days. If he was born around 7 a.m., this tendency is intensified. And he may in fact have made several such spontaneous proposals. This means that if you are married to this man, don't ever assume that his devotion also means exclusivity. He does not mean to be inconsistent. He simply has moved on to another phase. One woman is not necessarily enough to keep him busy. Often he will have two families, and be a decent father to both. It is the same with work. He may have an avocation that will consume a large part of his time. He is probably interested in the occult, has his own astrologer, is superstitious, and yet is not afraid to take a few risks in life. While he will pretty well work his way through the Zodiac, another Scorpio, and Aquarius, Pisces, or Cancer will have the best chances. A Gemini could be the one he snaps his cap for.

His illumination: Tremendous powers of persuasion.

His dark side: Superstitious.

SCORPIO-CANCER

This could be your knight in shining armor, riding across the desert on his fine Arabian charger. He could be your "Emotional Rescue"; he will be someone's. Even a one night stand with this man could change your life. He is dramatic, intense, considerate, and passionate. In fact, I am going to give him an eleven sexually. He will quite simply take you to places you've never been before, and I'm not talking about travel. This man is your every fantasy come to life. He is tall, dark, and handsome. He is a good money maker, and full of fun and surprises. He can cook, do the laundry, and give you advice on how to fix your hair and what to wear. Are you breathless yet? There is more. He will charm your friends, and your mother will think he is perfect. He isn't, of course, but he'll come close. He is impulsive, excessively physical, demanding and possessive. And, he is jealous. Even after he left you for someone else, to see you with someone else will make him see red. He is also in the top ten of possessiveness. If he had his way, he would never let go of anything. That may explain why he still keeps in touch with a lot of his former relationships (which drives you bats). It may also shed some light on the woman he eventually gives his heart and soul to. She will bear a striking resemblance to his mother. I hope he had a good relationship with her, or he'll make it rough for you. These little faults aside, he will make the woman of his choice silly with happiness. He will be a help mate, a friend, a fan, your partner in crime, if necessary. He will be an excellent father and husband. He can mix career and love fabulously. Speaking of his career, he will work hard and be very fair with his co-workers. When he plays he forgets work and vice versa. His concentration is tops. He will be most attracted to a woman he has to fight to control. A Capricorn or Cancer head his list. Everyone has a chance for a fling though, thank God.

His illumination: A wonderful mate.

His dark side: Still friends with the ex.

SCORPIO-LEO

This man has excessive pride and lust. . . a volatile temper, a white hot intensity. He is deep and intricate. This configuration rules both houses of sex in a chart, and he is therefore obsessed with sexual matters. A combination of fixed signs, he is rigid in his morality, and in yours. He will be measuring you against a set of standards that you may not even be aware of. And if you fall short, he will be quite angry with you. He places unnecessarily high expectations and standards on other people (his own may be more flexible). This means wife and children are also subject to his measures. He can handle life and death matters easily, and is in fact fascinated with both. This may account for his fields of work, as he is inclined towards medicine, research, investigation, math and science. His career goals are often interrupted by his affairs of the heart. He does have trouble keeping his feet on the ground with his excessive romantic life. His fascination with women is that of a detective trying to solve a crime. He wants to know everything about the woman in question. Once the mystery is pretty well solved, he is ready for another mystery. A beautiful one. This man looks for beauty in women first. He must find her unusually attractive and mysterious. He also likes a clinging vine. A hard bill to fill, but fill it he will. Once he finds the object of his affection he usually wines and dines her, takes her to the theatre, museums, art fairs, and the like. He is also a good gift giver. He will be generous and often lavish with gifts. He often slips into moods of infancy, wanting to be babied and catered too. If it means making peanut butter and jelly sandwiches at 4 a.m., you will be expected to do it. It may be a test. His grading is simple—pass or fail. A Leo, of course, understands him. An Aries matches his fires; a Pisces he can dream with.

His illumination: Commanding.

His dark side: Fixed emotions.

SCORPIO-VIRGO

He is good looking and masculine, and women are unusually attracted to him. His presence is one of strength. He is a macho man who can express his feelings. Alleged to be more mental than emotional, it has been my experience that the emotions run deep and powerful. He will try to conceal this with an intellectual rationalization, but truth is, if he loves you his devotion knows no bounds, even if you do not live up to all he expects from you. He also covers a multitude of worries and anxieties with a false bravado. Never puncture his ego with careless assumptions about his insecurities. His pride cannot handle it. He likes the rough and tumble type of woman, lusty and a little untamed. If you are the sexy librarian type, that is okay too, as long as you eventually lose control under his skilful hands. He will work long, hard hours for you. Hold down two jobs to support your extravagances. Sell his soul to buy you the best house he possibly can. He needs you, the object of his devotion. He will analyze you, penetrate your secrets, and challenge you. He will never intentionally criticize you beyond good taste. He will tease and play with you. He wants to entertain you, to befriend you, and to eventually adore you. Do not take his promise to feed you pablum in your old age lightly. He means it. He is deep still waters, and you know what that means. He will notice your new hairdo, pat your sagging fanny, and caress your over-permed hair. He will make you feel like a million dollars. He will tell you when your dieting has gone too far, and put his foot down that you have forgotten your vitamins again. He will be as attentive with his children. A Scorpio-Virgo combination always gives a few sexual kinks. Sex in the elevator, watching other men try to pick you up, a little spanking, are some of the stuff women of his choice might indulge in. Indulge she will if she is a Libra, Capricorn, Cancer, or Gemini of his choosing.

His illumination: Deep emotions.

His dark side: False bravado.

SCORPIO-LIBRA

This is one of the most charming men of the Sun-Moon combinations, and the romantic par excellence. He is magnetic, persuasive, ardent and loyal. In one hypnotic nod he gestures he understands your more complex emotions. He can dress and undress you, both physically and emotionally. No matter how preoccupied he is about other things, if he is interested in you, he will never let the slightest incident about your life go unnoticed. He lives to understand you. He will calm and reassure you in the midst of his own inner turmoil that you are totally oblivious to. He is friendly and genuinely interested in others, whether at home or at work. He is a defender of the underdog, and often ends up in a legal or service related field. While he makes friends easily, he wants only to surround himself with the most refined of the group. He has high standards and is prone to criticisms and analyses that tend to sting and smart. He is less abrasive with his children. What does he need to accomplish to balance out his life? To find the right partner. His every emotional fiber calls out for a mate. He needs to share his dreams, his goals, and every waking moment with someone. If you are that someone you will not have to worry about being left home alone a lot. He looks for beauty in a woman, and for style (yes you can splurge on that new leather dress) as well as elegance. The woman in the tacky plaid coat could give him nightmares for a week. Your four letter words will get you demerits on your score card. He will have no use for foul language (unless it is under covers, of course). The beautiful Libra snags him right off the bat, the Capricorn or Scorpio hangs in there for years. The Cancer or Pisces can relate to him. The Aries goes for his throat.

His illumination: Ardent.

His dark side: Inner turmoil.

SCORPIO-SCORPIO

Mesmerizing, compelling and dangerous. His desire to master is strong, just like his willpower. His sexual chemistry is overwhelming, and usually sane, conservative and prim women find themselves in the grip of uncontrollable urges to run their toes up his pant legs. Obsessions and compulsions explode with this double combination. You may have heard he was a bad boy. You won't care. He is caution to the wind and lace panties tossed in the back seat of cars. Once he sets his sights on you he will be relentless in his pursuit. He knows what he wants and may propose shortly after the introduction. While his eyes tear through your soul, he will be ever so cautious in revealing his true self to you. One of the most complex of the 144 combinations, there will be three levels of this combination. One is the Scorpion who likes to indulge in self-destructive behaviour, treat you nasty and marry your best friend to get even because you made him mad. Another is like the Eagle soaring high in business, protecting his family and working toward self mastery. The most evolved of the three combinations is the Dove who desires peace and harmony, strives to conquer self limitations and unravel the mysteries of life and afterlife. Since the third type is relativly rare, I'd suggest taking your blinders off before I got into anything permanent. He will want to possess you body and soul. Everything will come second to him if he has his way. And he usually has his way because he is hypnotic. And compelling. Remember this before you take your shoes off. You might be in over your head. Needless to say, not everyone is up to this. A Scorpio understands. The Pisces knows. The Aries can do battle. The Capricorn fascinates.

His illumination: Ability to transform.

His dark side: Tries to control destiny.

SCORPIO-SAGITTARIUS

This man is an elusive creature, always aspiring to another level of accomplishment, or relationship. His love for recreation, travel, sports, education and romance comes first in life. He changes jobs, residence and women frequently. He likes to remain as unencumbered as possible. This means children, too. A friend to everyone, he keeps his friendships at a distance. In other words, don't call him, he'll call you. Many people mistake his friendliness for more. Some women mistake his interest for something deeper, only to get their hearts broken. He was just being kind. His silence and unreadable thoughts confuse many people. Only count on what he tells you. He is usually quite forthright when he finally opens up to communicate. He is an unusual man who can do well in law, religion, teaching, arts, or music. He is not as able in business, because it does not appeal to his higher mind, but he is a decent co-worker. He likes women who are companions. A woman who can travel from boudoir to hockey field, from tennis to a poetry reading steals his heart. He wants a woman with tremendous backbone, one who cannot be bought in any way. One who is with him because of desire, not need. He wants to believe she is very selective about who she gets involved with. If you have a lesser relationship in your past, best not to let him hear too much about it. He will hold it against you for a long time. This man is a contradiction, he wants to possess you and yet be given total freedom. If you can manage this you are more than half way to meeting his rather hard and fast rules for a relationship. If I were you, I'd be so tough to tie down, that he gives up his freedom (in a sense) to keep you from going astray. Lots of charm, excitement and romance lure you to give it a try, especially if you are a Leo, Sagittarius, or a Scorpio.

His illumination: Inspiration and physical strength.

His dark side: Short on practicality.

SCORPIO-CAPRICORN

I don't care what his early environment was, how poor and pitiful, how lavish and secure, count on it only getting better. He will surmount all odds and make it to the top of the heap. He has one passion, and that is to make lots of money, which he knows buys power. Power is the other commodity he most desires in life. Cold? You bet. Underneath the sexual passions burns a love of money. There also burns a white hot fire to be recognized as a government or public figure. Only when he has achieved his goals will he mellow out and work on relationships. Before that, he is a troublesome husband, father, and co-worker. He may well be about 50 when his life change occurs. Oh, yes, another thing about his money. It's his. That means he won't lavish it on you. Cavalier in his youth about the use of money, he nearly worships it in old age. If you are into fondling bank deposits and see no value in diamonds and furs and other girls' best friends, he may be the one you want to spend your golden (I mean green) years with. You won't ever have to worry in his earlier years that he will have a lot of job changes, changes of heart, or residence. There is no floundering around trying to find himself. He knows what he wants early on and if you are part of his plan, he will be so ardent in his pursuit of you that it will make your head spin. You can be his co-partner (not stand passively by his side) and watch as he is promoted, and promoted. He will treat you as an inferior if you do not have a few advancements along the way. If your friends are tacky, well, you'd better set your sights on someone else. He doesn't want to spend his valuable time with lesser beings, unless it has been time specified for some good charity endeavor. Don't ask about his roots or early environment. He has put it all out of his mind. You'd better do the same. You may never meet his mother. Best bets: Capricorn, Cancer, or Libra.

His illumination: Climbs to the top.

His dark side: Can be miserly.

SCORPIO-AQUARIUS

This man is eccentric. He reminds me of a very pleasant and sociable visitor from another planet. He has relationships with "us," likes "us," and reads and studies "us," but never quite becomes one of "us." That we think him odd or peculiar is of little or no concern to him. His intellect is tuned in to the scientific and pseudo scientific. His first toy was probably a computer. His first word was "starship." He is often a loner amidst a crowd of adoring worshippers. He usually finds a devoted spouse who lets him wander around doing his own thing. He is entertaining, fun loving, exciting, unpredictable, and unfortunately, often unreliable. He is an inventor and if routine work is required to support the family, well, adios family. Unless you all pitch in together to support him and his latest discovery, he will leave. He is prophetic and can visualize the society in the next few decades. But the way he starts inventing for it leaves the more practical of us at a loss. I mean food on the table tonight comes first to the rest of the world, does it not? He is just as confused as to why you don't see it all his way as he is about your narrow, practical views, for he is a gentle soul, kind and sweet. All he wants is peace and lighthearted surroundings. Why is everyone yelling that he missed work again to sleep on a book and see if he could absorb its contents like Edgar Cayce did? Don't they understand the importance of his experiments? Emotionally pleasant, he acts like he is unsure as to who you and the children are. If work interferes with his projects he'll put the phone in the oven so he can't hear work calling. I mean it, this man can go off on some real tangents. Are you up to it? Be Aquarius, Pisces, maybe Cancer. Don't have your feet planted solidly on the ground, and be careful.

His illumination: Transforms others.

His dark side: Peculiar ideas.

SCORPIO-PISCES

This is the mystery man of the Zodiac. He is so appealing. His dreamy bedroom eyes are kind of watery blue. He is easily distracted and has a poetic nature. Blame it on his sixth sense. For all his mystery, he has you figured. He may still be confusing himself with his daydreams intruding upon his realities from time to time, however. Early in life he dreams of writing poetry, acting, being a war hero, or a surgeon. He gets bogged down in deep depressions that hinder his goals. His fantasies are more exciting than life, so he withdraws for a while. Romantic? Well, I have my suspicions that he invented Valentine's Day. Good looking? Ever so. Sensual? You bet.

Outgoing? No way. Nervous? Yes. Let me tell you a little about his nerves. He can glide through business ventures and board meetings, climbs (literally) the highest mountains; but sleeping without the night light scares the pants off him. Subjects like Instant Human Combustion will make him break out in a rash. This insecurity enables him to get along very well with children. He's usually faced a major trauma somewhere along the way in his life, and hasn't quite recovered yet. The secret is, he never really will. For all his macho man appearance and demeanor, he will tell you his innermost secret fears. He is a very anxious man. Probably smokes a bit too much. And, quite frankly, he needs someone to help him make it through the night. If you want that to be you, you must be soft spoken and the strength behind the scenes. You also need to have a set of morals and ethics and be able to dream with your feet on the ground as well. Don't play games with this man. Be as virtuous as possible. He has good father and husband potential. A Pisces, Libra, or Cancer are made for him. A Capricorn may surprise you and give you quite a run for your money.

His illumination: Romantic par excellence.

His dark side: Mysterious, pent up.

Sagittarius

November 23–December 22

SAGITTARIUS-ARIES

This is the typification of the Type A personality. He is on the go, hyperactive, energetic, outgoing, life in the fast lane, all fired up and ready to act. Impulsive and daring, this man aspires to live each and every waking moment as fully as possible. He is not selfish exactly, but you will have to put on your track shoes to run his races his way. He certainly doesn't have the time to explain his actions. Let me try. He is an overgrown, pleasant child. He loves to play. He wants to have fun. Along the way, he becomes a success. He is a natural born executive, and a fair minded boss. He leaves a string of broken hearts in his wake. He can stay up and party all night, come home, shave and shower, and head back to the office for a grinding 12 hour nonstop day. He is not even cranky before his coffee. But, if someone makes him angry, all hell will break out for a few minutes. He will recover and be as pleasant as can be afterwards. It was just his lightning fast way of expression. He can keep up this schedule for many a year, stay ruggedly involved in sports, and anything high risk. And then it happens. He wears himself out. He develops high blood pressure. He has tension headaches. His body may go a bit earlier than most, but the spirit remains as strong and vital, as youthful as ever. He will always delight you. He usually marries young. How or why he has very little memory of. He certainly didn't mean to. He never wanted to get married. He won't repent in leisure. Like everything else, he'll make a quick and final decision to divorce, and that will be that. The children will still adore

him—he is so much like them. He likes 'em all, but a Leo, Sagittarius, or Libra will top the list.

His illumination: Ready when opportunity knocks.

His dark side: Impulsive.

SAGITTARIUS-TAURUS

Here lucky Jupiter teams up with the money making moon in Taurus. This configuration also lends itself to an honest, kindly, sweet
tempered person who is easily impressed by his peer group and surroundings. Put him in the wrong environment and he tends to feel
weighted down, and eventually alienated from the entire situation.
But in the right atmosphere he thrives. He grows into a well balanced personality that just looks for love and affection. In other
words, this is one of the few men I can recommend for a remodelling
job, if you should so desire. Not that he needs to be altered from his
wonderful potential. Just keep him away from the negative, petty,
inharmonious situations that nearly destroy him. Keep him sunny
and bright, be honest and loyal, and feed him chocolates. You will
have in return a wonderful and loving companion. He can excel in
positions of personnel, banking, catering, counseling, teaching, or
negotiating. He will love his children and teach them true values
and ethics. He will provide a nice, comfortable home and a healthy
recreational life. No beer in front of the television set all day for him.
He will have a definite tendency to put on weight throughout the
years. Loyal and devoted, he will sacrifice most anything for his be-
loved. He will stand to be counted when times are rough. He will
usually have artistic outlets for his energies, like woodworking. He
should be encouraged to continue his education as much as possible; it not only makes him happy, but it enhances his talents and
earning potential. He is a wonderful, honest, and kindly co-worker.
Not everyone who continues his education leaves with such benefits. He's a nice man, offering you a nice life. You are undoubtedly a
Taurus, Libra, Leo, or another Sagittarian.

His illumination: A well balanced, nice man.

His dark side: Wrong environment shatters.

SAGITTARIUS-GEMINI

Can you imagine how his mother felt raising this half man half horse set of twins? The astrological symbols here give you a clue to his duality. From early childhood to mid years he's dashing about inhaling life. He spends many years not knowing what he wants, who he is, and often you'll be left wondering where he is. Not that this is all bad, especially if you like relationships that are punctuated with absences, changes of residence, and misplaced notes to each other as to your whereabouts. This man is not possessive even in the early throws of romance. If you're available when he swings by to pick you up on the spur of the moment, fine. If you should be out, he'll dash about to the next address in his black book and manage to have a great time without you. This doesn't mean he's not caring, he just doesn't get enmeshed. While his level of commitment is not the stuff romance novels are made of, he'll always be available to the woman of his life in her times of crisis. Other men may sneak out of town when your checks bounce and your cold sore flares up, but dilemmas serve as a mating call for this guy. If you don't try to obligate him or tie him down, or have him clock in, you'll find him quite reliable in his own fashion. He likes conquest and if you're too easily captured the affair will quickly lose its fascination for him. He is attractive in a loose, long legged way and usually has no problems on Saturday nights. He's famous for wine, women and song, and finds himself propositioned regularly. This, of course, is unsettling for the woman who is trying to raise his children. But nature has a way of taming this wild horse, and his middle to late years finds him approaching life with less urgency. He can put his roaming behind him, graze about and not jump fences. And you, old steady one, can enjoy a man of many talents who in his own fashion has strong ethics about higher issues and good will toward his fellow persons. A word of caution: don't mistake his contentment for complacency. You'll need to keep yourself in good shape mentally and physically, not lose you interest in things beyond your relationship, and never forget to aim for the stars with him. Since he often equates predictability with boredom you'll always need to intrigue him. This one is best with a Gemini-Sun or another Sagittarius. The Sagittarian Moon girls quite simply fascinate.

His illumination: There in a crisis.

His dark side: Gone a lot.

SAGITTARIUS-CANCER

Does he look like his mom, only taller? Did he worship her just a touch? Think maybe you can fill her shoes? Does he think that he was reincarnated from Robin Hood? Did he secretly believe in Santa Claus until he was twelve? There is a lot of wonderful child in this man. And he is looking, quite frankly, for a mother. Conversely, he is not the best father and husband material. To tell you the truth, he needs one. He is so idealistic that he sees almost everything with rose colored glasses. Lead him around, but don't attempt to remove his glasses. He can't live with the realities of the harsh, cruel world. The ugly truth about life hurts him. That is why he needs protection. Not that you could guess he needs such care the way he is so adept at surviving financially. This is especially true if he was born about 6 or 7 at night. This is a very fortunate configuration for financial success. He will be a fair co-worker. He is also possessed with a strange set of religious beliefs. What's so strange? Well, for all his ethics, he will think having a half dozen girls on the hook is perfectly moral. And so as not to hurt anyone, he tells them all he loves them. And then when it is time to leave, a little story like his work for the CIA requires him to move to Iowa in the morning and sever all ties, or he has just developed bone cancer and won't be able to attend your graduation tonight, usually does the trick. For him. Because so help me, you'll believe him. Or maybe you give him enough rope that he just leaves without hideous lies. He doesn't allow himself to think he lied, he was feeling bad and he did meet someone who lived in Iowa once. If you want to forgive this, do me a favor and sleep with his best friend while he's "out of town." An Aquarius, a Sagittarius, a Gemini, or the motherly Cancer are possible victims.

His illumination: Wonderful qualities.

His dark side: Needs protection.

SAGITTARIUS-LEO

Here are the configurations for happiness and success, excitement, adventure, and tall, good looks. This one is ambitious, popular, and definitely prone to love affairs. Important people, usually with political connections, are attracted to this man. Perhaps they admire his idealistic nature, his fair opinions, his concern for mankind. His faith in mankind rather rubs off on those around him. People feel his generosity of spirit, and in turn, behave better for it. He is, in fact, what is known as a good catch. One of the most faithful of the Sagittarians, he has every intention of being devoted as a father and husband. He may slip with all that attention and popularity; other women cannot leave this guy alone! But he can be easily forgiven. He is looking for a woman who is a companion, an intellectual equal, and with plenty of spirit, personality and independence. If your idea of marriage is his bringing home the bacon to his clinging vine wife who can only talk one syllable words, or acronyms like PTA, MADD, etc., you are in big trouble. Never let him see you with mud masks on your face. Don't parade around in dingy white bras and chipped fingernail polish. He will be repulsed. He wants all the finer qualities in a mate. Many of the same that he possesses. Keep your promises and don't let him down. You can probably find him relaxing with a glass of ale or wine after a hard day in marketing with his adoring co-workers. Any promotional fields will inspire him to his greatest heights. He has an uncanny sense for what other people want, whether in cars or oatmeal. It is this talent that can bring in some pretty exciting salary offers throughout his life. Another Sagittarius, or a Leo would be the ideal match. The impossible (for him) Scorpio woman fascinates. The impetuous Aries keeps him on his toes. Settle down time comes with a match to his Moon, or a Cancer with lots of Leo in her chart.

His illumination: One of the top 144.

His dark side: Needs space.

SAGITTARIUS-VIRGO

He comes on strong and brainy. Perhaps you think he might even border on genius. Regardless of how he makes his approach, he will proposition you in one breath and smoothly cover it with a long spiel about the latest protein wafer he is working on. Make no mistake, he is after your body. He won't grab for it, or do anything so overt, but he'll keep working on you until you give in. Since he is so focused on conquest, you might think he will be easy to please. Wrong. He wants you to be perched atop the highest pedestal. He wants someone above human frailties. He will pick at you to become more perfect until you either mend your ways or leave for a less demanding partner. He is not easy to live with. He'll drive you and the children nuts with his exactness. On the surface, he is witty, ambitious, daring, adventuresome, and "promising." He has such plans for going places. He could be an attorney, a preacher, a teacher, or an artist. He carefully shows his positive side at work. He has such strong ethics, so few morals. He goes after what he wants with a fierce intensity, whether it is a promotion or a fling. All this intensity leaves for a lot of nervous disorders. To say he is hyperactive is to make the understatement of the year. Sagittarius men are always on the go, full of vitality and vigor. His idea of a really fun weekend would be to camp out and do some serious hiking. You know, lots of wine and pine nut. If you are a nurse weekdays, you could be the one. He does have a streak of hypochondria. A Gemini would be great. A Virgo will at least understand him. An Aries or Leo could also be a good match. The Sagittarian is capable of several romances at once, so what the heck, this guy could have several of you on the string at the same time. So could his Gemini sweetie. He will, of course, think she is very tacky to be playing around.

His illumination: Promising in all areas.

His dark side: A streak of hypochondria.

SAGITTARIUS-LIBRA

This sociable, appealing man is the cause of many a woman running madly to her best friend about the "love at first sight" rush she felt when she first met him. One of the few Sagittarian men who want to be married (though all of them seem to marry too often), he comes on in a white hot fashion pursuing the woman of his dreams. Caution. This may be a very fleeting infatuation for this man, while the object of his current affections is ready for a lifetime commitment. He is impetuous. He is foolhardy. He does his best work in large groups, partly because of his business charisma. He may be wandering around hotels and banquet rooms, or a similar organization where he utilizes his skills to bring together large groups of people. Since partying is such a large part of his life, you can expect his work to revolve around it as much as his play. You will have to be both his perfect hostess and fun loving companion. If you require eight hours of sleep each night, better pass on this one. He'll age you faster than overexposure to the sun any day. The enchanting Libra Moon is a favorable position to the lucky Sagittarius Sun, and gives this man plenty of breaks in life. Good fortune comes to him, usually in the form of an influential set of friends. This good fortune can be wasted with his "easy come, easy go" attitude. The opportunities are there, the drive and persistence to succeed may not be. He is not emotionally deep, but he usually means well. His vices? He may be a bit of a gambler, a womanizer, and often a touch lazy. He's often a long distance father. Can you handle it? You'll want to try, I know. Especially if you are a Libra, Leo, Aquarius, or any female not short on hormones.

His illumination: Charismatic.

His dark side: Foolhardy.

SAGITTARIUS-SCORPIO

There is a side to the Sagittarian that is quiet, almost sulky, in spite of what you might have read in some publications. When you mix this with the secretive, intense Scorpio Moon, you get a man that can be very difficult to communicate with, whether at home or work. Downright nasty from time to time, to be exact. Demanding, possessive, and determined to have his own way about almost everything. He will not demand it; you either give him his way or he moves on to someone else. He's not always a good bet for a lifetime of co-partnering or parenting. If you are looking for a little less than the lifetime stuff, he could be the one for you. He has much innate insight and wisdom. You will not be able to put much over on this one. While he may act carefree about his money, you will have to explain every nickel and dime should you start to co-mingle finances. He can keep his secrets (like where he really was last Thursday night), yet learn all of yours. He won't stop at much in terms of obtaining his considerable goals. There is much power about this man. He quite simply gets what he goes after. He is aggressive and determined. His uncanny insights into people make him an excellent judge of character and an excellent listener. He is a champion for the underdog, and a sturdy friend. If, however, he feels betrayed in friendship, or rejected in a love relationship, you can count on a truly terrifying wrath. Never abuse his kindness. Don't try to be coy. And break your sexual kinks to him gently. He wants passion of a sizzling nature, but he needs to have it sneak up on him. If not, he has to struggle with the morality of it. Let him taint you. A sly Scorpio, a Capricorn, a Libra, or even a Cancer has the best chances of survival with this one.

His illumination: Wise.

His dark side: Sulky.

SAGITTARIUS-SAGITTARIUS

You probably met him at a function where he was a spokesman of sorts. He was touting something, sprinkling in bits and pieces of his goals for mankind. He'd be a wonderful minister if his interest in the opposite sex weren't so obsessive. At any rate, he is a spellbinding orator or spokesman. In business he is very energetic and ambitious, not afraid of expanding his duties or long hours. Therefore, he is management potential. He also has a wonderful knack for dealing fair and square with everyone. He will not manipulate or bait his co-workers. He is a man of exceptional integrity. He is not, however, warm and sensitive. He is a bit proud and aloof, and you find he relates best as a teacher even in a co-partnership situation. If you are a gossip or have little of his ethical beliefs, it won't matter who you are or what you have to offer. Sorry, but he will have to respect you in the morning. You, however, may find him to be paradoxical. He may leave you amazed at this double standard. Too much to drink and he doesn't have enough backbone to stand up for his own previously held ideas. And, when he wants to play, his best friend's wife will not necessarily be off limits. He is above all restless, hasty, and unpredictable. This is one reason why he isn't usually Father of the Year. Chances for his best success come through ventures outside the continental U.S. If your double Sagittarian was born about 1957 or 1958, his tendency for nervousness and restlessness is considerably lessened. Otherwise, this man is about the most hyperactive, energetic night owl you could pick. Keep your wits about you and be truly liberated and independent. Don't let him suck your life up in his and you will entice him like no one else. One of you will have to keep your feet on the ground. An Aquarius with a Sagittarius Moon would be great. A pretty little Leo is another good bet.

His illumination: Spellbinding orator.

His dark side: Reckless.

SAGITTARIUS-CAPRICORN

It is a rare man with this combination who is not unusually bright. He can talk himself into boardrooms and bedrooms of just about anyone. He is a little too shrewd for his own good and he can scale any heights to obtain his goal of success. He won't injure his co-workers in the process. He often finds himself more hardened and bitter than he had planned. This man can be very cynical given a few wrong turns. He detests human frailties and is quite the taskmaster. His own frailties can be quickly dismissed and rationalized away. As a husband and father he holds tight but loving reins. He values tradition and convention. If you can provide him the nest of comfort, and a white picket fence around it, he will adore it. He wants you to be fenced in however, and not him, so be prepared to have him wander a bit outside your domain. He can be cold and lay down some pretty hard rules for those closest to him in life. For those less important alliances, he really is very tolerant. Remarks like, "I'm so proud of you" go to the stumbling drunk who stayed off the sauce for a day. Not to you for years of dedication and hard work on your PhD. You will have to learn not to take his oversights seriously. It is easy to lend a helping hand to someone he has no commitment towards. It's tough logic to follow, but you'll get the hang of it. His rewards for you are in his being there for you whenever there is a real crisis in your life. He will not be offended at all by your ambition, social climbing, and desire to obtain. He is healthy, ruggedly handsome, somewhat dark, and impeccably dressed. You more aspiring females will trample each other to get to him. He'll just sort of sit back and pick and choose. He is definitely Capricorn girl material. A Gemini or another Sagittarius could do the trick.

His illumination: Bright and shrewd.

His dark side: Cynical.

SAGITTARIUS-AQUARIUS

When I think of this man, I think of changes. He changes opinions, crusades, businesses, and his residences. I also think of influence. He can lead, hypnotize, inspire, and transform others. He's a most unusual man. He can handle the burdens of immense responsibility and power and never be led astray by his sway over people. He is most trustworthy. Excellent in science and politics, his natural bent is in the arts and drama. Ahead of his time, visionary, to be exact, he can read or write science fiction like it was today's newspaper. His intelligence, integrity, and his individuality are his strong points. He is a wonderful, if absentminded, friend. Always busy and on the move, he occasionally lapses into peculiar moods. These are usually accompanied by little electric jolts in his brain that start off the intuitive, inventive, investigative process. During these times of insight, he may be difficult to understand as he is frenzied and fevered by some new concepts. People on a personal basis during these times of vision are secondary to him. It will be sort of like Thomas Edison took over his body and he's got a few more contributions to make for mankind. When he is not doing all of the above, you can bet he is unintentionally spellbinding many a fair maiden. The attraction is not mutual. He loves but a few. The few he loves possess the qualities of intelligence, vision, companionship, and independence. If you dream of a tract home in suburbia with lots of babies, don't even consider this man. It would be his nightmare. Another Sagittarius, maybe; an Aquarian or Gemini fair maiden, you bet. A Libra with lots of Aquarius influences could make it happen.

His illumination: Visionary, trustworthy.

His dark side: Change junkie.

SAGITTARIUS-PISCES

If the Sagittarian is half man and half horse, and the Pisces is the sign of dual fishes, can you imagine how complex this man is going to be? He is full of dreams for humanity. He sees the best in his visions of mankind. He has great powers of observation, is receptive, sympathetic, and caring. He is a nice neighbor, friend, or father. He is also oftentimes his own worst enemy. His love of excess, of over indulgence in food and drink (or worse), bring him down to the level of mortals he so often tries to rise above with yoga and the like. The most "delicate" of the Sagittarian men, his sturdy good looks are accentuated with a chiseled old fashioned quality. He is the Marlborough Man with stars in his eyes, and waves in his hair. This softness amidst rugged appeal lends a romantic, ethereal quality that many women pursue. He is forever the observer, and will sit back and watch the fuss with detachment while he fixes his sights on some beautiful little creature with a ton of emotional baggage. Throw in an illness or two and you've got him hook, line, and sinker. He is hopeless in his own best interests in love. He is therefore subject to many ups and downs in the courtship arena. Contradictory himself, he understands, indeed thrives on, a tangled mess of life in someone else. If you like to be on the receiving end of a relationship and be fawned over for your dependence, this is the one you have been waiting for. In turn, he will ask that you turn a blind eye to his erring ways. Meet him researching, writing, or teaching about hospitals or institutions. Drive him crazy with lacy blouses under your coveralls or blue jeans. Best bets are Scorpio, Cancer, or Pisces. A Virgo lady often fills the bill.

His illumination: Sympathetic, kindly.

His dark side: Given to excess.

Capricorn

December 22–January 21

CAPRICORN-ARIES

Look for him at the top and climbing still higher. He will never be successful enough or rich enough. And like George Burns, he can keep on succeeding long after others have retired into a life of achievement. He simply does not know the words STOP or QUIT. Example: Told of fame and fortune at 56, a 33 year old asks, "What will I become famous for?" "For everything that you have done. . . painting, writing, your profession, even your charitable activities." "What about my singing?" he replies. It had to be just one more piece of accomplishment. For all this determination you would guess him to be totally hard and devoid of other desires. Wrong. He is the man who taught women about having it all. He wants nice homes, a boat, several cars, and a decent relationship. Children? He's rather indifferent. Unless you get to know him well, he appears quick tempered (he is), and cold (he is not). This reserved exterior hides a pretty hot blooded man. He is a man who is insecure and worries himself to the point of exhaustion. Since he is not much of a sleeper (an insomniac oftentimes), add a few things to worry about and he overworks himself to the point of illness. If things get really good, he worries that something bad is about to happen. Sounds like he can't relax. Not necessarily; he can. Given the right companions he can party with the best of them. And he can even get pretty silly along the way. Practical jokes and all. He can also be romantic, though I suspect it does not come naturally. He simply knows how to play the game. When he falls in love, it is still not entirely. It is an extension of his deep need to share his life. He will have plenty of

113

girls to choose from. He prefers a practical, efficient, self-assured woman who knows what she wants from life—to arrive. And that they will, in style. A Taurus, Virgo, Leo, or Aries is his best bet.

His illumination: Can have it all.

His dark side: Practical in love.

CAPRICORN-TAURUS

Here the bull meets the goat. Both signs are sturdy, plodding little fellows with their feet firmly planted on the ground. Just like him. You won't see him dashing about, changing his mind, searching for universal truths. He's a steady, honest fellow at work or play. He is more concerned with the basic needs of life, served under a sturdy roof, and preferably on a silver platter. He doesn't want a bunch of junk in his castle. His plans are to be a banker, real estate broker, or veterinarian. He will invest wisely yet keep his priorities in order about using the available monies for fun and adventure as well. He will not be a miser with you; except of course, in regard to your sexual adventures. You will be allowed very few. He will be fair about this though. He in turn expects to be faithful to the one he loves without exceptions. And if any man can, this one will. He also wants children. He is slow to anger, yet his anger once evoked, is not a pretty sight. Picture the bull snorting. Never insult his pride, honesty, accomplishments, or his mother. Used to winning everything through hard work, the girl of his dreams needs to be sincere and not a pushover. The coy, hard to get routine will not last long with him. He really is too down to earth for such nonsense. He knows all about love and has a strongly passionate nature. Women sense this and respond as if by magic. His romantic life will be as full or as sparse as he decides. He is not easily led. He looks for good stock, good bone structure and teeth. Smile pretty and put your best earth sign forward. Surprise match: the Scorpio. Dynamic!

His illumination: Can invest wisely.

His dark side: Nasty when angered.

CAPRICORN-GEMINI

He is curious, glib, and expressive. This man is inclined to think with his head instead of his heart. About the only things he gets into are his younger women. He doesn't want to be reminded of his aging, primarily because he maintains youthful good looks longer than anyone else does. He is amazing in his boyish appearance well into his sixties. Therefore, he figures a few twenty or thirty year old companions can't hurt his image, but being caught with some old fogies his own age definitely will. This volatile part of his nature, his romantic inclinations, are offset by his level headed approach to business. He is shrewd and often times calculating. He has every intention of getting ahead and is aware of opportunities others miss. He wonders why his co-workers don't notice the many chances for advancement—he is always alert. He is very bright, especially in areas of communications, and excels in writing, interviewing, making presentations, etc. Used to getting attention early on as a child, he grows into a somewhat blatantly confident individual. He can get a little arrogant from time to time. He just needs a little coaxing to settle down. Once he does, he will be a surprisingly warm and loving husband and father. He is, after all, a rather nervous individual. And like most of the Capricorn Suns, he worries too much. He needs a bright, open environment, and to be surrounded with lighthearted (and younger) individuals. He needs a companion to drag him out of doors into the fresh air, and for a change of scene. He will shower his women with roses and attention, but he gets more miserly in his relationships once he feels he has won her hand. He uses his money carefully. He was, in his own way, buying you on the first few dates with all the romance stuff. If you are the dimpled Libra darling, you'll take the presents and run. An Aquarius, Gemini, or Taurus hangs in there.

His illumination: Confident.

His dark side: Nervous.

CAPRICORN-CANCER

This man is not the life of the party. He is not full of good cheer, fun, and frivolity. He is one of the most reserved fellows you are likely to meet. He is fully capable of taking care of himself, and his little reliance on others becomes more obvious with age. He will survive against all odds if necessary. He will not call on anyone for help. He can't really ask for help because he learned early on to look out for himself. Also, because he knows who he can and can't count on. His parents probably let him down as a child, and like the elephant he will never forget. In truth, his somber, reserved, often moody and sullen personality leave many a person feeling that he can't be trusted. His projection of mistrust is returned by those around him, and that gives him one more reason for self-pity; no one likes him. This is not true (you for one, or you'd be looking up someone else). Older people, influential people, and ambitious people like him for a confidant. They know he is not talking. This is a nice quality. Problem is, he sometimes does this with you, too. He just clams up and won't talk. He is serious but this doesn't mean that he can't be witty, intelligent, and sensitive to your needs. He does make money, and spending it on his family and loved ones is a first priority. He will not take lightly any slights, imagined or otherwise, from you. He is looking for a mother figure and you can be older, plump, and not too pretty and he'll still adore you. Like his other values, his ideas for womanhood are his own. He is an excellent psychotherapist, teacher, or counselor with an after hours flair for history and the fine arts. Libra makes him knuckle down; Cancer babies him; Scorpio sets him on fire.

His illumination: Can make money.

His dark side: Confused his role models.

CAPRICORN-LEO

Remember the Aries-Capricorn combination where he couldn't ever accomplish enough? Well, this is his brother who can't quite acquire enough. He wants power, money, and things. There is no modesty about this man, even false. He wants to show off his acquisitions. He is not being so much gaudy as proud of his personal measures of success. He usually comes from humble beginnings, parentage, background, and oftentimes a degree of ill health. He is forever climbing, not necessarily social, to scale his heights. There are often two types of Leo Moon combinations. One type is the men born in the 1940s often become socially reclusive for no apparent reason late in life. They still interact and have powerful, influential friends, but they just want to be more and more alone. For some you can chalk it up to the partying days being over (and could he ever party). For others it is the first sign that he is trying to save enough money to "drop out." He has better things to do with his time, like study, invent, create. Often submissive to a degree at home, he takes command everywhere else. His co-workers know instinctively that he's on his way to the top. In romance he takes the initiative. He is impulsive and knows instinctively what he is looking for from life and love. Women are so attracted to him, he often avoids the more aggressive types, preferring the quiet, confident girl who responds to his overtures. He wants someone to play with. As long as you don't miss work to plan an adventure, or compromise his prestige, he is highly attracted to a woman who helps him escape from the serious task of obtaining all his goals. His children can get in on the playful side of his personality. Picnics, amusement parks, theatres, and day long romps in bed with a fiery Leo, Sagittarius, or a kinky little Virgo girl are the best bets for this man's happiness.

His illumination: Knows what he wants.

His dark side: Obsession with purpose.

CAPRICORN-VIRGO

There he is. The slight, serious, somewhat dark corporate account- ant. He is practical and conventional. His co-workers think he is a genius. Nothing could ever throw him off balance. Wrong; one thing can and usually does—an unhappy marriage. A miserable marriage. A wife with a chronic illness or neurosis. You won't be- lieve me because he has such a pleasant, stable appearance. Trust me, it is a mask. His intelligence and insights are lost in the love rela- tionships department. The intellectual side of this man is strong, and he needs a bright partner. He also needs a clean one. No crum- pled sheets or dingy underwear for him. A classic bookworm, if you want to get his head out of the book, you will have to have a strong ability to talk knowingly on a number of subjects, and be a superb housekeeper and domestic engineer. His values in a relationship are strictly conventional. He will expect to be catered to, and will be until his basically unsteady partner unravels. At this point he will take over the more domestic role, including raising the children. Everything he does, he does well. Even his sexual habits are studied and perfected. Spontaneous passion is not his nature. Textbook study has no doubt come first. His choices in mates are surprising. A Pisces, a Gemini, a Cancer, or a Virgo are the most attractive of the Zodiac for him. He promises devotion, stability, pensions, cars in running order, taxes paid on time, and a well stocked freezer. He needs a Taurus, Virgo, Cancer, or Pisces to make him tick.

His illumination: Does most everything well.

His dark side: Choice of mate surprises.

CAPRICORN-LIBRA

Here is a man no one can resist. Everyone he meets is fascinated by his charm. He is the romantic of the Capricorns. He usually has experienced some domestic difficulties, even in childhood. Yet he is devoted to his family. His devotion will be shown in a grand fashion, rather than mundane things like keeping promises. He means well, but is easily distracted by The Good Life. He is the man in *The Days of Wine and Roses*. He gets by in life on his charms and innate talents (he is fabulous in the arts) rather than his persistence. He has a tendency to have things come his way early and easily, and then fall victim to excess in drink or drugs. Obtaining his goals too soon, or too easily, as often is the case, leaves him gloomy and aimless. He has a sad tendency to self-destruct in front of his friends and family. Not necessarily the most handsome of men, he has more appeal than most of the Zodiac combined. He will always be surrounded by admiring and beautiful women. His idea of a compliment is to say, "You look like you just got released from the fat farm." It will be music to your ears. They write romance novels about this guy. He can turn your heart into a fluttering butterfly. And if you are the one he has been looking for, he will tell you within the first few hours of meeting you. If he is involved with someone else when this happens, he will terminate the other relationship. This man does not play games. He will want the best in clothes, cars, and houses for you and his family. He will obtain it early on. He won't care if you are as frivolous with money as he is. He just wants happy, fun filled, successful days with his beautiful mate beside him. Capricorns, Libras, or possibly a Pisces stand the best chance. Try to catch him young, before he gets too successful for his own good.

His illumination: Takes your breath away.

His dark side: Does most eveything well.

CAPRICORN-SCORPIO

This is one of the most powerful combinations in the Zodiac. No telling quite how these energies will erupt. There is nothing vague or wishy-washy about this man. He has his opinions on just about everything, and will not be afraid to tell you so. He is tense, has a fiery temper, and days of deep, quiet depression. He has morose and morbid thoughts which often center around death. He may be in fact, death phobic. He comes across as severe and humorless. He is neither, really. His sense of humor is fantastic, but subtle, intelligent, and off-the-wall. It may quite simply be over most people's heads. As for severity, he can be the most sympathetic of listeners, and offer really good advice. He is a good friend. He is also a devoted, consistent, passionate lover. Just don't cross him or he will make your life hell. He will be relentless in his desire for revenge. It will not matter in the least that you are sorry, or that you have changed for the better. You're dead meat. If you are in competition with him say, for example, in business, prepare to lose. This is the combination that wins. No matter how the prospects look for him, if he wants something he will get it. Please don't try to stand in his way. On the other hand, he sounds a lot scarier than he is—if he loves you, he fairly purrs. There is nothing he won't sacrifice for the loved one he trusts, or for his children. Don't try to fool him, I think he reads minds. He has a dark side sexually. Sex is very important to him. He needs you to dominate him. You will have to find out by instinct what he wants sexually. He will never talk about it. A Scorpio here can decipher it all. A Pisces or Cancer can help him be gentle. Keep away, Aries!

His illumination: Off-the-wall humor.

His dark side: Opinionated.

CAPRICORN-SAGITTARIUS

Here is the combination of the old man and the young child. He needs to keep track of time, but wears a Mickey Mouse watch to do it. He is patient with his loved ones and a maniac if kept waiting at the post office. He is given to flights of fancy, but very few would ever guess. He is organized in order that he can spend his leisure hours working on his various schemes to become rich and famous. His deep dark secret is that *Lifestyles of the Rich and Famous* is his favorite show. He will only watch this when he is alone, I'm sure. He may be the most stable, efficient, and practical person you've ever worked with (that is probably how you met him), but he has an inconsistent streak. If he could afford it, he would probably never bother to so much as pick up his clothes. He would be studying, traveling, partying, and trying to cram a lifetime of fun into a few years. He also manages to worry a few hours of the day, even when having fun. Capricorn usually starts with the most impoverished of youth, emotionally and financially. He never forgets his beginnings. His constant goal is to get as far from these beginnings as possible. He pretends to accept less than the best in the most pleasant and charming manner. He does not for one moment accept anything less than spectacular accomplishments and surroundings for himself. Let him achieve his dreams and watch the change. He will still be loyal to his old friends and family, but the tract home and pickup truck are gone. He will spend his last cent to move to Bel-Air and buy his Rolls. Don't try to stop him or he'll never give you a second thought. Other than that, he's a good husband and he will gush over his children. When his ship comes in he's on it! A Sagittarian or Leo playmate is best. The sexy Scorpio is the dark horse he may dump his considerable others for.

His illumination: Spectacular feats.

His dark side: Early struggles.

CAPRICORN-CAPRICORN

An iron will, nerves of steel, and a heart of stone. He won't be flattered, cajoled, manipulated, or controlled. You know the odd part of all this? He would love to have his dream come true and have some fair maiden bring out his sweet, gentle side. I don't know what it will take, and neither does he, but he is like Scrooge at Christmas. He really wants to do something nice for other people. He just doesn't want to get hurt or to be taken advantage of. That is what makes his barriers so concrete hard. His defenses are elaborate. Try to compliment him. First you get the ice cold stare, then a stern nod, and finally the slight blush when he realizes you really mean it. Then he is delighted. He starts to like you. He is timid for all his ferocity. You could take your time and sneak up on him this way. Why bother? Because here is a man who knows what loyalty and devotion are all about. He is also a man who will keep the wolves away from your beautiful oak carved, stained glass door. He is an excellent provider, father, and a very decent human being. But, like I said earlier, he is going to have to have an awakening. And you know what? He can turn out to be a good companion. He has a silly side. Laughing makes him feel good, and once he gets hooked on that he is very sexually demanding. Like everything else he does for you, he will want to do it the best he possibly can. You will have to go after this man. One, he stays home a lot—he feels secure there. Two, he works obsessively. His secretary stands a strong chance. Especially if she is a Cancer, Pisces, or a Taurus who can be on time.

His illumination: Excellent provider.

His dark side: Elaborate defenses.

CAPRICORN-AQUARIUS

This is a very unusual, almost eccentric man. He won't fit into many categories (even mine), and will be very hard to predict. He is given to tremendous whims. He is the most capricious man of the Zodiac. He likes to be unrestricted and free spirited. He is a teacher, photographer, executive, restauranteur, antique dealer, or writer for Mother Earth. He often pursues several vocations at once. He wants to experience it all. He does not necessarily stick to all these professions and avocations. He is subject to many changes. He is ruled by his electric moods. He could read Shirley McLain's *Out on a Limb,* and take off to Peru for his own out of body experience. That he left his wife and kids and business appointments to fend for themselves will be of no concern to him. He is a student of life. He does exactly whatever makes him feel good. While he appears to be full of surprises, he is actually doing whatever he wants. That is the key to understanding this man. If all this excitement is for you, and you also hate traits like dependability and practicality, count on this: He will be ever so good at keeping his word to you. Once he has been snagged, and once he makes one of his rare promises, he will keep it to the ends of the earth. He needs a fellow adventurer, a confident, caring, leftover flower child to help him through this world. Once he settles down, he will be a good catch. If he was born in the early 1960s he'll be ready to settle in his late 20s and early 30s. Born in the 1940s, he undergoes his major changes within the decade. He needs you, pixie Gemini, wacky Aquarius, or Libra. Underneath it all is a sound fellow.

His illumination: Hot and sassy.

His dark side: Capricious.

CAPRICORN-PISCES

This man is a wonderful friend and co-worker. He is sympathetic and kind, and full of wisdom. He also knows, and keeps secret, where just about everyone's skeletons are hidden. Every person he knows calls on him for advice and friendship. This soft hearted, generous man has a sharp mind and a gentle soul. He carries a lot of emotional baggage. He himself keeps his problems hidden from others. He has, in fact, some deep, dark secrets that he carries literally to the grave. He usually has a secret marriage or relationship that he mentions to no one, even his current wife and children. He may also have an illegitimate child hidden away somewhere. Add to this at least one woman who broke his heart and made him turn to chemical escapes. Chronic ill health follows, and guess what? No one knows because he doesn't talk about what hurts him. If he could talk about it, he might not use drugs or drink. And as if all this weren't bad enough, he usually has a glandular problem that causes him to gain weight. He is by 40 usually quite heavy. This adds to his pain because he is a very attractive man. He is also usually found in some sort of limelight, often political or religious. He is very image conscious and, yes, vain. He will be the first to poke fun at himself, but not in connection with the word fat. Laughing and cheerful, he can pull up everyone by their bootstraps, except himself. He is oftentimes his own worst enemy. Rescue him if you can, because he could be a wonderful, exciting husband and father. This job calls for a drug free Pisces, a homemaking Cancer, or a Scorpio who has exorcised her own demons.

His illumination: Soft-hearted, and generous.

His dark side: Own worst enemy.

Aquarius

January 21–February 20

AQUARIUS-ARIES

His family was an immense help to him, not only materially, but physically. He comes from good stock. He was instilled early with a good sense of himself and common sense. He was the street smart kid who never had to hit the streets. He was the young man desperately bored with school, making excellent grades. As a result he understands his children instinctively. He is now the grown man with a definite direction and sense of purpose. Not especially charming, he comes across at first meeting as vain and arrogant. He is. But he is also witty, intelligent, and intense. He does not want to be pinned down and is one of the true bachelor combinations of the Zodiac. Even married, there is no question about his getting to race cars, staying out all night for his poker parties, or flying off to boxing matches. He is a man's man, and his own man. He will not be tied down to a mortgage and repairing refrigerators. He is pleased with his life and his circumstances from an early age. He isn't really looking for a relationship to round himself out. He is strong willed but careful not to offend the sensitive persons around him. Creative artistic ideas fairly pour out of his head. He is often a freelancer because he does not like the routine of checking in and out of offices. A time clock would be totally offensive to him. A house with frilly curtains and bedspreads will give him the heebie jeebies. If you want him to spend intimate time with you, keep your home eclectic, with clean open spaces. Put the ferns outside where he thinks they belong. An Aries, Leo, or Gemini are the best bets to capture his rather elusive heart.

His illumination: Creative, independent.

His dark side: Routine is abhorrent to him.

AQUARIUS-TAURUS

This Uranus/Venus ruled man has a sensitive nervous system and a plodding and calm emotional nature. These influences just don't harmonize in the same body. It is his basic nature to accept the unusual and unconventional. His emotions require tranquility. He never really gets it. The Aquarian can happily go off on one tangent after another, the Taurus just wanted to have wine with dinner. The Aquarian thinks money is the root of all evil, the Taurus needs roots. People sense this conflict as erratic and impulsive. But as he grows older he becomes a huge success, and falls more into sync with himself. Public acclaim comes looking for him, he does not pursue it, nor even dream of it. It will not turn his head. It, like money, is nice to have but his goals were always more directed towards humanitarian ventures. He would like to set up outer space travel tours, give lectures on how to gain self confidence, launch campaigns for social reforms. His *Psychology Today* personality can't figure how the *Wall Street Journal* got into his mail box. It was his Taurus Moon that ordered it. Every now and then that stubborn little moon gets his way. This moon gets its way with women too. Women are ever so attracted to this man. He in turn is a romantic, but in a space age sort of way. He will want all the elements of a hot romance without the commitments of yesteryear. He likes his girls curvy, frilly, and dainty. He wants to do the pursuing. But he will be ethical in his approach. He will not tell her wild stories and tales of devotion to get her into bed. He doesn't have to. He makes an eventual good husband, and a loving, accepting father. He won't ask that you follow in his footsteps. The lovely Libra, the misty eyed Pisces, and the cool Capricorn have the best chance of a long term relationship with this man.

His illumination: Can be a huge success.

His dark side: May forget his address.

AQUARIUS-GEMINI

Here is a real romantic. At least he is in his heart. His "I'll call you on Monday" that turns into Thursday is the biggest commitment he has made. Would you believe that he is crazy about you? And yet he forgets you so easily. I am not going to give any other man this excuse about not calling when he is supposed to. This guy is a passive spirit. A puff of air. Unless he was born between nine and ten in the morning, in which case he didn't call because he was with someone else. He is glib, and usually handsome, so he can get away with a lot of rotten things other men wouldn't even consider. If he was born about 1940 to 1946 and he pulls this forgetful act on you, get your track shoes on because he really, really was out with someone else. He is hot air when it comes to his beliefs on social reform and crusades. He will not actually be found fund raising or answering telephone hotlines. He will leave that to you. At any rate, he needs to develop a little more stability in his love relationships because he is so easily infatuated. As you can guess, he's not the most likeable husband or father. He also needs this stability in his professional life. His co-workers would like to be able to count on him. He can easily flit from job to job. He can alter his career from advertising, to construction, to real estate in the bat of your eyelash. He is adept at most of the trades, but he takes a rather long time to settle down. The early 1990s will settle him down plenty. He'll have a lot of responsibility from the planets, and will have no choice but to become more stable. If he's the one for you, I hope that you are a Libra of the most controlling sort. You could change this man. An Aquarius or a Sagittarius can entice and perhaps entrap. Everyone will eventually have a chance for a fling with this one though.

His illumination: Means well.

His dark side: Forgets your address.

AQUARIUS-CANCER

This man is tied to the past. Naturally, since he wants to hang on to every bit and part of his old life, it makes it difficult for him to go on with his new relationships. He will not change, so you will have to accept this little quirk in him. In his prior failed relationship he no doubt attributed assets to his loved one that quite simply did not exist. He just saw her in a light far more favorable than she deserved, and all this hanging on serves to complicate his life and his health. He develops stomach problems. Relaxation seems impossible to come by. Your nagging about any of this will not help the situation. What else? He has problems with his eyes and his mother. To compensate for all this, he is popular, friendly, sociable, sensitive, caring, and emotive. In fact, he could pretty well fit into the perfect man category. He is good natured, considerate, generous with the object of his affection, rational, conventional, capable of great business deals, and quite the money maker. Where do you find this man? First, he probably has wide spaced eyes hidden behind his glasses. Or else he is squinting a lot because he forgot to wear them. He either has his own small business or is in sales or brokering. He'll be the quiet one at the computer checking things out. Or after work he could be found at a yoga class, or a gourmet restaurant. He's probably out with his mother. Not that he couldn't get a date; he probably has two scheduled for later on tonight. It is just that mom has a special place in his heart and he is not too macho to show it. I think he's a honey. I hope he finds a Cancer, Pisces, or a Capricorn. I hope he finds happiness.

His illumination: He's a sweetie.

His dark side: Mom may move in.

AQUARIUS-LEO

In a word, he is stubborn. He is also always there if you need him, a strong handsome shoulder to cry on, understanding, gallant. And, for those of you into domination, he can be a real pushover in love. He is a little naive. I think he deserves much better than to be taken advantage of though. He is lovable and will share your life, hopes, dreams, and chores with you. He will meet you more than halfway to be sure. He is capable and responsible at home and at work. He is a good parent. He may talk a lot about discipline and, God forbid, a spanking, but he is very lenient. He usually has few children. Either one, or a set of twins. He is always wanting more, though. Courtship with this man could drive you crazy, but in marriage he is relatively dependable. One thing, either way, from the moment you meet him he needs attention. He has a fair amount of pride and yes, conceit.

He is ambitious. But he needs a supporter. He had a strong attachment to his mother, may even resemble her, and yet there is the basis
for his primary misunderstanding about relating to women. He
does have trouble with that. He has a tendency to over-idolize the
woman of the moment. And when the relationship falls flat on its
face from his unrealistic expectations, he can't figure it out. For all he
has to offer, he has a lot of trouble maintaining a relationship. He
means well, but you know about the road that was paved with good
intentions. If you are a strong actress, a professional gambler, a computer whiz, or a doctor, I think he'll behave. Otherwise, you'll have
some rough days ahead. He must have a challenge. A dramatic one.
A Leo, Sagittarius, or determined Libra stands the best chance with
this one.

His illumination: Gallant.

His dark side: Stubborn.

AQUARIUS-VIRGO

He belongs to MENSA, no doubt. This man is very smart. Some people build walls around them to protect themselves. His barrier is rational detachment. It gives me the chills just thinking about how
cold and aloof he can be. And yet, he has such strong skills in communicating, and presents such a pleasant demeanor, that some of
the less observant of us fail to notice that he continually distances
himself. He will not take much initiative in the pursuit of a relationship. He does well, however, in fields requiring high visibility and
public contact. He is good as a teacher, salesman, journalist, or
speech writer. People love him. His secret desire, no doubt, is to invent the computer that can replace the doctor or nutritionist. He has
some pretty far reaching, innovative, humanitarian ideas. He has
many friends for all his aloofness and outspokenness. That is because people can sense a basically good heart. His nervous system is
fragile, and if he smokes he compounds damage to his susceptible
lungs. He does not have the sort of good looks that drive women
crazy. But upon closer examination he has an earnest, decent sort of
good looks. Rather squeaky clean. Speaking of clean, you had better
be. He will not be the least offended if you stop to brush your teeth
before going to bed. If you take breaks from your romantic candlelight dinner to put the pans in the dishwasher it will not break the

spell for him. This is one of the few men who can deal with reality. He appreciates order and admires neatness. If I made him sound boring, he is not. He has a lot of exciting, unpredictable things happen to him in his life. Your days with him will never be dull. He just doesn't go around looking for adventure. Adventure comes to his door. You might also come to his door, especially if you are a Gemini, Aquarius, or Capricorn, and catch yourself a good man.

His illumination: Can deal with reality.

His dark side: Detatched emotionally.

AQUARIUS-LIBRA

Oftentimes this man is beautiful. His good looks are so startling one might think there is not much else to him. Romantically, he is unstable. A one night stand is usually pretty much all he is looking for. This is hard on the ladies. He is charming and nice, but he is very inconsistent in everything he does. I know this is falling on deaf ears, and that as you read my warnings about this womanizer all you can see is his gentle good looks, his almost silken hair and chiseled beauty. He is not deep. He was just practicing the art of flirting. When he has conquered you, and that is usually on the first date, he is gone just like the puff of air he is. His double Air signs leave him as restless as the wind. He just doesn't dream of marriage and children. He can fall in love though, but guess what? She'll break his heart. He will pick the most unusual, unreliable and strange girl he encounters. He didn't set about to do this to be difficult. It just works out that way, don't ask me why. This makes him cranky. He will run to other women for solace. They will do whatever they can to put a smile back on that sour little face. And guess who he will still love? Her. As he begins to recover, he will throw parties at his home. You may not even be invited. Speaking of his home and parties, the parties will be rather small in the number of guests. And even if his mother said he was the messiest child she ever raised, his own time will be neat and clean. He will not serve Hogie sandwiches, but some delicacy from the caterer. He hates cheap, ordinary things. All this artistic eye stuff leads him into a career in the arts, promotion, or sales. No sitting behind the CPA's desk for him. I know one who makes hundreds of thousands of dollars a day, and do you know how he keeps track of it? In a little red book by his nightstand where he doodles his outcome and outgo for the day. You know what? He keeps nearly perfect records. Remember, he is smart. A beautiful Taurus, Pisces, or Libra catches his eye. The Capricorn he admires.

His illumination: Artistic eye.

His dark side: Inconsistent.

AQUARIUS-SCORPIO

This man has a negative streak in him that distorts his view of reality. He also does not easily learn from his experiences. He has a chip on his shoulder. He likes his existence to be as spontaneous as possible, and hates to plan things in advance. Needless to say, you're not going to be able to make many changes in him. In fact, he is pretty pleased with himself as he is. Know why? Because he has the ability to command respect from people. He is also very intelligent and usually has a host of followers. This man could sway the masses. He is a man given to impulsive actions, and when they turn out to be hairbrained, as a few will, he will be the first to laugh at himself. If he does not laugh first, you be sure not to even crack a smile. He wants control over his co-workers, his lovers, his friends. Giggle at him when he is serious and he will verbally chew your hair off. I mean it, this man gets really cranky. He has a hidden interest in the occult, and will probably use some of its teachings to cure his few aches and pains. Some of his pains are due to problems in the reproductive area. Sometimes it will be of a hypertensive nature. Part of his health problems are with his excess sexuality, and part, like the hypertension, are due to his never being quite able to let go of a grudge. He probably still carries a grudge from grade school. Also, another thing not so good for his mental and physical health is his tendency to keep all his secrets locked up and filed away from probing eyes. There are some tragedies and personal heartbreaks he cannot share with anyone. Sometimes he does this because quite frankly, you would be appalled at some of the things he has done. The Capricorn/Pisces attracts him, but he needs the quietness of a Cancer of the lightness of the Gemini.

His illumination: Commands respect.

His dark side: Excess sexuality.

AQUARIUS-SAGITTARIUS

This man is pretty mellow and tranquil. No pent up secret emotions here. In fact when he has a heartbreak, he will tell you and, without brooding, let you know as to how he plans to have a happier future. He is an optimist. He has no intention of fretting over his losses forever. He won't need therapy to find out where he is going and what he expects out of life. He knew at a very early age. He has a very uncomplicated outlook on life. It is, simply put, nice. Extremely independent, he grows less emotionally high strung as he grows older. Even though he mellows out do not expect that he will account for his time. Loving, supportive, and decent with his loved one, he still wants to be left pretty much alone. He will not need you to travel with him, entertain him, or to have you as a companion. Nonetheless, he is a romantic, even if in an unconventional manner. He usually has several marriages, and can count at least five true loves in his life, and many loving children. As he gets older he gets better. He'll have every woman at Seniors' Bingo drooling over him. There is a spring in his step and a sparkle in his eyes that time cannot dim. This big hearted fellow will break hearts into his 90s. He loves to travel, and chances are he will have made his money in the import, export, legal, or teaching professions. Much of his monies came through his ventures in another country from his place of birth. He will have a few long distance romances in his life, and do you know what? He will usually list these as his most successful of romances. He will swim oceans to get to his overseas honey, but once she's nearby a lot of the glitter fades. Never mind, she will have enjoyed herself. Was she a Capricorn? Sagittarius, Libra and Leo play out some of his marital dramas.

His illumination: Optimistic and mellow.

His dark side: A loner in the relationship.

AQUARIUS-CAPRICORN

This man wants a few simple things out of life, like to be an astronaut, the President, or maybe a General. He has lots of integrity and determination. He is a workhorse, and has had problems with his father. He will not at all be above marrying to better himself. If all this drive doesn't pan out early, and it usually does not, depressions are likely. We are talking about deep, dark, gloomy days where he wonders if it is all worth it? It is, and he knows it. He knows he will eventually get what he wants, and that makes the bad times tolerable. Never for a moment will he lose faith in himself. Oh, he may worry and fret, but deep inside he knows. He knows that if he doesn't get to be General, he can settle happily for Colonel. He has a stern formality about him. Even, I suspect, when he is alone with his cat. Oftentimes you will feel that he is talking down to you; he probably is. Given to a feeling of superiority, he really can't help himself. He is used to executive positions at an early age, and takes naturally to leadership. He will make decent money, but your social life will always have a practical use, rather than being just for recreation. You will be his person, not his partner, if he decides that you are the one for him. You will be expected to be the political wife even when he is just starting out as a law student. You must be poised, calm under pressure, stately, and as ambitious as he is. Naturally, not many women are interested in filling this bill, nor could many meet the rigid demands. Who might want to give it a try? A Capricorn, naturally, or a Libra who has no plans of her own. Sometimes a bright little Aquarius will fit right into the softer side of this man.

His illumination: Integrity.

His dark side: May marry to better himself.

AQUARIUS-AQUARIUS

Pursuing whatever catches his fancy at the moment, this man is the Christopher Columbus of the Zodiac configurations. He wants to explore the world, all levels of mankind, every culture, and be free enough to follow his every whim. He is an idealist who makes no barriers about economic stratas, color, or creed. He is the ponderer who wants the answers to the universal and spiritual truths. I am tired just thinking about his need to experience. It is constant. His interests are so varied that it would take volumes to list them all. His abilities are also assorted, ranging from mechanics, philosophies, and physics to the occult. He is a leader in many organizations. He is electrifying air currents darting about. He has the natural talent to be one of the finest scientists. He just needs the stick-to-itiveness to make a success of himself. He will be found in the midst of his odd collections of artifacts and memorabilia. He prefers to work alone, but gets along fine in congested areas as well. He also is usually surrounded by some pretty peculiar acquaintances. His wife, however, will not be strange. Here in the selection of his mate, he is a snob. In any other area of life he is not. Something happens to him when he starts thinking about "the one." He becomes very conventional. He wants a self-sufficient, progressive woman who can appreciate the need for their mutual freedom. He is hoping that she comes from some decent economic situation. He is not being cold or greedy, he just wants to be doubly sure she won't need to count on him for financial security either. He really wants her liberated. He wants to encourage individuality and a sense of adventure in his children. Another Aquarius, Gemini, or even a Pisces will enable him to dream his dreams.

His illumination: A natural leader.

His dark side: Detached in love.

AQUARIUS-PISCES

Scared by the boogie man at an early age, he never fully recovered. He still has strange phobias. He had imaginary friends as a child and he still sees or hears things others do not. He is not a schizophrenic, but rather something of a mystic from time to time. He is both irrational and sane. He will believe in the Hollow Earth Theory (one gave me the book once) and fear the Bermuda Triangle. He also comes to the breakfast table telling you of the latest international news . . . before the newspaper is even delivered. He is very, very odd to say the least. He wants tranquil surroundings, and wouldn't you with all he has to contend with within himself? He is gentle. He hates arguments. Electrifying changes rule his life. He finds the house he really wants two days after he put another he thought he wanted in escrow, or he loses his passport on the way to the airport, maybe he had an encounter with a UFO. Everything seems to happen to him to create one crisis after the other in his life. Naturally, this does not set the stage for a prosperous dating life. Women are turned off by a man in a continued state of chaos who is never even phased by it. Who wouldn't be if it happened all your life? He's decent. He could be a fine husband, and the kind of father who understands the terrors of childhood. He tells the truth as he knows it. He never wants to hurt anyone's feelings. All his messages get garbled. It is a wonder he can find his way to work. He needs a steadfast woman who never has out of the ordinary things happen to her. A Cancer, a Libra, a Pisces can help him with all the little things, like finding his shoes.

His illumination: Prophetic.

His dark side: Phobic.

Pisces

February 20–March 21

PISCES-ARIES

Given a chance, the Pisces man would stay home, draw the drapes, and retire from life. But this Moon saves him. No way will the emotional Aries Moon get out of the mainstream. He wants action and often the Pisces wonders how it is that he is out there doing all these brave things, like sports car racing or scuba diving. In spite of himself, he finds that he is dashing, active, and involved with everything from the local political party to the company newsletter. He may mutter to himself when he is alone, but he is always secretly proud of the race he entered or his under water photos. He is proud because he overcame his inclination to avoid life, and he is determined to make the best of himself. He does things for his mental health. He wants to be strong and healthy enough to help others. He is a humanitarian at heart. He is an excellent fund raiser for a worthy cause. He would be a good researcher for some medical pursuit. He wants to help others because he has a wonderful heart. His face is usually round, and his head rather large. Aside from that, he is attractive. He is also a lot of fun. Not that you will know about that if you're not included in his inner circle where he can relax and be himself. If you don't know him well, you will swear that you have never even seen him smile. If you know him well, you will have countless memories of the times you laughed your mascara off with his antics. He can be found walking with his head down, as if plowing his way through life. He is. He is fragile and needs very badly to survive. He does not know that he doesn't have to give 200 percent to do it. This includes fatherhood—he is a fabulous parent. If he falls in love with you, he will work very hard to make your relationship the best it can be. If you do not put as much effort in it, he will put his head down and plow forward again, never looking back to even say goodbye. Oh yes, if you run into him some years later, and he seems to be stifling a laugh, it is because he heard you lost your job and your eyesight is failing. Now that he will find very amusing. A Taurus, an Aries, or the Scorpio can lead him on a merry chase. He will think he has been very daring indeed to be with a Scorpio.

His illumination: A good researcher.

His dark side: Fragile.

PISCES-TAURUS

This man is lucky. I can hear him now saying, "Oh sure," in total disbelief. Whatever money he needs is there for him. He is a good money maker, investor, and inheritor. He did not think luck had much to do with it because he is not afraid of hard work, is cautious about expenses, and has made himself sick worrying about what inflation will do to his retirement monies. Never mind that he is only 26. He is quite simply not sure of things. He is not even sure about himself, let alone you. But given the odds, he will figure he is his own best bet. Entry into his life, on more than a superficial level, is a rare gift he imparts to a few. For these lucky few, he is a wonderful friend, lover, husband, and father. He often over-extends his energies to help you paint your house, repair your car, and visit your ailing mother. He does not keep score exactly, but if in return you do not help him patch his roof, your friendship will become less intense. At work he is cooperative, even if he is your boss. Again, if you let him down, you can expect to have him start documenting your performance. He is going to go places in his career. He will do it modestly, and with little discussion. He will not brag, nor will he lord his promotions over his co-workers. He will instead try to help you advance as well. If he falls asleep in the movies with you, do not consider it a sign he was bored. He actually felt relaxed enough with you to let his defenses rest (literally) a moment. If he reeks of liquor on the first date, give him a second chance. He may have drank to have the courage to go out with you. When he falls in love it is instant and lasting. Since he knows this in advance of you, he had to drink to calm himself over the married life that he sees flashing before him. It wasn't something he'd planned, like his portfolio or planting his hedges next Saturday. Remember, he knows well in advance of the rest of us what is happening to him. He just doesn't want to talk about it. A steady little Taurus, a Virgo, a Capricorn, or Cancer all have a chance. He is adaptable no matter what he says about himself. A Leo will drive him wonderfully crazy, and he'll hang on until she finally gives him ulcers.

His illumination: Lucky.

His dark side: Unsure.

PISCES-GEMINI

Everything he does scares him. It ought to. He hasn't the slightest idea what he will be up to next. Like when he wakes up on his day off and begins remodeling the den, only to find himself wandering from the hardware store to a new subdivision, and to the not so local new car dealership. While he is not exactly aimless, he is easily distracted. This includes his career goals and relationships at work. This is all part of his restless, ever-changing mood, and his afflicted nervous system. It is not uncommon for this man to have trouble with the opposite sex; he just can't seem to get the hang of relationships. He also usually has several crises going on at the same time. These usually come about as the result of his having dropped the ball somewhere along the line. If he sounds like a handful, let me assure you he is. Speaking of a handful, he is a really cuddly sleeper, and will have handfuls of you as you sleep. He wants in turn for you to give lots of hugs and pats, as he does. Not especially consistent in love, he may murmur another name in his sleep. She doesn't mean a thing to him. Women are easy to come by; he is shallow and he only said her name because today and yesterday often get confused with this man. What he needs is help. A lot of gentle guidance. If he stays in a relationship, it may be only to have his laundry done and the refrigerator stocked. It may sound as though I don't like this man. That is not true. I just find him very difficult for the average woman of today to deal with, especially if there is a family involved. A Gemini or Aquarius is best. Who else could even attempt it?

His illumination: Adaptable.

His dark side: Ever changing moods.

PISCES-CANCER

The Sun and Moon are in a fortunate position here. While this person never really asserts himself, he is usually doing what he wants anyway. There is just no discussion, and God forbid, an argument about it. If ever anyone was ruled by the Moon, it is this man. His moods change often, at least every two and one half days, like the Moon does, and he is ruled by his ever changing emotions. He has some pretty raunchy sexual escapades at some point during his life, but will deny it with his last breath; he claims innocence to the end. Want to know why? Because if it was unpleasant or unpopular, he has put it out of his mind and it is as if nothing ever happened. He believes what he wants to. He cannot handle a lot of harsh reality. He is a gentle and sensitive soul. He wants everyone to like him, even when he has been naughty or cranky. Naturally, his co-workers do not always find him enchanting or trustworthy. If he is upset, he gets headaches, his stomach aches, or he overindulges in sweets (bad for his blood sugar) and alcohol. This overindulgence also applies to his falling in love. When he wants someone's love he will go to any lengths to try and please her. He is a wonderful sweetheart, and will remain that way until he becomes disenchanted. Then he will ignore, humiliate, and chill his partner to the bone. He will be astonished that you are hurt and bewildered. He also quite frankly will no longer care. He has lots of secret and multiple affairs until he meets the girl of his dreams. Literally. He may dream of her before he ever sets eyes on her. She may be older. He is a restless husband but a loving and attentive father. His dream may be a Scorpio or Capricorn, but if these are at the same time, pray they never met each other. The Cancer is what he needs.

His illumination: Sensitive and caring.

His dark side: Secret affairs.

PISCES-LEO

This man wears a mask. He is an actor. He is proud, commanding and majestic, and can take center stage. If he can't be center stage without much effort, or has to stand by and see another person take to the limelight, he will quietly walk off by himself. He wants admiration. He wants it without fanfare and open competition. There is a lot of inner turmoil in this man. He is a creature of complex needs. There is nothing to dislike about him though, even if he sometimes appears to be aloof, or worse yet, an outright snob. He would be an excellent nurse, playwright, a teacher of dramatics, a writer of children's stories, or inventor of gambling recreations. He's a hard-working, non-complaining co-worker. Many times emotional unhappiness results in an almost overwhelming loss of energy. He tries to take care of too many people, and his commitments romantically often leave him taxed and drained. He wants to take care of someone, and is so intense in his closest relationship that it becomes almost smothering for the woman of his dreams. This Moon, when coupled with the Pisces Sun, can be over-protective. This includes his relationships with the children. Part of the duality of his nature is that he radiates a lighthearted air of happy confidence when in truth, none of that is so. He needs some assistance. He will be appealing and hide his complexities well. You won't believe me. Commit yourself to him and be prepared for a life of ups and downs. Help him with a balanced, rational demeanor. Believe in stability and adore him. A Leo, Cancer, or Sagittarius could be the Rx for this man.

His illumination: Appealing.

His dark side: A life of ups and downs.

PISCES-VIRGO

This man has a real advantage—he has both a fine intellect and a wonderful insight. It certainly gives him an edge over the rest of us. You will never guess this unless you really look into his eyes. You see, he acts pretty befuddled and absentminded a lot of the time. He loves his ordered, routine and somewhat dull life. I say somewhat, because he thinks it is a wonderful way to live—work, home, work, home. And he does have some variety. Doctor's appointments, lawn maintenance, and bank deposits. Plus, he has to tend to his friends who are not feeling well, his failing plants, and his herbal garden. I am not being snide when I say this. I admire his ability to be all work and no play. I bring it up only to mention that his health often suffers just a tad. He has nervous disorders like skin rashes, colon and bladder problems. Then if he continues to push himself he has a tendency to get really moody and start drinking a bit too much. Then his routine will vary: home, work, home, drink. He is not a bad fellow though. He is a good provider, a sensitive husband and father, a wonderful worker bee. I think he deserves a happy helpmate who can spread a little sunshine into his life. She must be of top sterling qualities. His head will rule his heart. But then I imagine that you had that figured out already. He needs health foods, fresh air, exercise, lots of books, and mini-vacations. He won't stray too far from his ruts, but he will get used to a little variance. Think him over, he may have more possibilities than you guessed. He needs someone to turn him on. A Pisces, Virgo, Gemini, and of course, a Scorpio.

His illumination: Strong intellect.

His dark side: Intellect rules.

PISCES-LIBRA

Unless there is a lot of Aries in his chart, this man is a good example of the B-type personality. He avoids routines, tight schedules, and decision making. He lives instead in the world of dreams and plans. He often takes a long time making decisions, and cannot stand to be pressured. Charming and congenial, he seems also to be protected by the angels. He may or may not be, but chances are he is protected instead by the incredible intuition that he was born with. If you can get him to pay attention, he can see right through the motives and feelings of most everyone he meets. Most of the time, however, he keeps himself a bit aloof from the rest of the world. He also has a tendency to excesses, especially with food and drink. Those men with this configuration who were born in the early morning hours (6 to 8 a.m.), usually get in trouble with these tendencies to party, enjoy life, or drink a bit too much. He needs a lot of freedom and therefore often stands the best chance of success in an independent career; a career where he feels he is beautifying or bettering other people's lives makes him happiest. He is a delightful, creative co-worker. Give him a time clock and he can become quite despondent. Unharmonious surroundings can make him physically ill. While he needs a gracious sort of lifestyle, he is not materialistic. If you are wishing for a ball of fire in the business world, better pass this one up. When F. Scott Fitzgerald wrote of the tyranny of the weak, I think he may have been referring to this man. He needs a partner more than anything else in life. He needs it so much that he will never let you know what a relationship means to him. He worries and he feels insecure. Yet his ideas will become yours. No matter how odd his features, he will be very appealing. He looks to you for his answers. You will have to be the stronger of the two. Raise this husband as you do the rest of the children. Best matches are the beautiful Libras, Pisces, or Taurus. The Fire signs will leave him in the dust.

His illumination: Protected by angels.

His dark side: Needy in love.

PISCES-SCORPIO

He is handsome and magnetic. Try to look beyond that. He has more lives than the old cat ever dreamed of. He is the man they refer to when they talk about "Out of disaster rises the Phoenix." Mapped out, his life looks like the graph of an earthquake. If he feels like exploding at a dinner party, he will. He doesn't give a damn who thinks what. He just wants to express himself. Logic has very little place in his life. His emotions leave little room for reason, whether at home or work. His less volatile co-workers may shudder in his presence. He walks into a room and everyone else pales in comparison. Since he is also witty and usually has a fair degree of wealth and fame early on, he can pick and choose from a host of girls. He will dominate them all. She can be the most independent, sought after girl there, but he will win. If the lady of his choice does not buckle under, he will simply move on to another. He must have control. And if he has to fight for it, physically even, he will. He will have many battles in life to fight, personal, legal, emotional, and romantic. What then would one more be to this man? Chances are he will have many secrets, personal tragedies, and serial relationships. His children may cause him great anguish because he does love them. He may also marry several times. He may not be the most stable of husbands. He is a wonderful lover, though. He sees what he wants to see in his ladies—odd things that no other man notices. He may very well pick out the least physically attractive of the ladies because of the tilt of her head, or the sound of her voice. His choice will be a mystery to everyone else. Cancer, Aries, Scorpio, and some Tauruses have the best chance for a more serious relationship.

His illumination: Magnetic, hypnotic.

His dark side: Needs control.

PISCES-SAGITTARIUS

This man relates to people so well, and is so popular, you can hardly get near him. He has a well balanced attitude and knows how to make concessions. He doesn't have a lot of inner conflicts, though he is not petty or superficial. Outgoing, he loves to meet people and is a happy traveller. Remember a long time ago when I said that the Sagittarian will leave you home alone a lot? Well, this Moon position really will. He loves activity, not quiet little dinners at home. He is athletic and bright and would rather spend the evening playing tennis or preparing to study marine biology than with your new casserole and china. He will never, never change. If you begin to tie him down, he will find someone else. Do you know what? He will hardly even miss you. Like Barbie dolls, his women are interchangeable. His attachments are not all that deep. He will show his grief over you in odd little ways, like marrying someone else within a week. It is not a pretty picture. If you really must fall in love with this man, please protect yourself and promise not to tie him down. Your plans for dinner with the Harvey's next Monday are sure to be cancelled when he arises early one morning to announce his safari to Africa. Yes, he's known for months, but in truth, he preferred not to tell you. Why? He knew you'd be upset and he didn't want to argue. He just wanted to go in peace without a confrontation, and he wanted to go primarily without you. Even if you should be able to hunt better than he. The thing in question here is his freedom. Do not become predictable. Don't expect him to conform to the words "husband material" or "doting father." A Sagittarius will, of course, be made in Africa for him. A Gemini will delight him. A Capricorn will wring his thick neck.

His illumination: Athletic and bright.

His dark side: Does not conform.

PISCES-CAPRICORN

Was his mother a touch of a religious fanatic? Was there something severe in his background? Will he ever fully recover? There was a serious, wise old child in this man during his youth. As he grows older, he seems to grow younger emotionally. He will still be light years ahead of the rest of us in the understanding of human nature, and yet he will still worry. He can even worry about his successes. He will worry they are fly-by-night accomplishments, that the bank will fail (he doesn't really trust banks anyway). He will worry his hair will fall out, or that his eyesight will fail. He can't really help himself, it is the Pisces Sun that rules the subconscious emotions, for one thing. You might say with this combination he has a hyperactive subconscious. He needs to get away from his busy work schedule and dependent co-workers, and seclude himself near a large body of water. Sometimes a particular worry will leave him fixated. He could for example, make elaborate money burial arrangements in his back yard. For all his strength and usual good sense he often has a love affair with an inferior type of woman that leaves him totally out of control. He will not worry about this like he will everything else. He will think instead that he is some sort of a savior to the girl. He will get up at 4:30 a.m. to fix the little fool breakfast, because she finally got off drugs long enough to go to work for a week. Or he will loan her his car so she can drive into town to meet another man. I am not saying this man is a sap. But there is usually a time that he falls hard and ends up in a no-win situation. How does it end? She leaves. He will wait for her return. If you are a touch neurotic, or can affect a character disorder, you have your foot in the door. He has a lot to offer. He is kind, very kind. He is successful, and obtains a considerable amount of wealth at some time in his life. He could be a fabulous husband and father. A Capricorn, a Scorpio, or Cancer does best with him.

His illumination: Understands human nature.

His dark side: Attracted to neurotics.

PISCES-AQUARIUS

This man is a crusader. He could be the head of the local AA, the local MS society, or anything where he leads people in an almost missionary manner. His leadership will be easygoing, understanding and warm. His co-workers secretly admire him. If however, on the more intimate one to one basis he decides to take an instant liking to you, he will for all his love and admiration still seem cool and detached. He can forget his appointments and his children's birthdays. That he would remember that today is the anniversary of the day you met is out of the question. You will have to look for actions and more concrete declarations of his love and your standing as his wife. These actions could take the form of his allowing you to co-fund raise with him, or in his sharing his dream of leaving the world a better place. If you start to bore him during dinner, he will stare directly at you with his big, dreamy eyes, and try some astral travel between courses. He has a sweet tooth so he will return for dessert. While he does not actively seek attention in social situations, he does have a strong appeal for women and will not shrink from the prospects of a few numbers in his black book. He is looking for a mate made in heaven, so he is not very realistic in matters having to do with long term relationships. He can get really despondent when he finally realizes that his little sweetheart is less than divine. He may even make you another of his soul saving crusades. If you continue to falter, as humans do, he will have no choice but to try another. Your frailties make him nervous. Underneath it all he secretly fears he will slip a bit himself. A Libra girl, another Aquarian Sun or Moon, and of course another Pisces Sun may be able to help him make compromises in love.

His illumination: Wants to leave the world a better place.

His dark side: Befogged.

PISCES-PISCES

He is an unusual man with an odd habit of putting a peculiar twist or turn into almost every situation. This is the man who makes appearance in the body only. His mind is elsewhere. Actually, he'd prefer to be alone. He likes his daydreams just as well, if not better, than reality. His powerful emotions beg him to stay in familiar surroundings. He hates change. The bravest thing he ever did was buy, and actually move into, that new house. I'll bet he lost sleep over it. He has trouble with women because in part, he has trouble communicating. This man has a lowered physical energy and a rather frail constitution. Disharmony in his surroundings or at work could send him over the edge. During times of disharmony, he will need to escape into the positive energies of writing, perhaps poetry. His work, usually helping people, like a doctor, a bartender, or counsellor, asks for his undivided attention and sympathetic ear. A fellow can only take this for so long. He must be careful of his lungs (he no doubt smokes too much) and his tendencies to escape. Chemical abuse or an excessive craving for sweets is a common disorder. He could O.D. on chocolate cookies. He pays very little attention to his health problems. He seems to have little regard for medical advice for himself. He is a contradiction in many ways. He is a dual sign and given to mood swings. In love he gives his all. He will give far more than he is likely to receive. But it may take several years for him to give himself to a relationship. The girl will have to move very slowly and sort of sneak up on him. He will want a dainty, ultra feminine type of woman. He will give as much to his wife and children as he does to his co-workers. A Libra can attract him physically, the Virgo catches him between the ears, but the Cancer or Scorpio goes straight to his subconscious where he spends a good deal of his life.

His illumination: Willing to help.

His dark side: Mood swings.

Rising Signs
for Men

ARIES RISING
"Was I the first?"

Was he the first to make you feel this way, share your special secrets, meet the family, see you in that red bustier? Of course not. But while this man claims to be wild about honesty, he is far more crazed to hear how he has no predecessor and no equal. Aries is the first sign of the Zodiac and here you find a man who is all impulse, energy (unless he is hooked up to a ventilator), and raging enthusiasm for living. He is ambitious and in a hurry. If you want to poke along and smell the roses find yourself another rising sign. If you mosey out of bed, blow dry your hair for more than ten minutes, and simply must have that first cup of coffee before you start your day you will not be able to sustain his interest. And you will have more to sustain than his interest. While he is one of the four motivating Ascendants and can inspire others to almost anything, he sometimes cannot keep his own motor running at peak. Since he continually pours out his energies to others he often comes up short and his cup runs low. Enter the woman of his life. She will be his coach and his trainer. "Of course, you can sell the most stocks, get in the finals for Mr. Universe and start your own business before the end of the week." He knows his boundaries: infinity. Once you understand he wants to be the man from Krypton instead of Ohio you will begin to see the task ahead of you. He will have disappointments and setbacks from time to time as reality challenges him with swats on the nose like a frisky puppy in training. Get him to remove his imaginary cape and you will find an able bread winner, an innovative self-starter, a trusting co-partner and a sentimental softy. I know of one tough guy with boundless dreams who was nearly broke one Christmas. He gave his wife a record, "You Needed Me" by Anne Murray. They both cried and mushed it up. Then she went back to tap dancing in the kitchen. You can fall into the pit with him, but a good coach always knows when to pick up the pace. The secret of his success is that he always gravitates toward the top of infinity. Be ready to soar with him. And don't forget to tell him he is the only one you've flown with.

General Life Tendencies

Frequently with this man you find estrangements or difficulties with his family, perhaps the early loss of a sibling, and a problem with his mother. His father may not have been a good provider. All of this contributes to a certain harshness with his immediate family. Relatives hanging out for a casual Sunday brunch will not be a problem. A great deal of this man's determination for a strong family life, an enduring relationship and financial success stem from his early childhood experiences and disappointments.

TAURUS RISING
"I'm good with money."

Regardless of his humble beginnings or his obvious charm upon meeting you, if you don't meet his standards of style he won't embark upon a serious relationship with you. He may live with you, promise you something more in the future, meet your family, yet he will be saving himself for Ms. Right. His idea of perfect woman may lie in the fact that his favorite movie stars are Grace Kelly, Gene Tierney, and Greer Garson. Barely out of his teens he'll see an old movie and get fixated on the 40s woman with the sterling silver hairbrush, white gloves and the "Oh, my gosh, my dance card is full" expression. While he'll be delightfully playful with his MTV look alike acquaintances he longs for something more. His entire life is a series of wistful desires for the finer things. He's saving his money for the house on the hill, dreaming of the girl who'll dance cheek to cheek at the ball with him in his tuxedo, her gloved hand draped across his shoulder. These flights of fancy are like blueprints for life with him no matter how meager his finances. His outward calm hides his turmoil over a future where candle lit dinners are the norm. He can't take risks with his plans and he can't be with a woman who will embarrass him in public. This trait carries well into the golden years where he prefers a widow over a divorcee, old money versus new, and blue chip over blue sky. Taking the stroll through life at a leisurely pace, his footing steady and sturdy, you'll find he needs a lot of rest and time to roam free. Show him this profile and he'll snort, "That is not at all like me." Let him win the Lottery and watch the transformation. Wear lilac, lace, and the bearing of a lady, and tour the good life with a man of faithful heart and solid future.

General Life Tendencies

This man had a dominant father who left a lasting influence in his life. While he wants a conservative life and all the creature comforts and works doggedly towards them, he won't necessarily burn the midnight oil to get them. He'll find another way to acquire. The reason for this is that he's basically a B personality type. It's not until middle age that he begins to reap the harvest of his efforts. As if by some quirk of nature he is often attracted to women who live far away. He'll write lots of letters and yet lust for others with more than his heart. He is a very physical guy. Once married he has every intention of remaining faithful.

GEMINI RISING
"Let's go to both parties tonight."

Gemini Rising men are world class travelers even if confined to their own neighborhoods. They are restless and active and have some marvelous characteristics. They have the rare quality of being able to throw themselves into work, and yet totally forget work and shift into play with 100 percent abandon. Sometimes, after a late night of partying the alarm is ringing about the time they come in from play. Not a problem for this guy, he will shower, shave and proceed to work with his usual enthusiasm. That could explain why he often looks peculiar in the mornings. He is this way with women as well. And when "he's not near the one he loves, he loves the one he's near." If you can cope with that fact, or are of the same inclination, things should be cool. If not, brace yourself for some turmoil. Another thing, to cover his tracks he has a lot of stories to tell. Stories like the goat ate his divorce papers. Therefore, don't take his word as gospel. Speaking of his word, there will be lots of them, late into the night. Words are his foreplay, afterplay and surprisingly his verbal fantasies during can be a humdinger of an experience. Blind dates with Gemini Rising are not often regretted. He could show up at your door in any attire topped with a baseball cap and his beeper placed on his hip . . . or a tuxedo with a cummerbund that advertises his business. The real reason for his incongruity is he is always on the way from or to something else. He is fussy about the way he dresses no matter how odd it may appear to the rest of us. GQ he is not; but meaningful to him nonetheless. As for the girl of his dreams, she'd better be feminine in appearance and less scattered. If he really takes an interest he may buy you a matching cap or something he has bonded with in the way of apparel. He could take you anywhere, his destinations depend on his emotions. Even if you aren't interested in pursuing the relationship you will have had an exciting, memorable time. Relationships with this man are punctuated with periods of upheaval (he is still seeing his ex), disappearing acts (he is seeing someone new) and absentmindedness (he has two dates tonight). Somehow he is able to get away with these antics for quite a while, because he is fun. A lot of us grow up leaving the child in us behind. Gemini Rising is delightfully childlike. He even maintains a youthful appearance well into middle age. If you don't see the beauty of being swept off your feet to an amusement park or having barbecues in your living room on rainy days, hurry on to the old stodgy Capricorn Rising and leave room for the absolute tons of women who can't resist this man. The wonder of the Gemini Rising is in the delight he takes in the universe. Living is fascinating business for this man. He will always have a cause, a project, an adventure in the works. It's contagious. Get crazy with him and even when its over you can take the lessons in living with you. What better gift?

General Life Tendencies
     This man's life is filled with changes. Lots of women come and go in his parade of dates. There is a strong attraction to people from different backgrounds. He likes variety in food and experience. He accumulates money from other peoples' business expertise. This is fortunate because he has on occasion been duped in career and business. Business ventures are generally risky for the Gemini Rising. A

natural communicator he is a lover of art, science, and literature. He can excel in any of these professions.

CANCER RISING
"I'd rather stay at home."

Cancer Rising men almost go into shock when they hear other men say that home is where you go when there's nowhere else to go. It's all they can do to leave and yet once they are out there in the business world they're some of the best money makers, and like shooting stars soar through the skies of competition at work. There is really no contradiction here about home and work, they become attached to their surroundings. Habits are their roots, strong as crabgrass. At home he won't replace his old recliner, he'll reupholster it. At work he'll use words like "expand," not relocate. The Cancer man is clinging, things mean so much to him. They are part of where he's been and who he is. Garage sales should be listed before the obits in the paper in his way of thinking. It'll be a serious breech in your relationship with this man should you not appreciate his need to be surrounded by his habits. He hangs on to his people in much the same manner. Should a loved one leave his life for whatever reason, he'll still hang on to his feelings even when they cause him anguish. While he is an excellent counselor, he's not an excellent patient because he never lets go of the garbage he totes around. He is sensitive and you can share your innermost thoughts with him, he won't hurt you by using your weakness or abusing your trust. No matter. He will however insist on living exactly as he wants to live. It may be near his childhood home, his mother, or something of significance concerning his past. He will also have bouts with the blues. He worries about the end of the world. He worries about his health. Free floating anxiety is as much a part of his life as a Woody Allen character. So when he asks you "Why don't we just have dinner at home tonight?" he isn't really looking for an answer or debate, he's looking for more time under his 1600 square foot security blanket of stucco, and time to drop his shell away from the demands of the world. Since security, home, and hearth are so important to him, a woman who wants to pull up roots every few years and immerse herself in another culture for the sake of experience will not entice him. Changing your hair color every now and then will make him nervous, and when he gets nervous he gets crabby. And when he gets crabby my only suggestion is to pull the covers over both your heads until it passes. He won't be cajoled, consoled, or talked out of his moods. Remember that, if you think because he comes across so sweet and gentle that you can mold or manipulate him. While he is changeable, he does not change.

General Life Tendencies

Men with strong Cancer in their charts are often excellent money makers. I wouldn't count on those earnings though until he's in his middle 30s. This is a time when Cancer Rising men usually stabilize and put their creative imaginations to use. Also, they will have hardened their shells a little bit and will have a better grip on reality. In addition to this, they often lose materially through love affairs and children in the earlier parts of their lives. These men are found in marital relationships where they carry most of the burdens. They are attracted to women who, if not actually older, are mature in their actions.

LEO RISING
"Is this the top of the line?"

Leo Rising men come in two primary categories: the beautiful ones who don't have to roar to be heard, and a simple toss of the lion's mane will do (or the steady gaze of the hazel eyes); or the less magnificent ones who roar and bellow constantly striving for the limelight. These lesser Leo Risings don't have the animal magnetism and grace of the beautiful ones to charm their audience but this will not stop them in their pursuit of overwhelming everyone at any gathering. This is how you spot one. Another way to tell them apart from the other combinations is to ask them something about anything. They'll have an answer, have been there, or know the person the subject was named for. This sounds like it is a lot of baloney, but chances are he's telling the truth. It's as if nature conspired to introduce them to everyone of prominence, and educate them on all the glitzy conversational tidbits. If you want to bask in this for all eternity you'll have to make sure your orbital spin revolves around his. In other words, don't ever upstage him. That means in career matters as well. While he admires the two career family, he needs a one

man woman who allows him to dictate on matters of dress, and lifestyle. Not that this is all bad. He'll have better taste and sense of style
than your latest fashion magazine. In a recent movie Burt Reynolds
refers to his rival in romance as "His Gucciness." The rival is the
epitome of a Leo Rising. This man's relentlessness in excellence extends to the selection of a mate. He would tidy up his injuries for the
ambulance driver unless he was comatose. He is always perfecting
his image. Mohammed Ali's (a Leo Rising) constant pre-fight
speeches repeated the theme, "I am the greatest." Wonder how he's
going to be in romance? Fabulous, if you aren't offended by the mirrors above the bed. Heavenly, if you can honestly put him in the center of your universe. He'll certainly notice you; forget postponing
your pedicure. He'll be devoted. Never express your crush on the
men on the Chippendales calendar. And for your own safety don't
look for bargains from the local discount store for either of you. He is
beyond all this. He's also beyond petty, disloyal, mundane character flaws. He is bright rays of glamour, intrigue, drama, passion, excitement, and sweetness shining down on one special person.

General Life Tendencies

For all his desire to have a lasting marriage, a second marriage
is often indicated. He is attracted to an intelligent, often somewhat
eccentric marriage partner. You can bet his father had a few skeletons in his closet. At the very least, his father was not there for him
emotionally in his childhood. From austere beginnings he grows
into prominence and while not much for sure fire money making
schemes, he will acquire far more than he started with financially.
His background may surprise you for he has a style that spells superiority. His old age may surprise you even further if he was born in
the 40s. He may become more and more a recluse.

VIRGO RISING
"Let's finish working first."

Virgo Rising looks for the women in his life much like the horse
breeder looks for a future champion. He wants good sturdy stock,
nice teeth—not stained, good intellect, strong hands to hold the
plow. He's a sturdy, meticulous man who actually enjoys work and
worry. If you've got problems he won't hesitate to help if he judges

you to be someone worth rescuing. He doesn't wear rose colored glasses and doesn't delude himself. He deals with the facts and loves to sort through the data. Being precise, practical, and of service is exciting for him. While the rest of the world finds the laborious to be tedious and wants to put off such tasks for as long as humanly possible, the Virgo Rising finds this to be the stuff of which dreams are made. Not that he's boring. He is intelligent and has a lot more to say than he is given credit for in most cases. Not only is he choosy about how he deals with life and with women, but being alone for great periods of time doesn't bother him. He is therefore often overlooked in the dating scene. Getting him to warm up is another matter. He is slow to respond, and even when awe struck by beauty and intelligence he'll manage to find a flaw or two to dwell on—problem areas like a disturbing lack of knowledge in Greek history, or legs with cellulite. If you pass the majority of tests, wild instant abandon is foreign to him. He'll offer you a love that is unselfish, thoughtful, and committed. Aggressive, liberated women won't usually gain his admiration. Structured, subtle ladies who are in need of some sort of fixing up usually find him in quiet, steady pursuit. He won't write lavish poetry or send flowers; but he'll balance your checkbook and help you plant herbs. It's not the stuff that romance novels are made of, but it is the stuff that makes for long lasting relationships. Teach him that love doesn't mean sacrifice, simple reciprocal consideration will do, and he can excel as a mate.

General Life Tendencies

His childhood is often marked with poor health. Health, like money, has to be pursued actively by this man. Nothing seems to fall into his lap. He watches his diet and his money with a sharp eye because he has discovered he has to in order to survive. The lukewarm ties between his brothers and sisters are probably the result of a broken home rather than a defect on his part. He will undoubtedly travel to exotic lands and make most of his money from sources outside his natural place of birth. He is decidedly more interesting than given credit for. There's a sadness in his eyes because he is often most attracted to partners of an escapist nature. It's a hard road traveling with a partner who appears to take more than she gives.

LIBRA RISING
"I try to get along with everybody."

Lively and intelligent with a well chosen word or two, this man can convince you of almost anything. He is successful at work, popular with everyone, and has a reputation for changing his mind and his girlfriends in the bat of an eyelash. If you don't pay attention this may be confusing. Let me lay it out for you. Whatever he changes his mind about didn't involve a basic value. He can con anyone but when his emotions are involved he dwells on things like honor. Ashley Wilkes in *Gone with the Wind* is the epitome of a Libra Rising man. When he stands at the wood pile and Scarlet talks to him about running away she asks what there is to stop them. Ashley answers, "Nothing, except honor." Scarlet could have saved herself years of agony when he gave her longing looks and half promises of lust. Later, she is given another clue when he speaks of Melanie being the only dream that did not die in the face of reality. Dreams and honor, such are the things which bind and tie him. Yes, he is flirtatious, and yes, he will go from one relationship to another because he cannot stand to be alone. A connoisseur of beauty, he has been known to marry bone structure. But when he finds his dream he commits. Let me give you two examples of distorted honor. Upon meeting the woman of his dreams one Libra Rising man discovered that this woman had a child from another marriage. Out of respect for the child's loss of her father he refused to visit when the child was around. Only after he made his commitment to the woman in marriage did he establish a relationship with the daughter. His reasoning: he did not want the child to experience the loss of another father figure and wanted to make sure of his position first. Another man had several mistresses and kept lifelong contact with them even after their marriages. Why? His sense of honor required him to keep tabs on their well being since he felt guilty that he never offered them marriage. His motives twist and wind through the T Maze but he always curves back to respect and dignity. Share the dream of perfect mates, gracious living and getting along harmoniously with everyone and he will provide you a comfortable home with old world charm where love is gentle and sweet.

General Life Tendencies

His life is a quest for harmony. His relatives are abundant and he benefits from the association. His early environment has an oddity, his parents often were something of a role reversal. His mother was probably the dominant partner and may have contributed heavily to the marriage financially. She was also a little aloof and reserved with her affections. His father, on the other hand, was most demonstrative and nurturing. Because of this he's not sure of roles in marriage and oftentimes this leads to fierce quarrelling in his unions. He is apt to have many changes of address so memorize his social security number or something permanent. His children will fulfill many of his own hopes and wishes.

SCORPIO RISING
"I can do anything I put my mind to."

No point in mincing words, this man is strong willed. He's turbulent and volatile. He's also commanding and astute. He can excel in business where a take-control personality is needed. His intensity is shown in his line of work. He is attracted to danger and excels in investigative, political, religious, or medical careers. He's not timid in his choice of work. He can soar to the heights or fall to the depths depending on how involved he is and what his goals are. A sturdy friend, he's not the kind you classify as a buddy. He doesn't pal around and spends much time alone. But he'll always remember a kind deed from a friend. He's best at building and rebuilding, whether it's his business, his relationships or his list of things to master. Perhaps one of his strongest abilities to rebuild is shown in his recuperative powers. He can bounce back from years of abusing his health, a major accident or illness as if by pure willpower. And more than anything else, willpower is his key word. Detonating bombs won't scare him. Losing the object of his affections, however, is frightening and can lead to melancholy, brooding, and compulsive, obsessive behavior. His powers of persuasion with you are amazing. All your common sense is dissolved. Does he hypnotize you as you sleep? In your lucid moments you actually wonder how he can have such a hold on you. He prefers to dominate and control, even if only for a short time, even if the control is benevolent. When he concentrates on the woman of his choice it is total. He'll plan romantic days for you. If he misses work to take you sailing for lunch, so be it. He'll schedule your days and evenings so tightly you won't have time to sleep. The planets are in the process of changing him now, and he's more cautious and somewhat more leery than usual.

The rules he lives his life by are changing and hopefully he'll be less intense, more relaxed and cheerful in the next few years. Can he be faithful? Yes. Can he make money? Yes. Can he fulfill your every dream. Yes. But only if he wants to.

General Life Tendencies

Inclined towards extremes, the Scorpio Rising man has strong likes and dislikes, and is passionate about life. In a constant state of evolution he rises and falls again much like the Phoenix. Born with a strong physical body he can survive trauma, deprivation, and near fatal health setbacks; he is nearly fearless. In love and romance this man gives his all and seems to be blessed with many choices in mates who can offer him lasting happiness. Inclined to many secrets he can't hide his emotions for his chosen one. He reveals his feelings for his mate with steadfast and enduring love in his own quiet way; not necessarily in the popularized fashion of the media. Destined to follow paths of leadership, his career is often involved in the military, political, medical, or behind-the-scenes work which punctuates his home life with frequent absences.

SAGITTARIUS RISING
"I'm thinking about moving on."

Whatever his faults, there is no malice in this man. You might have to repeat this line over and over when you try and rebound from his cutting remarks and insensitive behavior toward you. He is difficult to understand, like the other dual Rising signs. Look at it from his point of view. He met someone new, or someone old, or maybe he just wanted to go hunting for the week. He never realized you'd take it so hard. He doesn't think in terms of commitment. Basically he is a man who likes friendship with women. He told you from the beginning that he just wanted to be friends; that he likes to hang loose, and believes that mankind was really designed for serial relationships. He is not vague about what he wants in a relationship with you. He told you what he was like, you just didn't listen. So what? Is it his fault now that two weeks after you applied for a new social security card with his last name he informs you he is moving to Idaho? Without you? He is as shocked as you are that you are in this mess. He told you right up front that he was a travelin' man and that he'd always thought about getting away from the city to a nice little place like Idaho. You kept thinking that you'd change him. That is why he is so dismayed. What more could he have done to make you realize he'd never meant to stay? "My god," he says, as his large hands fling about, "I told you we were friends and that one day I'd be moving on. But you never listened." Women never do listen to him and it confuses him no end. They don't fail to hear because they are hearing-impaired, but because they see him with their hearts. And their hearts are saying that this is a kind and gentle man. That he is baseball, Chevrolets and apple pie. There is a boyish charm with Sagittarius Rising that could melt Aunt Elvira's heart. No one is immune. No one. That is why someone in Idaho is waiting for him. But I'll tell you what happened to Idaho. He made it through California, but by the time he hit Nevada he found this cute little thing (Sagittarius Rising tends to like the petite ones . . . they can just sorta grab them up in their long dangling arms, you know) and thought he'd hang out with her awhile. He is easily distracted. I think the one way to have the best of him is to think of the words of a song . . . "It's just knowing that your door is always open and your path is free to walk, that keeps . . . you ever gentle on my mind." Don't ask a lot of questions, if this is the man for you. Give him space. Don't issue ultimatums unless you mean them. Don't give his already itchy feet a rash by having your cousins over for a spaghetti feed just so they can look him over. He is likely to hide in the bathtub until he can make his escape. If he feels unrestricted by your love, he'll be dragging you home for the holidays. What he wants is a companion. A commitment is something he falls into like a Black Hole. He doesn't give up his wanderings, but he does take a pal along the way. At this point in the relationship you discover that walking along side him beats trying to follow or lead. It can be a wondrous thing.

General Life Tendencies
    Several marriages are usually in store for the Sagittarius Rising man. He will have a few children and broken ties with them. His careers are long and serious as a rule. These men deal well with people and yet as managers won't miss a trick from staff. Their basically benevolent nature will keep them from mentioning the petty, although they have it stored in their minds. More than one set of parents is indicated here, or the ties with a grandparent are exception-

ally strong. A love affair with a relative is not unheard of. In his youth this man is involved in dual liaisons and many relationships. It is part of his sense of adventure.

CAPRICORN RISING
"My mother and I are really close."

Don't let the fact that earlier I called this man stodgy deter you, because even he can't stop the eventual limelight his accomplishments will bring. He is shy. Even when he runs for mayor. He'll make a few self depreciating jokes (it helps him psychologically to beat his detractors to the punch) and hee haw about his flaws. Fact is he is very sensitive to criticism and self conscious in public situations. Why do they push themselves? Because they must show everyone they can do anything. Accomplishment is what they breathe for. Nothing else matters if they cannot prove to themselves that they can scale the great heights just like their Zodiac symbol. Nothing is too great a price to pay to achieve and acquire. Ulcers? There are drugs for that. Broken relationships? They will settle for their memories. It's desperate, this need to produce. It is how they prove their self worth. For them, being is not enough. So why bother with anyone this driven? Because here you have quality. Good old fashioned values like honesty, dependability, sincerity. He may not always be faithful, but he will be devoted to his chosen one. This is an odd combination of standards. What it means to you is that he will always be there in spirit for the one he loves, but he won't spend a lot of time pining about when he is by himself. He is afraid of the dark and does not have any plans to endure long nights alone. If you have to spend the summer in the Himalayas with your Guru, his heart is the only part of himself he'll be saving for you. He makes money, he loves his mother (hope you resemble her), he takes responsibility better than most men, he is intelligent, reliable and a general non-nerd socially. Relaxed, he has a killer sense of humor. Very relaxed, he has a hearty sexual appetite. How do you get this guy to lighten up? You spin tales of his stocks increasing, his real estate appreciating and his agent selling his textbook for a bedtime story. When he feels secure he will express it with a well stocked pantry, prepaid insurance, and he'll get so crazy with glee he'll go the other way and party until you beg for mercy. Since capriciousness is a well hidden facet of his personality, you may find yourself regretting his swinging too far to the other side. If he has enough money he'll retreat into solitude and self indulgence. Your first tip off could be the trapeze in the bedroom. Watch for signs. Once he becomes a wild and crazy guy it will take a lot to get him back into mundanity again. He only needs to achieve the heights once. Getting there with him could bring you the most dizzying experiences of your life. He is not your ordinary man. His highs and lows are stupendous, but he never forgets the one who rode the crests with him. And the way he'll spend forever trying to show his appreciation can leave a girl pretty breathless. And don't forget what he said about his money.

General Life Tendencies

This man does well in corporations and government agencies. His talents for organization are second to none. As conservative as he is, he will take chances in monetary ventures and can achieve surprising success in original, innovative ways. This man will have strong, meaningful ties with his mate. This attachment often borders on co-dependency. He will want control of joint finances, and of the home environment, however. He gives up some of his need for control in the community where he excels in joint efforts and ventures. Because of this he usually has good standing in the community. His business partners and his friends are powerful and dynamic.

AQUARIUS RISING
"Let's be friends."

Cerebral, scientific, and flying his own time machine, the Aquarius Rising man does not have a great deal of time to dwell on emotion. His knack for understanding the connections between time and emotion allows for his not getting stuck in the moment and being able to move his mind to a point in the future where opportunities are better and brighter. Do you still wonder why he is so dispassionate when you cry over his forgetting to show for dinner? This cool and impersonal approach to all matters, including romance, leaves his acquaintances bewildered from time to time which is the way he wants it. This man's ruler is the planet of the unexpected and he has episodes where his actions are so unpredictable that it's as though he wants to be bad. In spite of the confusion on a personal level his intentions for the group or fellow man are usually good. He provides fascination, something many men are unable to spark in their relationships. He offers relationships based on a flow of communication and ideas. He is the free spirited prophet, forced to work as a radio repairman until he can prove his theories about the Greenhouse Effect, who captures many women in their mid-life crises. He is seductive change and intriguing adventure for the bored. His boldness is hypnotic for the shy. For himself he is independent, idealistic, unique. Yet, for all his unpredictable, unorthodox behavior, he is fixed. Determined. Because he has such incredible will power he is often emotionally blocked in discussions. Prepare to lose in the battle of wits with this man. Not because he is brighter, but because he cannot be penetrated. The spell this man can cast in spite of his oddities is one of the fourth dimension. You learn of vision, brotherhood, curiosity, and possibilities that are so quickly forgotten in the nine to five world. When he says, "Let's just be friends," and you head back to mundanity, remember the flights to the unknown aboard his fantastic time machine and your momentary insight into the land of tomorrow. Wasn't the glimpse worth it all?

General Life Tendencies

This man could collect friends while in a think tank. Not known for his practicality he is especially careless in money matters. Having experienced a loving early environment he is a caring father and inspires his children to intellectual heights. He is attracted to a marriage partner who is dynamic, powerful, and risk-taking. While he won't be dominated, he desires to have a mate who will provide a strong challenge. For all his scientific approach to life he has secret worries and fears. He is much more approachable in matters of the heart than is apparent on the surface.

PISCES RISING
"I've got this feeling."

Esoteric subjects, healing crystals, Tarot cards may sound like psycho-babble to your average man, but to Pisces Rising this can sound like a possible way to get in touch with his feelings. His efforts to get in touch with himself often lead to acquaintanceships with mystics, psychics and the modern day therapists. He feels with such intensity that he needs people in his life who share the quest for more than the material or mundane. While he is a delightful companion he can be enigmatic and dual. The slippery fish swimming in two directions is his sign ruler for a reason. Pleasant, caring, and sensitive, he is popular with nearly everyone. Popular, but not necessarily a part of the crowd. After all, he would really rather be experiencing something life altering than cheering with the guys over Monday Night Football. His mind is always searching for something more; oftentimes his body, too. Elusive women haunt him sexually. Something within his depths keeps him from open pursuit when his feelings are involved. The object of his affections, at a loss to understand his behavior after two emotion packed days together, does not hear from him and assumes he is no longer interested. He, playing the waiting game, assumes the same and he finds himself in another broken relationship. Must he punish himself? Yes. What he wants most is to be swept off his feet in romance, astral travel, or far-fetched dreams. The woman who captures him is bold enough to create seismographic excitement and understand his moods. This man needs to find companions who offer stability while encouraging emotional growth and responsibility. Companions who are highly evolved, yet fascinating and energetic. He bores easily and his attention span is very short. But he offers a rare gift of insight, sensitivity, and gentleness that is nearly irresistible. Also there is a magic about him, and the ability to make dreams come true that leaves the most daring of women slightly breathless.

General Life Tendencies

This man can often be found in the field of religion, education, and/or travel. Dual careers are common with him. He is impulsive with money and it will be his choice of a partner that will enable him to gain from joint finances. Lots of short distance excursions and the possibility of two residences are in his future. While his lovers remind him of his mother, his marriage partner is much more efficient and less idealized. Psychosomatic illness and low life vitality mark this man. His daily routines are fixed. Don't go rearranging his furniture. His children will have excellent chances for success.

Introduction to the Guide to Women

I know something: You men want romance as much as most women do. Maybe more. You really don't want someone you have to tackle and hog tie. The pursuit is great, but deep in every man's heart he wants to feel like his woman loves him beyond compare. Since this is downright embarrassing for most men to admit, I'll drop it right here. Only remember to look for the compatible Moon positions. Your Sun sign in the same sign as her Moon, your Moon and her Ascendant, your Moon in aspect to her Sun (or vice versa).

This portion of the book is about women: the agony and the ecstasy. For years woman has been labeled mysterious, inconsistent and unpredictable. I don't think she is. I just think she is evolving. Her needs are changing. And she is expressing herself more openly with less thought of negative judgement and consequences.

Twenty, even ten years ago, a man could appear on her horizon with blonde good looks, a red sports car and some of daddy's money, and be the catch of the year. Not today. Today's woman looks for heart, humor and honesty. She has seen her mother—possibly herself—saddled with the impossible job of being all things to all people. Wife, lover, mother, co-breadwinner. She no longer wants to exhaust herself carrying these burdens for a man who is sullen, disloyal or non-supportive.

I think every woman is entitled to—and indeed grows by—the inevitable "ex." That first disasterous man who shows her just what she can do in the name of love—but isn't willing to do again. So unless you catch her early on, you will need to have developed some sensitivity, positive qualities, and the ability to laugh at yourself and the world around you. Smashing the dishes instead of taking your turn, ditching your dirty clothes wherever you've undressed, being phobic about touching the knobs on the oven will probably not fly for today's woman. She wants a soulmate, a helpmate and a playmate.

Famous Lovers

Goldie Hawn and **Kurt Russell** present an interesting pair. His Cancer Moon and her Scorpio Sun work well together, but it is her Saturn aspect that ties the knot (whether or not they ever do). **Dennis Quaid** and **Meg Ryan** have a nice Sun and Moon aspect with her Scorpio Sun to his Cancer Moon. But it is **Farrah Fawcett**'s Sun in the same sign as **Ryan O'Neal**'s Moon that keeps this couple coming back for more. They may fight, and separate, but the chemistry is nearly overwhelming. So, if Farrah is the woman for you, you just might need to change your Moon. Nothing short of that will probably do.

Then General Types of Sun Sign Mothers

The **Aries Sun mother** will dominate and walk around a lot with her arms folded across her chest. She just wants to you to know she can be the boss. She is, however, at her best when camping, swimming, and playing like the rest of the children. Include her.

The **Taurus Sun mother** is quietly running the show. She will attempt to provide stability and security, and wants everyone cuddly, comfy and cozy. Her bouts of anger are not pretty, however.

The **Gemini Sun mother** is active, restless, energetic, and may alternate being the big sister and your favorite teacher. She stresses the importance of a child's need to experience, and the value of curiosity.

The **Cancer Sun mother** is receptive, intuitive and caring. Don't try to lie to her. Don't break her heart with cruel remarks. She could get real cranky to cover her wounds.

The **Leo Sun mother** was born to forever be a child. Loving and protective, she will be your best friend. Humor her with her fixed ideas and hasty decisions. She really has her heart in the right place.

The **Virgo Sun mother** won't take her task lightly. She will want to teach you every survival skill known to her. She will instruct you in the fine art of pinching pennies and picking vegetables. Mostly, however, she will teach you to respect the earth and all its living creatures.

The **Libra Sun mother** wants her children to remain close to her all of her life. She can alternate between strict or lax, depending on the day. But she will never waiver from her desire for her children to be the best they can and enjoy the beauty and wonder of life.

The **Scorpio Sun mother** wants to master. She can be stern, but she is part of her child's heart and devoted to her family. She knows your future, so don't try to hide your present. She, not you, will keep the secrets in the family.

The **Sagittarius Sun mother** may be a bit too freedom loving to commit to childrearing on a full time basis. She dreams of nannies. But, she is a delight, and since she has never fully grown up herself she can inspire her children to dream and reach for the stars.

The **Capricorn Sun mother** is a serious, somber mother who wants to do the right thing by her children. She probably read to you in the womb. She wants you to be a good citizen. Would asking you to be an astronaut or President be too much?

The **Aquarius Sun mother** is filled with adventure and love and the best of intentions. She may forget that you are well past your feeding schedule, or that the laundry is dirty. But she will never forget to teach you the value of friendships or universal love.

The **Pisces Sun mother** is able to read your mind, an unfortunate thing for most children. She can dream your dreams, dance your dance, and teach you about your meaning on this earth. Not often realistic, she is nonetheless a spiritual leader. Let her be your guide.

Aries

March 21–April 20

ARIES-ARIES

She's not subtle. She's not unstable, but living with her could be like being in the same room with a blow torch. She's easily angered into screaming fits and ugly little outbursts. When she's in her cooing mode she can do enchanting little things like read books on baby names. She's one of the most independent women of the Zodiac, and yet, if you give her a chance, she'll stay home to look after you. And I do mean look after, because she's a very jealous lady. I saw one of these in action one night when her boyfriend was out with another woman; it wasn't a pretty sound. Right then and there in front of a restaurant full of quietly dining patrons, she called the other woman any number of things. So warnings fair to both sexes: Mess with her and you can fully expect a confrontation. If by chance she was mistaken, she won't be too proud to apologize. She's also a survivor—your leaving her for another woman won't stunt her growth. She may fantasize about you for years, but she'll go on, and even do quite well without you, in fact. She simply puts herself and her needs first. In this respect she's very healthy emotionally. She doesn't know much about guilt or complicated needs to nurture. She won't be coy. Traditionally masculine careers like military pursuits, outdoor ranger, stock brokering work just as well for her as the traditionally female careers of modeling, etc. She can do just about whatever she puts her mind to. If she's interested in you she'll let you know. Not the most popular co-worker, she's efficient. As a wife and mother she'll be strict but caring and temperamental. The household will have to adjust—she won't. Best bets: She's usually attracted to Scorpios or Leos. I'd suggest a Libra. They may quarrel, but the Libra can calm her. Fire signs ignite her.

Her illumination: Emotional strength.

Her dark side: Easy to ignite.

ARIES-TAURUS

This is one of the sweetest Aries girls. She turns a lot of her fire into productive outlets like helping others, surviving life and getting her own way to everyone's satisfaction. She's appealing in a common sense fashion, a no-frills girl who can tackle the engine of her car as well as the dripping water faucets in the house. She'd be a wonderful wife and mother, but since she's not traditional in her expressions of romance, men often need to give her a second look. Her idea of a great Valentine's Day card is something that pokes fun of love or you. She has a love-hate relationship with sentiment. She wants to be vulnerable, but it scares the ramish part of her nature. So she does her best never to let her softer side show. At work she'll be a caring supervisor, with a strict set of rules that are quite simple: You are here to work, not to take breaks or read the *Wall Street Journal* (no doubt her very own favorite). If you have an emergency or illness that she feels prevents you from working, she'll carry your load and hers to keep you afloat. Never get yourself into the situation where she feels you have taken advantage of her generosity. She's a nasty enemy. She's an excellent judge of people and does well in managerial positions. She also excels in financial consulting or banking. She won't actively pursue a marriage for money, but one should fall into her life in later years. In her earlier years she has a tendency to marry in haste. Once that little episode is over, she'll never be so hasty again. She's an odd, independent little creature that few get to know well. She'll manage the office softball team and run home to cook a gourmet dinner served on a lace tablecloth—if she wants to. As one told me once, "I can bring home the bacon and fry it up. I can, but I don't." Look for a strong Taurus or Capricorn to show her her sentimental side, and for the Leo to set her heart a-flutter.

Her illumination: Can do most anything.

Her dark side: May not want to.

ARIES-GEMINI

Probably had a date with her tonight and she changed her mind, huh? Something really did come up—another speech to write, another commercial to tape, or it could very well have been another man. He got to her pheromones. Rest assured, whatever the reason, she's plenty excited about the project. You see, she's always at the mercy of her rather over-stimulated nervous system. She's usually physically and mentally over-taxed. She talks on both phones, she uses her hands to gesture, and she often does two things at once, like eat lunch and write ad copy. She'll probably end up on beta-blockers. She'll need something to slow down her racehorse mind in a plow horse body. The Gemini Moon lends itself to nervous disorders, and she really needs to heed her inner voice that screams, "One thing at a time." Not especially good wife and mother material, she's a super co-worker. She's sympathetic to their stories of woe, and hopes for their best success. Naturally the fault finders at the top who expect her creativity to pour out from 9 to 5 may find that they're in for some unpleasant surprises. Like she's usually a little tardy, or prefers to work "'til the wee small hours of the morning." Then she figures she has the right to pay back that time by taking an extra long lunch to get her nails done. Then jealousy rears its ugly head! The keeper of the time clock gets really cranky. Try to explain her time sheets to anyone—the time will be there, but like everything else it'll be in her own fashion, and with her own set of rules. If you want to be the one she gives her heart to, be as prepared as the rest of the world for her lack of punctuality, dependability, and conventional order to drive you right over the edge. An Aquarius or another Aries understands all this; a Sagittarius can at least give it a whirl.

Her illumination: Excitable.

Her dark side: Weird body clock.

ARIES-CANCER

She's a battler and has learned to stand alone. Much of this stems from some form of estrangement in the early environment. She'll continue to act out the disharmony with men and women who try to place restraints or control over her. For all this, she's usually well liked and pleasant. She's a nice wife and mother, showing much concern for the well-being of her loved ones. Artistic or creative fields are best suited to her, and a love of history or antiques can be a fascinating avocation. She can have some periods of anxiety and worry. If she experiences disharmony on the home front in her later years, she can become fearful, introverted, with an inclination for stomach troubles and headaches. She has a strange insight into people and can see right through many a man. She usually marries young and has her children early. She can overcome many obstacles to get whatever she desires out of life. She's difficult to get to know well, and will have few women friends. Maybe that's just as well since she has been known to chase a few husbands along the way. As a co-worker, she's mysterious, sweet, non-complaining and pleasant. You'll instinctively know when she's not leveling with you. Her approach to all matters is manipulation. If you're a man that interests her, she'll be ever so cute in her approach. She's afraid that her own personality isn't strong enough, when in actuality it's very strong. She'll eventually get her way. She deserves it too. She's had a lot to overcome no matter how effortless it looks from the outside. A Scorpio likes to do battle with her; a Pisces likes the fantasy; an Aries will allow her to be herself . . . when this happens, she can grow into the superwoman class.

Her illumination: Sugar and spice.

Her dark side: Faces many hardships.

ARIES-LEO

This is one woman who truly needs her recreation and relaxation— let her sail, soar, and play act. She's vivacious and vibrant, and she has more than enough sparkle and pizzazz for both herself and her lover. Adventures like making love in an abandoned boxcar are ordinary occurrences for her. She's the combination of the infant and the child, and approaches life and situations accordingly. She wants her needs met, but for her playmates to have fun also. Yes, she can be self-centered, and yes, she can over-dramatize every event. But ah, she's such a refreshing, enthusiast of life. She's smart enough to never mention that the refrigerator broke or that she has a few errands to run. She knows what a damper reality is to infatuation. She wants a life of play and excitement. She wants her man to desire the same. Capable in the arts, music and drama, she's an outstanding contributor in life. Her greatest talent comes from being able to make her dreams come true. Her positive, unwavering faith enables her to accomplish much. She's lucky, but I'm not sure if she made it happen by positive thinking and visualization, or if she was truly lucky in the traditional sense. Her Sun-Moon combination is fortunate for both success, happiness and popularity. It inclines to a happy childhood and a mutual understanding with the marriage partner. Her love of family extends to trying to blend career with children. A good wife and mother, if she has to work outside the family environment, she'll probably carry her babies on her hip. She's a woman all her own, and both sexes find her an enchanting addition to their lives. I'd like to see her with another Leo, Aries or Sagittarius, or a Cancer with lots of Leo in his chart.

Her illumination: Makes love in a boxcar.

Her dark side: A handful.

ARIES-VIRGO

You must be some kind of guy getting up the nerve to look up this one. Did she tell you you could? You need to clear these things with her first. She's strict with her people. You really should be more reverent. She's also your boss, right? I mean, when it really comes down to it, aren't you the one who makes all the concessions and gets the lectures? If all this sounds negative, well it is. And even though you know for sure now, you will probably want to hang in there for the finish because she's so romantic—but in the oddest sort of way. It comes in the form of loyalty, devotion, and eventually back rubs, shoe shining and quiet admiration. She's pretty intimidating at first though with her reserved manner. There's an immense pride about her. Her co-workers will automatically sit straighter in their chairs and work harder when she's around. They know she'll tell if they slip. They probably remember the neighborhood snitch from their own childhoods, and would prefer that the CEO didn't know about the liberal use of the Watts line. She won't be the most popular of the people you meet, and her lack of friends always seems to surprise her. Every now and then she'll get really friendly and ask a co-worker or a neighbor to lunch. They're all busy. She knows it's something personal, and yet she can't figure out what she could possibly have done to arouse such mistrust. Because while she can spot flaws in others, she really can't figure out her own shortcomings. Don't ever try to explain it to her it'll just show how much you lack in tact. She usually doesn't do much for fun; life is such serious business. But you can catch her out gardening, fishing, sculpting or at some other productive recreation. If this one is for you, don't plan on a lot of little ones—she 's usually not all that interested. You're probably a Virgo or you couldn't have gone this far; or you're perhaps a Gemini who needs to be disciplined.

Her illumination: Devoted.

Her dark side: Strict.

ARIES-LIBRA

She has two dreams—one to be independent, and one to find a soul mate. If it sounds conflicting, let me assure you it is. She over-idealizes this man she wants to identify with, so that it's nearly impossible to match her expectations. She wants you to share her dreams and goals, be her companion and lover, and yet she can't express herself well enough to compromise. She actually thinks that these perfect love relationships occur naturally, and I suppose they do if you have a few prior lifetimes together to iron out the wrinkles. Therefore, as things happen she creates these difficulties in forming a relationship that means the most to her. She also has a conflict over who's the boss, and "How can I be me and share my life with another?" Maybe therapy will help. She can drink and turn in a few promiscuous years and then, as if by magic, reform and ask that you, too, become a teetotaler, or whatever her betterment. She has another teeny little flaw: She likes to spend your (not her) money. She's usually active both socially and physically, and rather slender and attractive. She has a poise and grace about her that attracts many an admirer. She likes to pass the rejects of her Saturday nights on to her friends or co-workers. She loves to match-make. She can alternate between daring and insecure, tomboy and delicate child. It's an initial combination that few men can resist. A whiz at working with metals or machinery, she can also do well with fabric and design. Her eye for color is unusual. She really needs the financial stability of an older man, just as she needs his companionship. It steadies her nerves to know he is settled. Look to the sign of—surprise!— Capricorn (they act older even when young). A Libra is just a romantic fling. The Leo or Aries can help her find the perfect composite man if they have an Aquarius, Libra or Gemini Moon.

Her illumination: Poised.

Her dark side: Over-idealizes.

ARIES-SCORPIO

I hope you're serious here because she's nothing to toy with. She's intense. Look it up—you'll find words like "overpowering," "severe," "excessive," to define it, and her. She's very self-possessed, and isn't going to be sold a bill of goods. If she doesn't come looking for you, or you think you can get away with being glib with her, you'd better back off before she hisses. She's a decent person and has every intention of being an excellent wife and mother. Not everyone will understand the severity of this commitment to herself, though. Because she often leads a troubled, impetuous life that's quite different from her plans. No matter, she'll bounce back to original goals and find herself on the right track once again. Her life is never what you could call dull. She may have extremes in wealth or lifestyle. There are a number of Scorpio Moon ladies who have married very well, then been widowed. She may be one of them depending on the time of her birth. Now, don't you go worrying that her soup tasted funny last night, it's nothing like that. It just seems to be the way of the constellations to give her a few extra bucks and some notoriety. She can marry up. She can also do any number of other things like be a scientist, an investigator, a researcher, a sex therapist. Speaking of which, her sexuality is on low boil all the time. This simmering lady can find more ways to arouse, excite and take you by surprise than you could conjure up in your wildest fantasies. You're going to have to have a lot more going for you than good looks and a fat paycheck. She wants a provocative, stimulating, remarkable man with ethics. Sagittarius, Cancer and an evolved Scorpio stand the best chance, especially if you come from a noble family or good lineage.

Her illumination: Marries well.

Her dark side: May hiss.

ARIES-SAGITTARIUS

As you read this, she's probably out skydiving, flying, or on a cross country skiing adventure—if you're lucky. If not, she may have taken leave for the tennis matches at Wimbledon and left you to water her plants. This fiery lady goes off on some pretty wild tangents. She wants variety, adventure and excitement in her life. She lives each and every day to the fullest. She usually has long legs, no matter what her height, and they're in a constant state of motion. She probably thinks a soap opera is some exciting new form of theatre where you pitch your new crusade. She can't stand being tied down to household chores, and will fight you for the privilege of hauling the trash and repairing the roof. She often gets caught up in the double standards—yours, not hers. She can stray pretty far from home, and yet manage to expect fidelity on your part. This is one of the ways in which she is considerably naive. She has an impulsive, expansive, and childlike nature. Duty and responsibility come hard to her. Her intentions are good, but exciting things happen to detour her. A spirited co-worker, she can enthuse others on any project or task, and then totally lose interest herself. Her best chances for career success come from the fields of travel, exploration, or publishing. Her very own import-export business will be a good opportunity for success. She needs a man as adventurous as she is—no use trying to settle her down. She can stay happily unwedded for years with the same man. Being a mother will be another of her adventures in life. Her children will adore her. Look to another Sagittarius or a surprise match with a Gemini. A Scorpio fling is bound to happen, with stormy results.

Her illumination: Miss Excitement.

Her dark side: Detours easily.

ARIES-CAPRICORN

Let me guess—you met her at work; she was the owner; she's awfully young for such success and you're impressed. You should be. She knows everyone who could help her in business and guess what? They're friends. They can't wait to offer free advice or to come over and help her plan a party to woo prospective clients. She has such a fabulous sense of humor and a straight forward way of expression, who can resist? Besides, she's pretty in an unconventional way. Her head may be large for her body, or she's especially frail in stature. No matter, men and women alike agree on her attractiveness. She could write the book on using people, except she lives by a strict code that nearly forces her to pay back. So no one really gets taken advantage of. She'll talk you into a number of things that seem to benefit her, and then mysteriously you'll find yourself paid back at a crucial moment. She has a superb sense of timing. She can also change from the sweet, demure business woman in the prim dress, to the tough-talking wheeler-dealer. These are just her business suits, so to speak. Actually, she's given to bouts of near manic-depressive episodes of "I can't do it; yes, I can!" If she really starts to fall for you and opens up to her little quirks, you can expect a lot of surprises about her insecurities. She'll worry over her weight, her manner of dress, her ability at public speaking, and how long her success can last. She needs more innate confidence in herself. I can tell you her childhood may have been severe. She was probably handled rather strictly. She won't treat people in kind, and in fact bends over backwards to be gentle and lenient with her friends, husband and children. Speaking of husbands, you'll probably be thinking of it far sooner than she will. Changing diapers in the conference room isn't what she dreams of. Sneak up on her or she's apt to go traipsing off with someone else. She needs a Cancer, Capricorn, or a prominent Leo.

Her illumination: Born for success.

Her dark side: Needs reassurance.

ARIES-AQUARIUS

She sometimes gets the order of things a bit mixed up, and starts her family before she's ready to marry or settle down. And when she does decide to settle down, she wants a good provider who's not a penny-pinching sort. She'll have plenty of men to choose from, as she's witty and uncommonly bright. And because, while unusual, she's a good wife and mother. She encourages the growth of the children's imaginations and the expansion of the husband's horizons. That she's set in her ways and highly volatile will be compensated for in other ways. This lady needs to be tamed and if the man is up to it, he finds for himself a very different sort of femme fatale. She looks for the unusual in her mate. The average guy, in the run of the mill car, will leave her cold. The slightly off-beat, but an exceptionally well bred man in tennies sets her nerve endings on fire. More mathematically inclined than most women, more avant garde, she dreams of inventions, computers and test tubes, rather than other more usual pursuits. She can be found in the scientific fields, or the professions of fund raising or exploring the unknown. She probably thinks Jacques Cousteau lived the perfect life, except she likes sports involving the water the least. While she's popular, she's often misunderstood. Her frankness, her odd little ways, like trying to repair her own microwave, leave some people dazed. And, while she's one of the friendliest of the Zodiac, she has a maddening tendency to invade the average person's space as she talks. It's because she's open and outgoing. She's not intimidated by many people or things. Her wishes in life usually come true, and if you want to share this with her, give her lots of freedom and boutique credit cards. Look for the man with the Gemini Moon to lead her on a merry chase (it can be done). A Libra can force her to grow as a person, and a Sagittarius would just adore her.

Her illumination: Uncommonly bright.

Her dark side: Set in her ways.

ARIES-PISCES

This lively creature wants to bare her soul, but she's one of the more secretive women and can't, for the life of her, get into confidences. She's contradictory and lives on a deep emotional level most of us can't comprehend. Her emotional depth concerns her and not you, however. Because for all her love for another person, she can't fully integrate herself with another. She's emotionally absent in many respects. Her ideas are loftier and she wants to know herself in relation to the universe. In her physical relationships she doesn't ask for such exaltation. She's a pretty sexual lady and if you're a one night stand it'll be because she wanted it that way. Her loves and her finances will see quite a few changes in her life. She can work long and hard behind the scenes, and then come out with a very forceful project or piece of art. She's not a shrinking violet, and yet is content to work alone. When she wants attention (and she won't go too long without it), she comes out with all her ram force. As a wife and mother she's caring and ever so sympathetic. As a romantic partner she's less emotional than most women. Hard to pin down as she is, if she wants you, your friendship, or a particular job, she'll let you know—she'll quite simply go after it. She's happiest if she feels she's involved in serving or helping others, or in a field of communications where her ideas are exchanged or incorporated into social reforms, teaching or counseling. She can be the most soft spoken and most demanding of her Zodiac sisters. She has a natural interest in medicine, probably resulting from her tendency to infections like earaches, head wounds, etc. She is always advised to be exceedingly careful with medicines. Escapes through drugs or illness are not uncommon for her if she's unhappy. She needs the assertive signs of Leo, Sagittarius or Aries to help her deal with her emotional Moon. A man with a balanced Cancer Moon is also good mate potential.

Her illumination: Soft spoken.

Her dark side: Emotionally absent.

Taurus

April 20–May 21

TAURUS-ARIES

This woman spends a lot of time thinking about money and what it can do for her—like buy the freedom to pursue recreation and luxuries to add comfort to her existence. She's one of the love 'em and leave 'em ladies of the configurations. She's aggressive in her handling of the opposite sex, and is often considered pushy by men who aren't used to being pursued so intently. She likes to interfere in relationships where the man has someone else in his life. It's more often the challenge of disruption than the pursuit of love or of the man himself. She's a powerful lady. She is oftentimes her own worst enemy, for her headstrong actions can provoke the natural laws of consequence, like angering other women or overindulging in Venus pursuits. In middle age she may find she has little to show for her life in terms of money or stable relationships. She'll have had plenty of adventure though. After a turbulent teenage period and early adulthood, she has every chance of growing into a peace loving and suitable mate. Her children will have scrubbed little faces, live in shiny little houses, and yet she can be a mother of considerable detachment from time to time, depending on what adventures she has going on in her life. She usually marries young and has a fair amount of children. She will have experienced relationships where she's had very stormy days and nights. She's not afraid to scream loud and hard at any mistreatment. With great determination she'll eventually win her fair amount of wealth and material comfort. As a coworker she'll be neat, industrious and confusing. She can alternate between periods of near frenzy and plodding, slow work production. Since battles are part of her emotional makeup, she may as well pair up with a Capricorn, because he'll at least encourage her to grow. The Leo attracts and repels; the Sagittarius can handle it in stride.

Her illumination: Adventurous.

Her dark side: Headstrong.

TAURUS-TAURUS

Most of these ladies are very attractive. They usually have problems with their overactive taste buds, and have a tendency to gain weight. No matter, she'll have her share of admirers and yours, too. She's one of the stellar mixes who's in love with love at an early age. Wanting the best from life, and seeing the best in others she often has trouble accepting the cold hard fact that not everyone is as nice as she is. A few less than perfect romantic attachments can introduce her to the world of reality. She is so slow to make up her mind, that once she does it's going to take some tall talking to get her to change her position—this lady is very determined, yet she is very loving. Domestication comes easily to her, along with her career in banking, appraising, financial analysis, or anything that enhances other people's lives. She won't be afraid to tackle both career and home unless of course, you have tons of money, in which case she'll be content to stay home and make both your lives comfortable and cozy. If she works, the house may be a mess but she won't leave home without her decorating samples for the new bedroom, or a well planned menu for her husband and children. The old saying about the woman having to be good in only one room of the house was shattered by this woman. She is excellent in the bedroom, the kitchen, and the board room at the brokerage firm. Socially she's pleasant and kindly. She has a quiet charm and never forgets to ask how your family is doing. She won't be the life of the party but she'll enjoy herself just the same. Confident, she isn't shaken by the arrival of the most beautiful woman in the room. She doesn't question her place in a man's heart—oftentimes, for her own good, she should. The men best suited to her are the Earth signs of Virgo and Capricorn (she doesn't need any more Taurus in her life). A nice Libra would be delightful, or a Pisces who is stimulating in the area of life that she hasn't fully developed yet. A Scorpio brings out the peevish bull in her but she likes it.

Her illumination: Quiet charm.

Her dark side: Determined, determined.

TAURUS-GEMINI

Taurus women sometimes stray from their mates, so if you want this one for yours, and if fidelity is important to you, keep reading. She's a steady fixed sign, hooked up with an unsteady and very restless Moon. It gives her the "Frivolities." She won't be apt to impress you with her consistency or her stability. She will instead delight you with her love of the good times, and the pursuit of pleasure. She often makes leaping conclusions that lead to judgement errors that cause a great deal of trouble, legal and otherwise. She's well suited to fields of communication and oftentimes the arts. She's the morale booster at work, and her co-workers find her a determined little worker. She'll show up for work freshly showered and a bit too early on the days after the nights when she didn't bother to go home and go to bed. She's a whirlwind of social events, planning towards, or coming from one party to another in her younger years. Later on she can settle down to the more earthy pursuits like planting, and even farming—as long as she gets to run some machinery, tune the car and get out of the house on Friday nights. She isn't impressed with ambition in a man, nor intellect beyond common sense. Abstract formulas don't appeal to her. If she can't feel it, smell it, or touch it, it's too abstruse for her. Another thing, she hates to be alone. It's for this simple reason that many a man has shared the bed with her. She needs the comfort of another body. She needs a man who can keep her busy—her idle hands get into trouble. She'd be a wonderful travelling singer, and probably has a very melodious voice. If you want to keep it melodious, don't act as she does—when she gets jealous, she's very vocal. A Libra is perfect; an Aquarius can understand most of her contrasting needs. The Gemini of course has a strong chance.

Her illumination: Capable in arts.

Her dark side: Frivolous.

TAURUS-CANCER

Most Taurus women aren't manipulative—this one is. She can convince you that she needs your time, money, and attention, when she knows full well that she doesn't. She often does this just to get attention or to put you in a spot with a commitment of sorts. Like a test. She isn't docile or whimsical. She's a tough lady. She'll play the game however she deems it necessary to win. When she commits herself to someone she's a devoted spouse and a simply wonderful mother. She has her fits of doom and gloom, though, and then becomes almost obsessive about the children. Her choice of work is a profession where she can work from the home. She is given to bouts of laziness and self-indulgence. She hides these well, because she's proud of her image as a superior mother and wife once she decides to settle down. She usually has robust health, but poor vision and problems of sluggish digestion. She has a wealth of ideas to draw on for her professional use. And there's every indication that she can succeed. She'd be a wonderful song writer, or fashion designer. If you picture her executive appearance as briefcase in hand and wearing tailored clothes, you need to rethink. She has an unconventional manner of dress—casual and understated. Her ideas of fashion and beauty are off, but can set trends. Her impressions of people are fixed and should you ever slight or offend her, she'll quite simply never forgive you. Before her life is over, she will have shed many a silent tear over the loss of some of the men in her life. She's quite sentimental about the affairs. She has probably carried on some sort of secret correspondence with a few of them for years. The illusions of love oftentimes beat the real thing. Her fantasy men are the Libra, Taurus, Virgo. The Scorpio is too possessive for her—she wants to be adored, not restricted. The Cancer captures her soul.

Her illumination: Plays to win.

Her dark side: Has fits of doom.

TAURUS-LEO

This is one of the more financially ambitious women in the 144 positions. She wants money—money for luxury and extravagances and self-esteem. This combination by degrees can accentuate a need to realize that relationships can't be forced. At any rate, the men in her life face some difficulties in adjusting to her way. She does have a lot to offer, though. She's not afraid of hard work, she knows early on that life doesn't always hand you what you want, and so she can be very determined to follow her dream of success and financial excess. She's often overly concerned about her appearance and even if petite or not especially beautiful, she's a powerful, looming presence in a room—she has a queenly air about her. Her earth and fire combination enables her to accomplish much more than the other Taureans (except Cancer and Scorpio). She'll be impressed by friends of influence, by ambition and the trappings of success. Also, she won't be hesitant to express it. She doesn't deny her ambitions for herself or her husband or lover. Speaking of lover, he'll probably be all the more substantial things in life, and sexual in a narcissistic sort of way. She's attracted to people who admire themselves. She likes a man who wants to gaze into mirrors because, guess what? She does, too. A born executive, she can see through her co-workers and employees. She likes or dislikes people on sight, and pretty well sticks to these opinions regardless. Want to play around on this one? Try and get by with a few misdeeds? My advice: Expect a backlash. If she has let you get close to her, and you have fooled her once already, the second time will be your last. She has tremendous pride. Don't force her to confront you with your deception. The man who stands the best chance is the one born Leo, Capricorn, or Taurus.

Her illumination: Appreciates value.

Her dark side: Hates deception.

TAURUS-VIRGO

This is some lady. She's very appealing with a non-glamorous beauty in spite of the sequined dress she'll wear on occasion. She prefers a comfortable life and dress style. She's well suited to gardening clothes, dance leotards, or other productive clothing. This lack of pretense enables her to meet all people with the same spirit of enthusiasm, regardless of their status or of hers. She can obtain much success in her profession, which could be arts, nursing, gardening, ecology—anything that she puts her mind to. Most often, though, she tires of pursuits and moves on to another. She's less static than some of the earth sign combinations because of the busy Virgo Moon. She's capable in so many areas that she has a tendency to scatter herself in all directions. The most tactful of the Virgo Moons, she's very careful not to offend people with her views or opinions—she phrases it nicely. If you don't accept it, she'll smile and go merrily along unperturbed. She can keep records and write into the wee small hours of the morning. Her diary must be a lulu! She's a good mother, usually has one long lasting relationship, and before or after that, has numerous others. While not necessarily promiscuous, she has more admirers than she can be tempted with. Other women like her, and her co-workers find her a delight. She wants to have the material comforts in life, but if the pursuit of intellectual experiments calls for a bare existence, she'll experiment. She's a natural student. In some fashion or another, she works to better mankind. This work involves the geocentric matters. Her feet are planted firmly on terra cotta no matter how outrageous her new ventures sound. She can rattle off her bank balance while exploring ancient ruins. A Capricorn or Virgo catches her attention immediately. The Pisces Moon man gives her a challenge, especially if he's another Taurus—but then, she likes challenges.

Her illumination: Lacks pretense.

Her dark side: Mother Earth.

TAURUS-LIBRA

I think she's "The Lady in Red." This lady is a romantic par excellence and the ultra-feminine Sun-Moon combination leaves many a fluttering heart (yes, men's hearts flutter too) in her wake. She can have teeny little flaws like the not so perfect figure or face, and still be one of the most glamorous ladies of the Zodiac. Quite simply, there's this aura about her of romance and tantalizing sexuality. The fellows just can't keep away. In fact, they go very much overboard and actually send flowers. If they're lucky enough to get a date, they may even bring wine, make special dinner reservations, and in general go to great lengths to try and please this one. She seems to have the knack of smiling sweetly and listening to them beat on their chests while she punctuates with a great many "You don't say"s. Now you may think that this wouldn't be a very stimulating evening for those men who are so impressed by intelligence and wit. Believe me, this was all they were looking for—a woman who cared only about them. Suddenly the political science teacher could care less about the Middle East. This is the way she works her charm. Not especially an intellectual or an ambitious lady, she does look for these characteristics in a man. She's smart enough to know that these qualities are apt to bring in more money for her extravagant tastes. She does want a good provider. She also needs peace and harmony, and this is vital to her well being. The placement of the moon, however, suggests that she'll have a series of adjustments in life that alter her home base. Each time this happens, her inner stability is threatened. If she was born around noon, her creativity and tendency to drama increases. The rest of the ladies of this combination would be top notch real estate brokers. The general public loves her, and her co-workers find she loves teamwork. How to catch her? Be romantic, need her, cater to her, and provide luxury. Another Taurus could do this, or a Libra; the Capricorn can bring out her always ready sexuality. An Aquarius born to wealth has a good chance also.

Her illumination: Heart stopping.

Her dark side: Relationship junkie.

TAURUS-SCORPIO

This exciting lady needs one week at The Taming of the Shrew school because she has one of the nastiest tempers in the Zodiac. She is really hypersensitive and quick to defend herself against real or imagined slights. She's a wonderful, passionate, animated lover and playmate. Her long term wife material may leave a little to be desired though. If you're looking for lesser than a cosmic or spiritual relationship, this lady could be for you. She's affectionate between outbursts, and always has a nice touch or pat for you and the children. She smiles adoringly and manages to try and be a good companion to you in business or recreational pursuits. Her highly physical nature puts lust and desire above any other characteristics she dreams of in a man. Lucky for you, you don't have to be especially bright or successful; you don't even have to be witty and fun. You just need excessive sexual energy to make this lady happy. She's shrewd, resourceful and very courageous. If this sounds like your cup of tea (or in her case, love potion), then all you need to do is catch her eye. This shouldn't be a problem if you are attractive, musky and ardent in your pursuit. She can nearly read minds, so send your sexual messages through your brain waves. Surely she has other interests, you say. Of course. She's probably a whiz at investing other people's money, handling wills, estates, insurance claims, and could even be an outstanding investigator of most any sort. She's also very capable of making money. She's enchanted by the natural wonders of the world, and wonderful hiking and outdoor activities. She's also interested in her co-workers. So, she's not solely interested in sex, just primarily. If you're slightly breathless at the sound of this girl, I hope you're a Capricorn, Taurus, Scorpio or Aries. These combinations stand the best chance for a long term relationship.

Her illumination: Knows what she wants.

Her dark side: Hypersensitive.

TAURUS-SAGITTARIUS

I don't care if this woman was born in the early 1900s, she knew then about having it all. She's so likable, considerate, and pleasant, that hardly anyone could guess that she may find you a dullard. That friendly Sagittarius Moon gives her the most optimistic and sociable outlooks imaginable. Life can, and often does, hand her some really tough situations, but this Earth-Fire combination gives her the stamina to bounce back like some Socko toy. She can care for terminally ill family members and hold down the bank presidency job while raising her family. Okay, you say, surely she gets really nasty at work. No, she will not. She'll be a top flight boss, full of compassion and understanding. She has the ability to withstand. On the positive side this combination is given positions of authority, money, quiet fame, material acquisitions, and love of a great many people. She is one of the sweeties of the Zodiac. When life isn't burdening her with some pretty difficult matters, she's the first one ready to go out and party or plan exciting overseas travel. She'll eventually meet many an influential person, and most probably give them guidance through her profession. She keeps in touch with old neighbors and co-workers, and doesn't hesitate to lend a helping hand or check to anyone in need. The catch here though is need. If you aren't trying to better yourself, forget to bathe, or something equally icky, she'll be extending the helping hand right past you. As a lover she's passionate and expressive. Given to overindulgence with food or drink, she may create a few problems for herself along these lines. It was probably the only way she could escape some of the demands made on her throughout the years. In later years she gets the much needed and long overdue time for herself. She will relish it. If you want to be the object of her devotion, don't consider ever displaying less than desirable manners, breeding, or position—those are her most desired traits in a man. This is a job that calls for a Capricorn, Leo, or Sagittarius. The Sagittarius could excess with her.

Her illumination: Resilient.

Her dark side: Fussy about breeding.

TAURUS-CAPRICORN

She is just about tops as the wife and mother of the Zodiac. She's usually stable, loving, hardworking, and—can you beat this—ridiculously funny and astonishingly sexual. Sounds just like what you've been waiting for. Number one, you probably won't notice her right away—she's not out to market herself. She knows what she's got and if you can't see it, she figures you're a little too backward for her. Her idea of a great eye catching dress is one that is conservative—perhaps a nice little non-occasional suit. Like her, you have to know quality before you can possess it. If you think that glittery gold tasselled thing is snazzy, you won't even begin to understand her. She has a very real sense of purpose. Things are meant to wear well, to last, to stay in style, and that applies to her lifestyle and her men, just as it does to her dress code. Even if she was poverty stricken most of her life, she'll be offended by the nouveau riche. She's not frivolous, and is up to her neck in convention. The thing that saves her from being austere is her terrific sense of adventure and her wit. Her idea of the daring may not be riding the rapids, but it'll be the likes of a geology or anthropology expedition, or perhaps a nice little auction at Southeby's—now that's an adventure (if you've ever scratched your nose at an auction you'll know that auctions are indeed not for the timid). She is her own person. She does wonderfully well at work, but her co-workers know the Capricorn Moon propels her on to higher and better things, and they don't have great expectations for a long relationship with her. If you want a commitment out of her, leave your stock portfolio on the coffee table next to *Connoisseur* magazine, or bring her tickets to an old world art fair. Don't even think about gulping your wine, flirting with her friends, or wasting your money at the races. Your only excuse for being there in the first place is to see how your trotters are doing—yours, as in your very own. Who else but the earthy Virgo, Taurus or Capricorn? The Cancer or Pisces are the dark horses.

Her illumination: Class act.

Her dark side: Expects the best.

TAURUS-AQUARIUS

This one often gets an early start in attempting a conventional relationship, but as she grows older she may surprise everyone with her unconventional choice of the young poet or bohemian who has retired early in life. She's a sought after sweetheart, and she can certainly have her pick. She's one woman who can see the diamond in the rough when it comes to romance. Helpful and loving with everyone, it's no surprise that in her earlier years she may have been duped. She emerges wiser but not necessarily sadder. She still anages to see the best in everyone and will not hesitate to lend a helping hand when asked. This little ray of electric sunshine is everyone's favorite and she has many friends among her co-workers and neighbors. She appears delightful and uncomplicated. She's probably not that simple—she doesn't want to get bogged down in heavy debates, so her opinions are not necessarily all that well known. Intuitive and imaginative she has odd little hobbies that may drive you nuts. She's attracted to astrology and related fields, and in fact, may have bought you this book as a guide to your little black book. She could probably devise a new rating system for you. She's usually more of a friend than a lover at first. She comes by friendships quite naturally. And while you may become hooked early in the romance, she may not have made the transition from friend to lover as fast. Once she does she will quite simply knock your socks off with her sexuality. As a roommate, she's not apt to leave her nylons draped over the shower curtain rod. More likely, you'll be tripping over radios in need of repair, or some other odd little piece of debris. These are her treasures, do not touch. As a wife she'll try to tidy up a bit. Her unpredictability delights her children. If she's the one for you, I hope you're the Sun sign of Aquarius or

Taurus, or the Moon sign of Libra or Gemini. There may be a few other lesser signs before the main stellar combination.

Her illumination: Sought after.

Her dark side: Complicated.

TAURUS-PISCES

This is one of the prettiest women in the combinations. She has dimples, good teeth and large fluid eyes. When educated she's unusually bright. She may start off in life a little vacuous on the surface, but believe this: She'll grow as a person with each passing year. She'll become more and more involved in humanitarian pursuits. It wouldn't be unusual for her to start out as a model for I. Magnin's, and end up with a career in learning disabilities. She's a secretive, receptive, sensitive combination, and her direction is pretty much up to her. She doesn't brag or market herself (she's more apt to hide her considerable talents), but when she enters a room everyone's aware that a wunderkind is among them. She'll be an adoring wife and mother. Co-workers, once they get over the shock that she has wit and charm to boot and is non-threatening, will adore her. She has two teeny flaws: She is so extravagant that you'd better be able to earn a strong salary. No marked down sales bargains for her. And, she's dramatic. The way she holds her head, the way she lights her cigarette—all part of her natural expression for the arts. She'll probably be a superb dancer and you can either find her doing some marvelous charity work at the local hospital or toting her adopted ones to the supermarket between ballet lessons. In love she's gentle, poetic, and often the victim of love addiction or love at first sight. If the object of her affections is lazy or a bit shady, she can cope. If he's fooling around with someone else she'll drop him faster than a polyester blouse. He'll be amazed—no amount of pleading and promises to behave will assuage her. Look to a Taurus, Capricorn or gentle Pisces. If he happens to be a stockbroker, all the better.

Her illumination: Lots of things.

Her dark side: Addicted to love.

Gemini

May 21–June 22

GEMINI-ARIES

This little cutie can amuse you in more ways than you ever dreamed. She could make you a bizarre birthday video that pokes horrible fun at you, and have you laughing until your jaws ache. She can bring even the most serious person out of their blue moods. Her laughter is sheer delight; her presence is a tonic. Her energy is contagious. Oftentimes the men who are most attracted to her are serious professionals who find her a positive, sure-fire escape after a hard day at brain surgery. She's bright and well versed on many subjects, but isn't what you'd call an intellectual. Caught with a book of poetry under her arm, people may snicker that she's being pretentious. She isn't; she's genuinely curious on a surface level about a great many things. She's not terribly good at the follow through of attending school for the degree in a particular field. She hates to be tied down to a routine. This includes you and the children, though none of you will suffer for her disdain for order. She'll teach you the meaning of zest in your life, and that one can indeed survive life without always being punctual. While these are valuable lessons, she may encounter an unappreciative ex-husband or two along the way. She can be a big money maker in spite of her extravagances— she's shrewd underneath all that frivolity. She has friends from the janitor to the head of the corporation. Her co-workers have no doubt bailed her out of one of her delightful escapades at one time or another. She'll do the same for them should they ever loosen up and enjoy themselves. If this is the one for you, and she's a little doll, you'll need to give her plenty of walking room. She may forget to

193

come home at all (leave alone on time), if you tie her down too much. If you're a traveling salesman you have just met a woman who'll delight not only in your frequent absences, but in having to move around a lot. Wanderlust is inbred in her. Look to a Gemini or a Gemini Moon, an Aries or an Aquarius. The Sagittarius will fascinate her, but alas, he can't quite keep up with her.

Her illumination: Sparkling wit.

Her dark side: Lack of follow-through.

GEMINI-TAURUS

This delightful companion is a glib, smooth talking little money maker. She probably closed two deals while you were taking a shower. She doesn't like to waste time and can do more business on the phone in one afternoon than you can at your desk in a week. She excels in real estate or finance. She is no slouch in the singing department, either, so never ignore her artistic side. While important people don't fall into her path she is careful to cultivate the business contacts that she needs. If she suddenly gushes over a new friend you can be sure that she has a side interest in this person's business associates. She is mercury quick, and can change from feminine and frilly to tomboy or business executive in an astonishingly short amount of time. And while she's more reliable than most of the Gemini configurations she is still fully capable of taking off on some pretty exciting tangents. If you're a bit stodgy or a stick-in-the-mud, chances are she'll stifle a few yawns and move on to where there is more action. She'll entice many men with her attractive Taurus Moon, and in her early years she experiences many romances— she usually has a man in every city. That's the way she wants it. Under all the love of excitement lies a girl who can be exceedingly levelheaded and provide an unusual but reliable home base for the children and the man in her life. She'll no doubt want several children, and she's the kind of mother (surprisingly), who has trouble letting go. She usually has a number of marriages or relationships in which she lives with someone, but if her man is reliable himself, and lets her dream her sometimes unsteady dreams, he can snag himself a nice lifelong companion. She'll require a lot of your attention because she's surprisingly romantic for all her inconsistencies. Look to the signs of Libra, Taurus, Sagittarius and Virgo to entice her the longest. The Pisces could get hurt though it'll be fun while it lasts.

Her illumination: Money-maker.

Her dark side: Bores easily.

GEMINI-GEMINI

You've just met the mistress of contradictions! And you want my help. Well, I'll do the best I can but you can count on only one thing from her—surprises. Some of which may not be so pleasant, like when she falls madly in love with you, and then just as quickly falls madly out of love. Oh, she'll allow you to be her friend and let you know all about the new lover, but things will obviously never be quite the same. The thing that saves her from being vicious and unlikable with all her emotional disasters, is the fact that there's not really a malicious bone in her agile body. She has no more control of her fancies and whimsical behavior than you do. Like the delightful puff of air she is, she can blow in and out of your life with maddening force. She'll be a child in distress, a seductress in hiking shorts and the intellectual behind the wide framed glasses. Each and every lover and friend knows a different side of her—none can know the composite. She's social in a peculiar sort of way. She requires people and activity in order to survive. She detests being alone, and yet she can be in a group and have one of her more retiring moods take over hardly saying a word to a soul. She can write you long and gushy letters one week, and then not even respond to your most extravagant gift the next. She's fond of talking on the phone and her most frequent indulgence is the rather overwhelming telephone bill at the end of the month. You'll wish, should you ever have to pay one of these for her, that she was born to shop instead. Emotional turmoil over all her conflicting, fleeting and electrifying ideas causes everyone around her to suffer. She can't help this. Since obviously she is most difficult to settle down, maybe you ought to opt for a lifetime friendship with her instead of pursuing something of more substance. That way she could continue to delight you without disappointing you as a wife who skims over the role of mate, mother and partner just as easily as she does the rest of life's matters, from the company annual report to visiting her comatose friends. The Sagittarian will jump at a chance with this one, as will the Aquarian.

The Pisces really must get out fast. The Gemini will, of course, be drawn to her, but as a couple they make everyone crazy.

Her illumination: Not malicious.

Her dark side: Her phone bill.

GEMINI-CANCER

This is the most sensitive and emotional of the Gemini configurations. She's in near desperate need of someone to assure her everything will turn out all right. If she has a problem, she can get so worked up over it that she develops emotional problems running from inability to eat or sleep to periods of despondency. She's most often fearful under her bubbling personality. She's afraid of a great many things, some of which don't in reality exist. She may leave you uncertain as to which of her problems are indeed real. Nonetheless, she suffers from them. She's a delightful companion on her sunnier days, intelligent, intuitive, curious, and charming. She has a quiet resolve despite her appearing to be something of an airhead. She's fully capable of obtaining success in the worlds of finance, education, marketing, or in the field of writing. She is in near desperate need of roots, and yet obtaining them may be one of life's most trying concerns for her. She loves children and has many dreams of motherhood. She's one of the better Gemini mothers. Her sensitivity to her children's needs is acute but her ability to fulfill them is not always as reliable. She's capable of having more than one relationship at a time, so if you're a possessive man, you should know up front that she may cause you nothing but grief. Obviously she'll make the Scorpio man frenzied. Another Gemini, the Libra or Aquarius can attract and even understand her. But the best energies for harmony come with the Cancer Sun or Moon. She needs someone to show her a delicate balance and to provide the stable home life she can't arrange for herself.

Her illumination: Bubbles.

Her dark side: Fearful.

GEMINI-LEO

This woman is very sociable and in touch with current events, gossip, and who's who in office politics. One thing for sure, she's no wallflower. While this configuration is attractive and very appearance conscious, the women born during the middle 1940's have a commanding, compelling presence. They're also the least committed to their love relationships. Otherwise, this configuration leads to a strong desire for a mate with whom she feel a deep and lasting bond. She wants a devoted husband and children she can re-explore the wonders of childhood with. This lady is curious, resourceful and exciting in her approach to life. While she's normally inclined to study it'll be in her own fashion and in her own time. Therefore, she may not have excelled in school academics. But make no mistake about her intelligence. She'll be fully capable in sales, arts, poetry and music. She can be found in the fields of secretarial work, messenger services, and oftentimes newspaper work. Wherever she ends up professionally, her career is busy, exciting, and she's a talented and diligent co-worker. So able in fact, that the sky's the limit for her in all her endeavors. People in authority come to her for advice and counsel. I suppose, by now, that you realize just what a live wire you have an interest in. She's quite simply a nice lady who has every intention of getting the best out of life, including men and status. She's not afraid to buy out of the ordinary and expensive clothing and housing. She needs a daring, sociable co-partner who has just as much to offer as she does. Look to the Sagittarius, Leo or Aries Moons for the best chances of catching her attention. The Gemini Moon can capture her heart, and the Sagittarius man will come as close to causing her grief as she'll allow any mere mortal.

Her illumination: No wallflower.

Her dark side: You can't be, either.

GEMINI-VIRGO

This lady is a constant student, whether of human nature or other pursuits. Things fascinate her and people confuse her. She's one of the gloomiest of the Geminis but this isn't visible in facial expression to the casual observer. Inside, deep down, she's just not content. The project begun last spring with all its fascination now pales in contrast to the reality of the long hard work involved. Or the lovely friendship last year has now made too many demands on her time. Whether co-worker or friend, she's as inconsistent as the wind. She has trouble keeping her commitments, partly because she grows bored so easily, and partly because she's a prisoner to her over-stimulated emotions. Hyperactive, she likes to be on the go for the pure motion of it. One of her biggest expenses will be the gasoline bill, because she likes to travel to nearby places and get out of the house. She's one of the women of the Zodiac who prefers to be anywhere first and home last. While she's not particularly domestic, she does like to give parties. She likes to spend time with others on a detached basis, exchanging opinions and stories, but not sharing confidences or emotions. She's a perfect companion for a man who's looking for a part time but permanent arrangement. If he can wine and dine her, take her on trips and support her he'll have this lady waiting in the wings for a very long time. She was in no rush to get married anyway. She probably already did that once and found it wasn't quite the situation for her. Since she doesn't pout or display her gloomier side, she's a fun companion. I only wonder at how she can hide her feelings well into her 50s. Her nervous system usually betrays her by then, and the pent up emotions can surface. Never quite knowing what she was looking for, she never found it. She'll find you if you offer the challenge and intellectual stimulation, and the not too deep emotions, especially if you're a Sagittarian, Virgo, or Aquarian. The Capricorn as a rule will get out as fast as he can and it's a shame because she needs a good Earth sign.

Her illumination: Lively companion.

Her dark side: Detatched.

GEMINI-LIBRA

This is the combination of communication and partnerships. Therefore, communication about personal matters and concerns comes easily to her. While this isn't a lazy combination, it does provide an easy flow of life's energies. This woman is more psychologically and emotionally balanced than some of her fellow Gemini sisters. Daily life isn't ordinarily a chore or a challenging event for her. She gets along well with everyone, from the neighbors (where she's no doubt a favorite), to her co-workers who take an instant and often long lasting liking to her. In love things could run just as smoothly, except for one slight flaw—she's fickle. Part of her nature cries out for one long lasting, fated love. The other part is distracted by an occasional new man who offers some new excitement and challenge. Maybe he offers it along the lines of intellect, wit or pure sexual experimentation. For this reason she often finds herself in love with love for much of her life. She's a natural born flirt, and adores the pampering, flattering stages of new relationships. Truly believing that variety is the spice of life, she'll lead many a man on some not so merry chases. You really shouldn't mind, as she's exciting, fun, delectable and appealing to nearly every man she meets. She's just not wearing her heart on her sleeve for you to fool with. She's not deep; her commitments aren't long lasting; her values aren't conventional. She's a bright girl who spends a lot of time in her head. This means that while you may be gazing into her eyes the gaze back may be totally different than what you read. Her mind may be on a recently read book. Speaking of books, she's not an open one, nor can you judge her by her delightful cover. She's looking for a man of special qualities. She wants a man who can promise to make life an exploration for her, who'll be her buddy, who she can laugh and ponder with. An Aquarian, a Gemini, and often the Sagittarius man will tempt her. She could fool everyone and find a Virgo who gives her full rein for her life's choice.

Her illumination: Everyone's favorite.

Her dark side: Fickle.

GEMINI-SCORPIO

If she isn't an actress, she's acting anyway. There's a lot of drama and need to emote in this woman. The emoting ranges from tears, when necessary, to screaming exercises for the lungs. She can change personalities, clothes and hairstyles at least twice a day. She does know what she wants however, and she'll get it. She may come across as flighty or vacuous, but that's only her way of understatement. You see, she's guilty of not having many interests. It's not, however, because she's dull, she simply has a few specific interests and concentrates her energies there. In this respect she's not like other Geminis. One of her chief concerns will be herself. Were you honestly expecting me to say, "you"? Then you must be new in this relationship. Because only in the beginning will you get that kind of attention from her. Her attraction to you at first may be for something you can offer emotionally, financially or physically. Later on she gets back on center and concentrates on herself again. Now I'm going to stick up for her. It may well be the result of some earlier relationships that left her leery. Regardless, she's terrific fun—outdoorsy, rough and tumble one moment, feminine and dainty the next, and sexually aggressive later. She won't leave you looking for a companion. She'll be all you need. She can submit for a time, but count on this: She's going to have her own way. This is one of the reasons serial relationships appeal to her. Her theory is that you just move on after the honeymoon's over. Why waste time and energy on a dead horse? She knows a lot of people, but has few close friends. She's innately suspicious. She only lets her guard down with a few—like her babies. She's a loving mother and sort of a best friend with her daughters. As a co-worker she's distant. If she weren't she'd expose her mood swings and you'd wish you hadn't gotten to know her all that well. I admire her single-minded purpose. Best bets with this one for the long term: Libra with a Pisces Moon, or another Gemini.

Her illumination: Sense of purpose.

Her dark side: Sense of purpose.

GEMINI-SAGITTARIUS

Here is the bachelorette of the Zodiac. She usually marries young enough, and has commitments often enough, but she really never truly bonds. She enjoys adventure and romance, but can never quite settle down to more traditional relationships. She's also one of the full moon babies who grew up, no doubt, under some sort of estrangement from her parents. She keeps looking to other people for her answers but under a highly independent facade. Of course, this leads to some confusion on the part of the men in her life. The problem is, wherever she goes—she goes too, so the same inherent problems are there. Problems of restlessness, an almost reckless need for variety and adventures. Her daring is exciting, her ability to withstand and bounce back is admirable, but her lack of being able to keep a promise leaves many a friendship and romance on the rocks.

She'll stand you up, turn you out, ask you back, and maybe get her dates mixed up. You may find another guy waiting on her doorstep with the same problem as you. She'll have quite a story to tell, and you'll no doubt forgive her once or twice. This routine is as regular and normal to her as breathing is for you. This is her idea of romance: Stormy seas, high tides and uncharted courses. She opts for breathtaking scenes like two fellows at the door at the same time. Surprisingly you may not be quite able to get her out of your mind. You know you're in over your head and yet you'll try to continue to salvage yourself and the relationship. It can be done, but she needs some tight reins. She can manage career and home life well. She does need the guidance of someone she respects. You can find her wandering around travel agencies, libraries, hiking, or learning yoga. As a mate and wife she'll always pop in and out of your home and life like a stranger. She may be more at home at work where her co-workers find her energetic. She's not ungovernable. If you're good at dealing with the unruly, and have a good strong Sagittarius Sun, you're probably trying to train her already. Some Virgos can handle the task, and the Aries will actually wait at the door with the other fellow. Afterwards, he'll swear it never happened.

Her illumination: Unforgettable.

Her dark side: Unruly.

GEMINI-CAPRICORN

This is one of the more morose Gemini positions. She, like her Virgo Moon sisters, can alternate from fun, frivolous, flirting, to despondent, sullen and downright awful company. If you meet her in the party mode and she finds you totally enchanting, you might expect her to at least like you in a month. This isn't necessarily so. There's a secret to understanding this over and above the famous Gemini inconsistency. It's her hard, ambitious, shrewd little Moon. While you may have been good for the interim, what she wants long term is a man who can make money, provide security and status, and not ask for too much in return. She can be selfish, and if you don't fit the bill, don't expect her to be very committed to you. She's one of the women of the Zodiac who can have the longest list of ex-lovers and husbands imaginable. Ask her about it. She'll tell you that after a while they grew disinterested, or that she doesn't have too much luck with the opposite sex. She has plenty of luck, don't fool yourself. She can talk them right out of their bridgework and not bat an eye. What most likely happened is that their originality and independence became more and more unmanageable and she was losing control. Or their struggling artist career that was so enchanting, looked in retrospect, more like unpromising and floundering to her in the long run. If you think all this heartless, imagine how she feels about herself. She knows what she's up to. Try to make her your friend and maybe she'll stick around a little longer. She'll change jobs, schools, and life goals faster than you can change into your jogging clothes. She leaves everyone—lover, children, co-workers—confused and often angry. On the positive side, she won't be boring or try to possess you. Look for her to get tangled up with a Sagittarius or Aquarius, but she settles late in life for a Capricorn. Keep her away from the poor sweet Pisces or Cancer.

Her illumination: Captivating.

Her dark side: Yearns to wander.

GEMINI-AQUARIUS

Here is the flighty, ethereal woman who captures your imagination. She's light and airy, true, but she has substance; she has insight and intelligence. She may not have had enough education but she's smart—smart enough to use her facade to protect herself from men who think they can manipulate her. For all her elusiveness, romantically she knows what she's looking for: A man who can be both friend and lover; a man who can keep up with her intelligence and easy flow of ideas and facts. There's a certain amount of the wistful child in her, who sighs deeply about the last three men who loved her and how they misunderstood her. They did, and with reason. She never once came out and told them what she wanted. She asked a lot of questions and asked for a lot of advice, but she wasn't listening. She had her mind set on the answers and solutions long before they entered the picture. She just wanted to make them feel good. And then it happened. She got what she was looking for—the career break or another man—and she didn't even stop to check with them about any of it. She was gone like the celestial little puff of air she is. I rather admire her determination, for of all the Geminis she has one of the better grips on what she wants. "No," you say! I must be wrong. Surely then you clearly have the wrong birth data. No matter, you'll adore her 'til the last breath you draw. She's fun, witty, pretty, captivating. Even those of us who have her figured out as well as is humanly possible, we find her special indeed, and most adorable. Let her have her way. We all just want the best for her. She may not have many close friends, but almost everyone adores her, even when she's bad—like being thoughtless of her co- workers, her husband, and her children. It's easy to forgive her because she's so helpless. The joke is on us. A Libra will attract, the Aquarius will start to comprehend her, and a Sagittarius with a high IQ has the best chance of keeping her around.

Her illumination: A delight.

Her dark side: Celestial puff.

GEMINI-PISCES

The duality of this combination leaves a woman of conflicting, often contradictory emotional needs. She wants to be alone but also to be involved in every form of human contact and communication. Because of her extreme sensitivity and fascination with the intangible facets of her moods and life perceptions, she's not all that reliable in dealing with the more concrete aspects of life. She has a tendency to distort realities. Some who do not understand her, may take her flights of fantasy as pure fabrication on her part. In fact, she's as confused about her true self as you are. She often has alternating tales of her childhood, and these can range from pitiful to extraordinary. The most accurate conclusion that may be arrived at by herself or anyone else is that she's in a constant state of turmoil. She has a genuine caring for others, when her self concern is not at its peak from nervousness. During her times of less faltering interaction with others she is pure delight. Attractive to both men and women, there's a hesitant quality about her that makes others want to shelter and care for her. Since she's fully capable of attracting a wide variety of men, she should be doubly careful of her final choice. She needs a stable, rather self-assured man of keen intellect. She needs a caretaker of sorts. Men who don't fall into this category won't last long in her life. She'll not be timid about seeking a replacement for him either. She intuitively knows what she needs to keep her out of her often deep bouts of melancholy. Her childhood left scars that might confuse her, but that she won't forget. She's a delightful but troubling wife, mother, and co-worker. Look to the Cancer Moon, the Libra or Aquarius Sun or Moon.

Her illumination: Caring.

Her dark side: Needs a caretaker.

Cancer

June 22–July 23

CANCER-ARIES

She has survived some rounds that a heavyweight would shrink from but she can stand right back up and forgive the offender. While some people write the laws of order and proper conduct, and others contemplate such principles, this lady quite simply lives them. My hat is off to her for the lack of viciousness or bitterness that lesser women would display after what circumstances have dealt her. Proud and unpretentious, she has a sense of morality and honor that would leave the rest of us in awe. And yet, she'll tell you (if she is) that she's honored by your friendship. She could touch the very coldest of hearts. The ladies or men in her life should feel special indeed. She will, with her last breath, defend you, assist you, even jerk you out of the pub to keep you from hurting yourself. She didn't bother you with her troubles; she took every defeat and setback in stride; setbacks like failed marriages, the loss of children, deceptive relatives, and severe financial hardships. She's weathered some of the stuff soap operas are made of, and managed to find herself a decent husband, a good job, and become the mother of intelligent, fine human beings. If you meet her in her early years you may find her attached or unhinged—it depends—by a series of unfortunate circumstances. But as she grows, her problems become less malignant and her circumstances more rewarding. She'll even manage a fair degree of prominence and quiet admiration. She's a sweet wife and she deserves a decent man—one who can understand that some people can overcome their past. She would find forgetting her anniversary or birthday a near sin. She wants thoughtfulness in ro-

205

mance. She knows it's the thought that counts, so the guy who brings the banana and art book will actually score points with her. Look to the middle aged Aries or Leo to snag her. The Pisces is oftentimes the surprise catch.

Her illumination: Ethics.

Her dark side: A past to overcome.

CANCER-TAURUS

This is another one of the ideal sweethearts of the Zodiac. She's sincere and loyal to her family, her friends, and her co-workers. She reeks of professionalism at work, and with tenderness at home with her children, whom she finds nearly perfect. She has a healthy respect for money and won't spend you into the poor house. She knows the meaning of keeping her word, her promises, and your secrets. She can charm your in-laws and encourage errant children to behave themselves. Her manner is gentle. She doesn't like change, and wants security and stability above all. She doesn't want to quarrel to achieve her goals. She's an earth mother. Check her handbag and you'll find a small book of photos of her babies. She's attractive to boot, and is nice with everyone, from the mailman to her banker. Her banker, by the way, is delighted to see her because she's one of the most capable money makers of the 144 combinations. She reeks of decency and self respect. She's just as able in the arts as she is in the kitchen, where gourmet cooking is one of her added specialties. She won't be arrogant or boastful about her many accomplishments. She also won't go off on wild tangents, because she's down to earth and very realistic. She has a commanding sense of purpose, and you'd better have also if you want this one to be a part of your life. Infidelity, once she's settled, is nearly abhorrent to her. Little vices like gambling or drugs, or other not so hot character traits will send her packing. She won't buy a return ticket either. She's a special lady and deserves the best. If you can fill the bill and have a nice Capricorn, Taurus, or Cancer Moon, you stand a good chance. A Libra can sometimes be the surprise dark horse in this considerable race.

Her illumination: Money-maker.

Her dark side: Can be gullible.

CANCER-GEMINI

The Cancer woman is one of the most impressionable of the Zodiac, and one of the most easily touched by love. This Sun-Moon combination gives this gal an edge—she may cry at movies but won't have to be escorted out because she began to sob. She wants love and romance, but instead of being led on a merry chase, she can lead you around by the nose if she so desires. Yet she has had her share of failed romances, you can be sure. It's part and parcel of her chaotic self. From early childhood on she's impressionable, and easily confused by things she sees and hears. Most of her heart's bruises come from her misinterpretation of the facts. There's a part of her that enjoys being misunderstood, though she'll never admit it—it provides her with an easy out when she so desires. She's full of contradictions. She'll expect you to be there for her day and night, and yet she may well drop out of your sight for days, and figure she owes you no explanation. Since she's easily infatuated, you're probably better off not knowing the details or hearing her try to explain anyway. The pursuit of romance is often more enchanting than the actual reality of it. Despite her highly erratic romantic life in the early years, she can eventually settle into a solid relationship. She'll never be a top notch wife, housekeeper, or mother due to her lack of basic interest in these matters. She's one of the women who truly enjoy their career and harbor no secret desire to stay home and tend the babies. The man of her choice will have to be as challenging as she is, and enter marriage as a near experiment with few ground rules. Her emotional changes leave no room for too many rules. She's a favorite at work, and could have the boss mad about her. The Virgo could be the surprise mate here, even with his fault finding which will hurt her. The best bet besides the obvious Cancer or Gemini is the Capricorn with a Gemini Moon. A Scorpio with a Moon in the Air element has a strong chance.

Her illumination: Communicates well.

Her dark side: Impressionable/erratic.

CANCER-CANCER

This lovely little butterfly can flit from one love affair to another. She believes in romance at any cost early on and may jump into relationships too easily. This often results in an early marriage or two of short duration. Later on as she matures, she faces the cold hard fact about herself that she needs security and financial stability as much as romance. This may set off a series of attractions to older, more stable men. She's a loving wife and mother, and has the teeny flaw of switching her affections to her children. This mother par excellence can leave her lovers and husbands believing that they play second fiddle to the children—they do. In addition, she can transfer her affections to anyone nearby at the drop of the hat if she becomes disenchanted. She's one of the most imaginative of the Zodiac combinations, and she can excel in professions where she can put the creations of her mind to work. She's an overly sensitive boss, both to your feelings and to hers. It's for this reason that she holds herself back professionally. She's not a natural born leader; she lacks the necessary survivor spirit. Firing someone could make her physically ill so she therefore does best in entrepreneurial careers. She wants a practical, well balanced partner who can shower her with presents, flowers, romance, and attention. She can't stand a harsh word, so whatever rough edges he has, her mate had better file them down elsewhere—a coarse companion will not last long with her. The tears she sheds so easily over every imagined slight are real. Tread carefully or you can start waterworks on a daily basis. She craves the affection a Pisces could give, and is attracted to the Scorpio only when he's a good boy. A roving Sagittarius won't last long with her, and an Aries can give her a near breakdown. The Taurus stands an excellent chance. Carry a hankie.

Her illumination: Imaginative.

Her dark side: Touchy, easily offended.

CANCER-LEO

This lady is a real sweetheart with a sex appeal all her own. She's outgoing, vibrant and usually presents a happy, smiling face. She's constantly seeking contact with people, whether a hello from the neighbors or a kiss from her loved ones. She's one of the most affectionate, loving women of the Zodiac. Loyal herself, she imagines that everyone else is also. At first. Then she grows more cautious and develops the "I'm OK, you're not so hot" attitude. This rarely shows as she always manages to keep up her illusion of almost docile submission. She's not that way at all. She has quite a strong will of her own, but is rarely in need of displaying it, because she usually gets her way anyhow. She'll support her ailing mother, dote on her children, and bring tears to your eyes as you admire her sweet and adoring nature. She's an inspiration in the lesson of simple, honest, uncomplicated love. Since she's a natural money maker and a doting mother she is sought after as a friend by both sexes. She has a collection of recipes and a good stock portfolio. She's a well balanced person, even if her Moon and Sun are in reverse of the natural order of things. In love she'll have her share of heart breaks and disappointments. She's easily infatuated. She wants a tender lover with a more than average amount of ambition and common sense. Since this is not always easy to find, the quest leaves her discouraged from time to time. She cries at the movies, feels every emotion in the book, and when you're with her, you too experience a wider range of feelings. She'll settle after her late 20s into a woman of less emotional excess, but it will always be there. She enjoys both spending and making money, and if you try to play miser with her she could get really depressed. She's not putting you on—a shortage of money to splurge on her family, friends, or clothes can really take its emotional toll. Marriage plans may be delayed for her. It's for the best because she usually emerges with a real prize. Best bets for her happiness are the Capricorn, Leo, Cancer or Pisces. I didn't forget the Scorpio—she'll have discarded a few of them before she settles down to wedded bliss. She could marry a co-worker—he'd be in a position to get to know the real her.

Her illumination: Well balanced/admirable.

Her dark side: Extravagant.

CANCER-VIRGO

This lady has a well balanced temperament. At ease with herself, her life rarely offers obstacles she can't overcome with minimal effort. Her critical Moon is monitored by the Cancer Sun's sensitivity to others, giving her a soft, gentle approach to people which endears her to them. She can poke wonderful fun at her friends and children, because she's never unkind—she simply has a way of teasing and joking that is extraordinarily appealing. She's fun—not zany or wild—but lively. She's competent, but doesn't boast about her successes. Maybe this is why you're into your fourth date with her and you just now found out she heads up her own production company. She'll be as unassuming about her decent, middle class family and her grade point average. This is one lady who believes if you've got it, don't flaunt it. I must tell you if you haven't already guessed, you need to look more closely and pay attention so as not to miss a rare opportunity to find yourself a decent, loving, capable and talented spouse. You'll have little interest in her if you're looking for a lady of easy virtue, emotional baggage, or a complicated outlook on life. She has faith in herself and doesn't want to be used or abused. She also doesn't want a man who hasn't got his life in order. You don't have to impress her with your car, bank account or famous last date. She's looking for a nice man, one who both gives and receives in a relationship just as she does. If you're a macho man, you'll just tickle her funny bone. If you're sensitive but logical and have a nice Taurus Moon, or a Virgo Moon with a heart of gold, you stand a good chance of getting to the fifth or even sixth date with her. She knows early on in life what she wants: A nice home, stable children, devoted husband and fabulous career. She'll hold out to get it.

Her illumination: A prize.

Her dark side: Reads your mind.

CANCER-LIBRA

Now here's a competitor for the top ten femme fatales of the Zodiac. If she could have notches on her cute little waist cincher, she would. She can charm, dazzle, sweet talk, and out maneuver men in a way that leaves other women open mouthed. She can not only get her man, she can get her man to do just about whatever she wants, and that's quite a feat. She can also treat him a bit shabbily from time to time, and guess what? He'll dash back for more. The Moon position tells me that she had a troublesome childhood and suffered much emotionally. When you get her she'll probably come scarred from a prior failed relationship and she's just not up to giving herself one hundred percent. She's not self-destructive. Sometimes she may appear callous about your feelings by her unkept promises. This is a very emotional woman and she experiences some real highs and lows in life. You may never guess this upon meeting her as she is delightful socially. If she wants to party and you don't, she's fully capable of waiting until you fall asleep and then going out on her own. Maybe it was someone like her that inspired the song, *Ruby, Don't Take Your Love To Town*. Naturally every now and then the guy wakes up alone and runs right after her. You can bet he's feeling more like going out now. She's an inconsistent mother, and will let her love life interfere with her children. But, not to worry, her boyfriends will help tend them—like I said, she gets her way. Next time you're out shopping for her, bring her wine and a nice piece of art—she'd like that. Also, if she likes her co-workers but not her job, you might want to think about letting her stay home. Notice, I said "letting" her—she wants you to think you're in control of this relationship. A Scorpio, of course, can fill the sexual bill, but he'll be upset by her independence. A Cancer of Pisces could be a notcher. The Libra could make the match. Aquarians fascinate.

Her illumination: Charming.

Her dark side: Manipulative.

CANCER-SCORPIO

This lady is sexy. The usual Cancer reserve is overwhelmed by the Scorpio Moon, and she's not afraid to walk across the room emitting messages with the sway of her hips. She loves to play on the imagination of the men around her. If she finds you attractive, she'll make her intentions known—even when your girlfriend or wife is around. In this sense, she can be quite the trouble maker. Sometimes she behaves this way just to get attention, but if it's to show her interest in you, you can be sure more overtures will follow. She loves emotions other than romance. She loves to playact, or watch the real thing at theatres. She likes to create an atmosphere at home, whether with the aroma of freshly baked bread or the dimly lit boudoir and heavy air of Shalimar. It all depends on her mood, and these are subject to change at least every two and one half days. A bad temper is included in her repertoire of emotions, so don't let her occasional lapses into submission confuse you. She does know full well both what she wants in life, and the rules by which she's willing to play.

She wants romance and all of the good things. She needs security, a filled pantry, the promise of a pension, roses on a frequent basis, and a man who feels privileged to be in her company. She's an excellent keeper of the fires, and a protective, attentive mother. She's an exciting challenge for the man who spends all day doing repetitive work, has never had a crisis in his life, and would watch the soaps if given the chance. With her, he'll never miss much in the way of change, excitement and drama. If she was born around 5 in the morning she may possess an exceptional figure, full breasted and curvy. She'll be smart enough not to diet it away. The men she finds most attractive are the Scorpio (who else?), the adoring Pisces, the surprise attraction of the Capricorn, or the challenge of the Sagittarius who may not meet her ransoms.

Her illumination: Dramatic.

Her dark side: Emotional.

CANCER-SAGITTARIUS

She's one of the strong women that weak men are often drawn to. This complicates her life, as she's sensitive and hates to refuse anyone. For all her softness, she'll put her foot down if she feels imposed on by a lover or a co-worker. She wants a strong man and will not settle for less. She needs a man with ambition and self-assurance. She's excellent in career matters after furthering her education. She may lag a bit behind without formal training because she's acutely aware of her own shortcomings. She's sensitive about her liabilities. In a supervisory position she begins to excel. She truly cares about her staff and their potential, and can prove herself to be one of the best bosses of the Zodiac. Her life won't flow easily as she faces many an adjustment with this Sun-Moon position. She may get something in her mind like another lover, moving to a small island, or working on her PhD in mid-life, and set in motion a series of events like a disrupted marriage, a career change, or lifestyle variation. Since the Cancer Sun part of her nature hates to let go or to make drastic changes, she can wake up wondering how it all came about when parts of her life need total reconstruction. She's an emotive, caring, intelligent and fun loving woman, who likes the idea of creating a home environment for her loved ones. She needs roots, but can also express herself out of the home. She'd be an excellent counselor, a fabulous chef, and inspirational professor. She can do all the above at home, as well. If you're a Sagittarius, Cancer, Leo, or Scorpio you could get lucky with this nice, nice, lady.

Her illumination: Nice.

Her dark side: Midlife crisis.

CANCER-CAPRICORN

I can't think of anyone who's more family oriented than this lady when she matures. In her teen years and early adult life she's torn by family conflict, emotional trials and tribulations, and infatuations that bring pain. She learns from her early mistakes, and then beneath her quiet, unassuming manner, lies her inner core of strength. She's extraordinary at reassuring others and can calm the troubled waters for friends and family. Paradoxically, she upsets herself with needless fears, worries and anxieties. If you realize that she hides her near phobic reaction to life under a false bravado, you can step right up and become her security blanket as she rises to the top of some government office or agency. She's a top notch administrator, organizer, and co-partner in life. She'll take care of the children, balance the checkbook, and keep her home running smoothly. She'll deny herself many of the fine things she craves in order to give to her family. Some of this is her basic tendency to give too much to those she loves, and some of it is her basic good nature. While she can handle just about everything on a daily basis she's looking for the pieces to her puzzle. This is where the choice of her mate comes into the picture. She needs a man to help her fight the boogie man who lives deep in her heart. She needs someone to offer her answers and solutions to confirm her own ideas. She needs a Capricorn, a Taurus, a Pisces of strength and inner purpose. She's a star who needs to shine, and she needs someone to encourage her to step out into the spotlight.

Her illumination: Genuine.

Her dark side: Anxiety ridden.

CANCER-AQUARIUS

You really need my help trying to understand this one. You see it's her combination of planets, or the influence of the changing Cancer Sun and the erratic Uranus ruled Moon that causes her to change ideas and emotions faster than the speed of light. Did she tell you that she never wants to have children because the world is over-populated, and then in the next breath tell you that she wants to have four of her own? Did she tell you she wants to be a wife and mother more than anything in the world, and then switch quickly to how little time she has to invest in her latest humanitarian invention? Does she fight for her privacy and then steal the show at every social gathering within a hundred miles? Well, she means it all. She's a creature of varied moods and emotions, all sincere and all fleeting. She can be everywhere and yet a million years away. Therein lies both her fascination and your problem. I tell you this to help you cope, because once you understand that a lot of what she says is merely conversational you can relax and enjoy her. Plus, I have a secret for you: When she's about 28 years old the planets will do funny things to her and she'll mature very fast in her early thirties. She won't have a lot of time to invest in you if you're complicated. One thing uncomplicated about her is her love of fashion, and strongly individual appearance. She wants to stand out in a crowd so she can pretend not to care—and she succeeds. She'd be wonderful with another Aquarian who knows about changes. A Capricorn can help her to settle down to a more secure environment later in life, and the Pisces could be her playmate forever.

Her illumination: Fascinating.

Her dark side: Hard to understand.

CANCER-PISCES

This one was born cagey. She's a feminine delight, sweet natured, almost compliant and easy going on the surface. Back up and take another look. This sweet lady, and she is sweet, is also leary of you and your intentions. She's fully capable of taking care of herself, and can hold a grudge with the best of them—this little quirk doesn't happen often though. Truly she's the soul of optimism, but if she's hurt she can retreat back into her introverted shell faster than the bat of her lashes. She simply can't forgive someone who has deliberately tried to mislead or take advantage of her. It's always a set back for her to find that the world and the people in it are less than perfect. For this lady of rare sensitivity, it is doubly so. She's romantic and therefore vulnerable. While she may nod sweetly at an imagined insult, or turn her pouty lips down a notch, rest assured she's not about to forgive you, so don't bother to try and get back in her good graces. She's also not adventurous, and the mention of a trip to far away places may cause her to run for the Valium. This Sun-Moon combination lends itself to a fearful, insecure nature. Since she's timid, men often mistake her for a pushover and are very surprised to learn that they might not indeed be the boss in their house. Her moodiness may dictate lifestyles, and overrule what you had planned. When she's happily in a relationship she can be ferociously protective of her man. The same applies to her children. She's wonderful wife and mother material. You'll have to allow her her career interests though, because once familiar with her co-workers and surroundings, she becomes a top notch chemist, marine biologist or restauranteur. She's fully capable once she learns to get out and about on her own. Leos are often the most attractive to her, but the Scorpio of integrity, the Cancer or Pisces Sun or Moon stand the best chance. The only problem for the Pisces is when he is as near phobic as she is about making changes in life.

Her illumination: Capable.

Her dark side: She sees right through you.

Leo

July 23–August 23

LEO-ARIES

This lady is dynamic, daring, and courageous. She's also something of a loadstone to men and has an ardent, unconventional love life early on. She has no doubt entered, where others fear to tread, into a perverse relationship where the man was clearly an inferior. She has this wonderful, sunlit presence punctuated with periods of intemperance and foul temper. In someone of less pizzazz this would be nearly intolerable, but her swift episodes of anger are of not of lasting concern for anyone. Even when deeply in love, she can be a nasty, temperamental partner on a nearly daily basis. If you can stand up to that, you'll have an exceptional woman of substance. You'll also have a partner who can sky dive, pal around with the jet set, or inspire others with her appeal and regal bearing. She won't be a stranger to influential people, particularly in the realm of politics. She can't guarantee you success, but she can help you to be noticed (if for nothing else than your ability to capture her for a while). She has her own ideas of fidelity and marriage, and they will be strong. They may not coincide with yours—you'll have to adapt. While generous, she's not particularly thoughtful, and the idea of your having to travel an hour to pick her up for dinner and wait two hours to eat just to get a good night nod at the door, will never enter her head for a moment as being selfish or inconsiderate. She is, after all, gracing you with her presence. She's the whip cracker at work in her own queenly way. She loves to find shortcuts for everyone's work load, and to ask for more output as a result. She's not unkind, just impatient. Fast in her decisions she's expecting no less of

217

you.

If you hesitate over reports and projects, you'll be able to read her scorn in the flickering of an eye. If you're in hopes of being her life's passion, you need a steel core and a hard head. The ram in her will love to lock horns with you. An Aries is my number one choice. The Sagittarius, if he comes with a Leo Moon, will be my second. The Scorpio usually comes in the early sordid period of her life, and the Pisces is a nice occasional bedfellow. Gemini is the moth to her flame.

Her illumination: Sparkles and shines.

Her dark side: Hot headed.

LEO-TAURUS

"There must be more to life than having everything," may be this lady's motto. And indeed, there are times when she'll actively pursue interests other than acquisition, accomplishment, security and luxury. But, these interests will still be expressions of the good life— tennis at the country club, a cruise to the Bahamas, or fund-raising for the arts. If you absolutely have to talk about universal truths then please serve good wine with your discourse. She's one of the most beautifully adorned women of the Zodiac, even if she can only afford clothing from the local thrift shop. She wears jewelry, hairstyles and clothing as decorations to her person. She wants to be known, indeed remembered, as the lovely, successful lady you met at the charity wine tasting. And however humble her beginnings, she'll acquire, and move to the better address. Of course the thrift shops will then be out of the question. She's not tactful, but her opinions are honest. She has a strong sense of integrity. She's often powerful in her presence and strong in her ability to attract important people to her. If she was born between 1940 and 1953, these qualities are often enhanced, especially so if she was born around 5 a.m. What this means to you is that she won't stand for being bossed around, treated like a second class citizen, or receiving less than your full respect. She's a wonderful co-worker, full of ideas and loaded with ambition. She doesn't fear competition. She's a loving mother, devoted to raising healthy, upstanding little adults. She's a loyal wife, and she'll stand behind you through just about anything except betrayal to her or her values. Naturally, stepping on her public image will cost you. She's very selective in her choice of a mate. She's sensuous and yes, fun both in and out of the mono-grammed sheets. I wasn't trying to scare you away from her in the beginning of this profile, I just wanted to be sure you understand her values. Without that knowledge, even your moon in the right place won't matter to her. She does best with the Capricorn, or the Leo or Taurus Moons, and will most likely seek out the Aries for her less purposeful adventures in life.

Her illumination: Hot headed.

Her dasrk side: Strict values.

LEO-GEMINI

Leo rules the natural house of sex and recreation. Gemini rules a wisecracking, restless Moon. And so, in presenting this woman, I think of the one who most typified her combination of the il-luminaries: Mae West. Remember, when she was asked if she ever met a man who was man enough for her? She answered, "Why sure, honey, lotsa times." If ever a quip could describe this lively woman it's that. She has a sense of drama mingled with glib, exciting en-tendres, a lighthearted, capricious way of approaching life. She's not, therefore, merely a flirt who can't settle down. She goes deeper that this. She know she's too easily infatuated to settle on one man for long, and therefore doesn't like to make promises that leave her on the receiving end of waffle irons and tablecloths, at nice little bri-dal showers. She wants excitement, variety, and glamour in her life. She does well in public careers, public administration, public rela-tions, or sales. She isn't really domesticated and if she stays home at all, it's to read something for which she has suddenly developed a curiosity. She thinks children are wonderful creatures, made more loveable through upbringing by the grandparents or a nanny, if she can afford one. Speaking of affording, she's a luxury item. She'll want jewelry, fancy clothes, and a nice amount for traveling and en-tertaining expenses. You'll want her to be more, but she does best in a mistress situation. She has a lot of love to give in an open, affection-ate, often detached manner. She's not a cold wind, just a restless one. The talkative Geminis and Virgos do well with her, the Leo matches her sense of showmanship, and the Aries knows how to keep her stimulated. She's fickle and appealing enough to have a chance with almost every sign.

Her illumination: Delightful.

Her dark side: Hard to pin down.

LEO-CANCER

Here the Sun and Moon are in their true placements. This lady is the natural born mother of the Zodiac. She loves children and has an innate understanding of their needs and emotions. She's loving, kind, hospitable, and generous. She's dependable and honorable and is the kind of friend who'll stop everything to help someone in a crisis. She may not be as quick to ask for another's assistance, not wanting to burden people with her own problems. She's one of the genuine sweethearts of the Zodiac. She may not encounter fame and fortune, or be the most beautiful, but her harmonious nature, her giving and caring soul are just about tops in the 144 combinations. For all this she has very little conceit. She may appear vain to those who aren't concerned with their image or with fashion. She's a definite clothes horse. Her love of extravagant and elegant clothes is on her list of life's pleasures (you were hoping she placed home cooking and ironing shirts above all?), along with get togethers with dear and close friends. There's nothing not to like about this uncomplicated woman. She's the top confidant at work, capable enough to do her job and bail you out when yours is getting you down. She's the childhood sweetheart who marries her high school football hero and thinks he's still wonderful after all these years. If she marries more than once, she usually marries a man who manages with her partnership to excel in his profession to the point of prosperity. She's not a nag, petty or mean. The children will love her when she's old and other mothers are discarded. People rally to help her when she's as fragile as the wings of the birds she has cared for. She could lapse into an affair along the way if she felt true love and devotion were not hers at home. A Leo would be perfect, a Pisces would be adorable, and while the Cancer is good of course, the Libra could be the long shot.

Her illumination: A sweetheart.

Her dark side: Needs near adoration.

LEO-LEO

You'll know when you are in the presence of the queen for she wears her hair like a tiara. She's proud, haughty and elegant whether in a starched apron or a silk dress. She can choose to be giddy, subdued, or gregarious, but she'll always be the center of attention at any given function. She's the sort you say "excuse me" to in hushed tones when you accidentally bump her in the subway. The epitome of the word "class," men stop to apologize to her if they've just cussed in her presence. This will no doubt amuse her, as she's no stranger to a sailor's vocabulary when angered herself. Ah, but she'll never let on because she knows this inborn air of superiority has won her many a friend, job, or lover. Her husband and children will not be treated like subjects though, because she was born for mothering and romance. Notice I didn't say "wifing." This is because she's devoted and generous with her loved ones, but doesn't let herself be denegrated to lesser roles like caretaking for others. She'll demand that the family be clean and well behaved co-inheritors of the throne. She has a tremendous sense of humor and adventure under her exterior, and can poke wonderful fun at you or herself. She's not petty or malicious—as a rule. There is an exception and you should be made aware of it right away. If you offend her sense of honor or trust she'll take her long fingernails to your face. Or she may just freeze you out. She's an exciting companion, friend, co-worker and lover. She has a wonderful love of life and will lead you on a thrilling, merry chase of daily explorations. Things just seem to happen to this woman, like the Governor dialed her number by mistake, and after a fun chat he invited her to a dinner. She needs a strong man who can take a second seat (which is where he'll be), like a delightful Libra with a Leo Moon, or a Capricorn who understands that her flirting and extravagance are merely displays of drama. A Sagittarius could also be the one. She can't stand men who aren't terribly bright or who are indecisive, so if you want to be in the running don't take two weeks to decide where to go for your spontaneous weekend getaway.

Her illumination: Exceptional.

Her dark side: Vindictive.

LEO-VIRGO

This lioness is fastidious, intelligent and sound. She has a way of looking at problems and issues, and coming up with wonderful solutions that leave you wondering, "Now why didn't I think of that?" It's for this reason that she's so capable in business. Her primary talent is logic. Her drawbacks are her tendency to introspection, her strong opinions, and her exacting Virgo Moon. She may be much like her mother in this respect. She'll also pass on this demanding nature to her children. She wants her life ordered and to run like clockwork. She'll ask her family to pitch in and make sure everyone lives up to her expectations. She can alternate responsibilities around the house just to keep everything fair. She'll demand respect and high standards from her husband and children. If her mothering sounds cold, let me assure you she has a lightness of spirit that her children can sense under the reserve. They want nothing more than to gain her respect (they know they have her love), and as a result they turn out better than most children. In this respect she's often a wonderful mother. As a sweetheart, she's the least dramatic and outgoing of the Leo women, so don't expect to use her as your showpiece. She's much more substantial than that. She's not afraid of romance, however, and is a sexual lady. She's a worrier and she often has fears of an illness coming along and sapping her strength. Her health problems usually are of the intestinal sort. She needs lots of fresh air, sunshine and someone to drag her off on vacations where she can give her tired body a rest. Women of this configuration born in the late 1970s may be subject to depressions from time to time. She needs a playmate, a man with ambition, good sense, and a flair for adventure. Look to the Sun signs of the Virgo to bog her down, the Leo to buoy her spirits. The Capricorn can understand her, but the Aries can show her how to have fun.

Her illumination: Capable.

Her darkness: Exacting.

LEO-LIBRA

If you're in politics or a rising corporate executive this is the pick of the Zodiac for an outstanding political wife. This lady draws people of influence and power to her like a magnet. She is absolute charm and dignity, and usually one of the most lovely of ladies well into her golden years. She, like her male counterpart, is going to have so many admirers you'll have difficulty getting out of the stampede, because there will be many admirers for her other qualities. She'll be a devoted wife and mother. She has an elegance about every undertaking in life, including the pursuit of her man. That's right. She'll pursue him with the tilt of her majestic head, the gaze of her eyes and other subtle tricks of the queen. Never tacky enough to actually flirt overtly, she nevertheless gets the message across. She's the same in her career pursuits and in the handling of her children—she invented body language. Commanding nods and gestures take the place of hands on her tight reins. It's to everyone's delight that she gets what she goes after, for she's a wonderful companion, lover, mother and boss. She'll never be a co-worker even if she should be temporarily stuck at a factory job on an assembly line. Like cream she rises to the top. She has a fondness for clothes and was born looking rich. She'll no doubt know some heartache, because climbing to the top often brings perils, but she bears her disasters well. Her flaws: She doesn't really ever quite mix with the masses, and she doesn't take a back seat to anyone, I mean anyone, so that includes you. I don't care who you are, how rich or how famous, she gives the orders. Don't worry, you'll not even suspect that she has you in such control, so how can you be offended. The Leo who could be such a good match would fight for control, so I'm going to suggest a Taurus, Cancer or Libra for her.

Her illumination: Rises to the top.

Her darkness: Bossy.

LEO-SCORPIO

This is a powerful combination. She'll be commanding, nearly overbearing, and often irrestible. If she was born during the 1940s she'll also have one crisis after the other, especially if born in the early morning hours. She's excessive and rather inflexible. When she's working on a project, usually politics or research, she may forget to eat, sleep, or that you exist. This will apply to the children as well, though she's normally a devoted mother. She doesn't know the meaning of half way or half hearted. Since sex either for recreation or cosmic unions is so important to her, you can expect her to experiment a bit with the subject in her younger years. During these times she may also forget to eat or sleep. Her thoughts, to say the least, aren't scattered. She won't flail herself about in tears when things have run amuck—she'll dig her claws in and set about the task of making order out of chaos. She won't be your clinging vine either. Even at the peak of her devotion, she's not looking for someone to complete her parts, rather she's looking for a man who can handle the jungle queen. She's strong and protective of her friends, co-workers and loved ones. She'll be the first to offer a helping hand when someone has a problem. If you have too many, she'll be the first to tell you why she has withdrawn her assistance. She isn't hesitant about giving her opinion. She's strong, she's extreme, and she's worth the knowing. If you're a Leo or Scorpio you can deal with it, but the barometer at your house will frequently register stormy. Maybe a nice, not so strong Pisces can let her take the lead, or a Sagittarius can help her to lighten up. A Libra may offer the calming air she needs—she needs less intensity to save her from herself. Remind her as she's opening her fifth pack of cigarettes today.

Her illumination: Jungle queen.

Her darkness: Compulsive.

LEO-SAGITTARIUS

Whew! What a lot of energy this combination has. And what an enormous amount of luck, charm, and social savvy. This woman has a child's sense of adventure and love of life. She has creative talent and far reaching ideas. Love of the exchange of culture, experience and artistic expression runs high with her. If she was born around 8 or 9 p.m., she has outstanding chances for a career in an artistic field. She needs a strong birth time to help her to conserve, not scatter, her considerable talents and energies. This scattering of interests usually shows up in her work output, and leaves her co-workers a bit bewildered as to her aspirations, as she can change career goals suddenly. One of her work talents is to be able to accomplish more in a few hours than other people do in one day. She has a wide range of knowledge and is often intimidating to bosses who are easily threatened. She isn't what one might call a devoted sweetheart, mother or wife. She has a deep love for her family, but her need for freedom is so intense that she can be neglectful of the full attention they deserve. These ladies are the kiss-and-run mothers of the Zodiac. She'll be very affectionate, and lavish with praise and cuddling. She won't be, however, the type to sit at her children's sides and help with the multiplication tables. Her husband should also allow for this trait to show up when it comes to the mundane chore of dusting or the tedious task of dish washing. He should be able to balance her zest for living, her enthusiasm for sports, her love of travel and adventure, and her healthy approach to sex against her shortcomings. If he can, he may discover that she's quite a catch indeed, and he'll never be able to accuse her of being boring. She'll lead many a man on a merry chase and will be counted as the one who got away by nearly all the signs of the Zodiac. Another Leo or Sagittarius, and yes, the Aries too, stand a good chance of keeping up with her. The Libra may captivate her with his social grace, and the Aquarius may stand the best chance of understanding her less than personal approach to romance.

Her illumination: One of the best.

Her darkness: Scattered.

LEO-CAPRICORN

Here is the purposeful, determined, very witty woman who has never for one moment let heartache stand in her way. She'll go after whatever she truly desires in spite of setbacks that would send other women strolling near balcony ledges. This is an outstanding configuration for full fledged success and accomplishment. The relation of the sun to the Moon suggests however that whatever she achieves doesn't come without a price—the price being a near constant rearrangement of her life, living quarters, and family security. Her children may cause her much grief, which she'll bear quietly and with patience. She's a loving mother and wife—one of the best really, even with a business to run, or a career that leaves her nearly frayed. Her desire to excel is so strong that she gives her heart and soul to all her endeavors, and naturally this takes a toll on her health. The heart or the bones are usually the weak points that react to her stress. You, if you don't know her well, may be a little surprised at what I have to say about her, after all, she has this wonderful child-like sense of humor, she's gracious with her co-workers, and outstanding as a boss. You never remember her complaining about a thing—well, she did roll her eyes once when her husband fell down drunk at the company dinner. But surely that didn't upset her. Surely, it did. She needs a dear friend in a man. She needs respect and loyalty and someone to care for her for a change. A Cancer, Leo, Capricorn or Taurus would do nicely. She could fall hard for a Pisces or Scorpio but that might only add to her problems. Regardless, she'll convince everyone that she has a wonderful life. I hope she has indeed.

Her illumination: Endures.

Her darkness: Think of Scarlet at Fair Oaks.

LEO-AQUARIUS

This full Moon baby looks for creative channels to express her desire to work in the public eye, to organize and demonstrate her creative talents. Impish yet commanding, she never meets a stranger. She's sincerely interested in others, and if you're the jealous or possive sort she'll drive you very nearly crazy. She may or may not mean anything with her hugs and lavish attentions to all her friends. Either way, she considers her relationships her concern, and not yours. She doesn't deal in possessive, confining emotions. She's a ray of sunshine, and can't be captured or held still. If you dare to tread on her friendships, demand some sort of exclusivity, she'll stamp her feet LIKE THIS! She has a temper that can easily be enraged. But, being the loveable, humane and basically kind person that she is, she'll forgive you. You won't get your way, you'll merely be pardoned. She has no use in her life for the small or petty emotions that accompany many intimate relationships. For you men out there who're looking for a woman who has very little interest in the ties that bind, this one could be for you. If you can be as sensible about romance as she is, you'll have yourself a witty, sociable, intelligent companion who can teach you about higher spiritual consciouness. I can assure you this will not be a boring relationship. She is a nice co-worker, the kind people want to protect. She is an adoring mother, and can settle down into a stable marriage. There may be a slight problem in her later years, as she is highly attracted to younger men. She may be the one in the marriage to want to pack her bags and run off with the younger man and leave you at home to tend the kids and your toupee. Scorpios should clear out after the first date, Libra and Aquarius fare well. Some Sagittarians can manage to keep some sort of control.

Her illumination: Never boring.

Her darkness: Stubborn as a mule.

LEO-PISCES

This woman is not quite the humanitarian that her male counterpart is. She may find herself in the helping professions of medicine or social work, or even religion, but she'll have character flaws that are more apparent than those of the man of this Sun-Moon combination. One of them is near rage when not the center of attention, although she'll hide it well. The need for approval with Leo is always great, but with the sensitive Pisces Moon it's intensified. She can be very contradictory—she wants to compete and to win, but she doesn't want to run the risk of putting herself out, or of losing. Oftentimes as a result she has a tendency to live in a fantasy world. Some of her typical escapes are books, television and overindulgence in the bubbly. Shopping sprees can also be a favorite outlet. As a wife and mother she's caring and many times devoted beyond belief. Her need to feel superior often takes its toll on her work relationships where she finds it difficult to commit to a job unless she's very clearly the boss. She craves positions of power and prominence. This woman will always look her best—feminine and romantic. She's stalking the jungle looking for a man to rescue her from the beasts. In the area of romance, she's often sought after and usually winds up with quite a catch. Her catch will be the man who'll appreciate her need to look her best, and not complain about the manicurist costing more than the groceries. Since this is a rare sort of man, she needs someone who appreciates being admired for his pretty wife. She does have trouble in her romantic life regardless of the man, because she believes in the old childhood stories where the prince arrives in the nick of time to save the fair maiden. It's a heck of a shock to find that the prince is just the guy next door who gets five o'clock shadow and needs reassurance that he won't get fired next Friday. Look to the Pisces, Libra, or Aries to win her hand.

Her illumination: Aura of glamour.

Her darkness: Needs a prince.

Virgo

August 23–September 23

VIRGO-ARIES

Here is a demanding position of the Sun and Moon—this woman will stop at nothing to succeed. She'll help you with your goals unless, of course, yours and hers should ever collide. In that case she can be totally shameless in her trampling over you and stomping your heart into the ground, to say nothing of your career goals. She lays groundwork for her awards and public recognition even in the area of charity work. She does nothing without the thought of personal gain. She'll blow her own trumpet, or better yet, manipulate you into doing it for her. You won't catch on until it's to late, because she spends a great deal of time leaning on you for help—help with her personal life. It's midnight and she can't sleep as usual, could you listen to her problems again? What would she ever do without you? She'll survive, trust me. She can be the most manic, hyperactive person you've ever met when she's on a roll, and then she can fall into a slump and barely figure out how she can survive another day. When she's younger this is touching and nearly always considered a source for real concern. People tend to drop everything to come to her aid ("Would a raise help, or a promotion?"), but as she ages her antics leave one a little weary—she overstays her welcome in the sympathy department. She's critical and exacting. When she first meets you and offers to fry you the best chicken this side of Dixie, you can't imagine there's ice in her veins. I wouldn't want this woman for a co-worker or a boss; you may be able to handle it if you're thick skinned, however. As a mother, if you were jailed she'd bake you a cake with a file in it. She has, as you may have guessed, quite a time finding Mr. Right. Her life will bring many involvements, but she marries late in life. She's bright, she's a good conversationalist, a hard worker and a money maker. I don't know, maybe it beats dining alone. She needs another Virgo or Aries, a forceful Scorpio with a Leo Moon, or a Capricorn with a whip.

Her illumination: Obtains her goals.

Her dark side: Rigid.

VIRGO-TAURUS

This Virgo lady is sneaky about one thing—the lights bestowed upon her by the sun and moon often lend a helping hand in the department of beauty. You never think about the beautiful Virgo, but there seem to be two extremes of Virgo ladies. And when they're beautiful, as in the case of the Pisces, Taurus, and Scorpio Moons, they're stunning. There's a reserved, quiet, imposing manner, that is sedate, and non glittering. The Virgo doesn't have the magnetism of the Scorpio, or the drama of the Leo, but with this configuration, I find a commanding, no-nonsense, earthy sexuality that knocks men off their Gucci loafers. Notice I didn't say tennies or cowboy boots. These ladies are too "establishment" and old money (even when born to poverty, which is not unusual) to pay much attention to anyone who can't dress with taste and convention. She's strong, defiant, and enduring about her sex appeal. Lesser men back off unless they're very obtuse. Should they attempt casual conversation, she'll no doubt practically sniff in their faces and walk off. She's something of a snob. She also won't bother with silly little games. Actually she'd rather be home with a good book and a nice glass of wine. She likes to socialize alright, but the crowd is very select. She's as discriminating at work, where she's highly successful in whatever she set her mind to. She's an outstanding money maker. She's also a good wife and a positively fabulous mother. She can teach her children at home and put the modern school system to shame. Even with her appeal, she's not usually snapped up by some lucky man at an early age—she'll usually be well wedded and totally devoted later than her friends. She asks only that her mate be loving and stable, and of course hardworking. He won't have to be at all good looking—she looks into the very soul of men. Look to the rich Capricorn to appreciate this one, or the Taurus. The Aries or Aquarius can't usually relate to her at all.

Her illumination: Enduring beauty.

Her dark side: Makes few compromises.

VIRGO-GEMINI

While not exactly a chatter box, this combination is talkative and expressive. In fact, she can be quite charming. She's intelligent and fully capable in many areas. She's not, however, all that consistent. So while she's versatile and has many chances to excel, I can't say she'll exactly pounce on them or even be there to answer the door when opportunity knocks. She's one of the most glib, quietly persuasive women in the Zodiac. She makes a wonderful presentation (flow charts and all), and can do exceedingly well in interviews, but when it comes time to actually do the job. . . well, it might interfere with her current whim. Capable, she's not especially industrious. Breaking a promise means nothing to her—she'll feel no guilt or remorse, being childlike enough to think these things don't really matter. What? She's decided against having the family over for Christmas? Why, she was the one with the original idea, but her ideas are always better than her actions. Well, she's changed her mind. If you force her to go ahead with the plans, she'll sweetly smile and say, "Of course, dear." Then her overactive Virgo nerves get the best of her, and lo and behold she's sick on Christmas (she's also given to spells of fantasy and nervous disorders). Not to worry, she'll be better right after dinner time. Get the message? Like her male counterpart, she's more show than go. She can pull the wool over your eyes for years. But maybe you'd like to get this out in the open right up front. That way, you can make plans that you yourself can count on. She does offer sweet mothering and a good deal of attention to her husband. She's good in personnel, nursery work, or earth related fields like real estate. She'd be an excellent nutritionist or physician's assistant. Her co-workers will catch on to her in no time at all. It's just you fellows with the Gemini Sun or Moon that are a little slow. A Taurus or a Sagittarius would be great with her.

Her illumination: Smoothes over for others.

Her dark side: Broken promises.

VIRGO-CANCER

This woman finds exercise, health foods, and all those awful things come quite naturally to her. And on her they look good. While the early part of her life may not be so easy, as she ages she finds herself and obtains her security. Security is vital to her. Ask her to move about and she gets nervous. Her stomach will ache and ulcers could develop. She's deeply emotional, don't let her Virgo exterior fool you. Because she's logical and clear thinking on most matters, don't imagine she can't lose it over you, threatening her very existence. In spite of her reserve, and yes, dignity, upset her and you'll see her turbulent, excessive emotions explode. She can out seethe, out tantrum, and hold a grudge better than anyone alive. She won't care who knows about the outbursts when they're in progress, but she'll care later when her reserved side takes over. She's a natural with computers, nutrition, insurance matters, or social work. The boss will adore her, her co-workers have mixed feelings (she can be snappish). But no matter, she'll do well in her profession. She can advance rapidly. She'll keep the company secrets. She'll be on time, and she'll work hard. At home she's not the most industrious housekeeper, nor the most capable mother. Oftentimes her children get by with murder. Her husband won't have such leeway, however. In fact, he may have some real solid problems keeping her temper down and her domesticity up. She oftentimes becomes leary after the first relationship or marriage that didn't live up to its promise. The next man will pay. She'll be suspicious of the new man possessing not only his own flaws but the ones from the previous relationships. She was probably one of the women who told me, "There are not 144 types of men, there's only one—rotten." She's going to need you to be a man among men—tolerant, cooperative, and understanding of her quirks. If you pass the test you could have yourself quite a catch. Best chances are Cancer, Taurus, or Virgo. The Leo, Sagittarius, or Aries will make her act like an ugly witch.

Her illumination: Solid.

Her dark side: Suspicious.

VIRGO-LEO

This lady is the shopper who compares labels and prices, and thinks everything through in her purchase of the most quietly fashionable garments she can find. She's a good shopper, not your everyday shop-a-holic. She's also discriminating in life. For the lady of this configuration born around 5 a.m., her chances of getting the most out of her dollar are enhanced. She also becomes more physically appealing if born in the early morning. She can be something of a snob if you only know her superficially. She does have definite values, and expects everyone to be as loyal, steadfast, and hardworking as she is. While not a party animal by nature, she's given to spells of carefree, near giddy behavior when she feels she has met all her obligations and can afford the time to relax. She needs to be encouraged to alter her routine and lighten up, because she can easily overtax her nervous system and push herself to near physical exhaustion from time to time. During these periods she's most likely involved in trying to prepare the perfect annual report, produce the best children's documentary, or make the most sales for the hospital fundraiser. She looks for a man of substance, and as long as he's noble and self assured with good reason, he can be rather homely. It goes right back to being a good shopper. Once she's decided on her man, she'll have every intention of standing by him through thick and thin. She'll demand respect from her co-workers, and yet be rather meek around those who are her work superiors. She never quite has the confidence in her work that she should. I wish I could say she was more well-rounded, and less critical of herself because she could be such wonderful fun for everyone—she would be one of the more delightful companions of the Zodiac. But she really isn't. No matter, she's a top notch mother, who wants only the best life can offer for her children and for the man she'll quietly adore. He'll no doubt be a dashing Leo, a troublesome Sagittarius or Gemini, or a Capricorn Sun man with a Virgo Moon.

Her illumination: Steadfast.

Her dark side: Needs to have fun.

VIRGO-VIRGO

Gosh, I hope she's not your mother-in-law, but let's pretend she is, for the sake of understanding. She needs to know you first. That means to analyze and to, yes, pick apart and study. After all, you married her child. That alone may give her cause to investigate you as she didn't think her child was such a catch either. Get the idea? No one is exempt from her suspicious, exacting nature. This is not to say she's not a nice person— you just have to get into the way she thinks every little thing through. She's efficient and thorough, attending well to the details of life. She's stable and looks for the same with the people in her life—no fluff for her. Since she's able to get right to the heart of matters, she's hard to fool. Health concerns will be on her mind a lot throughout her life. While she doesn't have to be the health nut, she's often portrayed to be, but you can still expect a few bran muffins made from scratch during your relationship with her. As for the massive, almost Herculean task of getting romantically involved with this woman, you'll need to remember that while sticks and stones . . . you can't get upset by mere words. Words about your flaws, the color of your suit, the state of your finances may leave you shaken, but if she's the one for you, you only need to learn to endure phase 1, because after words come the less abusive glares. The not so subtle glances will chill you to the bone in the early years. After a while you can adjust and will have for a mate a dependable, punctual, orderly and practical wife who won't waste your money or hers. She'll share your burdens, listen to your problems and fight dragons for you. So what if she doesn't laugh when you tickle her. She'll be an earnest mother to your children. And guess what? She'll be popular with neighbors and with both her coworkers and yours. The general public won't swoon at the sight of her, however. I told you, she takes some getting used to. You really need to be a Virgo, Taurus or Capricorn, or a Gemini who can take direction.

Her illumination: Substantial.

Her dark side: Critical.

VIRGO-LIBRA

This self sufficient, assured, rather reserved lady is captivating with her aloofness and snob appeal. She's elusive and evasive and again, this coupled with the Libra Moon, adds to her charisma. She wants the finer things out of life, intellectual stimulation, enjoyment of the arts, refined friends and a harmonious family life. While men may trip over themselves to get to her, she's very critical about making the decision as to which man she'll get involved with. He must be a fair man with a highly evolved sense of justice. Their perspectives must match. If not, she can happily go her way alone. Capable in many professional areas, the arts or the communications media are most attractive to her. She'd be a fine lawyer intellectually, but her distaste for the tawdry stops her from getting too involved in that profession. This same sense of discrimination will prevent her from going to excess in regard to romance, emotion, or frivolity. She seeks moderation in life, and won't overdo in either work or play. She's a little like her own weights and measures system. If she's measuring you at work, you'd better be ambitious and hardworking. She'll be an extremely loyal and steadfast co-worker. She inspires admiration from her superiors on sight and they recognize her as one of their own. She has a quiet, steely determination and sense of purpose in life. She has undoubtedly seen many rough years as a child, and could tell a few stories to tear your heart out. But, having seen the worst she now looks forward to the best. If you like to sit by the television with a can of beer, or get crazy at the wrestling matches no amount of good looks, intelligence or money will entice her to your side. If you have presence and character, she'll be nearly the ideal sweetheart and wife. She'll want nothing more than to spare her own children the seedier side of life. The Libra man of course will appeal to her senses first. An occasional Leo who has some modesty, the Virgo Moon who is tactful in his appraisal of people, and the Taurus will at least get to walk her to her door. Geminis excite her.

Her illumination: Sense of moderation.

Her dark side: Evasive.

VIRGO-SCORPIO

Virgo is so often credited with such negative nit picking faults that it's hard to imagine that they often produce some of the most divinely beautiful women. Such is the case with this Scorpio Moon. It's the Water element that brings the intensity of a very sexual, earthy beauty. The features are often perfect, even if aided by the plastic surgeon's scalpel. She'll become the prettiest early on in life. She'll also arrive at the top of her profession against all odds. Her artistic expression is superb—she can sculpt, paint, and act—and if she can hold back her natural combativeness with co-workers, she can advance rapidly in the arts. Her personal life is also marked by her bouts of nastiness, and she has trouble doing what she likes best: staying married. She's not good at compromises. There is her way and no other. She won't be coy in her approach to men; she'll emit musk if she has to. If you happen to be married, she'll have little or no pity for you and your family and the havoc she'll cause. She's not indecisive or timid. Watch this gorgeous creature make mincemeat out of you and your life if she so desires. While the romance is on, however, she'll make your days memorable. Given to play acting she can do little housewife skits for months, and then drop the role. When she does, you too may be neglected. You'll probably find her busy at work, or planting exotic flowers in the greenhouse. She doesn't necessarily change her mind, rather she pursues different things from time to time, and other prior commitments fall by the wayside. She'll wound your pride and hurt your feelings. As a wife put one star on her apron, but as a lover she should rate about a ten. Best bets for attracting this one are the Scorpio, Gemini or Pisces. The Cancer is compelling.

Her illumination: Passionate.

Her dark side: Strict.

VIRGO-SAGITTARIUS

The Virgo Sun position finds itself in conflict with the Sagittarian Moon desire to obtain at most any cost, while the thoughtful Sun placement ponders over each step of the way. The Virgo Sun is discriminating, while the Sagittarius Moon is not. Therein lies this woman's dilemma. She may feel near schizophrenic as she finds herself making impulsive travel plans, or bedding a new man who is totally opposite from what she had been seeking intellectually. Why does she do these things? She hasn't a clue. She demands a lot of herself. She wants to be near perfect, and her daring, fun loving Moon keeps tripping her up. Actually her Moon should take the credit for saving her from becoming cold, demanding and exacting. She needs something to stir her inner fires, and to get her heart started in the mornings. She has exceptional intelligence. Her high standards, both for herself and her loved ones, are appealing to many a man. She's a good choice for a second wife, as most men won't appreciate her qualities until after they've experienced some of the more dishonest relationships that help them to grow. She's the sort you can enjoy your vacation with, who'll help you repay your bills, and put you through school without complaint. She'll command your respect, and sneak her way into your heart with her little oddities. You'll find her lack of possessive, heavy emotionalism a refreshing change from some of the more intense ladies of romance. When she gives in to her Moon, and winds up with a streak of orange in her hair, don't ask why she did it. She won't know. The Gemini could be the one she can't explain her yearning for, and the one she loves and hates. The Virgo, Capricorn and Sagittarius are good bets for helping her to lighten up. Give her a chance to grow on you.

Her illumination: High standards.

Her dark side: Self-centered.

VIRGO-CAPRICORN

You can take this woman's luckiest break and find even that wasn't such a big deal. Life comes hard for both the Capricorn and the Virgo, and even though this combination combines a certain innate amount of good fortune, her life will still have been a struggle at best. She's therefore a self sufficient person early on in life. No frivolous, carefree years of aimless wandering for her. No overcharged credit cards, either. She's moderate, sensible and rock solid in all her endeavors. She even ages well, like fine wine. For all this good common sense, you'd think that men would crash her door down. Wrong. She has an air of sternness and propriety about her that scares away numbers of less than substantial men. This is good be-cause she deserves better than the inferior sort. Once you give her the chance to express herself romantically you'll find a good and loving partner. She has an earthy sexuality. She's not afraid to give herself totally to intimacy. You as her mate, must first win her admi-ration and respect. Her friendship will follow, and finally she can become hopelessly devoted and amorous. She'll be as loving with the children but it'll be in the form of providing an ordered, well tended house. It'll come also in the form of helping them with their homework and science projects. Motherhood is serious business to her and she's therefore a more pleasant mother as her children grow older, more adult and more responsible. Little cooing creatures that need constant tending are not the stuff her life dreams are made of. But her intentions and nurturing are good, just the same. She finds the work place more comfortable than home, and while not a super-star, she's a good, honest co-worker and is very efficient with every assignment. She won't soar to the top, instead she'll inch her way step by step. If she's the one for you don't brag about your Porsche payments or you last six sexual conquests. Hope to have your Moon in Virgo, Gemini or Capricorn. The Sun sign of Capricorn should fare well also. The Pisces inspires.

Her illumination: No max'd credit cards.

Her dark side: Struggles in life.

VIRGO-AQUARIUS

This lady is one of the least romantic and emotional of the 144 com-binations. Watching people around her fall apart never seems to get under her skin. A constant student of human nature, she finds it fas-cinating but not very meaningful to her on an emotional level. For this reason she can excel in nursing or service work. She'll always keep her detachment, and can't figure people who bring their work home with them. There will be no emotional burnout for her. She's a decent person who'll help others with their problems, to a point. She's just not what you would call the gushy type. While she appre-ciates good looks in a man, she certainly won't trip over herself to get to know him. She isn't the aggressive type about career matters or romance. She's a good hard worker and can handle responsibility and routine. She's the rare type of wife who can tolerate her husband not coming home for the night with little or no explanation—she's glad for the time off. She's a very detached individual, and understands a less than ardent nature in her mate. Needless to say, she's not brimming over with social charm. She's blunt and direct, from her voice to her mannerisms. It often comes down to a lack of tact. She's happiest left to her small circle of acquaintances, her gardening or studies. She knows she's considered odd or different, and she's not at all bothered by that fact. Actually, she agrees with the consensus and is somewhat proud of it. She has a wonderful sense of humor that is her saving grace. Her appreciation for the unusual, her love of experimentation with life, attracts a particular sort of man. She may be found out in the backyard with her children trying to fly on homemade wings. She's definitely one of a kind. The Aquarian will snap her up. The Libra, the Cancer and the Leo don't appreciate her brand of femininity at all. The Gemini may find her appealing in a way he can't explain.

Her illumination: One of a kind.

Her dark side: Not romantic.

VIRGO-PISCES

This is one of the more interesting of the full Moon combinations. One reason for this is that she's not the typical critical Virgo, nor the full moon person who needs another to bail her out of situations, or to make her complete. She may in fact have the distinct problem of doing too many good deeds for another at the expense of her own best interests. She has a better chance for success if she was born around noon, but success, as it is usually defined isn't a concern to her. It may be for this reason that it somehow wanders to her door and nearly forces itself on her. While she may have considerable worry and strain on her own home front, she won't normally mention any of it to you—she's very quiet with her woes. This in one of her most admirable traits. Another wonderful trait is that she can find something nice to salvage in a not so decent fellow human being—she's very compassionate. You can fall publicly on your face and she'll give you the "Oh, it wasn't so bad, why everyone admires you so much for all the wonderful other things that you do," and your failure seems less significant. She is good therapy. She's also a good friend. But I've saved the best for last. She's also naturally beautiful, inside and out. It wouldn't be uncommon for someone to stop her on the street and announce to her that she should be in movies, and for her to nod "Thank you, but I'm too shy." She is. She's not vain, and really prefers to be left alone with her garden, her family, and her very delightfully spoiled children. She needs a nice man, the best, in my opinion, and she'll wait until eternity for him. A Pisces, Virgo, Libra, or Scorpio could be in the running. Treat her like the princess she is.

Her illumination: Wonderfully feminine.

Her dark side: Falls for troubled men.

Libra

September 23–October 23

LIBRA-ARIES

This is the most eccentric of the Libra ladies. She has odd interests, peculiar companions, and fiery emotions. She's also given to more instantaneous decisions than her Libra sisters. This makes her more fun, but gets her into a lot of trouble. She's so attractive to the opposite sex that she finds herself in one involvement after another, often with disastrous effects. She can marry too young, and find that all she really wanted was to be alone. Love and duty are a hard mix for her. She likes the idea of being in love and can chatter for hours about the wonders of romance, but she never quite gets the hang of the responsibilities that a commitment entails. She's a delightful companion on her own terms, and most of her relationships should not exceed the limits of friendship and casual commitment. She's one of the talented homemakers of the Zodiac who can decorate her home with her own pieces of art, hang her fabric wallpaper and cut her own carpet. She's both masculine and feminine in her capabilities, her interests and her self expression. She may appear soft and easily led, but I can assure you she'll end up doing everything her way, and with very little compromise. She often gets into power struggles with men. Just because she looks so gentle doesn't mean that she's meek and easily tamed. Assuming she's soft and docile seems to be the fatal mistake of her men. She'll get her way at any cost. She'll make up her own mind, and needs very little help from you about much of anything. She's an opinionated co-worker who hates taking orders. She'll be subordinate when she knows she has to be to survive, but she's planning an escape route from her work,

241

her lover, or even her children if they start to place too many restrictions on her. She's a handful for anyone, and the men in her life need to be big and hairy. I think she needs a Scorpio, Aries, or Sagittarius. She often sets her sights on an Aquarius, or Pisces just to test her powers.

Her illumination: Attraction.

Her dark side: Rebellion.

LIBRA-TAURUS

If she weren't so genuinely sweet we women would have to hate her, because she's lovely, gracious, exceptionally pretty and nearly irresible to the average man. She's one of the most appealing women of the combinations, and men can spot her at 140 feet. They'll leap over tall buildings to get near her, to say nothing of leaving the office should they spot her walking down the corridors of the building. She was born for romance and making men feel like they've been struck by lightning at the nearness of her. She's ultra feminine; and, while fully capable of running her own life, no man will believe it. Once involved with a man, and there will be plenty of men in her life, she'll never forget his mother's name, his brand of liquor, or his favorite story about his best friend, Jimmy. It's all part of her charm. You men will wish she was as able to remember her promise of love and fidelity, because she's easily infatuated. Believe me it's not entirely her fault. One, she has twice as many chances as the average woman in the dating game. Two, she's in love with love and not very realistic about the way relationships work. Three, she's looking for the nearly perfect man, and he's hard to find. Consider yourself lucky that you wandered into the path of her pursuit of the ideal. She'll be well worth the experience. She's gentle as the summer breeze, and sweet and charitable with nearly everyone. She's an outstanding mother. She'll be a soft touch for anyone with a problem. She won't however, involve her own emotions too much, except that if you're exceptionally good looking she can get caught up in a beautiful face. In that case, she may falter in her good judgement. She'll oftentimes get the nearly perfect man and the nearly perfect face mixed up and end up in relationships that aren't at all what she's looking for. If you're the handsome Libra-Leo, the appealing Taurus-Libra, or tall Sagittarius who's just as fickle, you stand a good chance of getting a kiss and a promise.

Her illumination: Charitable.

Her dark side: Looks are paramount.

LIBRA-GEMINI

This charming, witty woman, who's also very pretty and appealing, is mostly show. She prefers her man to support her financially, emotionally, and physically. She doesn't do this viciously. She's basically kind and decent, and she's also quite intelligent. Her mind is on many other things. They created the saying about it being a woman's prerogative to change her mind to describe this combination. She does this often. She has another little flaw: she's lazy. She often pretends she will do this or that, but you can bet she'll have a tummy ache on the day it's time to produce. She is, on the other hand, blessed with a wonderful sense of humor, and will make you laugh at the way you tripped over the dirty clothes and all the junk that came tumbling out of the closet. Since a sense of humor is a must for survival, she holds a good trump card. Speaking of trumps, she'll love to gamble, to have friends over, to host your poker nights, and watch football with you. It's one of the few times she'll prepare much in the way of food. She could live on air, it seems. What you do with this one is up to you. I like her. I just think she's better suited to broadcasting than to love and marriage. She's a decent parent, however. As a friend she's steadfast, thoughtful, and well-meaning. You Virgos and Geminis will fight over her (she'll just drive the Virgo nuts), but an Aquarian could be the ticket. If he'd wanted a housekeeper, he'd have hired one.

Her illumination: Witty.

Her dark side: Self-indulgent.

LIBRA-CANCER

You'll know her right away. She's the charming little thing who in her youth had all the men helping her carry her paycheck home from work. She had the looks and personality to win many a heart and the quest for a new sexual partner. I think she was looking for some constructive outlet like being a mother, and it got all mixed up. Life hands her so many bonuses and yet, she never seems to connect. She manages to turn the terrific job, the devoted husband, and the great family into shambles because she can't say no—to the opposite sex, or over-indulgence in drink, or shopping sprees. She never meant to hurt anybody, least of all herself, she was just directionless. About the age of thirty-five she'll have a major turning point in her life, a real awakening. If this doesn't shake her out of her dilemma, chances are she'll continue on her course of self-destruction. She's basically kind and gentle in nature. Her emotions are just too yielding for everyone's own good. She needs a good support group to keep her working on a solid footing within the home and professional community. If you're a very nurturing individual and have lots of energy to assist her in her everyday affairs, and can stand the sting of an infidelity now and then, I think you've found just the one for you. She can be fun and impish. Maybe you'll want to wait until after she's had her crisis. She'd be excellent in real estate (people do love her), or interior decorating. As a mother she's loving and yet undependable. She really needs her Cancer, or a Scorpio who has risen out of his own ashes. She seems to be most attracted to other Libras or Libra Moon men though.

Her illumination: Delightful.

Her dark side: Yielding.

LIBRA-LEO

This lovely creature has tons of dramatic appeal. She'll go out of her way to inspire others, build confidence and create harmony. Sunny and bright, she's not self-centered or demanding. She does, however, know what she wants and she's fully prepared to go after it. She'll have many friends, most of whom are influential. Her emotional needs are best met at work in a career of exchanging ideas or involving extensive travel. She'd excel in directing little children in the theatre. At any rate, she's a fair and just co-worker and can't figure dishonesty. You can count on her to be dependable and responsible. While she's an excellent mother, she's not traditional. She brings her personal interests into her home life, teaching her children a variety of subjects not learned in school. Her husband will find her enchanting and alluring long after her ardor for him has cooled. The man in her life will have to be sociable and possess a fair amount of flair himself. He'll also have to be tolerant of her extravagances. She's a clothes horse and dresses beautifully—it's part of her innate showmanship. She likes to do things on a grand scale and there's nothing petty about her. She possesses a solid faith that she can overcome almost any setback or problem, and she can. Never at a loss for male admirers, she's straightforward and not given to playing games. What you see is what you get, and you'll be all the luckier for it. Don't take advantage of her good nature—she feels a higher calling than to pick up your socks. Best chances for a lasting relationship comes with a Leo or a Sagittarius. The Libra Moon will catch her eye from time to time, though.

Her illumination: Alluring.

Her dark side: Won't wash your toupe.

LIBRA-VIRGO

She can drive the Fire signs of Aries, Leo and Sagittarius into screaming fits with her analyzing every itty bitty thing. She can never really enjoy herself for worrying over what she should have done instead. She may have been the first person to utter "Are we having fun yet?" She lives in fear of making a faux pas. It's the stuff her nightmares are made of . . . a typo on her memo to the CEO, her slip showing, making a rash decision (any decision made within twenty-four hours of laborious consideration). This is the least charming of the Libra configurations, and one of the reasons is her near neurotic need to not make a mistake. She's meticulous to a fault in her dedication to making all the right choices. Needless to say, spontaneity isn't her strong point. If she should happen to be your boss, you might as well start taking your stress tabs, because she'll expect you to be as faultless as she dreams she is. What it all gets down to is massive insecurities, and almost no creativity in her working environment. If you like to second guess another person's life and give advice that won't be taken, this little honey is for you. She'll tell you when you have lint on your coat, when your father over tipped, and when your boss first noticed the stain on your tie. You'll get a lot of her attention; I'm just not sure you're up to all of it. Another thing, be affectionate, not romantic. Too much overt romantic goings on makes her wonder if you have good sense. Roses make her sneeze. A good pocket calculator is really much more thoughtful. She'll dazzle you and the children with devotion as she understands it. She has a sense of decency that runs through to her very core. She doesn't want to be the belle of the ball, she wants to be the backbone of the family. Take your time getting to know her or she'll think you're too impulsive and lack substance. Could the Capricorn resist? The Taurus can plod along with her and admire her pretty face. The Aquarius wonders if therapy can cure her.

Her illumination: Roses make her sneeze.

Her dark side: Roses make her sneeze.

LIBRA-LIBRA

In the introduction, I promised to tell you who would care how handsome you are. Well, this lady is one of the women of the 144 configurations who places a high priority on good looks, right down to the shape of your nose. She may act flighty at times, and fall in and out of love on a regular basis, but in the final analysis she falls hardest for the man with savoir faire and wavy hair. If she has to wait for him to terminate other relationships she will. She can pursue her man for years with quiet intensity. If you like your ladies thin, she'll diet for you with great determination. If you like redheads, she'll become one. She'll spin romance and fantasy around you. The fact that she's very pretty to start with may help in her romantic pursuits, but what really gets to her men is the way she will hang in there for the one she gives her heart to. She's no doubt read and actually enjoyed *The Total Woman,* and has every intention of becoming one for the mate of her choice. It's just that there'll be quite a number of men who pass through her life before the Main One. She'll like to change you. She won't nag, but you'll have to make concessions to her gentle management. You may never even notice that you're losing a part of yourself to her manipulations. Further, you may not care. Look around your home, did you really want all the lace curtains, the wicker chairs and the lovely ferns? Did you really want to give up baseball to remodel the den? Probably not. Watch her at the office. Does she manage to weave the same magic on her superiors? Wil anyone ever catch on? Sometimes, but they won't care much. She needs beauty and harmony to survive life. Once she has it she'll want to pass it on to others. She's a divine puff of inspiration, she makes everyone feel good in her presence and better for having fallen under her spell. The Capricorn won't want to give in, the Cancer will, but he can cause her too much frustration with his moods. She needs a Sagittarius, or an Aquarius. She creates quite an odd team with the Pisces who can sometimes come out on top.

Her illumination: Ability to cast a spell.

Her dark side: Need for control.

LIBRA-SCORPIO

This lady is something of a novelty. She's a very different sort of woman. Normally sweet tempered and calm, she's very affected by her moon and can be one of the most irascible of the Zodiac. Her temper is memorable, mostly, I believe, because she's usually so nice. It seems odd for her to screech about. She's many a man's delight as she's very focused on romance and sex. She has a sexuality that can take over even the most logical and temperate of men. This sexual expression of hers is the combination of a spiritual union and the force and energy of a tidal wave. She's pure fantasy, romance and candlelight, and then raw, earthy passion. Never quite sure of what you mean to her, you'll keep coming back for more. Is it physical or cosmic? Are you the only one that makes her feel that way, or would telephone sex work as well? I'm going to let you figure that out for yourself. It's not fair for me to tell all her secrets. She's also talented, but not in the usual business ways. She's a researcher, an investigator, a soldier or a spy. I told you right up front she was a novelty, so if you're expecting a lover in the general sense look elsewhere. She'll be a baffling co-partner; she'll barely notice you one day and put you under a microscope the next. The children will receive the same sort of treatment. She's consistent about this: she's never dull, always exciting, exotic and alluring. If she pursues you, you'll find yourself in her fragile spider's web. It's going to take some doing to get yourself out. If you're a Scorpio, Cancer or Taurus, you'll like the weaving. The Virgos think she's the perfect answer to counterbalance an ordered day, but don't have the stamina for her long term. She's usually attracted to the Sagittarius, who is no match for her.

Her illumination: Sexual.

Her dark side: Baffling.

LIBRA-SAGITTARIUS

This lady is one of the shakers and movers of the Zodiac. She's also a thinker, but she doesn't want to get too deep into a subject. Debates are exciting for her. She wants a superficial knowledge of nearly every subject, from religion to foreign languages. If she was born around 3 in the afternoon she's apt to have numerous job changes and an accentuation of her oftentimes flighty nature. This woman doesn't know much about the meaning of discretion or moderation. She's a hard one to pin down to one relationship because of the foot-loose Sagittarius Moon that hates any sort of restriction. Those little words like, "Love, honor and obey" at wedding ceremonies can be repeated without much meaning. She isn't about to obey anyone. But she'll love and honor her man, or she wouldn't bother to be with him. She must respect a man, his mind and his ambitions. Since she aspires to a great many things, you need to have a series of long term goals yourself. She may be prone to wander, to change phone numbers and addresses, but her life's goal stays basically the same—she wants plenty of money to explore, to experiment, and to enjoy the fruits of her labors. She won't horde money. She knows it's a tool for barter and she's willing to exchange it for her various necessities. Basics like pedicures, raw linen trousers, and music lessons are part of her life's food. She's a delightful traveling companion, a fabulous date, and a great hostess. She's not a good checkbook balancer, or a mother of the utmost devotion. She may even consider the children a near nuisance. She wants to stay married to the right man so she can have her home base to hang her nylons from, but she may slip into an affair once or twice. It shouldn't interfere with her marriage, because it was really no more to her than an exercise in the art of courtship—she doesn't want to get out of practice. She was born for it. The Sagittarius is nearly perfect for her. The Leo is too demanding of her attentions, and a few Scorpios will fall by the bedside. The Capricorn may be her Waterloo.

Her illumination: A great date.

Her dark side: A Donna Juan.

LIBRA-CAPRICORN

This lady has a strong streak of self concern that borders on the selfish. She has less charm than her Libra counterparts, but she still has enough to capture the hearts of many men. Women also like her. She's witty; she's sociable; she's in control. Just in case you didn't catch that last line, let me repeat: she's in control. She has such a delightful demeanor that you may never suspect she can be a snob, that she'll use you to social climb, or that she'll put herself and her needs above anything else. She usually has giant obstacles to overcome to achieve her desires in life. She'll conquer all, rest assured. She may marry you and put you through school, allow you to trip up and remain unemployed too long and be ever so supporting. But the fact is, she thinks less of you for your failures. And, she'll never feel quite as enamored with you. She has a moon that allows her to shoulder all the responsibilities in marriage, most especially if she was born around 4 or 5 in the morning. But she has the sun that won't let her do it forever, and she can be known to leave a note to her husband saying that she'll be leaving and won't return. She usually has few children, and will make sure they are not left in the lurch, but she's going, nonetheless. A man can see it coming when the dinners aren't by candlelight anymore, or when she moves to another state to study for her doctorate. The next man she meets may be just as troublesome for her, but she falls in love rather quickly and will work out the details later. She has quite a number of youthful vices and a list of lovers. As she matures, she turns up her nose at women who behave as she did. She doesn't like to be reminded of anything tacky in her life. She stands the best chance for happiness with an Aquarian, or a Virgo. She'll lust after the Scorpios.

Her illumination: Determined to succeed.

Her dark side: Calculating in love.

LIBRA-AQUARIUS

This one is so romantic and captivating that right away you're hooked. Please stand back and take a good look. She has a way of spinning a tale of woe that may not be factual, but that leaves you ready to beat on your chest proclaiming how you, Tarzan, can take care of Jane. Believe me, this Jane can take care of herself—she can, but rarely has to. She usually marries well and lives a life of ease and comfort. She also tosses in a few tawdry little liaisons under oh, such proper cover. As a wife she's a chaotic. She puts her husband through some unhappy times indeed. As a mother, she can alternate between doting and total inattention, depending on the child. If she can get by, and she can, without working she will. If she were to have co-workers she'd consider them inferior on sight, and they'd know it instantly. She's not therefore immensely popular with females. Ah, but she should care! She's blessed with good fortune all her life, although she totally denies this because she considers living on the golf course a sad fate indeed. Anyone knows the correct address is in Beverly Hills. She'll spend your last dime to get her nails done. Why then are you so besotted? Because she's crafty and charming and funny, and you are defending her to me already, I know. Yes, I'm fully aware that she calls you Daddy, and that she needs you to help her with "things." She's just a helpless little girl at heart, and you're the best thing that has ever happened to her. You may very well be, or she'd be with someone else. I picture her in about 40 years coming down the staircase like Gloria Swanson in the classic Sunset Boulevard. Please give me this: Try two dates with a real person. It's not good for both of you to love the same body. Who she hooks easiest: An Aquarius or Libra Moon, or a Scorpio or Aries macho man.

Her illumination: Captivating.

Her dark side: Tricky.

LIBRA-PISCES

Open the car door for this one. Don't just reach across the car from the inside, but get up and get out and open the door. She's traditionally feminine, and wants to be pampered and loved and adored. She wants to see love in your pure little face as you gaze into her eyes. Bring her breakfast in bed, a single red rose and assure her she's safe with you. She's so competent in her career that she could be a top notch teacher, researcher, artist, or even your psychiatrist. Underneath all her social grace, poise and capabilities she needs tremendous ego boosting. She's not one of the strongest combinations physically, especially if born around 5 or 6 in the morning. She needs extra rest, attention to diet, and the avoidance of stimulants. She has a tendency to drive herself too hard and push herself too fast. She really should be living in a quiet area, away from a lot of traffic, noise and pollution. Most of her life may involve service to others, whether at work or home. She's a tireless defender of her co-workers, and a good and true friend. She excels best, however, when working alone, unlike most Libras. She's not to be taken lightly for all her mood swings, as she's a very sensitive and caring person. She's just tremendously affected by her surroundings. Discordant conditions make her a little crazy. She's a loving partner and wife. She's overly anxious to please, and your insensitive remarks about her capabilities will shatter her like fragile glass. If you want to get a chance to know this one better, forget your four letter words, leave the evidence of another woman well hidden, and don't break any promises to her. She wants the best from a man. Big biceps and pea hearts won't cut it. Look to the Pisces, Cancer, Taurus or Libra to win her fearful little heart.

Her illumination: Gentle.

Her dark side: Fragile.

Scorpio

October 23–November 23

SCORPIO-ARIES

Demanding, exacting, vain, compelling, she could be the woman who came and saw and conquered, except she has the personality of a bulldozer. She thrives on upheaval, and creating chaos. If her days and nights aren't strained and extreme she feels she hasn't really lived the day. She has excessive passion, whether for ideas or relationships. Her inner fires are stirred by new excitement in her affairs. At work she practices management by crisis. She's not popular, has few friends, and a list of ex-relationships and husbands. The smart ones of this configuration of Pluto and Mars will try and refrain from the vows of marriage until they're sure of their life's directions and values. One of the reasons for this is that she can turn her ardent, devoted love into deep uncontrollable hate in a matter of hours if she feels she was wronged. You won't be forgiven, and unfortunately not forgotten either. She can dwell on her negative feelings as easily as her positive ones. Best for you to move across town if you want to end the romance with her and she is angry. She, like the male of this configuration, looks over everyone she meets for spare parts. She isn't looking for a playmate, a helpmate or a copartner. She's looking for someone to provide her with opportunity at work, stability at home, and the ability to meet her needs at her time and place. She could be one of the prettier women of the Zodiac except for the scowling, cross lines on her face as she ages. Her walk, even in high heels, gives you the impression that she's wearing combat boots. She is. Life is a jungle to her and she's going to survive it at all costs. If you want dainty, frilly, easily touched and sentimental,

253

look to another configuration. She's an irresistible mother and wife. If she was born between 7 and 8 a.m., she lightens up and can be less demanding and considerably more fun. You Aries men will want to get into the power game with her. Another Scorpio takes her sexuality and runs, the Sagittarius may get involved, but will become a missing person if necessary to get out.

Her illumination: You can take her hunting.

Her dark side: Unforgiving.

SCORPIO-TAURUS

One thing about this woman, when she sets her mind to something, it's set. While not inflexible, she's committed. She's also not the least bit gullible in case you had any schemes you'd planned to put over on her. She learned early on about life and the unscrupulous few. She's one of the women who have endured much—loss of family, loved ones, a child, even. She doesn't dwell on these things. She intuitively knows that the only way to survive is to put the past behind her and keep her feet moving forward one step at a time. She's no saint though, and I must tell you, she's an awful nag with her husband even though she'll give him more devotion than he dreamed possible. She's practical and down to earth, but in her heart of hearts, she'd love to be a Libra, or wear the gaudy silver dress and spend the evening at the best restaurant with the most influential dining companions. This may never be for her because she usually comes from poverty or a lower social class, and often marries a difficult man. She acquires money eventually, but the style, breeding, and elegance she so much admires is always a touch out of reach. A conscientious co-worker, she's not afraid of hard work. As a mother she brings, quite naturally, some of her difficulties to the children. She'll try to be as protective as possible, but it may not always work. To describe her as a mother let me tell you a story: I read there was a mother who was raising her children alone. It was Thanksgiving and they didn't have enough money for a turkey, so the mother baked a meatloaf carefully shaped like a turkey. She asked her oldest son to carve it. It was the most memorable Thanksgiving the children would ever have. It was a holiday of spirit and pride and yes, love. It's rather like the silver dress she could never afford for herself. I hope a rich Cancer marries her. A Libra or a Taurus would understand the longing for beauty in an ugly world.

Her illumination: Dignified.

Her dark side: She rages.

SCORPIO-GEMINI

This is an unusual combination. This woman will publicly defend her man at any cost. She'll spin tales of her wedded bliss until even she believes them. But guess what? Left alone with the object of her devotion, she can screech to the top of her lungs about what a jerk she thinks he is. I really can't explain it. The fast-footed Gemini Moon usually gets out in situations like this, but the hang-in-there sign of Scorpio fights her man until the bitter end. And the end, if it does come, will be bitter. This woman doesn't have much of a middle ground. I admire her ability to keep her secrets and to never let the private woes show in public. This means then, that she's loaded with strength and resolve. This means that if she wants you, you can look forward to her dogged pursuit for years. Only she'll imitate the starry eyed romantic for you. It'll be an insidious pursuit, burning candles for you because you're away from her, sending lovely little poetic notes, calling you with heroic little stories about how she's surviving without you in spite of the pain. It gets to a fellow after a while. The fact that her failed marriages might have any connection with her personality won't register much with the object of her affections because she only married the others while waiting for the right one, you. She's attractive and rather solidly built, dark and compelling. She's normally a hard worker, neat and clean, and unusually interested in sex. She's a devoted parent, and while an intense wife, she's not one of the best of the Zodiac. Best chances for happiness: Virgo or Gemini, another Scorpio, or a Capricorn. The Leo may be the one who got away.

Her illumination: Compelling.

Her dark side: Can be sarcastic.

SCORPIO-CANCER

She, like her male counterpart, is one of the more choice picks of the configurations. She's no doubt beautiful, magnetic, and has a quiet sex appeal that leaves even the most aloof of men somewhat shaken in her presence. She'll be unusually feminine, normally rather petite, and dressed to the hilt. She doesn't flaunt her innate good looks. Women as well as men give her open admiration. She's a loyal friend and lover, but somewhat naive in general. She'll grow up fast, however. She won't express herself concerning her changes. Rather at about the age of 35, she'll begin to assert herself. Her pride, not vanity, won't permit her to be mistreated in her more mature years. If you want to hang on to this one, don't mess with her. You'll pay dearly. The price will be the loss of her extraordinary love. If you have a few other girlfriends still hanging around adoring you, you can find a rare patience in this one. She instinctively knows her place in your heart and is not easily threatened. She's a nice person. She has a fondness for money. She'll live lavishly. She may even expect you to help support her mother or maiden aunt. She's intensely loyal and generous to her loved ones. She's happiest at home, and she wants to be a wife and mother first. She may not get to have the number of children she dreams of, but she'll remember all the vows from her wedding day. If you get sick or need her to bring in some extra money, she'll be right by your side. Catch her young and treat her right. Give her lots of tender loving care, trust, and admiration. Be the strong shoulder for her to lean on, and she'll thrive in your care. Hope to be a Pisces, Cancer, or Taurus. The Capricorn understands her values.

Her illumination: Stirring beauty.

Her dark side: Inability to let go.

SCORPIO-LEO

The male of this combination wants sex and places a high priority on it. The female of this configuration uses her sexuality in the most constructive ways. There have been some top models and beauty contestants in this Sun-Moon position. They project both sexuality and drama. They also frequently make jokes about how they reached the top with their sex appeal. They know what they've got and they use it, but not in the casting couch fashion. They project this incredible aura of majestic voluptuousness. It's a big sentence and I really wouldn't use it on anyone else, but she deserves it. She's ambitious and she can stand on her own two feet. Yet, she can turn around and be a loving and devoted mother and wife. It just takes an exceptional man to domesticate her as it's not her natural instinct. She's daring and she can travel to the exotic, study for the bar, design jewelry, become a police woman or a coroner. She's her own breed of cat—the lioness. She's often self-destructive on the emotional side of her life. Passionate, her love affairs are often tainted by some undercurrent of the forbidden, sordid, or discredited. She will however, rise again from the pit she has plunged herself into. And while domestic harmony will never be what she gets, her own brand of marriage or partnership will be stable and often very lasting. There will be nothing dull or ordinary about her life—it'll take many a twist and turn. She'll undoubtedly endure all this to her credit, and end up with some financial security which she'll have earned for herself. To survive life with this one, you'd best not have too many plans about wearing the pants in your family. Look for a Scorpio, a Capricorn who wants to be bossed (there are a few), or a Sagittarius who doesn't get all that wrapped up in emotional scenes.

Her illumination: Magnetism.

Her dark side: Attracted to the forbidden.

SCORPIO-VIRGO

If this woman has set her sights on you, you're in for a lifetime of love and devotion. The extent of her dedication depends on you. If you want it in the form of brother or sister love, or husband-wife bonds, she'll offer it sweetly. It's not that she's subservient, but rather that she's capable of many different kinds of deep feeling for the people in her life. She's the good friend who pops in with pizza on the day of your divorce to tell you that to her you're still divine. When you are feeling like you're growing the waist that ate New York, she'll tell you that portly becomes you best and then put you on a diet. She's not one to hover about, and may not always be in your life on a daily basis, but she'll be there for you if you need her. And, if she loves you, she's probing and will get every last little secret out of you. She's blunt and can tell you what you need to do with your life, but she'll try to be positive in her approach. She's a sweetie in her own mysterious way. You, on the other hand, may not be so able to drive all the demons from her soul. She's a hard worker, and will work sweetly by your side. If she has her own place of employment, she'll be a discriminating boss who exacts her money's worth at the end of each payday. She'll also try to communicate with her co-workers. Her concern for people is genuine. The aloof, analytical moon will pick apart relationships of lesser values, but once she has become the mother to your children her commitment to you will be more solid. She'd consider separate housing before divorce. Unless, of course, you're a complete louse. In that case you'd better drop off the face of the earth. A handsome, sexy, man will always capture her attention. The man she can be proud of, she can admire, will be the one she finally settles down with. Don't expect her to give up some of the prior meaningful relationships, she still intends to be friends with the men she has loved. Another Scorpio, the Scorpio Moon, or the Virgo Sun are best long term. The Libra hunk, or the masterful Leo can catch her attention between relationships.

Her illumination: Sweet.

Her dark side: Analytical.

SCORPIO-LIBRA

This is the sultry, compelling, conquering beauty that begs for a man to chase after her, and let her give in to the pursuit. Everything she desires out of life revolves around love and romance. When she's younger, she's easily misled in romance, not only because of the many choices she has, but because of her rosy belief than people are better than they are. As she matures, she can become suspicious and more discriminating in matters of the heart. Of all the Scorpio women, she's the most easily fooled. Her stability is not inborn, for she can be frivolous, but grows with the years and her experience. She'll toughen up, but never become what you could call caustic and bitter. She loves the latest fashions and the excitement of most any social gathering. A dreary old Chamber of Commerce mixer will do if she can use the evening to be her gracious, well dressed self. She does well in interviews as she has a sincere, charming approach to others that comes across as employable. This trait works to her advantage in all matters dealing with the public. She does have a turbulent, stormy core, but it won't be something she normally displays outside her home perimeters. She's the sort of housekeeper who could have her home ready to be photographed for *House Beautiful* by 9 a.m. She has a flair for decorating and color, but her real talents lie in the service related fields, or in accounting and insurance, even law. She's pleasant and helpful as a co-worker or supervisor. She's a wife who, if you give her lots of attention and love, will grow to love you with near worship in her eyes. She needs in return for you to allow her to color coordinate your socks and serve you breakfast in bed. She has a lot of love to give to another human being, and her lucky family will benefit if they allow her to express herself. She won't stand for mistreatment, so be careful not to take advantage of her good intentions. She needs the wonderful characteristics of the Cancer or Pisces Moon, and the Libra Sun or Taurus Sun should be other good matches.

Her illumination: Irresistable.

Her dark side: Stormy.

SCORPIO-SCORPIO

This enigmatic, tumultuous lady is not one to have her nose tweaked. For all her femininity, she has the strength of General Patton. Nothing can defeat her except herself; she's a formidable opponent. To understand her you must know a little about her ruler, Pluto. Pluto is said to destroy to rebuild. The changes of Pluto cannot be prevented, and it seeks to control and revolutionize. What this lady wants, for all her display of fragility in seduction, is to control you. One way she does this is with something like hypnosis, done with the eyes. She's not overt and doesn't need to talk much about what she wants from you. She uses eye contact and body language (does she ever use body language!). She has a seamy side and can tell naughty little stories and create stormy scenes and quarrels. She has a fascination for the deep, forbidden, and the strange. If you're strange or forbidden, she may begin her campaign to fascinate you. You think it's happening, but then again, you're not sure. You feel yourself drowning in her murky eyes, and soon you're the captive. It was really quite simple for her. All she needed was to read your mind and tell you what you needed to hear—that you are the most handsome, most virile, most wonderful man she has ever known. She'll tell you that your wife doesn't understand, let alone deserve you. And as to your vices, well, you needed a flaw to make you less God-like. You'll spend your nights rushing to her, and your days planning to do whatever you have to do to live up to all her worshipping of you. She'll seemingly give up her life to you. Change jobs for you? Of course—she was having trouble with her co-workers anyway. Wait for the nasty divorce from your wife? Naturally. But the hooks get deeper. She needs some help with the children (she's a troubling mother), with her finances, with her personal problems (of which there are many). After you are consumed and have given all you have to give, the sultry whispers may cease. If you're thinking of saving some part of your life for yourself, better clear out now. A Capricorn can do battle; the Pisces is hypnotized; the Sagittarius moves to Toledo.

Her illumination: Reinstates your manhood.

Her dark side: Leaves you weak.

SCORPIO-SAGITTARIUS

This is the lady with the talk show hostess personality. She can lead, inspire, debate, and delve into your deep, dark secrets, and you feel like she becomes your friend in the process. She isn't afraid to share her thoughts and feelings with others. In this respect she's the least typical of the Scorpios. She wants to roam, not cling, to soar, not sting or crawl about. She's determined to get ahead, and romance may play second to her career. She wants power, and her determination and single-minded purpose is the currency she uses to pay her way. Yes, she'll use you to get ahead. She'll never admit it to you, but her Sagittarius Moon finds it unforgivable and picks at her conscience, denying her rationalizations. Even if it seems she doesn't pay for her misdeeds, her Moon keeps taunting her to strive to be a better person. This one will hunt and fish with you. You can take her to Africa and she'll outshoot you and the rest of the hunters. She's ardent in her approach to life, and she's blunt and opinionated. The 1980s have done more to create change in her life than the planets will do for decades. If you find her uprooting her life, making sweeping changes as a result, please bear with her. She should survive the transition all to the betterment of her and her relationships. Stormy weather is predicted for her most of her life, but she fares well whatever the climate because she can survive. She may be intemperate, dogmatic and nearly impossible from time to time, but she'll make it. If you work for or with her, brace yourself for lots of changes. In her own way she tries to be kind with everyone, however. As a wife, I suspect you've figured her for something less than a dependent, clinging vine sort. You may have lots of bowls of cereal for dinner. The children will be mostly your responsibility. The Aries falls hard, the Scorpio Moon or Sun feels compelled to be with her. The Pisces gets wiped out.

Her illumination: Lively companion.

Her dark side: Driven.

SCORPIO-CAPRICORN

The position of this lady's sun to her moon indicates a basic harmony in self expression and being able to put her ideas across to others. She'd be a good communicator or teacher. She could also excel in public administration. Just don't ask her to get too personally involved. Her chilly little Capricorn Moon won't permit it. She's one of the most goal oriented women of the configurations. She has a plan, Stan, and if you are an inferior being her interest in you will be minimal. If she's caught in early poverty, she may use you to escape her humble beginnings. But if you don't have your feet solidly planted on the ground she won't be there to celebrate your twentieth anniversary. Whatever her beginnings they'll be lightyears away from her current dreams and aspirations. In her 20s she may appear frivolous, and may get caught up in some minor flirtations and extravagances. In her 30s she may begin to express her real needs more, and start working toward the stability of a fixed residence, career, and sound financial planning. The lovely little bathing suit and diamond ring that were so fascinating in her twenties, pale in comparison to the price of six semester units in her thirties. Her forties find her deeply committed to her life's goals, to acquire, to accomplish and to amass considerable security. This can also be loosely translated as the burning desire for money. You have to admire her consistency, her hard work, her dedication to her goals. This lady is one of the Zodiac's all time champions of survival. As a wife and mother she's not the lighthearted, warm and tender mother of which fairy tales are made. She's steadfast and will stick by her children through thick and thin. If you're the Capricorn man who can't keep away from her, or the Cancer or Scorpio that wants to know more about her, remember not to have your hopes set on running the house and controlling this woman. She's her own person, and the best you can hope for is that she'll allow you to share her life's plan. Sagittarius brings out her higher side.

Her illumination: A survivor.

Her dark side: Cold Moon.

SCORPIO-AQUARIUS

Because of the complexities of the configuration, I have to explain this somewhat erratic woman to you in astrological terms. Scorpio and Aquarius are both fixed signs giving an inclination towards inflexibility. The rulers of these astrological signs however, are erratic and force changes. Now maybe you'll understand why, for all her determination not to make alterations in her life, she ends up with sweeping, electrifying twists and turns to her lifestyle. Life changes seem to build up slowly against her will, and then gain tremendous momentum. She is then faced with displacement and loss of structure in her life. She's therefore given to periods of emotional turmoil that are very distressing. She's nonetheless a strong personality, intelligent and artistic. She's intolerant of most general opinion and consensus. She has a peculiar, but outstanding, physical attractiveness. Usually she has an expressive face that's nearly enthralling. She hates the ordinary or routine. She's attracted to people from different cultures, with unorthodox ideas and backgrounds. Extremely gifted, she could reach the top of a number of professions, including medical research. She's given to periods of laziness however, so she's a most unreliable co-worker from time to time. During these periods she can be less than honest in her dealings with people, and her inner agitation is too great to concern herself with others. The rest of the time, she's an enchanting, curious, active, very sociable creature. She can be the most gentle and loving of mothers. Her husband will alternately receive near worship and total indifference from her during their relationship. Yes, she's difficult. She never quite merges with the rest of the world. But she's fascinating beyond belief. She reeks of the word conquer and it drives men mad. All she's really looking for is a gentle, loving, and understanding soul. Another Scorpio, a Pisces, or a nice Cancer Moon has the best chance. The attractive Aquarian would be too unsettling in the long run, but the fascination is there.

Her illumination: Intelligent.

Her dark side: Difficult.

SCORPIO-PISCES

This is one of the sexual sorceresses of the Zodiac. The intensity which nearly compels men to notice her is the very thing which drives them away. She's not especially ambitious for worldly things; her accomplishments are counted by the number of men in her wake. Oddly enough, for all her conquests, hanging onto one is quite a problem. "Compelling" turns into "complicated"; "alluring" turns into "possessive"; and "insatiable" turns out to be "demanding." She attacks every problem with, "Where there's a will, there's a way," never realizing where there's a way, there's a way out, and many men will eventually exit. Her reactions are very low periods of glum, and it shows on her face. She'll revert to scowling and howling if given the chance. In her early years she has a quiet, less formidable allure. The ladies of this combination born early evening have the best chances to turn all this emotion into something more ethereal and mystical. A sensationalist, she often finds herself in situations with some pretty shady characters. Women instinctively shy away from her. Given a few wrong turns, she can become the victim of over stimulated emotions that creates a need for alcohol and drugs. In life she'll be one of the youngest to experiment in the unknown and sexual activities. She usually marries young, has children young, and spends later years in subdued regret. Born with too much insight for her own good, she's a difficult wife (no fooling her!), and an exacting mother. She needs someone to offer her balance and to acquaint her with the niceties of friendship with her own sex. Not that I'd want to suggest many women try this friendship around their husbands. No point tempting fate. The same rule may apply to your job—she won't want it for the money or challenge, she wants it for the power it yields. Best bets: Scorpio or Pisces of course, or a Scorpio Moon. A Taurus can captivate her. The Fire signs make for steamy, heated liaisons.

Her illumination: Alluring.

Her dark side: Obsessive.

Sagittarius

November 23–December 22

SAGITTARIUS-ARIES

This woman is full of surprises, it just looks like her only interest is having fun and enjoying life. She never shows any outward concern for success or materialistic things, and she may not actually be concerned. The fact is however, she'll win at just about any race, and that includes the race to the top. She's so lucky that she could go hiking and fall into poison ivy, stumble to the road to hitch hike and be picked up by the owner of a chain of banks. She'll arrive at the doctor's office just as his secretary is leaving and find that he needs an immediate replacement. Naturally since she knows all about office management she begins the job right then and there, while the rich banker awaits her company for dinner that evening. This girl doesn't have much competition in the area of romance or ultimate gain. In a few years, ask this delightful lady how she became the multimillionairess and she'll tell you it all began with some innocent misadventure like a toothache, or a case of poison ivy. She won't have stepped on anyone in the process, nor have alienated any co-workers, or set about with any deliberate plans to get where she is. This configuration is fortunate and chance treats her well. She has abundant energy and can act as the recreation leader for her family when she decides to marry. She won't be a conventional wife, though she has been known to bake bread and plant gardens. She's more apt to be found nurturing others in the direction of jogging, sports of any kind, and a life full of wonderful, active adventures. She's also a fiery little companion in the bedroom, and will become quite nasty if you should ever suggest separate beds because she takes up all the

265

room flailing her arms and legs about all night—she wants her man right there beside her. If you doubt this for a moment, bring up the subject—the Aries Moon will start screaming. It's one of her few flaws of importance, this nasty temper. She needs, of course, an Aries or Leo. She may find her mate coming from the sign of Capricorn with the Fire Moons of Aries or Sagittarius.

Her illumination: Lucky.

Her dark side: Hot tempered.

SAGITTARIUS-TAURUS

This is a woman born to politics, theatre, public speaking, and the best of the best. Whether in clothes, houses, or her profession, look to exceptional attention to obtaining the finest. While born with luxurious appetites and ambitions, it may take years for her to obtain them. One reason is her spells of inactivity and despondency over the not so glittering bad times. If, to make matters worse, she's disillusioned in love she may become almost inactive and dismal. This is out of the ordinary for her, as she's usually sociable, vivacious, and lively. She's good in sports and the artistic avocations, so she's capable in many areas. She's the one Sagittarius woman who needs a stable relationship and a man of high ideals and spirits. She truly flounders without it. She's a wife and mother of the utmost devotion and steadfastness. She's probably the most favored employee in the company, and her co-workers find her kindness and caring unequaled. She won't be petty, quarrelsome, or mean. She wants everyone to be happy, and for life to be its rosy best all around. Her strong spiritual bent comes shining through in her actions. She's not only living this life to the best, she's trying to do all the right things for her karma. Teachings of the Far East aren't new to her. Unless she was born in the early morning hours, she'll most likely have one marriage. She knows tawdry things only happen to other people. She instinctively shies away from situations which may be shady or tacky. She does so with grace and good humor, as she doesn't moralize for others. She has a tendency to gain weight due to the love of fattening foods that both the Sagittarius and the Taurus are born with. A Leo, Taurus, or Aquarius will help her with her storybook romance. The Virgo is too mundane for her.

Her illumination: Goodwill.

Her dark side: Spells of despondency.

SAGITTARIUS-GEMINI

Like her male counterpart, she's a handful. In a man's chart the restlessness also implies unpredictability and the need for a lot of guess work on the part of his pursuer. Not so with this lady of duality. She makes no promises. She's in touch with her inconsistencies and tries to make them a part of her life. She may find it difficult to marry because she knows she's used to a man for every need. As I write, good old Hank is saving for her next dinner ring, Bill is making plans to remodel her bedroom, and John is dashing about making arrangements to take her away to Hawaii for the weekend. He really can't wait to see her tan those long legs and roll against the white sand. He probably even knows about Bill and likes the guy. She's neat about the order of her life and the men in it. They know possessive, heavy emotions are foreign to her. They can count on her sense of adventure and fun, and her love of freedom. They also know that she won't have her life uprooted by a mere man. All her men have their very own niches, on that you can depend. Naturally you can't expect her to be domestic with all this going on in her life. But you will get a home cooked meal once in a while. She usually has a child early in life, but her mothering is somewhat lax, and her child may seem to grow up without much assistance from anyone. She's a real find for you men who aren't too familiar with deep emotions yourselves. She's an ambitious lady, and even manages to work part time most of her life. Popular with most everyone (except the wives and girlfriends of her men), she also has a lot of women friends. The most lasting of her women friends learn not to entrust too much with her—she's at the mercy of her Moon. She'll look for the Leo, Sagittarius, Gemini and Libra to add to her collection. She probably felt the most for a Scorpio, but he just demanded too much from her emotionally.

Her illumination: Life of the party.

Her dark side: Problems in commitments.

SAGITTARIUS-CANCER

This is one of the natural adoptive mothers of the Zodiac. Did you say you knew of a homeless child across the globe from her? Just start the papers and send them over. This idealism and optimism is the theme of her life. That a lot of misfortunes can't be cured by her or anyone else, may never really sink in. In this respect she's unrealistic and too selfless for her own good. For often the idealism of her good deeds is shattered by the reality of the effects of poverty and ill health on her recipients. Things aren't always as happy and lovely as she imagined. While the rest of the world may benefit, she oftentimes suffers from her good intentions. Money is short again, the kids are sick, but so is she; she needs to rush to the store to get groceries for dinner tonight and as usual, there's no time left for herself. If this goes on for too long, she may become bitter and withdrawn. She can brood indefinitely over injustices and the fact that no matter how she tries, she just can't help everyone. This wonderful human being with the happy smiling and often pretty face, both at work and at home, lives in a world of torment. She isn't going to tell anyone about her problems, and that includes her husband, her best friend, or eventually her therapist. She talks, but won't reveal anything significant. Impressionable with the opposite sex, she may involve herself in a few situations that she later regrets. She made a mistake. She trusted him. He took advantage of her. But what the heck, the next guy couldn't be all that bad, huh? Hopefully not, for she deserves something nice here on this earth—never mind all those jewels on her crown in heaven. She just wants help making it through the day. She needs a caring man who can cuddle and soothe her. A Pisces, Cancer, Taurus, or Libra can take the ribbon from her hair.

Her illumination: Generous heart.

Her dark side: Gives too much to others.

SAGITTARIUS-LEO

Like the male with this configuration she's a lucky, lively, idealistic and simply wonderful human being. She understands the masses and can appeal to their needs whether emotional, as in crusades, or material, as in promotion. She can excel in most any undertaking from sweetheart, lover, wife, friend, mother or co-worker. She can inspire a new line of clothing, a new philosophy of morality, or the simple neighborhood birthday party. You simply feel better for having known her. She has courage of her convictions, and tremendous loyalty to her ideas. She's one of the most honest of the Zodiac, and is fearless in her protection of her loved ones—she'll have many. Her family, her parents, former lovers, childhood playmates, etc. can always count on her support, and she never loses contact with those she considers part of her extended family. When success comes her way, usually from an early age, she won't flaunt it, nor will people begrudge her her laurels. She's an admirable specimen. She's physical with her energies, and loves the outdoor life as well as the good life. She's not passive sexually and is usually sexually expressive. She's an exciting if challenging, match for her mate. While men are attracted to her, she's not an easy person to get a date with, let alone a commitment from. When settled she is often tempted, but rarely unfaithful. She'd rather get a divorce than sneak around on her husband. If you lose her respect it'll be replaced with pity and she'll be done with you. The best chances here are a noble Leo, another Sagittarius, or a high minded Capricorn who also reveres truth and honor.

Her illumination: Courageous.

Her dark side: Hyperactive.

SAGITTARIUS-VIRGO

The most amazing thing about this woman is her enormous insecurity and her total ability to hide it. She may think she's coyote ugly, obese and undesirable, yet project herself as the most poised and confident lady ever to enter the room. Her fright is mistaken for calm; her apprehension for thoughtfulness. It's a bluff. That she's starving herself to death or undergoing therapy over all her alleged shortcomings would never occur to anyone. Her exacting nature demands perfection of you, too. She'll remind you of your flaws and imperfections, and she'll wound you with her blunt and tactless assessment of you. The terrible thing is, she's usually very correct about the other fellow's defects. Knowing this makes the judgments even harder to take. You can't defend yourself with her misjudgments—"Ha! What do you know?" She knows plenty and it's a lot for a lover to withstand. It puts a real damper on a man's sexuality, too. When your lover comes with a built-in sexual director and critic, it's not an easy job to perform at your peak, unless of course you like the dominance of it all. This isn't to say she's unpleasant, just severe. For you bad little boys she may be the find of the year. In relationships other than sexual or romantic, she's less strict and actually shows her bright and cheerful, if somewhat reserved, exterior. She's pleasant and professional with her co-workers and friends. She may be slow to have children, but motherhood will be fulfilling for her and will soften her up considerably. Her off-limits persona is very alluring to many a man, and she won't have a shortage to choose from. She can also surprise herself and obtain much professional status. Best bets here are the Leo, Sagittarius or Capricorn; if your moon is in Sagittarius or Aries, all the better.

Her illumination: Talented.

Her dark side: Given to self-abuse.

SAGITTARIUS-LIBRA

This lucky, lively lady is one of the most socially active of the Zodiac. She's not sexually dormant either. She's witty and full of fun and adventure. Men swarm around her and women find her an inspiration. They like to ask her how she does it? How do you have so many admirers? She's hard to dislike and therefore immensely popular with both sexes. She's always searching for some higher truth, some better form of communication, some way to improve mankind. She's not, however, one to actively work at the betterment of mankind—she isn't that deep in her philosophies. She's a party animal by nature. She has the rare ability to stay young well into her middle years, and often beyond. She's one of the most enchanting co-workers, a fair and excellent supervisor, and a capable employee. The catch in the last sentence was capable. I didn't say persevering, dedicated or purposeful. She's one of the risk takers in life. Her gambles aren't the kind involving career moves, they're the kind of risks that involve trying not to get fired over taking an extra week of vacation to spend a few more days with her new lover. She's a top flight romantic. She's not, however, dedicated to the principle of one man fulfilling her every desire. She attracts people who give her what she wants from life. While she looks for love and romance it may not be on the deepest of levels. She'll break hearts and promises. She'll be fun and worth it if you can keep your wits about you. If you're looking to be one of her husbands, you'll need to have the Sagittarius Sun or Moon, or the Aquarius Moon. The Aries Moon is ever so attractive, and the Taurus who is so fascinating at first stands to get his heart broken.

Her illumination: Popular.

Her dark side: Lacks purpose.

SAGITTARIUS-SCORPIO

Her specialty is self sufficiency. She's fully able to attend to her life's realities and to yours. She can be counted on to take the ailing for a walk, listen to your problems (though she will rarely offer advice), and offer her assistance to any number of causes. She won't, however, be non-discriminating in her choice of good deeds. She thinks things through carefully and makes sound decisions based on facts, not emotions. She's a sturdy worker, and is determined to get along with her co-workers, even when she finds them unappealing. She wants to arrive, and success, she figures, doesn't come without able people to delegate her work to as she moves ahead. She'll be counting on you to help her succeed from the day she fills out her payroll information. She can make the best out of a bad situation if necessary, but if she can, she'll move mountains to improve any circumstance. She's one of the most serious and fixed of the Sagittarians, and her moon tends toward not letting go of her personal problems and secrets. For this reason, though she may need a shoulder to cry on, she won't give in to the urge to unload her problems. It's also for this reason that she gets herself into trouble with escapes of a troublesome nature. Her emotions are heavy, brooding and often self destructive since they can cause ill health. As a mother she's often disappointed in the outcome of her children, though she'll stand by them through almost everything, and nod "Don't say I didn't tell you so, son." That's about the extent of her criticism but it'll sting all the same. As a lover, she's very sexual, and you may end up being the one with the headache. Forget the apples—she thinks sex everyday keeps the doctor away. If you want to play doctor you'll probably get a chance regardless of your Moon. The nice Cancer and Pisces Moons, the Sagittarius Moon, and the Gemini Moons attract her the most. You wouldn't be surprised if I suggested the Scorpio for the long term relationship, would you? It's a natural.

Her illumination: Self-sufficient.

Her dark side: Brooding.

SAGITTARIUS-SAGITTARIUS

This lady loves her freedom and therefore she may not talk marriage until after the baby's first cry. Marriage and babies are usually delightful surprises to the double Sagittarian who only remembered it was a terrific party. She doesn't like her schedule being interrupted by having to pick up your cleaning or take the children to their dental appointment. She's had plans of her own for years now and isn't accustomed to sharing. She's also used to giving the orders, not taking them. She's simply wonderful at supervising others, and in handling long distance business deals. She lives in publishing, religion, and import export businesses. Can you honestly expect her to decipher grocery lists and cries for cookies and milk? Of course not. Before her version of marriage set in she was known for being the life of the party. She's usually well traveled and in a constant state of learning. She's not a starry-eyed romantic, rather a travelling nomad who enjoys the opposite sex like she does a good bottle of wine. She can hurt the sensitive types with her casual regard for them. Life is an adventure and she's fully capable of going it alone. That's the way she prefers it, even though like most Sagittarians she'll marry more than once. Her children may adore her childlike self-centeredness, for she'll be one of them. Her husbands may expect a bit more from her and therein lies the rub. She'll be attracted by the Aries, the Leo, and her fellow Sagittarian. If you're persuasive, maybe the Libra or the Aquarius can handle her lifestyle or temperament better. She'll never be at a loss for admirers or potential mates at any rate.

Her illumination: Full of surprises.

Her dark side: Constant motion.

SAGITTARIUS-CAPRICORN

This woman is ambitious and has the intelligence and timing to carry her dreams to their fullest. Whatever setbacks she may encounter, she's prepared. Image conscious, she can hide behind her green velvet drapes like Scarlet O'Hara to seek out a loan. She can be down to her last cent, but she'll never be without her passport and her American Express Card. If there's a business deal to be made, or a man around who's handy with a loan, she can bounce back like no one else in the Zodiac. She's so able and clever it's almost scary. She can be as flighty and wild as a hurricane, and with her inner eye never lose focus on what she needs to do to make her considerable dreams come true. This is no lady to take lightly, however giddy she may be acting today. She's keeping score with you, and while she may never comment, she's judging your appearance, your family, your friends (or lack of them), and primarily your marketability. If you meet all her standards, you'll be among the fold of her wondrously loved and nurtured extended family. She may be judgmental, but she's just. She won't trample on others for her success no matter how determined she is to accomplish. For her it not only matters if you win or lose, but how you play the game. She's superb with children, loving to explore their minds and instill her values along the way. She's still part child herself. Never forget that if you want to win her heart. Expect her to be original in everything she undertakes. Expect men to adore her 'til she's old and grey. Don't embarrass her in public. Once she has it all, and that includes the man of her heart, she settles into married life with just a few weeks of AWOL during her lifetime. The obvious bets are the Capricorn, Sagittarius, or Leo Sun or Moon.

Her illumination: Carries American Express.

Her dark side: Judgmental.

SAGITTARIUS-AQUARIUS

This is a nice Moon position for the Sagittarius Sun. This lady is cerebral without becoming boring or analytical. She's deliriously funny, and will know a little bit about everything in the most inoffensive way. She's full of changes, from the color of her hair to the latest live-in (bunkie to her). She's not what you could call a sentimentalist. Men are usually very attracted to her and her electric blue eyes, her uncommonly candid views on life, and her sense of adventure. There's very little she's afraid of, and mountain climbing, sky diving and channeling are all great forms of recreation to her. She has probably been everybody's favorite oddball since high school. She'll have a host of friends and admirers. She may not feel all that attached to them in return. Her love emotions are way out there beyond Jupiter and Mars. Charming nonetheless, she'll never be at a loss for men in her life. She excels in the communication fields, and is a very nice, very talented supervisor. She makes friends at work and play. She keeps in touch with her family but she won't exactly bake bread for the family reunion (unless she was born around 5 a.m.). As she ages and she has soaked up her environment, she can become quite the artist, the performer or the inventor. She can be really attracted to someone romantically and he may not have the slightest idea until she starts to unbutton his shirt. Don't tie her down too much, don't be upset that she makes more money than you do, and don't nag about her exercising to computer music, and she may let you in on the fun and excitement life brings to her. If you're a Libra, Gemini or an Aquarian you're probably already a friend. If your Moon is in Sagittarius you have a good chance at long term things like watching her playact with the children and spin tales of happiness for you all.

Her illumination: Sense of adventure.

Her dark side: Emotionally detached.

SAGITTARIUS-PISCES

This is the fragile, sensitive little creature at the Yoga class, or with a book on the Far East Religions tucked under her arm. She's long legged no matter her height, with fluid, almost watery eyes, and a beauty that comes from her brightly shining internal light. She's not your everyday typical woman in her approach to life. She sees life in broad, sweeping generalizations and with constant observation. While she's esoteric and fanciful, she's not a dim bulb. She's bright, humane and involved in everything, from current events to the secrets of the pyramids. She's a healer and a mystic. She's pure enchantment. She's not, however, the most steady of Sun-Moon combinations. She is given to changes of residence, changes of vocation, and often changes of husbands. She's never a petty or mean individual. She's almost incapable of holding a grudge, and her forgiving nature leaves the lesser of us mortals in pure bafflement. Let her be near the water, grow in the adventure of the great outdoors (she can see more in her walk around the farm than some people do on a trip around the world). Let her touch and feel, and soak in the Universe. She may be preparing for her work in publishing, nursing, or religion. She may be ready to embark on a temporary mission to help the handicapped, the oppressed, the imprisoned. Encourage her to flit like the little butterfly she is and she may be willing to share her peculiar, but usually correct, perception of reality with you. Friend or lover, you can't help but benefit from your relationship with her. She's a wonderful mother, because she was born to care for people who have trouble caring for themselves. She'll look after her husband with the instincts of a nurse, and hope to heal his every hurt. If you are an emotional wreck she'll run to your rescue. I hope she gets more out of life than constant nurturing for someone else. She needs someone to experience and enjoy the simple beauties of the sunrise with her. Another Pisces, or a Cancer Sun or Moon are the most attractive to her combination. The Gemini may make her his life's crusade.

Her illumination: No dim bulb.

Her dark side: Not terribly steady.

Capricorn

December 22–January 21

CAPRICORN-ARIES

Who wants to get to the top and first? This stellar configuration. This Sun and Moon combine the goat and the ram. If climbing the highest mountain and reaching the top alone ever meant anything to anyone, it does to this woman. She can feel discouragement to the depths of her soul when things go wrong, but being as determined as she is, she knows the only way to get ahead is to keep moving and put your setbacks behind you. Time is always of the essence with her, and she'll run her races fast and hard. She'll be as determined to accomplish at age 80 as she was at 20. If she sounds one-dimensional, she's not. She wants it all—the career, the family, the prestigious home and life. She wants it not for the money and power, which she certainly enjoys, but to validate her existence. She's her own toughest critic and she needs to prove herself to herself. She'll appreciate the fact that you're impressed, but she does what she does for herself. She can write, teach, organize, and work with metals. Her talents are nearly unlimited. So, fine, she's a worker bee. Can she relax and have fun? You bet. Between projects she uses fun and play to cleans her mind. She'll put just as much energy into partying as she does into her work. This means that her relaxation may appear near frenzied to the rest of the world. It is, but you'll have quite the companion. She'll tease you, pull jokes on your friends, and throw one party after the other. If you start to notice co-workers being invited over to the house, or some of her favorite clients, you can be sure her work phase is about to take over again. She won't be without friends. She's liked by everyone, from neighbors to supervisors, and if you're in her inner circle of loved ones, she'll have a wonderful way of sticking her nose into your business. Needless to say, her husband and children will get an energetic, caring mother and wife to be proud of. Look to the Capricorn Moon to snag this one, or the Leo or Sagittarius Moons as well. The Scorpio man can also find her appealing until her career starts to interfere.

Her illumination: Energetic.

Her dark side: Has trouble with men.

CAPRICORN-TAURUS

Want to know what her favorite book is? The software program *Financial Cookbook*. It makes her dizzy just to think of spending a few hours plugging in all the interest rates, inflation factors and those wonderful numbers. When she dates, try as she may to play dumb, men start talking banking, investments, and big business. You could guess that she isn't dating the tennis pro to start with, but still it's rather amazing how men of money and power are attracted to her. The reason is her uncommon good sense, her quick grasp of business risks, and appreciation for money and success. This is where her interests lie, and she won't pretend to care about football or what's under the hood of your car. She's not a gold digger, her dreams are to make it on her own terms, and win at the game of money and power. Surprisingly, for all her fascination with finance, she's a well rounded individual who can plan family get togethers, organize a mismatched office staff, and teach men the art of romance. She's a loving person who knows the importance of keeping her word and your secrets. She's one of the most trustworthy of the Zodiac. She's usually attractive, exceptionally well groomed, and fabulously lucky. She'll be a devoted wife and mother for a man of substance, consistency, and old fashioned values. She's often more sought after as a date than she cares to be. It goes back to her favorite book again. Time is important to her and she may consider a date a waste of her valuable energy. She's fun and witty, and does love to party but it must be with the right man. He may be older. His nickname won't be Silly Putty. Get to know her and you can find yourself babbling away 'til the wee small hours of the morning. About futures—yours, hers, and gold. A Taurus Sun or Capricorn Moon doubles both your chances for happiness, and the Virgo is a good bet for a shorter term relationship. The Cancer, her polar opposite, is a surprise match.

Her illumination: Clever, astute.

Her dark side: Determined.

CAPRICORN-GEMINI

Did she just get in from a round of golf with her boss, or is she being reclusive writing a play in the upstairs study? Was she up until all hours again, or did she go to bed early and get up at 3 a.m.? I bet you'd give just about anything for a bit more predictability from her. Let me tell you, she is predictable. You can count on her sticking close to home (she likes to keep her journeys short and not venture too far from home) and wanting you to be there too. She'll need a lot of space, and you'll need only a little. She has all this worked out, and if you watch her really closely, you too can count on a few basic things from her to be constant: She'll be curious, nervous, and impish. She'd be a wonderful teacher or technical writer. She needs to work in an independent capacity because interaction with her co-workers isn't always pleasurable for her, or them. At home she needs increasing freedom as she ages, and will be relieved to have the children move out and just visit occasionally. She's usually good looking and will have had a life of many changes and sudden reversals. But she has the stuff to survive the most troublesome of setbacks. Frequently, she can be imposed upon to help others to the point of overtaxing her own nervous system, (always fragile). She'd be better off volunteering her time to physical therapy or fund raising, and saving a few precious moments for her body to relax and recharge. She's basically a good person and yet she's very difficult on a day to day basis. Give her lots of independence. At the dating level, she's likely to give you quite a run for your money. Notice, I used the word money. That always gets into the picture with the Capricorn. Of course, another Capricorn could do well, but I'm going to bet on a Virgo, Aquarius, or Gemini.

Her illumination: Impish.

Her dark side: Sudden reversals.

CAPRICORN-CANCER

Remember the lady sobbing over E.T. when he got sick and couldn't seem to phone home? This is the Capricorn-Cancer combination who can't think of anything worse than being stranded, unable to be with her family, or being in a strange place. She was a fearful child and a timid adult. Oh, I know, she's probably an executive, a money maker, and she instills obedience in her co-workers. She comes across like the most secure of women, unless you get to know her strange little phobias and fears. When her moody personality emerges she can be as odd to you as she is to herself. She isn't the liveliest, most unconventional person you'll ever meet, I can assure you. But she's a good family member, whether parent or child, and devoted to wedding ceremonies, convention and her mother. If you haven't guessed by now, you'll need to court her mother as well as her along the way. She can live on her intuition alone, so if you think your potential mother-in-law is an old bat, this lady will read your mind and you won't have scored many points. Better to be sensitive and honest, with lots of common sense to capture her heart. Make any efforts at entering her family circle sincere rather than flamboyant. You won't have to fight off hordes of admirers or kidnap her from her tons of friends in order to spend time with her. She's not one of the most popular of women. She chooses friends carefully. If you like the child-like side of her that needs a near father figure to help through the gloomy spells, or if you're attracted to a woman of ambition and executive potential, this could be the one for you. Best matches: The Pisces, the Cancer, the Scorpio. Yes, the Scorpio could hold her tight while she sleeps. The Air signs just can't be bothered.

Her illumination: Kind.

Her dark side: Gets in ruts.

CAPRICORN-LEO

Now here is a nice wife. Sort of. I mean, she looks good at company functions, keeps a lovely home, raises the children well, and puts up a good front—even years after the bloom is off the rose. She does it for two reasons: One is pride. She hates to admit she made a mistake about anything. The other reason is money. She wouldn't have married you if you weren't going to be a good producer. She'll hang in there for another car, the new house, etc. Also for your reputation, because she epitomizes the woman behind the throne. She won't talk about her man's inadequacies, but he'll know. So will the children and the rest of the world. It's the way she dotes on him in public: really dutiful stuff. It doesn't fool too many for too long. Chances are she's loved and lost before, and her heart is just not all that charged up for you. Chances are also that she came from very humble beginnings and hasn't forgotten the feel of an empty stomach. You may not ignite her fires, but by the time you catch on to your real function in her life, you're celebrating your 25th anniversary and, what the heck, she's been dear in her own way. She helped you get to the top, the kids never spent a night in jail, and she can handle her liquor. Besides, she can be really playful and very earthy. She has a good head for the stock market, lands some pretty terrific jobs, leads you on some wonderful adventures, and is decent with your mother. She'll be dedicated to you. Rule number one on survival with her is: Never, never cheat on her—she could get really attracted to the matches by your bedside. A Libra, Capricorn, or Cancer does best with this one.

Her illumination: Great Mother.

Her dark side: Gets even.

CAPRICORN-VIRGO

The Capricorn woman often makes a valiant attempt to present herself as assured, confident and a touch above the crowd, like the goat on the hill, overseeing his valley. You'd sometimes like to take the woman with this combination and pull her off the hill and lecture her on smugness and aloofness. No use. Because you know what? Underneath all her reserve is a woman who's just as insecure as the rest of the world. Once you understand that she's bluffing, whistling in the dark, you have to admire her considerable efforts at covering her frailties. She's so good at keeping up this facade that, well, I wouldn't want to play poker with her. I also wouldn't want to hurt her feelings. She'll never, never forgive or forget. I know I've made her exterior sound harsh and unappealing, but she isn't. Further, she is attractive to men in a special sort of way. She makes them feel like winning her would be catching a real prize. They find the challenge, coupled with her considerable poise and good looks, irresistible. This woman knows hardship and heartbreak. She can be a nice co-worker and a top notch business woman. She works long and hard for everything she obtains in her career. How she survives depends a lot on the men in her life. If she is hurt excessively by misplaced love, she can turn out very bitter. If she gets lucky and finds her Mr. Right early, she'll be devoted, loving, generous and a real gem. Otherwise, she'll even be a tyrant with her babies. She won't be a hot ticket in the bedroom unless she finds the right man to make her understand about bells ringing and bombs bursting. If she finds him, he can count on some real surprises in the sexual area. She's a contradictory woman to start with. She'll be attracted to the Scorpio, the Sagittarius and the Virgo. A Libra or Taurus could light up her life.

Her illumination: A gem.

Her dark side: Complex emotions.

CAPRICORN-LIBRA

There are more similarities between the man and the woman of this configuration than are found elsewhere in the Zodiac. She can scale the heights and sink to the depths. Her relationships with men, beginning with her father, are strained. She looks for a strong man, an able man, and one who she can trust with her deep dark little secrets. Life is not easy for her, and her early childhood may be marked by unhappy, discordant episodes. Her need for a good, solid relationship is critical. She may fight you tooth and nail on giving her what she wants, because she's afraid to let her needy side show. She has faced rejection at one point that left scars. She may feel unworthy of love. She may try to scare you off with her little fits of intemperance or outlandish behavior. She may ache to be with only you and choose instead to have lunch with her group of admirers. Her Libra Moon logic slips, but the charm and allure of her moon is always intact. You, my dear man, are probably bewitched and have no idea what to do about your dilemma. Just wait out the strangeness, the determined to shock you behavior, and you'll get another chance to prove your worth. And she, miracle of all, may begin to cooperate with you. From that time on, she lets her guard down, and you'll find her all the more enchanting and loveable.

She'll be one of the more enticing ladies of the 144. Her career and her dedication to it may leave you a little awed. She'll find time to do something charitable and crusading, and will expect her friends to share in her efforts. She may remind you from time to time just how important she is (and she usually has some professional distinction), but she'll have a sense of humor about it. Her co-workers are magnetized by her charm. She's fair and talented. She's not necessarily the loveliest of the women of the Zodiac, but she trades on her charisma and can pick the most handsome, intelligent, and prize worthy of men for her very own. She'll even be a good mother. Who can capture her? The fellow Capricorn, the Taurus, or the strange Gemini she doesn't really feel all that comfortable with. The Cancer may be the one who breaks her heart—he doesn't mean to, they just stress each other out.

Her illumination: Talented.

Her dark side: Fits of intemperance.

CAPRICORN-SCORPIO

Here is a woman who can appear, amazingly, unlike her inner core. Her true character may be cleverly hidden but from a few. Socially, or on the surface, she's happy, energetic and self-confident. She's not a taskmaster and may even be considered something of a libertine. She isn't. She's not without the sternest of values, even though in her youth she may have been no stranger to sordid affairs and an involvement with drugs. She may come from a family of wealth and breeding and defy them all with her brazen lifestyle during her early adulthood. Then as if by magic (the magic of the Pluto ruled Moon) she'll change into a rather virtuous, conservative lady of the manor. She can and does attract many a man, and will catch someone of elegance, position, or wealth. He may be very surprised indeed to learn that she was ever less than the grand dame. She'll nag him if the fine points of his behavior or on being less than genteel. She may sound like a hypocrite, but she's not; she has changed. Her Moon and Sun combined together to raise her above her beginnings. Transformed, she wants nothing to do with the reminders of her less than perfect past, including you. She has an unconventional sort of attractiveness and appeal, and she's good looking long after other women have begun to fade. While she can laugh delightfully, be the perfect hostess, once the party is over she can go to her room and quietly sink into deep periods of gloom. She's therefore difficult to get to know as I'm sure you've guessed by now. Once she has undergone her transformation and achieved the status she desires, she becomes almost tolerant of her fellow man and his shortcomings. She may even surprise you and lend a helping hand on occasion. She didn't mean to be unkind or rigid, she was simply in the process of overcoming her insecurities and frailties. It's all very complex. Her knees turn to jelly over a good family name or an outstanding career accomplishment in a man. Once she's found him, she'll be a good wife and mother unless he fails to continue to measure up. Then the fireworks start. Look to another Capricorn, Scorpio, Taurus, or Cancer to tame this one.

Her illumination: Potential for growth.

Her dark side: Volitile.

CAPRICORN-SAGITTARIUS

The capricious Capricorn and the dual sign moon meet to give a woman a personality difficult to define. She may appear helpless and flighty from time to time, but she's not. She just wanted someone to carry her groceries, or she chose not to flaunt her intelligence for the day. She always has a genuine "Hello" and, "How are you today?" for everyone. Even little children open doors for her as the result of her special attention to others. Sometimes more special attention than she had intended because people often confide their deep dark secrets in her and men oftentimes mistake this interest as something more than casual. This is the result of a quite simple teaming up of two very people/public oriented planets. She has several little flaws, like she can keep your secret and yet not her own. Her secrets usually revolve around her worries over things that may never happen—it can drive you nuts. But then imagine how she feels! She has a tremendous drive for accomplishment and everything she does must reflect achievement. If you embarrass her in public, treat her friends badly, or jeopardize her standing in the community she'll make sure you're no longer a part of her life. Things have a purpose in her world and that includes you. She's not cold hearted outside these perimeters, however. She'll care for the sick and old, and dote on children. She'll be a pleasant and adoring mother. Efficient as a homemaker, she never quite has her mind on the domestic. Since her mind is fixed on career she's apt to drift off a bit and get a little of the salad lettuce in your martini. At work she's more centered and accomplishes much. Her co-workers may find her impressive but not necessarily charming—she's known to speak her mind. She needs a sunny man to dispel her fears. A Sagittarius Moon, a Cancer Moon, or the Leo Sun are the best bets for this. It's the Scorpio that arouses her sexuality the most.

Her illumination: Popular.

Her dark side: Driven.

CAPRICORN-CAPRICORN

This is a cold one. If you're the man she wants, she'll come to you. That it might jeopardize your careers or current relationships will be of no concern to her. She won't be subtle, and she'll take the lead sexually. She'll win in almost any contest, and there's not much of a match for her in her pursuits. She's the one who eventually causes her defeat down the line, with her own demanding, highly ambitious ways. She marries up; she marries older; and life gives her a few surprises along the way. She picks men because they can offer her something, and poof!, they lose it—their money, their challenge, and most often their good nature. This one will push her man right over the brink. She is given to bouts of ill health and very serious melancholy. She'll fight to bounce back. It'll be in her own unbending, iron-fisted fashion, however, so she'll not elicit much help along the way. Her Sun and Moon positions give her a constellation of characteristics that lacks perspective. The other person's needs will be forgotten. Her compulsive way of needing control and order leaves the strongest of men cringing in her shadow. The emotional insecurities resulting from a lack of love in early childhood have left her anxious and fearful. She won't admit this, nor show any indication of such inner turmoil due to this upbringing. She may be fearful of normal relationships; you should be fearful of her—she's going to give you quite a tumble. Found in executive, administrative, or governmental positions, she'll have stepped over many a body to get ahead. Being her own worst enemy occurs most often if this lady was born about 4 to 7 a.m. As a wife and co-worker she leaves a lot to be desired. As a mother, her temperament improves considerably. Best bets: A Scorpio (whew!), a Cancer, or a Leo. The Pisces is able to touch her heart.

Her illumination: Able.

Her dark side: Lacks perspective.

CAPRICORN-AQUARIUS

This lady's dilemma is "To be or not to be"... conventional, that is. She's hardworking, dependable and odd. On one hand she reveres convention, and on the other hand she mocks it. She's very bright and lightyears ahead of the rest of the world. She's also one of the most capricious women of the Zodiac. She has a lot of ability, but while interested in a great number of things, she doesn't market her talents. Her co-workers, her bosses, and most of all her friends would be surprised at how capable she could be if only she'd set her mind to it. In her own odd fashion she'll arrive at a station in life having considerable status, and she'll excel at some sort of organizational or governmental work. She'll also obtain a fair amount of money in her lifetime. Her friends, family and children can always count on her to be there for them. So, in spite of her odd way of working things to her advantage, she'll manage to live a decent, productive life. She'll be the traveling singer, the magician, and the tarot card reader in her spare time. While she loves to have periods of privacy, she'll manage to get more notoriety than she planned on. There's something intriguing about her, and nearly everyone wants to uncover her private side. There's a streak of genius in her, and she loves to mix with people in social settings where she can exchange ideas and insights. She's much in demand socially, but you can't count on her not to espouse her pet theories to your boss. She'll start to overcome her extremes of nature as she approaches her thirties. If this is the one for you, I hope you're an Aquarius, a Gemini, a Libra or Sagittarius. Sometimes the Scorpio fascinates in her youth, but it's something she can outgrow. She'll never outgrow her wonderfully odd little habits and attitudes, thank heavens.

Her illumination: Intriguing.

Her dark side: Extreme.

CAPRICORN-PISCES

She may or may not be beautiful, but her sex appeal will be more than enough to captivate many a man in her early years. Her later years often find her overweight, or a victim of alcohol and drug abuse. It takes a toll on her beauty. Never mind, she still has a husband or two out there who would dump Miss America for her. Once she gives herself to a man (is she ever hard to get down the aisle) he's never quite the same. There's a mysterious, brooding, sullen quality to her sexuality and it leaves a man a bit shaken. She may very well be the reason men ask, "Was it good for you?" I mean, the poor guy is used to a smile, a "Wow," or something, for Heaven's sake. I can see her now, taking a puff on her cigarette saying, with that appraising look in her eye, "Don't worry, darling, you were great." It's scary for her men. One of the reasons for his terror may be that she ran off with an artist a few years ago, or has a ten year gap in her life that she never discusses. That appraising look may crop up again from time to time as you ask about the father of her children. Funny, after four years with her, you still aren't sure of his name. She may confuse you, but this much I have figured out ... If she wanted you to know, she'd have told you. She reveres secrets. She has a biting, yet terribly funny sense of humor, and can laugh at herself. She's not all that serious about everything, just those other parts of her life. She can act (of course, or you wouldn't be so bewitched); she can dance; she can run a government research center. She's fully capable of any number of things. For all the men in her life, she never quite makes the connection in intimacy and often ends up in her last days alone, by choice. The Sagittarius will find her irresistible because she's so odd. She needs, however, a Pisces or a Scorpio. If the Moon were to be in Capricorn, it could help her considerably in life.

Her illumination: Sexy.

Her dark side: Sullen.

Aquarius

January 21–February 20

AQUARIUS-ARIES

This lady is smart and comes from a good family. She may be one of the few women you have met that impresses you with her good common sense. She's also dazzling with her talents and creativity. Hang on a minute and don't fall overboard. While she does have these and many other things to offer, she's a problem for many a man. She hates routine, has a fiery temper, and is not much for sentiment and hearts and flowers. Falling in love with her will be on par with bringing one of the guys home to live with you. She's not into matching towels or decorating the guest room. She's got a lot on her mind, and if you're really lucky you may get dinner served on a paper plate. If you expect, in any way, a conventional woman, lover or co-partner you really must look elsewhere. To try and push her into a mold of conventionality or normality would be cruel and unjust. She may very well be lightyears ahead of the rest of the world concerning the importance of ideas versus material acquisitions. She'd rather come up with ten good ideas than ten new credit cards or silk blouses. She's different in her appearance also. She's quick acting, fast moving, and has a athletic sort of appeal. She may have more friends than anyone you have ever met, in spite of the fact that she may also have the hottest temper in town. Everyone forgives her little outbursts, as they know there's no malice or grudge holding with her. And, if they didn't, it wouldn't really matter much to her. She has more important things to worry about than her social standing. She worries about mankind, ecology, karma, and ESP. Don't expect her to get all worked up over a recipe or who will drive the children to softball practice. How to catch her attention? Use phrases like "global impact." If you're another Aquarian, a Libra or Gemini, you'll find her enchanting. The Sagittarius also fares well with her. The Capricorn is truly baffled, and the Scorpio has probably never even noticed her.

Her illumination: No malice.

Her dark side: Volcanic temper.

AQUARIUS-TAURUS

What a nice person. She's so sweet, and she's not opinionated. But she's the most stubborn woman alive. And do you know what? It'll be over nothing or practically nothing. She'll let you have your way and bend over backwards to please everyone. Then suddenly she'll get this maniacal look in her eyes and boom! She's crossed her arms and is pretty darn mad. This lady is sensual and romantic. Even in her aging years she'll have that sparkle in her eye for many of the men in the retirement home. She needs companionship and wants a man who can work and play with her. She's truly the wife beside her man. Her children will receive the sympathetic ear and get a good hot meal to start their day. She's also caring in other ways that make her special. She accepts people or her family as they are, and doesn't make a big fuss over trying to change them. She lives by the Golden Rule. That's a lot to be said about one person. She can be eccentric in dress, loving odd little hats or other very personal statements of fashion. She's often progressive, unconventional in terms of romantic relationships. She can be the first woman on your block with a very young husband, or to live happily out of wedlock. She makes her own laws, and they're simple, fair, and just. She may not have come from the easiest childhood situation, and life may give her a few bad turns before she's 30, but she'll pull herself out of the slump and obtain her own brand of security—a peaceful home and enough money to pay the bills. Her love of luxury may be subdued to a small collection of Dresden and a well stocked refrigerator. She doesn't complain about her lot in life, because she knows there's more to obtain than material things on this earthly planet. This lady would rather have her rewards in heaven, and I for one, believe that she'll get them. An Aquarius, Gemini, Taurus, or Virgo will find a place in her heart.

Her illumination: Sweet nature.

Her dark side: Bullheaded.

AQUARIUS-GEMINI

This lady is fun, she's fabulously funny and full of adventure. She may be non compus mentus in romance, however. She quite simply is her own person and so involved with her own activities that she forgets to buy the dress for your parents' wedding anniversary celebration. It was unintentional—she thinks they're wonderful, and can't wait to attend, but she really was involved with her pursuits—things like writing an editorial to the local paper regarding their backward, inept reporting. Or maybe she was tied up at work—the xerox machine broke and she's the only one who can repair it. Schedules, order and propriety mean nothing to her. Frilly dresses and lace panties mean nothing to her. Intelligence, enterprise, contemplation and investigation mean the universe to her. If you were to give her a book on harmonics, I predict she would fairly swoon. She's bright but flighty. She doesn't bother with women's lib. She's been liberated since she was a child. If she was born around 3 a.m. she was probably the most precocious of children, aloof and adult amongst the others. She simply didn't know what all the fuss about stacking blocks was about—she was already admiring pyramids. As a mother she's divine, but she'll swear she's not. She's not doting, however, just a puff of pure inspiration. As a wife, well we touched on her romantic assets earlier. She means to be romantic, and many a man may have caught her eye. But, hey, guys, she's just as footloose and carefree as you are. Don't act like you don't understand it—she's beating you at your own game. A Leo could get her to at least pay attention; the Libra, Gemini or Aquarius can live with the full speed ahead intellect; the Scorpio or Capricorn better step back ten paces.

Her illumination: Great fun.

Her dark side: Nervous.

AQUARIUS-CANCER

This is the most emotional configuration of the Aquarian women, and she acts a lot like her Cancer Moon personality. She'll be less detached and rationalizing than her Aquarius sisters. She craves a stable home life, kids and a husband. She's not afraid to compete with the best of them in career pursuits, and is often a sizeable money maker. She could be a technical writer, a computer whiz, and a mother par excellence. She does well in careers that help other women—decorating, teaching, counseling, to name a few. She, like her male counterpart, is one of the better catches of the Zodiac. She'll gain strength in the 1990s and become even more sturdy and confident. This will be a time of struggle for her but she'll emerge all the better for it. When she's very young she doesn't get too involved in romance, but as she ages it's one of her top priorities. Several marriages wouldn't be uncommon for her. After the planets play with her before the beginning of the 21st century, she'll be more settled in her role as wife and mother. In her earlier years she tends to be too changeable and easily influenced. Her positive traits are her generosity, her sound judgment, her concern for others. She's also something of an inspiration to everyone she meets. Men are attracted to her sensitive, non-assertive qualities. She'll be a slow worker, but pleasant to get along with. She won't trample over people to get ahead. She won't have to—her success is written in the stars. The men who are most attracted to her are the Air signs of Libra, Aquarius and Gemini. She'll be looking for the emotive signs of Cancer, Pisces, or Scorpio. The Virgo could be the surprise match.

Her illumination: Generous, sound.

Her dark side: Emotive.

AQUARIUS-LEO

Imagine the ability to be queen of any situation and not really caring too much? That's this lady, because she has a commanding presence and could be very compelling and dramatic if she wanted to be. She could be the fashion designer that could sketch a new line of clothes while watching her husband tune the car. She could walk into a room and develop a hundred friendships without remembering anyone's name. But she doesn't care all that much about reaching the pinnacle of her career, or having everyone's adoration. What she really wants is a relationship, one relationship that gives to her. She's one of the children of the Zodiac, and with her full Moon, she wants to be babied. Like being fed in bed when she has a cold. She's into instant gratification also. She wants what she wants as soon as the Aquarian bolt of electricity hits her brain. No waiting, no explanations. If she was counting on you to meet her needs and you don't deliver, she can get pretty cranky. If you can deliver most of the time, you can count on her as a wife who really puts a lot of herself into the relationship. She'll be wonderful with everyone's children, a neighborhood favorite who'll spin tales of wonder and fantasy. But don't ask this of her for too long a time. She needs time for herself because she's independent and gives in to her own whims. She'll always be kind, and her humanitarian instincts are outstanding. But she's needy. Whether you're a friend or lover, when she drops by for attention and indulgence from you, she'll expect you to give as much as she would. She needs a man who's tender, strong, able to provide emotionally and financially. If you want to be the one I hope you have your sun in Leo and a nice Libra Moon. The Aquarius Moon or the Sagittarius Sun also have strong chances for creating the chemistry she could thrive on.

Her illumination: Dynamic.

Her dark side: Needy.

AQUARIUS-VIRGO

This lady is one of the more practical of the Aquarians. She's a nice person who likes to read, study, write and lead protest marches. Filled with common sense, she'll pass up a one carat diamond in favor of a nice, portable home computer any day. The position of her Moon to her Sun, and the ruler of her Sun, give her many sudden changes in her life. Some of these may be connected with travel, or residence, and many will be related to health matters. She's often the peculiar eater, who could live on nuts and cell salts from time to time. When she has a health problem, it's usually related to nervous disorders and poor circulation. Her own life's adjustments come to her through other people, and not crises she created herself. Perhaps that's why she has periods of health upsets—she's reacting to the unfairness of her situations. She really does try to have her life in order and not move about or make sudden and drastic life changes. She wants her house, office, romance, and life neat and tidy so she can concentrate on a freeze dried man formula. She has an extraordinary mind for inventions, research, facts and formulas. She approaches matters of the heart in the same fashion as does the scientist embarking upon a new species. This leaves a lot of men feeling out of their realm—it should. She's not exactly the starry eyed dreamer that romance novels are made of. She's a wonderful co-worker, always ready to help with the extra workload. She's a dutiful wife and mother who asks that everyone live up to their fullest potential. Emotional outbursts from anyone in her life will leave her bewildered. She may leave you all and buy herself a robot to co-partner her in life. It's logical in Spock fashion. Look to a delightful Libra to balance her scales, a Leo to get the most emotion out of her or a Gemini to take her into his starship.

Her illumination: Practical.

Her dark side: Sudden changes.

AQUARIUS-LIBRA

This lovely creature is always in love with love. She delights in every new catch. She falls in love fast and yet, never really commits. That's because she's fickle. She can fall right back out of the infatuation. She also has a little secret—she's really and truly in love with someone (she may even say she hates him), and he isn't interested in her. Or he may be interested but doesn't think she's quite worth the bother. She needs a lot of attention, and yet plenty of room to roam. Whatever his reason for his not being captured by her like everyone else is, he sets himself up as the unobtainable man, and therefore the one she wants. She may carry on for years with her little secret, making promises to love, honor, and even marry, but won't quite get around to it. If this man ever came around and wanted her I have the distinct feeling that she would reconsider. This little puff of steam has a wide variety and large numbers of friends. These friendships don't have to be long, enduring or especially close. A circle of admirers will do fine for her needs. In return she's a charming, sympathetic and caring friend and she's known to lend her time and money to help those in need. Very much ahead of her peers, she's still old fashioned in her taste in clothing and home decorating. She's a good worker and a pleasant co-worker. She has a scientific bent to her artistic talents. She'd also be a near perfect car or computer salesperson—people are naturally convinced by her. It's that lovely Libra Moon, again. You need to be dependable with her, nearly devoted after the pursuit in which you are rather hard to pin down yourself. Never let her be too sure of you in the beginning— she needs a challenge. Send her computer music, or a new hybrid of flowers you created yourself, she'll be enchanted. The Air signs of Gemini, Aquarius or Libra understand her inconsistency; the Sagittarius has the hard-to-catch quality she lusts after.

Her illumination: Gregarious.

Her dark side: Elusive.

AQUARIUS-SCORPIO

Here are two fixed signs. One is ruled by the planet of regeneration and the other is ruled by electrifying changes. The humanity loving Sun opposes the secretive emotions of the Moon. The only changes she'll make are the ones inclined by the stars. Some of her more noticeable changes occur during her midlife crisis, in which case she'll usually want to totally alter her lifestyle, often with a younger man and career switches, when she's about 40 to 42 years old. She's courageous and determined, and once motivated, very ambitious. The women of this configuration born during the 1940s are doubly intense and will have strong struggles for power in relationships all their lives. Their intensity will incline them to periods of ill health, usually problems related to nervous disorders resulting from hypertension, circulatory ailments, or overtaxed, over stimulated emotions. She's hardly ever still, very seldom tranquil, and often restless and hyperactive. Obviously, if your dream woman would never ruffle your feathers or campaign against your political choices, this is not the lady for you. If she's dreadfully unhappy in her marriage she can endure for years, with extended vacations, long hours at work, or whatever it takes to get keep you at a distance. Even then she'll defend you with her last breath, outside the privacy of your home. She's not as fierce as her energy makes her sound. She'll have a host of friends. Co-workers may find her dizzying but enjoyable. Her ambitions as a mother are often put aside for her own considerable needs. She's very susceptible to flattery and attention. If you want to be the one for her, you'll need to give her plenty of praise, affection, and time to herself. Who could understand this better than the Scorpio or the Gemini, or the Aquarian Moon? Sometimes the Aries Sun is the surprise mate for this lady of determination. A Cancer will be mystified.

Her illumination: Challenging.

Her dark side: Rarely tranquil.

AQUARIUS-SAGITTARIUS

This lady belongs to everyone in an elusive sort of way. She's a hail and farewell person who knows most everybody in town, but doesn't share her inner self with many. She's born with very little innate suspicion or mistrust, and looks for the best in everyone, regardless of their past or current social status. She's much more interested in a man's thoughts about black holes than how he acquired his millions. Her searing insight into personalities cuts right through many a man's facade, so you won't be able to fool her. You won't need to if you're inspirational, philosophical, humane and a bit zany. She probably won't even notice that your teeth are a little crooked. She's impulsive, and if she likes you she could end up in a whirlwind romance that lasts only a few days, followed by a marriage with a lot of years ahead. It's very important for her to have achieved something of importance in life. But what she considers important may be the very different from ordinary measures of success. She'll want to live life to the fullest everyday, to have the riches of love, to have the freedom to explore and communicate. She'll find great pleasure in living abroad or at least travelling to exotic places throughout her life. The idea of packing her family up and moving them to new places, new experiences, and even new cultures is very appealing to her. She's not timid about exploring the unknown, whether it's around the block, in outer space, or with an exchange of ideas. She's attractive to many men and interested in only a few. She'll be most attracted to the Sagittarius, the Aquarius, the Libra, and sometimes the Capricorn is the match made in heaven. There are a few Capricorns who offer the Aquarius and Sagittarius mix of planets to match her own.

Her illumination: Philosophical.

Her dark side: Not trusting.

AQUARIUS-CAPRICORN

This all American, unorthodox, and revolutionary lady who has led many a cause is going to fool you. You'll swear I have her all wrong and that she's really childlike and almost irresponsible. She is not. She's possessed of stern stuff. She's highly intelligent and is going after some wonderful, inspired things from life. She's fully capable of taking care of herself and making her own decisions. She can't help it that you're so slow to understand her. She has a lot on her mind, and her absence of explanation is often mistaken for not having an answer. She does indeed know what's going on. She's not as empty headed as she may appear to the less astute man. That she doesn't prefer frills in her attire, or satins and lace, doesn't mean she's not feminine. She's quite simply not concerned about her appearance or the impression she makes on you or anyone else. In spite of this indifference to the impact she makes on others, she is highly concerned about her own opinion of herself. She may be found at any number of self- improvement classes, and she may tote her children along. She may in fact take up child rearing as a near cause should she have a large family herself. It's her way of lending a universal helping hand. Men who can't see the importance of her concern with humanitarianism will leave her appalled at their self centeredness. She's a lot to contend with. You'll have to fit into her life plans, as she has no time to adjust to your needs. She's a big hearted person, but she's not the most romantic or typical of women. She aims high and looks for a man of considerable talent, ambition, and concern for the welfare of others. Her icy little Capricorn Moon will sort him out for her. She'd be a delight with a Gemini, Capricorn, or another Aquarius. The Virgo Moon, while in the same element as her Moon, better not need much mothering or she'll be looking elsewhere.

Her illumination: Intelligence.

Her dark side: Emotions can chill.

AQUARIUS-AQUARIUS

Better read this one quickly before she changes her mind about the date you had planned. She may decide to trot off to the local planetarium or whip out her books on Stonehenge. She's looking for ultimate truths, not a date on Saturday night. She's one of the more masculine women of the Zodiac, and is less interested in feminine pursuits and vocations than most. She's also no slave to fashion or man. That means you, no matter how attractive or appealing you are. She's no doubt looking for a good friend. She'll have numerous male friends, mostly platonic. From youth through old age, her emotions aren't heavy. She may never experience being boy crazy as a child or love sick as a woman. She won't get carried away with any emotions. If she sounds like she's not popular, think again. She's one of the few women you'll know who is friends with nearly everyone at work and within her family. One of the reasons is that she knows familiarity may breed contempt. This slightly impersonal approach to other people tends to attract rather than repel. While her co-workers and lovers see this detached side of her, once she finds her man, he and the children will find an idealistic, kind, and generally superior human being. And being a creature of whims she'll give in to yours as often as possible. Just don't expect her to build her life around yours. She'll fit in in her own way—detached, logical, and with respect for everyone's individuality. She likes a man with keen insight and a healthy emotional state, who can write or communicate ideas well. She won't be boring or confining. She'll be most attracted to the Libra, the Gemini or the Sagittarius. The Scorpio or Cancer may baffle her.

Her illumination: Whimsical.

Her dark side: Looks for an emotionally healthy man.

AQUARIUS-PISCES

Just as the man with this configuration eventually tries to do something for the betterment of mankind at his own expense and sacrifice, so will this lady. She's unassuming, friendly, yet intuitively wise about people and their motives. It's for this reason that her insights often lead her to spiritual pursuits, religious undertakings, or the fields of healing. Whatever her shortcomings personally, she gives more than she takes. She's a very decent human being who'll leave the world a better place for her having inhabited it. Not overly ambitious, she can in fact appear lazy. She's simply tuned in to higher things than career and salary increases. Fortunately, the universe has a way of lending her a helping hand, and she's often lucky in material affairs in spite of herself. This is especially fortunate because she has periods of near recluse during her life, along with periods of phobias and acute anxieties. Her whole life is an oddity of being too insightful and too fanciful. Blame this alternating on the troublesome Pisces Moon with all its shadings of intemperance. She's a warm co-worker and a delightful parent. As a wife she's elusive, with almost no pretenses or complications aside from her complex visions and insights. In social situations she's a shadowy figure that everyone notices by her vague presence there. This dichotomy leads to many misconceptions about her, as well as much gossip. She's simply light years ahead of the rest of us, although it doesn't manifest itself in the form of education. She can, in fact, be a poor student due to inattention. She has a spark of genius. Eventually the switch will be turned on and she can finally follow her own course in life. She may outgrow most men. She could use a match to her Sun or Moon, or a Cancer would be oh, so nice.

Her illumination: Spiritually inclined.

Her dark side: Vague presence.

Pisces

February 20–March 21

PISCES-ARIES

This combination is somehow backward in my way of thinking. The strong Sun, calling for action, is trapped in an emotional placement where the Pisces who wants emotional privacy is trapped in the position of strength. Strength it doesn't have. This complex woman can drown herself in her own sorrows. She's combative in areas that she should be gentle in, and vice versa. She appears to have more confidence than she has, and gives an air of false bravado. In actuality, she's easily offended, hurt or given to emotional lows. She often falls victim to her easily stimulated emotional nature and loves too many too hard, then turns her anger with these men inward. She looks for men who're exciting and a bit dangerous. The nice guy will finish last in the race for her. She's given to horrible tantrums with those closest to her. Like other Aries Moon positions, these quarrels may not last long, but they're pretty hideous while they're happening. She's the coldest of the Pisces and won't hesitate to step on you to get what she wants. She'll also not hesitate to let you know what her plans are. All this may even be accompanied by a lecture on how you deserve her competition. Have no fear, she's not usually a winner in such pursuits because she lacks fixity of purpose. She needs to work in a situation where she's an independent contractor, like a hairdresser or researcher. A little of her goes a long way with her co-workers. Several marriages are likely. Otherwise, she can be fun and imaginative with them. The men most apt to catch her attention can fight back. This calls for a Scorpio or another Aries who knows how to cope with women who pull hair. Pisces or Leo should run away as fast as their little legs can take them.

Her illumination: Not materialistic.

Her dark side: Pulls hair.

PISCES-TAURUS

This woman was a happy child, a friendly high school student, a more reserved young adult, and finally a introverted adult. The Pisces is ever trying to adjust to life and its realities. You see, there's a basically good, kind person behind the dark glasses and the quiet persona. She's probably had more than one someone take advantage of her good nature and is now on guard. This is a shame really, for it's easy for the Pisces to retire from life, and hard for the Taurus. While at ease at home and often alone, she's just as outgoing when given a chance to unwind socially with someone she cares for or with a small trusted group of friends. She's the pleasant co-worker who'll put in long twelve hour days to succeed. She'll stay for the gold watch, but underneath she's waiting for someone to free her jailed spirit. The man who can do this will have to overcome her tendency to be boss, and be able to put good times and fun in the place of order and fearfulness. I hope, to tell you the truth, she meets a silly sort of man who places laughter on the list of basic necessities. If he can do this, and yet maintain the lawn, the bank accounts, and auto engine for her, he can turn her into a near party animal. Then she's back to the happy child. The duality of the sun makes her impressionable and almost sponge like when it comes to picking up on her surroundings. She can absorb heartache from her fellow man, laughter from her co-workers, criticism from her mother, all in one day. It doesn't bounce off her psyche, it stays in there, all the hurts, feelings, and trials. There's a lot of emotion in this cool cookie. There's also a lot of good common sense, a fascinating sense of adventure and humor. She'd be a strict, but loving mother wanting nice clean conventional little children. After a couple of Zodiac mismatches she can find herself happily mated with a Libra, Taurus, or Cancer. She'll like the Leo and Sagittarius, but only in small doses.

Her illumination: Sweetness and light.

Her dark side: Jailed spirit.

PISCES-GEMINI

This is the combination of fishes swimming in opposite directions, and the twins. If she sounds like she has trouble with her life's direction, she does. She may say something one moment and totally change her mind the very next. "Now why did I do that?" she wonders. Get her into a job as a photo-journalist for a hospital and you begin to get her moving in a direction she'll stay with. She loves to talk, to photograph, to read, to write, and to be of service to other people. If she can't have a career with a lot of variety she'll become a job hopper. She's talented and she's nice to work with if you like chameleons. Ask several people to describe her—they won't even be able to agree on the color of her eyes. She can exhibit more emotions in one day than the average woman can in a month. Naturally relationships are a little difficult for her to handle. She's going to be troublesome. She may be having an affair with someone else while she's with you. But, the mystery and the delight of her is that you'll see what you want to see. I think that's a rather positive attribute. David Letterman made a statement about someone that seems to sum this lady up: "Sometimes when you look into her eyes you get the feeling someone else is driving." For a brief moment in time another of herselves can take over the wheel. If you can help her by being a steadying influence, you'll find she's handy around the house, crazy about the children (on some days), and wonderful to you (on some days). But she's always a woman and always a delight, even if absentminded. Naturally you can't be very complex yourself—she's enough for the both of you. The Pisces or the Libra has the best chance. The Sagittarius doesn't have much time to invest in her complexities. The Gemini usually isn't able to give the sort of attention she needs. The Cancer or Scorpio can come to her rescue and will at least get acquainted with one of her selves.

Her illumination: Chameleon.

Her dark side: Chameleon.

PISCES-CANCER

This woman is ultra-feminine, and has fine tuned extra-sensory perception. While you may not be able to put one over on her, she can put plenty over on you. She lives on sensation, emotion, and imagination. She has a mind of her own, although that's the last you'd suspect upon meeting her. She comes across as unusually agreeable, and perhaps a bit slow. True, she's no perpetual student or whiz in any particular field, but she's bright enough. Her intelligence is clouded, however, with strange apparitions, dreams, hunches, and feelings. Since this usually begins in early childhood, she's somewhat anxious, for she's had years of being "different." She knows things before they happen, and this is trying, especially when she's dealing with people who are more concrete than she is. It should, but it doesn't, add to her credibility, knowing when the phone is going to ring before it does; it should make her feel more secure, but it doesn't. She spends a lot of her time trying to not know what is about to happen, or to block out her intuition. She may be, therefore, prone to episodes like low blood sugar attacks that are actually rather like panic attacks. She scares herself silly with her imagination. Her children may grow up a little timid under her mothering, but she's a loving mother and a lot of fun with her children. She can use her own childlike characteristics to be a wonderful playmate, and is often found planning parties "just because" that are elaborate with balloons, drawings, and colorful streamers. As a wife or lover she's less adorable. She is given to very grown up bouts of unhappiness and gloom. During these times she won't allow you to talk or amuse her into a better frame of mind. She has a true artistic temperament, and when she unhinges, it's difficult for the men in her life. Impressionable, she is given to infatuations throughout her lifetime. Some of these will naturally interfere with other relationships, because she becomes so besotted with the new that she doesn't pretend to hide it from the old. Now if you're the husband, you're going to be hurt and may eventually demand a showdown at high noon. This is not advisable as she'll then deny any wrongdoing on her part, no matter how convicting the evidence. She, at this point, has some severe memory lapses, and really thinks she's innocent. It's all very confusing to the rest of us. Just take her as she is: loving, kind, imaginative, and a bit befuddled. All mysteries can't be solved. She needs a Cancer man or a Pisces to emote with her. She wants a Scorpio to excess with her. The Capricorn and Virgo find her too impractical for their long term tastes.

Her illumination: Wonderful playmate.

Her dark side: Befuddled.

PISCES-LEO

This woman is a glittering mist, strange and lonely, easily swayed, with a fragile shell of confidence to surround her. She, like her male counterpart with this combination, is an actor of sorts. She can effectively hide behind a mask that leaves no tell-tale sign of insecurity or episodes of frantic ups and downs. Subject to strongly motivated subconscious behavior, she often leads herself on hopeless romantic pursuits, believing in love from someone when it quite simply is not reciprocated. The Moon is in an outgoing, sexual, and romantic position overshadowed by a sensitive, receptive, yet basically withdrawn Sun. Therefore this Sun-Moon combination can often be out of touch in matters of the heart. From career choices to raising children, the heart decides the course of actions. This lady is not one to rely heavily on the facts or evidence. She uses instead, her heart on her sleeve as her geiger counter of life. She has many more admirers than she can cope with, and yet will most often fall for the one who has the least to offer her. A man, perhaps, who's in some way an inferior. There is in short, an abundance of emotionalism here that leads to trouble for her. She's a loving, good hearted person, with a. delicate presence and emotional balance. She looks for a man who's not too superficial in appearance, and who has inner strength and character. She wants a lavish home, preferably near water, and preferably with the mortgage paid off. She won't be hesitant to try and do this for herself. She can be a judge of sorts, a nurse, an actress, a television film maker, or a water ski professional. She'll be both mother and child to her children depending on her moods. If you can assure her everything will turn out right, and that you can provide for her without pounding on your chest, your. chances are much improved with this one. If you can, this coupled with a nice Pisces or Cancer Moon, a Leo Sun or possibly the Capricorn Sun, your chances are tops, for she'll be a faithful, loving friend, co-worker or wife.

Her illumination: Loving.

Her dark side: Wants the mortgage paid off.

PISCES-VIRGO

This lady is one of the natural nurses of the Zodiac. She's interested primarily in service to other people. She is given to the effect of the full moon emotionalism in her chart. You can watch her lose her good common sense from time to time as her sympathies get carried away and she invests her heart and soul in someone of inferior character or less than admirable intentions. She's drawn, as if my a magnet, into a relationship in which she is the caretaker, when in reality she needs to be cared for. She has problems with an easily stimulated nervous system and coping mechanisms that break down from time to time. She can therefore get into trouble with unhealthy escapes like drugs, alcohol and people who need her to carry them around like an albatross. She is good natured, sweet and trusting, and it's a shame these qualities aren't often met in kind. As she grows older, she learns from earlier mistakes of being duped, and can become quite discriminating. It may be that she swings to the other side of her nature and begins to stay clear of any relationship that asks her to give more than she is given. She asks only that someone remembers her needs. She can be so self effacing that her mate may not know for years what she takes in her coffee, because he was too busy being catered to by her. This being taken for granted backs up on her, and when she's had enough, she'll let go with a fury. I can only hope that she finds someone who'll let her nurture without pushing her to extremes and taking her for granted. She won't be so gullible with her children. She'll be a good mother, fair and loving. I hope she finds a wonderful Pisces man, or a sweet tempered Taurus. A sharing, caring Cancer would be a great match too.

Her illumination: Learns from mistakes.

Her dark side: Overloaded circuits.

PISCES-LIBRA

So you're tired of uptight women? You don't want an overachiever? What you do want is some lovely woman who places a high priority on having fun and enjoying life? I think you've found her in this fascinating combination of sun and moon. This lady loves the good life, won't stick to her diet, and once she finds her man she'll put him before the children, her friends or her job. She's popular with nearly everyone, and while she needs an independent sort of career she's a delight to work with. So what's the flaw? There aren't many really. She's a touch absent-minded in that schedules annoy her, and she can not only be late for her appointments, but may miss them altogether. She's slow to reach decisions. She can have multiple memberships to organizations like Overeaters, Gamblers and Alcoholics Anonymous. Her hobby may be collecting wine, and if you can afford ten thousand dollars for things like her fancies, and ignore the more typical needs like standard housing, you're in for the time of your life. One last thing, you'll need to go with her on all her dinners, parties and vacations, or she can soon forget that you, her partner in life, exist at all. She is a touch forgetful. Same goes for the children who'll get lots of hugs and kisses and very little solid evidence of typical mothering. Where do you find her? She may be sailing, or better yet out in someone's yacht. She'll try and locate herself near water. Then there is of course, her various organizations, or the hospital where she most probably works. She can be found wandering around familiar haunts—she won't be too innovative and experiment with new ones. She'll charm you, this one. And, yes, she'll appear pretty. In actuality she may or may not be, but she always leaves the impression of a lovely, misty, ethereal creature. You'll simply be enchanted, especially if you're a Libra, Taurus, or Pisces. The Sagittarius is often her dream man, but she drives him crazy with her lack of drive.

Her illumination: Loves to cuddle.

Her dark side: Absent-minded.

PISCES-SCORPIO

Beautiful? You bet. Mysterious, commanding, emotional and dramatic are all appropriate descriptions for her. She'll use every trick in the book to attract a desired man, except not showing a mind of her own. She's expressive and yes, volatile. Logic isn't her strong point. She's white hot in and out of the rack. Naturally, being on low boil night and day is going to be a tad rough on the body. Enter the world of excessive, compulsive behavior. She can out drink, smoke, and overindulge anyone she meets. She'll have the longest list of ex's, lawsuits and hospital stays. She'll also possess some of the best, most admirable qualities imaginable. She can lead wonderful fund raising causes for medical woes, or spend her spare hours visiting hospital wards. No matter what her station in life, she'll be the center of attention—controversial, considered adulterous, vice laden, and saintly. She's both saint and sinner. She'll be gossiped about long after she's gone. If you're troubled, married, or downright impossible, your chance of attracting her is upped about ten points. She loves the challenge. She's very feminine, yet masculine pursuits don't scare her. Yes, she'd love to go with you to Egypt. Of course her vision of the two of you going down the Nile together will be different from yours. She's conjuring up lavender voile, wide brimmed hats and jasmine perfume to make things more exotic. What looks good against the pyramids, reds or browns? No matter, you'll enjoy yourself. As a mother she's loving, but alternates between periods of over-protectiveness and inattention. As a wife she's a delightful, extravagant companion. Stock up on the aspirin before you attach yourself to this unforgettable roller coaster. Best bets: A Scorpio, of course, or a Cancer with some nice Earth planets.

Her illumination: A saint.

Her dark side: A sinner.

PISCES-SAGITTARIUS

The problem with this Sun-Moon combination is the desire for what she wants on one hand, and her drive to get it on the other. She's in motion either physically or mentally at all times, and the restlessness of this coupling of planets leaves her nervous and edgy. Other than that, you have yourself a lady who's outgoing, generally considerate and socially appealing. She'd much prefer to camp out in the wilderness than to feel the nylon plush from the local hotel underneath her feet. She wants to explore, learn and then teach. Her idea of teaching may be a little unusual, like channeling, or Sanskrit, but she'll love every minute she spends solving the mysteries of culture and mankind's relationship to space. You won't be apt to find her browsing through Spiegel's, planning which curtains to hang in the nursery. Not that she won't ever do anything like that. It's just clearly a secondary priority. In love and child raising she's usually too free with her reins. Oftentimes, she puts too much freedom in the wrong hands and it leaves her with a broken heart, when her loved ones don't quite measure up to all her trust. She can hold down two jobs, run two households, and still be something of a visionary. Her energy, both mentally and physically, is strong. Everyone around her admires her ability to juggle all this and still be a kindly, friendly sort. And friendly is how I would describe her relationship to her lovers or husband (future or past). She's loving in the most detached manner and yet, is romantic enough to appreciate flowers from you on occasion. She just won't lose herself in another person. This is perhaps what makes her so interesting. She has a healthy, well balanced approach to sex and love. If you want to search the planet for experiences with her you'll no doubt be the Sagittarian she dreams of. The Aquarian and the Gemini will also appeal strongly to her.

Her illumination: Loves to camp.

Her dark side: Won't get lost in love.

PISCES-CAPRICORN

This lady is one of the champion worriers of the Zodiac. As you read this, she's probably fretting about the hole in the ozone layer. Her values are also full of contradictions. She has the cold, hardworking Moon and the service oriented, sensitive Sun for her planetary lights. She may work for years to acquire affluence and prestige, and then in a weak moment her Pisces Sun, that loves the downtrodden, will give away large amounts of her money to charities. It was her way of getting even with her moon after all the years of slavery it imposed on her. She's the same way in love. She'll love with a devotion that's overwhelming, and then turn around and never forgive a hurt or injustice. It's baffling behavior to those of you who don't yet comprehend her conflicting needs. In her earlier years she may have been too much of a pushover in love to suit herself. She'll harbor her little secret and vow to never be such an easy touch again. If you reach her late in life, she'll be leary and hard to approach. Catch her young while she's still sensitive and susceptible to romance, but treat her right. She has trouble with despondent, negative, morbid moods. Still, in spite of it all, she's a trustworthy worker and a good employer. She won't be wearing her heart on her sleeve. With children she's strict and yet full of hugs and squeezes. Pisces knows how to love—often too much. Capricorn is cold. These two forces combine to give her problems with romance all her life. Don't delve too far into her secrets, but try to lighten her load. If you can instill a sense of security and calm her inner anxieties you'll stand a strong chance with this lady. She looks for inner beauty so your outer shell won't matter much. The Virgo attracts, often only to frustrate her more. The Cancer, or Scorpio are good bets for a long term match. The Taurus is also a nice steadying influence.

Her illumination: Looks to your heart.

Her dark side: Morose spells.

PISCES-AQUARIUS

Her potential lies in public life and public service; her liability lies in her need to set her own pace. She's the philosopher of the Zodiac, and she has odd ideas about every human condition and how to make it better. Guided by her intuition she can tell when you're going to call before you've reached for the phone. She may forget to answer because another insight just popped into her head. She may leave you wondering if you're her main man or whether you've reached a disconnected number. She's not the average woman found in your black book. She can see things before they happen. She knows more about humanity than just about anyone you'll ever meet, and yet she'll tell you less. If she has something to say you can read about it in the newspaper, or watch for her next crusade. She may start her career in leadership as the class president, but she'll move quietly along to the PTA and other causes later in life. She's in the process of evolving and she isn't into small talk or what Vogue has to say about anything. Her loftier side hits a few snags, however, when she discovers she's just as frail as the rest of us, and she slips into periods of depression, substance abuse or excesses in sex. If she has been unusually proud of herself prior to these lapses, her co-workers may be delighted. There was a smugness about her that bothered them from the beginning. If she's looking for love in all the wrong places and finds you, she can fall hard, and will rarely stray from you and the kids. That's if you have a Capricorn Moon, Cancer or Scorpio Sun, or are an irresistible, troublesome Gemini. You might have to remind her about the tax advantages of being married—that little piece of paper is unnecessary to this lady who knew the two of you were fated on sight.

Her illumination: A born leader.

Her dark side: Looks for love in all the wrong places.

PISCES-PISCES

This double Pisces woman has probably seen more trouble than you could ever imagine. She's so sensitive that she's subject to the moods of the truly despondent. She's probably spent many a day in her childhood playing with her imaginary friends. Since she's so emotive she finds escapes into the world of fantasy to be her best source of retreat. She has also, no doubt, been raised by one parent or family member who had their own brand of escape as well. Her life seems to be one struggle after the other for simple things like balance and temperance. She's not petty, malicious or unkind. Since many of the people she comes in contact with may be, she's always left a little sadder and wiser for her forgiving, loving personality— when in love she'll go that extra mile. She's deeply touched by the human condition. She wants a rosy world, where there's no starvation, illness, or any of life's injustices. After a few years in the real world she finds the true condition almost too hard to bear. She's not weak, and between 28 and 30 she may find herself getting better at coping with life and its disappointments. She's secretive, preferring to keep her melancholy to herself. If all this sounds like she's a bore, or can't be witty and yes, vibrant, let me assure you the duality of her nature can cover these character traits well. She may be in fact, the center of her circle of friends. While she may not always seek the limelight, she may end up nevertheless a leader in some humanitarian way, in spite of herself. Perhaps she can set an example on how to overcome. Unexplained, almost compulsive behavior comes naturally to her. Of course there are many ups and downs, reverses and good fortune that come her way. Any or all of this is hard on her already delicate health and her fragile nervous condition. She's been dealt some of the hardest of life's circumstances, and yet she can teach us all a lesson in charity, love of mankind, and surviving the hardest of knocks. Childlike in some respects, she needs a strong man who can relate. A Cancer would be great; the Capricorn will be there to pick up the pieces; the Scorpio will probably have the best chance of experiencing her sensitive approach to sex.

Her illumination: Has faith, hope, and charity.

Her dark side: Surrounded by the weak.

Rising Signs for Women

ARIES RISING
"I'm pretty independent."

Shining, sunny, bright, there's a teeny touch of arrogance about the Aries Rising woman. Sounds of "I am woman" thunder in her heart. She likes to trespass into traditional male-dominated tasks, from plant management to her own auto maintenance. She likes to win, to be first. She can tackle sports, mechanics and most left brain functions. What she can't do is relax and let things happen naturally. In romance her mating call is "I'm installing my lawn sprinklers Saturday, wanna help?" Her values are in her accomplishments, competence, mastery. She looks for a man who is impressed by this. Not all are. Naturally this creates a few relationship problems for her. Quite frankly, she's very capable of living her life without a man and she flaunts that ability. Underneath all this self confidence and independence flutters a heart that fears domination and control. She isn't timid about romance, nor is she cold hearted. What she longs for is a man who can run his own race and allow her spirit to roam about a bit. She wants a man who prefers a tank top and shorts to lacy lingerie. Feminine wiles are out of the question with an Aries Rising. She could never respect a man who couldn't see through silly games, and above all, she needs a man she can admire and respect. When she finally finds such a knight, she'll happily give her heart, barbecue his steaks, and if necessary, fight to defend him against the world.

General Life Tendencies

There's a lot to be said for this natural placement of the houses. Some of the favorable tendencies are the ability to attract money and the stamina to spend it. Not afraid to go it alone, the Aries Rising woman attracts partnerships. Men are beneficial to her, even if her father was somehow lacking in the financial department. Brothers can create disappointments and even estrangement. She's not afraid to break convention and is more than able in all career matters. She has a host of friends and a wonderful sense of adventure. She really wants a life long mate but won't hesitate to hold out for the Prince. She faces hardships with an iron will and will always end the race at the front of the line.

TAURUS RISING
"I'm good with money."

The steel magnolia of the Rising signs, the Taurus Rising woman has a strong backbone and an iron will. Possessed of an extraordinary amount of self control, she can contain her emotions admirably and yield to a man's apparent domination. Here's one ascendant that's happy to let her man beat his chest. She'll let you be your eccentric self, notice the pretty passing ladies, and listen enchantedly to all your stories of bygone days. But while she may seem to know no bounds in her quiet adoration of you, she does indeed have her limits. Push her too far and she'll dig in her heels, create a cloud of sullen, white hot dust, and simmer for days. Her anger, though not easily aroused, is an unforgettable sight. Most of her emotions aren't squandered on causes and concerns, but saved for the practical issues of her life like enticing meals for her man, sensuous fabrics next to her body and the appeasement of her strong sexual nature. Money is also an issue in her life. Since money affords creature comforts it holds a strong attraction for her. Like her temper, she hides the extent of her lust for material things, and steadily plods along on the acquisition path. Calm and surefooted, she's willing to wait for her good fortune. She's not flighty, flashy or whimsical. She's mother earth, the smell of fresh baked bread, and lazy afternoons on white cotton sheets.

General Life Tendencies

Robust health, two sources of income, steady, slow progress in life, and children who volunteer to clean their rooms are part of the stellar offerings with a Taurus Rising. While she may experience difficulty with delivery of her first child (did she stay in bed for months?) her otherwise lifelong health is usually one of her best assets. Her life's mate may be willful, passionate and problematic, but she endures. Values are important to her and she's the first to disapprove of her own shortcomings. Excessive appetites for many things create some of her personal problems. She plays her cards close to her chest and reveals her secrets only when necessary.

GEMINI RISING
"I'm busy tonight."

The Gemini Rising woman is still delightfully part child. She jabbers, she jiggles, she jogs. She doesn't sit still for long stretches unless, of course, she's talking on the phone. Entertaining, she's often the best of hostesses, throwing parties extraordinaire. Her enthusiasm is contagious and her charm offsets the harsh feelings over her flirtatious eye. A possessive man will simply be driven nuts by her restless nature. The best of companions, she has a host of friends. She was born for fun and adventure. She's witty and can keep you up all night talking. SurpRisingly, family is important to her and she's a ready friend in a crisis. Her money is spent on action, travel, entertainment, and life's pleasures. The man who attracts her must be energetic (nearly frantic is alright), sociable, intelligent and be committed to an idea or cause. He won't mind having his house invaded by new friends, old family, neighbors and stray dogs. He'll submit to endless photographs of their life together and to telephones in the cars. He'll enjoy her becoming a blond, redhead or brunette sooner or later, depending on her moods. It may be for this reason alone that most men find her the most irresistible of the Rising signs. If you don't treat her right she'll move on quietly, taking only memories.

General Life Tendencies

Great fluctuations in her personal financial status, peculiar ethics and morality, adoring children, and several marriages are in store for the Gemini Rising woman. A whirlwind who can videotape the family album while stirring the pasta, she lives a life full of variety, communication and intrigue. People of vast background differences are drawn into her inner circle. In fact, one of her husbands may be from a different background or culture. She'll do many things in her life, packing excitement and adventure into every waking moment. While all this makes for quality time on the mortal plane she needs to give her overstimulated nervous system a break from time to time.

CANCER RISING
"I'm close to my family."

This is the woman of principles, the mistress of change. Looking for Mr. Right is almost an obsession and she'll travel to China to be with him. She is nearly rooted to her home base, however, so he can expect to end right back in the midwest where it all began with daddy and mum. Nearly crazed for decorating and remodeling, she turns her home or apartment into a showplace. Since she attracts men of money, her apartment may be at the Plaza where she'll drag in pumpkins and fix her own turkey for her honey on Thanksgiving. She has one of the strongest nesting instincts of the Rising signs. She's intuitive, a natural therapist, and finds men nestling up to her with long, tall tales of woe about former relationships. You won't leave this relationship unchanged. She has a knack for remodeling, remember, and that means you too. She's not shallow, but her anxiety over everything from flash floods to broken fingernails may make it appear so. One of the most attractive in a fragile, translucent sort of way, she nonetheless has her share of disappointments in love and gets really complicated in romance. Complicated like after a year of what you think is a good relationship she stops taking your calls because of an imagined slight. Or after you settle down and start a career, she decides she needs more security. Sweet talk her with words like security, roots, mortgages. She doesn't sparkle or shine, she glows. She isn't action, but reaction. She doesn't adorn, but she clings. She's déjà vu and warm memories.

General Life Tendencies

Clever, initiating, manipulating, this woman has an unsteady early life. A few failed relationships along the way leave her with a scarred heart and a flood of tears. But she rises above it and finds herself a stable, conservative, moneymaking man in the end. The problem is, she may find the marriage isn't fifty-fifty and that she carries the weight of the relationship on her dainty little shoulders. There are many life changes in store for this woman—impulsive career changes, passionate love affairs, children with wills stronger than her own, and men who rain on her parade. No matter, she makes a life change in the 30s and may end up with everything her heart desires.

LEO RISING
"I love jewelry."

A mane of hair glistening in the sunlight, a sunny smile, and an abundance of baubles and jewels are part of the aura of Leo Rising, the star of the Rising signs. If she sounds spoiled, she is. Attention comes to her naturally, and she inspires and leads as if by birthright. She's not a standard model, but a luxury one. Men who need to dominate or manipulate had better steer clear. She has only icy contempt for such attempts at control. She requires equal billing in her relationships. She's capable in many fields but will always manage to perform even the most mundane chores in some sort of creative, dramatic fashion. She prides herself on being a breed apart. For all her drama and excitement, she has the wonderful ability to enjoy life like a child; laughing, frolicking, and playful. In relationships she's generous and loving to those she admits into her inner circle; but aloof to those she does not. Those exiled from her court can expect the bone chilling indifference that comes after dismissal. She's determined, headstrong and a challenge few men can resist. But there's a surprise for the man who wins her respect—she can be tamed. Tamed, but never conquered. As long as she believes her mate is admirable and worthy she'll be his most steadfast and loyal friend. She can be dragged through the mud, she can weather marital storms few women could endure. You can be a brief tornado in her life; but her mate cannot be cheap, petty or unimaginative. And the man of her dreams can't spend too many Friday nights at Joe's Bar and Grill.

General Life Tendencies

This woman has such generosity of soul that despite some of her hardships life may impose upon her she sees her glass as half full. And indeed it is, because many important people and events conspire to fill her glass. It's not unusual for Leo Rising to end up with some degree of authority, wealth and recognition for her efforts. Even her children are fortunate for her. In affairs of the heart she's most attracted to unconventional partners. There are sudden endings and beginnings with relationships for her. This woman won't have conventional marriages, and will do best with an independent, intelligent sort of man.

VIRGO RISING
"I need a routine."

Here is the woman who puts you back in touch with the earth. Her values lie in work and nature. She writes Haiku, reads *Prevention*, rides bicycles, and reminds you you don't do too many things quite right. Curious, delving, asking for perfection, she has a wonderful flaw: she idealizes her mate. Lucky for you, even though you mess up her kitchen, botch the roofing and hum off key, she thinks you're a wonderful human being. She won't commit to "you're adorable" (only children are), she won't admire your buns, but she'll appreciate that you work out. She has no intention of fawning over you, but she'll take great care in watching your cholesterol count, typing your exam papers and knitting funny things for your mother. The "Virgo the Virgin" stuff is only symbolic so you may as well forget it and come to terms with the fact that she'll leave you for someone else if you don't love and appreciate her in return. She wants romance as much as any of her Zodiac sisters, but she expresses it differently. Her passion commingles with devotion and unity. She is what she appears to be, determined to pursue solid, lasting happiness and the simple things in life. Not realizing how difficult and complex relationships can become, her expectations are not easily met. She's wonderful for the man who is secure enough to appreciate the beauty of a sturdy, solid rock and forsake the glitter of fool's gold.

General Life Tendencies

The Virgo Rising woman is discriminating in all matters, yet has near blind faith in her marriage partner. He can be ill, neurotic, emotionally needy. In healthier conditions the man will be of strong spiritual qualities, and will be idolized by her. Often this woman will choose not to marry because she has experienced long term deception by a lover and will never quite get over it. A natural mother she'll be conventional and somewhat strict with her children. Subject to spells of ill health her circulatory system, and immune system are often her weak spots. She normally has a long and successful career and an easy time attracting money.

LIBRA RISING
"I'm not afraid of relationships."

Dimpled and delightful, she comes across pliant and compromising. She may be unsure, even indecisive. She'll call on you, her "friend," "daddy," "squizzle toes," to help her through the week's crisis. She's unable to manage by herself. Whoa! Get a grip on yourself, fella. Isn't she running her own business? Isn't she the doctoral candidate? This is part of her seduction. It's wonderful to play the game, but never mistake her helplessness for anything less than her carefully calculated plan to entrap you. This woman is very strong. Not that she isn't desirable, or even a terrific catch. But she's going to have you jumping through hoops if that's what she wants. She's an expert at persuasion and will have no qualms at getting you to marry her, move to another city, change your religion, your vocation. There is no woman in the Rising signs that can compare to her when it comes to taming her man. If you dream of a benevolent dictator, look no further. In turn you'll get a home that's cozy, a wife who's unusually attractive and intelligent, and a top notch hostess. She'll never admit to her manipulations, and no one will ever guess that you're not guiding her through life. You can even play boss in front of your friends. She won't talk bad about you to her friends unless she's in crisis. Of course by that time she may be ready to leave. She idealizes her mate, is in love with love, and offers you dinner by candlelight. She'll camp with you, ride on your motorcycle, help you study for your exams, make herself indispensable. When she offers her affection it is without reserve. She does this because life without a mate for the Libra Rising is unbearable. She quite simply exists for love.

General Life Tendencies
Naturally attractive to everyone, Libra Rising has some advantages early on. Since relationships are critical to her, it's not surprising that she usually has large numbers of relatives. While her marriage may be a stormy one, she's in constant search for an ideal, harmonious relationship. There's a possibility of an inheritance and many changes in career matters. Her children are usually successful, highly individual people. Subject to medical misdiagnosis or confusion, she often needs second medical opinions for her illnesses. She has a lifelong fascination with travel and education.

SCORPIO RISING
"Where there's a will, there's a way."

Sensuous, alluring, mysterious, she is the predator of the Zodiac. She's not afraid of life or death, and therefore the most exotic man in the room won't phase her. She'll go after what she wants from life with the strategy of a general, the daring of a skydiver. If, upon meeting her, she doesn't lock eyes with you, chances are that you, even at your most enticing best, won't get to first base. She's the steam from fire and ice, the allure of musk, the sexual chemist. She has the power to take you to the depths of despair and send you soaring back to ecstacy. She can read your mind, leave you in a sexual stupor, solicit your secrets, and yet you may not know her past, her friends, her family. She doesn't invite you over for roast dinners, or to sleep on cotton sheets. She is love potions, smoked oysters, and fur rugs before crackling fires. She is screaming fights and stupendous lovemaking. When she mates she wants it to be for life. She'll stop at nothing to defend you, to honor you, and to stand by you. Infidelities on your part are simply out of the question. While she has the strongest endurance of the Rising signs, your involvement with another woman may leave her shattered and nearly beyond repair. Temporarily. She'll recover, mumble curses about your grave, and rise again. Her will power is a magnificent thing.

General Life Tendencies

This woman has the strongest physical body of the Zodiac in terms of resistance to illness. As if attempting to test her robustness, mother nature usually gives her a health crisis that she is able to overcome at some point in her life. She's just as fixed when it comes to her marriage—this woman will be one of the most determined to make hers work. She'll be inclined to a career of prominence and often glamour. She works hard for her success and it usually comes in the second half of her life. She's forever transforming herself, and has most likely had an unusual early family environment.

SAGITTARIUS RISING
"I need a lot of freedom."

It's not that she forgot her Girl Scout oath about being clean and tidy and good, but she really won't have time for a lot of the wifey things. Scattered energies and her enthusiasm for life override her desire to bake you carrot cake or start the war on dust balls. Here is the woman of enthusiasm, the bubbles in the champagne of life. If I had to pick the most outstanding characteristic of this Rising sign I would say it is her love of living live to the fullest. Naturally with this being her priority, she may have episodes of adventure that get her in some trouble, like forgetting to come back from her two week vacation, hiding her new sale dresses under dry cleaning bags ("I stayed on my budget, but cleaning costs have just gone sky high"), selling her heirloom china to pay for dance costumes. When it's all said and done, she'll have had a host of friends and twenty jobs, attracted the most admirers, and loved a dozen men. Who can resist the genuinely good natured, the eternal optimist, the prom queen who stayed home with her best friend who had the measles? She never quite grows older, refusing to accept limitations on fun or adventure. She's hard to resist, harder yet to pin down. She does a lot of things in haste, and while marrying is not usually one of them, several marriages are in store for this firecracker.

General Life Tendencies

Born with traveling feet this woman is one of the most lively of the Zodiac. Life is generally good to the woman with the Sagittarius Rising, but she'll still have periods of despondency during her lifetime. Given to quiet times alone, no one can guess that much of her outgoing personality is a response to her environment and not necessarily an inborn trait. There is a strong possibility of dual sets of family in her early years. Popular early on, she marries young and has several relationships before she settles into a strong commitment. She has a few children of her own who are as impulsive and headstrong as she has been. A joy to be around she does very well in her career. Inheritances and legacies are probable.

CAPRICORN RISING
"I like to set goals."

Setting goals, writing lists, stocking the pantry, but still asking her mom go to the mall to help her pick out clothes, even though she's already in her thirties. She's the woman of substance. Anxiety ridden, no stranger to the night crazies, she's fearful and timid underneath the layers of control. She loves Woody Allen movies because he voices her fears. She's afraid to make the wrong choice, to love the wrong man, to present a paper with a dangling participle. Yet despite this, she exudes supreme confidence. Understanding this dichotomy allows you to proceed into the sacred territory of her heart. Verbalizing her fears, assessing her shortcomings, demeaning her plans excludes you from her life. Once you understand the formula for friendship with her she's an easy friend, a loyal and loving partner. She'll keep your trust, share your dreams. She's aloof, distant, but never cold or uncaring. Slow in romance, she unfolds like a flower in spring, gently. Men sense this hesitancy and therein lies her allure. What better mating call than reluctance? Convincing her is half the excitement. She may or may not be the prettiest, men seldom notice. Refusing to market herself, she won't tell you she has an MBA, is also an interior decorator, and is one of the wittiest people you'll ever meet. Here is the woman of depth. Shallow men repel her. Aimless, unsteady men leave her chilled to the bone. She is high cheekbones and high aspirations. She looks for sincerity, decency, and yes, some money in the bank.

General Life Tendencies
Despite a life of obstacles she steadily rises above her original economic situation. A stormy, but solid relationship with her father

leaves her strong and determined with her own children, and nurturing with her husband. Her desire for status, her appreciation of values, inclines her to work excessively long and hard in her career. Wrapped in the cloth of normalcy, she has a streak of inconsistencies and is subject to many changes. While her course may baffle those around her, remember her final path is upward. Subject to early ill health and constant strain due to nervous disorders she nonetheless improves with age and is one of the longest living of the Rising signs.

AQUARIUS RISING
"I'm a bit of a visionary."

She doesn't pay attention, yet she notices everything. Paradoxical, she never sways from loyalty, humanitarian ideals, and her basic good nature. You can be poor in material things, but the man of her dreams must be rich in talent, ideas, and achievements. Detached romantically she can forget your anniversary, what you take in your coffee, but she'll never doubt you or ask you to compromise your beliefs. She's a banker in love, tallying your intellectual assets and good breeding against your liabilities. Feminine wiles and fits of passion are foreign to her. If she heads off for an exotic adventure you may not hear from her until she returns. She rarely suffers from homesickness or loneliness. If you haven't gathered by now, I can tell you that she is the most unusual of the Rising signs. Needless to say, she doesn't seek a conventional man, nor will she endure a coupling that is not punctuated with excitement, chemistry or good solid friendship. For all this, she has sudden endings or beginnings in her relationships with the opposite sex. So warnings fair, while she doesn't want to be possessed or fenced in, she does require attention. If you become detached or preoccupied (like she is) she may decide you're not worth the effort. Remember, she's a paradox. But she's witty, fun, intelligent, and progressive. Strains of H.G. Wells are in her genes. Boring she will never be.

General Life Tendencies
Attracted to the scientific, electronics, the arts and literature this woman can carve some unusual careers for herself. Except for her free spirited episodes and her out of body tendencies, she is

fixed in her approach to life and probably came from a solid, loving early childhood. Determined in matters regarding her home life, her marriage, and her career she is loyal and can endure much to make things work. The rest of her life is more rambling, the children are hyperactive, money matters elude her, health and vitality are inconsistent, and her mate demands attention. The eccentric of the Rising signs, she is humane, kind, and has hopes for mankind to better itself. A visit from E.T. may not be unusual.

PISCES RISING
"I have ESP."

Here's a woman who wants to be loved, protected and cared for. Eternally feminine and devastatingly appealing, she's the hope of spring, the romance of summer and the beauty of fall. She may not make it all the way until winter, however, because she doesn't bear up under the strain of reality very well. She can and will endure many hardships, heartbreaks, and crises, but they'll take their toll. She believes in ideals and dreams, and dreams can and do shatter in the face of reality. She'll stand by you when you lose your job or your car, but not when you lose your self respect. The enormity of her faith in you is what you find so enduring in the beginning and so crushing in the end. Who can live up to men on the silver screen, men who don't get sick, who fill the house with flowers and bring boxes from Tiffany's? She's short on practicality, so if you don't mind providing her shelter from the harsher realities of life, and you can supply a nearly endless source of affection and attention, you can get a woman not altered by today's standards. She is eternal, not trendy. She is ethereal and volatile. She can rise above and sink to the depths, fascinating you all the while. Her attraction lies in her vagueness. Men reach out wanting to capture the illusive. Count the seasons and secure her in winter.

General Life Tendencies
Impressionable, romantic and procrastinating, this woman is the psychic of the Rising signs. Her inner voice is strong and she is better off following it. She'll usually have a large family of her own, two sets of parents for herself, and a husband who is meticulous and exacting. Friends of status and position come to her aid throughout

her life helping her over hurdles in work. A career involving import, export, publishing or overseas is probable. She'll be fortunate in these matters. Impulsive with money, her choice of a partner gives her an opportunity to learn discrimination and control. Two residences are possible as well as a tiny inheritance. While her life isn't Utopia, it isn't bad.

Tables

How to Find the Sun/Moon Position
For Your Combinations

The astrological year begins around the 21st of March, with the sign Aries, and every month the Zodiac signs change positions to another sign. This is your "Sun sign."

Approximate dates for the Zodiac signs are shown here to serve as an illustration but the dates given on the following pages of tables are more exact.

The approximate dates for each Sun sign with its abbreviation are:

Sign	Dates From/To	Abbr.	Sign
Aries	March 21 to April 21	ARI	♈
Taurus	April 21 to May 21	TAU	♉
Gemini	May 21 to June 21	GEM	♊
Cancer	June 21 to July 21	CAN	♋
Leo	July 21 to August 21	LEO	♌
Virgo	August 21 to September 21	VIR	♍
Libra	September 21 to October 21	LIB	♎
Scorpio	October 21 to November 21	SCO	♏
Sagittarius	November 21 to December 21	SAG	♐
Capricorn	December 21 to January 21	CAP	♑
Aquarius	January 21 to February 21	AQU	♒
Pisces	February 21 to March 21	PIS	♓

This sign rotation also happens with the Moon positions but the Moon moves into a different Zodiac sign every 2 to 2-1/2 days. In order to find your exact combination you will need to follow the tables in the back of the book to the year you are looking up, then proceed to the month column and down to the day column. For example: to look up February 3, 1957, you go to the Sun Ingresses to determine your Sun sign. The Sun Ingresses gives the date in which the Sun enters one sign and moves out of a previous sign; thus in 1957, the Sun entered Aquarius at 2:39 a.m, Jan 20; and moved into the next Sun sign, Pisces, on February 18 at 16:59 (4:59 p.m.). Since February 3rd falls within those dates you can determine that this person is an Aquarius.

To determine the person's Moon sign, simply turn to the Moon Ingresses and find the table which corresponds to your year, month and date. From this table you can tell that this person's Moon is in Aries, provided that he or she was born after 19:42 (7:42 p.m.) EST. The Moon will remain in Aries until the 6th of February.

All times are given in Eastern Standard Time (EST). You will need to convert your birth time into EST in order to obtain an accurate reading. (Convenient time conversion tables can be found in several Llewellyn Publications Annuals, such as the Llewellyn Astrological Calendar, Llewellyn's Moon Sign Book, and Llewellyn's Daily Planetary Guide.)

MOON INGRESSES

1900–2000

Use these tables to find your Moon Sign. The day listed is the day on which the Moon moved into the sign indicated in the table.

— 1900 —

JAN
2	16:26	AQU
4	17:09	PIS
6	18:46	ARI
8	22:26	TAU
11	4:37	GEM
13	13:06	CAN
15	23:31	LEO
18	11:27	VIR
21	0:07	LIB
23	11:55	SCO
25	20:50	SAG
28	1:47	CAP
30	3:13	AQU

FEB
1	2:48	PIS
3	2:38	ARI
5	4:42	TAU
7	10:08	GEM
9	18:50	CAN
12	5:49	LEO
14	18:00	VIR
17	6:37	LIB
19	18:45	SCO
22	4:54	SAG
24	11:33	CAP
26	14:16	AQU
28	14:05	AQU

MAR
2	13:02	ARI
4	13:25	TAU
6	17:05	GEM
9	0:46	CAN
11	11:39	LEO
14	0:04	VIR
16	12:39	LIB
19	0:35	SCO
21	11:03	SAG
23	18:57	CAP
25	23:25	AQU
28	0:42	PIS
30	0:13	ARI

APR
1	0:01	TAU
3	2:14	GEM
5	8 :17	CAN
7	18:11	LEO
10	6:25	VIR
12	19:01	LIB
15	6:38	SCO
17	16:39	SAG
20	0:37	CAP
22	6:06	AQU
24	8:59	PIS
26	10:00	ARI
28	10:34	TAU
30	12:30	GEM

MAY
2	17:24	CAN
5	2:01	LEO
7	13:36	VIR
10	2:10	LIB
12	13:42	SCO
14	23:08	SAG
17	6:20	CAP
19	11:31	AQU
21	15:01	PIS
23	17:22	ARI
25	19:21	TAU
27	22:06	GEM
30	2:55	CAN

JUN
1	10:45	LEO
3	21:34	VIR
6	10:00	LIB
8	21:46	SCO
11	7:06	SAG
13	13:31	CAP
15	17:38	AQU
17	20:27	PIS
19	22:57	ARI
22	1:54	TAU
24	5:52	GEM
26	11:28	CAN
28	19:19	LEO

JUL
1	5:43	VIR
3	17:59	LIB
6	6:12	SCO
8	16:05	SAG
10	22:27	CAP
13	1:41	AQU
15	3:12	PIS
17	4:38	ARI
19	7:17	TAU
21	11:48	GEM
23	18:20	CAN
26	2:49	LEO
28	13:18	VIR
31	1:30	LIB

AUG
2	14:09	SCO
5	1:01	SAG
7	8:14	CAP
9	11:32	AQU
11	12:10	PIS
13	12:09	ARI
15	13:25	TAU
17	17:14	GEM
19	23:56	CAN
22	9:03	LEO
24	19:57	VIR
27	8:13	LIB
29	21:03	SCO

SEP
1	8:49	SAG
3	17:27	CAP
5	21:53	AQU
7	22:47	PIS
9	22:00	ARI
11	21:45	TAU
13	23:58	GEM
16	5:40	CAN
18	14:39	LEO
21	1:53	VIR
23	14:19	LIB
26	3:06	SCO
28	15:10	SAG

OCT
1	0:57	CAP
3	7:04	AQU
5	9:22	PIS
7	9:06	ARI
9	8:17	TAU
11	9:02	GEM
13	13:02	CAN
15	20:53	LEO
18	7:52	VIR
20	20:25	LIB
23	9:05	SCO
25	20:50	SAG
28	6:47	CAP
30	14:02	AQU

NOV
1	18:06	PIS
3	19:27	ARI
5	19:25	TAU
7	19:50	GEM
9	22:32	CAN
12	4:49	LEO
14	14:48	VIR
17	3:09	LIB
19	15:48	SCO
22	3:09	SAG
24	12:26	CAP
26	19:30	AQU
29	0:24	PIS

DEC
1	3:22	ARI
3	5:01	TAU
5	6:27	GEM
7	9:04	CAN
9	14:19	LEO
11	23:04	VIR
14	10:49	LIB
16	23:34	SCO
19	10:54	SAG
21	19:33	CAP
24	1:34	AQU
26	5:47	PIS
28	9:02	ARI
30	11:55	TAU

— 1901 —

JAN
1	14:54	GEM
3	18:36	CAN
5	23:59	LEO
8	8:04	VIR
10	19:07	LIB
13	7:52	SCO
15	19:43	SAG
18	4:30	CAP
20	9:47	AQU
22	12:41	PIS
24	14:45	ARI
26	17:16	TAU
28	20:54	GEM
31	1:50	CAN

FEB
2	8:12	LEO
4	16:33	VIR
7	3:18	LIB
9	15:56	SCO
12	4:26	SAG
14	14:10	CAP
16	19:50	AQU
18	22:06	PIS
20	22:44	ARI
22	23:41	TAU
25	2:22	GEM
27	7:20	CAN

MAR
1	14:30	LEO
3	23:37	VIR
6	10:37	LIB
8	23:12	SCO
11	12:04	SAG
13	22:56	CAP
16	5:56	AQU
18	8:52	PIS
20	9:06	ARI
22	8:41	TAU
24	9:37	GEM
26	13:15	CAN
28	20:00	LEO
31	5:29	VIR

APR
2	16:57	LIB
5	5:38	SCO
7	18:31	SAG
10	6:02	CAP
12	14:27	AQU
14	18:56	PIS
16	20:06	ARI
18	19:33	TAU
20	19:18	GEM
22	21:11	CAN
25	2:28	LEO
27	11:20	VIR
29	22:54	LIB

MAY
2	11:43	SCO
5	0:27	SAG
7	11:54	CAP
9	20:58	AQU
12	2:55	PIS
14	5:43	ARI
16	6:16	TAU
18	6:07	GEM
20	7:03	CAN
22	10:47	LEO
24	18:18	VIR
27	5:18	LIB
29	18:07	SCO

JUN
1	6:44	SAG
3	17:43	CAP
6	2:30	AQU
8	8:55	PIS
10	13:01	ARI
12	15:10	TAU
14	16:10	GEM
16	17:22	CAN
18	20:23	LEO
21	2:41	VIR
23	12:42	LIB
26	1:14	SCO
28	13:51	SAG

JUL
1	0:31	CAP
3	8:34	AQU
5	14:22	PIS
7	18:36	ARI
9	21:45	TAU
12	0:10	GEM
14	2:31	CAN
16	5:54	LEO
18	11:43	VIR
20	20:55	LIB
23	9:00	SCO
25	21:45	SAG
28	8:33	CAP
30	16:09	AQU

AUG
1	20:59	PIS
4	0:16	ARI
6	3:07	TAU
8	6:08	GEM
10	9:37	CAN
12	14:04	LEO
14	20:17	VIR
17	5:14	LIB
19	16:58	SCO
22	5:54	SAG
24	17:18	CAP
27	1:13	AQU
29	5:36	PIS
31	7:44	ARI

SEP
2	9:17	TAU
4	11:32	GEM
6	15:11	CAN
8	20:26	LEO
11	3:33	VIR
13	12:52	LIB
16	0:31	SCO
18	13:33	SAG
21	1:44	CAP
23	10:45	AQU
25	15:43	PIS
27	17:29	ARI
29	17:47	TAU

OCT
1	18:28	GEM
3	20:54	CAN
6	1:52	LEO
8	9:28	VIR
10	19:26	LIB
13	7:19	SCO
15	20:22	SAG
18	9:01	CAP
20	19:18	AQU
23	1:46	PIS
25	4:26	ARI
27	4:34	TAU
29	4:01	GEM
31	4:42	CAN

NOV
2	8:09	LEO
4	15:06	VIR
7	1:15	LIB
9	13:30	SCO
12	2:32	SAG
14	15:09	CAP
17	2:04	AQU
19	10:04	PIS
21	14:31	ARI
23	15:52	TAU
25	15:24	GEM
27	15:02	CAN
29	16:43	LEO

DEC
1	22:02	VIR
4	7:24	LIB
6	19:38	SCO
9	8:45	SAG
11	21:04	CAP
14	7:42	AQU
16	16:12	PIS
18	22:09	ARI
21	1:23	TAU
23	2:22	GEM
25	2:23	CAN
27	3:18	LEO
29	7:04	VIR
31	14:56	LIB

— 1902 —

JAN		
3	2:30	SCO
5	15:36	SAG
8	3:47	CAP
10	13:48	AQU
12	21:40	PIS
15	3:44	ARI
17	8:06	TAU
19	10:49	GEM
21	12:21	CAN
23	13:56	LEO
25	17:16	VIR
27	23:58	LIB
30	10:28	SCO

FEB		
1	23:17	SAG
4	11:38	CAP
6	21:27	AQU
9	4:29	PIS
11	9:31	ARI
13	13:26	TAU
15	16:43	GEM
17	19:37	CAN
19	22:37	LEO
22	2:44	VIR
24	9:18	LIB
26	19:05	SCO

MAR		
1	7:27	SAG
3	20:04	CAP
6	6:22	AQU
8	13:16	PIS
10	17:21	ARI
12	19:55	TAU
14	22:13	GEM
17	1:04	CAN
19	4:54	LEO
21	10:12	VIR
23	17:31	LIB
26	3:20	SCO
28	15:24	SAG
31	4:12	CAP

APR		
2	15:20	AQU
4	23:03	PIS
7	3:11	ARI
9	4:50	TAU
11	5:37	GEM
13	7:04	CAN
15	10:18	LEO
17	15:57	VIR
20	0:05	LIB
22	10:28	SCO
24	22:36	SAG
27	11:26	CAP
29	23:16	AQU

MAY		
2	8:16	PIS
4	13:30	ARI
6	15:23	TAU
8	15:21	GEM
10	15:15	CAN
12	16:54	LEO
14	21:36	VIR
17	5:42	LIB
19	16:33	SCO
22	4:58	SAG
24	17:47	CAP
27	5:50	AQU
29	15:50	PIS
31	22:35	ARI

JUN		
3	1:46	TAU
5	2:10	GEM
7	1:26	CAN
9	1:39	LEO
11	4:44	VIR
13	11:45	LIB
15	22:22	SCO
18	10:58	SAG
20	23:46	CAP
23	11:37	AQU
25	21:50	PIS
28	5:39	ARI
30	10:26	TAU

JUL		
2	12:14	GEM
4	12:07	CAN
6	11:54	LEO
8	13:43	VIR
10	19:16	LIB
13	4:56	SCO
15	17:17	SAG
18	6:04	CAP
20	17:38	AQU
23	3:24	PIS
25	11:15	ARI
27	16:57	TAU
29	20:16	GEM
31	21:34	CAN

AUG		
2	22:06	LEO
4	23:43	VIR
7	4:15	LIB
9	12:43	SCO
12	0:26	SAG
14	13:10	CAP
17	0:38	AQU
19	9:51	PIS
21	16:57	ARI
23	22:20	TAU
26	2:13	GEM
28	4:50	CAN
30	6:45	LEO

SEP		
1	9:13	VIR
3	13:42	LIB
5	21:26	SCO
8	8:25	SAG
10	21:01	CAP
13	8:44	AQU
15	17:53	PIS
18	0:14	ARI
20	4:31	TAU
22	7:39	GEM
24	10:23	CAN
26	13:16	LEO
28	16:58	VIR
30	22:19	LIB

OCT		
3	6:07	SCO
5	16:40	SAG
8	5:06	CAP
10	17:19	AQU
13	3:07	PIS
15	9:30	ARI
17	12:56	TAU
19	14:40	GEM
21	16:10	CAN
23	18:39	LEO
25	22:53	VIR
28	5:14	LIB
30	13:46	SCO

NOV		
2	0:26	SAG
4	12:44	CAP
7	1:22	AQU
9	12:16	PIS
11	19:44	ARI
13	23:24	TAU
16	0:19	GEM
18	0:14	CAN
20	1:06	LEO
22	4:24	VIR
24	10:49	LIB
26	20:01	SCO
29	7:12	SAG

DEC		
1	19:33	CAP
4	8:16	AQU
6	20:01	PIS
9	5:03	ARI
11	10:11	TAU
13	11:38	GEM
15	10:55	CAN
17	10:13	LEO
19	11:40	VIR
21	16:46	LIB
24	1:39	SCO
26	13:09	SAG
29	1:44	CAP
31	14:20	AQU

— 1903 —

JAN		
3	2:12	PIS
5	12:14	ARI
7	19:09	TAU
9	22:19	GEM
11	22:28	CAN
13	21:27	LEO
15	21:32	VIR
18	0:47	LIB
20	8:14	SCO
22	19:15	SAG
25	7:55	CAP
27	20:27	AQU
30	7:55	PIS

FEB		
1	17:52	ARI
4	1:36	TAU
6	6:27	GEM
8	8:25	CAN
10	8:33	LEO
12	8:41	VIR
14	10:53	LIB
16	16:43	SCO
19	2:29	SAG
21	14:46	CAP
24	3:20	AQU
26	14:31	PIS
28	23:45	ARI

MAR		
3	7:00	TAU
5	12:16	GEM
7	15:34	CAN
9	17:23	LEO
11	18:47	VIR
13	21:18	LIB
16	2:26	SCO
18	11:01	SAG
20	22:33	CAP
23	11:06	AQU
25	22:24	PIS
28	7:13	ARI
30	13:29	TAU

APR		
1	17:50	GEM
3	21:00	CAN
5	23:39	LEO
8	2:27	VIR
10	6:11	LIB
12	11:45	SCO
14	19:56	SAG
17	6:49	CAP
19	19:15	AQU
22	7:01	PIS
24	16:07	ARI
26	21:55	TAU
29	1:07	GEM

MAY		
1	3:02	CAN
3	5:02	LEO
5	8:08	VIR
7	12:52	LIB
9	19:26	SCO
12	4:02	SAG
14	14:46	CAP
17	3:05	AQU
19	15:21	PIS
22	1:22	ARI
24	7:40	TAU
26	10:27	GEM
28	11:10	CAN
30	11:42	LEO

JUN		
1	13:45	VIR
3	18:18	LIB
6	1:28	SCO
8	10:46	SAG
10	21:47	CAP
13	10:06	AQU
15	22:42	PIS
18	9:43	ARI
20	17:17	TAU
22	20:46	GEM
24	21:12	CAN
26	20:35	LEO
28	21:04	VIR

JUL		
1	0:19	LIB
3	6:58	SCO
5	16:31	SAG
8	3:56	CAP
10	16:21	AQU
13	5:00	PIS
15	16:36	ARI
18	1:28	TAU
20	6:26	GEM
22	7:47	CAN
24	7:06	LEO
26	6:33	VIR
28	8:13	LIB
30	13:27	SCO

AUG		
1	22:21	SAG
4	9:49	CAP
6	22:21	AQU
9	10:50	PIS
11	22:23	ARI
14	7:52	TAU
16	14:15	GEM
18	17:12	CAN
20	17:37	LEO
22	17:13	VIR
24	18:01	LIB
26	21:46	SCO
29	5:22	SAG
31	16:14	CAP

SEP		
3	4:45	AQU
5	17:07	PIS
8	4:12	ARI
10	13:22	TAU
12	20:11	GEM
15	0:27	CAN
17	2:30	LEO
19	3:20	VIR
21	4:28	LIB
23	7:33	SCO
25	13:53	SAG
27	23:45	CAP
30	11:59	AQU

OCT		
3	0:24	PIS
5	11:11	ARI
7	19:34	TAU
10	1:41	GEM
12	6:00	CAN
14	9:03	LEO
16	11:24	VIR
18	13:49	LIB
20	17:23	SCO
22	23:15	SAG
25	8:14	CAP
27	19:58	AQU
30	8:35	AQU

NOV		
1	19:37	ARI
4	3:36	TAU
6	8:39	GEM
8	11:50	CAN
10	14:24	LEO
12	17:16	VIR
14	20:55	LIB
17	1:42	SCO
19	8:06	SAG
21	16:50	CAP
24	4:09	AQU
26	16:55	PIS
29	4:42	ARI

DEC		
1	13:14	TAU
3	17:56	GEM
5	19:55	CAN
7	20:58	LEO
9	22:47	VIR
12	2:22	LIB
14	7:56	SCO
16	15:19	SAG
19	0:34	CAP
21	11:48	AQU
24	0:35	PIS
26	13:08	ARI
28	22:57	TAU
31	4:33	GEM

— 1904 —

JAN		
2	6:25	CAN
4	6:18	LEO
6	6:23	VIR
8	8:25	LIB
10	13:20	SCO
12	21:03	SAG
15	6:58	CAP
17	18:32	AQU
20	7:18	PIS
22	20:10	ARI
25	7:09	TAU
27	14:26	GEM
29	17:32	CAN
31	17:38	LEO

FEB		
2	16:45	VIR
4	17:01	LIB
6	20:08	SCO
9	2:49	SAG
11	12:41	CAP
14	0:37	AQU
16	13:27	PIS
19	2:10	ARI
21	13:31	TAU
23	22:05	GEM
26	3:00	CAN
28	4:36	LEO

MAR		
1	4:16	VIR
3	3:53	LIB
5	5:24	SCO
7	10:18	SAG
9	19:03	CAP
12	6:47	AQU
14	19:43	PIS
17	8:13	ARI
19	19:09	TAU
22	3:52	GEM
24	9:55	CAN
26	13:16	LEO
28	14:31	VIR
30	14:54	LIB

APR		
1	16:04	SCO
3	19:41	SAG
6	2:57	CAP
8	13:49	AQU
11	2:38	PIS
13	15:04	ARI
16	1:31	TAU
18	9:31	GEM
20	15:22	CAN
22	19:27	LEO
24	22:10	VIR
27	0:05	LIB
29	2:07	SCO

MAY		
1	5:36	SAG
3	11:58	CAP
5	21:50	AQU
8	10:17	PIS
10	22:51	ARI
13	9:12	TAU
15	16:30	GEM
17	21:21	CAN
20	0:50	LEO
22	3:49	VIR
24	6:48	LIB
26	10:08	SCO
28	14:29	SAG
30	20:53	CAP

JUN		
2	6:13	AQU
4	18:15	PIS
7	7:02	ARI
9	17:50	TAU
12	1:06	GEM
14	5:10	CAN
16	7:26	LEO
18	9:26	VIR
20	12:11	LIB
22	16:09	SCO
24	21:31	SAG
27	4:40	CAP
29	14:07	AQU

JUL		
2	1:58	PIS
4	14:55	ARI
7	2:29	TAU
9	10:32	GEM
11	14:41	CAN
13	16:10	LEO
15	16:48	VIR
17	18:14	LIB
19	21:34	SCO
22	3:10	SAG
24	11:01	CAP
26	21:01	AQU
29	8:58	PIS
31	21:59	ARI

AUG		
3	10:13	TAU
5	19:30	GEM
8	0:44	CAN
10	2:30	LEO
12	2:25	VIR
14	2:25	LIB
16	4:12	SCO
18	8:51	SAG
20	16:37	CAP
23	3:02	AQU
25	15:16	PIS
28	4:17	ARI
30	16:44	TAU

SEP		
2	2:59	GEM
4	9:46	CAN
6	12:53	LEO
8	13:18	VIR
10	12:44	LIB
12	13:05	SCO
14	16:05	SAG
16	22:45	CAP
19	8:55	AQU
21	21:20	PIS
24	10:20	ARI
26	22:33	TAU
29	8:59	GEM

OCT		
1	16:50	CAN
3	21:38	LEO
5	23:36	VIR
7	23:45	LIB
9	23:43	SCO
12	1:25	SAG
14	6:31	CAP
16	15:39	AQU
19	3:50	PIS
21	16:51	ARI
24	4:44	TAU
26	14:38	GEM
28	22:24	CAN
31	4:04	LEO

NOV		
2	7:40	VIR
4	9:27	LIB
6	10:20	SCO
8	11:54	SAG
10	15:56	CAP
12	23:47	AQU
15	11:14	PIS
18	0:14	ARI
20	12:06	TAU
22	1:25	GEM
25	4:17	CAN
27	9:26	LEO
29	13:27	VIR

DEC		
1	16:33	LIB
3	19:01	SCO
5	21:38	SAG
8	1:46	CAP
10	8:53	AQU
12	19:30	PIS
15	8:19	ARI
17	20:33	TAU
20	5:57	GEM
22	12:08	CAN
24	16:04	LEO
26	19:01	VIR
28	21:56	LIB
31	1:12	SCO

— 1905 —

JAN		
2	5:08	SAG
4	10:20	CAP
6	17:43	AQU
9	3:57	PIS
11	16:29	ARI
14	5:11	TAU
16	15:25	GEM
18	21:56	CAN
21	1:13	LEO
23	2:46	VIR
25	4:09	LIB
27	6:35	SCO
29	10:44	SAG
31	16:51	CAP

FEB		
3	1:08	AQU
5	11:39	PIS
8	0:03	ARI
10	13:00	TAU
13	0:17	GEM
15	8:05	CAN
17	12:00	LEO
19	13:05	VIR
21	13:03	LIB
23	13:42	SCO
25	16:31	SAG
27	22:19	CAP

MAR		
2	7:05	AQU
4	18:12	PIS
7	6:46	ARI
9	19:42	TAU
12	7:35	GEM
14	16:48	CAN
16	22:19	LEO
19	0:18	VIR
21	0:03	LIB
22	23:26	SCO
25	0:26	SAG
27	4:40	CAP
29	12:47	AQU

APR		
1	0:03	PIS
3	12:52	ARI
6	1:44	TAU
8	13:35	GEM
10	23:28	CAN
13	6:30	LEO
15	10:13	VIR
17	11:04	LIB
19	10:30	SCO
21	10:28	SAG
23	13:04	CAP
25	19:41	AQU
28	6:15	PIS
30	19:03	ARI

MAY		
3	7:52	TAU
5	19:21	GEM
8	5:01	CAN
10	12:34	LEO
12	17:40	VIR
14	20:12	LIB
16	20:50	SCO
18	21:05	SAG
20	22:56	CAP
23	4:12	AQU
25	13:34	PIS
28	1:53	ARI
30	14:41	TAU

JUN		
2	1:55	GEM
4	10:57	CAN
6	17:59	LEO
8	23:17	VIR
11	2:53	LIB
13	5:01	SCO
15	6:29	SAG
17	8:47	CAP
19	13:34	AQU
21	21:57	PIS
24	9:33	ARI
26	22:16	TAU
29	9:37	GEM

JUL		
1	18:17	CAN
4	0:27	LEO
6	4:53	VIR
8	8:16	LIB
10	11:04	SCO
12	13:46	SAG
14	17:12	CAP
16	22:29	AQU
19	6:36	PIS
21	17:39	ARI
24	6:16	TAU
26	18:01	GEM
29	3:00	CAN
31	8:47	LEO

AUG		
2	12:09	VIR
4	14:20	LIB
6	16:28	SCO
8	19:24	SAG
10	23:45	CAP
13	6:00	AQU
15	14:34	PIS
18	1:30	ARI
20	14:02	TAU
23	2:18	GEM
25	12:12	CAN
27	18:31	LEO
29	21:32	VIR
31	22:33	LIB

SEP		
2	23:12	SCO
5	1:04	SAG
7	5:13	CAP
9	12:02	AQU
11	21:20	PIS
14	8:35	ARI
16	21:05	TAU
19	9:40	GEM
21	20:37	CAN
24	4:17	LEO
26	8:07	VIR
28	8:54	LIB
30	8:22	SCO

OCT		
2	8:35	SAG
4	11:20	CAP
6	17:36	AQU
9	3:09	PIS
11	14:49	ARI
14	3:25	TAU
16	15:59	GEM
19	3:29	CAN
21	12:33	LEO
23	18:03	VIR
25	19:55	LIB
27	19:24	SCO
29	18:34	SAG
31	19:37	CAP

NOV		
3	0:19	AQU
5	9:06	PIS
7	20:48	ARI
10	9:32	TAU
12	21:54	GEM
15	9:14	CAN
17	18:50	LEO
20	1:47	VIR
22	5:29	LIB
24	6:18	SCO
26	5:47	SAG
28	6:03	CAP
30	9:11	AQU

DEC		
2	16:26	PIS
5	3:24	ARI
7	16:06	TAU
10	4:25	GEM
12	15:14	CAN
15	0:19	LEO
17	7:30	VIR
19	12:25	LIB
21	15:01	SCO
23	16:00	SAG
25	16:53	CAP
27	19:32	AQU
30	1:30	PIS

— 1906 —

JAN		
1	11:16	ARI
3	23:33	TAU
6	11:58	GEM
8	22:38	CAN
11	6:57	LEO
13	13:11	VIR
15	17:48	LIB
17	21:08	SCO
19	23:36	SAG
22	1:59	CAP
24	5:26	AQU
26	11:13	PIS
28	20:06	ARI
31	7:45	TAU

FEB		
2	20:17	GEM
5	7:21	CAN
7	15:32	LEO
9	20:50	VIR
12	0:08	LIB
14	2:34	SCO
16	5:08	SAG
18	8:32	CAP
20	13:17	AQU
22	19:52	PIS
25	4:45	ARI
27	15:58	TAU

MAR		
2	4:31	GEM
4	16:19	CAN
7	1:16	LEO
9	6:34	VIR
11	8:53	LIB
13	9:48	SCO
15	11:01	SAG
17	13:54	CAP
19	19:07	AQU
22	2:38	PIS
24	12:10	ARI
26	23:27	TAU
29	11:58	GEM

APR		
1	0:20	CAN
3	10:31	LEO
5	16:53	VIR
7	19:26	LIB
9	19:29	SCO
11	19:08	SAG
13	20:23	CAP
16	0:39	AQU
18	8:10	PIS
20	18:15	ARI
23	5:56	TAU
25	18:28	GEM
28	7:02	CAN
30	18:09	LEO

MAY		
3	2:03	VIR
5	5:53	LIB
7	6:23	SCO
9	5:25	SAG
11	5:12	CAP
13	7:45	AQU
15	14:06	PIS
17	23:54	ARI
20	11:49	TAU
23	0:27	GEM
25	12:54	CAN
28	0:14	LEO
30	9:11	VIR

JUN		
1	14:38	LIB
3	16:35	SCO
5	16:15	SAG
7	15:40	CAP
9	16:56	AQU
11	21:40	PIS
14	6:21	ARI
16	17:55	TAU
19	6:35	GEM
21	18:51	CAN
24	5:50	LEO
26	14:50	VIR
28	21:13	LIB

JUL		
1	0:43	SCO
3	1:53	SAG
5	2:06	CAP
7	3:12	AQU
9	6:52	PIS
11	14:12	ARI
14	0:55	TAU
16	13:25	GEM
19	1:38	CAN
21	12:09	LEO
23	20:29	VIR
26	2:38	LIB
28	6:46	SCO
30	9:17	CAP

AUG		
1	10:58	CAP
3	12:57	AQU
5	16:37	PIS
7	23:07	ARI
10	8:55	TAU
12	21:03	GEM
15	9:23	CAN
17	19:50	LEO
20	3:31	VIR
22	8:40	LIB
24	12:10	SCO
26	14:55	SAG
28	17:39	CAP
30	20:56	AQU

SEP		
2	1:28	PIS
4	8:04	ARI
6	17:21	TAU
9	5:05	GEM
11	17:40	CAN
14	4:37	LEO
16	12:18	VIR
18	16:39	LIB
20	18:53	SCO
22	20:35	SAG
24	23:02	CAP
27	2:58	AQU
29	8:34	PIS

OCT		
1	15:56	ARI
4	1:21	TAU
6	12:53	GEM
9	1:38	CAN
11	13:27	LEO
13	22:02	VIR
16	2:34	LIB
18	4:00	SCO
20	4:14	SAG
22	5:14	CAP
24	8:24	AQU
26	14:11	PIS
28	22:18	ARI
31	8:18	TAU

NOV		
2	19:56	GEM
5	8:44	CAN
7	21:13	LEO
10	7:10	VIR
12	13:00	LIB
14	14:54	SCO
16	14:29	SAG
18	13:58	CAP
20	15:23	AQU
22	19:59	PIS
25	3:53	ARI
27	14:18	TAU
30	2:16	GEM

DEC		
2	15:01	CAN
5	3:37	LEO
7	14:30	VIR
9	22:00	LIB
12	1:31	SCO
14	1:55	SAG
16	1:02	CAP
18	1:03	AQU
20	3:48	PIS
22	10:17	ARI
24	20:15	TAU
27	8:23	GEM
29	21:11	CAN

— 1907 —

JAN			FEB			MAR			APR		
1	9:29	LEO	2	10:10	LIB	1	16:31	LIB	2	6:59	SAG
3	20:19	VIR	4	15:55	SCO	3	21:26	SCO	4	9:24	CAP
6	4:41	LIB	6	19:34	SAG	6	1:04	SAG	6	12:35	AQU
8	9:55	SCO	8	21:35	AQU	8	4:04	CAP	8	16:47	PIS
10	12:07	SAG	10	22:51	CAP	10	6:50	AQU	10	22:16	ARI
12	12:21	CAP	13	0:41	PIS	12	9:56	PIS	13	5:36	TAU
14	12:20	AQU	15	4:39	ARI	14	14:20	ARI	15	15:24	GEM
16	13:55	PIS	17	11:58	TAU	16	21:10	TAU	18	3:34	CAN
18	18:42	ARI	19	22:46	GEM	19	7:10	GEM	20	16:25	LEO
21	3:21	TAU	22	11:31	CAN	21	19:36	CAN	23	3:17	VIR
23	15:04	GEM	24	23:41	LEO	24	8:07	LEO	25	10:22	LIB
26	3:56	CAN	27	9:29	VIR	26	18:11	VIR	27	13:47	SCO
28	16:00	LEO				29	0:46	LIB	29	15:02	SAG
31	2:12	VIR				31	4:33	SCO			

MAY			JUN			JUL			AUG		
1	15:59	CAP	2	4:10	PIS	1	16:14	ARI	2	16:56	GEM
3	18:07	AQU	4	9:47	ARI	3	23:56	TAU	5	5:27	CAN
5	22:12	PIS	6	18:12	TAU	6	10:41	GEM	7	18:26	LEO
8	4:20	ARI	9	4:55	GEM	8	23:16	CAN	10	6:17	VIR
10	12:29	TAU	11	17:16	CAN	11	12:18	LEO	12	16:07	LIB
12	22:41	GEM	14	6:21	LEO	14	0:29	VIR	14	23:35	SCO
15	10:50	CAN	16	18:35	VIR	16	10:35	LIB	17	4:32	SAG
17	23:53	LEO	19	4:05	LIB	18	17:34	SCO	19	7:05	CAP
20	11:37	VIR	21	9:43	SCO	20	21:11	SAG	21	8:00	AQU
22	19:54	LIB	23	11:42	SAG	22	22:06	CAP	23	8:33	PIS
25	0:03	SCO	25	11:30	CAP	24	21:46	AQU	25	10:28	ARI
27	1:05	SAG	27	11:00	AQU	26	22:00	PIS	27	15:26	TAU
29	0:54	CAP	29	12:07	PIS	29	0:37	ARI	30	0:19	GEM
31	1:26	AQU				31	6:53	TAU			

SEP			OCT			NOV			DEC		
1	12:22	CAN	1	9:05	LEO	2	14:43	LIB	2	6:35	SCO
4	1:20	LEO	3	20:49	VIR	4	20:23	SCO	4	9:28	SAG
6	12:56	VIR	6	5:40	LIB	6	23:25	SAG	6	10:18	CAP
8	22:07	LIB	8	11:38	SCO	9	1:24	CAP	12	16:49	AQU
11	5:01	SCO	10	15:47	SAG	11	3:38	AQU	14	23:24	PIS
13	10:07	SAG	12	19:07	CAP	13	6:52	PIS	17	8:25	ARI
15	13:46	CAP	14	22:13	AQU	15	11:24	ARI	19	19:31	TAU
17	16:12	AQU	17	1:20	PIS	17	17:31	TAU	22	8:09	GEM
19	18:02	PIS	19	4:57	ARI	20	1:43	GEM	24	21:06	CAN
21	20:25	ARI	21	10:00	TAU	22	12:24	CAN	27	8:27	LEO
24	0:55	TAU	23	17:39	GEM	25	1:04	LEO	29	10:26	VIR
26	8:49	GEM	26	4:25	CAN	27	13:50	VIR	31	20:28	LIB
28	20:09	CAN	28	17:14	LEO	30	0:09	LIB			
			31	5:28	VIR						

— 1908 —

JAN			FEB			MAR			APR		
2	21:25	CAP	1	8:32	AQU	1	19:05	PIS	2	8:04	TAU
4	20:58	AQU	3	7:50	PIS	3	19:20	ARI	4	13:26	GEM
6	21:03	PIS	5	8:31	ARI	5	21:50	TAU	6	22:43	CAN
8	23:24	ARI	7	12:24	TAU	8	4:13	GEM	9	10:58	LEO
11	5:05	TAU	9	20:23	GEM	10	14:39	CAN	11	23:41	VIR
13	14:10	GEM	12	7:48	CAN	13	3:28	LEO	14	10:33	LIB
16	1:45	CAN	14	20:47	LEO	15	16:09	VIR	16	18:44	SCO
18	14:33	LEO	17	9:28	VIR	18	3:04	LIB	19	0:41	SAG
21	3:23	VIR	19	20:48	LIB	20	11:52	SCO	21	5:10	CAP
23	15:03	LIB	22	6:14	SCO	22	18:45	SAG	23	8:40	AQU
26	0:17	SCO	24	13:15	SAG	24	23:48	CAP	25	11:25	PIS
28	6:08	SAG	26	17:29	CAP	27	2:57	AQU	27	13:57	ARI
30	8:33	CAP	28	19:04	AQU	29	4:33	PIS	29	17:16	TAU
						31	5:41	ARI			

MAY			JUN			JUL			AUG		
1	22:44	GEM	3	2:59	LEO	2	22:58	VIR	1	17:56	LIB
4	7:23	CAN	5	15:42	VIR	5	11:20	LIB	4	4:53	SCO
6	19:01	LEO	8	3:34	LIB	7	21:23	SCO	6	12:47	SAG
9	7:46	VIR	10	12:30	SCO	10	3:49	SAG	8	16:57	CAP
11	19:00	LIB	12	17:52	SAG	12	6:40	CAP	10	17:53	AQU
14	3:12	SCO	14	20:25	CAP	14	7:07	AQU	12	17:09	PIS
16	8:26	SAG	16	21:35	AQU	16	6:58	PIS	14	16:50	ARI
18	11:44	CAP	18	22:51	PIS	18	8:02	ARI	16	18:56	TAU
20	14:15	AQU	21	1:27	ARI	20	11:46	TAU	19	0:48	GEM
22	16:49	PIS	23	6:10	TAU	22	18:48	GEM	21	10:26	CAN
24	20:04	ARI	25	13:16	GEM	25	4:45	CAN	23	22:32	LEO
27	0:30	TAU	27	22:44	CAN	27	16:38	LEO	26	11:23	VIR
29	6:48	GEM	30	10:14	LEO	30	5:24	VIR	28	23:47	LIB
31	15:38	CAN							31	10:56	SCO

SEP			OCT			NOV			DEC		
2	19:52	SAG	2	8:13	CAP	2	21:10	PIS	2	5:26	ARI
5	1:40	CAP	4	12:16	CAP	4	22:58	ARI	4	8:37	TAU
7	4:06	AQU	6	13:50	PIS	7	0:43	TAU	6	13:01	GEM
9	4:04	PIS	8	14:01	ARI	9	4:01	GEM	8	19:33	CAN
11	3:22	ARI	10	14:43	TAU	11	10:18	CAN	11	4:52	LEO
13	4:11	TAU	12	17:55	GEM	13	20:07	LEO	13	16:39	VIR
15	8:28	GEM	15	1:00	CAN	16	8:23	VIR	16	5:12	LIB
17	16:57	CAN	17	11:51	LEO	18	20:44	LIB	18	16:12	SCO
20	4:42	LEO	20	0:33	VIR	21	7:04	SCO	21	0:02	SAG
22	17:35	VIR	22	12:43	LIB	23	14:39	SAG	23	4:38	CAP
25	5:46	LIB	24	22:59	SCO	25	19:55	CAP	25	7:01	AQU
27	16:31	SCO	27	7:12	SAG	27	23:40	AQU	27	8:38	PIS
30	1:28	SAG	29	13:34	CAP	30	2:39	PIS	29	10:48	ARI
			31	18:12	AQU				31	14:24	TAU

— 1909 —

JAN
2	19:54	GEM
5	3:25	CAN
7	13:01	LEO
10	0:34	VIR
12	13:11	LIB
15	1:02	SCO
17	10:02	SAG
19	15:09	CAP
21	17:00	AQU
23	17:09	PIS
25	17:36	ARI
27	20:02	TAU
30	1:22	GEM

FEB
1	9:32	CAN
3	19:50	LEO
6	7:36	VIR
8	20:10	LIB
11	8:30	SCO
13	18:48	SAG
16	1:28	CAP
18	4:08	AQU
20	4:00	PIS
22	3:08	ARI
24	3:45	TAU
26	7:33	GEM
28	15:08	CAN

MAR
3	1:41	LEO
5	13:48	VIR
8	2:23	LIB
10	14:41	SCO
13	1:37	SAG
15	9:46	CAP
17	14:09	AQU
19	15:08	PIS
21	14:17	ARI
23	13:50	TAU
25	15:55	GEM
27	21:55	CAN
30	7:44	LEO

APR
1	19:51	VIR
4	8:31	LIB
6	20:33	SCO
9	7:17	SAG
11	15:57	CAP
13	21:44	AQU
16	0:26	PIS
18	0:51	ARI
20	0:43	TAU
22	2:03	GEM
24	6:35	CAN
26	15:02	LEO
29	2:33	VIR

MAY
1	15:11	LIB
4	3:05	SCO
6	13:16	SAG
8	21:26	CAP
11	3:26	AQU
13	7:14	PIS
15	9:13	ARI
17	10:24	TAU
19	12:13	GEM
21	16:15	CAN
23	23:36	LEO
26	10:14	VIR
28	22:39	LIB
31	10:38	SCO

JUN
2	20:32	SAG
5	3:54	CAP
7	9:04	AQU
9	12:40	PIS
11	15:22	ARI
13	17:50	TAU
15	20:53	GEM
18	1:28	CAN
20	8:32	LEO
22	18:29	VIR
25	6:36	LIB
27	18:52	SCO
30	5:03	SAG

JUL
2	12:04	CAP
4	16:14	AQU
6	18:41	PIS
8	20:45	ARI
10	23:29	TAU
13	3:30	GEM
15	9:08	CAN
17	16:42	LEO
20	2:32	VIR
22	14:26	LIB
25	3:01	SCO
27	14:00	SAG
29	21:32	CAP

AUG
1	1:22	AQU
3	2:42	PIS
5	3:22	ARI
7	5:05	TAU
9	8:55	GEM
11	15:08	CAN
13	23:29	LEO
16	9:42	VIR
18	21:36	LIB
21	10:24	SCO
23	22:17	SAG
26	7:02	CAP
28	11:37	AQU
30	12:45	PIS

SEP
1	12:19	ARI
3	12:27	TAU
5	14:55	GEM
7	20:35	CAN
10	5:12	LEO
12	15:55	VIR
15	4:00	LIB
17	16:50	SCO
20	5:11	SAG
22	15:13	CAP
24	21:22	AQU
26	23:32	PIS
28	23:07	ARI
30	22:14	TAU

OCT
2	23:04	GEM
5	3:10	CAN
7	10:58	LEO
9	21:42	VIR
12	10:01	LIB
14	22:47	SCO
17	11:02	SAG
19	21:37	CAP
22	5:13	AQU
24	9:09	PIS
26	10:02	ARI
28	9:27	TAU
30	9:27	GEM

NOV
1	11:57	CAN
3	18:10	LEO
6	4:04	VIR
8	16:19	LIB
11	5:04	SCO
13	16:58	SAG
16	3:09	CAP
18	11:05	AQU
20	16:20	PIS
22	19:02	ARI
24	19:57	TAU
26	20:31	GEM
28	22:27	CAN

DEC
1	3:17	LEO
3	11:50	VIR
5	23:30	LIB
8	12:17	SCO
11	0:01	SAG
13	9:31	CAP
15	16:39	CAP
17	21:48	PIS
20	1:25	ARI
22	3:57	TAU
24	6:05	GEM
26	8:46	CAN
28	13:17	LEO
30	20:50	VIR

— 1910 —

JAN		
2	7:38	LIB
4	20:19	SCO
7	8:20	SAG
9	17:40	CAP
11	23:53	AQU
14	3:51	PIS
16	6:46	ARI
18	9:39	TAU
20	12:58	GEM
22	17:03	CAN
24	22:24	LEO
27	5:52	VIR
29	16:05	LIB

FEB		
1	4:33	SCO
3	17:05	SAG
6	3:04	CAP
8	9:14	AQU
10	12:13	PIS
12	13:41	ARI
14	15:20	TAU
16	18:19	GEM
18	23:03	CAN
21	5:29	LEO
23	13:41	VIR
25	23:59	LIB
28	12:16	SCO

MAR		
3	1:10	SAG
5	12:12	CAP
7	19:23	AQU
9	22:33	PIS
11	23:10	ARI
13	23:15	TAU
16	0:39	GEM
18	4:31	CAN
20	11:04	LEO
22	19:57	VIR
25	6:46	LIB
27	19:07	SCO
30	8:06	SAG

APR		
1	19:56	CAP
4	4:32	AQU
6	9:01	PIS
8	10:05	ARI
10	9:33	TAU
12	9:27	GEM
14	11:34	CAN
16	16:56	LEO
19	1:35	VIR
21	12:44	LIB
24	1:19	SCO
26	14:14	SAG
29	2:12	CAP

MAY		
1	11:46	AQU
3	17:51	PIS
5	20:24	ARI
7	20:33	TAU
9	20:03	GEM
11	20:50	CAN
14	0:32	LEO
16	7:58	VIR
18	18:46	LIB
21	7:27	SCO
23	20:17	SAG
26	7:57	CAP
28	17:33	AQU
31	0:31	PIS

JUN		
2	4:38	ARI
4	6:19	TAU
6	6:40	GEM
8	7:16	CAN
10	9:52	LEO
12	15:52	VIR
15	1:42	LIB
17	14:08	SCO
20	2:57	SAG
22	14:15	CAP
24	23:15	AQU
27	5:59	PIS
29	10:44	ARI

JUL		
1	13:48	TAU
3	15:38	GEM
5	17:09	CAN
7	19:44	LEO
10	0:55	VIR
12	9:41	LIB
14	21:35	SCO
17	10:26	SAG
19	21:41	CAP
22	6:06	AQU
24	11:57	PIS
26	16:08	ARI
28	19:27	TAU
30	22:21	GEM

AUG		
2	1:11	CAN
4	4:40	LEO
6	9:58	VIR
8	18:13	LIB
11	5:34	SCO
13	18:27	SAG
16	6:05	CAP
18	14:31	AQU
20	19:40	PIS
22	22:42	ARI
25	1:02	TAU
27	3:44	GEM
29	7:14	CAN
31	11:49	LEO

SEP		
2	17:57	VIR
5	2:22	LIB
7	13:29	SCO
10	2:22	SAG
12	14:39	CAP
14	23:53	AQU
17	5:12	PIS
19	7:30	ARI
21	8:29	TAU
23	9:49	GEM
25	12:37	CAN
27	17:26	LEO
30	0:22	VIR

OCT		
2	9:29	LIB
4	20:45	SCO
7	9:37	SAG
9	22:26	CAP
12	8:51	AQU
14	15:22	PIS
16	18:06	ARI
18	18:27	TAU
20	18:18	GEM
22	19:26	CAN
24	23:08	LEO
27	5:54	VIR
29	15:30	LIB

NOV		
1	3:12	SCO
3	16:06	SAG
6	5:01	CAP
8	16:19	AQU
11	0:26	PIS
13	4:43	ARI
15	5:47	TAU
17	5:12	GEM
19	4:53	CAN
21	6:45	LEO
23	12:08	VIR
25	21:17	LIB
28	9:13	SCO
30	22:15	SAG

DEC		
3	10:57	CAP
5	22:17	AQU
8	7:20	PIS
10	13:22	ARI
12	16:14	TAU
14	16:39	GEM
16	16:12	CAN
18	16:48	LEO
20	20:25	VIR
23	4:10	LIB
25	15:36	SCO
28	4:41	SAG
30	17:14	CAP

—1911—

JAN			FEB			MAR			APR		
2	4:02	AQU	3	0:58	ARI	2	7:49	ARI	2	20:49	GEM
4	12:50	PIS	5	5:36	TAU	4	11:22	TAU	4	22:53	CAN
6	19:33	ARI	7	9:03	GEM	6	14:23	GEM	7	2:15	LEO
9	0:01	TAU	9	11:28	CAN	8	17:24	CAN	9	7:23	VIR
11	2:17	GEM	11	13:33	LEO	10	20:45	LEO	11	14:36	LIB
13	3:03	CAN	13	16:39	VIR	13	1:05	VIR	14	0:07	SCO
15	3:50	LEO	15	22:22	LIB	15	7:19	LIB	16	11:46	SAG
17	6:31	VIR	18	7:39	SCO	17	16:21	SCO	19	0:34	CAN
19	12:47	LIB	20	19:53	SAG	20	4:05	SAG	21	12:33	AQU
21	23:06	SCO	23	8:38	CAN	22	16:54	CAN	23	21:41	PIS
24	11:54	SAG	25	19:18	AQU	25	4:13	AQU	26	3:03	ARI
27	0:30	CAN	28	2:51	PIS	27	12:14	PIS	28	5:13	TAU
29	10:57	AQU				29	16:52	ARI	30	5:39	GEM
31	18:55	PIS				31	19:14	TAU			

MAY			JUN			JUL			AUG		
2	6:07	CAN	2	19:14	VIR	2	8:59	LIB	1	1:44	SCO
4	8:09	LEO	5	2:07	LIB	4	18:27	SCO	3	13:21	SAG
6	12:50	VIR	7	12:21	SCO	7	6:39	SAG	6	2:10	CAN
8	20:26	LIB	10	0:37	SAG	9	19:32	CAN	8	14:02	AQU
11	6:36	SCO	12	13:28	CAN	12	7:34	AQU	11	0:01	PIS
13	18:33	SAG	15	1:44	AQU	14	18:04	PIS	13	8:02	ARI
16	7:21	CAN	17	12:27	PIS	17	2:35	ARI	15	14:12	TAU
18	19:40	AQU	19	20:32	ARI	19	8:34	TAU	17	18:24	GEM
21	5:53	PIS	22	1:14	TAU	21	11:42	GEM	19	20:43	CAN
23	12:41	ARI	24	2:46	GEM	23	12:30	CAN	21	21:54	LEO
25	15:48	TAU	26	2:20	CAN	25	12:25	LEO	23	23:26	VIR
27	16:12	GEM	28	1:54	LEO	27	13:26	VIR	26	3:06	LIB
29	15:37	CAN	30	3:35	VIR	29	17:32	LIB	28	10:16	SCO
31	16:03	LEO							30	21:01	SAG

SEP			OCT			NOV			DEC		
2	9:37	CAN	2	5:56	AQU	1	1:12	PIS	2	23:43	TAU
4	21:35	AQU	4	16:00	PIS	3	8:49	ARI	5	1:18	GEM
7	7:17	PIS	6	22:56	ARI	5	12:54	TAU	7	0:55	CAN
9	14:31	ARI	9	3:13	TAU	7	14:29	GEM	9	0:39	LEO
11	19:49	TAU	11	5:56	GEM	9	15:11	CAN	11	2:27	VIR
13	23:47	GEM	13	8:12	CAN	11	16:39	LEO	13	7:36	LIB
16	2:48	CAN	15	10:55	LEO	13	20:06	VIR	15	16:09	SCO
18	5:18	LEO	17	14:42	VIR	16	2:04	LIB	18	3:08	SAG
20	8:05	VIR	19	20:05	LIB	18	10:28	SCO	20	15:24	CAN
22	12:22	LIB	22	3:37	SCO	20	20:54	SAG	23	4:06	AQU
24	19:17	SCO	24	13:34	SAG	23	8:55	CAN	25	16:18	PIS
27	5:21	SAG	27	1:37	CAN	25	21:40	AQU	28	2:37	ARI
29	17:39	CAN	29	14:14	AQU	28	9:32	PIS	30	9:31	TAU
						30	18:36	ARI			

—1912—

JAN
1	12:29	GEM
3	12:25	CAN
5	11:17	LEO
7	11:23	VIR
9	14:42	LIB
11	22:07	SCO
14	8:57	SAG
16	21:28	CAN
19	10:07	AQU
21	22:06	PIS
24	8:41	ARI
26	16:52	TAU
28	21:42	GEM
30	23:15	CAN

FEB
1	22:47	LEO
3	22:23	VIR
6	0:13	LIB
8	5:53	SCO
10	15:36	SAG
13	3:52	CAN
15	16:34	AQU
18	4:13	PIS
20	14:17	ARI
22	22:26	TAU
25	4:15	GEM
27	7:30	CAN
29	8:43	LEO

MAR
2	9:14	VIR
4	10:54	LIB
6	15:25	SCO
8	23:44	SAG
11	11:12	CAN
13	23:50	AQU
16	11:28	PIS
18	20:59	ARI
21	4:16	TAU
23	9:37	GEM
25	13:22	CAN
27	15:54	LEO
29	17:59	VIR
31	20:40	LIB

APR
3	1:16	SCO
5	8:48	SAG
7	19:24	CAN
10	7:48	AQU
12	19:42	PIS
15	5:15	ARI
17	11:51	TAU
19	16:03	GEM
21	18:53	CAN
23	21:22	LEO
26	0:18	VIR
28	4:15	LIB
30	9:48	SCO

MAY
2	17:30	SAG
5	3:42	CAN
7	15:50	AQU
10	4:08	PIS
12	14:20	ARI
14	21:04	TAU
17	0:33	GEM
19	2:04	CAN
21	3:18	LEO
23	5:41	VIR
25	10:00	LIB
27	16:27	SCO
30	0:54	SAG

JUN
1	11:17	CAN
3	23:19	AQU
6	11:55	PIS
8	23:03	ARI
11	6:47	TAU
13	10:33	GEM
15	11:24	CAN
17	11:16	LEO
19	12:09	VIR
21	15:33	LIB
23	21:58	SCO
26	6:58	SAG
28	17:50	CAN

JUL
1	5:58	AQU
3	18:40	PIS
6	6:30	ARI
8	15:33	TAU
10	20:34	GEM
12	21:55	CAN
14	21:16	LEO
16	20:49	VIR
18	22:37	LIB
21	3:52	SCO
23	12:34	SAG
25	23:41	CAN
28	12:01	AQU
31	0:40	PIS

AUG
2	12:40	ARI
4	22:37	TAU
7	5:10	GEM
9	7:57	CAN
11	8:00	LEO
13	7:14	VIR
15	7:48	LIB
17	11:28	SCO
19	18:59	SAG
22	5:43	CAN
24	18:07	AQU
27	6:40	PIS
29	18:21	ARI

SEP
1	4:20	TAU
3	11:45	GEM
5	16:06	CAN
7	17:43	LEO
9	17:51	VIR
11	18:18	LIB
13	20:54	SCO
16	2:59	SAG
18	12:43	CAN
21	0:52	AQU
23	13:25	PIS
26	0:45	ARI
28	10:04	TAU
30	17:12	GEM

OCT
2	22:09	CAN
5	1:11	LEO
7	2:55	VIR
9	4:25	LIB
11	7:05	SCO
13	12:19	SAG
15	20:56	CAN
18	8:31	AQU
20	21:08	PIS
23	8:29	ARI
25	17:15	TAU
27	23:23	GEM
30	3:36	CAN

NOV
1	6:46	LEO
3	9:34	VIR
5	12:32	LIB
7	16:17	SCO
9	21:44	SAG
12	5:48	CAN
14	16:45	AQU
17	5:24	PIS
19	17:17	ARI
22	2:13	TAU
24	7:41	GEM
26	10:37	CAN
28	12:34	LEO
30	14:55	VIR

DEC
2	18:26	LIB
4	23:22	SCO
7	5:48	SAG
9	14:10	CAN
12	0:51	AQU
14	13:26	PIS
17	2:00	ARI
19	11:57	TAU
21	17:51	GEM
23	20:11	CAN
25	20:44	LEO
27	21:27	VIR
29	23:56	LIB

—1913—

JAN
1	4:50	SCO
3	12:02	SAG
5	21:10	CAN
8	8:07	AQU
10	20:39	PIS
13	9:36	ARI
15	20:46	TAU
18	4:07	GEM
20	7:14	CAN
22	7:26	LEO
24	6:48	VIR
26	7:26	LIB
28	10:50	SCO
30	17:30	SAG

FEB
2	2:59	CAN
4	14:25	AQU
7	3:03	PIS
9	16:00	ARI
12	3:47	TAU
14	12:38	GEM
16	17:29	CAN
18	18:47	LEO
20	18:08	VIR
22	17:37	LIB
24	19:11	SCO
27	0:11	SAG

MAR
1	8:52	CAN
3	20:22	AQU
6	9 :10	PIS
8	21:57	ARI
11	9:35	TAU
13	19:00	GEM
16	1:21	CAN
18	4:28	LEO
20	5:08	VIR
22	4:55	LIB
24	5:37	SCO
26	9:00	SAG
28	16:09	CAN
31	2:54	AQU

APR
2	15:39	PIS
5	4:22	ARI
7	15:32	TAU
10	0:31	GEM
12	7:09	CAN
14	11:31	LEO
16	13:53	VIR
18	15:03	LIB
20	16:14	SCO
22	19:03	SAG
25	0:56	CAN
27	10:33	AQU
29	22:54	PIS

MAY
2	11:39	ARI
4	22:35	TAU
7	6:50	GEM
9	12:43	CAN
11	16:58	LEO
13	20:10	VIR
15	22:44	LIB
18	1:15	SCO
20	4:38	SAG
22	10:13	CAN
24	19:00	AQU
27	6:47	PIS
29	19:36	ARI

JUN
1	6:46	TAU
3	14:43	GEM
5	19:41	CAN
7	22:52	LEO
10	1:31	VIR
12	4:27	LIB
14	8:01	SCO
16	12:31	SAG
18	18:41	CAN
21	3:21	AQU
23	14:46	PIS
26	3:38	ARI
28	15:23	TAU
30	23:47	GEM

JUL
3	4:30	CAN
5	6:40	LEO
7	8:01	VIR
9	10:00	LIB
11	13:26	SCO
13	18:37	SAG
16	1:39	CAN
18	10:48	AQU
20	22:13	PIS
23	11:07	ARI
25	23:30	TAU
28	8:58	GEM
30	14:23	CAN

AUG
1	16:25	LEO
3	16:44	VIR
5	17:13	LIB
7	19:23	SCO
10	0:03	SAG
12	7:25	CAN
14	17:10	AQU
17	4:52	PIS
19	17:47	ARI
22	6:31	TAU
24	17:03	GEM
26	23:54	CAN
29	2:55	LEO
31	3:16	VIR

SEP
2	2:47	LIB
4	3:21	SCO
6	6:32	SAG
8	13:07	CAN
10	22:56	AQU
13	10:58	PIS
15	23:56	ARI
18	12:34	TAU
20	23:35	GEM
23	7:45	CAN
25	12:27	LEO
27	14:02	VIR
29	13:47	LIB

OCT
1	13:31	SCO
3	15:08	SAG
5	20:11	CAN
8	5:09	AQU
10	17:07	PIS
13	6:09	ARI
15	18:31	TAU
18	5:13	GEM
20	13:45	CAN
22	19:45	LEO
24	23:07	VIR
27	0:18	LIB
29	0:30	SCO
31	1:30	SAG

NOV
2	5:09	CAN
4	12:44	AQU
7	0:02	PIS
9	13:02	ARI
12	1:17	TAU
14	11:24	GEM
16	19:17	CAN
19	1:18	LEO
21	5:40	VIR
23	8:30	LIB
25	10:13	SCO
27	11:54	SAG
29	15:12	CAN

DEC
1	21:43	AQU
4	8:01	PIS
6	20:46	ARI
9	9:12	TAU
11	19:09	GEM
14	2:12	CAN
16	7:09	LEO
18	11:00	VIR
20	14:19	LIB
22	17:21	SCO
24	20:28	SAG
27	0:36	CAN
29	7:01	AQU
31	16:38	PIS

—1914—

JAN		
3	4:58	ARI
5	17:44	TAU
8	4:13	GEM
10	11:12	CAN
12	15:13	LEO
14	17:40	VIR
16	19:53	LIB
18	22:44	SCO
21	2:40	SAG
23	7:59	CAN
25	15:13	AQU
28	0:54	PIS
30	12:57	ARI

FEB		
2	1:55	TAU
4	13:20	GEM
6	21:16	CAN
9	1:27	LEO
11	3:00	VIR
13	3:37	LIB
15	4:55	SCO
17	8:04	SAG
19	13:38	CAN
21	21:41	AQU
24	8:01	PIS
26	20:09	ARI

MAR		
1	9:08	TAU
3	21:15	GEM
6	6:34	CAN
8	12:03	LEO
10	14:02	VIR
12	13:57	LIB
14	13:40	SCO
16	15:01	SAG
18	19:23	CAN
21	3:15	AQU
23	14:01	PIS
26	2:30	ARI
28	15:27	TAU
31	3:42	GEM

APR		
2	13:59	CAN
4	21:06	LEO
7	0:37	VIR
9	1:12	LIB
11	0:27	SCO
13	0:23	SAG
15	2:59	CAN
17	9:31	AQU
19	19:53	PIS
22	8:30	ARI
24	21:28	TAU
27	9:29	GEM
29	19:50	CAN

MAY		
2	3:53	LEO
4	9:02	VIR
6	11:14	LIB
8	11:20	SCO
10	11:04	SAG
12	12:31	CAN
14	17:29	AQU
17	2:40	PIS
19	14:54	ARI
22	3:52	TAU
24	15:37	GEM
27	1:28	CAN
29	9:22	LEO
31	15:13	VIR

JUN		
2	18:51	LIB
4	20:30	SCO
6	21:13	SAG
8	22:41	CAN
11	2:47	AQU
13	10:45	PIS
15	22:12	ARI
18	11:01	TAU
20	22:44	GEM
23	8:07	CAN
25	15:14	LEO
27	20:35	VIR
30	0:33	LIB

JUL		
2	3:20	SCO
4	5:26	SAG
6	7:54	CAN
8	12:11	AQU
10	19:33	PIS
13	6:15	ARI
15	18:49	TAU
18	6:47	GEM
20	16:12	CAN
22	22:43	LEO
25	3:01	VIR
27	6:05	LIB
29	8:45	SCO
31	11:36	SAG

AUG		
2	15:14	CAN
4	20:27	AQU
7	4:04	PIS
9	14:25	ARI
12	2:46	TAU
14	15:07	GEM
17	1:11	CAN
19	7:52	LEO
21	11:30	VIR
23	13:19	LIB
25	14:44	SCO
27	17:00	SAG
29	20:58	CAN

SEP		
1	3:04	AQU
3	11:26	PIS
5	22:00	ARI
8	10:15	TAU
10	22:54	GEM
13	9:56	CAN
15	17:41	LEO
17	21:42	VIR
19	22:52	LIB
21	22:53	SCO
23	23:36	SAG
26	2:35	CAN
28	8:37	AQU
30	17:33	PIS

OCT		
3	4:38	ARI
5	16:58	TAU
8	5:40	GEM
10	17:26	CAN
13	2:37	LEO
15	8:02	VIR
17	9:49	LIB
19	9:21	SCO
21	8:41	SAG
23	9:55	CAN
25	14:40	AQU
27	23:14	PIS
30	10:35	ARI

NOV		
1	23:08	TAU
4	11:44	GEM
6	23:33	CAN
9	9:37	LEO
11	16:42	VIR
13	20:10	LIB
15	20:36	SCO
17	19:43	SAG
19	19:42	CAN
21	22:43	AQU
24	5:53	PIS
26	16:44	ARI
29	5:22	TAU

DEC		
1	17:54	GEM
4	5:19	CAN
6	15:13	LEO
8	23:03	VIR
11	4:09	LIB
13	6:23	SCO
15	6:40	SAG
17	6:46	CAN
19	8:48	AQU
21	14:25	PIS
24	0:03	ARI
26	12:19	TAU
29	0:53	GEM
31	12:02	CAN

—1915—

JAN			FEB			MAR			APR		
2	21:12	LEO	1	11:10	VIR	2	23:15	LIB	1	9:49	SCO
5	4:28	VIR	3	15:33	LIB	5	1:05	SCO	3	10:05	SAG
7	9:53	LIB	5	18:48	SCO	7	2:59	SAG	5	11:47	CAN
9	13:25	SCO	7	21:33	SAG	9	5:59	CAN	7	16:04	AQU
11	15:25	SAG	10	0:25	CAN	11	10:41	AQU	9	23:08	PIS
13	16:52	CAN	12	4:09	AQU	13	17:17	PIS	12	8:32	ARI
15	19:17	AQU	14	9:40	PIS	16	1:55	ARI	14	19:38	TAU
18	0:15	PIS	16	17:46	ARI	18	12:38	TAU	17	7:57	GEM
20	8:42	ARI	19	4:37	TAU	21	0:58	GEM	19	20:37	CAN
22	20:13	TAU	21	17:05	GEM	23	13:22	CAN	22	7:54	LEO
25	8:48	GEM	24	4:58	CAN	25	23:38	LEO	24	15:53	VIR
27	20:08	CAN	26	14:11	LEO	28	6:13	VIR	26	19:47	LIB
30	4:55	LEO	28	20:04	VIR	30	9:10	LIB	28	20:24	SCO
									30	19:37	SAG

MAY			JUN			JUL			AUG		
2	19:40	CAN	1	6:49	AQU	3	3:24	ARI	1	21:40	TAU
4	22:23	AQU	3	11:32	PIS	5	14:02	TAU	4	9:43	GEM
7	4:41	PIS	5	20:07	ARI	8	2:30	GEM	6	22:11	CAN
9	14:10	ARI	8	7:31	TAU	10	14:57	CAN	9	9:08	LEO
12	1:41	TAU	10	20:07	GEM	13	2:06	LEO	11	17:42	VIR
14	14:09	GEM	13	8:38	CAN	15	11:22	VIR	13	23:56	LIB
17	2:48	CAN	15	20:12	LEO	17	18:21	LIB	16	4:17	SCO
19	14:32	LEO	18	5:53	VIR	19	22:51	SCO	18	7:19	SAG
21	23:47	VIR	20	12:39	LIB	22	1:06	SAG	20	9:38	CAN
24	5:16	LIB	22	16:03	SCO	24	2:04	CAN	22	12:03	AQU
26	7:02	SCO	24	16:45	SAG	26	3:10	AQU	24	15:35	PIS
28	6:27	SAG	26	16:22	CAN	28	6:04	PIS	26	21:21	ARI
30	5:39	CAN	28	16:55	AQU	30	12:06	ARI	29	6:08	TAU
			30	20:15	PIS				31	17:39	GEM

SEP			OCT			NOV			DEC		
3	6:12	CAN	3	2:13	LEO	1	20:31	VIR	1	12:09	LIB
5	17:25	LEO	5	11:05	VIR	4	2:29	LIB	3	15:33	SCO
8	1:42	VIR	7	16:09	LIB	6	4:37	SCO	5	15:47	SAG
10	7:00	LIB	9	18:20	SCO	8	4:36	SAG	7	14:53	CAN
12	10:15	SCO	11	19:21	SAG	10	4:34	CAN	9	15:01	AQU
14	12:41	SAG	13	20:57	CAN	12	6:23	AQU	11	17:57	PIS
16	15:21	CAN	16	0:15	AQU	14	11:05	PIS	14	0:30	ARI
18	18:50	AQU	18	5:38	PIS	16	18:40	ARI	16	10:15	TAU
20	23:32	PIS	20	12:57	ARI	19	4:29	TAU	18	22:03	GEM
23	5:56	ARI	22	22:09	TAU	21	15:57	GEM	21	10:45	CAN
25	14:35	TAU	25	9:15	GEM	24	4:34	CAN	23	23:24	LEO
28	1:43	GEM	27	21:53	CAN	26	17:23	LEO	26	10:51	VIR
30	14:21	CAN	30	10:27	LEO	29	4:33	VIR	28	19:42	LIB
									31	0:56	SCO

—1916—

JAN			FEB			MAR			APR		
2	2:44	SAG	2	13:09	AQU	3	0:27	PIS	1	12:49	ARI
4	2:26	CAN	4	14:16	PIS	5	3:56	ARI	3	19:11	TAU
6	1:58	AQU	6	17:45	ARI	7	10:08	TAU	6	4:20	GEM
8	3:22	PIS	9	0:50	TAU	9	19:46	GEM	8	16:11	CAN
10	8:07	ARI	11	11:30	GEM	12	8:04	CAN	11	5:01	LEO
12	16:43	TAU	14	0:13	CAN	14	20:41	LEO	13	16:07	VIR
15	4:18	GEM	16	12:39	LEO	17	7:13	VIR	15	23:41	LIB
17	17:07	CAN	18	23:09	VIR	19	14:38	LIB	18	3:48	SCO
20	5:33	LEO	21	7:14	LIB	21	19:27	SCO	20	5:53	SAG
22	16:33	VIR	23	13:09	SCO	23	22:48	SAG	22	7:34	CAN
25	1:26	LIB	25	17:21	SAG	26	1:44	CAN	24	10:07	AQU
27	7:43	SCO	27	20:13	CAN	28	4:47	AQU	26	14:05	PIS
29	11:18	SAG	29	22:18	AQU	30	8:19	PIS	28	19:35	ARI
31	12:43	CAN									

MAY			JUN			JUL			AUG		
1	2:49	TAU	2	6:46	CAN	2	1:57	LEO	3	6:54	LIB
3	12:12	GEM	4	19:47	LEO	4	14:33	VIR	5	14:56	SCO
5	23:53	CAN	7	8:15	VIR	7	1:06	LIB	7	19:57	SAG
8	12:52	LEO	9	17:59	LIB	9	8:16	SCO	9	22:08	CAN
11	0:45	VIR	11	23:40	SCO	11	11:44	SAG	11	22:28	AQU
13	9:15	LIB	14	1:40	SAG	13	12:21	CAN	13	22:30	PIS
15	13:42	SCO	16	1:33	CAN	15	11:46	AQU	16	0:02	ARI
17	15:10	SAG	18	1:17	AQU	17	11:55	PIS	18	4:46	TAU
19	15:31	CAN	20	2:40	PIS	19	14:33	ARI	20	13:27	GEM
21	16:34	AQU	22	6:55	ARI	21	20:46	TAU	23	1:21	CAN
23	19:35	PIS	24	14:26	TAU	24	6:36	GEM	25	14:24	LEO
26	1:04	ARI	27	0:44	GEM	26	18:53	CAN	28	2:30	VIR
28	8:54	TAU	29	12:55	CAN	29	7:56	LEO	30	12:34	LIB
30	18:54	GEM				31	20:18	VIR			

SEP			OCT			NOV			DEC		
1	20:25	SCO	1	7:28	SAG	1	19:50	AQU	1	4:30	PIS
4	2:06	SAG	3	11:23	CAN	3	23:05	PIS	3	8:35	ARI
6	5:44	CAN	5	14:28	AQU	6	3:00	ARI	5	14:35	TAU
8	7:39	AQU	7	17:00	PIS	8	8:07	TAU	7	22:41	GEM
10	8:42	PIS	9	19:41	ARI	10	15:19	GEM	10	9:00	CAN
12	10:18	ARI	11	23:45	TAU	13	1:20	CAN	12	21:18	LEO
14	14:09	TAU	14	6:38	GEM	15	13:45	LEO	15	10:19	VIR
16	21:38	GEM	16	16:58	CAN	18	2:33	VIR	17	21:50	LIB
19	8:45	CAN	19	5:40	LEO	20	13:03	LIB	20	5:53	SCO
21	21:41	LEO	21	18:04	VIR	22	19:48	SCO	22	9:58	SAG
24	9:47	VIR	24	3:46	LIB	24	23:12	SAG	24	11:07	CAN
26	19:22	LIB	26	10:09	SCO	27	0:45	CAN	26	11:05	AQU
29	2:21	SCO	28	14:07	SAG	29	2:06	AQU	28	11:42	PIS
			30	17:01	CAN				30	14:26	ARI

—1917—

JAN

1	20:04	TAU
4	4:39	GEM
6	15:35	CAN
9	4:03	LEO
11	17:02	VIR
14	5:05	LIB
16	14:32	SCO
18	20:18	SAG
20	22:28	CAN
22	22:19	AQU
24	21:41	PIS
26	22:34	ARI
29	2:35	TAU
31	10:26	GEM

FEB

2	21:31	CAN
5	10:16	LEO
7	23:09	VIR
10	11:04	LIB
12	21:06	SCO
15	4:23	SAG
17	8:24	CAN
19	9:32	AQU
21	9:06	PIS
23	9:00	ARI
25	11:20	TAU
27	17:35	GEM

MAR

2	3:52	CAN
4	16:36	LEO
7	5:29	VIR
9	17:01	LIB
12	2:41	SCO
14	10:18	SAG
16	15:39	CAN
18	18:33	AQU
20	19:31	PIS
22	19:54	ARI
24	21:35	TAU
27	2:29	GEM
29	11:28	CAN
31	23:39	LEO

APR

3	12:33	VIR
5	23:54	LIB
8	8:55	SCO
10	15:51	SAG
12	21:08	CAN
15	0:57	AQU
17	3:25	PIS
19	5:10	ARI
21	7:31	TAU
23	12:05	GEM
25	20:08	CAN
28	7:32	LEO
30	20:19	VIR

MAY

3	7:52	LIB
5	16:39	SCO
7	22:44	SAG
10	3:00	CAN
12	6:18	AQU
14	9:11	PIS
16	12:04	ARI
18	15:38	TAU
20	20:53	GEM
23	4:49	CAN
25	15:43	LEO
28	4:21	VIR
30	16:20	LIB

JUN

2	1:35	SCO
4	7:28	SAG
6	10:45	CAN
8	12:46	AQU
10	14:43	PIS
12	17:31	ARI
14	21:49	TAU
17	4:02	GEM
19	12:34	CAN
21	23:27	LEO
24	12:00	VIR
27	0:26	LIB
29	10:37	SCO

JUL

1	17:14	SAG
3	20:25	CAN
5	21:25	AQU
7	21:53	PIS
9	23:25	ARI
12	3:13	TAU
14	9:48	GEM
16	19:00	CAN
19	6:17	LEO
21	18:52	VIR
24	7:33	LIB
26	18:41	SCO
29	2:39	SAG
31	6:48	CAN

AUG

2	7:50	AQU
4	7:20	PIS
6	7:19	ARI
8	9:37	TAU
10	15:24	GEM
13	0:40	CAN
15	12:19	LEO
18	1:02	VIR
20	13:42	LIB
23	1:16	SCO
25	10:28	SAG
27	16:15	CAN
29	18:28	AQU
31	18:11	PIS

SEP

2	17:20	ARI
4	18:06	TAU
6	22:19	GEM
9	6:40	CAN
11	18:13	LEO
14	7:02	VIR
16	19:33	LIB
19	6:55	SCO
21	16:32	SAG
23	23:37	CAN
26	3:34	AQU
28	4:39	PIS
30	4:16	ARI

OCT

2	4:25	TAU
4	7:14	GEM
6	14:06	CAN
9	0:50	LEO
11	13:32	VIR
14	1:59	LIB
16	12:54	SCO
18	22:01	SAG
21	5:14	CAN
23	10:17	AQU
25	13:03	PIS
27	14:09	ARI
29	14:59	TAU
31	17:26	GEM

NOV

2	23:09	CAN
5	8:43	LEO
7	20:56	VIR
10	9:27	LIB
12	20:13	SCO
15	4:36	SAG
17	10:55	CAN
19	15:38	AQU
21	19:04	PIS
23	21:36	ARI
25	23:56	TAU
28	3:13	GEM
30	8:48	CAN

DEC

2	17:32	LEO
5	5:07	VIR
7	17:42	LIB
10	4:53	SCO
12	13:11	SAG
14	18:35	CAN
16	22:00	AQU
19	0:31	PIS
21	3:07	ARI
23	6:26	TAU
25	11:03	GEM
27	17:29	CAN
30	2:15	LEO

—1918—

JAN
1	13:24	VIR
4	1:57	LIB
6	13:50	SCO
8	22:58	SAG
11	4:27	CAN
13	6:56	AQU
15	7:54	PIS
17	9:04	ARI1
9	11:49	TAU
21	16:52	GEM
24	0:17	CAN
26	9:45	LEO
28	20:59	VIR
31	9:27	LIB

FEB
2	21:52	SCO
5	8:15	SAG
7	14:57	CAN
9	17:46	AQU
11	17:57	PIS
13	17:31	ARI
15	18:31	TAU
17	22:30	GEM
20	5:51	CAN
22	15:53	LEO
25	3:33	VIR
27	16:01	LIB

MAR
2	4:33	SCO
4	15:48	SAG
7	0:05	CAN
9	4:23	AQU
11	5:12	PIS
13	4:15	ARI
15	3:48	TAU
17	5:58	GEM
19	11:58	CAN
21	21:37	LEO
24	9:31	VIR
26	22:07	LIB
29	10:28	SCO
31	21:47	SAG

APR
3	6:59	CAN
5	12:56	AQU
7	15:22	PIS
9	15:19	ARI
11	14:40	TAU
13	15:37	GEM
15	19:58	CAN
18	4:19	LEO
20	15:46	VIR
23	4:25	LIB
25	16:37	SCO
28	3:31	SAG
30	12:33	CAN

MAY
2	19:13	AQU
4	23:08	PIS
7	0:41	ARI
9	1:05	TAU
11	2:06	GEM
13	5:31	CAN
15	12:31	LEO
17	23:01	VIR
20	11:26	LIB
22	23:38	SCO
25	10:09	SAG
27	18:28	CAN
30	0:38	AQU

JUN
1	4:54	PIS
3	7:37	ARI
5	9:30	TAU
7	11:36	GEM
9	15:14	CAN
11	21:36	LEO
14	7:11	VIR
16	19:10	LIB
19	7:30	SCO
21	18:05	SAG
24	1:51	CAN
26	7:01	AQU
28	10:27	PIS
30	13:05	ARI

JUL
2	15:44	TAU
4	19:04	GEM
6	23:42	CAN
9	6:21	LEO
11	15:33	VIR
14	3:09	LIB
16	15:41	SCO
19	2:49	SAG
21	10:46	CAN
23	15:20	AQU
25	17:32	PIS
27	18:59	ARI
29	21:07	TAU

AUG
1	0:48	GEM
3	6:22	CAN
5	13:49	LEO
7	23:17	VIR
10	10:46	LIB
12	23:27	SCO
15	11:23	SAG
17	20:17	CAN
20	1:11	AQU
22	2:48	PIS
24	2:56	ARI
26	3:35	TAU
28	6:20	GEM
30	11:50	CAN

SEP
1	19:53	LEO
4	5:56	VIR
6	17:35	LIB
9	6:20	SCO
11	18:51	SAG
14	5:02	CAN
16	11:15	AQU
18	13:27	PIS
20	13:07	ARI
22	12:27	TAU
24	13:31	GEM
26	17:45	CAN
29	1:25	LEO

OCT
1	11:46	VIR
3	23:44	LIB
6	12:28	SCO
9	1:05	SAG
11	12:07	CAN
13	19:54	AQU
15	23:42	PIS
18	0:14	ARI
19	23:21	TAU
21	23:11	GEM
24	1:40	CAN
26	7:55	LEO
28	17:42	VIR
31	5:45	LIB

NOV
2	18:32	SCO
5	6:52	SAG
7	17:50	CAN
10	2:26	AQU
12	7:52	PIS
14	10:12	ARI
16	10:27	TAU
18	10:20	GEM
20	11:47	CAN
22	16:23	LEO
25	0:51	VIR
27	12:25	LIB
30	1:13	SCO

DEC
2	13:21	SAG
4	23:41	CAN
7	7:52	AQU
9	13:48	PIS
11	17:33	ARI
13	19:36	TAU
15	20:49	GEM
17	22:35	CAN
20	2:25	LEO
22	9:33	VIR
24	20:10	LIB
27	8:49	SCO
29	21:04	SAG

—1919—

<table>
<tr><td colspan="3">JAN</td><td colspan="3">FEB</td><td colspan="3">MAR</td><td colspan="3">APR</td></tr>
<tr><td>1</td><td>7:02</td><td>CAN</td><td>2</td><td>2:38</td><td>PIS</td><td>1</td><td>12:15</td><td>PIS</td><td>1</td><td>23:40</td><td>TAU</td></tr>
<tr><td>3</td><td>14:16</td><td>AQU</td><td>4</td><td>5:02</td><td>ARI</td><td>3</td><td>13:29</td><td>ARI</td><td>3</td><td>23:56</td><td>GEM</td></tr>
<tr><td>5</td><td>19:19</td><td>PIS</td><td>6</td><td>7:22</td><td>TAU</td><td>5</td><td>14:14</td><td>TAU</td><td>6</td><td>2:23</td><td>CAN</td></tr>
<tr><td>7</td><td>23:01</td><td>ARI</td><td>8</td><td>10:31</td><td>GEM</td><td>7</td><td>16:10</td><td>GEM</td><td>8</td><td>7:48</td><td>LEO</td></tr>
<tr><td>10</td><td>2:02</td><td>TAU</td><td>10</td><td>14:46</td><td>CAN</td><td>9</td><td>20:09</td><td>CAN</td><td>10</td><td>16:07</td><td>VIR</td></tr>
<tr><td>12</td><td>4:49</td><td>GEM</td><td>12</td><td>20:18</td><td>LEO</td><td>12</td><td>2:19</td><td>LEO</td><td>13</td><td>2:43</td><td>LIB</td></tr>
<tr><td>14</td><td>7:56</td><td>CAN</td><td>15</td><td>3:32</td><td>VIR</td><td>14</td><td>10:26</td><td>VIR</td><td>15</td><td>14:54</td><td>SCO</td></tr>
<tr><td>16</td><td>12:16</td><td>LEO</td><td>17</td><td>13:07</td><td>LIB</td><td>16</td><td>20:29</td><td>LIB</td><td>18</td><td>3:52</td><td>SAG</td></tr>
<tr><td>18</td><td>18:57</td><td>VIR</td><td>20</td><td>1:04</td><td>SCO</td><td>19</td><td>8:25</td><td>SCO</td><td>20</td><td>16:14</td><td>CAN</td></tr>
<tr><td>21</td><td>4:43</td><td>LIB</td><td>22</td><td>13:57</td><td>SAG</td><td>21</td><td>21:24</td><td>SAG</td><td>23</td><td>2:09</td><td>AQU</td></tr>
<tr><td>23</td><td>17:00</td><td>SCO</td><td>25</td><td>1:08</td><td>CAN</td><td>24</td><td>9:25</td><td>CAN</td><td>25</td><td>8:17</td><td>PIS</td></tr>
<tr><td>26</td><td>5:35</td><td>SAG</td><td>27</td><td>8:36</td><td>AQU</td><td>26</td><td>18:12</td><td>AQU</td><td>27</td><td>10:40</td><td>ARI</td></tr>
<tr><td>28</td><td>15:54</td><td>CAN</td><td></td><td></td><td></td><td>28</td><td>22:46</td><td>PIS</td><td>29</td><td>10:36</td><td>TAU</td></tr>
<tr><td>30</td><td>22:44</td><td>AQU</td><td></td><td></td><td></td><td>30</td><td>23:58</td><td>ARI</td><td></td><td></td><td></td></tr>
</table>

<table>
<tr><td colspan="3">MAY</td><td colspan="3">JUN</td><td colspan="3">JUL</td><td colspan="3">AUG</td></tr>
<tr><td>1</td><td>10:01</td><td>GEM</td><td>1</td><td>23:26</td><td>LEO</td><td>1</td><td>14:06</td><td>VIR</td><td>2</td><td>18:08</td><td>SCO</td></tr>
<tr><td>3</td><td>10:51</td><td>CAN</td><td>4</td><td>5:19</td><td>VIR</td><td>3</td><td>22:35</td><td>LIB</td><td>5</td><td>6:58</td><td>SAG</td></tr>
<tr><td>5</td><td>14:38</td><td>LEO</td><td>6</td><td>14:58</td><td>LIB</td><td>6</td><td>10:19</td><td>SCO</td><td>7</td><td>18:52</td><td>CAN</td></tr>
<tr><td>7</td><td>22:01</td><td>VIR</td><td>9</td><td>3:16</td><td>SCO</td><td>8</td><td>23:13</td><td>SAG</td><td>10</td><td>3:57</td><td>AQU</td></tr>
<tr><td>10</td><td>8:32</td><td>LIB</td><td>11</td><td>16:12</td><td>SAG</td><td>11</td><td>10:57</td><td>CAN</td><td>12</td><td>9:59</td><td>PIS</td></tr>
<tr><td>12</td><td>20:58</td><td>SCO</td><td>14</td><td>4:05</td><td>CAN</td><td>13</td><td>20:14</td><td>AQU</td><td>14</td><td>13:59</td><td>ARI</td></tr>
<tr><td>15</td><td>9:54</td><td>SAG</td><td>16</td><td>13:59</td><td>AQU</td><td>16</td><td>3:06</td><td>PIS</td><td>16</td><td>17:05</td><td>TAU</td></tr>
<tr><td>17</td><td>22:07</td><td>CAN</td><td>18</td><td>21:32</td><td>PIS</td><td>18</td><td>8:06</td><td>ARI</td><td>18</td><td>20:03</td><td>GEM</td></tr>
<tr><td>20</td><td>8:24</td><td>AQU</td><td>21</td><td>2:38</td><td>ARI</td><td>20</td><td>11:44</td><td>TAU</td><td>20</td><td>23:14</td><td>CAN</td></tr>
<tr><td>22</td><td>15:45</td><td>PIS</td><td>23</td><td>5:29</td><td>TAU</td><td>22</td><td>14:20</td><td>GEM</td><td>23</td><td>3:00</td><td>LEO</td></tr>
<tr><td>24</td><td>19:47</td><td>ARI</td><td>25</td><td>6:42</td><td>GEM</td><td>24</td><td>16:25</td><td>CAN</td><td>25</td><td>8:08</td><td>VIR</td></tr>
<tr><td>26</td><td>21:03</td><td>TAU</td><td>27</td><td>7:28</td><td>CAN</td><td>26</td><td>19:00</td><td>LEO</td><td>27</td><td>15:42</td><td>LIB</td></tr>
<tr><td>28</td><td>20:53</td><td>GEM</td><td>29</td><td>9:24</td><td>LEO</td><td>28</td><td>23:28</td><td>VIR</td><td>30</td><td>2:16</td><td>SCO</td></tr>
<tr><td>30</td><td>21:05</td><td>CAN</td><td></td><td></td><td></td><td>31</td><td>7:06</td><td>LIB</td><td></td><td></td><td></td></tr>
</table>

<table>
<tr><td colspan="3">SEP</td><td colspan="3">OCT</td><td colspan="3">NOV</td><td colspan="3">DEC</td></tr>
<tr><td>1</td><td>14:58</td><td>SAG</td><td>1</td><td>11:29</td><td>CAN</td><td>2</td><td>14:19</td><td>PIS</td><td>2</td><td>4:03</td><td>ARI</td></tr>
<tr><td>4</td><td>3:21</td><td>CAN</td><td>3</td><td>22:03</td><td>AQU</td><td>4</td><td>18:31</td><td>ARI</td><td>4</td><td>6:34</td><td>TAU</td></tr>
<tr><td>6</td><td>12:54</td><td>AQU</td><td>6</td><td>4:44</td><td>PIS</td><td>6</td><td>19:31</td><td>TAU</td><td>6</td><td>6:36</td><td>GEM</td></tr>
<tr><td>8</td><td>18:46</td><td>PIS</td><td>8</td><td>7:44</td><td>ARI</td><td>8</td><td>19:04</td><td>GEM</td><td>8</td><td>5:55</td><td>CAN</td></tr>
<tr><td>10</td><td>21:48</td><td>ARI</td><td>10</td><td>8:33</td><td>TAU</td><td>10</td><td>19:03</td><td>CAN</td><td>10</td><td>6:28</td><td>LEO</td></tr>
<tr><td>12</td><td>23:36</td><td>TAU</td><td>12</td><td>8:59</td><td>GEM</td><td>12</td><td>21:14</td><td>LEO</td><td>12</td><td>10:07</td><td>VIR</td></tr>
<tr><td>15</td><td>1:35</td><td>GEM</td><td>14</td><td>10:39</td><td>CAN</td><td>15</td><td>2:41</td><td>VIR</td><td>14</td><td>17:48</td><td>LIB</td></tr>
<tr><td>17</td><td>4:39</td><td>CAN</td><td>16</td><td>14:32</td><td>LEO</td><td>17</td><td>11:32</td><td>LIB</td><td>17</td><td>5:01</td><td>SCO</td></tr>
<tr><td>19</td><td>9:08</td><td>LEO</td><td>18</td><td>20:59</td><td>VIR</td><td>19</td><td>22:59</td><td>SCO</td><td>19</td><td>17:59</td><td>SAG</td></tr>
<tr><td>21</td><td>15:15</td><td>VIR</td><td>21</td><td>5:51</td><td>LIB</td><td>22</td><td>11:48</td><td>SAG</td><td>22</td><td>6:49</td><td>CAN</td></tr>
<tr><td>23</td><td>23:25</td><td>LIB</td><td>23</td><td>16:53</td><td>SCO</td><td>25</td><td>0:46</td><td>CAN</td><td>24</td><td>18:20</td><td>AQU</td></tr>
<tr><td>26</td><td>10:00</td><td>SCO</td><td>26</td><td>5:31</td><td>SAG</td><td>27</td><td>12:38</td><td>AQU</td><td>27</td><td>3:56</td><td>PIS</td></tr>
<tr><td>28</td><td>22:37</td><td>SAG</td><td>28</td><td>18:35</td><td>CAN</td><td>29</td><td>22:03</td><td>PIS</td><td>29</td><td>11:06</td><td>ARI</td></tr>
<tr><td></td><td></td><td></td><td>31</td><td>6:08</td><td>AQU</td><td></td><td></td><td></td><td>31</td><td>15:29</td><td>TAU</td></tr>
</table>

—1920—

JAN			FEB			MAR			APR		
2	17:13	GEM	1	2:54	CAN	1	12:23	LEO	2	5:00	LIB
4	17:19	CAN	3	4:06	LEO	3	15:41	VIR	4	13:34	SCO
6	17:30	LEO	5	6:18	VIR	5	20:53	LIB	7	0:42	SAG
8	19:46	VIR	7	11:20	LIB	8	5:10	SCO	9	13:25	CAN
11	1:48	LIB	9	20:14	SCO	10	16:35	SAG	12	1:32	AQU
13	11:58	SCO	12	8:21	SAG	13	5:25	CAN	14	10:50	PIS
16	0:44	SAG	14	21:14	CAN	15	16:58	AQU	16	16:29	ARI
18	13:34	CAN	17	8:20	AQU	18	1:25	PIS	18	19:08	TAU
21	0:40	AQU	19	16:39	PIS	20	6:43	ARI	20	20:15	GEM
23	9:34	PIS	21	22:37	ARI	22	9:58	TAU	22	21:22	CAN
25	16:32	ARI	24	3:06	TAU	24	12:26	GEM	24	23:49	LEO
27	21:43	TAU	26	6:42	GEM	26	15:02	CAN	27	4:22	VIR
30	1:06	GEM	28	9:41	CAN	28	18:21	LEO	29	11:19	LIB
						30	22:48	VIR			

MAY			JUN			JUL			AUG		
1	20:37	SCO	3	3:05	CAN	2	21:31	AQU	1	14:18	PIS
4	8:00	SAG	5	15:38	AQU	5	8:37	PIS	3	23:10	ARI
6	20:39	CAN	8	2:43	PIS	7	17:39	ARI	6	5:56	TAU
9	9:09	AQU	10	10:58	ARI	9	23:46	TAU	8	10:15	GEM
11	19:32	PIS	12	15:35	TAU	12	2:40	GEM	10	12:11	CAN
14	2:24	ARI	14	16:57	GEM	14	3:03	CAN	12	12:41	LEO
16	5:35	TAU	16	16:27	CAN	16	2:32	LEO	14	13:28	VIR
18	6:13	GEM	18	16:02	LEO	18	3:12	VIR	16	16:28	LIB
20	6:01	CAN	20	17:45	VIR	20	7:03	LIB	18	23:13	SCO
22	6:50	LEO	22	23:06	LIB	22	15:03	SCO	21	9:45	SAG
24	10:11	VIR	25	8:19	SCO	25	2:31	SAG	23	22:22	CAN
26	16:50	LIB	27	20:15	SAG	27	15:22	CAN	26	10:36	AQU
29	2:33	SCO	30	9:06	CAN	30	3:37	AQU	28	20:55	PIS
31	14:21	SAG							31	5:03	ARI

SEP			OCT			NOV			DEC		
2	11:20	TAU	1	21:32	GEM	2	8:37	LEO	1	17:45	VIR
4	15:58	GEM	4	0:29	CAN	4	12:04	VIR	3	22:50	LIB
6	19:04	CAN	6	3:14	LEO	6	17:23	LIB	6	6:51	SCO
8	21:02	LEO	8	6:23	VIR	9	0:50	SCO	8	17:10	SAG
10	22:55	VIR	10	10:44	LIB	11	10:27	SAG	11	5:00	CAN
13	2:11	LIB	12	17:14	SCO	13	22:03	CAN	13	17:39	AQU
15	8:19	SCO	15	2:31	SAG	16	10:45	AQU	16	6:04	PIS
17	17:58	SAG	17	14:17	CAN	18	22:40	PIS	18	16:30	ARI
20	6:09	CAN	20	2:53	AQU	21	7:46	ARI	20	23:22	TAU
22	18:33	AQU	22	13:57	PIS	23	13:02	TAU	23	2:15	GEM
25	4:58	PIS	24	21:53	ARI	25	15:00	GEM	25	2:13	CAN
27	12:35	ARI	27	2:34	TAU	27	15:12	CAN	27	1:16	LEO
29	17:49	TAU	29	5:00	GEM	29	15:33	LEO	29	1:38	VIR
			31	6:35	CAN				31	5:07	LIB

—1921—

JAN			FEB			MAR			APR		
2	12:27	SCO	1	5:04	SAG	3	0:04	CAP	1	20:22	AQU
4	22:58	SAG	3	17:14	CAP	5	12:46	AQU	4	8:28	PIS
7	11:10	CAP	6	5:59	AQU	8	0:44	PIS	6	18:31	ARI
9	23:50	AQU	8	18:04	PIS	10	10:58	ARI	9	2:00	TAU
12	12:11	PIS	11	4:52	ARI	12	19:15	TAU	11	7:16	GEM
14	23:15	ARI	13	13:45	TAU	15	1:29	GEM	13	10:59	CAN
17	7:40	TAU	15	19:55	GEM	17	5:36	CAN	15	13:48	LEO
19	12:24	GEM	17	22:58	CAN	19	7:52	LEO	17	16:21	VIR
21	13:36	CAN	19	23:34	LEO	21	9:08	VIR	19	19:25	LIB
23	12:45	LEO	21	23:21	VIR	23	10:50	LIB	21	23:54	SCO
25	12:04	VIR	24	0:21	LIB	25	14:34	SCO	24	6:45	SAG
27	13:47	LIB	26	4:28	SCO	27	21:34	SAG	26	16:28	CAP
29	19:25	SCO	28	12:37	SAG	30	7:58	CAP	29	4:26	AQU

MAY			JUN			JUL			AUG		
1	16:47	PIS	2	20:04	TAU	2	10:23	GEM	2	22:11	LEO
4	3:14	ARI	5	0:17	GEM	4	11:56	CAN	4	21:19	VIR
6	10:32	TAU	7	1:47	CAN	6	11:34	LEO	6	21:52	LIB
8	14:51	GEM	9	2:19	LEO	8	11:26	VIR	9	1:33	SCO
10	17:19	CAN	11	3:41	VIR	10	13:28	LIB	11	9:00	SAG
12	19:17	LEO	13	7:10	LIB	12	18:43	SCO	13	19:30	CAP
14	21:52	VIR	15	13:11	SCO	15	3:05	SAG	16	7:42	AQU
17	1:47	LIB	17	21:28	SAG	17	13:43	CAP	18	20:20	PIS
19	7:22	SCO	20	7:39	CAP	20	1:44	AQU	21	8:30	ARI
21	14:53	SAG	22	19:24	AQU	22	14:24	PIS	23	19:07	TAU
24	0:35	CAP	25	8:04	PIS	25	2:42	ARI	26	2:58	GEM
26	12:17	AQU	27	20:03	ARI	27	12:58	TAU	28	7:18	CAN
29	0:51	PIS	30	5:14	TAU	29	19:37	GEM	30	8:31	LEO
31	12:05	ARI				31	22:18	CAN			

SEP			OCT			NOV			DEC		
1	8:07	VIR	2	20:37	SCO	1	11:08	SAG	1	3:32	CAP
3	8:06	LIB	5	1:22	SAG	3	18:38	CAP	3	13:42	AQU
5	10:24	SCO	7	9:45	CAP	6	5:18	AQU	6	2:04	PIS
7	16:21	SAG	9	21:13	AQU	8	17:51	PIS	8	14:37	ARI
10	1:58	CAP	12	9:51	PIS	11	5:52	ARI	11	0:46	TAU
12	14:01	AQU	14	21:34	ARI	13	15:20	TAU	13	7:08	GEM
15	2:39	PIS	17	7:08	TAU	15	21:41	GEM	15	10:12	CAN
17	14:29	ARI	19	14:21	GEM	18	1:41	CAN	17	11:35	LEO
20	0:41	TAU	21	19:32	CAN	20	4:32	LEO	19	13:03	VIR
22	8:42	GEM	23	23:08	LEO	22	7:17	VIR	21	15:52	LIB
24	14:06	CAN	26	1:40	VIR	24	10:32	LIB	23	20:33	SCO
26	16:58	LEO	28	3:49	LIB	26	14:38	SCO	26	3:02	SAG
28	18:02	VIR	30	6:34	SCO	28	20:03	SAG	28	11:17	CAP
30	18:41	LIB							30	21:32	AQU

—1922—

JAN
2	9:45	PIS
4	22:42	ARI
7	9:59	TAU
9	17:27	GEM
11	20:47	CAN
13	21:21	LEO
15	21:13	VIR
17	22:21	LIB
20	2:02	SCO
22	8:33	SAG
24	17:29	CAP
27	4:17	AQU
29	16:34	PIS

FEB
1	5:36	ARI
3	17:41	TAU
6	2:42	GEM
8	7:30	CAN
10	8:40	LEO
12	7:58	VIR
14	7:35	LIB
16	9:23	SCO
18	14:32	SAG
20	23:05	CAP
23	10:12	AQU
25	22:45	PIS
28	11:42	ARI

MAR
2	23:52	TAU
5	9:49	GEM
7	16:19	CAN
9	19:10	LEO
11	19:23	VIR
13	18:44	LIB
15	19:13	SCO
17	22:34	SAG
20	5:41	CAP
22	16:18	AQU
25	4:56	PIS
27	17:50	ARI
30	5:38	TAU

APR
1	15:29	GEM
3	22:46	CAN
6	3:13	LEO
8	5:09	VIR
10	5:36	LIB
12	6:07	SCO
14	8:26	SAG
16	14:02	CAP
18	23:28	AQU
21	11:44	PIS
24	0:38	ARI
26	12:08	TAU
28	21:20	GEM

MAY
1	4:12	CAN
3	9:05	LEO
5	12:19	VIR
7	14:22	LIB
9	16:01	SCO
11	18:32	SAG
13	23:26	CAP
16	7:46	AQU
18	19:21	PIS
21	8:13	ARI
23	19:46	TAU
26	4:29	GEM
28	10:27	CAN
30	14:34	LEO

JUN
1	17:48	VIR
3	20:44	LIB
5	23:42	SCO
8	3:18	SAG
10	8:30	CAP
12	16:25	AQU
15	3:25	PIS
17	16:13	ARI
20	4:09	TAU
22	13:02	GEM
24	18:27	CAN
26	21:28	LEO
28	23:37	VIR

JUL
1	2:05	LIB
3	5:30	SCO
5	10:05	SAG
7	16:12	CAP
10	0:27	AQU
12	11:16	PIS
14	23:59	ARI
17	12:28	TAU
19	22:10	GEM
22	3:56	CAN
24	6:27	LEO
26	7:22	VIR
28	8:27	LIB
30	10:59	SCO

AUG
1	15:35	SAG
3	22:22	CAP
6	7:19	AQU
8	18:23	PIS
11	7:06	ARI
13	19:57	TAU
16	6:43	GEM
18	13:40	CAN
20	16:45	LEO
22	17:16	VIR
24	17:05	LIB
26	18:02	SCO
28	21:26	SAG
31	3:54	CAP

SEP
2	13:12	AQU
5	0:42	PIS
7	13:29	ARI
10	2:24	TAU
12	13:51	GEM
14	22:13	CAN
17	2:48	LEO
19	4:08	VIR
21	3:44	LIB
23	3:28	SCO
25	5:11	SAG
27	10:16	CAP
29	19:03	AQU

OCT
2	6:41	PIS
4	19:36	ARI
7	8:20	TAU
9	19:44	GEM
12	4:52	CAN
14	11:02	LEO
16	14:04	VIR
18	14:43	LIB
20	14:26	SCO
22	15:06	SAG
24	18:34	CAP
27	2:00	AQU
29	13:07	PIS

NOV
1	2:05	ARI
3	14:40	TAU
6	1:34	GEM
8	10:23	CAN
10	17:06	LEO
12	21:37	VIR
15	0:01	LIB
17	0:59	SCO
19	1:53	SAG
21	4:32	CAP
23	10:36	AQU
25	20:40	PIS
28	9:21	ARI
30	22:00	TAU

DEC
3	8:34	GEM
5	16:34	CAN
7	22:33	LEO
10	3:09	VIR
12	6:40	LIB
14	9:14	SCO
16	11:28	SAG
18	14:35	CAP
20	20:08	AQU
23	5:14	PIS
25	17:23	ARI
28	6:13	TAU
30	17:03	GEM

—1923—

JAN

2	0:40	CAN
4	5:34	LEO
6	9:00	VIR
8	11:59	LIB
10	15:05	SCO
12	18:34	SAG
14	22:57	CAP
17	5:06	AQU
19	13:58	PIS
22	1:37	ARI
24	14:34	TAU
27	2:08	GEM
29	10:19	CAN
31	14:57	LEO

FEB

2	17:12	VIR
4	18:39	LIB
6	20:37	SCO
8	23:59	SAG
11	5:08	CAP
13	12:19	AQU
15	21:44	PIS
18	9:20	ARI
20	22:15	TAU
23	10:31	GEM
25	19:58	CAN
28	1:31	LEO

MAR

2	3:42	VIR
4	4:01	LIB
6	4:16	SCO
8	6:06	SAG
10	10:34	CAP
12	18:02	AQU
15	4:08	PIS
17	16:06	ARI
20	5:00	TAU
22	17:33	GEM
25	4:06	CAN
27	11:14	LEO
29	14:37	VIR
31	15:07	LIB

APR

2	14:26	SCO
4	14:34	SAG
6	17:19	CAP
8	23:49	AQU
11	9:51	PIS
13	22:09	ARI
16	11:07	TAU
18	23:33	GEM
21	10:28	CAN
23	18:51	LEO
25	23:56	VIR
28	1:49	LIB
30	1:33	SCO

MAY

2	0:59	SAG
4	2:15	CAP
6	7:05	AQU
8	16:07	PIS
11	4:13	ARI
13	17:15	TAU
16	5:27	GEM
18	16:03	CAN
21	0:41	LEO
23	6:54	VIR
25	10:25	LIB
27	11:35	SCO
29	11:38	SAG
31	12:28	CAP

JUN

2	16:04	AQU
4	23:43	PIS
7	11:03	ARI
9	23:57	TAU
12	12:03	GEM
14	22:10	CAN
17	6:12	LEO
19	12:23	VIR
21	16:44	LIB
23	19:21	SCO
25	20:47	SAG
27	22:20	CAP
30	1:44	AQU

JUL

2	8:28	PIS
4	18:51	ARI
7	7:25	TAU
9	19:37	GEM
12	5:34	CAN
14	12:54	LEO
16	18:10	VIR
18	22:06	LIB
21	1:09	SCO
23	3:43	SAG
25	6:33	CAP
27	10:43	AQU
29	17:23	PIS

AUG

1	3:11	ARI
3	15:22	TAU
6	3:48	GEM
8	14:08	CAN
10	21:19	LEO
13	1:44	VIR
15	4:27	LIB
17	6:38	SCO
19	9:12	SAG
21	12:49	CAP
23	18:03	AQU
26	1:25	PIS
28	11:15	ARI
30	23:12	TAU

SEP

2	11:51	GEM
4	22:59	CAN
7	6:54	LEO
9	11:17	VIR
11	13:03	LIB
13	13:47	SCO
15	15:06	SAG
17	18:14	CAP
19	23:53	AQU
22	8:03	PIS
24	18:24	ARI
27	6:23	TAU
29	19:06	GEM

OCT

2	7:01	CAN
4	16:15	LEO
6	21:41	VIR
8	23:36	LIB
10	23:25	SCO
12	23:09	SAG
15	0:43	CAP
17	5:30	AQU
19	13:43	PIS
22	0:33	ARI
24	12:48	TAU
27	1:29	GEM
29	13:39	CAN

NOV

1	0:00	LEO
3	7:07	VIR
5	10:24	LIB
7	10:38	SCO
9	9:37	SAG
11	9:38	CAP
13	12:40	AQU
15	19:47	PIS
18	6:25	ARI
20	18:53	TAU
23	7:32	GEM
25	19:28	CAN
28	6:02	LEO
30	14:19	VIR

DEC

2	19:25	LIB
4	21:15	SCO
6	20:57	SAG
8	20:31	CAP
10	22:10	AQU
13	3:36	PIS
15	13:08	ARI
18	1:22	TAU
20	14:03	GEM
23	1:40	CAN
25	11:40	LEO
27	19:51	VIR
30	1:52	LIB

—1924—

JAN			FEB			MAR			APR		
1	5:23	SCO	1	16:03	CAP	2	2:11	AQU	2	22:46	ARI
3	6:48	SAG	3	18:43	AQU	4	7:45	PIS	5	9:12	TAU
5	7:22	CAP	5	23:12	PIS	6	15:26	ARI	7	21:13	GEM
7	8:54	AQU	8	6:37	ARI	9	1:36	TAU	10	9:53	CAN
9	13:14	PIS	10	17:10	TAU	11	13:44	GEM	12	21:15	LEO
11	21:23	ARI	13	5:35	GEM	14	2:08	CAN	15	5:21	VIR
14	8:49	TAU	15	17:34	CAN	16	12:32	LEO	17	9:27	LIB
16	21:28	GEM	18	3:09	LEO	18	19:27	VIR	19	10:24	SCO
19	9:06	CAN	20	9:46	VIR	20	23:00	LIB	21	10:05	SAG
21	18:34	LEO	22	13:57	LIB	23	0:28	SCO	23	10:33	CAP
24	1:49	VIR	24	16:47	SCO	25	1:29	SAG	25	13:30	AQU
26	7:14	LIB	26	19:16	SAG	27	3:37	CAP	27	19:39	PIS
28	11:09	SCO	28	22:13	CAP	29	7:47	AQU	30	4:39	ARI
30	13:53	SAG				31	14:13	PIS			

MAY			JUN			JUL			AUG		
2	15:37	TAU	1	9:48	GEM	1	4:28	CAN	2	8:05	VIR
5	3:48	GEM	3	22:27	CAN	3	16:11	LEO	4	15:20	LIB
7	16:31	CAN	6	10:29	LEO	6	2:16	VIR	6	20:24	SCO
10	4:30	LEO	8	20:41	VIR	8	9:55	LIB	8	23:32	SAG
12	13:57	VIR	11	3:41	LIB	10	14:37	SCO	11	1:21	CAP
14	19:29	LIB	13	6:57	SCO	12	16:32	SAG	13	2:52	AQU
16	21:11	SCO	15	7:17	SAG	14	16:49	CAP	15	5:29	PIS
18	20:34	SAG	17	6:29	CAP	16	17:11	AQU	17	10:32	ARI
20	19:49	CAP	19	6:43	AQU	18	19:31	PIS	19	18:54	TAU
22	21:05	AQU	21	9:52	PIS	21	1:12	ARI	22	6:15	GEM
25	1:50	PIS	23	16:56	ARI	23	10:37	TAU	24	18:48	CAN
27	10:16	ARI	26	3:28	TAU	25	22:37	GEM	27	6:19	LEO
29	21:23	TAU	28	15:52	GEM	28	11:12	CAN	29	15:19	VIR
						30	22:38	LEO	31	21:38	LIB

SEP			OCT			NOV			DEC		
3	1:55	SCO	2	10:55	SAG	2	21:53	AQU	2	8:39	PIS
5	5:01	SAG	4	13:03	CAP	5	2:35	PIS	4	15:11	ARI
7	7:41	CAP	6	16:20	AQU	7	9:40	ARI	7	0:34	TAU
9	10:33	AQU	8	21:07	PIS	9	18:44	TAU	9	11:53	GEM
11	14:17	PIS	11	3:31	ARI	12	5:35	GEM	12	0:21	CAN
13	19:42	ARI	13	11:50	TAU	14	17:57	CAN	14	13:13	LEO
16	3:39	TAU	15	22:23	GEM	17	6:51	LEO	17	1:07	VIR
18	14:24	GEM	18	10:48	CAN	19	18:11	VIR	19	10:15	LIB
21	2:55	CAN	20	23:22	LEO	22	1:52	LIB	21	15:26	SCO
23	14:53	LEO	23	9:33	VIR	24	5:18	SCO	23	16:56	SAG
26	0:07	VIR	25	15:49	LIB	26	5:38	SAG	25	16:19	CAP
28	5:54	LIB	27	18:27	SCO	28	4:58	CAP	27	15:41	AQU
30	9:00	SCO	29	19:03	SAG	30	5:26	AQU	29	17:06	PIS
			31	19:39	CAP				31	21:57	ARI

—1925—

JAN			FEB			MAR			APR		
3	6:31	TAU	2	0:33	GEM	1	8:26	GEM	2	17:33	LEO
5	17:53	GEM	4	13:11	CAN	3	20:38	CAN	5	4:55	VIR
8	6:33	CAN	7	1:50	LEO	6	9:23	LEO	7	13:05	LIB
10	19:14	LEO	9	13:01	VIR	8	20:24	VIR	9	18:04	SCO
13	6:55	VIR	11	22:06	LIB	11	4:44	LIB	11	21:06	SAG
15	16:33	LIB	14	4:55	SCO	13	10:38	SCO	13	23:32	CAP
17	23:12	SCO	16	9:28	SAG	15	14:52	SAG	16	2:23	AQU
20	2:34	SAG	18	12:02	CAP	17	18:07	CAP	18	6:03	PIS
22	3:23	CAP	20	13:21	AQU	19	20:51	AQU	20	10:45	ARI
24	3:09	AQU	22	14:37	PIS	21	23:34	PIS	22	17:00	TAU
26	3:46	PIS	24	17:22	ARI	24	3:04	ARI	25	1:33	GEM
28	7:00	ARI	26	23:04	TAU	26	8:35	TAU	27	12:46	CAN
30	13:58	TAU				28	17:08	GEM	30	1:37	LEO
						31	4:43	CAN			

MAY			JUN			JUL			AUG		
2	13:38	VIR	1	7:31	LIB	3	1:55	SAG	1	12:47	CAP
4	22:26	LIB	3	13:22	SCO	5	2:24	CAP	3	12:41	AQU
7	3:22	SCO	5	15:34	SAG	7	1:49	AQU	5	12:23	PIS
9	5:28	SAG	7	15:45	CAP	9	2:06	PIS	7	13:46	ARI
11	6:30	CAP	9	15:54	AQU	11	4:53	ARI	9	18:25	TAU
13	8:09	AQU	11	17:40	PIS	13	11:05	TAU	12	2:57	GEM
15	11:24	PIS	13	22:03	ARI	15	20:38	GEM	14	14:39	CAN
17	16:35	ARI	16	5:16	TAU	18	8:33	CAN	17	3:41	LEO
19	23:42	TAU	18	14:57	GEM	20	21:32	LEO	19	16:13	VIR
22	8:51	GEM	21	2:37	CAN	23	10:18	VIR	22	3:06	LIB
24	20:08	CAN	23	15:31	LEO	25	21:30	LIB	24	11:45	SCO
27	8:59	LEO	26	4:22	VIR	28	5:57	SCO	26	17:50	SAG
29	21:36	VIR	28	15:15	LIB	30	10:56	SAG	28	21:19	CAP
			30	22:33	SCO				30	22:41	AQU

SEP			OCT			NOV			DEC		
1	23:03	PIS	1	10:06	ARI	2	4:44	GEM	1	22:19	CAN
4	0:02	ARI	3	13:20	TAU	4	14:06	CAN	4	10:13	LEO
6	3:28	TAU	5	19:35	GEM	7	2:16	LEO	6	23:14	VIR
8	10:39	GEM	8	5:33	CAN	9	15:07	VIR	9	10:53	LIB
10	21:35	CAN	10	18:09	LEO	12	1:52	LIB	11	19:04	SCO
13	10:30	LEO	13	6:44	VIR	14	9:06	SCO	13	23:23	SAG
15	22:57	VIR	15	16:58	LIB	16	13:13	SAG	16	0:59	CAP
18	9:18	LIB	18	0:13	SCO	18	15:39	CAP	18	1:36	AQU
20	17:18	SCO	20	5:12	SAG	20	17:48	AQU	20	2:52	PIS
22	23:17	SAG	22	8:58	CAP	22	20:38	PIS	22	5:57	ARI
25	3:37	CAP	24	12:13	AQU	25	0:32	ARI	24	11:25	TAU
27	6:29	AQU	26	15:15	PIS	27	5:46	TAU	26	19:19	GEM
29	8:19	PIS	28	18:24	ARI	29	12:51	GEM	29	5:27	CAN
			30	22:29	TAU				31	17:27	LEO

—1926—

xJAN		
3	6:26	VIR
5	18:44	LIB
8	4:20	SCO
10	10:02	SAG
12	12:09	CAP
14	12:07	AQU
16	11:48	PIS
18	13:04	ARI
20	17:16	TAU
23	0:55	GEM
25	11:30	CAN
27	23:52	LEO
30	12:49	VIR

FEB		
2	1:11	LIB
4	11:40	SCO
6	19:02	SAG
8	22:50	CAP
10	23:37	AQU
12	22:57	PIS
14	22:48	ARI
17	1:09	TAU
19	7:22	GEM
21	17:28	CAN
24	6:00	LEO
26	19:00	VIR

MAR		
1	7:04	LIB
3	17:28	SCO
6	1:40	SAG
8	7:07	CAP
10	9:40	AQU
12	10:04	PIS
14	9:52	ARI
16	11:07	TAU
18	15:42	GEM
21	0:31	CAN
23	12:36	LEO
26	1:37	VIR
28	13:27	LIB
30	23:17	SCO

APR		
2	7:08	SAG
4	13:05	CAP
6	17:01	AQU
8	19:04	PIS
10	20:03	ARI
12	21:31	TAU
15	1:21	GEM
17	8:55	CAN
19	20:07	LEO
22	8:59	VIR
24	20:52	LIB
27	6:19	SCO
29	13:19	SAG

MAY		
1	18:33	CAP
3	22:32	AQU
6	1:32	PIS
8	3:55	ARI
10	6:34	TAU
12	10:46	GEM
14	17:53	CAN
17	4:20	LEO
19	16:55	VIR
22	5:04	LIB
24	14:42	SCO
26	21:14	SAG
29	1:24	CAP
31	4:19	AQU

JUN		
2	6:53	PIS
4	9:46	ARI
6	13:29	TAU
8	18:43	GEM
11	2:15	CAN
13	12:29	LEO
16	0:49	VIR
18	13:19	LIB
20	23:40	SCO
23	6:35	SAG
25	10:18	CAP
27	12:01	AQU
29	13:14	PIS

JUL		
1	15:14	ARI
3	18:59	TAU
6	0:57	GEM
8	9:17	CAN
10	19:51	LEO
13	8:08	VIR
15	20:52	LIB
18	8:08	SCO
20	16:11	SAG
22	20:28	CAP
24	21:48	AQU
26	21:46	PIS
28	22:13	ARI
31	0:47	TAU

AUG		
2	6:25	GEM
4	15:08	CAN
7	2:13	LEO
9	14:39	VIR
12	3:27	LIB
14	15:18	SCO
17	0:40	SAG
19	6:24	CAP
21	8:31	AQU
23	8:14	PIS
25	7:30	ARI
27	8:25	TAU
29	12:40	GEM
31	20:49	CAN

SEP		
3	8:01	LEO
5	20:41	VIR
8	9:23	LIB
10	21:16	SCO
13	7:22	SAG
15	14:37	CAP
17	18:23	AQU
19	19:07	PIS
21	18:20	ARI
23	18:13	TAU
25	20:51	GEM
28	3:35	CAN
30	14:11	LEO

OCT		
3	2:49	VIR
5	15:29	LIB
8	2:59	SCO
10	12:54	SAG
12	20:47	CAP
15	2:03	AQU
17	4:30	PIS
19	4:56	ARI
21	5:01	TAU
23	6:50	GEM
25	12:09	CAN
27	21:31	LEO
30	9:43	VIR

NOV		
1	22:23	LIB
4	9:38	SCO
6	18:52	SAG
9	2:11	CAP
11	7:42	AQU
13	11:22	PIS
15	13:28	ARI
17	14:54	TAU
19	17:10	GEM
21	21:55	CAN
24	6:10	LEO
26	17:36	VIR
29	6:14	LIB

DEC		
1	17:40	SCO
4	2:32	SAG
6	8:53	CAP
8	13:22	AQU
10	16:44	PIS
12	19:33	ARI
14	22:23	TAU
17	2:00	GEM
19	7:20	CAN
21	15:17	LEO
24	2:03	VIR
26	14:31	LIB
29	2:29	SCO
31	11:50	SAG

—1927—

JAN		
2	17:52	CAP
4	21:11	AQU
6	23:06	PIS
9	1:00	ARI
11	3:56	TAU
13	8:31	GEM
15	14:59	CAN
17	23:32	LEO
20	10:10	VIR
22	22:27	LIB
25	10:54	SCO
27	21:21	SAG
30	4:12	CAP

FEB		
1	7:22	AQU
3	8:07	PIS
5	8:20	ARI
7	9:51	TAU
9	13:55	GEM
11	20:51	CAN
14	6:12	LEO
16	17:16	VIR
19	5:31	LIB
21	18:09	SCO
24	5:35	SAG
26	13:56	CAP
28	18:14	AQU

MAR		
2	19:06	PIS
4	18:19	ARI
6	18:07	TAU
8	20:29	GEM
11	2:30	CAN
13	11:52	LEO
15	23:23	VIR
18	11:49	LIB
21	0:21	SCO
23	12:07	SAG
25	21:39	CAP
28	3:39	AQU
30	5:53	PIS

APR		
1	5:31	ARI
3	4:36	TAU
5	5:25	GEM
7	9:43	CAN
9	18:00	LEO
12	5:19	VIR
14	17:54	LIB
17	6:20	SCO
19	17:49	SAG
22	3:36	CAP
24	10:43	AQU
26	14:38	PIS
28	15:44	ARI
30	15:29	TAU

MAY		
2	15:53	GEM
4	18:52	CAN
7	1:39	LEO
9	12:03	VIR
12	0:27	LIB
14	12:52	SCO
16	23:58	SAG
19	9:11	CAP
21	16:16	AQU
23	21:02	PIS
25	23:38	ARI
28	0:51	TAU
30	2:03	GEM

JUN		
1	4:50	CAN
3	10:38	LEO
5	19:56	VIR
8	7:50	LIB
10	20:16	SCO
13	7:16	SAG
15	15:52	CAP
17	22:05	AQU
20	2:25	PIS
22	5:29	ARI
24	7:54	TAU
26	10:27	GEM
28	14:04	CAN
30	19:49	LEO

JUL		
3	4:27	VIR
5	15:48	LIB
8	4:17	SCO
10	15:37	SAG
13	0:07	CAP
15	5:31	AQU
17	8:43	PIS
19	10:58	ARI
21	13:24	TAU
23	16:46	GEM
25	21:31	CAN
28	4:01	LEO
30	12:42	VIR

AUG		
1	23:44	LIB
4	12:16	SCO
7	0:14	SAG
9	9:23	CAP
11	14:46	AQU
13	17:05	PIS
15	17:58	ARI
17	19:12	TAU
19	22:09	GEM
22	3:19	CAN
24	10:39	LEO
26	19:56	VIR
29	7:03	LIB
31	19:36	SCO

SEP		
3	8:10	SAG
5	18:29	CAP
8	0:50	AQU
10	3:16	PIS
12	3:18	ARI
14	3:03	TAU
16	4:29	GEM
18	8:50	CAN
20	16:13	LEO
23	2:02	VIR
25	13:30	LIB
28	2:06	SCO
30	14:54	SAG

OCT		
3	2:13	CAP
5	10:07	AQU
7	13:50	PIS
9	14:15	ARI
11	13:18	TAU
13	13:12	GEM
15	15:50	CAN
17	22:07	LEO
20	7:43	VIR
22	19:28	LIB
25	8:09	SCO
27	20:48	SAG
30	8:23	CAP

NOV		
1	17:27	AQU
3	22:56	PIS
6	0:54	ARI
8	0:37	TAU
10	0:04	GEM
12	1:16	CAN
14	5:49	LEO
16	14:14	VIR
19	1:41	LIB
21	14:26	SCO
24	2:54	SAG
26	14:01	CAP
28	23:07	AQU

DEC		
1	5:37	PIS
3	9:20	ARI
5	10:47	TAU
7	11:11	GEM
9	12:11	CAN
11	15:32	LEO
13	22:25	VIR
16	8:55	LIB
18	21:32	SCO
21	9:59	SAG
23	20:38	CAP
26	4:55	AQU
28	11:00	PIS
30	15:19	ARI

—1928—

JAN			FEB			MAR			APR		
1	18:15	TAU	2	6:22	CAN	2	17:38	LEO	1	6:54	VIR
3	20:20	GEM	4	10:53	LEO	5	0:52	VIR	3	16:47	LIB
5	22:28	CAN	6	17:10	VIR	7	10:05	LIB	6	4:28	SCO
8	1:53	LEO	9	2:04	LIB	9	21:31	SCO	8	17:20	SAG
10	7:54	VIR	11	13:42	SCO	12	10:25	SAG	11	5:57	CAP
12	17:18	LIB	14	2:32	SAG	14	22:34	CAP	13	16:07	AQU
15	5:27	SCO	16	13:54	CAP	17	7:31	AQU	15	22:20	PIS
17	18:07	SAG	18	21:47	AQU	19	12:20	PIS	18	0:40	ARI
20	4:50	CAP	21	2:06	PIS	21	13:54	ARI	20	0:36	TAU
22	12:28	AQU	23	4:09	ARI	23	14:06	TAU	22	0:09	GEM
24	17:25	PIS	25	5:42	TAU	25	14:54	GEM	24	1:14	CAN
26	20:48	ARI	27	8:08	GEM	27	17:42	CAN	26	5:12	LEO
28	23:43	TAU	29	12:05	CAN	29	23:05	LEO	28	12:29	VIR
31	2:47	GEM							30	22:36	LIB

MAY			JUN			JUL			AUG		
3	10:38	SCO	2	5:38	SAG	2	0:24	CAP	3	0:35	PIS
5	23:33	SAG	4	18:00	CAP	4	10:32	AQU	5	5:33	ARI
8	12:09	CAP	7	4:41	AQU	6	18:23	PIS	7	9:19	TAU
10	22:58	AQU	9	12:55	PIS	9	0:04	ARI	9	12:22	GEM
13	6:35	PIS	11	18:14	ARI	11	3:49	TAU	11	15:04	CAN
15	10:30	ARI	13	20:46	TAU	13	6:00	GEM	13	17:57	LEO
17	11:26	TAU	15	21:24	GEM	15	7:20	CAN	15	22:08	VIR
19	10:57	GEM	17	21:35	CAN	17	9:06	LEO	18	4:53	LIB
21	10:58	CAN	19	23:03	LEO	19	12:53	VIR	20	14:57	SCO
23	13:17	LEO	22	3:27	VIR	21	20:02	LIB	23	3:29	SAG
25	19:07	VIR	24	11:43	LIB	24	6:48	SCO	25	15:59	CAP
28	4:37	LIB	26	23:17	SCO	26	19:35	SAG	28	1:57	AQU
30	16:41	SCO	29	12:14	SAG	29	7:47	CAP	30	8:31	PIS
						31	17:34	AQU			

SEP			OCT			NOV			DEC		
1	12:27	ARI	3	0:10	GEM	1	9:41	CAN	3	0:17	VIR
3	15:07	TAU	5	2:21	CAN	3	12:14	LEO	5	7:53	LIB
5	17:43	GEM	7	6:18	LEO	5	17:42	VIR	7	18:46	SCO
7	20:52	CAN	9	12:14	VIR	8	2:05	LIB	10	7:30	SAG
10	0:50	LEO	11	20:15	LIB	10	12:54	SCO	12	20:30	CAP
12	6:02	VIR	14	6:29	SCO	13	1:21	SAG	15	8:36	AQU
14	13:13	LIB	16	18:45	SAG	15	14:26	CAP	17	18:49	PIS
16	23:05	SCO	19	7:51	CAP	18	2:40	AQU	20	2:16	ARI
19	11:24	SAG	21	19:34	AQU	20	12:20	PIS	22	6:25	TAU
22	0:16	CAP	24	3:50	PIS	22	18:14	ARI	24	7:40	GEM
24	11:02	AQU	26	8:05	ARI	24	20:31	TAU	26	7:17	CAN
26	18:02	PIS	28	9:16	TAU	26	20:24	GEM	28	7:07	LEO
28	21:31	ARI	30	9:11	GEM	28	19:44	CAN	30	9:13	VIR
30	23:00	TAU				30	20:29	LEO			

—1929—

	JAN			FEB			MAR			APR	
1	15:09	LIB	2	20:59	SAG	2	5:03	SAG	1	2:03	CAP
4	1:10	SCO	5	10:01	CAP	4	17:55	CAP	3	14:18	AQU
6	13:50	SAG	7	21:35	AQU	7	5:45	AQU	5	23:52	PIS
9	2:51	CAP	10	6:43	PIS	9	14:44	PIS	8	5:58	ARI
11	14:33	AQU	12	13:41	ARI	11	20:52	ARI	10	9:17	TAU
14	0:22	PIS	14	19:02	TAU	14	1:05	TAU	12	11:13	GEM
16	8:07	ARI	16	23:02	GEM	16	4:24	GEM	14	13:05	CAN
18	13:37	TAU	19	1:45	CAN	18	7:24	CAN	16	15:51	LEO
20	16:44	GEM	21	3:41	LEO	20	10:28	LEO	18	20:06	VIR
22	17:52	CAN	23	5:59	VIR	22	14:05	VIR	21	2:14	LIB
24	18:17	LEO	25	10:15	LIB	24	19:12	LIB	23	10:35	SCO
26	19:48	VIR	27	17:54	SCO	27	2:50	SCO	25	21:16	SAG
29	0:19	LIB				29	13:26	SAG	28	9:43	CAP
31	8:57	SCO							30	22:19	AQU

	MAY			JUN			JUL			AUG	
3	8:51	PIS	2	0:58	ARI	1	14:32	TAU	2	3:16	CAN
5	15:51	ARI	4	5:35	TAU	3	17:14	GEM	4	3:11	LEO
7	19:18	TAU	6	6:57	GEM	5	17:21	CAN	6	3:23	VIR
9	20:22	GEM	8	6:35	CAN	7	16:37	LEO	8	5:56	LIB
11	20:45	CAN	10	6:25	LEO	9	17:10	VIR	10	12:22	SCO
13	22:03	LEO	12	8:20	VIR	11	20:54	LIB	12	22:45	SAG
16	1:34	VIR	14	13:39	LIB	14	4:45	SCO	15	11:21	CAP
18	7:53	LIB	16	22:33	SCO	16	16:00	SAG	17	23:50	AQU
20	16:54	SCO	19	10:03	SAG	19	4:48	CAP	20	10:46	PIS
23	4:04	SAG	21	22:45	CAP	21	17:20	AQU	22	19:47	ARI
25	16:35	CAP	24	11:24	AQU	24	4:40	PIS	25	2:56	TAU
28	5:18	AQU	26	22:59	PIS	26	14:13	ARI	27	8:03	GEM
30	16:38	PIS	29	8:22	ARI	28	21:25	TAU	29	11:04	CAN
						31	1:43	GEM	31	12:27	LEO

	SEP			OCT			NOV			DEC	
2	13:27	VIR	2	1:10	LIB	2	23:47	SAG	2	18:26	CAP
4	15:51	LIB	4	6:40	SCO	5	10:57	CAP	5	6:58	AQU
6	21:21	SCO	6	15:19	SAG	7	23:33	AQU	S7	19:28	PIS
9	6:39	SAG	9	2:50	CAP	10	11:31	PIS	10	5:58	ARI
11	18:45	CAP	11	15:26	AQU	12	20:43	ARI	12	12:50	TAU
14	7:17	AQU	14	2:40	PIS	15	2:19	TAU	14	15:49	GEM
16	18:07	PIS	16	11:02	ARI	17	4:53	GEM	16	16:05	CAN
19	2:31	ARI	18	16:29	TAU	19	5:53	CAN	18	15:35	LEO
21	8:46	TAU	20	19:55	GEM	21	6:58	LEO	20	16:22	VIR
23	13:25	GEM	22	22:24	CAN	23	9:32	VIR	22	20:03	LIB
25	16:52	CAN	25	0:55	LEO	25	14:23	LIB	25	3:12	SCO
27	19:28	LEO	27	4:09	VIR	27	21:40	SCO	27	13:12	SAG
29	21:52	VIR	29	8:39	LIB	30	7:08	SAG	30	0:56	CAP
			31	15:02	SCO						

—1930—

JAN			FEB			MAR			APR		
1	13:30	AQU	2	19:23	ARI	2	1:09	ARI	2	22:43	GEM
4	2:05	PIS	5	4:49	TAU	4	10:19	TAU	5	3:11	CAN
6	13:28	ARI	7	11:08	GEM	6	17:16	GEM	7	6:09	LEO
8	21:59	TAU	9	13:56	CAN	8	21:35	CAN	9	8:11	VIR
11	2:35	GEM	11	14:01	LEO	10	23:26	LEO	11	10:17	LIB
13	3:35	CAN	13	13:14	VIR	12	23:54	VIR	13	13:45	SCO
15	2:38	LEO	15	13:51	LIB	15	0:44	LIB	15	19:50	SAG
17	1:57	VIR	17	17:45	SCO	17	3:46	SCO	18	5:08	CAP
19	3:45	LIB	20	1:49	SAG	19	10:24	SAG	20	16:59	AQU
21	9:25	SCO	22	13:13	CAP	21	20:40	CAP	23	5:24	PIS
23	18:56	SAG	25	1:57	AQU	24	9:05	AQU	25	16:10	ARI
26	6:53	CAP	27	14:13	PIS	26	21:24	PIS	28	0:09	TAU
28	19:35	AQU				29	8:00	ARI	30	5:26	GEM
31	7:59	PIS				31	16:24	TAU			

MAY			JUN			JUL			AUG		
2	8:54	CAN	2	19:37	VIR	2	4:47	LIB	2	23:25	SAG
4	11:32	LEO	4	23:04	LIB	4	9:56	SCO	5	9:35	CAP
6	14:11	VIR	7	4:30	SCO	6	17:50	SAG	7	21:27	AQU
8	17:30	LIB	9	11:56	SAG	9	3:50	CAP	10	10:03	PIS
10	22:07	SCO	11	21:21	CAP	11	15:23	AQU	12	22:33	ARI
13	4:39	SAG	14	8:39	AQU	14	3:58	PIS	15	9:38	TAU
15	13:40	CAP	16	21:12	PIS	16	16:26	ARI	17	17:46	GEM
18	1:04	AQU	19	9:15	ARI	19	2:55	TAU	19	22:02	CAN
20	13:34	PIS	21	18:36	TAU	21	9:40	GEM	21	22:58	LEO
23	0:56	ARI	24	0:01	GEM	23	12:23	CAN	23	22:14	VIR
25	9:16	TAU	26	1:58	CAN	25	12:19	LEO	25	21:58	LIB
27	14:07	GEM	28	2:07	LEO	27	11:35	VIR	28	0:11	SCO
29	16:26	CAN	30	2:29	VIR	29	12:18	LIB	30	6:05	SAG
31	17:45	LEO				31	16:05	SCO			

SEP			OCT			NOV			DEC		
1	15:36	CAP	1	10:10	AQU	2	18:35	ARI	2	13:32	TAU
4	3:28	AQU	3	22:48	PIS	5	4:38	TAU	4	20:32	GEM
6	16:07	PIS	6	10:52	ARI	7	11:59	GEM	7	0:32	CAN
9	4:22	ARI	8	21:15	TAU	9	17:05	CAN	9	2:53	LEO
11	15:18	TAU	11	5:30	GEM	11	20:46	LEO	11	5:04	VIR
14	0:01	GEM	13	11:30	CAN	13	23:42	VIR	13	8:05	LIB
16	5:43	CAN	15	15:20	LEO	16	2:27	LIB	15	12:20	SCO
18	8:19	LEO	17	17:26	VIR	18	5:37	SCO	17	17:55	SAG
20	8:46	VIR	19	18:44	LIB	20	10:01	SAG	20	1:12	CAP
22	8:44	LIB	21	20:33	SCO	22	16:42	CAP	22	10:44	AQU
24	10:08	SCO	24	0:24	SAG	25	2:23	AQU	24	22:36	PIS
26	14:35	SAG	26	7:27	CAP	27	14:33	PIS	27	11:30	ARI
28	22:49	CAP	28	17:54	AQU	30	3:07	ARI	29	22:52	TAU
			31	6:23	PIS						

—1931—

JAN

1	6:35	GEM
3	10:21	CAN
5	11:32	LEO
7	12:06	VIR
9	13:49	LIB
11	17:41	SCO
13	23:51	SAG
16	8:02	CAP
18	18:04	AQU
21	5:55	PIS
23	18:55	ARI
26	7:10	TAU
28	16:19	GEM
30	21:10	CAN

FEB

1	22:25	LEO
3	21:57	VIR
5	21:55	LIB
8	0:05	SCO
10	5:22	SAG
12	13:39	CAP
15	0:15	AQU
17	12:24	PIS
20	1:21	ARI
22	13:54	TAU
25	0:13	GEM
27	6:47	CAN

MAR

1	9:25	LEO
3	9:21	VIR
5	8:33	LIB
7	9:03	SCO
9	12:30	SAG
11	19:39	CAP
14	6:04	AQU
16	18:27	PIS
19	7:24	ARI
21	19:45	TAU
24	6:19	GEM
26	14:05	CAN
28	18:29	LEO
30	19:58	VIR

APR

1	19:50	LIB
3	19:51	SCO
5	21:52	SAG
8	3:21	CAP
10	12:40	AQU
13	0:49	PIS
15	13:48	ARI
18	1:51	TAU
20	11:56	GEM
22	19:43	CAN
25	1:04	LEO
27	4:10	VIR
29	5:35	LIB

MAY

1	6:26	SCO
3	8:14	SAG
5	12:36	CAP
7	20:37	AQU
10	8:02	PIS
12	20:57	ARI
15	8:55	TAU
17	18:27	GEM
20	1:26	CAN
22	6:28	LEO
24	10:07	VIR
26	12:51	LIB
28	15:08	SCO
30	17:48	SAG

JUN

1	22:08	CAP
4	5:24	AQU
6	16:01	PIS
9	4:44	ARI
11	16:55	TAU
14	2:22	GEM
16	8:38	CAN
18	12:37	LEO
20	15:33	VIR
22	18:23	LIB
24	21:35	SCO
27	1:27	SAG
29	6:35	CAP

JUL

1	13:57	AQU
4	0:10	PIS
6	12:40	ARI
9	1:14	TAU
11	11:14	GEM
13	17:31	CAN
15	20:42	LEO
17	22:22	VIR
20	0:06	LIB
22	2:57	SCO
24	7:19	SAG
26	13:23	CAP
28	21:25	AQU
31	7:46	PIS

AUG

2	20:10	ARI
5	9:05	TAU
7	20:02	GEM
10	3:11	CAN
12	6:31	LEO
14	7:26	VIR
16	7:45	LIB
18	9:11	SCO
20	12:47	SAG
22	18:59	CAP
25	3:38	AQU
27	14:28	PIS
30	2:57	ARI

SEP

1	15:59	TAU
4	3:44	GEM
6	12:15	CAN
8	16:48	LEO
10	18:04	VIR
12	17:43	LIB
14	17:41	SCO
16	19:40	SAG
19	0:48	CAP
21	9:18	AQU
23	20:29	PIS
26	9:10	ARI
28	22:07	TAU

OCT

1	10:04	GEM
3	19:38	CAN
6	1:50	LEO
8	4:35	VIR
10	4:50	LIB
12	4:17	SCO
14	4:51	SAG
16	8:19	CAP
18	15:39	AQU
21	2:33	PIS
23	15:21	ARI
26	4:12	TAU
28	15:48	GEM
31	1:27	CAN

NOV

2	8:40	LEO
4	13:08	VIR
6	15:03	LIB
8	15:21	SCO
10	15:39	SAG
12	17:52	CAP
14	23:41	AQU
17	9:33	PIS
19	22:09	ARI
22	11:00	TAU
24	22:12	GEM
27	7:10	CAN
29	14:06	LEO

DEC

1	19:17	VIR
3	22:45	LIB
6	0:43	SCO
8	2:04	SAG
10	4:18	CAP
12	9:10	AQU
14	17:51	PIS
17	5:50	ARI
19	18:46	TAU
22	6:00	GEM
24	14:22	CAN
26	20:17	LEO
29	0:41	VIR
31	4:18	LIB

—1932—

JAN			FEB			MAR			APR		
2	7:24	SCO	2	20:39	CAP	1	2:07	CAP	2	0:05	PIS
4	10:16	SAG	5	2:49	AQU	3	9:01	AQU	4	11:53	ARI
6	13:37	CAP	7	11:15	PIS	5	18:16	PIS	7	0:44	TAU
8	18:44	AQU	9	22:18	ARI	8	5:36	ARI	9	13:27	GEM
11	2:50	PIS	12	11:05	TAU	10	18:20	TAU	12	0:47	CAN
13	14:08	ARI	14	23:28	GEM	13	7:03	GEM	14	9:22	LEO
16	3:03	TAU	17	9:03	CAN	15	17:46	CAN	16	14:22	VIR
18	14:48	GEM	19	14:49	LEO	18	0:56	LEO	18	16:00	LIB
20	23:23	CAN	21	17:25	VIR	20	4:19	VIR	20	15:34	SCO
23	4:40	LEO	23	18:22	LIB	22	4:57	LIB	22	14:58	SAG
25	7:47	VIR	25	19:20	SCO	24	4:35	SCO	24	16:15	CAP
27	10:08	LIB	27	21:39	SAG	26	5:07	SAG	26	21:05	AQU
29	12:43	SCO				28	8:08	CAP	29	5:56	PIS
31	16:07	SAG				30	14:31	AQU			

MAY			JUN			JUL			AUG		
1	17:47	ARI	3	1:33	GEM	2	19:07	CAN	1	10:57	LEO
4	6:46	TAU	5	12:21	CAN	5	3:19	LEO	3	16:15	VIR
6	19:20	GEM	7	21:15	LEO	7	9:33	VIR	5	19:56	LIB
9	6:35	CAN	10	4:07	VIR	9	14:13	LIB	7	22:50	SCO
11	15:47	LEO	12	8:42	LIB	11	17:28	SCO	10	1:32	SAG
13	22:14	VIR	14	11:00	SCO	13	19:38	SAG	12	4:39	CAP
16	1:33	LIB	16	11:46	SAG	15	21:36	CAP	14	8:54	AQU
18	2:15	SCO	18	12:31	CAP	18	0:45	AQU	16	15:14	PIS
20	1:48	SAG	20	15:12	AQU	20	6:35	PIS	19	0:18	ARI
22	2:13	CAP	22	21:26	PIS	22	15:52	ARI	21	11:56	TAU
24	5:31	AQU	25	7:34	ARI	25	3:55	TAU	24	0:34	GEM
26	12:58	PIS	27	20:08	TAU	27	16:27	GEM	26	11:50	CAN
29	0:09	ARI	30	8:35	GEM	30	3:08	CAN	28	20:03	LEO
31	13:05	TAU							31	0:59	VIR

SEP			OCT			NOV			DEC		
2	3:32	LIB	1	13:44	SCO	1	23:55	CAP	1	11:47	AQU
4	5:06	SCO	3	14:03	SAG	4	3:06	AQU	3	17:08	PIS
6	7:00	SAG	5	16:00	CAP	6	10:07	PIS	6	2:35	ARI
8	10:12	CAP	7	20:44	AQU	8	20:25	ARI	8	14:42	TAU
10	15:16	AQU	10	4:27	PIS	11	8:34	TAU	11	3:26	GEM
12	22:31	PIS	12	14:36	ARI	13	21:14	GEM	13	15:28	CAN
15	8:01	ARI	15	2:24	TAU	16	9:32	CAN	16	2:13	LEO
17	19:34	TAU	17	15:03	GEM	18	20:36	LEO	18	11:09	VIR
20	8:14	GEM	20	3:27	CAN	21	5:09	VIR	20	17:32	LIB
22	20:14	CAN	22	13:57	LEO	23	10:08	LIB	22	20:53	SCO
25	5:32	LEO	24	21:03	VIR	25	11:38	SCO	24	21:43	SAG
27	11:07	VIR	27	0:16	LIB	27	10:59	SAG	26	21:31	CAP
29	13:22	LIB	29	0:31	SCO	29	10:17	CAP	28	22:23	AQU
			30	23:40	SAG				31	2:17	PIS

—1933—

JAN

2	10:14	ARI
4	21:37	TAU
7	10:20	GEM
9	22:17	CAN
12	8:27	LEO
14	16:42	VIR
16	23:03	LIB
19	3:25	SCO
21	5:55	SAG
23	7:18	CAP
25	8:57	AQU
27	12:31	PIS
29	19:21	ARI

FEB

1	5:40	TAU
3	18:05	GEM
6	6:14	CAN
8	16:17	LEO
10	23:43	VIR
13	4:59	LIB
15	8:47	SCO
17	11:43	SAG
19	14:23	CAP
21	17:29	AQU
23	21:56	PIS
26	4:43	ARI
28	14:20	TAU

MAR

3	2:18	GEM
5	14:43	CAN
8	1:18	LEO
10	8:42	VIR
12	13:03	LIB
14	15:28	SCO
16	17:19	SAG
18	19:47	CAP
20	23:39	AQU
23	5:16	PIS
25	12:50	ARI
27	22:32	TAU
30	10:14	GEM

APR

1	22:50	CAN
4	10:17	LEO
6	18:33	VIR
8	23:01	LIB
11	0:32	SCO
13	0:52	SAG
15	1:54	CAP
17	5:03	AQU
19	10:54	PIS
21	19:14	ARI
24	5:31	TAU
26	17:18	GEM
29	5:59	CAN

MAY

1	18:07	LEO
4	3:41	VIR
6	9:17	LIB
8	11:07	SCO
10	10:43	SAG
12	10:15	CAP
14	11:46	AQU
16	16:34	PIS
19	0:46	ARI
21	11:27	TAU
23	23:32	GEM
26	12:12	CAN
29	0:34	LEO
31	11:06	VIR

JUN

2	18:15	LIB
4	21:25	SCO
6	21:32	SAG
8	20:33	CAP
10	20:41	AQU
12	23:50	PIS
15	6:51	ARI
17	17:12	TAU
20	5:26	GEM
22	18:07	CAN
25	6:17	LEO
27	17:01	VIR
30	1:11	LIB

JUL

2	5:57	SCO
4	7:32	SAG
6	7:16	CAP
8	7:05	AQU
10	9:02	PIS
12	14:31	ARI
14	23:49	TAU
17	11:45	GEM
20	0:25	CAN
22	12:19	LEO
24	22:36	VIR
27	6:45	LIB
29	12:22	SCO
31	15:27	SAG

AUG

2	16:41	CAP
4	17:22	AQU
6	19:11	PIS
8	23:41	ARI
11	7:45	TAU
13	18:58	GEM
16	7:33	CAN
18	19:23	LEO
21	5:08	VIR
23	12:30	LIB
25	17:45	SCO
27	21:21	SAG
29	23:52	CAP

SEP

1	2:00	AQU
3	4:44	PIS
5	9:15	ARI
7	16:35	TAU
10	3:01	GEM
12	15:25	CAN
15	3:31	LEO
17	13:14	VIR
19	19:52	LIB
22	0:00	SCO
24	2:49	SAG
26	5:23	CAP
28	8:27	AQU
30	12:27	PIS

OCT

2	17:51	ARI
5	1:18	TAU
7	11:18	GEM
9	23:30	CAN
12	12:02	LEO
14	22:25	VIR
17	5:08	LIB
19	8:28	SCO
21	9:54	SAG
23	11:14	CAP
25	13:49	AQU
27	18:18	PIS
30	0:41	ARI

NOV

1	8:53	TAU
3	19:02	GEM
6	7:05	CAN
8	19:58	LEO
11	7:24	VIR
13	15:13	LIB
15	18:52	SCO
17	19:35	SAG
19	19:24	CAP
21	20:21	AQU
23	23:50	PIS
26	6:13	ARI
28	15:03	TAU

DEC

1	1:45	GEM
3	13:53	CAN
6	2:49	LEO
8	15:00	VIR
11	0:19	LIB
13	5:27	SCO
15	6:49	SAG
17	6:08	CAP
19	5:38	AQU
21	7:15	PIS
23	12:16	ARI
25	20:43	TAU
28	7:43	GEM
30	20:07	CAN

—1934—

JAN

2	8:56	LEO
4	21:09	VIR
7	7:21	LIB
9	14:11	SCO
11	17:18	SAG
13	17:37	CAP
15	16:56	AQU
17	17:18	PIS
19	20:28	ARI
22	3:27	TAU
24	13:54	GEM
27	2:24	CAN
29	15:12	LEO

FEB

1	3:01	VIR
3	13:00	LIB
5	20:32	SCO
8	1:15	SAG
10	3:24	CAP
12	3:57	AQU
14	4:28	PIS
16	6:40	ARI
18	12:04	TAU
20	21:17	GEM
23	9:23	CAN
25	22:14	LEO
28	9:46	VIR

MAR

2	19:02	LIB
5	1:59	SCO
7	6:59	SAG
9	10:22	CAP
11	12:36	AQU
13	14:26	PIS
15	17:00	ARI
17	21:46	TAU
20	5:52	GEM
22	17:13	CAN
25	6:03	LEO
27	17:45	VIR
30	2:37	LIB

APR

1	8:36	SCO
3	12:37	SAG
5	15:46	CAP
7	18:43	AQU
9	21:52	PIS
12	1:40	ARI
14	6:56	TAU
16	14:42	GEM
19	1:27	CAN
21	14:10	LEO
24	2:20	VIR
26	11:33	LIB
28	17:07	SCO
30	20:02	SAG

MAY

2	21:54	CAP
5	0:06	AQU
7	3:26	PIS
9	8:09	ARI
11	14:24	TAU
13	22:38	GEM
16	9:18	CAN
18	21:55	LEO
21	10:36	VIR
23	20:43	LIB
26	2:52	SCO
28	5:29	SAG
30	6:12	CAP

JUN

1	6:56	AQU
3	9:07	PIS
5	13:32	ARI
7	20:17	TAU
10	5:14	GEM
12	16:14	CAN
15	4:53	LEO
17	17:52	VIR
20	4:59	LIB
22	12:25	SCO
24	15:50	SAG
26	16:25	CAP
28	16:03	AQU
30	16:38	PIS

JUL

2	19:39	ARI
5	1:48	TAU
7	10:56	GEM
9	22:21	CAN
12	11:08	LEO
15	0:07	VIR
17	11:48	LIB
19	20:31	SCO
22	1:28	SAG
24	3:04	CAP
26	2:44	AQU
28	2:21	PIS
30	3:46	ARI

AUG

1	8:25	TAU
3	16:49	GEM
6	4:13	CAN
8	17:08	LEO
11	5:59	VIR
13	17:33	LIB
16	2:51	SCO
18	9:12	SAG
20	12:27	CAP
22	13:19	AQU
24	13:08	PIS
26	13:44	ARI
28	16:55	TAU
30	23:56	GEM

SEP

2	10:41	CAN
4	23:32	LEO
7	12:17	VIR
9	23:23	LIB
12	8:20	SCO
14	15:04	SAG
16	19:36	CAP
18	22:07	AQU
20	23:14	PIS
23	0:13	ARI
25	2:47	TAU
27	8:34	GEM
29	18:15	CAN

OCT

2	6:45	LEO
4	19:31	VIR
7	6:21	LIB
9	14:32	SCO
11	20:32	SAG
14	1:04	CAP
16	4:32	AQU
18	7:10	PIS
20	9:29	ARI
22	12:35	TAU
24	17:58	GEM
27	2:46	CAN
29	14:43	LEO

NOV

1	3:36	VIR
3	14:41	LIB
5	22:33	SCO
8	3:33	SAG
10	6:57	CAP
12	9:52	AQU
14	12:57	PIS
16	16:26	ARI
18	20:47	TAU
21	2:48	GEM
23	11:26	CAN
25	22:54	LEO
28	11:52	VIR
30	23:39	LIB

DEC

3	8:06	SCO
5	12:53	SAG
7	15:09	CAP
9	16:34	AQU
11	18:31	PIS
13	21:51	ARI
16	2:57	TAU
18	9:58	GEM
20	19:11	CAN
23	6:38	LEO
25	19:32	VIR
28	8:00	LIB
30	17:42	SCO

—1935—

JAN			FEB			MAR			APR		
1	23:27	SAG	2	13:26	AQU	2	0:16	AQU	2	10:32	ARI
4	1:44	CAP	4	12:47	PIS	4	0:13	PIS	4	11:18	TAU
6	2:04	AQU	6	12:49	ARI	5	23:41	ARI	6	14:35	GEM
8	2:18	PIS	8	15:23	TAU	8	0:43	TAU	8	21:49	CAN
10	4:03	ARI	10	21:36	GEM	10	5:12	GEM	11	8:52	LEO
12	8:25	TAU	13	7:24	CAN	12	13:52	CAN	13	21:47	VIR
14	15:43	GEM	15	19:35	LEO	15	1:48	LEO	16	10:01	LIB
17	1:38	CAN	18	8:33	VIR	17	14:52	VIR	18	20:10	SCO
19	13:27	LEO	20	21:03	LIB	20	3:08	LIB	21	4:06	SAG
22	2:20	VIR	23	8:05	SCO	22	13:45	SCO	23	10:14	CAP
24	15:00	LIB	25	16:41	SAG	24	22:24	SAG	25	14:44	AQU
27	1:46	SCO	27	22:05	CAP	27	4:49	CAP	27	17:40	PIS
29	9:11	SAG				29	8:42	AQU	29	19:27	ARI
31	12:48	CAP				31	10:15	PIS			

MAY			JUN			JUL			AUG		
1	21:10	TAU	2	15:44	CAN	2	9:13	LEO	1	4:07	VIR
4	0:26	GEM	5	1:20	LEO	4	21:09	VIR	3	16:55	LIB
6	6:51	CAN	7	13:26	VIR	7	9:53	LIB	6	4:57	SCO
8	16:55	LEO	10	2:00	LIB	9	21:15	SCO	8	14:25	SAG
11	5:26	VIR	12	12:36	SCO	12	5:28	SAG	10	20:10	CAP
13	17:48	LIB	14	19:57	SAG	14	10:03	CAP	12	22:22	AQU
16	3:55	SCO	17	0:21	CAP	16	11:54	AQU	14	22:19	PIS
18	11:13	SAG	19	2:56	AQU	18	12:31	PIS	16	21:55	ARI
20	16:21	CAP	21	4:56	PIS	20	13:33	ARI	18	23:08	TAU
22	20:09	AQU	23	7:21	ARI	22	16:21	TAU	21	3:26	GEM
24	23:14	PIS	25	10:54	TAU	24	21:42	GEM	23	11:17	CAN
27	1:59	ARI	27	16:07	GEM	27	5:44	CAN	25	22:01	LEO
29	4:59	TAU	29	23:27	CAN	29	16:04	LEO	28	10:21	VIR
31	9:11	GEM							30	23:08	LIB

SEP			OCT			NOV			DEC		
2	11:22	SCO	2	3:41	SAG	2	23:38	AQU	2	9:03	PIS
4	21:49	SAG	4	12:03	CAP	5	3:21	PIS	4	11:53	ARI
7	5:08	CAP	6	17:21	AQU	7	4:54	ARI	6	14:04	TAU
9	8:44	AQU	8	19:27	PIS	9	5:29	TAU	8	16:37	GEM
11	9:15	PIS	10	19:21	ARI	11	6:53	GEM	10	20:54	CAN
13	8:21	ARI	12	18:54	TAU	13	10:57	CAN	13	4:07	LEO
15	8:11	TAU	14	20:18	GEM	15	18:51	LEO	15	14:33	VIR
17	10:48	GEM	17	1:21	CAN	18	6:11	VIR	18	2:59	LIB
19	17:27	CAN	19	10:36	LEO	20	18:53	LIB	20	15:03	SCO
22	3:50	LEO	21	22:45	VIR	23	6:36	SCO	23	0:45	SAG
24	16:19	VIR	24	11:32	LIB	25	16:09	SAG	25	7:28	CAP
27	5:06	LIB	26	23:15	SCO	27	23:29	CAP	27	11:46	AQU
29	17:06	SCO	29	9:18	SAG	30	5:00	AQU	29	14:42	PIS
			31	17:31	CAP				31	17:16	ARI

—1936—

JAN			FEB			MAR			APR		
2	20:11	TAU	1	5:39	GEM	1	17:26	CAN	2	19:08	VIR
5	0:04	GEM	3	11:58	CAN	4	2:21	LEO	5	7:31	LIB
7	5:29	CAN	5	20:26	LEO	6	13:18	VIR	7	20:05	SCO
9	13:02	LEO	8	6:48	VIR	9	1:26	LIB	10	8:03	SAG
11	23:05	VIR	10	18:46	LIB	11	14:04	SCO	12	18:23	CAP
14	11:11	LIB	13	7:25	SCO	14	2:06	SAG	15	1:49	AQU
16	23:39	SCO	15	18:57	SAG	16	11:52	CAP	17	5:38	PIS
19	10:12	SAG	18	3:21	CAP	18	17:52	AQU	19	6:21	ARI
21	17:19	CAP	20	7:47	AQU	20	19:59	PIS	21	5:37	TAU
23	21:03	AQU	22	8:56	PIS	22	19:32	ARI	23	5:38	GEM
25	22:35	PIS	24	8:35	ARI	24	18:38	TAU	25	8:23	CAN
27	23:36	ARI	26	8:51	TAU	26	19:32	GEM	27	15:04	LEO
30	1:38	TAU	28	11:30	GEM	28	23:52	CAN	30	1:22	VIR
						31	8:04	LEO			

MAY			JUN			JUL			AUG		
2	13:43	LIB	1	9:12	SCO	1	4:27	SAG	2	4:26	AQU
5	2:17	SCO	3	20:38	SAG	3	13:34	CAP	4	7:36	PIS
7	13:54	SAG	6	6:03	CAP	5	19:57	AQU	6	9:22	ARI
9	23:57	CAP	8	13:18	AQU	8	0:11	PIS	8	11:12	TAU
12	7:48	AQU	10	18:27	PIS	10	3:10	ARI	10	14:12	GEM
14	12:53	PIS	12	21:47	ARI	12	5:46	TAU	12	18:52	CAN
16	15:14	ARI	14	23:49	TAU	14	8:39	GEM	15	1:20	LEO
18	15:48	TAU	17	1:30	GEM	16	12:28	CAN	17	9:45	VIR
20	16:12	GEM	19	4:09	CAN	18	17:58	LEO	19	20:17	LIB
22	18:20	CAN	21	9:06	LEO	21	1:54	VIR	22	8:36	SCO
24	23:42	LEO	23	17:16	VIR	23	12:31	LIB	24	21:10	SAG
27	8:48	VIR	26	4:24	LIB	26	0:54	SCO	27	7:35	CAP
29	20:39	LIB	28	16:53	SCO	28	12:56	SAG	29	14:13	AQU
						30	22:24	CAP	31	17:06	PIS

SEP			OCT			NOV			DEC		
2	17:43	ARI	2	3:25	TAU	2	15:01	CAN	2	4:44	LEO
4	18:04	TAU	4	3:37	GEM	4	19:37	LEO	4	11:31	VIR
6	19:55	GEM	6	6:29	CAN	7	4:00	VIR	6	21:56	LIB
9	0:16	CAN	8	12:45	LEO	9	15:15	LIB	9	10:28	SCO
11	7:13	LEO	10	22:02	VIR	12	3:52	SCO	11	23:07	SAG
13	16:20	VIR	13	9:19	LIB	14	16:34	SAG	14	10:26	CAP
16	3:13	LIB	15	21:47	SCO	17	4:21	CAP	16	19:43	AQU
18	15:33	SCO	18	10:38	SAG	19	14:11	AQU	19	2:44	PIS
21	4:25	SAG	20	22:38	CAP	21	21:04	PIS	21	7:27	ARI
23	15:53	CAP	23	8:00	AQU	24	0:37	ARI	23	10:06	TAU
25	23:53	AQU	25	13:28	PIS	26	1:29	TAU	25	11:25	GEM
28	3:39	PIS	27	15:10	ARI	28	1:12	GEM	27	12:37	CAN
30	4:10	ARI	29	14:34	TAU	30	1:40	CAN	29	15:14	LEO
			31	13:50	GEM				31	20:46	VIR

—1937—

JAN

3	5:55	LIB
5	17:58	SCO
8	6:43	SAG
10	17:54	CAP
13	2:25	AQU
15	8:29	PIS
17	12:49	ARI
19	16:07	TAU
21	18:54	GEM
23	21:38	CAN
26	1:08	LEO
28	6:31	VIR
30	14:50	LIB

FEB

2	2:11	SCO
4	14:59	SAG
7	2:34	CAP
9	11:00	AQU
11	16:10	PIS
13	19:12	ARI
15	21:35	TAU
18	0:23	GEM
20	4:04	CAN
22	8:51	LEO
24	15:05	VIR
26	23:27	LIB

MAR

1	10:23	SCO
3	23:08	SAG
6	11:23	CAP
8	20:36	AQU
11	1:50	PIS
13	4:00	ARI
15	4:54	TAU
17	6:19	GEM
19	9:26	CAN
21	14:36	LEO
23	21:44	VIR
26	6:47	LIB
28	17:51	SCO
31	6:33	SAG

APR

2	19:17	CAP
5	5:39	AQU
7	12:00	PIS
9	14:29	ARI
11	14:40	TAU
13	14:35	GEM
15	16:03	CAN
17	20:12	LEO
20	3:16	VIR
22	12:51	LIB
25	0:21	SCO
27	13:05	SAG
30	1:57	CAP

MAY

2	13:09	AQU
4	20:57	PIS
7	0:48	ARI
9	1:32	TAU
11	0:57	GEM
13	1:01	CAN
15	3:28	LEO
17	9:19	VIR
19	18:35	LIB
22	6:18	SCO
24	19:10	SAG
27	7:54	CAP
29	19:13	AQU

JUN

1	3:58	PIS
3	9:22	ARI
5	11:36	TAU
7	11:46	GEM
9	11:32	CAN
11	12:45	LEO
13	17:01	VIR
16	1:08	LIB
18	12:31	SCO
21	1:26	SAG
23	13:58	CAP
26	0:54	AQU
28	9:37	PIS
30	15:51	ARI

JUL

2	19:35	TAU
4	21:16	GEM
6	21:54	CAN
8	22:59	LEO
11	2:16	VIR
13	9:04	LIB
15	19:36	SCO
18	8:20	SAG
20	20:51	CAP
23	7:20	AQU
25	15:21	PIS
27	21:16	ARI
30	1:32	TAU

AUG

1	4:29	GEM
3	6:34	CAN
5	8:36	LEO
7	11:54	VIR
9	17:59	LIB
12	3:37	SCO
14	15:59	SAG
17	4:38	CAP
19	15:05	AQU
21	22:29	PIS
24	3:24	ARI
26	6:57	TAU
28	10:02	GEM
30	13:04	CAN

SEP

1	16:21	LEO
3	20:35	VIR
6	2:48	LIB
8	12:00	SCO
10	23:59	SAG
13	12:52	CAP
15	23:51	AQU
18	7:19	PIS
20	11:31	ARI
22	13:50	TAU
24	15:46	GEM
26	18:25	CAN
28	22:14	LEO

OCT

1	3:29	VIR
3	10:32	LIB
5	19:55	SCO
8	7:44	SAG
10	20:47	CAP
13	8:38	AQU
15	17:04	PIS
17	21:33	ARI
19	23:10	TAU
21	23:40	GEM
24	0:47	CAN
26	3:43	LEO
28	9:02	VIR
30	16:47	LIB

NOV

2	2:49	SCO
4	14:46	SAG
7	3:50	CAP
9	16:19	AQU
12	2:08	PIS
14	8:00	ARI
16	10:12	TAU
18	10:10	GEM
20	9:48	CAN
22	10:55	LEO
24	14:56	VIR
26	22:22	LIB
29	8:46	SCO

DEC

1	21:06	SAG
4	10:08	CAP
6	22:41	AQU
9	9:22	PIS
11	16:55	ARI
13	20:50	TAU
15	21:43	GEM
17	21:03	CAN
19	20:49	LEO
21	22:57	VIR
24	4:53	LIB
26	14:45	SCO
29	3:12	SAG
31	16:17	CAP

—1938—

JAN		
3	4:32	AQU
5	15:07	PIS
7	23:29	ARI
10	5:06	TAU
12	7:50	GEM
14	8:22	CAN
16	8:10	LEO
18	9:13	VIR
20	13:28	LIB
22	21:55	SCO
25	9:52	SAG
27	22:58	CAP
30	11:00	AQU

FEB		
1	20:59	PIS
4	4:55	ARI
6	10:59	TAU
8	15:08	GEM
10	17:26	CAN
12	18:34	LEO
14	19:57	VIR
16	23:28	LIB
19	6:37	SCO
21	17:34	SAG
24	6:28	CAP
26	18:36	AQU

MAR		
1	4:14	PIS
3	11:17	ARI
5	16:30	TAU
7	20:34	GEM
9	23:46	CAN
12	2:23	LEO
14	5:06	VIR
16	9:08	LIB
18	15:54	SCO
21	2:01	SAG
23	14:32	CAP
26	2:56	AQU
28	12:52	PIS
30	19:34	ARI

APR		
1	23:43	TAU
4	2:34	GEM
6	5:08	CAN
8	8:05	LEO
10	11:51	VIR
12	17:02	LIB
15	0:21	SCO
17	10:20	SAG
19	22:32	CAP
22	11:11	AQU
24	21:54	PIS
27	5:09	ARI
29	9:02	TAU

MAY		
1	10:45	GEM
3	11:51	CAN
5	13:42	LEO
7	17:17	VIR
9	23:06	LIB
12	7:16	SCO
14	17:41	SAG
17	5:51	CAP
19	18:38	AQU
22	6:09	PIS
24	14:36	ARI
26	19:17	TAU
28	20:52	GEM
30	20:53	CAN

JUN		
1	21:09	LEO
3	23:22	VIR
6	4:36	LIB
8	13:01	SCO
10	23:58	SAG
13	12:21	CAP
16	1:08	AQU
18	13:03	PIS
20	22:40	ARI
23	4:50	TAU
25	7:25	GEM
27	7:28	CAN
29	6:46	LEO

JUL		
1	7:24	VIR
3	11:09	LIB
5	18:49	SCO
8	5:46	SAG
10	18:22	CAP
13	7:06	AQU
15	18:56	PIS
18	5:03	ARI
20	12:31	TAU
22	16:43	GEM
24	17:55	CAN
26	17:26	LEO
28	17:17	VIR
30	19:35	LIB

AUG		
2	1:50	SCO
4	12:02	SAG
7	0:34	CAP
9	13:15	AQU
12	0 :45	PIS
14	10:35	ARI
16	18:26	TAU
18	23:51	GEM
21	2:40	CAN
23	3:27	LEO
25	3:43	VIR
27	5:26	LIB
29	10:26	SCO
31	19:28	SAG

SEP		
3	7:30	CAP
5	20:11	AQU
8	7:29	PIS
10	16:41	ARI
12	23:54	TAU
15	5:23	GEM
17	9:10	CAN
19	11:26	LEO
21	13:01	VIR
23	15:19	LIB
25	19:57	SCO
28	4:02	SAG
30	15:21	CAP

OCT		
3	3:58	AQU
5	15:27	PIS
8	0:23	ARI
10	6:43	TAU
12	11:11	GEM
14	14:31	CAN
16	17:20	LEO
18	20:09	VIR
20	23:43	LIB
23	5:00	SCO
25	12:54	SAG
27	23:39	CAP
30	12:09	AQU

NOV		
2	0:09	PIS
4	9:35	ARI
6	15:41	TAU
8	19:04	GEM
10	21:00	CAN
12	22:50	LEO
15	1:38	VIR
17	6:04	LIB
19	12:26	SCO
21	20:57	SAG
24	7:38	CAP
26	19:59	AQU
29	8:30	PIS

DEC		
1	19:03	ARI
4	2:01	TAU
6	5:19	GEM
8	6:08	CAN
10	6:18	LEO
12	7:38	VIR
14	11:28	LIB
16	18:13	SCO
19	3:31	SAG
21	14:39	CAP
24	2:59	AQU
26	15:41	PIS
29	3:15	ARI
31	11:48	TAU

—1939—

JAN

2	16:20	GEM
4	17:20	CAN
6	16:32	LEO
8	16:08	VIR
10	18:11	LIB
12	23:54	SCO
15	9:10	SAG
17	20:44	CAP
20	9:15	AQU
22	21:51	PIS
25	9:42	ARI
27	19:29	TAU
30	1:50	GEM

FEB

1	4:22	CAN
3	4:06	LEO
5	3:03	VIR
7	3:30	LIB
9	7:22	SCO
11	15:24	SAG
14	2:42	CAP
16	15:22	AQU
19	3:52	PIS
21	15:24	ARI
24	1:19	TAU
26	8:48	GEM
28	13:07	CAN

MAR

2	14:30	LEO
4	14:17	VIR
6	14:26	LIB
8	17:00	SCO
10	23:23	SAG
13	9:36	CAP
15	22:02	AQU
18	10:32	PIS
20	21:41	ARI
23	6:59	TAU
25	14:15	GEM
27	19:20	CAN
29	22:15	LEO
31	23:39	VIR

APR

3	0:49	LIB
5	3:22	SCO
7	8:48	SAG
9	17:47	CAP
12	5:34	AQU
14	18:05	PIS
17	5:14	ARI
19	13:57	TAU
21	20:17	GEM
24	0:44	CAN
26	3:55	LEO
28	6:27	VIR
30	9:02	LIB

MAY

2	12:36	SCO
4	18:11	SAG
7	2:34	CAP
9	13:41	AQU
12	2:10	PIS
14	13:41	ARI
16	22:28	TAU
19	4:07	GEM
21	7:23	CAN
23	9:34	LEO
25	11:51	VIR
27	15:06	LIB
29	19:48	SCO

JUN

1	2:15	SAG
3	10:50	CAP
5	21:41	AQU
8	10:05	PIS
10	22:11	ARI
13	7:43	TAU
15	13:33	GEM
17	16:07	CAN
19	16:58	LEO
21	17:57	VIR
23	20:31	LIB
26	1:25	SCO
28	8:39	SAG
30	17:54	CAP

JUL

3	4:54	AQU
5	17:18	PIS
8	5:50	ARI
10	16:27	TAU
12	23:21	GEM
15	2:16	CAN
17	2:31	LEO
19	2:08	VIR
21	3:11	LIB
23	7:04	SCO
25	14:10	SAG
27	23:51	CAP
30	11:15	AQU

AUG

1	23:42	PIS
4	12:23	ARI
6	23:48	TAU
9	8:06	GEM
11	12:21	CAN
13	13:10	LEO
15	12:19	VIR
17	12:04	LIB
19	14:20	SCO
21	20:14	SAG
24	5:34	CAP
26	17:09	AQU
29	5:43	PIS
31	18:15	ARI

SEP

3	5:48	TAU
5	15:02	GEM
7	20:52	CAN
9	23:12	LEO
11	23:09	VIR
13	22:39	LIB
15	23:44	SCO
18	4:02	SAG
20	12:11	CAP
22	23:24	AQU
25	12:00	PIS
28	0:22	ARI
30	11:29	TAU

OCT

2	20:38	GEM
5	3:17	CAN
7	7:10	LEO
9	8:46	VIR
11	9:16	LIB
13	10:19	SCO
15	13:36	SAG
17	20:22	CAP
20	6:40	AQU
22	19:06	PIS
25	7:28	ARI
27	18:09	TAU
30	2:31	GEM

NOV

1	8:42	CAN
3	13:02	LEO
5	15:57	VIR
7	18:03	LIB
9	20:14	SCO
11	23:42	SAG
14	5:42	CAP
16	15:01	AQU
19	3:00	PIS
21	15:36	ARI
24	2:23	TAU
26	10:09	GEM
28	15:12	CAN
30	18:34	LEO

DEC

2	21:23	VIR
5	0:23	LIB
7	3:57	SCO
9	8:33	SAG
11	14:51	CAP
13	23:43	AQU
16	11:14	PIS
19	0:03	ARI
21	11:32	TAU
23	19:37	GEM
26	0:03	CAN
28	2:05	LEO
30	3:29	VIR

—1940—

JAN			FEB			MAR			APR		
1	5:44	LIB	1	20:36	SAG	2	10:03	CAP	1	2:14	AQU
3	9:36	SCO	4	4:27	CAP	4	20:08	AQU	3	14:11	PIS
5	15:13	SAG	6	14:22	AQU	7	8:08	PIS	6	3:10	ARI
7	22:30	CAP	9	1:59	PIS	9	21:01	ARI	8	15:39	TAU
10	7:42	AQU	11	14:50	ARI	12	9:45	TAU	11	2:33	GEM
12	19:03	PIS	14	3:36	TAU	14	20:53	GEM	13	11:04	CAN
15	7:56	ARI	16	14:10	GEM	17	4:57	CAN	15	16:44	LEO
17	20:16	TAU	18	20:47	CAN	19	9:15	LEO	17	19:35	VIR
20	5:32	GEM	20	23:19	LEO	21	10:21	VIR	19	20:23	LIB
22	10:35	CAN	22	23:12	VIR	23	9:48	LIB	21	20:33	SCO
24	12:11	LEO	24	22:29	LIB	25	9:34	SCO	23	21:49	SAG
26	12:12	VIR	26	23:14	SCO	27	11:31	SAG	26	1:50	CAP
28	12:43	LIB	29	2:55	SAG	29	17:00	CAP	28	9:39	AQU
30	15:18	SCO							30	20:56	PIS

MAY			JUN			JUL			AUG		
3	9:52	ARI	2	5:44	TAU	2	0:16	GEM	2	20:20	LEO
5	22:13	TAU	4	15:50	GEM	4	7:11	CAN	4	21:51	VIR
8	8:34	GEM	6	23:02	CAN	6	11:13	LEO	6	22:50	LIB
10	16:34	CAN	9	4:01	LEO	8	13:45	VIR	9	0:46	SCO
12	22:23	LEO	11	7:41	VIR	10	16:07	LIB	11	4:29	SAG
15	2:18	VIR	13	10:44	LIB	12	19:07	SCO	13	10:15	CAP
17	4:41	LIB	15	13:32	SCO	14	23:05	SAG	15	18:08	AQU
19	6:12	SCO	17	16:34	SAG	17	4:18	CAP	18	4:10	PIS
21	8:00	SAG	19	20:45	CAP	19	11:22	AQU	20	16:14	ARI
23	11:35	CAP	22	3:15	AQU	21	20:59	PIS	23	5:17	TAU
25	18:19	AQU	24	12:56	PIS	24	9:02	ARI	25	17:13	GEM
28	4:39	PIS	27	1:13	ARI	26	21:57	TAU	28	1:54	CAN
30	17:19	ARI	29	13:53	TAU	29	9:04	GEM	30	6:32	LEO
						31	16:32	CAN			

SEP			OCT			NOV			DEC		
1	7:57	VIR	2	18:12	SCO	1	5:21	SAG	2	22:13	AQU
3	7:54	LIB	4	18:54	SAG	3	7:23	CAP	5	6:36	PIS
5	8:17	SCO	6	22:29	CAP	5	13:04	AQU	7	18:27	ARI
7	10:36	SAG	9	5:44	AQU	7	22:46	PIS	10	7:28	TAU
9	15:46	CAP	11	16:18	PIS	10	11:13	ARI	12	19:08	GEM
11	23:52	AQU	14	4:50	ARI	13	0:13	TAU	15	4:20	CAN
14	10:26	PIS	16	17:50	TAU	15	12:01	GEM	17	11:17	LEO
16	22:43	ARI	19	6:00	GEM	17	21:53	CAN	19	16:35	VIR
19	11:46	TAU	21	16:18	CAN	20	5:39	LEO	21	20:37	LIB
22	0:06	GEM	23	23:51	LEO	22	11:11	VIR	23	23:30	SCO
24	9:58	CAN	26	4:10	VIR	24	14:25	LIB	26	1:37	SAG
26	16:09	LEO	28	5:37	LIB	26	15:45	SCO	28	3:59	CAP
28	18:42	VIR	30	5:25	SCO	28	16:19	SAG	30	8:09	AQU
30	18:47	LIB				30	17:51	CAP			

—1941—

JAN

1	15:35	PIS
4	2:35	ARI
6	15:29	TAU
9	3:27	GEM
11	12:34	CAN
13	18:40	LEO
15	22:46	VIR
18	2:00	LIB
20	5:04	SCO
22	8:17	SAG
24	12:01	CAP
26	17:06	AQU
29	0:35	PIS
31	11:02	ARI

FEB

2	23:41	TAU
5	12:10	GEM
7	21:58	CAN
10	4:08	LEO
12	7:22	VIR
14	9:08	LIB
16	10:53	SCO
18	13:37	SAG
20	17:54	CAP
23	0:02	AQU
25	8:19	PIS
27	18:55	ARI

MAR

2	7:24	TAU
4	20:12	GEM
7	7:04	CAN
9	14:19	LEO
11	17:52	VIR
13	18:52	LIB
15	19:03	SCO
17	20:08	SAG
19	23:25	CAP
22	5:34	AQU
24	14:30	PIS
27	1:40	ARI
29	14:14	TAU

APR

1	3:07	GEM
3	14:44	CAN
5	23:26	LEO
8	4:21	VIR
10	5:55	LIB
12	5:32	SCO
14	5:08	SAG
16	6:39	CAP
18	11:31	AQU
20	20:07	PIS
23	7:35	ARI
25	20:23	TAU
28	9:11	GEM
30	20:56	CAN

MAY

3	6:34	LEO
5	13:06	VIR
7	16:12	LIB
9	16:34	SCO
11	15:50	SAG
13	16:04	CAP
15	19:15	AQU
18	2:34	PIS
20	13:34	ARI
23	2:27	TAU
25	15:10	GEM
28	2:37	CAN
30	12:16	LEO

JUN

1	19:39	VIR
4	0:17	LIB
6	2:14	SCO
8	2:24	SAG
10	2:32	CAP
12	4:42	AQU
14	10:34	PIS
16	20:31	ARI
19	9:03	TAU
21	21:45	GEM
24	8:51	CAN
26	17:55	LEO
29	1:03	VIR

JUL

1	6:17	LIB
3	9:34	SCO
5	11:14	SAG
7	12:21	CAP
9	14:36	AQU
11	19:42	PIS
14	4:35	ARI
16	16:30	TAU
19	5:10	GEM
21	16:15	CAN
24	0:48	LEO
26	7:04	VIR
28	11:41	LIB
30	15:09	SCO

AUG

1	17:50	SAG
3	20:17	CAP
5	23:32	AQU
8	4:51	PIS
10	13:13	ARI
13	0:32	TAU
15	13:10	GEM
18	0:38	CAN
20	9:16	LEO
22	14:53	VIR
24	18:22	LIB
26	20:49	SCO
28	23:13	SAG
31	2:18	CAP

SEP

2	6:39	AQU
4	12:52	PIS
6	21:29	ARI
9	8:32	TAU
11	21:06	GEM
14	9:09	CAN
16	18:36	LEO
19	0:29	VIR
21	3:18	LIB
23	4:24	SCO
25	5:25	SAG
27	7:45	CAP
29	12:17	AQU

OCT

1	19:18	PIS
4	4:38	ARI
6	15:52	TAU
9	4:23	GEM
11	16:53	CAN
14	3:29	LEO
16	10:36	VIR
18	13:54	LIB
20	14:26	SCO
22	14:01	SAG
24	14:40	CAP
26	18:03	AQU
29	0:51	PIS
31	10:38	ARI

NOV

2	22:19	TAU
5	10:53	GEM
7	23:26	CAN
10	10:49	LEO
12	19:29	VIR
15	0:22	LIB
17	1:40	SCO
19	0:54	SAG
21	0:12	CAP
23	1:47	AQU
25	7:09	PIS
27	16:27	ARI
30	4:19	TAU

DEC

2	17:00	GEM
5	5:22	CAN
7	16:43	LEO
10	2:13	VIR
12	8:46	LIB
14	11:52	SCO
16	12:10	SAG
18	11:27	CAP
20	11:54	AQU
22	15:33	PIS
24	23:24	ARI
27	10:43	TAU
29	23:27	GEM

—1942—

JAN

1	11:42	CAN
3	22:33	LEO
6	7:43	VIR
8	14:49	LIB
10	19:25	SCO
12	21:32	SAG
14	22:07	CAP
16	22:53	AQU
19	1:43	PIS
21	8:08	ARI
23	18:19	TAU
26	6:44	GEM
28	19:04	CAN
31	5:37	LEO

FEB

2	13:58	VIR
4	20:18	LIB
7	0:56	SCO
9	4:07	SAG
11	6:19	CAP
13	8:28	AQU
15	11:51	PIS
17	17:47	ARI
20	2:58	TAU
22	14:48	GEM
25	3:16	CAN
27	14:06	LEO

MAR

1	22:06	VIR
4	3:23	LIB
6	6:50	SCO
8	9:28	SAG
10	12:09	CAP
12	15:31	AQU
14	20:09	PIS
17	2:41	ARI
19	11:39	TAU
21	23:01	GEM
24	11:33	CAN
26	23:05	LEO
29	7:37	VIR
31	12:37	LIB

APR

2	14:55	SCO
4	16:05	SAG
6	17:42	CAP
8	20:57	AQU
11	2:20	PIS
13	9:49	ARI
15	19:18	TAU
18	6:37	GEM
20	19:10	CAN
23	7:22	LEO
25	17:03	VIR
27	22:50	LIB
30	0:59	SCO

MAY

2	1:03	SAG
4	1:05	CAP
6	2:56	AQU
8	7:44	PIS
10	15:32	ARI
13	1:37	TAU
15	13:15	GEM
18	1:49	CAN
20	14:21	LEO
23	1:08	VIR
25	8:22	LIB
27	11:32	SCO
29	11:39	SAG
31	10:44	CAP

JUN

2	11:00	AQU
4	14:14	PIS
6	21:11	ARI
9	7:16	TAU
11	19:12	GEM
14	7:50	CAN
16	20:20	LEO
19	7:34	VIR
21	16:05	LIB
23	20:51	SCO
25	22:09	SAG
27	21:30	CAP
29	21:01	AQU

JUL

1	22:46	PIS
4	4:11	ARI
6	13:23	TAU
9	1:10	GEM
11	13:52	CAN
14	2:08	LEO
16	13:09	VIR
18	22:02	LIB
21	4:02	SCO
23	6:58	SAG
25	7:38	CAP
27	7:37	AQU
29	8:49	PIS
31	12:56	ARI

AUG

2	20:48	TAU
5	7:55	GEM
7	20:31	CAN
10	8:40	LEO
12	19:09	VIR
15	3:31	LIB
17	9:38	SCO
19	13:35	SAG
21	15:47	CAP
23	17:07	AQU
25	18:56	PIS
27	22:39	ARI
30	5:29	TAU

SEP

1	15:41	GEM
4	4:01	CAN
6	16:16	LEO
9	2:31	VIR
11	10:05	LIB
13	15:19	SCO
15	18:58	SAG
17	21:48	CAP
20	0:27	AQU
22	3:34	PIS
24	7:57	ARI
26	14:35	TAU
29	0:05	GEM

OCT

1	12:04	CAN
4	0:36	LEO
6	11:14	VIR
8	18:33	LIB
10	22:47	SCO
13	1:11	SAG
15	3:14	CAP
17	6:01	AQU
19	10:05	PIS
21	15:37	ARI
23	22:52	TAU
26	8:19	GEM
28	20:00	CAN
31	8:49	LEO

NOV

2	20:19	VIR
5	4:22	LIB
7	8:27	SCO
9	9:47	SAG
11	10:18	CAP
13	11:49	AQU
15	15:28	PIS
17	21:31	ARI
20	5:38	TAU
22	15:35	GEM
25	3:17	CAN
27	16:10	LEO
30	4:30	VIR

DEC

2	13:56	LIB
4	19:07	SCO
6	20:34	SAG
8	20:07	CAP
10	19:57	AQU
12	21:56	PIS
15	3:05	ARI
17	11:17	TAU
19	21:46	GEM
22	9:46	CAN
24	22:36	LEO
27	11:11	VIR
29	21:45	LIB

—1943—

JAN

1	4:40	SCO
3	7:34	SAG
5	7:35	CAP
7	6:42	AQU
9	7:03	PIS
11	10:21	ARI
13	17:22	TAU
16	3:39	GEM
18	15:54	CAN
21	4:44	LEO
23	17:03	VIR
26	3:47	LIB
28	11:51	SCO
30	16:34	SAG

FEB

1	18:16	CAP
3	18:11	AQU
5	18:08	PIS
7	20:01	ARI
10	1:18	TAU
12	10:25	GEM
14	22:25	CAN
17	11:19	LEO
19	23:20	VIR
22	9:30	LIB
24	17:25	SCO
26	22:59	SAG

MAR

1	2:19	CAP
3	3:57	AQU
5	4:55	PIS
7	6:42	ARI
9	10:54	TAU
11	18:39	GEM
14	5:51	CAN
16	18:41	LEO
19	6:43	VIR
21	16:21	LIB
23	23:23	SCO
26	4:24	SAG
28	8:05	CAP
30	10:57	AQU

APR

1	13:27	PIS
3	16:18	ARI
5	20:38	TAU
8	3:42	GEM
10	14:03	CAN
13	2:40	LEO
15	14:59	VIR
18	0:41	LIB
20	7:04	SCO
22	10:57	SAG
24	13:40	CAP
26	16:21	AQU
28	19:36	PIS
30	23:40	ARI

MAY

3	4:57	TAU
5	12:16	GEM
7	22:17	CAN
10	10:39	LEO
12	23:22	VIR
15	9:45	LIB
17	16:20	SCO
19	19:33	SAG
21	21:00	CAP
23	22:23	AQU
26	0:58	PIS
28	5:17	ARI
30	11:25	TAU

JUN

1	19:30	GEM
4	5:46	CAN
6	18:03	LEO
9	7:04	VIR
11	18:22	LIB
14	1:59	SCO
16	5:36	SAG
18	6:30	CAP
20	6:34	AQU
22	7:37	PIS
24	10:53	ARI
26	16:52	TAU
29	1:27	GEM

JUL

1	12:14	CAN
4	0:40	LEO
6	13:45	VIR
9	1:45	LIB
11	10:41	SCO
13	15:37	SAG
15	17:07	CAP
17	16:46	AQU
19	16:31	PIS
21	18:09	ARI
23	22:53	TAU
26	7:04	GEM
28	18:04	CAN
31	6:43	LEO

AUG

2	19:46	VIR
5	7:52	LIB
7	17:40	SCO
10	0:09	SAG
12	3:10	CAP
14	3:37	AQU
16	3:07	PIS
18	3:33	ARI
20	6:40	TAU
22	13:35	GEM
25	0:07	CAN
27	12:50	LEO
30	1:47	VIR

SEP

1	13:34	LIB
3	23:21	SCO
6	6:39	SAG
8	11:14	CAP
10	13:18	AQU
12	13:47	PIS
14	14:09	ARI
16	16:15	TAU
18	21:43	GEM
21	7:11	CAN
23	19:34	LEO
26	8:31	VIR
28	19:57	LIB

OCT

1	5:05	SCO
3	12:03	SAG
5	17:11	CAP
7	20:40	AQU
9	22:45	PIS
12	0:12	ARI
14	2:26	TAU
16	7:07	GEM
18	15:28	CAN
21	3:13	LEO
23	16:10	VIR
26	3:38	LIB
28	12:15	SCO
30	18:15	SAG

NOV

1	22:37	CAP
4	2:10	AQU
6	5:16	PIS
8	8:11	ARI
10	11:33	TAU
12	16:32	GEM
15	0:23	CAN
17	11:28	LEO
20	0:22	VIR
22	12:19	LIB
24	21:09	SCO
27	2:35	SAG
29	5:43	CAP

DEC

1	8:02	AQU
3	10:36	PIS
5	14:00	ARI
7	18:30	TAU
10	0:33	GEM
12	8:47	CAN
14	19:37	LEO
17	8:23	VIR
19	20:56	LIB
22	6:46	SCO
24	12:44	SAG
26	15:24	CAP
28	16:21	AQU
30	17:17	PIS

—1944—

JAN			FEB			MAR			APR		
1	19:34	ARI	2	12:18	GEM	3	3:38	CAN	1	21:54	LEO
3	23:59	TAU	4	21:40	CAN	5	15:20	LEO	4	10:49	VIR
6	6:45	GEM	7	9:20	LEO	8	4:19	VIR	6	23:22	LIB
8	15:48	CAN	9	22:08	VIR	10	16:56	LIB	9	10:12	SCO
11	2:58	LEO	12	10:55	LIB	13	4:12	SCO	11	19:03	SAG
13	15:39	VIR	14	22:24	SCO	15	13:31	SAG	14	1:56	CAP
16	4:29	LIB	17	7:15	SAG	17	20:14	CAP	16	6:46	AQU
18	15:28	SCO	19	12:33	CAP	19	23:55	AQU	18	9:28	PIS
20	22:54	SAG	21	14:27	AQU	22	0:59	PIS	20	10:36	ARI
23	2:27	CAP	23	14:09	PIS	24	0:42	ARI	22	11:29	TAU
25	3:10	AQU	25	13:31	ARI	26	1:01	TAU	24	13:59	GEM
27	2:48	PIS	27	14:36	TAU	28	3:59	GEM	26	19:49	CAN
29	3:15	ARI	29	19:06	GEM	30	11:00	CAN	29	5:36	LEO
31	6:07	TAU									

MAY			JUN			JUL			AUG		
1	18:05	VIR	3	1:32	SCO	2	18:39	SAG	1	9:43	CAP
4	6:40	LIB	5	9:28	SAG	4	23:42	CAP	3	12:11	AQU
6	17:18	SCO	7	14:41	CAP	7	2:14	AQU	5	12:35	PIS
9	1:27	SAG	9	18:12	AQU	9	3:39	PIS	7	12:44	ARI
11	7:33	CAP	11	20:59	PIS	11	5:19	ARI	9	14:20	TAU
13	12:10	AQU	13	23:41	ARI	13	8:17	TAU	11	18:39	GEM
15	15:35	PIS	16	2:52	TAU	15	13:12	GEM	14	2:04	CAN
17	18:04	ARI	18	7:11	GEM	17	20:22	CAN	16	12:08	LEO
19	20:16	TAU	20	13:29	CAN	20	5:51	LEO	19	0:01	VIR
21	23:27	GEM	22	22:26	LEO	22	17:25	VIR	21	12:46	LIB
24	5:04	CAN	25	9:58	VIR	25	6:08	LIB	24	1:13	SCO
26	14:05	LEO	27	22:40	LIB	27	18:17	SCO	26	11:52	SAG
29	1:59	VIR	30	10:11	SCO	30	3:50	SAG	28	19:13	CAP
31	14:38	LIB							30	22:45	AQU

SEP			OCT			NOV			DEC		
1	23:15	PIS	1	9:30	ARI	1	20:29	GEM	1	10:17	CAN
3	22:27	ARI	3	8:46	TAU	4	0:05	CAN	3	16:53	LEO
5	22:29	TAU	5	10:00	GEM	6	7:45	LEO	6	3:04	VIR
8	1:14	GEM	7	14:57	CAN	8	18:59	VIR	8	15:29	LIB
10	7:47	CAN	10	0:04	LEO	11	7:45	LIB	11	3:42	SCO
12	17:51	LEO	12	12:05	VIR	13	19:48	SCO	13	13:51	SAG
15	6:01	VIR	15	0:56	LIB	16	6:02	SAG	15	21:22	CAP
17	18:48	LIB	17	13:04	SCO	18	14:20	CAP	18	2:44	AQU
20	7:11	SCO	19	23:50	SAG	20	20:47	AQU	20	6:40	PIS
22	18:17	SAG	22	8:49	CAP	23	1:19	PIS	22	9:43	ARI
25	2:56	CAP	24	15:19	AQU	25	3:57	ARI	24	12:25	TAU
27	8:10	AQU	26	18:54	PIS	27	5:23	TAU	26	15:26	GEM
29	9:58	PIS	28	19:54	ARI	29	6:55	GEM	28	19:44	CAN
			30	19:45	TAU				31	2:20	LEO

—1945—

JAN

2	11:49	VIR
4	23:44	LIB
7	12:13	SCO
9	22:56	SAG
12	6:28	CAP
14	10:57	AQU
16	13:28	PIS
18	15:21	ARI
20	17:48	TAU
22	21:35	GEM
25	3:05	CAN
27	10:33	LEO
29	20:09	VIR

FEB

1	7:46	LIB
3	20:23	SCO
6	7:58	SAG
8	16:30	CAP
10	21:12	AQU
12	22:53	PIS
14	23:13	ARI
17	0:05	TAU
19	3:01	GEM
21	8:43	CAN
23	16:59	LEO
26	3:14	VIR
28	14:57	LIB

MAR

3	3:33	SCO
5	15:45	SAG
8	1:38	CAP
10	7:40	AQU
12	9:50	PIS
14	9:33	ARI
16	8:55	TAU
18	10:05	GEM
20	14:32	CAN
22	22:32	LEO
25	9:11	VIR
27	21:15	LIB
30	9:50	SCO

APR

1	22:08	SAG
4	8:52	CAP
6	16:29	AQU
8	20:11	PIS
10	20:38	ARI
12	19:40	TAU
14	19:31	GEM
16	22:14	CAN
19	4:52	LEO
21	15:04	VIR
24	3:15	LIB
26	15:53	SCO
29	3:56	SAG

MAY

1	14:40	CAP
3	23:06	AQU
6	4:21	PIS
8	6:25	ARI
10	6:25	TAU
12	6:12	GEM
14	7:51	CAN
16	12:57	LEO
18	21:56	VIR
21	9:43	LIB
23	22:21	SCO
26	10:12	SAG
28	20:25	CAP
31	4:35	AQU

JUN

2	10:26	PIS
4	13:51	ARI
6	15:24	TAU
8	16:15	GEM
10	18:02	CAN
12	22:20	LEO
15	6:08	VIR
17	17:07	LIB
20	5:36	SCO
22	17:28	SAG
25	3:15	CAP
27	10:37	AQU
29	15:52	PIS

JUL

1	19:30	ARI
3	22:05	TAU
6	0:20	GEM
8	3:11	CAN
10	7:44	LEO
12	14:58	VIR
15	1:13	LIB
17	13:29	SCO
20	1:36	SAG
22	11:29	CAP
24	18:17	AQU
26	22:27	PIS
29	1:08	ARI
31	3:29	TAU

AUG

2	6:24	GEM
4	10:23	CAN
6	15:53	LEO
8	23:24	VIR
11	9:21	LIB
13	21:25	SCO
16	9:56	SAG
18	20:31	CAP
21	3:33	AQU
23	7:05	PIS
25	8:30	ARI
27	9:34	TAU
29	11:47	GEM
31	16:00	CAN

SEP

2	22:20	LEO
5	6:37	VIR
7	16:49	LIB
10	4:48	SCO
12	17:38	SAG
15	5:12	CAP
17	13:20	AQU
19	17:19	PIS
21	18:11	ARI
23	17:54	TAU
25	18:32	GEM
27	21:39	CAN
30	3:47	LEO

OCT

2	12:34	VIR
4	23:17	LIB
7	11:24	SCO
10	0:18	SAG
12	12:33	CAP
14	22:07	AQU
17	3:34	PIS
19	5:09	ARI
21	4:31	TAU
23	3:50	GEM
25	5:11	CAN
27	9:56	LEO
29	18:12	VIR

NOV

1	5:08	LIB
3	17:30	SCO
6	6:19	SAG
8	18:36	CAP
11	4:59	AQU
13	12:05	PIS
15	15:25	ARI
17	15:48	TAU
19	15:03	GEM
21	15:14	CAN
23	18:12	LEO
26	1:00	VIR
28	11:19	LIB
30	23:43	SCO

DEC

3	12:30	SAG
6	0:24	CAP
8	10:35	AQU
10	18:21	PIS
12	23:16	ARI
15	1:30	TAU
17	2:03	GEM
19	2:28	CAN
21	4:31	LEO
23	9:44	VIR
25	18:45	LIB
28	6:43	SCO
30	19:33	SAG

—1946—

JAN		
2	7:11	CAP
4	16:38	AQU
6	23:47	PIS
9	4:56	ARI
11	8:26	TAU
13	10:43	GEM
15	12:33	CAN
17	15:04	LEO
19	19:41	VIR
22	3:32	LIB
24	14:40	SCO
27	3:28	SAG
29	15:18	CAP

FEB		
1	0:24	AQU
3	6:33	PIS
5	10:38	ARI
7	13:47	TAU
9	16:46	GEM
11	19:59	CAN
13	23:51	LEO
16	5:03	VIR
18	12:36	LIB
20	23:05	SCO
23	11:41	SAG
26	0:02	CAP
28	9:35	AQU

MAR		
2	15:25	PIS
4	18:24	ARI
6	20:09	TAU
8	22:12	GEM
11	1:29	CAN
13	6:15	LEO
15	12:33	VIR
17	20:41	LIB
20	7:05	SCO
22	19:31	SAG
25	8:18	CAP
27	18:51	AQU
30	1:26	PIS

APR		
1	4:17	ARI
3	4:57	TAU
5	5:25	GEM
7	7:21	CAN
9	11:38	LEO
11	18:21	VIR
14	3:14	LIB
16	14:04	SCO
19	2:30	SAG
21	15:29	CAP
24	2:57	AQU
26	10:55	PIS
28	14:46	ARI
30	15:31	TAU

MAY		
2	15:04	GEM
4	15:23	CAN
6	18:05	LEO
8	23:58	VIR
11	8:54	LIB
13	20:09	SCO
16	8:46	SAG
18	21:42	CAP
21	9:32	AQU
23	18:39	PIS
26	0:05	ARI
28	2:04	TAU
30	1:55	GEM

JUN		
1	1:29	CAN
3	2:40	LEO
5	6:57	VIR
7	14:57	LIB
10	2:05	SCO
12	14:51	SAG
15	3:40	CAP
17	15:16	AQU
20	0:43	PIS
22	7:20	ARI
24	10:56	TAU
26	12:08	GEM
28	12:11	CAN
30	12:48	LEO

JUL		
2	15:45	VIR
4	22:21	LIB
7	8:42	SCO
9	21:21	SAG
12	10:06	CAP
14	21:17	AQU
17	6:16	PIS
19	12:59	ARI
21	17:36	TAU
23	20:19	GEM
25	21:44	CAN
27	22:58	LEO
30	1:33	VIR

AUG		
1	7:05	LIB
3	16:23	SCO
6	4:37	SAG
8	17:24	CAP
11	4:24	AQU
13	12:41	PIS
15	18:37	ARI
17	23:00	TAU
20	2:23	GEM
22	5:07	CAN
24	7:38	LEO
26	10:54	VIR
28	16:15	LIB
31	0:50	SCO

SEP		
2	12:32	SAG
5	1:24	CAP
7	12:42	AQU
9	20:46	PIS
12	1:49	ARI
14	5:04	TAU
16	7:46	GEM
18	10:42	CAN
20	14:13	LEO
22	18:38	VIR
25	0:40	LIB
27	9:13	SCO
29	20:33	SAG

OCT		
2	9:30	CAP
4	21:28	AQU
7	6:09	PIS
9	11:05	ARI
11	13:21	TAU
13	14:37	GEM
15	16:23	CAN
17	19:35	LEO
20	0:36	VIR
22	7:34	LIB
24	16:41	SCO
27	4:04	SAG
29	17:00	CAP

NOV		
1	5:37	AQU
3	15:32	PIS
5	21:28	ARI
7	23:49	TAU
10	0:08	GEM
12	0:16	CAN
14	1:53	LEO
16	6:05	VIR
18	13:13	LIB
20	22:58	SCO
23	10:44	SAG
25	23:40	CAP
28	12:30	AQU
30	23:30	PIS

DEC		
3	7:06	ARI
5	10:49	TAU
7	11:30	GEM
9	10:50	CAN
11	10:47	LEO
13	13:09	VIR
15	19:08	LIB
18	4:43	SCO
20	16:49	SAG
23	5:51	CAP
25	18:30	AQU
28	5:44	PIS
30	14:31	ARI

—1947—

JAN			FEB			MAR			APR		
1	20:06	TAU	2	8:39	CAN	1	15:59	CAN	2	3:31	VIR
3	22:26	GEM	4	9:02	LEO	3	18:00	LEO	4	7:40	LIB
5	22:28	CAN	6	9:42	VIR	5	19:47	VIR	6	13:57	SCO
7	21:54	LEO	8	12:40	LIB	7	22:51	LIB	8	23:13	SAG
9	22:45	VIR	10	19:29	SCO	10	4:51	SCO	11	11:09	CAP
12	2:54	LIB	13	6:16	SAG	12	14:34	SAG	13	23:52	AQU
14	11:16	SCO	15	19:12	CAP	15	3:01	CAP	16	10:48	PIS
16	23:03	SAG	18	7:39	AQU	17	15:36	AQU	18	18:26	ARI
19	12:11	CAP	20	17:58	PIS	20	1:58	PIS	20	22:56	TAU
22	0:37	AQU	23	1:58	ARI	22	9:23	ARI	23	1:28	GEM
24	11:23	PIS	25	8:08	TAU	24	14:29	TAU	25	3:23	CAN
26	20:11	ARI	27	12:47	GEM	26	18:16	GEM	27	5:44	LEO
29	2:46	TAU				28	21:26	CAN	29	9:16	VIR
31	6:52	GEM				31	0:22	LEO			

MAY			JUN			JUL			AUG		
1	14:24	LIB	2	13:54	SAG	2	8:03	CAP	1	2:50	AQU
3	21:36	SCO	5	1:52	CAP	4	20:50	AQU	3	14:49	PIS
6	7:10	SAG	7	14:38	AQU	7	9:03	PIS	6	1:20	ARI
8	18:55	CAP	10	2:47	PIS	9	19:35	ARI	8	9:44	TAU
11	7:41	AQU	12	12:34	ARI	12	3:12	TAU	10	15:18	GEM
13	19:21	PIS	14	18:46	TAU	14	7:17	GEM	12	17:50	CAN
16	3:57	ARI	16	21:22	GEM	16	8:15	CAN	14	18:07	LEO
18	8:52	TAU	18	21:33	CAN	18	7:35	LEO	16	17:49	VIR
20	10:52	GEM	20	21:07	LEO	20	7:19	VIR	18	19:04	LIB
22	11:27	CAN	22	22:02	VIR	22	9:34	LIB	20	23:45	SCO
24	12:18	LEO	25	1:52	LIB	24	15:41	SCO	23	8:35	SAG
26	14:50	VIR	27	9:17	SCO	27	1:41	SAG	25	20:31	CAP
28	19:54	LIB	29	19:46	SAG	29	14:02	CAP	28	9:18	AQU
31	3:43	SCO							30	21:04	PIS

SEP			OCT			NOV			DEC		
2	7:03	ARI	1	21:16	TAU	2	12:32	CAN	1	21:30	LEO
4	15:11	TAU	4	2:44	GEM	4	15:04	LEO	3	23:24	VIR
6	21:19	GEM	6	6:47	CAN	6	17:55	VIR	6	3:14	LIB
9	1:12	CAN	8	9:42	LEO	8	21:43	LIB	8	9:25	SCO
11	3:03	LEO	10	11:57	VIR	11	3:03	SCO	10	17:50	SAG
13	3:51	VIR	12	14:32	LIB	13	10:34	SAG	13	4:14	CAP
15	5:17	LIB	14	18:46	SCO	15	20:37	CAP	15	16:16	AQU
17	9:11	SCO	17	1:53	SAG	18	8:45	AQU	18	4:59	PIS
19	16:50	SAG	19	12:14	CAP	20	21:17	PIS	20	16:37	ARI
22	3:58	CAP	22	0:39	AQU	23	7:54	ARI	23	1:12	TAU
24	16:38	AQU	24	12:46	PIS	25	15:06	TAU	25	5:47	GEM
27	4:25	PIS	26	22:31	ARI	27	18:56	GEM	27	7:03	CAN
29	13:59	ARI	29	5:16	TAU	29	20:31	CAN	29	6:42	LEO
			31	9:36	GEM				31	6:47	VIR

—1948—

JAN		
2	9:10	LIB
4	14:51	SCO
6	23:41	SAG
9	10:41	CAP
11	22:54	AQU
14	11:36	PIS
16	23:44	ARI
19	9:43	TAU
21	16:02	GEM
23	18:24	CAN
25	18:00	LEO
27	16:56	VIR
29	17:30	LIB
31	21:28	SCO

FEB		
3	5:26	SAG
5	16:30	CAP
8	4:59	AQU
10	17:37	PIS
13	5:38	ARI
15	16:09	TAU
17	23:56	GEM
20	4:09	CAN
22	5:07	LEO
24	4:23	VIR
26	4:06	LIB
28	6:24	SCO

MAR		
1	12:42	SAG
3	22:51	CAP
6	11:15	AQU
8	23:54	PIS
11	11:33	ARI
13	21:41	TAU
16	5:46	GEM
18	11:14	CAN
20	13:58	LEO
22	14:43	VIR
24	15:02	LIB
26	16:50	SCO
28	21:47	SAG
31	6:34	CAP

APR		
2	18:19	AQU
5	6:56	PIS
7	18:29	ARI
10	3:59	TAU
12	11:20	GEM
14	16:42	CAN
16	20:16	LEO
18	22:31	VIR
21	0:17	LIB
23	2:50	SCO
25	7:32	SAG
27	15:22	CAP
30	2:16	AQU

MAY		
2	14:44	PIS
5	2:29	ARI
7	11:48	TAU
9	18:20	GEM
11	22:39	CAN
14	1:39	LEO
16	4:15	VIR
18	7:07	LIB
20	10:56	SCO
22	16:22	SAG
25	0:08	CAP
27	10:31	AQU
29	22:46	PIS

JUN		
1	10:55	ARI
3	20:44	TAU
6	3:07	GEM
8	6:29	CAN
10	8:12	LEO
12	9:49	VIR
14	12:34	LIB
16	17:04	SCO
18	23:29	SAG
21	7:51	CAP
23	18:16	AQU
26	6:24	PIS
28	18:56	ARI

JUL		
1	5:40	TAU
3	12:48	GEM
5	16:07	CAN
7	16:53	LEO
9	17:04	VIR
11	18:31	LIB
13	22:28	SCO
16	5:11	SAG
18	14:14	CAP
21	1:03	AQU
23	13:13	PIS
26	1:58	ARI
28	13:34	TAU
30	22:02	GEM

AUG		
2	2:21	CAN
4	3:14	LEO
6	2:33	VIR
8	2:30	LIB
10	4:57	SCO
12	10:50	SAG
14	19:52	CAP
17	7:03	AQU
19	19:23	PIS
22	8:06	ARI
24	20:04	TAU
27	5:40	GEM
29	11:34	CAN
31	13:42	LEO

SEP		
2	13:21	VIR
4	12:36	LIB
6	13:35	SCO
8	17:52	SAG
11	1:57	CAP
13	12:59	AQU
16	1:27	PIS
18	14:02	ARI
21	1:46	TAU
23	11:40	GEM
25	18:46	CAN
27	22:35	LEO
29	23:41	VIR

OCT		
1	23:30	LIB
3	23:59	SCO
6	2:55	SAG
8	9:31	CAP
10	19:43	AQU
13	8:04	PIS
15	20:37	ARI
18	7:54	TAU
20	17:15	GEM
23	0:22	CAN
25	5:10	LEO
27	7:54	VIR
29	9:16	LIB
31	10:32	SCO

NOV		
2	13:11	SAG
4	18:40	CAP
7	3:42	AQU
9	15:34	PIS
12	4:13	ARI
14	15:24	TAU
17	0:02	GEM
19	6:12	CAN
21	10:33	LEO
23	13:49	VIR
25	16:33	LIB
27	19:19	SCO
29	22:52	SAG

DEC		
2	4:17	CAP
4	12:32	AQU
6	23:46	PIS
9	12:30	ARI
12	0:09	TAU
14	8:45	GEM
16	14:01	CAN
18	17:03	LEO
20	19:19	VIR
22	22:00	LIB
25	1:39	SCO
27	6:29	SAG
29	12:47	CAP
31	21:08	AQU

—1949—

JAN			FEB			MAR			APR		
3	7:59	PIS	2	4:05	ARI	1	10:36	ARI	2	17:03	GEM
5	20:41	ARI	4	16:57	TAU	3	23:33	TAU	5	2:10	CAN
8	9:03	TAU	7	3:41	GEM	6	11:06	GEM	7	8:00	LEO
10	18:31	GEM	9	10:23	CAN	8	19:22	CAN	9	10:32	VIR
12	23:57	CAN	11	13:01	LEO	10	23:34	LEO	11	10:48	LIB
15	2:08	LEO	13	13:06	VIR	13	0:24	VIR	13	10:28	SCO
17	2:53	VIR	15	12:44	LIB	14	23:40	LIB	15	11:24	SAG
19	4:03	LIB	17	13:53	SCO	16	23:26	SCO	17	15:16	CAP
21	7:00	SCO	19	17:50	SAG	19	1:31	SAG	19	23:00	AQU
23	12:09	SAG	22	0:51	CAP	21	7:05	CAP	22	10:08	PIS
25	19:22	CAP	24	10:26	AQU	23	16:11	AQU	24	23:01	ARI
28	4:27	AQU	26	21:54	PIS	26	3:50	PIS	27	11:41	TAU
30	15:27	PIS				28	16:42	ARI	29	22:48	GEM
						31	5:30	TAU			

MAY			JUN			JUL			AUG		
2	7:44	CAN	2	23:54	VIR	2	8:22	LIB	2	20:25	SAG
4	14:12	LEO	5	2:58	LIB	4	11:22	SCO	5	1:36	CAP
6	18:12	VIR	7	5:14	SCO	6	14:45	SAG	7	8:34	AQU
8	20:07	LIB	9	7:24	SAG	8	19:03	CAP	9	17:46	PIS
10	20:54	SCO	11	10:40	CAP	11	1:09	AQU	12	5:20	ARI
12	21:57	SAG	13	16:27	AQU	13	10:02	PIS	14	18:18	TAU
15	0:57	CAP	16	1:39	PIS	15	21:43	ARI	17	6:23	GEM
17	7:19	AQU	18	13:45	ARI	18	10:36	TAU	19	15:15	CAN
19	17:27	PIS	21	2:31	TAU	20	21:58	GEM	21	20:08	LEO
22	6:02	ARI	23	13:20	GEM	23	5:52	CAN	23	21:56	VIR
24	18:42	TAU	25	21:02	CAN	25	10:19	LEO	25	22:25	LIB
27	5:27	GEM	28	2:01	LEO	27	12:36	VIR	27	23:20	SCO
29	13:39	CAN	30	5:27	VIR	29	14:20	LIB	30	2:01	SAG
31	19:36	LEO				31	16:44	SCO			

SEP			OCT			NOV			DEC		
1	7:05	CAP	3	6:20	PIS	2	0:35	ARI	1	20:22	TAU
3	14:37	AQU	5	18:28	ARI	4	13:37	TAU	4	8:29	GEM
6	0:27	PIS	8	7:27	TAU	7	1:55	GEM	6	18:32	CAN
8	12:14	ARI	10	20:03	GEM	9	12:35	CAN	9	2:28	LEO
11	1:13	TAU	13	6:51	CAN	11	21:01	LEO	11	8:32	VIR
13	13:47	GEM	15	14:35	LEO	14	2:43	VIR	13	12:45	LIB
15	23:52	CAN	17	18:43	VIR	16	5:36	LIB	15	15:14	SCO
18	6:05	LEO	19	19:48	LIB	18	6:19	SCO	17	16:32	SAG
20	8:34	VIR	21	19:19	SCO	20	6:16	SAG	19	18:00	CAP
22	8:42	LIB	23	19:08	SAG	22	7:20	CAP	21	21:25	AQU
24	8:21	SCO	25	21:11	CAP	24	11:25	AQU	24	4:20	PIS
26	9:22	SAG	28	2:51	AQU	26	19:36	PIS	26	15:05	ARI
28	13:07	CAP	30	12:22	PIS	29	7:18	ARI	29	3:58	TAU
30	20:14	AQU							31	16:13	GEM

—1950—

JAN

3	1:57	CAN
5	8:58	LEO
7	14:06	VIR
9	18:09	LIB
11	21:28	SCO
14	0:16	SAG
16	3:07	CAP
18	7:07	AQU
20	13:42	PIS
22	23:38	ARI
25	12:08	TAU
28	0:43	GEM
30	10:50	CAN

FEB

1	17:34	LEO
3	21:37	VIR
6	0:19	LIB
8	2:51	SCO
10	5:52	SAG
12	9:45	CAP
14	14:58	AQU
16	22:11	PIS
19	8:01	ARI
21	20:12	TAU
24	9:03	GEM
26	20:03	CAN

MAR

1	3:31	LEO
3	7:25	VIR
5	9:01	LIB
7	9:56	SCO
9	11:38	SAG
11	15:07	CAP
13	20:53	AQU
16	5:00	PIS
18	15:21	ARI
21	3:33	TAU
23	16:28	GEM
26	4:17	CAN
28	13:05	LEO
30	18:01	VIR

APR

1	19:41	LIB
3	19:36	SCO
5	19:37	SAG
7	21:30	CAP
10	2:25	AQU
12	10:38	PIS
14	21:32	ARI
17	10:00	TAU
19	22:55	GEM
22	11:02	CAN
24	20:58	LEO
27	3:30	VIR
29	6:25	LIB

MAY

1	6:38	SCO
3	5:51	SAG
5	6:08	CAP
7	9:22	AQU
9	16:34	PIS
12	3:18	ARI
14	15:59	TAU
17	4:53	GEM
19	16:51	CAN
22	3:07	LEO
24	10:51	VIR
26	15:26	LIB
28	17:01	SCO
30	16:44	SAG

JUN

1	16:27	CAP
3	18:18	AQU
5	23:57	PIS
8	9:44	ARI
10	22:13	TAU
13	11:05	GEM
15	22:45	CAN
18	8:38	LEO
20	16:32	VIR
22	22:10	LIB
25	1:19	SCO
27	2:26	SAG
29	2:49	CAP

JUL

1	4:20	AQU
3	8:52	PIS
5	17:25	ARI
8	5:14	TAU
10	18:02	GEM
13	5:34	CAN
15	14:53	LEO
17	22:06	VIR
20	3:34	LIB
22	7:27	SCO
24	9:56	SAG
26	11:40	CAP
28	13:56	AQU
30	18:19	PIS

AUG

2	2:03	ARI
4	13:06	TAU
7	1:44	GEM
9	13:27	CAN
11	22:37	LEO
14	5:04	VIR
16	9:31	LIB
18	12:49	SCO
20	15:36	SAG
22	18:23	CAP
24	21:53	AQU
27	3:02	PIS
29	10:45	ARI
31	21:19	TAU

SEP

3	9:46	GEM
5	21:54	CAN
8	7:34	LEO
10	13:55	VIR
12	17:28	LIB
14	19:27	SCO
16	21:13	SAG
18	23:49	CAP
21	4:00	AQU
23	10:10	PIS
25	18:32	ARI
28	5:09	TAU
30	17:27	GEM

OCT

3	6:00	CAN
5	16:40	LEO
7	23:54	VIR
10	3:29	LIB
12	4:31	SCO
14	4:44	SAG
16	5:56	CAP
18	9:27	AQU
20	15:53	PIS
23	0:59	ARI
25	12:03	TAU
28	0:23	GEM
30	13:04	CAN

NOV

2	0:38	LEO
4	9:21	VIR
6	14:10	LIB
8	15:29	SCO
10	14:52	SAG
12	14:26	CAP
14	16:15	AQU
16	21:39	PIS
19	6:40	ARI
21	18:08	TAU
24	6:39	GEM
26	19:14	CAN
29	7:02	LEO

DEC

1	16:54	VIR
3	23:29	LIB
6	2:20	SCO
8	2:17	SAG
10	1:17	CAP
12	1:35	AQU
14	5:11	PIS
16	12:59	ARI
19	0:10	TAU
21	12:50	GEM
24	1:18	CAN
26	12:46	LEO
28	22:42	VIR
31	6:20	LIB

—1951—

JAN

2	10:58	SCO
4	12:39	SAG
6	12:32	CAP
8	12:36	AQU
10	14:56	PIS
12	21:06	ARI
15	7:11	TAU
17	19:36	GEM
20	8:06	CAN
22	19:12	LEO
25	4:26	VIR
27	11:46	LIB
29	17:04	SCO
31	20:17	SAG

FEB

2	21:53	CAP
4	23:04	AQU
7	1:29	PIS
9	6:43	ARI
11	15:34	TAU
14	3:19	GEM
16	15:52	CAN
19	3:01	LEO
21	11:43	VIR
23	18:01	LIB
25	22:31	SCO
28	1:50	SAG

MAR

2	4:30	CAP
4	7:11	AQU
6	10:46	PIS
8	16:16	ARI
11	0:33	TAU
13	11:36	GEM
16	0:06	CAN
18	11:45	LEO
20	20:39	VIR
23	2:21	LIB
25	5:36	SCO
27	7:41	SAG
29	9:51	CAP
31	13:03	AQU

APR

2	17:45	PIS
5	0:16	ARI
7	8:53	TAU
9	19:41	GEM
12	8:05	CAN
14	20:18	LEO
17	6:07	VIR
19	12:14	LIB
21	14:55	SCO
23	15:40	SAG
25	16:20	CAP
27	18:33	AQU
29	23:14	PIS

MAY

2	6:27	ARI
4	15:47	TAU
7	2:51	GEM
9	15:13	CAN
12	3:50	LEO
14	14:44	VIR
16	22:06	LIB
19	1:24	SCO
21	1:44	SAG
23	1:08	CAP
25	1:42	AQU
27	5:06	PIS
29	11:54	ARI
31	21:34	TAU

JUN

3	9:03	GEM
5	21:32	CAN
8	10:12	LEO
10	21:47	VIR
13	6:31	LIB
15	11:17	SCO
17	12:27	SAG
19	11:38	CAP
21	11:04	AQU
23	12:50	PIS
25	18:14	ARI
28	3:18	TAU
30	14:52	GEM

JUL

3	3:28	CAN
5	16:01	LEO
8	3:36	VIR
10	13:05	LIB
12	19:19	SCO
14	22:03	SAG
16	22:15	CAP
18	21:42	AQU
20	22:29	PIS
23	2:22	ARI
25	10:07	TAU
27	21:08	GEM
30	9:43	CAN

AUG

1	22:08	LEO
4	9:19	VIR
6	18:35	LIB
9	1:24	SCO
11	5:31	SAG
13	7:19	CAP
15	7:53	AQU
17	8:53	PIS
19	11:59	ARI
21	18:27	TAU
24	4:28	GEM
26	16:45	CAN
29	5:10	LEO
31	16:00	VIR

SEP

3	0:32	LIB
5	6:49	SCO
7	11:12	SAG
9	14:07	CAP
11	16:12	AQU
13	18:22	PIS
15	21:48	ARI
18	3:42	TAU
20	12:47	GEM
23	0:35	CAN
25	13:08	LEO
28	0:06	VIR
30	8:09	LIB

OCT

2	13:24	SCO
4	16:49	SAG
6	19:30	CAP
8	22:19	AQU
11	1:47	PIS
13	6:20	ARI
15	12:37	TAU
17	21:22	GEM
20	8:43	CAN
22	21:25	LEO
25	9:02	VIR
27	17:26	LIB
29	22:10	SCO

NOV

1	0:20	SAG
3	1:40	CAP
5	3:43	AQU
7	7:23	PIS
9	12:53	ARI
11	20:08	TAU
14	5:16	GEM
16	16:28	CAN
19	5:12	LEO
21	17:36	VIR
24	3:09	LIB
26	8:32	SCO
28	10:20	SAG
30	10:23	CAP

DEC

2	10:45	AQU
4	13:08	PIS
6	18:18	ARI
9	2:05	TAU
11	11:54	GEM
13	23:23	CAN
16	12:05	LEO
19	0:53	VIR
21	11:41	LIB
23	18:39	SCO
25	21:27	SAG
27	21:24	CAP
29	20:36	AQU
31	21:11	PIS

—1952—

JAN

3	0:42	ARI
5	7:44	TAU
7	17:43	GEM
10	5:35	CAN
12	18:20	LEO
15	7:01	VIR
17	18:20	LIB
20	2:44	SCO
22	7:22	SAG
24	8:39	CAP
26	8:07	AQU
28	7:46	PIS
30	9:33	ARI

FEB

1	14:51	TAU
3	23:55	GEM
6	11:44	CAN
9	0:36	LEO
11	13:02	VIR
14	0:01	LIB
16	8:45	SCO
18	14:43	SAG
20	17:50	CAP
22	18:49	AQU
24	19:01	PIS
26	20:12	ARI
29	0:02	TAU

MAR

2	7:37	GEM
4	18:41	CAN
7	7:31	LEO
9	19:52	VIR
12	6:17	LIB
14	14:21	SCO
16	20:16	SAG
19	0:20	CAP
21	2:55	AQU
23	4:39	PIS
25	6:34	ARI
27	10:06	TAU
29	16:36	GEM

APR

1	2:39	CAN
3	15:10	LEO
6	3:41	VIR
8	13:56	LIB
10	21:14	SCO
13	2:08	SAG
15	5:42	CAP
17	8:44	AQU
19	11:41	PIS
21	14:57	ARI
23	19:15	TAU
26	1:41	GEM
28	11:06	CAN
30	23:13	LEO

MAY

3	11:58	VIR
5	22:39	LIB
8	5:49	SCO
10	9:51	SAG
12	12:09	CAP
14	14:15	AQU
16	17:06	PIS
18	21:07	ARI
21	2:30	TAU
23	9:38	GEM
25	19:06	CAN
28	7:00	LEO
30	19:57	VIR

JUN

2	7:26	LIB
4	15:20	SCO
6	19:21	SAG
8	20:47	CAP
10	21:27	AQU
12	23:01	PIS
15	2:29	ARI
17	8:11	TAU
19	16:04	GEM
22	2:04	CAN
24	14:03	LEO
27	3:07	VIR
29	15:19	LIB

JUL

2	0:26	SCO
4	5:27	SAG
6	7:03	CAP
8	6:55	AQU
10	7:00	PIS
12	8:56	ARI
14	13:46	TAU
16	21:38	GEM
19	8:05	CAN
21	20:21	LEO
24	9:25	VIR
26	21:54	LIB
29	8:05	SCO
31	14:38	SAG

AUG

2	17:28	CAP
4	17:42	AQU
6	17:05	PIS
8	17:34	ARI
10	20:46	TAU
13	3:37	GEM
15	13:53	CAN
18	2:19	LEO
20	15:23	VIR
23	3:42	LIB
25	14:11	SCO
27	21:54	SAG
30	2:24	CAP

SEP

1	4:03	AQU
3	4:00	PIS
5	3:58	ARI
7	5:48	TAU
9	11:06	GEM
11	20:24	CAN
14	8:39	LEO
16	21:42	VIR
19	9:42	LIB
21	19:44	SCO
24	3:33	SAG
26	9:06	CAP
28	12:25	AQU
30	13:53	PIS

OCT

2	14:34	ARI
4	16:06	TAU
6	20:15	GEM
9	4:16	CAN
11	15:51	LEO
14	4:51	VIR
16	16:45	LIB
19	2:10	SCO
21	9:12	SAG
23	14:29	CAP
25	18:28	AQU
27	21:23	PIS
29	23:35	ARI

NOV

1	1:59	TAU
3	6:02	GEM
5	13:13	CAN
7	23:57	LEO
10	12:47	VIR
13	0:58	LIB
15	10:19	SCO
17	16:34	SAG
19	20:41	CAP
21	23:52	AQU
24	2:55	PIS
26	6:10	ARI
28	9:55	TAU
30	14:53	GEM

DEC

2	22:09	CAN
5	8:23	LEO
7	20:58	VIR
10	9:36	LIB
12	19:39	SCO
15	2:00	SAG
17	5:18	CAP
19	7:03	AQU
21	8:46	PIS
23	11:30	ARI
25	15:46	TAU
27	21:48	GEM
30	5:54	CAN

—1953—

JAN			FEB			MAR			APR		
1	16:18	LEO	3	0:32	LIB	2	6:41	LIB	1	0:20	SCO
4	4:41	VIR	5	12:21	SCO	4	18:31	SCO	3	9:59	SAG
6	17:37	LIB	7	21:21	SAG	7	4:20	SAG	5	17:29	CAP
9	4:44	SCO	10	2:32	CAP	9	11:10	CAP	7	22:28	AQU
11	12:15	SAG	12	4:17	AQU	11	14:38	AQU	10	0:50	PIS
13	15:55	CAP	14	3:58	PIS	13	15:17	PIS	12	1:19	ARI
15	16:58	AQU	16	3:31	ARI	15	14:39	ARI	14	1:32	TAU
17	17:07	PIS	18	4:51	TAU	17	14:45	TAU	16	3:27	GEM
19	18:09	ARI	20	9:27	GEM	19	17:35	GEM	18	8:53	CAN
21	21:21	TAU	22	17:48	CAN	22	0:30	CAN	20	18:27	LEO
24	3:21	GEM	25	5:06	LEO	24	11:15	LEO	23	6:53	VIR
26	12:07	CAN	27	17:51	VIR	27	0:04	VIR	25	19:41	LIB
28	23:06	LEO				29	12:52	LIB	28	6:52	SCO
31	11:36	VIR							30	15:53	SAG

MAY			JUN			JUL			AUG		
2	22:55	CAP	1	9:46	AQU	2	21:24	ARI	1	5:57	TAU
5	4:13	AQU	3	13:12	PIS	5	0:24	TAU	3	10:11	GEM
7	7:47	PIS	5	16:02	ARI	7	4:43	GEM	5	17:00	CAN
9	9:49	ARI	7	18:42	TAU	9	10:55	CAN	8	2:16	LEO
11	11:12	TAU	9	22:03	GEM	11	19:28	LEO	10	13:34	VIR
13	13:27	GEM	12	3:18	CAN	14	6:29	VIR	13	2:09	LIB
15	18:17	CAN	14	11:28	LEO	16	19:04	LIB	15	14:44	SCO
18	2:47	LEO	16	22:37	VIR	19	7:17	SCO	18	1:30	SAG
20	14:31	VIR	19	11:17	LIB	21	16:59	SAG	20	8:53	CAP
23	3:16	LIB	21	22:58	SCO	23	23:07	CAP	22	12:29	AQU
25	14:33	SCO	24	7:48	SAG	26	2:03	AQU	24	13:12	PIS
27	23:09	SAG	26	13:29	CAP	28	3:07	PIS	26	12:46	ARI
30	5:17	CAP	28	16:52	AQU	30	3:56	ARI	28	13:11	TAU
			30	19:09	PIS				30	16:07	GEM

SEP			OCT			NOV			DEC		
1	22:30	CAN	1	13:54	LEO	2	20:51	LIB	2	16:31	SCO
4	8:05	LEO	4	1:41	VIR	5	9:12	SCO	5	3:09	SAG
6	19:48	VIR	6	14:28	LIB	7	20:07	SAG	7	11:33	CAP
9	8:28	LIB	9	2:57	SCO	10	5:19	CAP	9	18:00	AQU
11	21:06	SCO	11	14:20	SAG	12	12:31	AQU	11	22:47	PIS
14	8:32	SAG	13	23:52	CAP	14	17:18	PIS	14	2:07	ARI
16	17:21	CAP	16	6:35	AQU	16	19:36	ARI	16	4:23	TAU
18	22:30	AQU	18	9:56	PIS	18	20:15	TAU	18	6:28	GEM
21	0:07	PIS	20	10:27	ARI	20	20:55	GEM	20	9:40	CAN
22	23:31	ARI	22	9:47	TAU	22	23:32	CAN	22	15:23	LEO
24	22:45	TAU	24	10:05	GEM	25	5:41	LEO	25	0:24	VIR
27	0:01	GEM	26	13:24	CAN	27	15:41	VIR	27	12:11	LIB
29	4:57	CAN	28	20:55	LEO	30	4:06	LIB	30	0:43	SCO
			31	8:05	VIR						

—1954—

JAN

1	11:40	SAG
3	19:46	CAP
6	1:10	AQU
8	4:43	PIS
10	7:27	ARI
12	10:10	TAU
14	13:30	GEM
16	18:01	CAN
19	0:25	LEO
21	9:14	VIR
23	20:30	LIB
26	9:04	SCO
28	20:43	SAG
31	5:27	CAP

FEB

2	10:38	AQU
4	13:04	PIS
6	14:15	ARI
8	15:47	TAU
10	18:55	GEM
13	0:10	CAN
15	7:36	LEO
17	17:01	VIR
20	4:15	LIB
22	16:44	SCO
25	5:01	SAG
27	14:58	CAP

MAR

1	21:07	AQU
3	23:33	PIS
5	23:41	ARI
7	23:33	TAU
10	1:07	GEM
12	5:38	CAN
14	13:17	LEO
16	23:22	VIR
19	10:58	LIB
21	23:27	SCO
24	11:57	SAG
26	22:56	CAP
29	6:38	AQU
31	10:17	PIS

APR

2	10:40	ARI
4	9:43	TAU
6	9:40	GEM
8	12:29	CAN
10	19:06	LEO
13	5:03	VIR
15	16:58	LIB
18	5:33	SCO
20	17:55	SAG
23	5:12	CAP
25	14:03	AQU
27	19:22	PIS
29	21:09	ARI

MAY

1	20:43	TAU
3	20:07	GEM
5	21:30	CAN
8	2:29	LEO
10	11:23	VIR
12	23:04	LIB
15	11:42	SCO
17	23:54	SAG
20	10:49	CAP
22	19:49	AQU
25	2:09	PIS
27	5:32	ARI
29	6:34	TAU
31	6:41	GEM

JUN

2	7:46	CAN
4	11:35	LEO
6	19:07	VIR
9	5:59	LIB
11	18:30	SCO
14	6:38	SAG
16	17:06	CAP
19	1:26	AQU
21	7:37	PIS
23	11:44	ARI
25	14:09	TAU
27	15:42	GEM
29	17:36	CAN

JUL

1	21:17	LEO
4	3:56	VIR
6	13:54	LIB
9	2:04	SCO
11	14:19	SAG
14	0:40	CAP
16	8:20	AQU
18	13:33	PIS
20	17:08	ARI
22	19:53	TAU
24	22:31	GEM
27	1:42	CAN
29	6:11	LEO
31	12:50	VIR

AUG

2	22:14	LIB
5	10:03	SCO
7	22:33	SAG
10	9:21	CAP
12	16:55	AQU
14	21:17	PIS
16	23:38	ARI
19	1:26	TAU
21	3:57	GEM
23	7:50	CAN
25	13:23	LEO
27	20:44	VIR
30	6:12	LIB

SEP

1	17:49	SCO
4	6:33	SAG
6	18:10	CAP
9	2:31	AQU
11	6:55	PIS
13	8:23	ARI
15	8:45	TAU
17	9:55	GEM
19	13:13	CAN
21	19:04	LEO
24	3:11	VIR
26	13:11	LIB
29	0:52	SCO

OCT

1	13:42	SAG
4	2:05	CAP
6	11:46	AQU
8	17:17	PIS
10	18:59	ARI
12	18:32	TAU
14	18:10	GEM
16	19:50	CAN
19	0:41	LEO
21	8:45	VIR
23	19:12	LIB
26	7:11	SCO
28	19:59	SAG
31	8:37	CAP

NOV

2	19:23	AQU
5	2:35	PIS
7	5:43	ARI
9	5:49	TAU
11	4:51	GEM
13	5:00	CAN
15	8:03	LEO
17	14:53	VIR
20	1:03	LIB
22	13:13	SCO
25	2:02	SAG
27	14:24	CAP
30	1:20	AQU

DEC

2	9:39	PIS
4	14:35	ARI
6	16:23	TAU
8	16:17	GEM
10	16:07	CAN
12	17:49	LEO
14	22:54	VIR
17	7:52	LIB
19	19:44	SCO
22	8:35	SAG
24	20:41	CAP
27	7:01	AQU
29	15:10	PIS
31	20:57	ARI

—1955—

JAN			FEB			MAR			APR		
3	0:25	TAU	1	9:03	GEM	2	17:40	CAN	1	3:21	LEO
5	2:05	GEM	3	11:37	CAN	4	21:49	LEO	3	9:31	VIR
7	3:01	CAN	5	14:29	LEO	7	3:09	VIR	5	17:34	LIB
9	4:42	LEO	7	18:43	VIR	9	10:20	LIB	8	3:38	SCO
11	8:43	VIR	10	1:34	LIB	11	20:05	SCO	10	15:42	SAG
13	16:15	LIB	12	11:39	SCO	14	8:14	SAG	13	4:41	CAP
16	3:15	SCO	15	0:08	SAG	16	21:02	CAP	15	16:20	AQU
18	16:02	SAG	17	12:35	CAP	19	7:47	AQU	18	0:29	PIS
21	4:10	CAP	19	22:33	AQU	21	14:45	PIS	20	4:30	ARI
23	13:59	AQU	22	5:10	PIS	23	18:10	ARI	22	5:30	TAU
25	21:11	PIS	24	9:06	ARI	25	19:32	TAU	24	5:24	GEM
28	2:20	ARI	26	11:47	TAU	27	20:42	GEM	26	6:09	CAN
30	6:06	TAU	28	14:24	GEM	29	23:06	CAN	28	9:09	LEO
									30	14:58	VIR

MAY			JUN			JUL			AUG		
2	23:26	LIB	1	15:54	SCO	1	10:34	SAG	2	17:52	AQU
5	10:04	SCO	4	4:24	SAG	3	23:30	CAP	5	3:04	PIS
7	22:19	SAG	6	17:21	CAP	6	11:19	AQU	7	10:00	ARI
10	11:19	CAP	9	5:30	AQU	8	21:09	PIS	9	15:03	TAU
12	23:30	AQU	11	15:32	PIS	11	4:33	ARI	11	18:34	GEM
15	8:54	PIS	13	22:24	ARI	13	9:21	TAU	13	20:51	CAN
17	14:21	ARI	16	1:50	TAU	15	11:43	GEM	15	22:34	LEO
19	16:12	TAU	18	2:37	GEM	17	12:30	CAN	18	0:58	VIR
21	15:57	GEM	20	2:16	CAN	19	13:04	LEO	20	5:34	LIB
23	15:33	CAN	22	2:37	LEO	21	15:07	VIR	22	13:38	SCO
25	16:53	LEO	24	5:27	VIR	23	20:16	LIB	25	1:04	SAG
27	21:16	VIR	26	11:56	LIB	26	5:19	SCO	27	13:57	CAP
30	5:08	LIB	28	22:05	SCO	28	17:24	SAG	30	1:36	AQU
						31	6:19	CAP			

SEP			OCT			NOV			DEC		
1	10:23	PIS	1	0:47	ARI	1	14:23	GEM	1	0:47	CAN
3	16:24	ARI	3	3:52	TAU	3	15:12	CAN	3	1:08	LEO
5	20:37	TAU	5	6:00	GEM	5	17:20	LEO	5	3:50	VIR
7	23:59	GEM	7	8:23	CAN	7	21:37	VIR	7	9:49	LIB
10	3:01	CAN	9	11:42	LEO	10	4:16	LIB	9	19:00	SCO
12	6:02	LEO	11	16:12	VIR	12	13:13	SCO	12	6:34	SAG
14	9:34	VIR	13	22:14	LIB	15	0:17	SAG	14	19:24	CAP
16	14:36	LIB	16	6:24	SCO	17	12:59	CAP	17	8:20	AQU
18	22:19	SCO	18	17:08	SAG	20	1:59	AQU	19	20:02	PIS
21	9:12	SAG	21	5:52	CAP	22	13:11	PIS	22	5:06	ARI
23	22:01	CAP	23	18:33	AQU	24	20:48	ARI	24	10:33	TAU
26	10:08	AQU	26	4:38	PIS	27	0:27	TAU	26	12:33	GEM
28	19:13	PIS	28	10:47	ARI	29	1:11	GEM	28	12:18	CAN
			30	13:30	TAU				30	11:37	LEO

—1956—

JAN		
1	12:31	VIR
3	16:44	LIB
6	1:00	SCO
8	12:33	SAG
11	1:34	CAP
13	14:20	AQU
16	1:48	PIS
18	11:18	ARI
20	18:12	TAU
22	22:06	GEM
24	23:20	CAN
26	23:07	LEO
28	23:18	VIR
31	1:56	LIB

FEB		
2	8:34	SCO
4	19:13	SAG
7	8:09	CAP
9	20:52	AQU
12	7:52	PIS
14	16:49	ARI
16	23:49	TAU
19	4:51	GEM
21	7:50	CAN
23	9:11	LEO
25	10:05	VIR
27	12:21	LIB
29	17:45	SCO

MAR		
3	3:10	SAG
5	15:33	CAP
8	4:20	AQU
10	15:12	PIS
12	23:27	ARI
15	5:33	TAU
17	10:12	GEM
19	13:48	CAN
21	16:31	LEO
23	18:53	VIR
25	22:00	LIB
28	3:19	SCO
30	11:56	SAG

APR		
1	23:38	CAP
4	12:25	AQU
6	23:38	PIS
9	7:47	ARI
11	13:04	TAU
13	16:31	GEM
15	19:15	CAN
17	22:01	LEO
20	1:17	VIR
22	5:37	LIB
24	11:45	SCO
26	20:26	SAG
29	7:45	CAP

MAY		
1	20:28	AQU
4	8:16	PIS
6	17:06	ARI
8	22:24	TAU
11	1:01	GEM
13	2:21	CAN
15	3:52	LEO
17	6:40	VIR
19	11:26	LIB
21	18:27	SCO
24	3:47	SAG
26	15:12	CAP
29	3:52	AQU
31	16:10	PIS

JUN		
3	2:05	ARI
5	8:22	TAU
7	11:10	GEM
9	11:42	CAN
11	11:45	LEO
13	13:04	VIR
15	16:59	LIB
18	0:03	SCO
20	9:56	SAG
22	21:43	CAP
25	10:26	AQU
27	22:55	PIS
30	9:43	ARI

JUL		
2	17:26	TAU
4	21:26	GEM
6	22:20	CAN
8	21:42	LEO
10	21:35	VIR
12	23:55	LIB
15	5:57	SCO
17	15:38	SAG
20	3:41	CAP
22	16:29	AQU
25	4:51	PIS
27	15:54	ARI
30	0:41	TAU

AUG		
1	6:16	GEM
3	8:33	CAN
5	8:27	LEO
7	7:50	VIR
9	8:51	LIB
11	13:21	SCO
13	22:00	SAG
16	9:48	CAP
18	22:38	AQU
21	10:48	PIS
23	21:30	ARI
26	6:24	TAU
28	13:00	GEM
30	16:52	CAN

SEP		
1	18:14	LEO
3	18:21	VIR
5	19:05	LIB
7	22:27	SCO
10	5:46	SAG
12	16:46	CAP
15	5:28	AQU
17	17:34	PIS
20	3:48	ARI
22	12:01	TAU
24	18:25	GEM
26	23:00	CAN
29	1:49	LEO

OCT		
1	3:25	VIR
3	5:02	LIB
5	8:19	SCO
7	14:46	SAG
10	0:48	CAP
12	13:10	AQU
15	1:25	PIS
17	11:36	ARI
19	19:08	TAU
22	0:29	GEM
24	4:24	CAN
26	7:27	LEO
28	10:10	VIR
30	13:10	LIB

NOV		
1	17:25	SCO
3	23:57	SAG
6	9:24	CAP
8	21:20	AQU
11	9:51	PIS
13	20:37	ARI
16	4:13	TAU
18	8:45	GEM
20	11:18	CAN
22	13:10	LEO
24	15:32	VIR
26	19:11	LIB
29	0:35	SCO

DEC		
1	7:59	SAG
3	17:36	CAP
6	5:17	AQU
8	17:57	PIS
11	5:37	ARI
13	14:16	TAU
15	19:07	GEM
17	20:52	CAN
19	21:12	LEO
21	21:56	VIR
24	0:39	LIB
26	6:09	SCO
28	14:20	SAG
31	0:37	CAP

—1957—

JAN

2	12:25	AQU
5	1:05	PIS
7	13:23	ARI
9	23:27	TAU
12	5:44	GEM
14	8:06	CAN
16	7:51	LEO
18	7:04	VIR
20	7:55	LIB
22	12:03	SCO
24	19:52	SAG
27	6:33	CAP
29	18:42	AQU

FEB

1	7:21	PIS
3	19:42	ARI
6	6:38	TAU
8	14:35	GEM
10	18:39	CAN
12	19:19	LEO
14	18:17	VIR
16	17:50	LIB
18	20:06	SCO
21	2:23	SAG
23	12:27	CAP
26	0:43	AQU
28	13:25	PIS

MAR

3	1:31	ARI
5	12:21	TAU
7	21:04	GEM
10	2:45	CAN
12	5:12	LEO
14	5:20	VIR
16	4:59	LIB
18	6:15	SCO
20	10:54	SAG
22	19:35	CAP
25	7:18	AQU
27	20:00	PIS
30	7:55	ARI

APR

1	18:11	TAU
4	2:31	GEM
6	8:38	CAN
8	12:25	LEO
10	14:13	VIR
12	15:09	LIB
14	16:46	SCO
16	20:43	SAG
19	4:09	CAP
21	14:54	AQU
24	3:23	PIS
26	15:22	ARI
29	1:18	TAU

MAY

1	8:47	GEM
3	14:09	CAN
5	17:54	LEO
7	20:37	VIR
9	22:58	LIB
12	1:49	SCO
14	6:14	SAG
16	13:14	CAP
18	23:13	AQU
21	11:21	PIS
23	23:34	ARI
26	9:43	TAU
28	16:47	GEM
30	21:06	CAN

JUN

1	23:46	LEO
4	2:00	VIR
6	4:46	LIB
8	8:41	SCO
10	14:10	SAG
12	21:37	CAP
15	7:24	AQU
17	19:15	PIS
20	7:46	ARI
22	18:39	TAU
25	2:07	GEM
27	6:01	CAN
29	7:31	LEO

JUL

1	8:24	VIR
3	10:17	LIB
5	14:10	SCO
7	20:21	SAG
10	4:35	CAP
12	14:43	AQU
15	2:33	PIS
17	15:15	ARI
20	2:58	TAU
22	11:34	GEM
24	16:05	CAN
26	17:17	LEO
28	17:00	VIR
30	17:20	LIB

AUG

1	20:01	SCO
4	1:48	SAG
6	10:24	CAP
8	21:02	AQU
11	9:02	PIS
13	21:46	ARI
16	10:01	TAU
18	19:52	GEM
21	1:49	CAN
23	3:51	LEO
25	3:26	VIR
27	2:42	LIB
29	3:46	SCO
31	8:08	SAG

SEP

2	16:06	CAP
5	2:50	AQU
7	15:04	PIS
10	3:45	ARI
12	15:58	TAU
15	2:27	GEM
17	9:50	CAN
19	13:31	LEO
21	14:12	VIR
23	13:33	LIB
25	13:41	SCO
27	16:28	SAG
29	23:00	CAP

OCT

2	9:04	AQU
4	21:18	PIS
7	9:57	ARI
9	21:48	TAU
12	8:01	GEM
14	15:55	CAN
16	21:00	LEO
18	23:24	VIR
21	0:04	LIB
23	0:31	SCO
25	2:34	SAG
27	7:41	CAP
29	16:33	AQU

NOV

1	4:19	PIS
3	17:00	ARI
6	4:38	TAU
8	14:09	GEM
10	21:24	CAN
13	2:37	LEO
15	6:07	VIR
17	8:26	LIB
19	10:18	SCO
21	12:52	SAG
23	17:30	CAP
26	1:17	AQU
28	12:16	PIS

DEC

1	0:57	ARI
3	12:48	TAU
5	22:01	GEM
8	4:16	CAN
10	8:24	LEO
12	11:29	VIR
14	14:23	LIB
16	17:36	SCO
18	21:31	SAG
21	2:47	CAP
23	10:19	AQU
25	20:41	PIS
28	9:13	ARI
30	21:38	TAU

—1958—

JAN
2	7:22	GEM
4	13:22	CAN
6	16:22	LEO
8	17:59	VIR
10	19:52	LIB
12	23:03	SCO
15	3:50	SAG
17	10:13	CAP
19	18:23	AQU
22	4:42	PIS
24	17:03	ARI
27	5:57	TAU
29	16:48	GEM
31	23:41	CAN

FEB
3	2:38	LEO
5	3:11	VIR
7	3:24	LIB
9	5:04	SCO
11	9:12	SAG
13	15:56	CAP
16	0:52	AQU
18	11:40	PIS
21	0:02	ARI
23	13:05	TAU
26	0:53	GEM
28	9:17	CAN

MAR
2	13:27	LEO
4	14:15	VIR
6	13:36	LIB
8	13:35	SCO
10	15:57	SAG
12	21:37	CAP
15	6:28	AQU
17	17:42	PIS
20	6:17	ARI
22	19:16	TAU
25	7:20	GEM
27	16:53	CAN
29	22:46	LEO

APR
1	1:01	VIR
3	0:54	LIB
5	0:17	SCO
7	1:07	SAG
9	5:01	CAP
11	12:42	AQU
13	23:39	PIS
16	12:23	ARI
19	1:17	TAU
21	13:03	GEM
23	22:47	CAN
26	5:44	LEO
28	9:41	VIR
30	11:07	LIB

MAY
2	11:15	SCO
4	11:44	SAG
6	14:21	CAP
8	20:30	AQU
11	6:27	PIS
13	18:58	ARI
16	7:50	TAU
18	19:14	GEM
21	4:23	CAN
23	11:15	LEO
25	16:00	VIR
27	18:56	LIB
29	20:34	SCO
31	21:54	SAG

JUN
3	0:23	CAP
5	5:34	AQU
7	14:24	PIS
10	2:21	ARI
12	15:13	TAU
15	2:31	GEM
17	11:04	CAN
19	17:04	LEO
21	21:23	VIR
24	0:43	LIB
26	3:31	SCO
28	6:12	SAG
30	9:33	CAP

JUL
2	14:45	AQU
4	22:57	PIS
7	10:18	ARI
9	23:10	TAU
12	10:47	GEM
14	19:16	CAN
17	0:31	LEO
19	3:42	VIR
21	6:12	LIB
23	8:58	SCO
25	12:26	SAG
27	16:53	CAP
29	22:53	AQU

AUG
1	7:12	PIS
3	18:15	ARI
6	7:05	TAU
8	19:17	GEM
11	4:26	CAN
13	9:44	LEO
15	12:07	VIR
17	13:17	LIB
19	14:50	SCO
21	17:48	SAG
23	22:39	CAP
26	5:28	AQU
28	14:25	PIS
31	1:36	ARI

SEP
2	14:24	TAU
5	3:07	GEM
7	13:23	CAN
9	19:42	LEO
11	22:20	VIR
13	22:45	LIB
15	22:50	SCO
18	0:17	SAG
20	4:13	CAP
22	11:04	AQU
24	20:34	PIS
27	8:08	ARI
29	20:58	TAU

OCT
2	9:51	GEM
4	21:01	CAN
7	4:51	LEO
9	8:50	VIR
11	9:44	LIB
13	9:12	SCO
15	9:09	SAG
17	11:23	CAP
19	17:04	AQU
22	2:20	PIS
24	14:11	ARI
27	3:08	TAU
29	15:50	GEM

NOV
1	3:09	CAN
3	12:03	LEO
5	17:46	VIR
7	20:17	LIB
9	20:30	SCO
11	20:03	SAG
13	20:55	CAP
16	0:53	AQU
18	8:57	PIS
20	20:29	ARI
23	9:31	TAU
25	22:01	GEM
28	8:52	CAN
30	17:41	LEO

DEC
3	0:18	VIR
5	4:31	LIB
7	6:29	SCO
9	7:02	SAG
11	7:47	CAP
13	10:38	AQU
15	17:12	PIS
18	3:46	ARI
20	16:38	TAU
23	5:09	GEM
25	15:33	CAN
27	23:34	LEO
30	5:41	VIR

—1959—

JAN			FEB			MAR			APR		
1	10:22	LIB	1	22:11	SAG	1	3:33	SAG	1	17:42	AQU
3	13:42	SCO	4	1:29	CAP	3	7:06	CAP	4	1:23	PIS
5	15:56	SAG	6	5:41	AQU	5	12:17	AQU	6	11:33	ARI
7	17:50	CAP	8	11:51	PIS	7	19:26	PIS	8	23:32	TAU
9	20:52	AQU	10	20:55	ARI	10	4:54	ARI	11	12:25	GEM
12	2:40	PIS	13	8:48	TAU	12	16:37	TAU	14	0:48	CAN
14	12:10	ARI	15	21:40	GEM	15	5:31	GEM	16	10:55	LEO
17	0:33	TAU	18	8:51	CAN	17	17:28	CAN	18	17:28	VIR
19	13:16	GEM	20	16:38	LEO	20	2:23	LEO	20	20:19	LIB
21	23:47	CAN	22	21:06	VIR	22	7:28	VIR	22	20:34	SCO
24	7:14	LEO	24	23:29	LIB	24	9:27	LIB	24	19:59	SAG
26	12:14	VIR	27	1:15	SCO	26	9:54	SCO	26	20:33	CAP
28	15:55	LIB				28	10:32	SAG	28	23:56	AQU
30	19:06	SCO				30	12:49	CAP			

MAY			JUN			JUL			AUG		
1	6:59	PIS	2	11:37	TAU	2	7:06	GEM	1	2:24	CAN
3	17:19	ARI	5	0:36	GEM	4	19:04	CAN	3	12:10	LEO
6	5:39	TAU	7	12:44	CAN	7	5:08	LEO	5	19:30	VIR
8	18:35	GEM	9	23:19	LEO	9	13:16	VIR	8	0:57	LIB
11	6:57	CAN	12	7:51	VIR	11	19:27	LIB	10	5:00	SCO
13	17:41	LEO	14	13:42	LIB	13	23:34	SCO	12	7:59	SAG
16	1:38	VIR	16	16:39	SCO	16	1:42	SAG	14	10:19	CAP
18	6:07	LIB	18	17:15	SAG	18	2:42	CAP	16	12:54	AQU
20	7:25	SCO	20	17:02	CAP	20	4:05	AQU	18	17:00	PIS
22	6:51	SAG	22	18:01	AQU	22	7:41	PIS	20	23:52	ARI
24	6:24	CAP	24	22:10	PIS	24	14:54	ARI	23	9:59	TAU
26	8:10	AQU	27	6:28	ARI	27	1:44	TAU	25	22:19	GEM
28	13:43	PIS	29	18:11	TAU	29	14:24	GEM	28	10:34	CAN
30	23:19	ARI							30	20:34	LEO

SEP			OCT			NOV			DEC		
2	3:31	VIR	1	17:09	LIB	2	5:02	SAG	1	15:11	CAP
4	7:57	LIB	3	18:54	SCO	4	5:05	CAP	3	15:35	AQU
6	10:53	SCO	5	19:55	SAG	6	7:14	AQU	5	19:17	PIS
8	13:21	SAG	7	21:39	CAP	8	12:36	PIS	8	3:00	ARI
10	16:05	CAP	10	1:13	AQU	10	21:10	ARI	10	13:56	TAU
12	19:44	AQU	12	7:06	PIS	13	8:05	TAU	13	2:25	GEM
15	0:54	PIS	14	15:20	ARI	15	20:17	GEM	15	15:01	CAN
17	8:17	ARI	17	1:40	TAU	18	8:57	CAN	18	2:58	LEO
19	18:13	TAU	19	13:40	GEM	20	21:04	LEO	20	13:30	VIR
22	6:16	GEM	22	2:23	CAN	23	7:08	VIR	22	21:29	LIB
24	18:50	CAN	24	14:04	LEO	25	13:42	LIB	25	2:01	SCO
27	5:37	LEO	26	22:49	VIR	27	16:22	SCO	27	3:16	SAG
29	13:04	VIR	29	3:42	LIB	29	16:12	SAG	29	2:38	CAP
			31	5:14	SCO				31	2:15	AQU

—1960—

JAN			FEB			MAR			APR		
2	4:19	PIS	3	4:17	TAU	1	13:19	TAU	2	20:46	CAN
4	10:22	ARI	5	15:59	GEM	4	0:08	GEM	5	9:01	LEO
6	20:23	TAU	8	4:38	CAN	6	12:37	CAN	7	19:02	VIR
9	8:46	GEM	10	16:09	LEO	9	0:25	LEO	10	1:36	LIB
11	21:24	CAN	13	1:35	VIR	11	9:48	VIR	12	5:02	SCO
14	9:00	LEO	15	8:56	LIB	13	16:20	LIB	14	6:38	SAG
16	19:04	VIR	17	14:24	SCO	15	20:38	SCO	16	8:01	CAP
19	3:15	LIB	19	18:12	SAG	17	23:38	SAG	18	10:32	AQU
21	9:00	SCO	21	20:40	CAP	20	2:15	CAP	20	14:56	PIS
23	12:03	SAG	23	22:33	AQU	22	5:11	AQU	22	21:23	ARI
25	13:00	CAP	26	1:04	PIS	24	9:02	PIS	25	5:51	TAU
27	13:19	AQU	28	5:38	ARI	26	14:30	ARI	27	16:17	GEM
29	14:57	PIS				28	22:14	TAU	30	4:23	CAN
31	19:40	ARI				31	8:32	GEM			

MAY			JUN			JUL			AUG		
2	16:59	LEO	1	11:38	VIR	1	3:47	LIB	1	21:05	SAG
5	3:59	VIR	3	20:32	LIB	3	10:09	SCO	3	22:26	CAP
7	11:31	LIB	6	1:20	SCO	5	12:43	SAG	5	22:21	AQU
9	15:07	SCO	8	2:31	SAG	7	12:35	CAP	7	22:43	PIS
11	15:56	SAG	10	1:48	CAP	9	11:43	AQU	10	1:22	ARI
13	15:51	CAP	12	1:23	AQU	11	12:19	PIS	12	7:36	TAU
15	16:52	AQU	14	3:18	PIS	13	16:07	ARI	14	17:30	GEM
17	20:24	PIS	16	8:43	ARI	15	23:49	TAU	17	5:43	CAN
20	2:56	ARI	18	17:34	TAU	18	10:41	GEM	19	18:18	LEO
22	12:00	TAU	21	4:46	GEM	20	23:09	CAN	22	5:42	VIR
24	22:55	GEM	23	17:10	CAN	23	11:46	LEO	24	15:10	LIB
27	11:07	CAN	26	5:52	LEO	25	23:32	VIR	26	22:24	SCO
29	23:51	LEO	28	17:53	VIR	28	9:34	LIB	29	3:20	SAG
						30	16:55	SCO	31	6:09	CAP

SEP			OCT			NOV			DEC		
2	7:36	AQU	1	17:15	PIS	2	10:28	TAU	2	2:01	GEM
4	8:51	PIS	3	20:47	ARI	4	18:45	GEM	4	12:53	CAN
6	11:26	ARI	6	2:09	TAU	7	5:26	CAN	7	1:22	LEO
8	16:45	TAU	8	10:17	GEM	9	18:00	LEO	9	14:14	VIR
11	1:32	GEM	10	21:19	CAN	12	6:24	VIR	12	1:11	LIB
13	13:11	CAN	13	9:55	LEO	14	16:08	LIB	14	8:14	SCO
16	1:47	LEO	15	21:41	VIR	16	21:54	SCO	16	11:07	SAG
18	13:07	VIR	18	6:33	LIB	19	0:17	SAG	18	11:17	CAP
20	21:59	LIB	20	12:06	SCO	21	1:03	CAP	20	10:49	AQU
23	4:18	SCO	22	15:16	SAG	23	2:05	AQU	22	11:48	PIS
25	8:42	SAG	24	17:29	CAP	25	4:50	PIS	24	15:35	ARI
27	11:54	CAP	26	19:58	AQU	27	9:51	ARI	26	22:31	TAU
29	14:33	AQU	28	23:27	PIS	29	17:00	TAU	29	8:02	GEM
			31	4:12	ARI				31	19:22	CAN

—1961—

JAN			FEB			MAR			APR		
3	7:54	LEO	2	2:49	VIR	1	9:12	VIR	2	11:37	SCO
5	20:49	VIR	4	14:28	LIB	3	20:22	LIB	4	17:34	SAG
8	8:32	LIB	6	23:51	SCO	6	5:24	SCO	6	21:52	CAP
10	17:09	SCO	9	6:02	SAG	8	12:04	SAG	9	1:03	AQU
12	21:41	SAG	11	8:51	CAP	10	16:19	CAP	11	3:32	PIS
14	22:42	CAP	13	9:15	AQU	12	18:29	AQU	13	5:56	ARI
16	21:56	AQU	15	8:53	PIS	14	19:27	PIS	15	9:17	TAU
18	21:32	PIS	17	9:41	ARI	16	20:33	ARI	17	14:55	GEM
20	23:27	ARI	19	13:22	TAU	18	23:26	TAU	19	23:50	CAN
23	4:52	TAU	21	20:52	GEM	21	5:33	GEM	22	11:43	LEO
25	13:50	GEM	24	7:49	CAN	23	15:23	CAN	25	0:31	VIR
28	1:22	CAN	26	20:35	LEO	26	3:49	LEO	27	11:35	LIB
30	14:06	LEO				28	16:30	VIR	29	19:27	SCO
						31	3:22	LIB			

MAY			JUN			JUL			AUG		
2	0:25	SAG	2	12:45	AQU	1	21:53	PIS	2	11:19	TAU
4	3:40	CAP	4	14:51	PIS	4	0:12	ARI	4	18:04	GEM
6	6:24	AQU	6	18:24	ARI	6	5:02	TAU	7	3:57	CAN
8	9:23	PIS	8	23:38	TAU	8	12:28	GEM	9	16:00	LEO
10	12:56	ARI	11	6:41	GEM	10	22:13	CAN	12	5:01	VIR
12	17:26	TAU	13	15:50	CAN	13	9:57	LEO	14	17:44	LIB
14	23:35	GEM	16	3:16	LEO	15	22:55	VIR	17	4:45	SCO
17	8:17	CAN	18	16:12	VIR	18	11:39	LIB	19	12:44	SAG
19	19:45	LEO	21	4:32	LIB	20	22:05	SCO	21	17:08	CAP
22	8:39	VIR	23	13:51	SCO	23	4:42	SAG	23	18:26	AQU
24	20:18	LIB	25	19:06	SAG	25	7:29	CAP	25	18:03	PIS
27	4:35	SCO	27	21:00	CAP	27	7:42	AQU	27	17:49	ARI
29	9:11	SAG	29	21:18	AQU	29	7:13	PIS	29	19:37	TAU
31	11:21	CAP				31	7:56	ARI			

SEP			OCT			NOV			DEC		
1	0:53	GEM	3	4:44	LEO	2	1:18	VIR	1	22:08	LIB
3	10:01	CAN	5	17:46	VIR	4	13:43	LIB	4	8:30	SCO
5	22:01	LEO	8	6:04	LIB	6	23:41	SCO	6	15:25	SAG
8	11:05	VIR	10	16:20	SCO	9	6:51	SAG	8	19:31	CAP
10	23:34	LIB	13	0:21	SAG	11	12:00	CAP	10	22:12	AQU
13	10:23	SCO	15	6:24	CAP	13	16:00	AQU	13	0:42	PIS
15	18:55	SAG	17	10:37	AQU	15	19:19	PIS	15	3:45	ARI
18	0:42	CAP	19	13:10	PIS	17	22:11	ARI	17	7:39	TAU
20	3:44	AQU	21	14:36	ARI	20	1:03	TAU	19	12:48	GEM
22	4:36	PIS	23	16:07	TAU	22	4:59	GEM	21	19:50	CAN
24	4:40	ARI	25	19:25	GEM	24	11:21	CAN	24	5:26	LEO
26	5:42	TAU	28	2:03	CAN	26	21:02	LEO	26	17:30	VIR
28	9:32	GEM	30	12:30	LEO	29	9:26	VIR	29	6:27	LIB
30	17:20	CAN							31	17:42	SCO

—1962—

JAN

3	1:24	SAG
5	5:24	CAP
7	7:00	AQU
9	7:54	PIS
11	9:34	ARI
13	13:02	TAU
15	18:42	GEM
18	2:40	CAN
20	12:50	LEO
23	0:54	VIR
25	13:52	LIB
28	1:55	SCO
30	11:00	SAG

FEB

1	16:10	CAP
3	17:57	AQU
5	17:53	PIS
7	17:51	ARI
9	19:35	TAU
12	0:19	GEM
14	8:20	CAN
16	19:04	LEO
19	7:27	VIR
21	20:22	LIB
24	8:37	SCO
26	18:47	SAG

MAR

1	1:39	CAP
3	4:52	AQU
5	5:17	PIS
7	4:32	ARI
9	4:41	TAU
11	7:36	GEM
13	14:26	CAN
16	0:56	LEO
18	13:33	VIR
21	2:29	LIB
23	14:29	SCO
26	0:49	SAG
28	8:46	CAP
30	13:44	AQU

APR

1	15:43	PIS
3	15:42	ARI
5	15:26	TAU
7	17:00	GEM
9	22:12	CAN
12	7:37	LEO
14	19:57	VIR
17	8:54	LIB
19	20:37	SCO
22	6:27	SAG
24	14:20	CAP
26	20:08	AQU
28	23:40	PIS

MAY

1	1:12	ARI
3	1:50	TAU
5	3:17	GEM
7	7:28	CAN
9	15:36	LEO
12	3:12	VIR
14	16:03	LIB
17	3:43	SCO
19	13:03	SAG
21	20:09	CAP
24	1:31	AQU
26	5:30	PIS
28	8:15	ARI
30	10:17	TAU

JUN

1	12:41	GEM
3	16:57	CAN
6	0:24	LEO
8	11:13	VIR
10	23:51	LIB
13	11:45	SCO
15	21:04	SAG
18	3:30	CAP
20	7:49	AQU
22	10:59	PIS
24	13:43	ARI
26	16:35	TAU
28	20:10	GEM

JUL

1	1:19	CAN
3	8:56	LEO
5	19:23	VIR
8	7:48	LIB
10	20:06	SCO
13	6:01	SAG
15	12:32	CAP
17	16:08	AQU
19	18:01	PIS
21	19:34	ARI
23	21:57	TAU
26	1:57	GEM
28	8:01	CAN
30	16:21	LEO

AUG

2	2:58	VIR
4	15:18	LIB
7	3:56	SCO
9	14:49	SAG
11	22:18	CAP
14	2:08	AQU
16	3:17	PIS
18	3:26	ARI
20	4:20	TAU
22	7:28	GEM
24	13:34	CAN
26	22:30	LEO
29	9:36	VIR
31	22:01	LIB

SEP

3	10:47	SCO
5	22:27	SAG
8	7:20	CAP
10	12:27	AQU
12	14:02	PIS
14	13:33	ARI
16	13:01	TAU
18	14:29	GEM
20	19:26	CAN
23	4:07	LEO
25	15:31	VIR
28	4:08	LIB
30	16:49	SCO

OCT

3	4:40	SAG
5	14:35	CAP
7	21:22	AQU
10	0:29	PIS
12	0:41	ARI
13	23:44	TAU
15	23:51	GEM
18	3:05	CAN
20	10:31	LEO
22	21:32	VIR
25	10:14	LIB
27	22:49	SCO
30	10:20	SAG

NOV

1	20:18	CAP
4	4:03	AQU
6	8:53	PIS
8	10:46	ARI
10	10:45	TAU
12	10:44	GEM
14	12:49	CAN
16	18:40	LEO
19	4:34	VIR
21	16:58	LIB
24	5:34	SCO
26	16:44	SAG
29	2:01	CAP

DEC

1	9:26	AQU
3	14:54	PIS
5	18:18	ARI
7	20:00	TAU
9	21:08	GEM
11	23:22	CAN
14	4:21	LEO
16	13:00	VIR
19	0:42	LIB
21	13:18	SCO
24	0:33	SAG
26	9:19	CAP
28	15:43	AQU
30	20:21	PIS

—1963—

JAN

1	23:48	ARI
4	2:34	TAU
6	5:14	GEM
8	8:42	CAN
10	14:01	LEO
12	22:07	VIR
15	9:05	LIB
17	21:36	SCO
20	9:21	SAG
22	18:24	CAP
25	0:14	AQU
27	3:35	PIS
29	5:44	ARI
31	7:55	TAU

FEB

2	11:03	GEM
4	15:41	CAN
6	22:06	LEO
9	6:36	VIR
11	17:19	LIB
14	5:39	SCO
16	17:58	SAG
19	4:01	CAP
21	10:24	AQU
23	13:18	PIS
25	14:06	ARI
27	14:39	TAU

MAR

1	16:39	GEM
3	21:08	CAN
6	4:15	LEO
8	13:34	VIR
11	0:35	LIB
13	12:52	SCO
16	1:27	SAG
18	12:35	CAP
20	20:22	AQU
23	0:05	PIS
25	0:38	ARI
26	23:57	TAU
29	0:13	GEM
31	3:14	CAN

APR

2	9:46	LEO
4	19:21	VIR
7	6:50	LIB
9	19:14	SCO
12	7:49	SAG
14	19:27	CAP
17	4:35	AQU
19	9:54	PIS
21	11:30	ARI
23	10:51	TAU
25	10:07	GEM
27	11:28	CAN
29	16:25	LEO

MAY

2	1:13	VIR
4	12:43	LIB
7	1:16	SCO
9	13:43	SAG
12	1:14	CAP
14	10:52	AQU
16	17:32	PIS
18	20:48	ARI
20	21:22	TAU
22	20:54	GEM
24	21:29	CAN
27	0:59	LEO
29	8:22	VIR
31	19:10	LIB

JUN

3	7:39	SCO
5	20:01	SAG
8	7:07	CAP
10	16:22	AQU
12	23:21	PIS
15	3:47	ARI
17	5:55	TAU
19	6:44	GEM
21	7:47	CAN
23	10:45	LEO
25	16:57	VIR
28	2:41	LIB
30	14:48	SCO

JUL

3	3:12	SAG
5	14:03	CAP
7	22:37	AQU
10	4:53	PIS
12	9:17	ARI
14	12:15	TAU
16	14:28	GEM
18	16:45	CAN
20	20:16	LEO
23	2:07	VIR
25	11:03	LIB
27	22:39	SCO
30	11:08	SAG

AUG

1	22:13	CAP
4	6:26	AQU
6	11:46	PIS
8	15:07	ARI
10	17:38	TAU
12	20:16	GEM
14	23:40	CAN
17	4:17	LEO
19	10:41	VIR
21	19:26	LIB
24	6:39	SCO
26	19:16	SAG
29	6:58	CAP
31	15:38	AQU

SEP

2	20:38	PIS
4	22:53	ARI
7	0:03	TAU
9	1:46	GEM
11	5:08	CAN
13	10:30	LEO
15	17:48	VIR
18	3:00	LIB
20	14:11	SCO
23	2:50	SAG
25	15:16	CAP
28	1:04	AQU
30	6:47	PIS

OCT

2	8:48	ARI
4	8:50	TAU
6	8:59	GEM
8	11:01	CAN
10	15:55	LEO
12	23:35	VIR
15	9:25	LIB
17	20:53	SCO
20	9:33	SAG
22	22:21	CAP
25	9:21	AQU
27	16:37	PIS
29	19:40	ARI
31	19:43	TAU

NOV

2	18:49	GEM
4	19:09	CAN
6	22:24	LEO
9	5:14	VIR
11	15:08	LIB
14	2:57	SCO
16	15:40	SAG
19	4:23	CAP
21	15:52	AQU
24	0:33	PIS
26	5:25	ARI
28	6:50	TAU
30	6:15	GEM

DEC

2	5:45	CAN
4	7:20	LEO
6	12:27	VIR
8	21:22	LIB
11	9:05	SCO
13	21:54	SAG
16	10:22	CAP
18	21:29	AQU
21	6:29	PIS
23	12:41	ARI
25	15:58	TAU
27	16:59	GEM
29	17:07	CAN
31	18:09	LEO

—1964—

JAN		
2	21:48	VIR
5	5:10	LIB
7	16:04	SCO
10	4:50	SAG
12	17:14	CAP
15	3:48	AQU
17	12:04	PIS
19	18:11	ARI
21	22:24	TAU
24	1:05	GEM
26	2:52	CAN
28	4:46	LEO
30	8:09	VIR

FEB		
1	14:26	LIB
4	0:13	SCO
6	12:36	SAG
9	1:11	CAP
11	11:40	AQU
13	19:09	PIS
16	0:10	ARI
18	3:46	TAU
20	6:48	GEM
22	9:50	CAN
24	13:11	LEO
26	17:30	VIR
28	23:47	LIB

MAR		
2	8:54	SCO
4	20:47	SAG
7	9:36	CAP
9	20:36	AQU
12	4:06	PIS
14	8:16	ARI
16	10:31	TAU
18	12:26	GEM
20	15:12	CAN
22	19:15	LEO
25	0:42	VIR
27	7:48	LIB
29	17:04	SCO

APR		
1	4:41	SAG
3	17:37	CAP
6	5:25	AQU
8	13:47	PIS
10	18:09	ARI
12	19:37	TAU
14	20:06	GEM
16	21:24	CAN
19	0:40	LEO
21	6:18	VIR
23	14:09	LIB
26	0:01	SCO
28	11:46	SAG

MAY		
1	0:43	CAP
3	13:07	AQU
5	22:44	PIS
8	4:16	ARI
10	6:09	TAU
12	6:02	GEM
14	5:54	CAN
16	7:32	LEO
18	12:03	VIR
20	19:42	LIB
23	5:58	SCO
25	18:04	SAG
28	7:01	CAP
30	19:33	AQU

JUN		
2	6:02	PIS
4	13:03	ARI
6	16:20	TAU
8	16:50	GEM
10	16:17	CAN
12	16:35	LEO
14	19:28	VIR
17	1:54	LIB
19	11:50	SCO
22	0:04	SAG
24	13:02	CAP
27	1:22	AQU
29	11:57	PIS

JUL		
1	19:53	ARI
4	0:43	TAU
6	2:43	GEM
8	2:57	CAN
10	3:01	LEO
12	4:45	VIR
14	9:42	LIB
16	18:33	SCO
19	6:29	SAG
21	19:27	CAP
24	7:31	AQU
26	17:36	PIS
29	1:26	ARI
31	7:01	TAU

AUG		
2	10:29	GEM
4	12:13	CAN
6	13:11	LEO
8	14:51	VIR
10	18:52	LIB
13	2:32	SCO
15	13:45	SAG
18	2:39	CAP
20	14:40	AQU
23	0:14	PIS
25	7:16	ARI
27	12:24	TAU
29	16:16	GEM
31	19:14	CAN

SEP		
2	21:37	LEO
5	0:13	VIR
7	4:20	LIB
9	11:20	SCO
11	21:48	SAG
14	10:31	CAP
16	22:48	AQU
19	8:23	PIS
21	14:44	ARI
23	18:47	TAU
25	21:47	GEM
28	0:40	CAN
30	3:53	LEO

OCT		
2	7:43	VIR
4	12:45	LIB
6	19:57	SCO
9	6:03	SAG
11	18:32	CAP
14	7:16	AQU
16	17:33	PIS
19	0:05	ARI
21	3:25	TAU
23	5:04	GEM
25	6:38	CAN
27	9:14	LEO
29	13:26	VIR
31	19:25	LIB

NOV		
3	3:25	SCO
5	13:44	SAG
8	2:06	CAP
10	15:09	AQU
13	2:29	PIS
15	10:11	ARI
17	13:57	TAU
19	14:59	GEM
21	15:04	CAN
23	15:59	LEO
25	19:03	VIR
28	0:55	LIB
30	9:31	SCO

DEC		
2	20:24	SAG
5	8:54	CAP
7	21:58	AQU
10	10:00	PIS
12	19:13	ARI
15	0:33	TAU
17	2:22	GEM
19	2:03	CAN
21	1:31	LEO
23	2:42	VIR
25	7:05	LIB
27	15:12	SCO
30	2:21	SAG

—1965—

JAN

1	15:07	CAP
4	4:05	AQU
6	16:07	PIS
9	2:09	ARI
11	9:11	TAU
13	12:49	GEM
15	13:35	CAN
17	12:58	LEO
19	12:55	VIR
21	15:28	LIB
23	22:01	SCO
26	8:33	SAG
28	21:22	CAP
31	10:18	AQU

FEB

2	21:56	PIS
5	7:44	ARI
7	15:24	TAU
9	20:37	GEM
11	23:14	CAN
13	23:55	LEO
16	0:06	VIR
18	1:46	LIB
20	6:46	SCO
22	15:58	SAG
25	4:17	CAP
27	17:15	AQU

MAR

2	4:39	PIS
4	13:45	ARI
6	20:50	TAU
9	2:15	GEM
11	6:03	CAN
13	8:23	LEO
15	9:56	VIR
17	12:04	LIB
19	16:33	SCO
22	0:37	SAG
24	12:07	CAP
27	0:59	AQU
29	12:32	PIS
31	21:19	ARI

APR

3	3:29	TAU
5	7:55	GEM
7	11:25	CAN
9	14:24	LEO
11	17:15	VIR
13	20:39	LIB
16	1:42	SCO
18	9:32	SAG
20	20:24	CAP
23	9:05	AQU
25	21:03	PIS
28	6:13	ARI
30	12:04	TAU

MAY

2	15:27	GEM
4	17:39	CAN
6	19:50	LEO
8	22:48	VIR
11	3:05	LIB
13	9:10	SCO
15	17:32	SAG
18	4:20	CAP
20	16:51	AQU
23	5:15	PIS
25	15:19	ARI
27	21:49	TAU
30	0:59	GEM

JUN

1	2:06	CAN
3	2:47	LEO
5	4:34	VIR
7	8:30	LIB
9	15:04	SCO
12	0:10	SAG
14	11:21	CAP
16	23:52	AQU
19	12:29	PIS
21	23:30	ARI
24	7:17	TAU
26	11:19	GEM
28	12:20	CAN
30	11:59	LEO

JUL

2	12:12	VIR
4	14:43	LIB
6	20:38	SCO
9	5:54	SAG
11	17:29	CAP
14	6:08	AQU
16	18:45	PIS
19	6:13	ARI
21	15:14	TAU
23	20:49	GEM
25	22:54	CAN
27	22:38	LEO
29	21:55	VIR
31	22:55	LIB

AUG

3	3:21	SCO
5	11:50	SAG
7	23:23	CAP
10	12:10	AQU
13	0:38	PIS
15	11:57	ARI
17	21:28	TAU
20	4:21	GEM
22	8:05	CAN
24	9:02	LEO
26	8:37	VIR
28	8:53	LIB
30	11:54	SCO

SEP

1	19:00	SAG
4	5:52	CAP
6	18:34	AQU
9	6:57	PIS
11	17:50	ARI
14	2:57	TAU
16	10:07	GEM
18	15:01	CAN
20	17:36	LEO
22	18:30	VIR
24	19:16	LIB
26	21:47	SCO
29	3:43	SAG

OCT

1	13:29	CAP
4	1:49	AQU
6	14:14	PIS
9	0:54	ARI
11	9:17	TAU
13	15:40	GEM
15	20:27	CAN
17	23:52	LEO
20	2:14	VIR
22	4:21	LIB
24	7:32	SCO
26	13:10	SAG
28	22:05	CAP
31	9:50	AQU

NOV

2	22:23	PIS
5	9:22	ARI
7	17:30	TAU
9	22:55	GEM
12	2:30	CAN
14	5:14	LEO
16	7:55	VIR
18	11:11	LIB
20	15:37	SCO
22	21:57	SAG
25	6:46	CAP
27	18:04	AQU
30	6:40	PIS

DEC

2	18:23	ARI
5	3:12	TAU
7	8:28	GEM
9	10:57	CAN
11	12:09	LEO
13	13:36	VIR
15	16:34	LIB
17	21:41	SCO
20	5:02	SAG
22	14:27	CAP
25	1:45	AQU
27	14:18	PIS
30	2:40	ARI

—1966—

JAN

1	12:47	TAU
3	19:07	GEM
5	21:41	CAN
7	21:50	LEO
9	21:35	VIR
11	22:53	LIB
14	3:09	SCO
16	10:40	SAG
18	20:45	CAP
21	8:27	AQU
23	20:59	PIS
26	9:33	ARI
28	20:43	TAU
31	4:44	GEM

FEB

2	8:41	CAN
4	9:14	LEO
6	8:12	VIR
8	7:51	LIB
10	10:15	SCO
12	16:34	SAG
15	2:26	CAP
17	14:26	AQU
20	3:06	PIS
22	15:31	ARI
25	2:54	TAU
27	12:03	GEM

MAR

1	17:48	CAN
3	19:57	LEO
5	19:37	VIR
7	18:49	LIB
9	19:47	SCO
12	0:19	SAG
14	8:56	CAP
16	20:35	AQU
19	9:19	PIS
21	21:34	ARI
24	8:32	TAU
26	17:42	GEM
29	0:24	CAN
31	4:12	LEO

APR

2	5:31	VIR
4	5:40	LIB
6	6:31	SCO
8	9:54	SAG
10	17:02	CAP
13	3:43	AQU
15	16:14	PIS
18	4:28	ARI
20	15:01	TAU
22	23:28	GEM
25	5:48	CAN
27	10:10	LEO
29	12:50	VIR

MAY

1	14:31	LIB
3	16:24	SCO
5	19:53	SAG
8	2:13	CAP
10	11:52	AQU
12	23:55	PIS
15	12:16	ARI
17	22:50	TAU
20	6:40	GEM
22	12:01	CAN
24	15:37	LEO
26	18:23	VIR
28	21:00	LIB
31	0:12	SCO

JUN

2	4:39	SAG
4	11:11	CAP
6	20:21	AQU
9	7:57	PIS
11	20:27	ARI
14	7:30	TAU
16	15:27	GEM
18	20:06	CAN
20	22:29	LEO
23	0:08	VIR
25	2:23	LIB
27	6:04	SCO
29	11:32	SAG

JUL

1	18:52	CAP
4	4:15	AQU
6	15:40	PIS
9	4:16	ARI
11	16:04	TAU
14	0:52	GEM
16	5:45	CAN
18	7:28	LEO
20	7:47	VIR
22	8:39	LIB
24	11:32	SCO
26	17:05	SAG
29	1:05	CAP
31	11:02	AQU

AUG

2	22:36	PIS
5	11:15	ARI
7	23:38	TAU
10	9:39	GEM
12	15:42	CAN
14	17:51	LEO
16	17:35	VIR
18	17:06	LIB
20	18:25	SCO
22	22:51	SAG
25	6:37	CAP
27	16:56	AQU
30	4:49	PIS

SEP

1	17:28	ARI
4	6:00	TAU
6	16:53	GEM
9	0:27	CAN
11	4:01	LEO
13	4:26	VIR
15	3:33	LIB
17	3:35	SCO
19	6:22	SAG
21	12:53	CAP
23	22:48	AQU
26	10:49	PIS
28	23:30	ARI

OCT

1	11:48	TAU
3	22:44	GEM
6	7:13	CAN
8	12:25	LEO
10	14:27	VIR
12	14:30	LIB
14	14:22	SCO
16	16:00	SAG
18	20:56	CAP
21	5:41	AQU
23	17:21	PIS
26	6:04	ARI
28	18:06	TAU
31	4:28	GEM

NOV

2	12:43	CAN
4	18:37	LEO
6	22:10	VIR
8	23:55	LIB
11	0:54	SCO
13	2:37	SAG
15	6:37	CAP
17	14:04	AQU
20	0:53	PIS
22	13:32	ARI
25	1:37	TAU
27	11:31	GEM
29	18:50	CAN

DEC

2	0:02	LEO
4	3:49	VIR
6	6:44	LIB
8	9:18	SCO
10	12:14	SAG
12	16:31	CAP
14	23:20	AQU
17	9:18	PIS
19	21:40	ARI
22	10:08	TAU
24	20:14	GEM
27	2:59	CAN
29	6:58	LEO
31	9:34	VIR

—1967—

JAN			FEB			MAR			APR		
2	12:04	LIB	3	0:56	SAG	2	6:53	SAG	3	2:49	AQU
4	15:17	SCO	5	7:11	CAP	4	12:36	CAP	5	13:29	PIS
6	19:28	SAG	7	15:17	AQU	6	21:04	AQU	8	1:57	ARI
9	0:54	CAP	10	1:19	PIS	9	7:42	PIS	10	14:57	TAU
11	8:06	AQU	12	13:17	ARI	11	19:53	ARI	13	3:15	GEM
13	17:45	PIS	15	2:19	TAU	14	8:55	TAU	15	13:37	CAN
16	5:48	ARI	17	14:16	GEM	16	21:20	GEM	17	20:55	LEO
18	18:40	TAU	19	22:48	CAN	19	7:10	CAN	20	0:43	VIR
21	5:39	GEM	22	3:05	LEO	21	13:04	LEO	22	1:42	LIB
23	12:51	CAN	24	4:04	VIR	23	15:09	VIR	24	1:19	SCO
25	16:21	LEO	26	3:45	LIB	25	14:51	LIB	26	1:27	SAG
27	17:37	VIR	28	4:10	SCO	27	14:11	SCO	28	3:54	CAP
29	18:33	LIB				29	15:09	SAG	30	9:58	AQU
31	20:44	SCO				31	19:11	CAP			

MAY			JUN			JUL			AUG		
2	19:48	PIS	1	15:07	ARI	1	11:43	TAU	2	17:32	CAN
5	8:10	ARI	4	4:05	TAU	3	23:39	GEM	4	23:27	LEO
7	21:10	TAU	6	15:53	GEM	6	8:48	CAN	7	2:36	VIR
10	9:09	GEM	9	1:18	CAN	8	14:59	LEO	9	4:35	LIB
12	19:11	CAN	11	8:19	LEO	10	19:08	VIR	11	6:45	SCO
15	2:49	LEO	13	13:24	VIR	12	22:20	LIB	13	9:53	SAG
17	7:52	VIR	15	16:59	LIB	15	1:18	SCO	15	14:19	CAP
19	10:31	LIB	17	19:26	SCO	17	4:23	SAG	17	20:17	AQU
21	11:30	SCO	19	21:20	SAG	19	8:00	CAP	20	4:18	PIS
23	12:06	SAG	21	23:47	CAP	21	13:00	AQU	22	14:48	ARI
25	13:59	CAP	24	4:11	AQU	23	20:29	PIS	25	3:22	TAU
27	18:44	AQU	26	11:50	PIS	26	7:01	ARI	27	16:09	GEM
30	3:19	PIS	28	22:53	ARI	28	19:41	TAU	30	2:35	CAN
						31	8:01	GEM			

SEP			OCT			NOV			DEC		
1	9:09	LEO	2	23:35	LIB	1	10:27	SCO	2	21:25	CAP
3	12:08	VIR	4	23:15	SCO	3	9:52	SAG	4	23:57	AQU
5	13:04	LIB	6	23:33	SAG	5	10:45	CAP	7	6:20	PIS
7	13:45	SCO	9	2:04	CAP	7	14:46	AQU	9	16:44	ARI
9	15:40	SAG	11	7:46	AQU	9	22:43	PIS	12	5:32	TAU
11	19:43	CAP	13	16:38	PIS	12	9:59	ARI	14	18:19	GEM
14	2:09	AQU	16	3:58	ARI	14	22:53	TAU	17	5:23	CAN
16	10:53	PIS	18	16:42	TAU	17	11:41	GEM	19	14:21	LEO
18	21:47	ARI	21	5:39	GEM	19	23:13	CAN	21	21:22	VIR
21	10:21	TAU	23	17:28	CAN	22	8:48	LEO	24	2:27	LIB
23	23:22	GEM	26	2:41	LEO	24	15:46	VIR	26	5:36	SCO
26	10:46	CAN	28	8:20	VIR	26	19:49	LIB	28	7:10	SAG
28	18:42	LEO	30	10:32	LIB	28	21:14	SCO	30	8:11	CAP
30	22:39	VIR				30	21:11	SAG			

—1968—

JAN			FEB			MAR			APR		
1	10:24	AQU	2	9:40	ARI	3	5:28	TAU	2	1:41	GEM
3	15:36	PIS	4	21:16	TAU	5	18:17	GEM	4	14:13	CAN
6	0:46	ARI	7	10:09	GEM	8	6:22	CAN	7	0:29	LEO
8	13:03	TAU	9	21:35	CAN	10	15:28	LEO	9	7:04	VIR
11	1:55	GEM	12	5:50	LEO	12	20:52	VIR	11	10:01	LIB
13	12:54	CAN	14	11:03	VIR	14	23:24	LIB	13	10:32	SCO
15	21:10	LEO	16	14:22	LIB	17	0:34	SCO	15	10:24	SAG
18	3:11	VIR	18	17:00	SCO	19	1:54	SAG	17	11:23	CAP
20	7:48	LIB	20	19:48	SAG	21	4:35	CAP	19	14:58	AQU
22	11:28	SCO	22	23:12	CAP	23	9:17	AQU	21	21:46	PIS
24	14:24	SAG	25	3:37	AQU	25	16:16	PIS	24	7:33	ARI
26	16:57	CAP	27	9:43	PIS	28	1:32	ARI	26	19:23	TAU
28	20:06	AQU	29	18:15	ARI	30	12:55	TAU	29	8:12	GEM
31	1:16	PIS									

MAY			JUN			JUL			AUG		
1	20:50	CAN	2	22:53	VIR	2	11:10	LIB	3	0:11	SAG
4	7:54	LEO	5	4:50	LIB	4	15:21	SCO	5	1:58	CAP
6	15:59	VIR	7	7:31	SCO	6	17:05	SAG	7	3:38	AQU
8	20:21	LIB	9	7:43	SAG	8	17:24	CAP	9	6:46	PIS
10	21:30	SCO	11	7:06	CAP	10	18:04	AQU	11	12:54	ARI
12	20:54	SAG	13	7:47	AQU	12	21:03	PIS	13	22:36	TAU
14	20:31	CAP	15	11:43	PIS	15	3:52	ARI	16	10:52	GEM
16	22:22	AQU	17	19:50	ARI	17	14:31	TAU	18	23:16	CAN
19	3:53	PIS	20	7:26	TAU	20	3:13	GEM	21	9:40	LEO
21	13:15	ARI	22	20:23	GEM	22	15:32	CAN	23	17:21	VIR
24	1:16	TAU	25	8:43	CAN	25	1:55	LEO	25	22:45	LIB
26	14:13	GEM	27	19:31	LEO	27	10:10	VIR	28	2:39	SCO
29	2:43	CAN	30	4:27	VIR	29	16:33	LIB	30	5:41	SAG
31	13:54	LEO				31	21:12	SCO			

SEP			OCT			NOV			DEC		
1	8:22	CAP	2	22:21	PIS	1	11:51	ARI	1	3:58	TAU
3	11:20	AQU	5	5:36	ARI	3	22:02	TAU	3	16:06	GEM
5	15:28	PIS	7	15:07	TAU	6	9:48	GEM	6	4:44	CAN
7	21:50	ARI	10	2:44	GEM	8	22:27	CAN	8	17:03	LEO
10	7:06	TAU	12	15:24	CAN	11	10:45	LEO	11	4:00	VIR
12	18:55	GEM	15	3:09	LEO	13	20:55	VIR	13	12:09	LIB
15	7:29	CAN	17	11:59	VIR	16	3:27	LIB	15	16:32	SCO
17	18:26	LEO	19	17:06	LIB	18	6:06	SCO	17	17:28	SAG
20	2:16	VIR	21	19:06	SCO	20	6:04	SAG	19	16:33	CAP
22	7:00	LIB	23	19:33	SAG	22	5:20	CAP	21	16:00	AQU
24	9:39	SCO	25	20:14	CAP	24	6:03	AQU	23	18:01	PIS
26	11:31	SAG	27	22:43	AQU	26	9:53	PIS	26	0:03	ARI
28	13:45	CAP	30	3:55	PIS	28	17:26	ARI	28	9:57	TAU
30	17:11	AQU							30	22:12	GEM

—1969—

JAN		
2	10:53	CAN
4	22:55	LEO
7	9:43	VIR
9	18:33	LIB
12	0:32	SCO
14	3:19	SAG
16	3:40	CAP
18	3:17	AQU
20	4:21	PIS
22	8:44	ARI
24	17:13	TAU
27	4:54	GEM
29	17:37	CAN

FEB		
1	5:29	LEO
3	15:41	VIR
6	0:01	LIB
8	6:19	SCO
10	10:24	SAG
12	12:29	CAP
14	13:31	AQU
16	15:04	PIS
18	18:49	ARI
21	2:02	TAU
23	12:42	GEM
26	1:12	CAN
28	13:12	LEO

MAR		
2	23:07	VIR
5	6:34	LIB
7	11:57	SCO
9	15:48	SAG
11	18:41	CAP
13	21:10	AQU
16	0:04	PIS
18	4:27	ARI
20	11:21	TAU
22	21:13	GEM
25	9:19	CAN
27	21:37	LEO
30	7:54	VIR

APR		
1	15:04	LIB
3	19:23	SCO
5	21:58	SAG
8	0:05	CAP
10	2:47	AQU
12	6:42	PIS
14	12:14	ARI
16	19:44	TAU
19	5:29	GEM
21	17:18	CAN
24	5:51	LEO
26	16:57	VIR
29	0:44	LIB

MAY		
1	4:50	SCO
3	6:19	SAG
5	6:57	CAP
7	8:28	AQU
9	12:05	PIS
11	18:09	ARI
14	2:29	TAU
16	12:42	GEM
19	0:31	CAN
21	13:13	LEO
24	1:07	VIR
26	10:08	LIB
28	15:05	SCO
30	16:31	SAG

JUN		
1	16:07	CAP
3	16:04	AQU
5	18:14	PIS
7	23:37	ARI
10	8:06	TAU
12	18:49	GEM
15	6:53	CAN
17	19:36	LEO
20	7:54	VIR
22	18:04	LIB
25	0:31	SCO
27	3:00	SAG
29	2:45	CAP

JUL		
1	1:50	AQU
3	2:27	PIS
5	6:17	ARI
7	13:54	TAU
10	0:32	GEM
12	12:48	CAN
15	1:30	LEO
17	13:43	VIR
20	0:20	LIB
22	8:04	SCO
24	12:11	SAG
26	13:10	CAP
28	12:35	AQU
30	12:31	PIS

AUG		
1	14:55	ARI
3	21:02	TAU
6	6:50	GEM
8	18:58	CAN
11	7:39	LEO
13	19:33	VIR
16	5:51	LIB
18	13:54	SCO
20	19:13	SAG
22	21:49	CAP
24	22:36	AQU
26	23:04	PIS
29	0:58	ARI
31	5:51	TAU

SEP		
2	14:24	GEM
5	1:58	CAN
7	14:37	LEO
10	2:21	VIR
12	12:02	LIB
14	19:26	SCO
17	0:43	SAG
19	4:14	CAP
21	6:32	AQU
23	8:23	PIS
25	10:56	ARI
27	15:29	TAU
29	23:06	GEM

OCT		
2	9:53	CAN
4	22:26	LEO
7	10:22	VIR
9	19:49	LIB
12	2:19	SCO
14	6:34	SAG
16	9:36	CAP
18	12:22	AQU
20	15:26	PIS
22	19:18	ARI
25	0:33	TAU
27	8:01	GEM
29	18:13	CAN

NOV		
1	6:35	LEO
3	19:01	VIR
6	4:59	LIB
8	11:18	SCO
10	14:31	SAG
12	16:09	CAP
14	17:53	AQU
16	20:53	PIS
19	1:32	ARI
21	7:53	TAU
23	15:59	GEM
26	2:11	CAN
28	14:23	LEO

DEC		
1	3:14	VIR
3	14:17	LIB
5	21:31	SCO
8	0:43	SAG
10	1:21	CAP
12	1:28	AQU
14	2:57	PIS
16	6:56	ARI
18	13:36	TAU
20	22:28	GEM
23	9:09	CAN
25	21:22	LEO
28	10:21	VIR
30	22:19	LIB

—1970—

JAN			FEB			MAR			APR		
2	7:04	SCO	2	23:22	CAP	2	7:55	CAP	2	19:01	PIS
4	11:33	SAG	4	23:20	AQU	4	9:35	AQU	4	20:32	ARI
6	12:30	CAP	6	22:38	PIS	6	9:49	PIS	6	23:03	TAU
8	11:48	AQU	8	23:18	ARI	8	10:17	ARI	9	4:02	GEM
10	11:37	PIS	11	3:00	TAU	10	12:44	TAU	11	12:34	CAN
12	13:48	ARI	13	10:30	GEM	12	18:37	GEM	14	0:16	LEO
14	19:21	TAU	15	21:17	CAN	15	4:19	CAN	16	13:08	VIR
17	4:07	GEM	18	9:54	LEO	17	16:40	LEO	19	0:35	LIB
19	15:14	CAN	20	22:42	VIR	20	5:30	VIR	21	9:16	SCO
22	3:41	LEO	23	10:30	LIB	22	16:57	LIB	23	15:15	SAG
24	16:33	VIR	25	20:24	SCO	25	2:11	SCO	25	19:27	CAP
27	4:43	LIB	28	3:39	SAG	27	9:07	SAG	27	22:44	AQU
29	14:35	SCO				29	14:01	CAP	30	1:38	PIS
31	20:50	SAG				31	17:09	AQU			

MAY			JUN			JUL			AUG		
2	4:33	ARI	2	21:10	GEM	2	12:21	CAN	1	5:45	LEO
4	8:05	TAU	5	5:26	CAN	4	23:26	LEO	3	18:35	VIR
6	13:18	GEM	7	16:17	LEO	7	12:12	VIR	6	7:33	LIB
8	21:17	CAN	10	5:02	VIR	10	1:03	LIB	8	18:57	SCO
11	8:22	LEO	12	17:28	LIB	12	11:41	SCO	11	3:08	SAG
13	21:11	VIR	15	3:02	SCO	14	18:26	SAG	13	7:25	CAP
16	9:03	LIB	17	8:39	SAG	16	21:20	CAP	15	8:31	AQU
18	17:50	SCO	19	11:05	CAP	18	21:45	AQU	17	8:02	PIS
20	23:12	SAG	21	12:01	AQU	20	21:37	PIS	19	7:51	ARI
23	2:14	CAP	23	13:12	PIS	22	22:43	ARI	21	9:46	TAU
25	4:26	AQU	25	15:53	ARI	25	2:19	TAU	23	15:04	GEM
27	6:59	PIS	27	20:35	TAU	27	8:53	GEM	25	23:59	CAN
29	10:27	ARI	30	3:25	GEM	29	18:14	CAN	28	11:39	LEO
31	15:04	TAU							31	0:36	VIR

SEP			OCT			NOV			DEC		
2	13:26	LIB	2	6:36	SCO	3	3:33	CAP	2	13:45	AQU
5	0:55	SCO	4	15:32	SAG	5	8:11	AQU	4	16:56	PIS
7	9:59	SAG	6	22:11	CAP	7	11:33	PIS	6	20:04	ARI
9	15:52	CAP	9	2:26	AQU	9	13:52	ARI	8	23:25	TAU
11	18:34	AQU	11	4:31	PIS	11	15:51	TAU	11	3:34	GEM
13	18:58	PIS	13	5:13	ARI	13	18:49	GEM	13	9:33	CAN
15	18:36	ARI	15	6:00	TAU	16	0:24	CAN	15	18:22	LEO
17	19:21	TAU	17	8:44	GEM	18	9:36	LEO	18	6:05	VIR
19	23:02	GEM	19	14:59	CAN	20	21:50	VIR	20	19:02	LIB
22	6:41	CAN	22	1:13	LEO	23	10:40	LIB	23	6:28	SCO
24	17:55	LEO	24	13:58	VIR	25	21:25	SCO	25	14:28	SAG
27	6:54	VIR	27	2:37	LIB	28	5:03	SAG	27	19:02	CAP
29	19:34	LIB	29	13:15	SCO	30	10:06	CAP	29	21:24	AQU
			31	21:25	SAG				31	23:08	PIS

—1971—

JAN		
3	1:27	ARI
5	5:01	TAU
7	10:09	GEM
9	17:09	CAN
12	2:25	LEO
14	13:58	VIR
17	2:54	LIB
19	15:04	SCO
22	0:16	SAG
24	5:33	CAP
26	7:37	AQU
28	8:02	PIS
30	8:37	ARI

FEB		
1	10:49	TAU
3	15:35	GEM
5	23:07	CAN
8	9:07	LEO
10	20:58	VIR
13	9:51	LIB
15	22:22	SCO
18	8:46	SAG
20	15:37	CAP
22	18:44	AQU
24	19:06	PIS
26	18:30	ARI
28	18:55	TAU

MAR		
2	22:02	GEM
5	4:48	CAN
7	14:56	LEO
10	3:11	VIR
12	16:06	LIB
15	4:32	SCO
17	15:24	SAG
19	23:38	CAP
22	4:29	AQU
24	6:08	PIS
26	5:46	ARI
28	5:16	TAU
30	6:44	GEM

APR		
1	11:51	CAN
3	21:06	LEO
6	9:17	VIR
8	22:17	LIB
11	10:28	SCO
13	21:04	SAG
16	5:39	CAP
18	11:46	AQU
20	15:08	PIS
22	16:09	ARI
24	16:07	TAU
26	16:59	GEM
28	20:44	CAN

MAY		
1	4:35	LEO
3	16:04	VIR
6	5:00	LIB
8	17:04	SCO
11	3:08	SAG
13	11:10	CAP
15	17:20	AQU
17	21:40	PIS
20	0:12	ARI
22	1:32	TAU
24	3:02	GEM
26	6:27	CAN
28	13:17	LEO
30	23:49	VIR

JUN		
2	12:27	LIB
5	0:37	SCO
7	10:29	SAG
9	17:46	CAP
11	23:03	AQU
14	3:02	PIS
16	6:06	ARI
18	8:39	TAU
20	11:24	GEM
22	15:31	CAN
24	22:13	LEO
27	8:07	VIR
29	20:23	LIB

JUL		
2	8:47	SCO
4	18:59	SAG
7	2:04	CAP
9	6:27	AQU
11	9:15	PIS
13	11:33	ARI
15	14:11	TAU
17	17:47	GEM
19	22:57	CAN
22	6:17	LEO
24	16:10	VIR
27	4:12	LIB
29	16:51	SCO

AUG		
1	3:50	SAG
3	11:32	CAP
5	15:47	AQU
7	17:35	PIS
9	18:27	ARI
11	19:56	TAU
13	23:11	GEM
16	4:50	CAN
18	12:58	LEO
20	23:19	VIR
23	11:23	LIB
26	0:10	SCO
28	11:57	SAG
30	20:55	CAP

SEP		
2	2:05	AQU
4	3:51	PIS
6	3:44	ARI
8	3:38	TAU
10	5:26	GEM
12	10:21	CAN
14	18:38	LEO
17	5:29	VIR
19	17:48	LIB
22	6:34	SCO
24	18:44	SAG
27	4:53	CAP
29	11:39	AQU

OCT		
1	14:37	PIS
3	14:41	ARI
5	13:42	TAU
7	13:54	GEM
9	17:11	CAN
12	0:31	LEO
14	11:17	VIR
16	23:48	LIB
19	12:31	SCO
22	0:32	SAG
24	11:06	CAP
26	19:12	AQU
28	23:57	PIS
31	1:27	ARI

NOV		
2	0:56	TAU
4	0:28	GEM
6	2:15	CAN
8	7:57	LEO
10	17:45	VIR
13	6:06	LIB
15	18:50	SCO
18	6:30	SAG
20	16:37	CAP
23	0:53	AQU
25	6:48	PIS
27	10:04	ARI
29	11:09	TAU

DEC		
1	11:26	GEM
3	12:52	CAN
5	17:17	LEO
8	1:41	VIR
10	13:20	LIB
13	2:02	SCO
15	13:38	SAG
17	23:08	CAP
20	6:33	AQU
22	12:10	PIS
24	16:10	ARI
26	18:46	TAU
28	20:39	GEM
30	23:02	CAN

—1972—

JAN

2	3:22	LEO
4	10:51	VIR
6	21:34	LIB
9	10:04	SCO
11	21:58	SAG
14	7:26	CAP
16	14:04	AQU
18	18:29	PIS
20	21:36	ARI
23	0:18	TAU
25	3:14	GEM
27	7:02	CAN
29	12:22	LEO
31	19:56	VIR

FEB

3	6:07	LIB
5	18:18	SCO
8	6:38	SAG
10	16:51	CAP
12	23:37	AQU
15	3:11	PIS
17	4:51	ARI
19	6:12	TAU
21	8:36	GEM
23	12:53	CAN
25	19:15	LEO
28	3:40	VIR

MAR

1	14:01	LIB
4	2:01	SCO
6	14:37	SAG
9	1:50	CAP
11	9:43	AQU
13	13:40	PIS
15	14:38	ARI
17	14:28	TAU
19	15:13	GEM
21	18:27	CAN
24	0:47	LEO
26	9:48	VIR
28	20:42	LIB
31	8:49	SCO

APR

2	21:28	SAG
5	9:21	CAP
7	18:38	AQU
9	23:58	PIS
12	1:33	ARI
14	0:55	TAU
16	0:17	GEM
18	1:47	CAN
20	6:47	LEO
22	15:25	VIR
25	2:35	LIB
27	14:56	SCO
30	3:31	SAG

MAY

2	15:29	CAP
5	1:36	AQU
7	8:28	PIS
9	11:35	ARI
11	11:48	TAU
13	10:58	GEM
15	11:17	CAN
17	14:38	LEO
19	21:57	VIR
22	8:37	LIB
24	21:01	SCO
27	9:34	SAG
29	21:13	CAP

JUN

1	7:16	AQU
3	14:53	PIS
5	19:28	ARI
7	21:15	TAU
9	21:25	GEM
11	21:45	CAN
14	0:10	LEO
16	6:04	VIR
18	15:39	LIB
21	3:43	SCO
23	16:15	SAG
26	3:37	CAP
28	13:03	AQU
30	20:19	PIS

JUL

3	1:23	ARI
5	4:25	TAU
7	6:05	GEM
9	7:30	CAN
11	10:06	LEO
13	15:17	VIR
15	23:49	LIB
18	11:16	SCO
20	23:47	SAG
23	11:11	CAP
25	20:08	AQU
28	2:29	PIS
30	6:51	ARI

AUG

1	9:58	TAU
3	12:34	GEM
5	15:18	CAN
7	18:57	LEO
10	0:23	VIR
12	8:28	LIB
14	19:20	SCO
17	7:50	SAG
19	19:38	CAP
22	4:44	AQU
24	10:29	PIS
26	13:41	ARI
28	15:43	TAU
30	17:56	GEM

SEP

1	21:12	CAN
4	1:54	LEO
6	8:16	VIR
8	16:37	LIB
11	3:16	SCO
13	15:43	SAG
16	4:08	CAP
18	14:05	AQU
20	20:10	PIS
22	22:45	ARI
24	23:28	TAU
27	0:15	GEM
29	2:39	CAN

OCT

1	7:26	LEO
3	14:31	VIR
5	23:35	LIB
8	10:28	SCO
10	22:53	SAG
13	11:45	CAP
15	22:52	AQU
18	6:13	PIS
20	9:23	ARI
22	9:38	TAU
24	9:03	GEM
26	9:45	CAN
28	13:15	LEO
30	20:00	VIR

NOV

2	5:28	LIB
4	16:47	SCO
7	5:17	SAG
9	18:12	CAP
12	6:03	AQU
14	14:57	PIS
16	19:45	ARI
18	20:53	TAU
20	20:06	GEM
22	19:32	CAN
24	21:12	LEO
27	2:25	VIR
29	11:16	LIB

DEC

1	22:43	SCO
4	11:23	SAG
7	0:07	CAP
9	11:54	AQU
11	21:33	PIS
14	4:00	ARI
16	7:00	TAU
18	7:25	GEM
20	6:57	CAN
22	7:35	LEO
24	11:03	VIR
26	18:22	LIB
29	5:11	SCO
31	17:52	SAG

—1973—

JAN

3	6:31	CAP
5	17:48	AQU
8	3:03	PIS
10	9:58	ARI
12	14:25	TAU
14	16:42	GEM
16	17:39	CAN
18	18:41	LEO
20	21:24	VIR
23	3:17	LIB
25	12:53	SCO
28	1:11	SAG
30	13:55	CAP

FEB

2	0:56	AQU
4	9:23	PIS
6	15:29	ARI
8	19:54	TAU
10	23:11	GEM
13	1:45	CAN
15	4:13	LEO
17	7:32	VIR
19	12:59	LIB
21	21:36	SCO
24	9:15	SAG
26	22:04	CAP

MAR

1	9:23	AQU
3	17:32	PIS
5	22:38	ARI
8	1:51	TAU
10	4:31	GEM
12	7:30	CAN
14	11:08	LEO
16	15:43	VIR
18	21:49	LIB
21	6:16	SCO
23	17:27	SAG
26	6:16	CAP
28	18:13	AQU
31	2:55	PIS

APR

2	7:49	ARI
4	9:59	TAU
6	11:13	GEM
8	13:05	CAN
10	16:32	LEO
12	21:47	VIR
15	4:51	LIB
17	13:52	SCO
20	1:02	SAG
22	13:50	CAP
25	2:22	AQU
27	12:10	PIS
29	17:54	ARI

MAY

1	20:02	TAU
3	20:16	GEM
5	20:36	CAN
7	22:37	LEO
10	3:13	VIR
12	10:31	LIB
14	20:10	SCO
17	7:42	SAG
19	20:31	CAP
22	9:18	AQU
24	20:06	PIS
27	3:15	ARI
29	6:28	TAU
31	6:53	GEM

JUN

2	6:22	CAN
4	6:50	LEO
6	9:52	VIR
8	16:16	LIB
11	1:52	SCO
13	13:43	SAG
16	2:37	CAP
18	15:20	AQU
21	2:29	PIS
23	10:49	ARI
25	15:38	TAU
27	17:18	GEM
29	17:09	CAN

JUL

1	16:56	LEO
3	18:32	VIR
5	23:24	LIB
8	8:06	SCO
10	19:48	SAG
13	8:46	CAP
15	21:15	AQU
18	8:08	PIS
20	16:44	ARI
22	22:41	TAU
25	1:59	GEM
27	3:11	CAN
29	3:30	LEO
31	4:35	VIR

AUG

2	8:13	LIB
4	15:36	SCO
7	2:37	SAG
9	15:30	CAP
12	3:53	AQU
14	14:15	PIS
16	22:16	ARI
19	4:14	TAU
21	8:27	GEM
23	11:08	CAN
25	12:50	LEO
27	14:34	VIR
29	17:53	LIB

SEP

1	0:18	SCO
3	10:25	SAG
5	23:02	CAP
8	11:31	AQU
10	21:41	PIS
13	4:57	ARI
15	10:00	TAU
17	13:48	GEM
19	17:02	CAN
21	19:57	LEO
23	22:59	VIR
26	3:01	LIB
28	9:19	SCO
30	18:48	SAG

OCT

3	7:03	CAP
5	19:49	AQU
8	6:24	PIS
10	13:29	ARI
12	17:37	TAU
14	20:09	GEM
16	22:29	CAN
19	1:25	LEO
21	5:19	VIR
23	10:29	LIB
25	17:28	SCO
28	2:58	SAG
30	14:58	CAP

NOV

2	3:59	AQU
4	15:27	PIS
6	23:20	ARI
9	3:26	TAU
11	5:00	GEM
13	5:47	CAN
15	7:20	LEO
17	10:42	VIR
19	16:16	LIB
22	0:07	SCO
24	10:11	SAG
26	22:13	CAP
29	11:18	AQU

DEC

1	23:33	PIS
4	8:51	ARI
6	14:09	TAU
8	15:58	GEM
10	15:52	CAN
12	15:45	LEO
14	17:21	VIR
16	21:54	LIB
19	5:44	SCO
21	16:20	SAG
24	4:42	CAP
26	17:43	AQU
29	6:10	PIS
31	16:35	ARI

—1974—

JAN			FEB			MAR			APR		
2	23:38	TAU	1	11:54	GEM	2	22:00	CAN	1	6:41	LEO
5	3:00	GEM	3	14:06	CAN	4	23:49	LEO	3	8:57	VIR
7	3:29	CAN	5	14:12	LEO	7	0:34	VIR	5	11:23	LIB
9	2:43	LEO	7	13:52	VIR	9	1:52	LIB	7	15:26	SCO
11	2:42	VIR	9	15:11	LIB	11	5:40	SCO	9	22:28	SAG
13	5:22	LIB	11	19:58	SCO	13	13:21	SAG	12	8:57	CAP
15	11:55	SCO	14	5:02	SAG	16	0:42	CAP	14	21:35	AQU
17	22:13	SAG	16	17:16	CAP	18	13:39	AQU	17	9:45	PIS
20	10:48	CAP	19	6:21	AQU	21	1:34	PIS	19	19:21	ARI
22	23:50	AQU	21	18:16	PIS	23	11:03	ARI	22	1:54	TAU
25	12:01	PIS	24	4:13	ARI	25	18:10	TAU	24	6:12	GEM
27	22:32	ARI	26	12:12	TAU	27	23:34	GEM	26	9:18	CAN
30	6:42	TAU	28	18:11	GEM	30	3:40	CAN	28	12:04	LEO
									30	15:01	VIR

MAY			JUN			JUL			AUG		
2	18:40	LIB	1	6:11	SCO	3	7:20	CAP	2	1:47	AQU
4	23:44	SCO	3	14:22	SAG	5	19:42	AQU	4	14:27	PIS
7	7:06	SAG	6	0:49	CAP	8	8:26	PIS	7	2:16	ARI
9	17:16	CAP	8	13:03	AQU	10	20:11	ARI	9	12:13	TAU
12	5:35	AQU	11	1:44	PIS	13	5:22	TAU	11	19:16	GEM
14	18:04	PIS	13	12:53	ARI	15	10:55	GEM	13	22:49	CAN
17	4:20	ARI	15	20:47	TAU	17	12:57	CAN	15	23:27	LEO
19	11:11	TAU	18	0:59	GEM	19	12:44	LEO	17	22:43	VIR
21	14:55	GEM	20	2:22	CAN	21	12:10	VIR	19	22:45	LIB
23	16:46	CAN	22	2:30	LEO	23	13:20	LIB	22	1:38	SCO
25	18:13	LEO	24	3:12	VIR	25	17:46	SCO	24	8:35	SAG
27	20:26	VIR	26	5:58	LIB	28	2:00	SAG	26	19:16	CAP
30	0:17	LIB	28	11:41	SCO	30	13:11	CAP	29	7:53	AQU
			30	20:21	SAG				31	20:30	PIS

SEP			OCT			NOV			DEC		
3	7:59	ARI	2	23:40	TAU	1	13:24	GEM	1	1:22	CAN
5	17:51	TAU	5	7:01	GEM	3	18:02	CAN	3	3:32	LEO
8	1:37	GEM	7	12:31	CAN	5	21:31	LEO	5	5:41	VIR
10	6:40	CAN	9	16:03	LEO	8	0:19	VIR	7	8:43	LIB
12	8:55	LEO	11	17:57	VIR	10	2:59	LIB	9	13:14	SCO
14	9:13	VIR	13	19:11	LIB	12	6:24	SCO	11	19:35	SAG
16	9:18	LIB	15	21:24	SCO	14	11:40	SAG	14	4:04	CAP
18	11:15	SCO	18	2:15	SAG	16	19:42	CAP	16	14:49	AQU
20	16:47	SAG	20	10:45	CAP	19	6:39	AQU	19	3:13	PIS
23	2:22	CAP	22	22:21	AQU	21	19:12	PIS	21	15:36	ARI
25	14:39	AQU	25	10:57	PIS	24	7:00	ARI	24	1:45	TAU
28	3:15	PIS	27	22:14	ARI	26	16:05	TAU	26	8:16	GEM
30	14:26	ARI	30	7:01	TAU	28	21:59	GEM	28	11:16	CAN
									30	12:05	LEO

—1975—

JAN

1	12:33	VIR
3	14:22	LIB
5	18:39	SCO
8	1:40	SAG
10	10:59	CAP
12	22:04	AQU
15	10:24	PIS
17	23:04	ARI
20	10:22	TAU
22	18:23	GEM
24	22:21	CAN
26	23:01	LEO
28	22:14	VIR
30	22:14	LIB

FEB

2	0:54	SCO
4	7:11	SAG
6	16:43	CAP
9	4:17	AQU
11	16:46	PIS
14	5:23	ARI
16	17:10	TAU
19	2:35	GEM
21	8:19	CAN
23	10:14	LEO
25	9:38	VIR
27	8:39	LIB

MAR

1	9:34	SCO
3	14:06	SAG
5	22:40	CAP
8	10:10	AQU
10	22:50	PIS
13	11:19	ARI
15	22:53	TAU
18	8:44	GEM
20	15:49	CAN
22	19:32	LEO
24	20:22	VIR
26	19:52	LIB
28	20:08	SCO
30	23:10	SAG

APR

2	6:09	CAP
4	16:46	AQU
7	5:17	PIS
9	17:45	ARI
12	4:54	TAU
14	14:15	GEM
16	21:28	CAN
19	2:15	LEO
21	4:43	VIR
23	5:42	LIB
25	6:40	SCO
27	9:20	SAG
29	15:09	CAP

MAY

2	0:34	AQU
4	12:35	PIS
7	1:03	ARI
9	12:04	TAU
11	20:45	GEM
14	3:08	CAN
16	7:39	LEO
18	10:46	VIR
20	13:06	LIB
22	15:26	SCO
24	18:52	SAG
27	0:31	CAP
29	9:10	AQU
31	20:33	PIS

JUN

3	9:02	ARI
5	20:19	TAU
8	4:50	GEM
10	10:22	CAN
12	13:46	LEO
14	16:11	VIR
16	18:41	LIB
18	22:00	SCO
21	2:35	SAG
23	8:57	CAP
25	17:34	AQU
28	4:34	PIS
30	17:03	ARI

JUL

3	4:55	TAU
5	13:59	GEM
7	19:24	CAN
9	21:51	LEO
11	22:56	VIR
14	0:22	LIB
16	3:24	SCO
18	8:33	SAG
20	15:46	CAP
23	0:56	AQU
25	11:59	PIS
28	0:28	ARI
30	12:54	TAU

AUG

1	23:03	GEM
4	5:18	CAN
6	7:44	LEO
8	7:54	VIR
10	7:52	LIB
12	9:31	SCO
14	14:00	SAG
16	21:26	CAP
19	7:10	AQU
21	18:33	PIS
24	7:03	ARI
26	19:45	TAU
29	6:54	GEM
31	14:36	CAN

SEP

2	18:09	LEO
4	18:30	VIR
6	17:38	LIB
8	17:46	SCO
10	20:41	SAG
13	3:12	CAP
15	12:52	AQU
18	0:32	PIS
20	13:08	ARI
23	1:44	TAU
25	13:14	GEM
27	22:08	CAN
30	3:21	LEO

OCT

2	5:04	VIR
4	4:39	LIB
6	4:09	SCO
8	5:36	SAG
10	10:29	CAP
12	19:10	AQU
15	6:41	PIS
17	19:21	ARI
20	7:44	TAU
22	18:52	GEM
25	3:58	CAN
27	10:20	LEO
29	13:47	VIR
31	14:56	LIB

NOV

2	15:08	SCO
4	16:11	SAG
6	19:46	CAP
9	3:00	AQU
11	13:43	PIS
14	2:18	ARI
16	14:38	TAU
19	1:15	GEM
21	9:37	CAN
23	15:49	LEO
25	20:05	VIR
27	22:48	LIB
30	0:37	SCO

DEC

2	2:34	SAG
4	5:59	CAP
6	12:13	AQU
8	21:52	PIS
11	10:07	ARI
13	22:40	TAU
16	9:13	GEM
18	16:50	CAN
20	21:54	LEO
23	1:28	VIR
25	4:28	LIB
27	7:29	SCO
29	10:53	SAG
31	15:17	CAP

—1976—

JAN

2	21:34	AQU
5	6:36	PIS
7	18:22	ARI
10	7:10	TAU
12	18:20	GEM
15	2:01	CAN
17	6:16	LEO
19	8:26	VIR
21	10:11	LIB
23	12:49	SCO
25	16:52	SAG
27	22:25	CAP
30	5:35	AQU

FEB

1	14:47	PIS
4	2:18	ARI
6	15:14	TAU
9	3:17	GEM
11	11:59	CAN
13	16:33	LEO
15	18:00	VIR
17	18:15	LIB
19	19:14	SCO
21	22:19	SAG
24	3:55	CAP
26	11:49	AQU
28	21:42	PIS

MAR

2	9:23	ARI
4	22:19	TAU
7	10:56	GEM
9	20:59	CAN
12	2:56	LEO
14	4:59	VIR
16	4:45	LIB
18	4:18	SCO
20	5:34	SAG
22	9:49	CAP
24	17:20	AQU
27	3:34	PIS
29	15:38	ARI

APR

1	4:35	TAU
3	17:16	GEM
6	4:07	CAN
8	11:37	LEO
10	15:16	VIR
12	15:55	LIB
14	15:15	SCO
16	15:16	SAG
18	17:44	CAP
20	23:48	AQU
23	9:28	PIS
25	21:37	ARI
28	10:38	TAU
30	23:06	GEM

MAY

3	9:54	CAN
5	18:10	LEO
7	23:22	VIR
10	1:40	LIB
12	2:03	SCO
14	2:05	SAG
16	3:32	CAP
18	8:03	AQU
20	16:27	PIS
23	4:08	ARI
25	17:08	TAU
28	5:23	GEM
30	15:40	CAN

JUN

1	23:38	LEO
4	5:22	VIR
6	9:00	LIB
8	10:59	SCO
10	12:07	SAG
12	13:46	CAP
14	17:32	AQU
17	0:44	PIS
19	11:33	ARI
22	0:22	TAU
24	12:37	GEM
26	22:30	CAN
29	5:40	LEO

JUL

1	10:47	VIR
3	14:35	LIB
5	17:34	SCO
7	20:06	SAG
9	22:50	CAP
12	2:54	AQU
14	9:37	PIS
16	19:40	ARI
19	8:12	TAU
21	20:41	GEM
24	6:40	CAN
26	13:19	LEO
28	17:24	VIR
30	20:14	LIB

AUG

1	22:56	SCO
4	2:04	SAG
6	5:55	CAP
8	10:58	AQU
10	18:01	PIS
13	3:50	ARI
15	16:06	TAU
18	4:55	GEM
20	15:34	CAN
22	22:31	LEO
25	2:04	VIR
27	3:42	LIB
29	5:06	SCO
31	7:29	SAG

SEP

2	11:30	CAP
4	17:21	AQU
7	1:12	PIS
9	11:19	ARI
11	23:31	TAU
14	12:33	GEM
17	0:07	CAN
19	8:11	LEO
21	12:17	VIR
23	13:28	LIB
25	13:34	SCO
27	14:22	SAG
29	17:14	CAP

OCT

1	22:50	AQU
4	7:10	PIS
6	17:50	ARI
9	6:12	TAU
11	19:15	GEM
14	7:25	CAN
16	16:50	LEO
18	22:25	VIR
21	0:27	LIB
23	0:18	SCO
24	23:49	SAG
27	0:56	CAP
29	5:06	AQU
31	12:54	PIS

NOV

2	23:46	ARI
5	12:24	TAU
8	1:22	GEM
10	13:29	CAN
12	23:37	LEO
15	6:47	VIR
17	10:35	LIB
19	11:32	SCO
21	11:04	SAG
23	11:04	CAP
25	13:31	AQU
27	19:48	PIS
30	6:02	ARI

DEC

2	18:42	TAU
5	7:39	GEM
7	19:22	CAN
10	5:13	LEO
12	12:56	VIR
14	18:14	LIB
16	21:02	SCO
18	21:55	SAG
20	22:12	CAP
22	23:49	AQU
25	4:37	PIS
27	13:32	ARI
30	1:44	TAU

—1977—

JAN

1	14:43	GEM
4	2:13	CAN
6	11:21	LEO
8	18:24	VIR
10	23:48	LIB
13	3:45	SCO
15	6:19	SAG
17	8:03	CAP
19	10:13	AQU
21	14:31	PIS
23	22:20	ARI
26	9:42	TAU
28	22:38	GEM
31	10:21	CAN

FEB

2	19:12	LEO
5	1:18	VIR
7	5:37	LIB
9	9:05	SCO
11	12:12	SAG
13	15:14	CAP
15	18:46	AQU
17	23:45	PIS
20	7:23	ARI
22	18:07	TAU
25	6:51	GEM
27	19:03	CAN

MAR

2	4:26	LEO
4	10:19	VIR
6	13:35	LIB
8	15:38	SCO
10	17:42	SAG
12	20:40	CAP
15	1:01	AQU
17	7:06	PIS
19	15:24	ARI
22	2:06	TAU
24	14:39	GEM
27	3:17	CAN
29	13:41	LEO
31	20:26	VIR

APR

2	23:40	LIB
5	0:40	SCO
7	1:09	SAG
9	2:41	CAP
11	6:25	AQU
13	12:50	PIS
15	21:53	ARI
18	9:03	TAU
20	21:38	GEM
23	10:26	CAN
25	21:44	LEO
28	5:53	VIR
30	10:13	LIB

MAY

2	11:24	SCO
4	10:59	SAG
6	10:55	CAP
8	13:00	AQU
10	18:30	PIS
13	3:30	ARI
15	15:05	TAU
18	3:51	GEM
20	16:36	CAN
23	4:14	LEO
25	13:32	VIR
27	19:29	LIB
29	21:57	SCO
31	21:55	SAG

JUN

2	21:08	CAP
4	21:44	AQU
7	1:36	PIS
9	9:35	ARI
11	20:57	TAU
14	9:50	GEM
16	22:29	CAN
19	9:54	LEO
21	19:30	VIR
24	2:36	LIB
26	6:43	SCO
28	8:03	SAG
30	7:49	CAP

JUL

2	7:57	AQU
4	10:32	PIS
6	17:04	ARI
9	3:34	TAU
11	16:16	GEM
14	4:50	CAN
16	15:52	LEO
19	0:59	VIR
21	8:10	LIB
23	13:14	SCO
25	16:05	SAG
27	17:15	CAP
29	18:05	AQU
31	20:24	PIS

AUG

3	1:55	ARI
5	11:19	TAU
7	23:30	GEM
10	12:05	CAN
12	22:57	LEO
15	7:26	VIR
17	13:50	LIB
19	18:36	SCO
21	22:03	SAG
24	0:31	CAP
26	2:41	AQU
28	5:47	PIS
30	11:12	ARI

SEP

1	19:52	TAU
4	7:28	GEM
6	20:04	CAN
9	7:14	LEO
11	15:35	VIR
13	21:08	LIB
16	0:46	SCO
18	3:29	SAG
20	6:05	CAP
22	9:13	AQU
24	13:30	PIS
26	19:41	ARI
29	4:22	TAU

OCT

1	15:34	GEM
4	4:10	CAN
6	15:58	LEO
9	0:59	VIR
11	6:30	LIB
13	9:11	SCO
15	10:28	SAG
17	11:51	CAP
19	14:37	AQU
21	19:27	PIS
24	2:35	ARI
26	11:54	TAU
28	23:09	GEM
31	11:41	CAN

NOV

3	0:04	LEO
5	10:17	VIR
7	16:52	LIB
9	19:43	SCO
11	20:04	SAG
13	19:51	CAP
15	21:01	AQU
18	0:59	PIS
20	8:14	ARI
22	18:10	TAU
25	5:49	GEM
27	18:21	CAN
30	6:54	LEO

DEC

2	18:06	VIR
5	2:18	LIB
7	6:34	SCO
9	7:22	SAG
11	6:27	CAP
13	6:00	AQU
15	8:10	PIS
17	14:12	ARI
19	23:55	TAU
22	11:52	GEM
25	0:31	CAN
27	12:52	LEO
30	0:14	VIR

—1978—

JAN		
1	9:32	LIB
3	15:36	SCO
5	18:04	SAG
7	17:55	CAP
9	17:06	AQU
11	17:51	PIS
13	22:06	ARI
16	6:31	TAU
18	18:07	GEM
21	6:51	CAN
23	19:03	LEO
26	5:57	VIR
28	15:08	LIB
30	22:04	SCO

FEB		
2	2:14	SAG
4	3:51	CAP
6	4:05	AQU
8	4:48	PIS
10	7:57	ARI
12	14:51	TAU
15	1:25	GEM
17	13:56	CAN
20	2:10	LEO
22	12:40	VIR
24	21:04	LIB
27	3:29	SCO

MAR		
1	8:03	SAG
3	10:59	CAP
5	12:51	AQU
7	14:46	PIS
9	18:09	ARI
12	0:19	TAU
14	9:49	GEM
16	21:50	CAN
19	10:13	LEO
21	20:50	VIR
24	4:42	LIB
26	10:02	SCO
28	13:38	SAG
30	16:24	CAP

APR		
1	19:06	AQU
3	22:21	PIS
6	2:52	ARI
8	9:22	TAU
10	18:28	GEM
13	6:00	CAN
15	18:31	LEO
18	5:45	VIR
20	13:54	LIB
22	18:40	SCO
24	21:01	SAG
26	22:28	CAP
29	0:29	AQU

MAY		
1	4:01	PIS
3	9:28	ARI
5	16:53	TAU
8	2:19	GEM
10	13:42	CAN
13	2:18	LEO
15	14:16	VIR
17	23:25	LIB
20	4:39	SCO
22	6:32	SAG
24	6:42	CAP
26	7:11	AQU
28	9:37	PIS
30	14:53	ARI

JUN		
1	22:51	TAU
4	8:54	GEM
6	20:31	CAN
9	9:08	LEO
11	21:35	VIR
14	7:56	LIB
16	14:29	SCO
18	17:02	SAG
20	16:53	CAP
22	16:08	AQU
24	16:58	PIS
26	20:54	ARI
29	4:22	TAU

JUL		
1	14:38	GEM
4	2:34	CAN
6	15:14	LEO
9	3:45	VIR
11	14:49	LIB
13	22:48	SCO
16	2:50	SAG
18	3:34	CAP
20	2:42	AQU
22	2:27	PIS
24	4:47	ARI
26	10:51	TAU
28	20:31	GEM
31	8:29	CAN

AUG		
2	21:11	LEO
5	9:30	VIR
7	20:30	LIB
10	5:12	SCO
12	10:43	SAG
14	13:04	CAP
16	13:16	AQU
18	13:05	PIS
20	14:30	ARI
22	19:06	TAU
25	3:32	GEM
27	15:00	CAN
30	3:40	LEO

SEP		
1	15:47	VIR
4	2:16	LIB
6	10:39	SCO
8	16:40	SAG
10	20:20	CAP
12	22:09	AQU
14	23:10	PIS
17	0:51	ARI
19	4:44	TAU
21	11:57	GEM
23	22:32	CAN
26	11:02	LEO
28	23:12	VIR

OCT		
1	9:17	LIB
3	16:49	SCO
5	22:07	SAG
8	1:53	CAP
10	4:43	AQU
12	7:13	PIS
14	10:07	ARI
16	14:23	TAU
18	21:06	GEM
21	6:53	CAN
23	19:05	LEO
26	7:33	VIR
28	17:52	LIB
31	0:53	SCO

NOV		
2	5:04	SAG
4	7:41	CAP
6	10:04	AQU
8	13:07	PIS
10	17:12	ARI
12	22:36	TAU
15	5:45	GEM
17	15:17	CAN
20	3:10	LEO
22	15:58	VIR
25	3:08	LIB
27	10:39	SCO
29	14:24	SAG

DEC		
1	15:45	CAP
3	16:36	AQU
5	18:37	PIS
7	22:40	ARI
10	4:51	TAU
12	12:55	GEM
14	22:51	CAN
17	10:38	LEO
19	23:35	VIR
22	11:41	LIB
24	20:33	SCO
27	1:08	SAG
29	2:16	CAP
31	1:54	AQU

—1979—

JAN

2	2:09	PIS
4	4:42	ARI
6	10:18	TAU
8	18:43	GEM
11	5:15	CAN
13	17:17	LEO
16	6:11	VIR
18	18:41	LIB
21	4:51	SCO
23	11:09	SAG
25	13:28	CAP
27	13:13	AQU
29	12:26	PIS
31	13:12	ARI

FEB

2	17:04	TAU
5	0:34	GEM
7	11:06	CAN
9	23:26	LEO
12	12:18	VIR
15	0:38	LIB
17	11:13	SCO
19	18:52	SAG
21	23:01	CAP
24	0:13	AQU
25	23:53	PIS
27	23:55	ARI

MAR

2	2:10	TAU
4	7:59	GEM
6	17:35	CAN
9	5:48	LEO
11	18:43	VIR
14	6:42	LIB
16	16:50	SCO
19	0:39	SAG
21	5:57	CAP
23	8:53	AQU
25	10:05	PIS
27	10:48	ARI
29	12:37	TAU
31	17:09	GEM

APR

3	1:25	CAN
5	12:58	LEO
8	1:53	VIR
10	13:46	LIB
12	23:16	SCO
15	6:19	SAG
17	11:24	CAP
19	15:03	AQU
21	17:42	PIS
23	19:52	ARI
25	22:28	TAU
28	2:49	GEM
30	10:12	CAN

MAY

2	20:57	LEO
5	9:42	VIR
7	21:48	LIB
10	7:11	SCO
12	13:25	SAG
14	17:26	CAP
16	20:26	AQU
18	23:19	PIS
21	2:31	ARI
23	6:21	TAU
25	11:29	GEM
27	18:51	CAN
30	5:09	LEO

JUN

1	17:41	VIR
4	6:12	LIB
6	16:06	SCO
8	22:15	SAG
11	1:24	CAP
13	3:07	AQU
15	4:57	PIS
17	7:53	ARI
19	12:19	TAU
21	18:23	GEM
24	2:25	CAN
26	12:48	LEO
29	1:15	VIR

JUL

1	14:09	LIB
4	0:58	SCO
6	7:56	SAG
8	11:08	CAP
10	12:00	AQU
12	12:23	PIS
14	13:58	ARI
16	17:44	TAU
19	0:00	GEM
21	8:41	CAN
23	19:31	LEO
26	8:02	VIR
28	21:07	LIB
31	8:47	SCO

AUG

2	17:06	SAG
4	21:23	CAP
6	22:29	AQU
8	22:06	PIS
10	22:11	ARI
13	0:22	TAU
15	5:42	GEM
17	14:18	CAN
20	1:29	LEO
22	14:12	VIR
25	3:14	LIB
27	15:13	SCO
30	0:40	SAG

SEP

1	6:34	CAP
3	9:00	AQU
5	9:04	PIS
7	8:30	ARI
9	9:13	TAU
11	12:55	GEM
13	20:28	CAN
16	7:26	LEO
18	20:16	VIR
21	9:11	LIB
23	20:55	SCO
26	6:36	SAG
28	13:41	CAP
30	17:50	AQU

OCT

2	19:24	PIS
4	19:29	ARI
6	19:45	TAU
8	22:08	GEM
11	4:10	CAN
13	14:12	LEO
16	2:52	VIR
18	15:45	LIB
21	3:03	SCO
23	12:10	SAG
25	19:12	CAP
28	0:17	AQU
30	3:30	PIS

NOV

1	5:10	ARI
3	6:17	TAU
5	8:26	GEM
7	13:24	CAN
9	22:15	LEO
12	10:21	VIR
14	23:17	LIB
17	10:30	SCO
19	18:57	SAG
22	1:02	CAP
24	5:37	AQU
26	9:18	PIS
28	12:17	ARI
30	14:55	TAU

DEC

2	18:03	GEM
4	23:02	CAN
7	7:10	LEO
9	18:34	VIR
12	7:30	LIB
14	19:09	SCO
17	3:37	SAG
19	8:55	CAP
21	12:13	AQU
23	14:51	PIS
25	17:41	ARI
27	21:08	TAU
30	1:33	GEM

—1980—

JAN

1	7:30	CAN
3	15:48	LEO
6	2:49	VIR
8	15:39	LIB
11	3:56	SCO
13	13:18	SAG
15	18:52	CAP
17	21:26	AQU
19	22:34	PIS
21	23:52	ARI
24	2:32	TAU
26	7:12	GEM
28	14:03	CAN
30	23:09	LEO

FEB

2	10:22	VIR
4	23:05	LIB
7	11:47	SCO
9	22:20	SAG
12	5:13	CAP
14	8:20	AQU
16	8:55	PIS
18	8:43	ARI
20	9:36	TAU
22	12:59	GEM
24	19:35	CAN
27	5:11	LEO
29	16:54	VIR

MAR

3	5:41	LIB
5	18:23	SCO
8	5:39	SAG
10	14:03	CAP
12	18:46	AQU
14	20:11	PIS
16	19:42	ARI
18	19:14	TAU
20	20:48	GEM
23	1:56	CAN
25	10:59	LEO
27	22:53	VIR
30	11:50	LIB

APR

2	0:22	SCO
4	11:35	SAG
6	20:43	CAP
9	3:00	AQU
11	6:07	PIS
13	6:41	ARI
15	6:11	TAU
17	6:42	GEM
19	10:12	CAN
21	17:53	LEO
24	5:13	VIR
26	18:10	LIB
29	6:36	SCO

MAY

1	17:22	SAG
4	2:15	CAP
6	9:04	AQU
8	13:34	PIS
10	15:45	ARI
12	16:25	TAU
14	17:08	GEM
16	19:53	CAN
19	2:15	LEO
21	12:33	VIR
24	1:12	LIB
26	13:37	SCO
29	0:05	SAG
31	8:15	CAP

JUN

2	14:30	AQU
4	19:11	PIS
6	22:24	ARI
9	0:30	TAU
11	2:23	GEM
13	5:30	CAN
15	11:23	LEO
17	20:48	VIR
20	8:56	LIB
22	21:27	SCO
25	8:02	SAG
27	15:47	CAP
29	21:04	AQU

JUL

2	0:49	PIS
4	3:47	ARI
6	6:31	TAU
8	9:34	GEM
10	13:45	CAN
12	20:03	LEO
15	5:12	VIR
17	16:56	LIB
20	5:34	SCO
22	16:43	SAG
25	0:45	CAP
27	5:35	AQU
29	8:11	PIS
31	9:54	ARI

AUG

2	11:56	TAU
4	15:10	GEM
6	20:13	CAN
9	3:24	LEO
11	12:55	VIR
14	0:33	LIB
16	13:16	SCO
19	1:08	SAG
21	10:12	CAP
23	15:33	AQU
25	17:44	PIS
27	18:12	ARI
29	18:42	TAU
31	20:51	GEM

SEP

3	1:40	CAN
5	9:23	LEO
7	19:32	VIR
10	7:23	LIB
12	20:07	SCO
15	8:29	SAG
17	18:46	CAP
20	1:31	AQU
22	4:28	PIS
24	4:38	ARI
26	3:54	TAU
28	4:22	GEM
30	7:47	CAN

OCT

2	14:58	LEO
5	1:20	VIR
7	13:31	LIB
10	2:16	SCO
12	14:38	SAG
15	1:37	CAP
17	9:54	AQU
19	14:32	PIS
21	15:44	ARI
23	14:56	TAU
25	14:18	GEM
27	16:01	CAN
29	21:39	LEO

NOV

1	7:19	VIR
3	19:32	LIB
6	8:20	SCO
8	20:26	SAG
11	7:16	CAP
13	16:11	AQU
15	22:22	PIS
18	1:22	ARI
20	1:52	TAU
22	1:28	GEM
24	2:19	CAN
26	6:24	LEO
28	14:38	VIR

DEC

1	2:14	LIB
3	15:01	SCO
6	2:58	SAG
8	13:13	CAP
10	21:37	AQU
13	4:04	PIS
15	8:22	ARI
17	10:37	TAU
19	11:40	GEM
21	13:04	CAN
23	16:34	LEO
25	23:33	VIR
28	10:06	LIB
30	22:37	SCO

—1981—

JAN			FEB			MAR			APR		
2	10:43	SAG	1	5:38	CAP	2	22:51	AQU	1	13:42	PIS
4	20:42	CAP	3	12:56	AQU	5	3:13	PIS	3	15:26	ARI
7	4:13	AQU	5	17:22	PIS	7	4:49	ARI	5	15:05	TAU
9	9:43	PIS	7	20:02	ARI	9	5:23	TAU	7	14:48	GEM
11	13:44	ARI	9	22:11	TAU	11	6:43	GEM	9	16:34	CAN
13	16:46	TAU	12	0:52	GEM	13	10:06	CAN	11	21:37	LEO
15	19:18	GEM	14	4:43	CAN	15	16:03	LEO	14	5:57	VIR
17	22:08	CAN	16	10:11	LEO	18	0:20	VIR	16	16:39	LIB
20	2:22	LEO	18	17:35	VIR	20	10:31	LIB	19	4:40	SCO
22	9:03	VIR	21	3:13	LIB	22	22:15	SCO	21	17:16	SAG
24	18:46	LIB	23	14:55	SCO	25	10:52	SAG	24	5:32	CAP
27	6:49	SCO	26	3:30	SAG	27	22:53	CAP	26	15:58	AQU
29	19:12	SAG	28	14:47	CAP	30	8:16	AQU	28	22:57	PIS

MAY			JUN			JUL			AUG		
1	1:58	ARI	1	11:49	GEM	2	23:48	LEO	1	13:55	VIR
3	2:00	TAU	3	11:39	CAN	5	4:27	VIR	3	21:25	LIB
5	1:02	GEM	5	13:44	LEO	7	12:43	LIB	6	7:59	SCO
7	1:18	CAN	7	19:26	VIR	10	0:02	SCO	8	20:23	SAG
9	4:41	LEO	10	4:56	LIB	12	12:36	SAG	11	8:21	CAP
11	11:56	VIR	12	16:55	SCO	15	0:20	CAP	13	17:57	AQU
13	22:25	LIB	15	5:32	SAG	17	10:03	AQU	16	0:35	PIS
16	10:38	SCO	17	17:22	CAP	19	17:26	PIS	18	4:50	ARI
18	23:15	SAG	20	3:37	AQU	21	22:44	ARI	20	7:44	TAU
21	11:21	CAP	22	11:45	PIS	24	2:19	TAU	22	10:19	GEM
23	22:01	AQU	24	17:19	ARI	26	4:42	GEM	24	13:17	CAN
26	6:06	PIS	26	20:17	TAU	28	6:42	CAN	26	17:11	LEO
28	10:44	ARI	28	21:22	GEM	30	9:21	LEO	28	22:32	VIR
30	12:11	TAU	30	21:58	CAN				31	6:03	LIB

SEP			OCT			NOV			DEC		
2	16:11	SCO	2	12:00	SAG	1	7:47	CAP	1	2:10	AQU
5	4:24	SAG	5	0:50	CAP	3	19:52	AQU	3	12:17	PIS
7	16:49	CAP	7	12:02	AQU	6	4:53	PIS	5	18:50	ARI
10	2:59	AQU	9	19:33	PIS	8	9:39	ARI	7	21:32	TAU
12	9:35	PIS	11	23:02	ARI	10	10:45	TAU	9	21:31	GEM
14	12:56	ARI	13	23:44	TAU	12	10:00	GEM	11	20:41	CAN
16	14:31	TAU	15	23:42	GEM	14	9:38	CAN	13	21:09	LEO
18	16:00	GEM	18	0:53	CAN	16	11:33	LEO	16	0:39	VIR
20	18:40	CAN	20	4:35	LEO	18	16:54	VIR	18	7:59	LIB
22	23:09	LEO	22	11:06	VIR	21	1:34	LIB	20	18:40	SCO
25	5:29	VIR	24	19:57	LIB	23	12:37	SCO	23	7:12	SAG
27	13:41	LIB	27	6:39	SCO	26	1:01	SAG	25	20:00	CAP
29	23:54	SCO	29	18:49	SAG	28	13:53	CAP	28	7:54	AQU
									30	18:02	PIS

—1982—

JAN

2	1:34	ARI
4	6:03	TAU
6	7:49	GEM
8	8:02	CAN
10	8:22	LEO
12	10:38	VIR
14	16:18	LIB
17	1:47	SCO
19	14:01	SAG
22	2:51	CAP
24	14:26	AQU
26	23:50	PIS
29	6:59	ARI
31	12:04	TAU

FEB

2	15:21	GEM
4	17:19	CAN
6	18:51	LEO
8	21:16	VIR
11	2:03	LIB
13	10:17	SCO
15	21:46	SAG
18	10:37	CAP
20	22:16	AQU
23	7:10	PIS
25	13:18	ARI
27	17:33	TAU

MAR

1	20:51	GEM
3	23:49	CAN
6	2:51	LEO
8	6:28	VIR
10	11:35	LIB
12	19:17	SCO
15	6:04	SAG
17	18:48	CAP
20	6:54	AQU
22	16:02	PIS
24	21:38	ARI
27	0:40	TAU
29	2:45	GEM
31	5:10	CAN

APR

2	8:37	LEO
4	13:19	VIR
6	19:27	LIB
9	3:34	SCO
11	14:08	SAG
14	2:42	CAP
16	15:19	AQU
19	1:20	PIS
21	7:24	ARI
23	9:59	TAU
25	10:49	GEM
27	11:44	CAN
29	14:10	LEO

MAY

1	18:46	VIR
4	1:33	LIB
6	10:25	SCO
8	21:17	SAG
11	9:50	CAP
13	22:45	AQU
16	9:47	PIS
18	17:05	ARI
20	20:23	TAU
22	20:55	GEM
24	20:39	CAN
26	21:28	LEO
29	0:44	VIR
31	7:03	LIB

JUN

2	16:13	SCO
5	3:32	SAG
7	16:13	CAP
10	5:09	AQU
12	16:45	PIS
15	1:21	ARI
17	6:07	TAU
19	7:35	GEM
21	7:13	CAN
23	6:58	LEO
25	8:37	VIR
27	13:31	LIB
29	22:02	SCO

JUL

2	9:26	SAG
4	22:16	CAP
7	11:04	AQU
9	22:36	PIS
12	7:50	ARI
14	14:01	TAU
16	17:04	GEM
18	17:47	CAN
20	17:36	LEO
22	18:21	VIR
24	21:46	LIB
27	4:59	SCO
29	15:48	SAG

AUG

1	4:37	CAP
3	17:18	AQU
6	4:24	PIS
8	13:21	ARI
10	20:01	TAU
13	0:23	GEM
15	2:41	CAN
17	3:41	LEO
19	4:41	VIR
21	7:23	LIB
23	13:22	SCO
25	23:12	SAG
28	11:42	CAP
31	0:24	AQU

SEP

2	11:11	PIS
4	19:25	ARI
7	1:28	TAU
9	5:58	GEM
11	9:19	CAN
13	11:47	LEO
15	13:58	VIR
17	17:04	LIB
19	22:33	SCO
22	7:31	SAG
24	19:32	CAP
27	8:22	AQU
29	19:19	PIS

OCT

2	3:07	ARI
4	8:10	TAU
6	11:40	GEM
8	14:40	CAN
10	17:45	LEO
12	21:10	VIR
15	1:23	LIB
17	7:21	SCO
19	16:03	SAG
22	3:39	CAP
24	16:37	AQU
27	4:13	PIS
29	12:26	ARI
31	17:04	TAU

NOV

2	19:23	GEM
4	21:00	CAN
6	23:11	LEO
9	2:41	VIR
11	7:46	LIB
13	14:43	SCO
15	23:52	SAG
18	11:22	CAP
21	0:21	AQU
23	12:43	PIS
25	22:08	ARI
28	3:32	TAU
30	5:36	GEM

DEC

2	5:58	CAN
4	6:27	LEO
6	8:33	VIR
8	13:11	LIB
10	20:35	SCO
13	6:28	SAG
15	18:16	CAP
18	7:13	AQU
20	19:57	PIS
23	6:35	ARI
25	13:38	TAU
27	16:49	GEM
29	17:13	CAN
31	16:34	LEO

—1983—

JAN

2	16:50	VIR
4	19:45	LIB
7	2:17	SCO
9	12:14	SAG
12	0:27	CAP
14	13:27	AQU
17	2:03	PIS
19	13:09	ARI
21	21:37	TAU
24	2:41	GEM
26	4:29	CAN
28	4:11	LEO
30	3:35	VIR

FEB

1	4:48	LIB
3	9:33	SCO
5	18:29	SAG
8	6:34	CAP
10	19:41	AQU
13	8:02	PIS
15	18:47	ARI
18	3:31	TAU
20	9:53	GEM
22	13:32	CAN
24	14:47	LEO
26	14:50	VIR
28	15:31	LIB

MAR

2	18:51	SCO
5	2:16	SAG
7	13:30	CAP
10	2:31	AQU
12	14:48	PIS
15	1:01	ARI
17	9:05	TAU
19	15:21	GEM
21	19:53	CAN
23	22:44	LEO
26	0:19	VIR
28	1:49	LIB
30	4:58	SCO

APR

1	11:21	SAG
3	21:30	CAP
6	10:07	AQU
8	22:31	PIS
11	8:38	ARI
13	16:00	TAU
15	21:16	GEM
18	1:15	CAN
20	4:27	LEO
22	7:12	VIR
24	10:05	LIB
26	14:05	SCO
28	20:29	SAG

MAY

1	6:02	CAP
3	18:10	AQU
6	6:44	PIS
8	17:17	ARI
11	0:37	TAU
13	5:04	GEM
15	7:49	CAN
17	10:02	LEO
19	12:37	VIR
21	16:12	LIB
23	21:18	SCO
26	4:28	SAG
28	14:08	CAP
31	2:00	AQU

JUN

2	14:43	PIS
5	2:00	ARI
7	10:06	TAU
9	14:38	GEM
11	16:33	CAN
13	17:22	LEO
15	18:39	VIR
17	21:37	LIB
20	3:00	SCO
22	10:56	SAG
24	21:09	CAP
27	9:07	AQU
29	21:52	PIS

JUL

2	9:48	ARI
4	19:06	TAU
7	0:42	GEM
9	2:51	CAN
11	2:54	LEO
13	2:44	VIR
15	4:11	LIB
17	8:39	SCO
19	16:32	SAG
22	3:12	CAP
24	15:27	AQU
27	4:12	PIS
29	16:22	ARI

AUG

1	2:38	TAU
3	9:44	GEM
5	13:10	CAN
7	13:38	LEO
9	12:50	VIR
11	12:52	LIB
13	15:45	SCO
15	22:34	SAG
18	9:00	CAP
20	21:26	AQU
23	10:11	PIS
25	22:09	ARI
28	8:39	TAU
30	16:50	GEM

SEP

1	21:54	CAN
3	23:48	LEO
5	23:37	VIR
7	23:14	LIB
10	0:50	SCO
12	6:09	SAG
14	15:34	CAP
17	3:46	AQU
19	16:31	PIS
22	4:11	ARI
24	14:13	TAU
26	22:25	GEM
29	4:25	CAN

OCT

1	7:55	LEO
3	9:16	VIR
5	9:43	LIB
7	11:07	SCO
9	15:21	SAG
11	23:31	CAP
14	11:01	AQU
16	23:42	PIS
19	11:19	ARI
21	20:48	TAU
24	4:11	GEM
26	9:48	CAN
28	13:51	LEO
30	16:34	VIR

NOV

1	18:31	LIB
3	20:54	SCO
6	1:10	SAG
8	8:32	CAP
10	19:11	AQU
13	7:42	PIS
15	19:37	ARI
18	5:07	TAU
20	11:46	GEM
22	16:11	CAN
24	19:20	LEO
26	22:03	VIR
29	0:58	LIB

DEC

1	4:41	SCO
3	9:57	SAG
5	17:29	CAP
8	3:40	AQU
10	15:54	PIS
13	4:17	ARI
15	14:34	TAU
17	21:24	GEM
20	1:03	CAN
22	2:45	LEO
24	4:02	VIR
26	6:19	LIB
28	10:27	SCO
30	16:45	SAG

—1984—

JAN

2	1:08	CAP
4	11:31	AQU
6	23:35	PIS
9	12:16	ARI
11	23:37	TAU
14	7:41	GEM
16	11:48	CAN
18	12:50	LEO
20	12:36	VIR
22	13:08	LIB
24	16:05	SCO
26	22:13	SAG
29	7:13	CAP
31	18:12	AQU

FEB

3	6:23	PIS
5	19:05	ARI
8	7:06	TAU
10	16:40	GEM
12	22:21	CAN
15	0:10	LEO
16	23:33	VIR
18	22:40	LIB
20	23:45	SCO
23	4:23	SAG
25	12:50	CAP
28	0:03	AQU

MAR

1	12:30	PIS
4	1:08	ARI
6	13:10	TAU
8	23:30	GEM
11	6:49	CAN
13	10:22	LEO
15	10:48	VIR
17	9:52	LIB
19	9:50	SCO
21	12:42	SAG
23	19:37	CAP
26	6:10	AQU
28	18:38	PIS
31	7:15	ARI

APR

2	18:56	TAU
5	5:05	GEM
7	13:00	CAN
9	18:02	LEO
11	20:12	VIR
13	20:30	LIB
15	20:42	SCO
17	22:45	SAG
20	4:11	CAP
22	13:28	AQU
25	1:27	PIS
27	14:03	ARI
30	1:31	TAU

MAY

2	11:03	GEM
4	18:27	CAN
6	23:44	LEO
9	3:03	VIR
11	4:55	LIB
13	6:23	SCO
15	8:51	SAG
17	13:44	CAP
19	21:56	AQU
22	9:09	PIS
24	21:40	ARI
27	9:14	TAU
29	18:24	GEM

JUN

1	0:54	CAN
3	5:20	LEO
5	8:28	VIR
7	11:04	LIB
9	13:49	SCO
11	17:27	SAG
13	22:49	CAP
16	6:42	AQU
18	17:19	PIS
21	5:41	ARI
23	17:39	TAU
26	3:05	GEM
28	9:10	CAN
30	12:31	LEO

JUL

2	14:28	VIR
4	16:28	LIB
6	19:29	SCO
9	0:04	SAG
11	6:24	CAP
13	14:42	AQU
16	1:11	PIS
18	13:27	ARI
21	1:53	TAU
23	12:11	GEM
25	18:45	CAN
27	21:42	LEO
29	22:30	VIR
31	23:04	LIB

AUG

3	1:05	SCO
5	5:30	SAG
7	12:25	CAP
9	21:26	AQU
12	8:14	PIS
14	20:29	ARI
17	9:14	TAU
19	20:32	GEM
22	4:21	CAN
24	8:01	LEO
26	8:33	VIR
28	7:58	LIB
30	8:24	SCO

SEP

1	11:30	SAG
3	17:56	CAP
6	3:12	AQU
8	14:25	PIS
11	2:47	ARI
13	15:34	TAU
16	3:27	GEM
18	12:37	CAN
20	17:50	LEO
22	19:20	VIR
24	18:42	LIB
26	18:05	SCO
28	19:33	SAG

OCT

1	0:29	CAP
3	9:04	AQU
5	20:20	PIS
8	8:52	ARI
10	21:29	TAU
13	9:15	GEM
15	19:01	CAN
18	1:42	LEO
20	4:57	VIR
22	5:32	LIB
24	5:09	SCO
26	5:44	SAG
28	9:06	CAP
30	16:14	AQU

NOV

2	2:50	PIS
4	15:21	ARI
7	3:54	TAU
9	15:11	GEM
12	0:32	CAN
14	7:34	LEO
16	12:09	VIR
18	14:30	LIB
20	15:31	SCO
22	16:35	SAG
24	19:18	CAP
27	1:07	AQU
29	10:34	PIS

DEC

1	22:43	ARI
4	11:21	TAU
6	22:25	GEM
9	6:57	CAN
11	13:09	LEO
13	17:36	VIR
15	20:53	LIB
17	23:28	SCO
20	1:59	SAG
22	5:22	CAP
24	10:48	AQU
26	19:19	PIS
29	6:50	ARI
31	19:37	TAU

—1985—

JAN		
3	7:01	GEM
5	15:18	CAN
7	20:29	LEO
9	23:40	VIR
12	2:14	LIB
14	5:08	SCO
16	8:49	SAG
18	13:30	CAP
20	19:39	AQU
23	4:03	PIS
25	15:06	ARI
28	3:54	TAU
30	16:01	GEM

FEB		
2	1:00	CAN
4	6:03	LEO
6	8:10	VIR
8	9:11	LIB
10	10:50	SCO
12	14:10	SAG
14	19:28	CAP
17	2:37	AQU
19	11:39	PIS
21	22:43	ARI
24	11:28	TAU
27	0:12	GEM

MAR		
1	10:24	CAN
3	16:29	LEO
5	18:43	VIR
7	18:48	LIB
9	18:48	SCO
11	20:30	SAG
14	0:55	CAP
16	8:12	AQU
18	17:51	PIS
21	5:21	ARI
23	18:07	TAU
26	7:03	GEM
28	18:14	CAN
31	1:52	LEO

APR		
2	5:26	VIR
4	5:54	LIB
6	5:11	SCO
8	5:18	SAG
10	7:58	CAP
12	14:05	AQU
14	23:31	PIS
17	11:19	ARI
20	0:13	TAU
22	13:01	GEM
25	0:27	CAN
27	9:11	LEO
29	14:25	VIR

MAY		
1	16:23	LIB
3	16:18	SCO
5	15:57	SAG
7	17:12	CAP
9	21:39	AQU
12	5:57	PIS
14	17:26	ARI
17	6:24	TAU
19	19:02	GEM
22	6:06	CAN
24	14:55	LEO
26	21:07	VIR
29	0:41	LIB
31	2:08	SCO

JUN		
2	2:34	SAG
4	3:35	CAP
6	6:53	AQU
8	13:47	PIS
11	0:25	ARI
13	13:12	TAU
16	1:46	GEM
18	12:23	CAN
20	20:33	LEO
23	2:33	VIR
25	6:48	LIB
27	9:38	SCO
29	11:31	SAG

JUL		
1	13:23	CAP
3	16:37	AQU
5	22:41	PIS
8	8:21	ARI
10	20:45	TAU
13	9:24	GEM
15	19:55	CAN
18	3:26	LEO
20	8:30	VIR
22	12:11	LIB
24	15:17	SCO
26	18:13	SAG
28	21:22	CAP
31	1:26	AQU

AUG		
2	7:34	PIS
4	16:44	ARI
7	4:42	TAU
9	17:32	GEM
12	4:29	CAN
14	11:58	LEO
16	16:16	VIR
18	18:45	LIB
20	20:52	SCO
22	23:37	SAG
25	3:25	CAP
27	8:32	AQU
29	15:26	PIS

SEP		
1	0:43	ARI
3	12:29	TAU
6	1:28	GEM
8	13:11	CAN
10	21:28	LEO
13	1:53	VIR
15	3:35	LIB
17	4:18	SCO
19	5:41	SAG
21	8:50	CAP
23	14:12	AQU
25	21:51	PIS
28	7:43	ARI
30	19:36	TAU

OCT		
3	8:37	GEM
5	21:00	CAN
8	6:34	LEO
10	12:10	VIR
12	14:13	LIB
14	14:14	SCO
16	14:06	SAG
18	15:36	CAP
20	19:55	AQU
23	3:28	PIS
25	13:48	ARI
28	2:00	TAU
30	15:00	GEM

NOV		
2	3:32	CAN
4	14:04	LEO
6	21:19	VIR
9	0:53	LIB
11	1:32	SCO
13	0:53	SAG
15	0:54	CAP
17	3:26	AQU
19	9:43	PIS
21	19:43	ARI
24	8:08	TAU
26	21:09	GEM
29	9:24	CAN

DEC		
1	20:00	LEO
4	4:15	VIR
6	9:34	LIB
8	11:57	SCO
10	12:14	SAG
12	12:00	CAP
14	13:16	AQU
16	17:51	PIS
19	2:37	ARI
21	14:41	TAU
24	3:46	GEM
26	15:45	CAN
29	1:45	LEO
31	9:44	VIR

—1986—

JAN		
2	15:46	LIB
4	19:45	SCO
6	21:48	SAG
8	22:43	CAP
11	0:02	AQU
13	3:40	PIS
15	11:04	ARI
17	22:14	TAU
20	11:13	GEM
22	23:15	CAN
25	8:48	LEO
27	15:52	VIR
29	21:11	LIB

FEB		
1	1:20	SCO
3	4:32	SAG
5	7:02	CAP
7	9:36	AQU
9	13:33	PIS
11	20:22	ARI
14	6:39	TAU
16	19:18	GEM
19	7:40	CAN
21	17:26	LEO
23	23:59	VIR
26	4:08	LIB
28	7:07	SCO

MAR		
2	9:52	SAG
4	12:57	CAP
6	16:43	AQU
8	21:49	PIS
11	5:04	ARI
13	15:05	TAU
16	3:24	GEM
18	16:05	CAN
21	2:39	LEO
23	9:40	VIR
25	13:23	LIB
27	15:06	SCO
29	16:21	SAG
31	18:26	CAP

APR		
2	22:12	AQU
5	4:04	PIS
7	12:13	ARI
9	22:37	TAU
12	10:52	GEM
14	23:43	CAN
17	11:11	LEO
19	19:25	VIR
21	23:51	LIB
24	1:16	SCO
26	1:17	SAG
28	1:42	CAP
30	4:07	AQU

MAY		
2	9:31	PIS
4	18:02	ARI
7	5:00	TAU
9	17:27	GEM
12	6:19	CAN
14	18:16	LEO
17	3:46	VIR
19	9:42	LIB
21	12:03	SCO
23	11:58	SAG
25	11:16	CAP
27	12:01	AQU
29	15:55	PIS
31	23:44	ARI

JUN		
3	10:46	TAU
5	23:27	GEM
8	12:17	CAN
11	0:12	LEO
13	10:19	VIR
15	17:39	LIB
17	21:37	SCO
19	22:37	SAG
21	22:01	CAP
23	21:51	AQU
26	0:13	PIS
28	6:35	ARI
30	16:55	TAU

JUL		
3	5:33	GEM
5	18:20	CAN
8	5:57	LEO
10	15:51	VIR
12	23:41	LIB
15	4:59	SCO
17	7:35	SAG
19	8:11	CAP
21	8:18	AQU
23	10:00	PIS
25	15:03	ARI
28	0:12	TAU
30	12:20	GEM

AUG		
2	1:05	CAN
4	12:27	LEO
6	21:45	VIR
9	5:05	LIB
11	10:37	SCO
13	14:18	SAG
15	16:23	CAP
17	17:45	AQU
19	19:53	PIS
22	0:28	ARI
24	8:37	TAU
26	20:01	GEM
29	8:41	CAN
31	20:09	LEO

SEP		
3	5:07	VIR
5	11:34	LIB
7	16:13	SCO
9	19:41	SAG
11	22:29	CAP
14	1:08	AQU
16	4:28	PIS
18	9:34	ARI
20	17:26	TAU
23	4:14	GEM
25	16:45	CAN
28	4:40	LEO
30	13:58	VIR

OCT		
2	20:04	LIB
4	23:36	SCO
7	1:49	SAG
9	3:53	CAP
11	6:46	AQU
13	11:04	PIS
15	17:14	ARI
18	1:36	TAU
20	12:16	GEM
23	0:38	CAN
25	13:03	LEO
27	23:21	VIR
30	6:05	LIB

NOV		
1	9:20	SCO
3	10:20	SAG
5	10:49	CAP
7	12:29	AQU
9	16:30	PIS
11	23:15	ARI
14	8:25	TAU
16	19:27	GEM
19	7:47	CAN
21	20:26	LEO
24	7:47	VIR
26	16:00	LIB
28	20:14	SCO
30	21:09	SAG

DEC		
2	20:29	CAP
4	20:24	AQU
6	22:49	PIS
9	4:50	ARI
11	14:11	TAU
14	1:42	GEM
16	14:10	CAN
19	2:45	LEO
21	14:31	VIR
24	0:06	LIB
26	6:07	SCO
28	8:20	SAG
30	7:55	CAP

—1987—

JAN

1	6:54	AQU
3	7:37	PIS
5	11:52	ARI
7	20:14	TAU
10	7:40	GEM
12	20:19	CAN
15	8:46	LEO
17	20:16	VIR
20	6:10	LIB
22	13:31	SCO
24	17:36	SAG
26	18:43	CAP
28	18:18	AQU
30	18:25	PIS

FEB

1	21:10	ARI
4	3:54	TAU
6	14:24	GEM
9	2:56	CAN
11	15:22	LEO
14	2:27	VIR
16	11:45	LIB
18	19:05	SCO
21	0:10	SAG
23	2:58	CAP
25	4:09	AQU
27	5:08	PIS

MAR

1	7:38	ARI
3	13:12	TAU
5	22:27	GEM
8	10:25	CAN
10	22:55	LEO
13	9:56	VIR
15	18:35	LIB
18	0:58	SCO
20	5:33	SAG
22	8:49	CAP
24	11:19	AQU
26	13:46	PIS
28	17:13	ARI
30	22:47	TAU

APR

2	7:17	GEM
4	18:34	CAN
7	7:05	LEO
9	18:29	VIR
12	3:06	LIB
14	8:41	SCO
16	12:02	SAG
18	14:22	CAP
20	16:46	AQU
22	20:03	PIS
25	0:41	ARI
27	7:07	TAU
29	15:44	GEM

MAY

2	2:40	CAN
4	15:07	LEO
7	3:08	VIR
9	12:30	LIB
11	18:10	SCO
13	20:42	SAG
15	21:37	CAP
17	22:43	AQU
20	1:25	PIS
22	6:24	ARI
24	13:40	TAU
26	22:56	GEM
29	10:00	CAN
31	22:26	LEO

JUN

3	10:57	VIR
5	21:25	LIB
8	4:07	SCO
10	6:54	SAG
12	7:06	CAP
14	6:46	AQU
16	7:55	PIS
18	11:57	ARI
20	19:10	TAU
23	4:55	GEM
25	16:23	CAN
28	4:53	LEO
30	17:35	VIR

JUL

3	4:56	LIB
5	13:04	SCO
7	17:06	SAG
9	17:44	CAP
11	16:50	AQU
13	16:37	PIS
15	19:01	ARI
18	1:05	TAU
20	10:33	GEM
22	22:14	CAN
25	10:51	LEO
27	23:27	VIR
30	11:00	LIB

AUG

1	20:10	SCO
4	1:48	SAG
6	3:52	CAP
8	3:38	AQU
10	3:02	PIS
12	4:10	ARI
14	8:39	TAU
16	17:00	GEM
19	4:20	CAN
21	16:59	LEO
24	5:24	VIR
26	16:36	LIB
29	1:50	SCO
31	8:25	SAG

SEP

2	12:05	CAP
4	13:22	AQU
6	13:38	PIS
8	14:35	ARI
10	17:58	TAU
13	0:55	GEM
15	11:23	CAN
17	23:51	LEO
20	12:14	VIR
22	22:59	LIB
25	7:31	SCO
27	13:50	SAG
29	18:09	CAP

OCT

1	20:52	AQU
3	22:40	PIS
6	0:36	ARI
8	3:58	TAU
10	10:04	GEM
12	19:32	CAN
15	7:35	LEO
17	20:07	VIR
20	6:51	LIB
22	14:42	SCO
24	19:58	SAG
26	23:34	CAP
29	2:28	AQU
31	5:20	PIS

NOV

2	8:41	ARI
4	13:03	TAU
6	19:17	GEM
9	4:11	CAN
11	15:46	LEO
14	4:30	VIR
16	15:49	LIB
18	23:48	SCO
21	4:17	SAG
23	6:33	CAP
25	8:14	AQU
27	10:41	PIS
29	14:37	ARI

DEC

1	20:06	TAU
4	3:14	GEM
6	12:21	CAN
8	23:41	LEO
11	12:31	VIR
14	0:41	LIB
16	9:42	SCO
18	14:34	SAG
20	16:08	CAP
22	16:21	AQU
24	17:11	PIS
26	20:06	ARI
29	1:37	TAU
31	9:30	GEM

—1988—

JAN		
2	19:17	CAN
5	6:;48	LEO
7	19:36	VIR
10	8:18	LIB
12	18:40	SCO
15	0:59	SAG
17	3:16	CAP
19	3:03	AQU
21	2:28	PIS
23	3:32	ARI
25	7:37	TAU
27	15:03	GEM
30	1:12	CAN

FEB		
1	13:07	LEO
4	1:55	VIR
6	14:37	LIB
9	1:43	SCO
11	9:37	SAG
13	13:37	CAP
15	14:26	AQU
17	13:45	PIS
19	13:36	ARI
21	15:51	TAU
23	21:43	GEM
26	7:13	CAN
28	19:13	LEO

MAR		
2	8:07	VIR
4	20:33	LIB
7	7:28	SCO
9	16:00	SAG
11	21:32	CAP
14	0:09	AQU
16	0:43	PIS
18	0:46	ARI
20	2:06	TAU
22	6:22	GEM
24	14:28	CAN
27	1:55	LEO
29	14:50	VIR

APR		
1	3:06	LIB
3	13:27	SCO
5	21:30	SAG
8	3:20	CAP
10	7:11	AQU
12	9:25	PIS
14	10:48	ARI
16	12:32	TAU
18	16:11	GEM
20	23:05	CAN
23	9:35	LEO
25	22:17	VIR
28	10:38	LIB
30	20:40	SCO

MAY		
3	3:53	SAG
5	8:55	CAP
7	12:38	AQU
9	15:40	PIS
11	18:24	ARI
13	21:23	TAU
16	1:32	GEM
18	8:06	CAN
20	17:52	LEO
23	6:13	VIR
25	18:50	LIB
28	5:07	SCO
30	11:58	SAG

JUN		
1	15:59	CAP
3	18:35	AQU
5	21:01	PIS
8	0:05	ARI
10	4:03	TAU
12	9:15	GEM
14	16:20	CAN
17	1:58	LEO
19	14:04	VIR
22	2:58	LIB
24	13:59	SCO
26	21:19	SAG
29	1:01	CAP

JUL		
1	2:30	AQU
3	3:34	PIS
5	5:38	ARI
7	9:28	TAU
9	15:17	GEM
11	23:09	CAN
14	9:12	LEO
16	21:18	VIR
19	10:23	LIB
21	22:14	SCO
24	6:;43	SAG
26	11:08	CAP
28	12:26	AQU
30	12:24	PIS

AUG		
1	12:54	ARI
3	15:25	TAU
5	20:44	GEM
8	4:53	CAN
10	15:27	LEO
13	3:47	VIR
15	16:53	LIB
18	5:13	SCO
20	14:56	SAG
22	20:50	CAP
24	23:06	AQU
26	23:02	PIS
28	22:30	ARI
30	23:23	TAU

SEP		
2	3:12	GEM
4	10:38	CAN
6	21:15	LEO
9	9:49	VIR
11	22:52	LIB
14	11:08	SCO
16	21:26	SAG
19	4:46	CAP
21	8:44	AQU
23	9:52	PIS
25	9:30	ARI
27	9:30	TAU
29	11:44	GEM

OCT		
1	17:39	CAN
4	3:32	LEO
6	16:02	VIR
9	5:04	LIB
11	16:59	SCO
14	2:59	SAG
16	10:45	CAP
18	16:06	AQU
20	18:59	PIS
22	20:00	ARI
24	20:23	TAU
26	21:56	GEM
29	2:29	CAN
31	11:04	LEO

NOV		
2	23:03	VIR
5	12:05	LIB
7	23:47	SCO
10	9:07	SAG
12	16:13	CAP
14	21:37	AQU
17	1:35	PIS
19	4:13	ARI
21	6:03	TAU
23	8:13	GEM
25	12:20	CAN
27	19:53	LEO
30	7:00	VIR

DEC		
2	19:57	LIB
5	7:52	SCO
7	16:56	SAG
9	23:08	CAP
12	3:26	AQU
14	6:;54	PIS
16	10:04	ARI
18	13:12	TAU
20	16:44	GEM
22	21:36	CAN
25	4:58	LEO
27	15:28	VIR
30	4:10	LIB

—1989—

JAN

1	16:35	SCO
4	2:12	SAG
6	8:15	CAP
8	11:31	AQU
10	13:32	PIS
12	15:36	ARI
14	18:37	TAU
16	22:58	GEM
19	4:58	CAN
21	13:03	LEO
23	23:33	VIR
26	12:02	LIB
29	0:50	SCO
31	11:31	SAG

FEB

2	18:31	CAP
4	21:52	AQU
6	22:53	PIS
8	23:19	ARI
11	0:46	TAU
13	4:23	GEM
15	10:41	CAN
17	19:34	LEO
20	6:35	VIR
22	19:06	LIB
25	7:58	SCO
27	19:30	SAG

MAR

2	3:59	CAP
4	8:37	AQU
6	10:00	PIS
8	9:37	ARI
10	9:26	TAU
12	11:17	GEM
14	16:28	CAN
17	1:14	LEO
19	12:40	VIR
22	1:25	LIB
24	14:11	SCO
27	1:55	SAG
29	11:26	CAP
31	17:46	AQU

APR

2	20:38	PIS
4	20:52	ARI
6	20:08	TAU
8	20:32	GEM
10	23:59	CAN
13	7:32	LEO
15	18:40	VIR
18	7:32	LIB
20	20:14	SCO
23	7:39	SAG
25	17:16	CAP
28	0:34	AQU
30	5:04	PIS

MAY

2	6:51	ARI
4	6;56	TAU
6	7:04	GEM
8	9:20	CAN
10	15:24	LEO
13	1:31	VIR
15	14:08	LIB
18	2:48	SCO
20	13:53	SAG
22	22:55	CAP
25	6:02	AQU
27	11:14	PIS
29	14:26	ARI
31	16:00	TAU

JUN

2	17:03	GEM
4	19:18	CAN
7	0:29	LEO
9	9:30	VIR
11	21:32	LIB
14	10:12	SCO
16	21:13	SAG
19	5:42	CAP
21	11:58	AQU
23	16:37	PIS
25	20:07	ARI
27	22:46	TAU
30	1:09	GEM

JUL

2	4:20	CAN
4	9:38	LEO
6	18:05	VIR
9	5:31	LIB
11	18:10	SCO
14	5:32	SAG
16	14:02	CAP
18	19:36	AQU
20	23:08	PIS
23	1:41	ARI
25	4:11	TAU
27	7:16	GEM
29	11:33	CAN
31	17:42	LEO

AUG

3	2:20	VIR
5	13:29	LIB
8	2:06	SCO
10	14:03	SAG
12	23:17	CAP
15	5:00	AQU
17	7:46	PIS
19	9:00	ARI
21	10:11	TAU
23	12:40	GEM
25	17:14	CAN
28	0:12	LEO
30	9:30	VIR

SEP

1	20:48	LIB
4	9:24	SCO
6	21:52	SAG
9	8:14	CAP
11	15:03	AQU
13	18:08	PIS
15	18:39	ARI
17	18:23	TAU
19	19:17	GEM
21	22:51	CAN
24	5:45	LEO
26	15:33	VIR
29	3:16	LIB

OCT

1	15:54	SCO
4	4:30	SAG
6	15:46	CAP
9	0:07	AQU
11	4:38	PIS
13	5:42	ARI
15	4:53	TAU
17	4:20	GEM
19	6:10	CAN
21	11:48	LEO
23	21:16	VIR
26	9:12	LIB
28	21:57	SCO
31	10:24	SAG

NOV

2	21:47	CAP
5	7:10	AQU
7	13:26	PIS
9	16:09	ARI
11	16:10	TAU
13	15:20	GEM
15	15:52	CAN
17	19:46	LEO
20	3:55	VIR
22	15:26	LIB
25	4:14	SCO
27	16:31	SAG
30	3:27	CAP

DEC

2	12:43	AQU
4	19:49	PIS
7	0:12	ARI
9	2:00	TAU
11	2:16	GEM
13	2:50	CAN
15	5:42	LEO
17	12:20	VIR
19	22:46	LIB
22	11:19	SCO
24	23:38	SAG
27	10:11	CAP
29	18:39	AQU

—1990—

JAN

1	1:11	PIS
3	5:57	ARI
5	9:05	TAU
7	11:02	GEM
9	12:53	CAN
11	16:03	LEO
13	21:58	VIR
16	7:18	LIB
18	19:17	SCO
21	7:45	SAG
23	18:28	CAP
26	2:26	AQU
28	7:52	PIS
30	11:35	ARI

FEB

1	14:28	TAU
3	17:13	GEM
5	20:28	CAN
8	0:52	LEO
10	7:14	VIR
12	16:10	LIB
15	3:35	SCO
17	16:08	SAG
20	3:31	CAP
22	11:53	AQU
24	16:50	PIS
26	19:17	ARI
28	20:44	TAU

MAR

2	22:38	GEM
5	2:03	CAN
7	7:25	LEO
9	14:48	VIR
12	0:10	LIB
14	11:26	SCO
16	23:57	SAG
19	12:02	CAP
21	21:32	AQU
24	3:09	PIS
26	5:16	ARI
28	5:27	TAU
30	5:43	GEM

APR

1	7:51	CAN
3	12:51	LEO
5	20:43	VIR
8	6:45	LIB
10	18:19	SCO
13	6:49	SAG
15	19:16	CAP
18	5:54	AQU
20	12:58	PIS
22	15:59	ARI
24	16:04	TAU
26	15:13	GEM
28	15:40	CAN
30	19:09	LEO

MAY

3	2:19	VIR
5	12:29	LIB
8	0:23	SCO
10	12:57	SAG
13	1:22	CAP
15	12:31	AQU
17	20:55	PIS
20	1:32	ARI
22	2:43	TAU
24	2:01	GEM
26	1:35	CAN
28	3:30	LEO
30	9:09	VIR

JUN

1	18:32	LIB
4	6:;22	SCO
6	19:00	SAG
9	7:13	CAP
11	18:10	AQU
14	3:01	PIS
16	8:56	ARI
18	11:44	TAU
20	12:15	GEM
22	12:10	CAN
24	13:26	LEO
26	17:43	VIR
29	1:48	LIB

JUL

1	13:02	SCO
4	1:36	SAG
6	13:40	CAP
9	0:07	AQU
11	8:30	PIS
13	14:37	ARI
15	18:30	TAU
17	20:33	GEM
19	21:45	CAN
21	23:30	LEO
24	3:18	VIR
26	10:19	LIB
28	20:40	SCO
31	9:01	SAG

AUG

2	21:09	CAP
5	7:20	AQU
7	14:55	PIS
9	20:14	ARI
11	23:56	TAU
14	2:42	GEM
16	5:13	CAN
18	8:12	LEO
20	12:34	VIR
22	19:18	LIB
25	4:57	SCO
27	16:58	SAG
30	5:24	CAP

SEP

1	15:52	AQU
3	23:06	PIS
6	3:24	ARI
8	5:56	TAU
10	8:06	GEM
12	10:54	CAN
14	14:53	LEO
16	20:19	VIR
19	3:35	LIB
21	13:07	SCO
24	0:53	SAG
26	13:37	CAP
29	0:55	AQU

OCT

1	8:43	PIS
3	12:43	ARI
5	14:07	TAU
7	14:48	GEM
9	16:30	CAN
11	20:17	LEO
14	2:21	VIR
16	10:27	LIB
18	20:25	SCO
21	8:10	SAG
23	21:04	CAP
26	9:15	AQU
28	18:23	PIS
30	23:15	ARI

NOV

2	0:32	TAU
4	0:07	GEM
6	0:08	CAN
8	2:25	LEO
10	7:49	VIR
12	16:09	LIB
15	2:40	SCO
17	14:40	SAG
20	3:32	CAP
22	16:08	AQU
25	2:33	PIS
27	9:07	ARI
29	11:38	TAU

DEC

1	11:23	GEM
3	10:28	CAN
5	11:01	LEO
7	14:40	VIR
9	22:01	LIB
12	8:29	SCO
14	20:45	SAG
17	9:36	CAP
19	22:00	AQU
22	8:49	PIS
24	16:46	ARI
26	21:10	TAU
28	22:27	GEM
30	22:03	CAN

—1991—

JAN

1	21:55	LEO
3	23:58	VIR
6	5:34	LIB
8	15:00	SCO
11	3:07	SAG
13	16:01	CAP
16	4:05	AQU
18	14:24	PIS
20	22:28	ARI
23	4:02	TAU
25	7:07	GEM
27	8:24	CAN
29	9:04	LEO
31	10:45	VIR

FEB

2	15:03	LIB
4	23:02	SCO
7	10:24	SAG
9	23:17	CAP
12	11:17	AQU
14	21:00	PIS
17	4:12	ARI
19	9:25	TAU
21	13:11	GEM
23	15:57	CAN
25	18:13	LEO
27	20:51	VIR

MAR

2	1:04	LIB
4	8:09	SCO
6	18:36	SAG
9	7:15	CAP
11	19:32	AQU
14	5:12	PIS
16	11:38	ARI
18	15:41	TAU
20	18:38	GEM
22	21:28	CAN
25	0:44	LEO
27	4:42	VIR
29	9:50	LIB
31	17:02	SCO

APR

3	3:00	SAG
5	15:20	CAP
8	4:00	AQU
10	14:18	PIS
12	20:50	ARI
15	0:06	TAU
17	1:42	GEM
19	3:18	CAN
21	6:05	LEO
23	10:30	VIR
25	16:37	LIB
28	0:35	SCO
30	10:43	SAG

MAY

2	22:55	CAP
5	11:52	AQU
7	23:05	PIS
10	6:35	ARI
12	10:08	TAU
14	11:03	GEM
16	11:15	CAN
18	12:31	LEO
20	16:01	VIR
22	22:09	LIB
25	6:42	SCO
27	17:22	SAG
30	5:41	CAP

JUN

1	18:42	AQU
4	6:37	PIS
6	15:26	ARI
8	20:14	TAU
10	21:37	GEM
12	21:17	CAN
14	21:11	LEO
16	23:04	VIR
19	4:02	LIB
21	12:19	SCO
23	23:17	SAG
26	11:50	CAP
29	0:48	AQU

JUL

1	12:52	PIS
3	22:34	ARI
6	4:53	TAU
8	7:43	GEM
10	8:04	CAN
12	7:36	LEO
14	8:13	VIR
16	11:35	LIB
18	18:42	SCO
21	5:17	SAG
23	17:56	CAP
26	6:50	AQU
28	18:36	PIS
31	4:21	ARI

AUG

2	11:33	TAU
4	15:55	GEM
6	17:48	CAN
8	18:10	LEO
10	18:36	VIR
12	20:53	LIB
15	2:35	SCO
17	12:12	SAG
20	0:35	CAP
22	13:28	AQU
25	0:52	PIS
27	10:02	ARI
29	17:01	TAU
31	22:03	GEM

SEP

3	1:20	CAN
5	3:14	LEO
7	4:36	VIR
9	6:52	LIB
11	11:43	SCO
13	20:15	SAG
16	8:05	CAP
18	20:59	AQU
21	8:21	PIS
23	16:57	ARI
25	23:00	TAU
28	3:26	GEM
30	6:59	CAN

OCT

2	9:59	LEO
4	12:46	VIR
6	16:01	LIB
8	21:01	SCO
11	4:59	SAG
13	16:11	CAP
16	5:05	AQU
18	16:54	PIS
21	1:34	ARI
23	6:56	TAU
25	10:10	GEM
27	12:38	CAN
29	15:21	LEO
31	18:48	VIR

NOV

2	23:13	LIB
5	5:10	SCO
7	13:22	SAG
10	0:17	CAP
12	13:07	AQU
15	1:34	PIS
17	11:08	ARI
19	16:50	TAU
21	19:23	GEM
23	20:26	CAN
25	21:38	LEO
28	0:13	VIR
30	4:48	LIB

DEC

2	11:34	SCO
4	20:33	SAG
7	7:42	CAP
9	20:28	AQU
12	9:20	PIS
14	20:07	ARI
17	3:11	TAU
19	6:22	GEM
21	6:55	CAN
23	6:39	LEO
25	7:25	VIR
27	10:38	LIB
29	17:04	SCO

—1992—

JAN			FEB			MAR			APR		
1	2:31	SAG	2	9:10	AQU	3	4:12	PIS	1	22:05	ARI
3	14:10	CAP	4	21:52	PIS	5	15:08	ARI	4	6:19	TAU
6	3:00	AQU	7	9:16	ARI	8	0:06	TAU	6	12:34	GEM
8	15:53	PIS	9	18:37	TAU	10	7:04	GEM	8	17:19	CAN
11	3:23	ARI	12	1:09	GEM	12	11:51	CAN	10	20:47	LEO
13	12:01	TAU	14	4:32	CAN	14	14:21	LEO	12	23:10	VIR
15	16:56	GEM	16	5:16	LEO	16	15:14	VIR	15	1:11	LIB
17	18:27	CAN	18	4:48	VIR	18	15:56	LIB	17	4:11	SCO
19	17:58	LEO	20	5:06	LIB	20	18:21	SCO	19	9:41	SAG
21	17:23	VIR	22	8:12	SCO	23	0:14	SAG	21	18:41	CAP
23	18:43	LIB	24	15:27	SAG	25	10:09	CAP	24	6:39	AQU
25	23:33	SCO	27	2:34	CAP	27	22:45	AQU	26	19:21	PIS
28	8:21	SAG	29	15:35	AQU	30	11:24	PIS	29	6:14	ARI
30	20:08	CAP									

MAY			JUN			JUL			AUG		
1	14:10	TAU	2	6:58	CAN	1	17:16	LEO	2	3:18	LIB
3	19:29	GEM	4	8:36	LEO	3	17:38	VIR	4	6:17	SCO
5	23:10	CAN	6	10:29	VIR	5	19:28	LIB	6	12:58	SAG
8	2:08	LEO	8	13:34	LIB	7	23:54	SCO	8	23:01	CAP
10	4:57	VIR	10	18:28	SCO	10	7:18	SAG	11	11:07	AQU
12	8:06	LIB	13	1:30	SAG	12	17:16	CAP	13	23:52	PIS
14	12:16	SCO	15	10:51	CAP	15	5:04	AQU	16	12:12	ARI
16	18:23	SAG	17	22:20	AQU	17	17:45	PIS	18	23:11	TAU
19	3:14	CAP	20	11:01	PIS	20	6:08	ARI	21	7:37	GEM
21	14:44	AQU	22	23:04	ARI	22	16:37	TAU	23	12:37	CAN
24	3:26	PIS	25	8:29	TAU	24	23:45	GEM	25	14:16	LEO
26	14:53	ARI	27	14:15	GEM	27	3:09	CAN	27	13:47	VIR
28	23:17	TAU	29	16:43	CAN	29	3:40	LEO	29	13:12	LIB
31	4:20	GEM				31	3:02	VIR	31	14:39	SCO

SEP			OCT			NOV			DEC		
2	19:51	SAG	2	12:30	CAP	1	7:44	AQU	1	4:24	PIS
5	5:07	CAP	4	23:54	AQU	3	20:14	PIS	3	16:50	ARI
7	17:09	AQU	7	12:39	PIS	6	8:20	ARI	6	3:17	TAU
10	5:57	PIS	10	0:37	ARI	8	18:20	TAU	8	10:38	GEM
12	18:03	ARI	12	10:49	TAU	11	1:50	GEM	10	15:06	CAN
15	4:48	TAU	14	19:09	GEM	13	7:20	CAN	12	17:48	LEO
17	13:41	GEM	17	1:37	CAN	15	11:24	LEO	14	19:57	VIR
19	20:00	CAN	19	6:02	LEO	17	14:29	VIR	16	22:34	LIB
21	23:20	LEO	21	8:28	VIR	19	17:04	LIB	19	2:21	SCO
24	0:09	VIR	23	9:40	LIB	21	19:53	SCO	21	7:43	SAG
25	23:56	LIB	25	11:05	SCO	24	0:02	SAG	23	15:05	CAP
28	0:45	SCO	27	14:30	SAG	26	6:39	CAP	26	0:44	AQU
30	4:34	SAG	29	21:19	CA	28	16:20	AQU	28	12:29	PIS
									31	1:08	ARI

—1993—

JAN

2	12:31	TAU
4	20:43	GEM
7	1:11	CAN
9	2:50	LEO
11	3:21	VIR
13	4:31	LIB
15	7:43	SCO
17	13:31	SAG
19	21:47	CAP
22	8:01	AQU
24	19:48	PIS
27	8:29	ARI
29	20:38	TAU

FEB

1	6:15	GEM
3	11:57	CAN
5	13:52	LEO
7	13:30	VIR
9	12:59	LIB
11	14:24	SCO
13	19:09	SAG
16	3:21	CAP
18	14:06	AQU
21	2:13	PIS
23	14:51	ARI
26	3:12	TAU
28	13:53	GEM

MAR

2	21:17	CAN
5	0:41	LEO
7	0:53	VIR
8	23:47	LIB
10	23:41	SCO
13	2:34	SAG
15	9:29	CAP
17	19:53	AQU
20	8:12	PIS
22	20:52	ARI
25	9:00	TAU
27	19:49	GEM
30	4:15	CAN

APR

1	9:22	LEO
3	11:11	VIR
5	10:55	LIB
7	10:33	SCO
9	12:11	SAG
11	17:25	CAP
14	2:37	AQU
16	14:33	PIS
19	3:15	ARI
21	15:09	TAU
24	1:28	GEM
26	9:46	CAN
28	15:40	LEO
30	19:01	VIR

MAY

2	20:21	LIB
4	20:58	SCO
6	22:35	SAG
9	2:52	CAP
11	10:45	AQU
13	21:51	PIS
16	10:25	ARI
18	22:17	TAU
21	8:08	GEM
23	15:39	CAN
25	21:04	LEO
28	0:47	VIR
30	3:19	LIB

JUN

1	5:23	SCO
3	8:02	SAG
5	12:27	CAP
7	19:40	AQU
10	5:58	PIS
12	18:15	ARI
15	6:20	TAU
17	16:13	GEM
19	23:06	CAN
22	3:27	LEO
24	6:19	VIR
26	8:46	LIB
28	11:38	SCO
30	15:29	SAG

JUL

2	20:49	CAP
5	4:15	AQU
7	14:11	PIS
10	2:12	ARI
12	14:38	TAU
15	1:08	GEM
17	8:09	CAN
19	11:48	LEO
21	13:25	VIR
23	14:40	LIB
25	17:01	SCO
27	21:14	SAG
30	3:28	CAP

AUG

1	11:37	AQU
3	21:45	PIS
6	9:40	ARI
8	22:23	TAU
11	9:48	GEM
13	17:47	CAN
15	21:44	LEO
17	22:42	VIR
19	22:36	LIB
21	23:28	SCO
24	2:46	SAG
26	8:59	CAP
28	17:43	AQU
31	4:19	PIS

SEP

2	16:22	ARI
5	5:10	TAU
7	17:17	GEM
10	2:38	CAN
12	7:52	LEO
14	9:21	VIR
16	8:45	LIB
18	8:16	SCO
20	9:54	SAG
22	14:55	CAP
24	23:20	AQU
27	10:14	PIS
29	22:30	ARI

OCT

2	11:14	TAU
4	23:28	GEM
7	9:43	CAN
9	16:35	LEO
11	19:37	VIR
13	19:48	LIB
15	19:02	SCO
17	19:24	SAG
19	22:43	CAP
22	5:50	AQU
24	16:18	PIS
27	4:40	ARI
29	17:21	TAU

NOV

1	5:14	GEM
3	15:26	CAN
5	23:07	LEO
8	3:48	VIR
10	5:43	LIB
12	6:01	SCO
14	6:21	SAG
16	8:35	CAP
18	14:09	AQU
20	23:28	PIS
23	11:31	ARI
26	0:15	TAU
28	11:49	GEM
30	21:18	CAN

DEC

3	4:34	LEO
5	9:44	VIR
7	13:04	LIB
9	15:05	SCO
11	16:40	SAG
13	19:07	CAP
15	23:52	AQU
18	8:00	PIS
20	19:20	ARI
23	8:06	TAU
25	19:47	GEM
28	4:47	CAN
30	11:00	LEO

—1994—

JAN		
1	15:16	VIR
3	18:32	LIB
5	21:30	SCO
8	0:35	SAG
10	4:17	CAP
12	9:26	AQU
14	17:05	PIS
17	3:43	ARI
19	16:23	TAU
22	4:35	GEM
24	13:56	CAN
26	19:39	LEO
28	22:40	VIR
31	0:35	LIB

FEB		
2	2:50	SCO
4	6:15	SAG
6	11:03	CAP
8	17:17	AQU
11	1:24	PIS
13	11:50	ARI
16	0:21	TAU
18	13:06	GEM
20	23:28	CAN
23	5:48	LEO
25	8:28	VIR
27	9:07	LIB

MAR		
1	9:44	SCO
3	11:55	SAG
5	16:25	CAP
7	23:16	AQU
10	8:10	PIS
12	19:00	ARI
15	7:28	TAU
17	20:30	GEM
20	7:55	CAN
22	15:40	LEO
24	19:15	VIR
26	19:47	LIB
28	19:16	SCO
30	19:42	SAG

APR		
1	22:39	CAP
4	4:46	AQU
6	13:52	PIS
9	1:10	ARI
11	13:49	TAU
14	2:49	GEM
16	14:42	CAN
18	23:46	LEO
21	4:59	VIR
23	6:41	LIB
25	6:19	SCO
27	5:49	SAG
29	7:06	CAP

MAY		
1	11:35	AQU
3	19:48	PIS
6	7:02	ARI
8	19:51	TAU
11	8:44	GEM
13	20:28	CAN
16	5:59	LEO
18	12:32	VIR
20	15:55	LIB
22	16:52	SCO
24	16:44	SAG
26	17:18	CAP
28	20:20	AQU
31	3:04	PIS

JUN		
2	13:32	ARI
5	2:15	TAU
7	15:04	GEM
10	2:23	CAN
12	11:30	LEO
14	18:17	VIR
16	22:49	LIB
19	1:21	SCO
21	2:33	SAG
23	3:38	CAP
25	6:11	AQU
27	11:45	PIS
29	21:08	ARI

JUL		
2	9:24	TAU
4	22:13	GEM
7	9:18	CAN
9	17:44	LEO
11	23:49	VIR
14	4:16	LIB
16	7:36	SCO
18	10:10	SAG
20	12:31	CAP
22	15:39	AQU
24	20:57	PIS
27	5:32	ARI
29	17:14	TAU

AUG		
1	6:06	GEM
3	17:23	CAN
6	1:32	LEO
8	6:43	VIR
10	10:08	LIB
12	12:57	SCO
14	15:54	SAG
16	19:19	CAP
18	23:35	AQU
21	5:28	PIS
23	13:56	ARI
26	1:14	TAU
28	14:08	GEM
31	2:01	CAN

SEP		
2	10:38	LEO
4	15:34	VIR
6	17:58	LIB
8	19:27	SCO
10	21:26	SAG
13	0:45	CAP
15	5:43	AQU
17	12:32	PIS
19	21:31	ARI
22	8:48	TAU
24	21:42	GEM
27	10:13	CAN
29	19:56	LEO

OCT		
2	1:40	VIR
4	3:57	LIB
6	4:23	SCO
8	4:48	SAG
10	6:45	CAP
12	11:10	AQU
14	18:19	PIS
17	3:57	ARI
19	15:35	TAU
22	4:29	GEM
24	17:16	CAN
27	4:06	LEO
29	11:22	VIR
31	14:47	LIB

NOV		
2	15:20	SCO
4	14:47	SAG
6	15:03	CAP
8	17:49	AQU
11	0:05	PIS
13	9:45	ARI
15	21:45	TAU
18	10:42	GEM
20	23:22	CAN
23	10:34	LEO
25	19:10	VIR
28	0:23	LIB
30	2:22	SCO

DEC		
2	2:14	SAG
4	1:43	CAP
6	2:53	AQU
8	7:25	PIS
10	16:04	ARI
13	3:57	TAU
15	17:01	GEM
18	5:26	CAN
20	16:14	LEO
23	1:02	VIR
25	7:28	LIB
27	11:18	SCO
29	12:46	SAG
31	12:58	CAP

—1995—

JAN		
2	13:40	AQU
4	16:50	PIS
6	23:57	ARI
9	10:59	TAU
11	23:58	GEM
14	12:21	CAN
16	22:37	LEO
19	6:40	VIR
21	12:55	LIB
23	17:33	SCO
25	20:38	SAG
27	22:27	CAP
30	0:04	AQU

FEB		
1	3:06	PIS
3	9:13	ARI
5	19:10	TAU
8	7:45	GEM
10	20:18	CAN
13	6:32	LEO
15	13:53	VIR
17	19:01	LIB
19	22:56	SCO
22	2:14	SAG
24	5:12	CAP
26	8:15	AQU
28	12:17	PIS

MAR		
2	18:31	ARI
5	3:51	TAU
7	15:56	GEM
10	4:41	CAN
12	15:29	LEO
14	22:55	VIR
17	3:19	LIB
19	5:53	SCO
21	7:58	SAG
23	10:32	CAP
25	14:11	AQU
27	19:19	PIS
30	2:27	ARI

APR		
1	12:00	TAU
3	23:50	GEM
6	12:41	CAN
9	0:16	LEO
11	8:40	VIR
13	13:21	LIB
15	15:14	SCO
17	15:52	SAG
19	16:55	CAP
21	19:39	AQU
24	0:52	PIS
26	8:42	ARI
28	18:54	TAU

MAY		
1	6:54	GEM
3	19:46	CAN
6	7:56	LEO
8	17:34	VIR
10	23:31	LIB
13	1:54	SCO
15	1:59	SAG
17	1:37	CAP
19	2:40	AQU
21	6:41	PIS
23	14:14	ARI
26	0:47	TAU
28	13:08	GEM
31	2:00	CAN

JUN		
2	14:18	LEO
5	0:47	VIR
7	8:14	LIB
9	12:04	SCO
11	12:51	SAG
13	12:06	CAP
15	11:53	AQU
17	14:14	PIS
19	20:30	ARI
22	6:36	TAU
24	19:03	GEM
27	7:57	CAN
29	20:03	LEO

JUL		
2	6:36	VIR
4	14:56	LIB
6	20:20	SCO
8	22:38	SAG
10	22:44	CAP
12	22:22	AQU
14	23:38	PIS
17	4:24	ARI
19	13:21	TAU
22	1:24	GEM
24	14:17	CAN
27	2:08	LEO
29	12:13	VIR
31	20:24	LIB

AUG		
3	2:30	SCO
5	6:15	SAG
7	7:53	CAP
9	8:29	AQU
11	9:47	PIS
13	13:42	ARI
15	21:26	TAU
18	8:41	GEM
20	21:25	CAN
23	9:14	LEO
25	18:51	VIR
28	2:16	LIB
30	7:52	SCO

SEP		
1	11:58	SAG
3	14:46	CAP
5	16:48	AQU
7	19:09	PIS
9	23:15	ARI
12	6:22	TAU
14	16:49	GEM
17	5:17	CAN
19	17:20	LEO
22	3:02	VIR
24	9:51	LIB
26	14:21	SCO
28	17:31	SAG
30	20:11	CAP

OCT		
2	23:00	AQU
5	2:36	PIS
7	7:43	ARI
9	15:06	TAU
12	1:11	GEM
14	13:21	CAN
17	1:47	LEO
19	12:12	VIR
21	19:16	LIB
23	23:07	SCO
26	0:57	SAG
28	2:16	CAP
30	4:24	AQU

NOV		
1	8:18	PIS
3	14:22	ARI
5	22:36	TAU
8	8:56	GEM
10	20:58	CAN
13	9:38	LEO
15	21:03	VIR
18	5:19	LIB
20	9:41	SCO
22	10:57	SAG
24	10:49	CAP
26	11:16	AQU
28	14:00	PIS
30	19:52	ARI

DEC		
3	4:41	TAU
5	15:36	GEM
8	3:45	CAN
10	16:25	LEO
13	4:27	VIR
15	14:10	LIB
17	20:08	SCO
19	22:14	SAG
21	21:47	CAP
23	20:53	AQU
25	21:46	PIS
28	2:07	ARI
30	10:22	TAU

—1996—

JAN			FEB			MAR			APR		
1	21:30	GEM	3	4:47	LEO	1	11:48	LEO	2	16:27	LIB
4	9:57	CAN	5	16:23	VIR	3	23:14	VIR	4	22:58	SCO
6	22:31	LEO	8	2:31	LIB	6	8:41	LIB	7	3:22	SAG
9	10:30	VIR	10	10:36	SCO	8	16:06	SCO	9	6:31	CAP
11	20:56	LIB	12	15:59	SAG	10	21:33	SAG	11	9:10	AQU
14	4:31	SCO	14	18:30	CAP	13	1:09	CAP	13	12:01	PIS
16	8:26	SAG	16	19:01	AQU	15	3:16	AQU	15	15:44	ARI
18	9:08	CAP	18	19:10	PIS	17	4:51	PIS	17	21:06	TAU
20	8:16	AQU	20	20:59	ARI	19	7:16	ARI	20	4:55	GEM
22	8:03	PIS	23	2:09	TAU	21	12:00	TAU	22	15:26	CAN
24	10:38	ARI	25	11:15	GEM	23	20:00	GEM	25	3:45	LEO
26	17:17	TAU	27	23:11	CAN	26	7:07	CAN	27	15:50	VIR
29	3:43	GEM				28	19:38	LEO	30	1:28	LIB
31	16:12	CAN				31	7:16	VIR			

MAY			JUN			JUL			AUG		
2	7:43	SCO	2	21:30	CAP	2	7:06	AQU	2	18:06	ARI
4	11:06	SAG	4	21:46	AQU	4	7:08	PIS	4	22:34	TAU
6	12:55	CAP	6	23:20	PIS	6	9:43	ARI	7	6:50	GEM
8	14:40	AQU	9	3:24	ARI	8	15:44	TAU	9	17:58	CAN
10	17:30	PIS	11	10:12	TAU	11	0:53	GEM	12	6:30	LEO
12	22:01	ARI	13	19:17	GEM	13	12:09	CAN	14	19:08	VIR
15	4:26	TAU	16	6:09	CAN	16	0:32	LEO	17	6:56	LIB
17	12:49	GEM	18	18:23	LEO	18	13:17	VIR	19	16:51	SCO
19	23:17	CAN	21	7:08	VIR	21	1:15	LIB	21	23:49	SAG
22	11:29	LEO	23	18:38	LIB	23	10:44	SCO	24	3:23	CAP
24	23:59	VIR	26	2:54	SCO	25	16:25	SAG	26	4:11	AQU
27	10:34	LIB	28	7:02	SAG	27	18:18	CAP	28	3:50	PIS
29	17:31	SCO	30	7:48	CAP	29	17:48	AQU	30	4:16	ARI
31	20:44	SAG				31	17:02	PIS			

SEP			OCT			NOV			DEC		
1	7:21	TAU	3	8:15	CAN	2	4:17	LEO	2	1:12	VIR
3	14:09	GEM	5	20:13	LEO	4	16:58	VIR	4	13:24	LIB
6	0:30	CAN	8	8:50	VIR	7	4:30	LIB	6	22:40	SCO
8	12:55	LEO	10	20:01	LIB	9	13:03	SCO	9	3:59	SAG
11	1:29	VIR	13	4:47	SCO	11	18:27	SAG	11	6:16	CAP
13	12:52	LIB	15	11:08	SAG	13	21:45	CAP	13	7:15	AQU
15	22:21	SCO	17	15:38	CAP	16	0:15	AQU	15	8:45	PIS
18	5:32	SAG	19	18:52	AQU	18	3:01	PIS	17	11:56	ARI
20	10:13	CAP	21	21:23	PIS	20	6:35	ARI	19	17:11	TAU
22	12:40	AQU	23	23:51	ARI	22	11:13	TAU	22	0:18	GEM
24	13:44	PIS	26	3:12	TAU	24	17:21	GEM	24	9:15	CAN
26	14:47	ARI	28	8:36	GEM	27	1:38	CAN	26	20:10	LEO
28	17:25	TAU	30	16:57	CAN	29	12:31	LEO	29	8:46	VIR
30	23:02	GEM							31	21:33	LIB

—1997—

JAN
3	8:03	SCO
5	14:28	SAG
7	16:56	CAP
9	17:01	AQU
11	16:52	PIS
13	18:23	ARI
15	22:41	TAU
18	5:54	GEM
20	15:30	CAN
23	2:51	LEO
25	15:27	VIR
28	4:22	LIB
30	15:49	SCO

FEB
1	23:52	SAG
4	3:45	CAP
6	4:22	AQU
8	3:35	PIS
10	3:30	ARI
12	5:57	TAU
14	11:54	GEM
16	21:14	CAN
19	8:53	LEO
21	21:39	VIR
24	10:24	LIB
26	21:58	SCO

MAR
1	7:02	SAG
3	12:39	CAP
5	14:55	AQU
7	14:58	PIS
9	14:34	ARI
11	15:38	TAU
13	19:49	GEM
16	3:52	CAN
18	15:09	LEO
21	4:00	VIR
23	16:36	LIB
26	3:43	SCO
28	12:41	SAG
30	19:08	CAP

APR
1	23:00	AQU
4	0:43	PIS
6	1:20	ARI
8	2:21	TAU
10	5:29	GEM
12	12:04	CAN
14	22:23	LEO
17	11:01	VIR
19	23:37	LIB
22	10:20	SCO
24	18:33	SAG
27	0:33	CAP
29	4:51	AQU

MAY
1	7:51	PIS
3	10:00	ARI
5	12:05	TAU
7	15:22	GEM
9	21:14	CAN
12	6:34	LEO
14	18:44	VIR
17	7:28	LIB
19	18:13	SCO
22	1:52	SAG
24	6:52	CAP
26	10:21	AQU
28	13:19	PIS
30	16:19	ARI

JUN
1	19:40	TAU
3	23:56	GEM
6	6:03	CAN
8	14:59	LEO
11	2:44	VIR
13	15:36	LIB
16	2:52	SCO
18	10:40	SAG
20	15:03	CAP
22	17:21	AQU
24	19:10	PIS
26	21:39	ARI
29	1:24	TAU

JUL
1	6:36	GEM
3	13:34	CAN
5	22:46	LEO
8	10:23	VIR
10	23:22	LIB
13	11:21	SCO
15	20:03	SAG
18	0:46	CAP
20	2:30	AQU
22	3:01	PIS
24	4:04	ARI
26	6:54	TAU
28	12:05	GEM
30	19:39	CAN

AUG
2	5:28	LEO
4	17:16	VIR
7	6:18	LIB
9	18:51	SCO
12	4:46	SAG
14	10:43	CAP
16	12:59	AQU
18	13:02	PIS
20	12:46	ARI
22	13:58	TAU
24	17:57	GEM
27	1:12	CAN
29	11:20	LEO
31	23:28	VIR

SEP
3	12:31	LIB
6	1:11	SCO
8	11:55	SAG
10	19:24	CAP
12	23:11	AQU
15	0:00	PIS
16	23:26	ARI
18	23:22	TAU
21	1:40	GEM
23	7:34	CAN
25	17:13	LEO
28	5:28	VIR
30	18:33	LIB

OCT
3	6:58	SCO
5	17:44	SAG
8	2:05	CAP
10	7:30	AQU
12	10:00	PIS
14	10:26	ARI
16	10:17	TAU
18	11:27	GEM
20	15:46	CAN
23	0:11	LEO
25	12:00	VIR
28	1:06	LIB
30	13:16	SCO

NOV
1	23:28	SAG
4	7:32	CAP
6	13:34	AQU
8	17:36	PIS
10	19:45	ARI
12	20:46	TAU
14	22:06	GEM
17	1:33	CAN
19	8:39	LEO
21	19:34	VIR
24	8:30	LIB
26	20:44	SCO
29	6:29	SAG

DEC
1	13:39	CAP
3	18:59	AQU
5	23:08	PIS
8	2:25	ARI
10	5:01	TAU
12	7:36	GEM
14	11:26	CAN
16	17:59	LEO
19	4:01	VIR
21	16:36	LIB
24	5:08	SCO
26	15:08	SAG
28	21:49	CAP
31	1:59	AQU

—1998—

JAN

2	4:57	PIS
4	7:44	ARI
6	10:53	TAU
8	14:43	GEM
10	19:44	CAN
13	2:46	LEO
15	12:32	VIR
18	0:45	LIB
20	13:35	SCO
23	0:26	SAG
25	7:40	CAP
27	11:28	AQU
29	13:09	PIS
31	14:22	ARI

FEB

2	16:26	TAU
4	20:10	GEM
7	1:58	CAN
9	9:58	LEO
11	20:11	VIR
14	8:18	LIB
16	21:14	SCO
19	8:57	SAG
21	17:31	CAP
23	22:11	AQU
25	23:43	PIS
27	23:43	ARI

MAR

2	0:01	TAU
4	2:16	GEM
6	7:28	CAN
8	15:47	LEO
11	2:36	VIR
13	14:59	LIB
16	3:52	SCO
18	15:57	SAG
21	1:44	CAP
23	8:02	AQU
25	10:44	PIS
27	10:50	ARI
29	10:07	TAU
31	10:39	GEM

APR

2	14:11	CAN
4	21:37	LEO
7	8:26	VIR
9	21:05	LIB
12	9:57	SCO
14	21:53	SAG
17	8:06	CAP
19	15:42	AQU
21	20:07	PIS
23	21:31	ARI
25	21:10	TAU
27	20:56	GEM
29	22:58	CAN

MAY

2	4:50	LEO
4	14:48	VIR
7	3:20	LIB
9	16:11	SCO
12	3:49	SAG
14	13:40	CAP
16	21:31	AQU
19	3:04	PIS
21	6:07	ARI
23	7:07	TAU
25	7:26	GEM
27	8:59	CAN
29	13:39	LEO
31	22:22	VIR

JUN

3	10:18	LIB
5	23:07	SCO
8	10:35	SAG
10	19:51	CAP
13	3:04	AQU
15	8:32	PIS
17	12:24	ARI
19	14:48	TAU
21	16:27	GEM
23	18:40	CAN
25	23:05	LEO
28	6:55	VIR
30	18:06	LIB

JUL

3	6:46	SCO
5	18:25	SAG
8	3:28	CAP
10	9:53	AQU
12	14:23	PIS
14	17:46	ARI
16	20:34	TAU
18	23:19	GEM
21	2:44	CAN
23	7:50	LEO
25	15:35	VIR
28	2:15	LIB
30	14:45	SCO

AUG

2	2:49	SAG
4	12:19	CAP
6	18:32	AQU
8	22:05	PIS
11	0:11	ARI
13	2:05	TAU
15	4:47	GEM
17	8:56	CAN
19	15:02	LEO
21	23:22	VIR
24	10:03	LIB
26	22:26	SCO
29	10:56	SAG
31	21:24	CAP

SEP

3	4:22	AQU
5	7:49	PIS
7	8:53	ARI
9	9:17	TAU
11	10:41	GEM
13	14:21	CAN
15	20:49	LEO
18	5:53	VIR
20	16:58	LIB
23	5:23	SCO
25	18:06	SAG
28	5:31	CAP
30	13:54	AQU

OCT

2	18:24	PIS
4	19:33	ARI
6	18:58	TAU
8	18:45	GEM
10	20:49	CAN
13	2:26	LEO
15	11:33	VIR
17	23:03	LIB
20	11:37	SCO
23	0:17	SAG
25	12:06	CAP
27	21:45	AQU
30	3:59	PIS

NOV

1	6:28	ARI
3	6:13	TAU
5	5:12	GEM
7	5:40	CAN
9	9:34	LEO
11	17:38	VIR
14	4:59	LIB
16	17:42	SCO
19	6:14	SAG
21	17:46	CAP
24	3:44	AQU
26	11:15	PIS
28	15:35	ARI
30	16:54	TAU

DEC

2	16:31	GEM
4	16:29	CAN
6	18:56	LEO
9	1:22	VIR
11	11:44	LIB
14	0:17	SCO
16	12:48	SAG
18	23:56	CAP
21	9:18	AQU
23	16:46	PIS
25	22:05	ARI
28	1:06	TAU
30	2:23	GEM

—1999—

JAN			FEB			MAR			APR		
1	3:16	CAN	1	20:38	VIR	1	5:06	VIR	2	7:50	SCO
3	5:32	LEO	4	4:57	LIB	3	13:35	LIB	4	20:08	SAG
5	10:50	VIR	6	16:07	SCO	6	0:23	SCO	7	8:40	CAP
7	19:54	LIB	9	4:39	SAG	8	12:47	SAG	9	19:25	AQU
10	7:50	SCO	11	16:11	CAP	11	0:55	CAP	12	2:36	PIS
12	20:24	SAG	14	0:58	AQU	13	10:33	AQU	14	5:47	ARI
15	7:30	CAP	16	6:41	PIS	15	16:31	PIS	16	6:08	TAU
17	16:12	AQU	18	10:07	ARI	17	19:14	ARI	18	5:40	GEM
19	22:41	PIS	20	12:30	TAU	19	20:10	TAU	20	6:28	CAN
22	3:26	ARI	22	14:55	GEM	21	21:06	GEM	22	10:07	LEO
24	6:53	TAU	24	18:10	CAN	23	23:34	CAN	24	17:05	VIR
26	9:30	GEM	26	22:45	LEO	26	4:23	LEO	27	2:47	LIB
28	11:58	CAN				28	11:35	VIR	29	14:13	SCO
30	15:17	LEO				30	20:50	LIB			

MAY			JUN			JUL			AUG		
2	2:37	SAG	3	8:38	AQU	2	23:35	PIS	1	11:48	ARI
4	15:13	CAP	5	18:02	PIS	5	6:22	ARI	3	16:10	TAU
7	2:41	AQU	8	0:09	ARI	7	10:23	TAU	5	18:58	GEM
9	11:17	PIS	10	2:45	TAU	9	12:01	GEM	7	20:54	CAN
11	15:54	ARI	12	2:49	GEM	11	12:28	CAN	9	22:57	LEO
13	16:57	TAU	14	2:15	CAN	13	13:27	LEO	12	2:23	VIR
15	16:08	GEM	16	3:08	LEO	15	16:40	VIR	14	8:25	LIB
17	15:40	CAN	18	7:13	VIR	17	23:20	LIB	16	17:41	SCO
19	17:38	LEO	20	15:11	LIB	20	9:31	SCO	19	5:33	SAG
21	23:16	VIR	23	2:19	SCO	22	21:49	SAG	21	18:00	CAP
24	8:30	LIB	25	14:52	SAG	25	10:09	CAP	24	4:50	AQU
26	20:06	SCO	28	3:13	CAP	27	20:55	AQU	26	12:51	PIS
29	8:38	SAG	30	14:20	AQU	30	5:28	PIS	28	18:10	ARI
31	21:07	CAP							30	21:42	TAU

SEP			OCT			NOV			DEC		
2	0:26	GEM	1	8:32	CAN	1	23:08	VIR	1	12:30	LIB
4	3:11	CAN	3	12:14	LEO	4	6:58	LIB	3	22:36	SCO
6	6:30	LEO	5	17:41	VIR	6	16:47	SCO	6	10:28	SAG
8	10:58	VIR	8	0:53	LIB	9	4:16	SAG	8	23:15	CAP
10	17:17	LIB	10	10:02	SCO	11	17:01	CAP	11	12:00	AQU
13	2:09	SCO	12	21:20	SAG	14	5:47	AQU	13	23:19	PIS
15	13:36	SAG	15	10:05	CAP	16	16:22	PIS	16	7:31	ARI
18	2:15	CAP	17	22:18	AQU	18	22:58	ARI	18	11:46	TAU
20	13:39	AQU	20	7:34	PIS	21	1:27	TAU	20	12:40	GEM
22	21:52	PIS	22	12:42	ARI	23	1:15	GEM	22	11:53	CAN
25	2:35	ARI	24	14:26	TAU	25	0:30	CAN	24	11:33	LEO
27	4:52	TAU	26	14:34	GEM	27	1:20	LEO	26	13:35	VIR
29	6:22	GEM	28	15:10	CAN	29	5:12	VIR	28	19:15	LIB
			30	17:48	LEO				31	4:37	SCO

—2000—

JAN			FEB			MAR			APR		
2	16:33	SAG	1	12:11	CAP	2	8:15	AQU	1	3:13	PIS
5	5:25	CAP	4	0:32	AQU	4	18:31	PIS	3	10:23	ARI
7	17:54	AQU	6	11:03	PIS	7	1:55	ARI	5	14:30	TAU
10	5:00	PIS	8	19:18	ARI	9	7:02	TAU	7	16:59	GEM
12	13:49	ARI	11	1:22	TAU	11	10:47	GEM	9	19:17	CAN
14	19:39	TAU	13	5:24	GEM	13	13:52	CAN	11	22:17	LEO
16	22:26	GEM	15	7:46	CAN	15	16:44	LEO	14	2:20	VIR
18	23:02	CAN	17	9:12	LEO	17	19:49	VIR	16	7:37	LIB
20	22:59	LEO	19	10:54	VIR	19	23:58	LIB	18	14:36	SCO
23	0:08	VIR	21	14:22	LIB	22	6:19	SCO	20	23:59	SAG
25	4:10	LIB	23	20:59	SCO	24	15:44	SAG	23	11:48	CAP
27	12:02	SCO	26	7:11	SAG	27	3:52	CAP	26	0:43	AQU
29	23:19	SAG	28	19:46	CAP	29	16:35	AQU	28	12:07	PIS
									30	19:56	ARI

MAY			JUN			JUL			AUG		
2	23:55	TAU	1	11:35	GEM	2	21:39	LEO	1	8:28	VIR
5	1:24	GEM	3	11:31	CAN	4	22:20	VIR	3	10:32	LIB
7	2:15	CAN	5	11:47	LEO	7	1:48	LIB	5	16:05	SCO
9	4:02	LEO	7	13:58	VIR	9	8:49	SCO	8	1:31	SAG
11	7:42	VIR	9	19:00	LIB	11	19:07	SAG	10	13:45	CAP
13	13:28	LIB	12	2:56	SCO	14	7:29	CAP	13	2:44	AQU
15	21:17	SCO	14	13:19	SAG	16	20:28	AQU	15	14:42	PIS
18	7:10	SAG	17	1:28	CAP	19	8:45	PIS	18	0:45	ARI
20	19:02	CAP	19	14:27	AQU	21	19:10	ARI	20	8:32	TAU
23	8:01	AQU	22	2:53	PIS	24	2:45	TAU	22	13:56	GEM
25	20:08	PIS	24	12:56	ARI	26	7:02	GEM	24	17:01	CAN
28	5:09	ARI	26	19:20	TAU	28	8:31	CAN	26	18:18	LEO
30	10:03	TAU	28	22:00	GEM	30	8:25	LEO	28	18:56	VIR
			30	22:10	CAN				30	20:34	LIB

SEP			OCT			NOV			DEC		
2	0:56	SCO	1	17:51	SAG	3	1:42	AQU	2	22:24	PIS
4	9:09	SAG	4	4:43	CAP	5	14:14	PIS	5	9:18	ARI
6	20:48	CAP	6	17:34	AQU	8	0:03	ARI	7	16:28	TAU
9	9:45	AQU	9	5:37	PIS	10	6:13	TAU	9	19:51	GEM
11	21:35	PIS	11	14:52	ARI	12	9:28	GEM	11	20:50	CAN
14	7:01	ARI	13	21:07	TAU	14	11:22	CAN	13	21:10	LEO
16	14:06	TAU	16	1:20	GEM	16	13:20	LEO	15	22:31	VIR
18	19:23	GEM	18	4:38	CAN	18	16:16	VIR	18	2:02	LIB
20	23:17	CAN	20	7:43	LEO	20	20:36	LIB	20	8:13	SCO
23	2:01	LEO	22	10:53	VIR	23	2:34	SCO	22	16:58	SAG
25	4:03	VIR	24	14:31	LIB	25	10:34	SAG	25	3:55	CAP
27	6:23	LIB	26	19:24	SCO	27	20:58	CAP	27	16:26	AQU
29	10:31	SCO	29	2:41	SAG	30	9:28	AQU	30	5:28	PIS
			31	13:03	CAP						

SUN INGRESSES

1900–2000

Use these tables to find your Sun Sign. The day listed is the day on which the Sun moved into the sign indicated in the table. The Sun remains in that sign until the next day shown.

YEAR	JAN/AQU	FEB/PIS	MAR/ARI	APR/TAU	MAY/GEM	JUN/CAN	JUL/LEO	AUG/VIR	SEP/LIB	OCT/SCO	NOV/SAG	DEC/CAP
1900	20 6:32	18 21:01	20 20:39	20 8:27	21 8:17	21 16:40	23 3:36	23 10:20	23 7:20	23 15:55	22 12:48	22 1:42
1901	20 12:17	19 2:45	21 2:24	20 14:14	21 14:05	21 22:28	23 9:24	23 16:08	23 13:09	23 21:46	22 18:41	22 7:37
1902	20 18:12	19 8:40	21 8:17	20 20:04	21 19:54	22 4:15	23 15:10	23 21:53	23 18:55	24 3:36	23 0:36	22 13:36
1903	21 0:14	19 14:41	21 14:15	21 1:59	22 1:45	22 10:05	23 20:59	24 3:42	24 0:44	24 9:23	23 6:22	22 19:21
1904	21 5:58	19 20:25	20 19:59	20 7:42	21 7:29	21 15:51	23 2:50	23 9:37	23 6:40	23 15:19	22 12:16	22 1:14
1905	20 11:52	19 2:21	21 1:58	20 13:44	21 13:31	21 21:52	23 8:46	23 15:29	23 12:30	23 21:08	22 18:05	22 7:04
1906	20 17:43	19 8:15	21 7:53	20 19:39	21 19:25	22 3:42	23 14:33	23 21:14	23 18:15	24 2:55	22 23:54	22 12:53
1907	20 23:31	19 13:58	21 13:33	21 1:17	22 1:03	22 9:23	23 20:18	24 3:04	24 0:09	24 8:52	23 5:52	22 18:52
1908	21 5:28	19 19:54	20 19:27	20 7:11	21 6:58	21 15:19	23 2:14	23 8:57	23 5:58	23 14:37	22 11:35	22 0:34
1909	20 11:11	19 1:39	21 1:13	20 12:58	21 12:45	21 21:06	23 8:01	23 14:44	23 11:45	23 20:23	22 17:20	22 6:20
1910	20 16:59	19 7:28	21 7:03	20 18:46	21 18:30	22 2:49	23 13:43	23 20:28	23 17:31	24 2:11	22 23:11	22 12:12

YEAR	JAN/AQU	FEB/PIS	MAR/ARI	APR/TAU	MAY/GEM	JUN/CAN	JUL/LEO	AUG/VIR	SEP/LIB	OCT/SCO	NOV/SAG	DEC/CAP
1911	20 22:52	19 13:21	21 12:55	21 0:36	22 0:19	22 8:36	23 19:29	24 2:13	23 23:18	24 7:58	23 4:56	22 17:53
1912	21 4:29	19 18:56	20 18:30	20 6:13	21 5:57	21 14:17	23 1:14	23 8:02	23 5:08	23 13:50	22 10:48	21 23:45
1913	20 10:19	19 0:45	21 0:18	20 12:03	21 11:50	21 20:10	23 7:04	23 13:49	23 10:53	23 19:35	22 16:36	22 5:35
1914	20 16:12	19 6:38	21 6:11	20 17:54	21 17:38	22 1:55	23 12:47	23 19:30	23 16:34	24 1:18	22 22:21	22 11:23
1915	20 22:00	19 12:23	21 11:52	20 23:29	21 23:11	22 7:30	23 18:27	24 1:15	23 22:24	24 7:10	23 4:14	22 17:16
1916	21 3:54	19 18:18	20 17:47	20 5:25	21 5:06	21 13:25	23 0:22	23 7:09	23 4:15	23 12:58	22 9:58	21 22:59
1917	20 9:38	19 0:05	20 23:38	20 11:18	21 10:59	21 19:15	23 6:08	23 12:54	23 10:01	23 18:44	22 15:45	22 4:46
1918	20 15:25	19 5:53	21 5:26	20 17:06	21 16:46	22 1:00	23 11:52	23 18:38	23 15:46	24 0:33	22 21:38	22 10:42
1919	20 21:21	19 11:48	21 11:20	20 22:59	21 22:40	22 6:54	23 17:45	24 0:29	23 21:36	24 6:22	23 3:26	22 16:27
1920	21 3:05	19 17:29	20 17:00	20 4:40	21 4:22	21 12:40	22 23:35	23 6:22	23 3:29	23 12:13	22 9:16	21 22:17

YEAR	JAN/AQU	FEB/PIS	MAR/ARI	APR/TAU	MAY/GEM	JUN/CAN	JUL/LEO	AUG/VIR	SEP/LIB	OCT/SCO	NOV/SAG	DEC/CAP
1921	20 8:55	18 23:20	20 22:51	20 10:33	21 10:17	21 18:36	23 5:31	23 12:16	23 9:20	23 18:03	22 15:05	22 4:08
1922	20 14:48	19 5:17	21 4:49	20 16:29	21 16:11	22 0:27	23 11:20	23 18:05	23 15:10	23 23:53	22 20:56	22 9:57
1923	20 20:35	19 11:00	21 10:29	20 22:06	21 21:46	22 6:03	23 17:01	23 23:52	23 21:04	24 5:51	23 2:54	22 15:54
1924	21 2:29	19 16:52	20 16:21	20 3:59	21 3:41	21 12:00	22 22:58	23 5:48	23 2:59	23 11:45	22 8:47	21 21:46
1925	20 8:21	18 22:43	20 22:13	20 9:52	21 9:33	21 17:50	23 4:45	23 11:34	23 8:44	23 17:32	22 14:36	22 3:37
1926	20 14:13	19 4:35	21 4:02	20 15:37	21 15:15	21 23:30	23 10:25	23 17:14	23 14:27	23 23:19	22 20:28	22 9:34
1927	20 20:12	19 10:35	21 10:00	20 21:32	21 21:08	22 5:23	23 16:17	23 23:06	23 20:17	24 5:07	23 2:14	22 15:19
1928	21 1:57	19 16:20	20 15:45	20 3:17	21 2:53	21 11:07	22 22:03	23 4:54	23 2:06	23 10:55	22 8:01	21 21:04
1929	20 7:43	18 22:07	20 21:35	20 9:11	21 8:48	21 17:01	23 3:54	23 10:42	23 7:53	23 16:42	22 13:49	22 2:53
1930	20 13:33	19 4:00	21 3:30	20 15:06	21 14:42	21 22:53	23 9:42	23 16:27	23 13:36	23 22:26	22 19:35	22 8:40

YEAR	JAN/AQU	FEB/PIS	MAR/ARI	APR/TAU	MAY/GEM	JUN/CAN	JUL/LEO	AUG/VIR	SEP/LIB	OCT/SCO	NOV/SAG	DEC/CAP
1931	20 19:18	19 9:41	21 9:07	20 20:40	21 20:16	22 4:28	23 15:22	23 22:11	23 19:24	24 4:16	23 1:25	22 14:30
1932	21 1:07	19 15:29	20 14:54	20 2:28	21 2:07	21 10:23	22 21:18	23 4:07	23 1:16	23 10:04	22 7:11	21 20:15
1933	20 6:53	18 21:17	20 20:44	20 8:19	21 7:57	21 16:12	23 3:06	23 9:53	23 7:02	23 15:49	22 12:54	22 1:58
1934	20 12:37	19 3:02	21 2:28	20 14:01	21 13:35	21 21:48	23 8:43	23 15:32	23 12:46	23 21:37	22 18:45	22 7:50
1935	20 18:29	19 8:52	21 8:18	20 19:51	21 19:25	22 3:38	23 14:33	23 21:24	23 18:39	24 3:30	23 0:36	22 13:38
1936	21 0:13	19 14:33	20 13:58	20 1:32	21 1:08	21 9:22	22 20:18	23 3:11	23 0:26	23 9:19	22 6:25	21 19:27
1937	20 6:01	18 20:21	20 19:45	20 7:20	21 6:58	21 15:12	23 2:07	23 8:58	23 6:13	23 15:07	22 12:17	22 1:22
1938	20 11:59	19 2:20	21 1:43	20 13:15	21 12:51	21 21:04	23 7:58	23 14:46	23 12:00	23 20:54	22 18:07	22 7:14
1939	20 17:51	19 8:10	21 7:29	20 18:56	21 18:27	22 2:40	23 13:37	23 20:32	23 17:50	24 2:46	22 23:59	22 13:06
1940	20 23:45	19 14:04	20 13:24	20 0:51	21 0:23	21 8:37	22 19:35	23 2:29	22 23:46	23 8:40	22 5:49	21 18:55

YEAR	JAN/AQU	FEB/PIS	MAR/ARI	APR/TAU	MAY/GEM	JUN/CAN	JUL/LEO	AUG/VIR	SEP/LIB	OCT/SCO	NOV/SAG	DEC/CAP
1941	20 5:34	18 19:57	20 19:21	20 6:51	21 6:23	21 14:34	23 1:27	23 8:17	23 5:33	23 14:28	22 11:38	22 0:45
1942	20 11:24	19 1:47	21 1:11	20 12:40	21 12:09	21 20:17	23 7:08	23 13:59	23 11:17	23 20:16	22 17:31	22 6:40
1943	20 17:19	19 7:41	21 7:03	20 18:32	21 18:03	22 2:13	23 13:05	23 19:55	23 17:12	24 2:09	22 23:22	22 12:30
1944	20 23:08	19 13:28	20 12:49	20 0:18	20 23:51	21 8:03	22 18:56	23 1:47	22 23:02	23 7:56	22 5:08	21 18:15
1945	20 4:54	18 19:15	20 18:38	20 6:07	21 5:41	21 13:53	23 0:46	23 7:36	23 4:50	23 13:44	22 10:56	22 0:04
1946	20 10:45	19 1:09	21 0:33	20 12:03	21 11:34	21 19:45	23 6:38	23 13:27	23 10:41	23 19:35	22 16:47	22 5:54
1947	20 16:32	19 6:52	21 6:13	20 17:40	21 17:10	22 1:19	23 12:15	23 19:09	23 16:29	24 1:26	22 22:38	22 11:43
1948	20 22:19	19 12:37	20 11:57	19 23:25	20 22:58	21 7:11	22 18:08	23 1:03	22 22:22	23 7:18	22 4:29	21 17:34
1949	20 4:09	18 18:28	20 17:49	20 5:18	21 4:51	21 13:03	22 23:57	23 6:49	23 4:06	23 13:03	22 10:17	21 23:23
1950	20 10:00	19 0:18	20 23:36	20 11:00	21 10:28	21 18:37	23 5:30	23 12:24	23 9:44	23 18:45	22 16:03	22 5:14

YEAR	JAN/AQU	FEB/PIS	MAR/ARI	APR/TAU	MAY/GEM	JUN/CAN	JUL/LEO	AUG/VIR	SEP/LIB	OCT/SCO	NOV/SAG	DEC/CAP
1951	20 15:53	19 6:10	21 5:26	20 16:49	21 16:16	22 0:25	23 11:21	23 18:17	23 15:37	24 0:37	22 21:52	22 11:01
1952	20 21:39	19 11:57	20 11:14	19 22:37	20 22:04	21 6:13	22 17:08	23 0:03	22 21:24	23 6:23	22 3:36	21 16:44
1953	20 3:22	18 17:42	20 17:01	20 4:26	21 3:53	21 12:00	22 22:53	23 5:46	23 3:06	23 12:07	22 9:23	21 22:32
1954	20 9:12	18 23:33	20 22:54	20 10:20	21 9:48	21 17:55	23 4:45	23 11:36	23 8:56	23 17:57	22 15:15	22 4:25
1955	20 15:02	19 5:19	21 4:36	20 15:58	21 15:25	21 23:32	23 10:25	23 17:19	23 14:41	23 23:44	22 21:01	22 10:11
1956	20 20:49	19 11:05	20 10:21	19 21:44	20 21:13	21 5:24	22 16:20	22 23:15	22 20:36	23 5:35	22 2:50	21 16:00
1957	20 2:39	18 16:59	20 16:17	20 3:42	21 3:11	21 11:21	22 22:15	23 5:08	23 2:27	23 11:25	22 8:40	21 21:49
1958	20 8:29	18 22:49	20 22:06	20 9:28	21 8:52	21 16:57	23 3:51	23 10:46	23 8:09	23 17:12	22 14:30	22 3:40
1959	20 14:19	19 4:38	21 3:55	20 15:17	21 14:43	21 22:50	23 9:46	23 16:44	23 14:09	23 23:12	22 20:28	22 9:35
1960	20 20:11	19 10:27	20 9:43	19 21:06	20 20:34	21 4:43	22 15:38	22 22:35	22 19:59	23 5:02	22 2:19	21 15:26

YEAR	JAN/AQU	FEB/PIS	MAR/ARI	APR/TAU	MAY/GEM	JUN/CAN	JUL/LEO	AUG/VIR	SEP/LIB	OCT/SCO	NOV/SAG	DEC/CAP
1961	20 2:02	18 16:17	20 15:33	20 2:56	21 2:23	21 10:31	22 21:24	23 4:19	23 1:43	23 10:48	22 8:08	21 21:20
1962	20 7:58	18 22:15	20 21:30	20 8:51	21 8:17	21 16:25	23 3:19	23 10:13	23 7:36	23 16:41	22 14:02	22 3:16
1963	20 13:54	19 4:09	21 3:20	20 14:37	21 13:59	21 22:05	23 9:00	23 15:58	23 13:24	23 22:29	22 19:50	22 9:02
1964	20 19:42	19 9:58	20 9:10	19 20:28	20 19:50	21 3:57	22 14:53	22 21:52	22 19:17	23 4:21	22 1:40	21 14:50
1965	20 1:29	18 15:48	20 15:05	20 2:27	21 1:51	21 9:56	22 20:49	23 3:43	23 1:07	23 10:11	22 7:30	21 20:41
1966	20 7:20	18 21:38	20 20:54	20 8:12	21 7:33	21 15:34	23 2:24	23 9:18	23 6:44	23 15:51	22 13:15	22 2:29
1967	20 13:08	19 3:24	21 2:37	20 13:56	21 13:19	21 21:23	23 8:16	23 15:13	23 12:39	23 21:44	22 19:05	22 8:17
1968	20 18:55	19 9:10	20 8:23	19 19:42	20 19:07	21 3:14	22 14:08	22 21:04	22 18:27	23 3:30	22 0:49	21 14:00
1969	20 0:39	18 14:55	20 14:09	20 1:28	21 0:50	21 8:56	22 19:49	23 2:44	23 0:08	23 9:12	22 6:32	21 19:44
1970	20 6:25	18 20:42	20 19:57	20 7:16	21 6:38	21 14:43	23 1:38	23 8:35	23 6:00	23 15:05	22 12:25	22 1:36

YEAR	JAN/AQU	FEB/PIS	MAR/ARI	APR/TAU	MAY/GEM	JUN/CAN	JUL/LEO	AUG/VIR	SEP/LIB	OCT/SCO	NOV/SAG	DEC/CAP
1971	20 12:13	19 2:28	21 1:39	20 12:55	21 12:16	21 20:20	23 7:15	23 14:16	23 11:46	23 20:54	22 18:15	22 7:25
1972	20 18:00	19 8:12	20 7:22	19 18:38	20 18:00	21 2:07	22 13:03	22 20:04	22 17:33	23 2:42	22 0:03	21 13:14
1973	19 23:49	18 14:02	20 13:13	20 0:31	20 23:55	21 8:01	22 18:56	23 1:54	22 23:22	23 8:31	22 5:55	21 19:08
1974	20 5:46	18 19:59	20 19:07	20 6:20	21 5:37	21 13:38	23 0:31	23 7:29	23 4:59	23 14:11	22 11:39	22 0:57
1975	20 11:37	19 1:50	21 0:57	20 12:08	21 11:24	21 19:27	23 6:23	23 13:24	23 10:56	23 20:07	22 17:32	22 6:46
1976	20 17:26	19 7:41	20 6:50	19 18:04	20 17:22	21 1:25	22 12:19	22 19:19	22 16:49	23 1:59	21 23:22	21 12:36
1977	19 23:15	18 13:31	20 12:43	19 23:58	20 23:15	21 7:15	22 18:04	23 1:01	22 22:30	23 7:41	22 5:08	21 18:24
1978	20 5:05	18 19:22	20 18:34	20 5:50	21 5:09	21 13:10	23 0:01	23 6:58	23 4:26	23 13:38	22 11:05	22 0:22
1979	20 11:01	19 1:14	21 0:23	20 11:36	21 10:55	21 18:57	23 5:49	23 12:48	23 10:17	23 19:29	22 16:55	22 6:11
1980	20 16:49	19 7:03	20 6:11	19 17:24	20 16:43	21 0:48	22 11:43	22 18:42	22 16:10	23 1:18	21 22:42	21 11:57

YEAR	JAN/AQU	FEB/PIS	MAR/ARI	APR/TAU	MAY/GEM	JUN/CAN	JUL/LEO	AUG/VIR	SEP/LIB	OCT/SCO	NOV/SAG	DEC/CAP
1981	19 22:37	18 12:53	20 12:04	19 23:19	20 22:40	21 6:46	22 17:41	23 0:39	22 22:06	23 7:14	22 4:37	21 17:51
1982	20 4:32	18 18:47	20 17:57	20 5:08	21 4:24	21 12:24	22 23:16	23 6:16	23 3:47	23 12:59	22 10:24	21 23:39
1983	20 10:18	19 0:31	20 23:40	20 10:51	21 10:07	21 18:10	23 5:05	23 12:08	23 9:43	23 18:55	22 16:19	22 5:31
1984	20 16:06	19 6:17	20 5:25	19 16:39	20 15:59	21 0:03	22 10:59	22 18:01	22 15:34	23 0:47	21 22:12	21 11:24
1985	19 21:58	18 12:08	20 11:15	19 22:27	20 21:44	21 5:45	22 16:37	22 23:37	22 21:08	23 6:23	22 3:52	21 17:09
1986	20 3:47	18 17:58	20 17:04	20 4:13	21 3:29	21 11:31	22 22:25	23 5:27	23 3:00	23 12:15	22 9:45	21 23:03
1987	20 9:41	18 23:51	20 22:53	20 9:58	21 9:11	21 17:12	23 4:07	23 11:11	23 8:46	23 18:02	22 15:30	22 4:47
1988	20 15:25	19 5:36	20 4:40	19 15:46	20 14:58	20 22:57	22 9:52	22 16:55	22 14:30	22 23:45	22 21:13	21 10:29
1989	19 21:08	18 11:21	20 10:29	19 21:40	20 20:54	21 4:54	22 15:46	22 22:47	22 20:21	23 5:36	22 3:06	21 16:23
1990	20 3:03	18 17:15	20 16:20	20 3:28	21 2:38	21 10:34	22 21:22	23 4:22	23 1:56	23 11:15	22 8:48	21 22:08

YEAR	JAN/AQU	FEB/PIS	MAR/ARI	APR/TAU	MAY/GEM	JUN/CAN	JUL/LEO	AUG/VIR	SEP/LIB	OCT/SCO	NOV/SAG	DEC/CAP
1991	20 8:48	18 22:59	20 22:03	20 9:09	21 8:21	21 16:20	23 3:12	23 10:14	23 7:49	23 17:06	22 14:37	22 3:55
1992	20 14:33	19 4:44	20 3:49	19 14:58	20 14:13	20 22:15	22 9:10	22 16:11	22 13:44	22 22:58	21 20:27	21 9:44
1993	19 20:24	18 10:36	20 9:42	19 20:50	20 20:03	21 4:01	22 14:52	22 21:51	22 19:23	23 4:38	22 2:08	21 15:27
1994	20 2:08	18 16:23	20 15:29	20 2:37	21 1:49	21 9:49	22 20:42	23 3:45	23 1:20	23 10:37	22 8:07	21 21:24
1995	20 8:01	18 22:12	20 21:15	20 8:22	21 7:35	21 15:35	23 2:31	23 9:36	23 7:14	23 16:33	22 14:02	22 3:18
1995	20 8:01	18 22:12	20 21:15	20 8:22	21 7:35	21 15:35	23 2:31	23 9:36	23 7:14	23 16:33	22 14:02	22 3:18
1996	20 13:54	19 4:02	20 3:04	19 14:11	20 13:24	20 21:25	22 8:20	22 15:24	22 13:01	22 22:20	21 19:50	21 9:07
1997	19 19:44	18 9:53	20 8:56	19 20:04	20 19:19	21 3:21	22 14:16	22 21:20	22 18:57	23 4:16	22 1:49	21 15:08
1998	20 1:47	18 15:56	20 14:56	20 1:58	21 1:06	21 9:04	22 19:56	23 3:00	23 0:38	23 10:00	22 7:35	21 20:58
1999	20 7:38	18 21:48	20 20:47	20 7:47	21 6:53	21 14:50	23 1:45	23 8:52	23 6:33	23 15:53	22 13:26	22 2:45
2000	20 13:24	19 3:34	20 2:36	19 13:41	20 12:50	20 20:49	22 7:44	22 14:50	22 12:29	22 21:49	21 19:20	21 8:38

ASCENDANT TABLES

Use these tables to
find your Ascendant
or Rising Sign

Key to the Astrological Symbols

Aries	♈
Taurus	♉
Gemini	♊
Cancer	♋
Leo	♌
Virgo	♍
Libra	♎
Scorpio	♏
Sagittarius	♐
Capricorn	♑
Aquarius	♒
Pisces	♓

How to Use the Ascendant Tables

If the Sun sign is the character of a person, and the Moon sign is where we find the emotional needs of a person, then the third most important aspect of a person's birth combination is the Rising sign or Ascendant sign. This is taken from the time a person was born and sets in motion the personality characteristics of an individual. The following table will show you how to convert your birth time into the Ascendant sign. You simply look up your birth time and find where your personality traits lie. The importance of this Ascendant sign is the fact that oftentimes a person marries or commits to another when their Moon and ascendant are in the same sign.

The Table of Ascendants which follows is given for 0 degrees latitude, called GMT. The Ascendants or Rising signs are given to the nearest whole degree, and Military time is used throughout the table.

To convert GMT to the birthplace, first subtract one hour for Daylight Savings Time, if it applied at the time of the birth data. Next, subtract four minutes for each degree of longitude a birthplace is West of this time...75 EST, 90 CST, 105 MST, 120 PST...or add four minutes for each degree East of the standard meridian.

Ascendant Table

	0 hr	2 hr	4 hr	6 hr	8 hr	10 hr	12 hr	14 hr	16 hr	18 hr	20 hr	22 hr
1/1	8♎	2♏	25♏	20♐	19♑	28♒	17♈	0♊	16♋	27♋	22♌	14♍
1/10	17♎	10♏	4♐	29♐	00♒	13♓	3♉	10♊	10♋	6♌	29♌	23♍
1/21	24♎	18♏	12♐	8♑	13♒	1♈	17♉	22♊	18♋	13♌	8♍	1♒
1/31	2♏	26♏	21♐	19♑	28♒	17♈	1♊	16♋	28♋	21♌	14♍	9♒
2/9	9♏	3♐	30♐	30♑	13♓	2♉	10♊	10♋	5♌	29♌	24♍	17♒
2/20	17♏	11♐	8♑	12♒	30♓	17♉	26♊	17♋	13♌	7♍	1♒	25♒
3/1	25♏	20♐	18♑	26♒	16♈	29♉	1♋	27♋	20♌	13♍	8♎	2♏
3/11	3♐	29♐	30♑	12♓	2♉	11♊	9♋	4♌	29♌	22♍	15♎	9♏
3/22	11♐	7♑	12♒	29♓	16♉	21♊	18♋	12♌	6♍	29♍	22♎	16♏

Ascendant Table
(Continued)

	0 hr	2 hr	4 hr	6 hr	8 hr	10 hr	12 hr	14 hr	16 hr	18 hr	20 hr	22 hr
4/1	19♐	17♑	26♒	15♈	29♉	1♋	26♋	21♌	13♍	6♎	1♏	25♏
4/11	29♐	30♑	1♓	1♉	10♊	10♋	3♌	28♍	21♍	15♎	9♏	2♐
4/21	7♑	11♒	28♓	16♉	21♊	17♋	10♌	5♍	28♍	24♎	17♏	10♐
5/1	16♑	25♒	15♈	28♉	30♊	25♋	19♌	13♍	7♎	1♏	25♏	20♐
5/10	29♑	10♓	1♉	11♊	8♋	3♌	27♌	21♍	15♎	7♏	1♐	27♐
5/20	10♒	27♓	16♉	21♊	17♋	10♌	5♍	29♍	24♎	16♏	10♐	6♑
5/31	24♒	14♈	28♉	30♊	25♋	20♌	13♍	8♎	1♏	24♏	18♐	18♑
6/10	10♓	30♈	9♊	8♋	2♌	2♌	21♍	14♎	7♏	2♐	27♐	27♑
6/20	26♓	14♉	20♊	17♋	10♌	4♍	29♍	22♎	15♏	10♐	6♑	10♒
6/30	13♈	28♉	30♊	25♋	20♌	13♍	6♎	0♏	24♏	18♐	15♑	24♒
7/10	29♈	9♊	8♋	3♌	27♌	21♍	14♎	8♏	1♐	26♐	26♑	8♓
7/20	14♉	20♊	16♋	10♌	5♍	29♍	22♎	15♏	9♐	5♑	8♒	25♓
7/30	27♉	30♊	25♋	18♌	12♍	5♎	30♎	27♏	17♐	15♑	23♒	12♈
8/8	9♊	8♋	2♌	27♌	20♍	13♎	8♏	2♐	26♐	26♑	8♓	29♈
8/19	19♊	16♋	4♍	29♍	22♎	22♎	15♏	8♐	5♑	9♒	26♓	13♉
8/29	20♊	24♋	13♍	5♎	29♎	29♎	23♏	17♐	15♑	22♒	12♈	26♉
9/8	7♋	1♌	19♍	13♎	7♏	7♏	2♐	26♐	26♑	9♓	28♈	8♊
9/18	17♋	10♌	27♍	21♎	16♏	15♏	9♐	5♑	8♒	24♓	13♉	18♊
9/28	25♋	18♌	5♎	29♎	23♏	23♏	17♐	15♑	22♒	10♊	26♉	28♊
10/8	2♌	25♌	13♎	8♏	1♐	0♐	25♐	25♐	6♓	27♈	6♊	6♋
10/17	9♌	3♍	21♎	15♏	8♐	8♐	5♑	8♒	23♓	12♉	18♊	16♋
10/28	18♌	11♍	29♎	22♏	18♐	17♐	14♑	21♒	9♈	24♉	28♊	23♋
11/7	25♌	20♍	5♏	0♐	25♐	26♐	25♑	6♓	26♈	7♊	6♋	1♌
11/17	3♍	27♍	15♐	8♐	5♑	3♑	8♒	23♓	11♉	18♊	16♋	8♌
11/28	11♍	4♎	24♏	17♐	15♑	13♑	22♒	11♈	24♉	27♊	23♋	17♌
12/7	18♍	12♎	30♏	26♐	25♑	25♑	6♓	26♈	6♊	6♋	1♌	26♌
12/17	26♍	21♎	8♐	5♑	7♒	6♒	22♓	12♉	16♊	15♋	9♌	2♍
12/27	4♎	29♎	16♐	14♑	21♒	20♒	9♈	23♉	27♊	23♋	17♌	10♍

442

STAY IN TOUCH

On the following pages you will find listed, with their current prices, some of the books and tapes now available on related subjects. Your book dealer stocks most of these, and will stock new titles in the Llewellyn series as they become available. We urge your patronage.

However, to obtain our full catalog, to keep informed of new titles as they are released and to benefit from informative articles and helpful news, you are invited to write for our bi-monthly news magazine/catalog. A sample copy is free, and it will continue coming to you at no cost as long as you are an active mail customer. Or you may keep it coming for a full year with a donation of just $7.00 in U.S.A. and Canada ($20.00 overseas, first class mail). Many bookstores also have *The Llewellyn New Times* available to their customers. Ask for it.

Stay in touch! In *The Llewellyn New Times'* pages you will find news and reviews of new books, tapes and services, announcements of meetings and seminars, articles helpful to our readers, news of authors, advertising of products and services, special money-making opportunities, and much more.

The Llewellyn New Times
P.O. Box 64383-Dept. 289, St. Paul, MN 55164-0383, U.S.A.
• • •

TO ORDER BOOKS AND TAPES

If your book dealer does not have the books and tapes described on the following pages readily available, you may order them directly from the publisher by sending full price in U.S. funds, plus $3.00 for postage and handling for orders *under* $10.00; $4.00 for orders *over* $10.00. There are no postage and handling charges for orders over $50.00. UPS Delivery: We ship UPS whenever possible. Delivery guaranteed. Provide your street address as UPS does not deliver to P.O. Boxes. UPS to Canada requires a $50.00 minimum order. Allow 4-6 weeks for delivery. Orders outside the U.S.A. and Canada: Airmail—add retail price of book; add $5.00 for each non-book item (tapes, etc.); add $1.00 per item for surface mail.

FOR GROUP STUDY AND PURCHASE

Because there is a great deal of interest in group discussion and study of the subject matter of this book, we feel that we should encourage the adoption and use of this particular book by such groups by offering a special "quantity" price to group leaders or "agents."

Our Special Quantity Price for a minimum order of five copies of *The Book of Lovers* is $38.85 cash-with-order. This price includes postage and handling within the United States. Minnesota residents must add 6.5% sales tax. For additional quantities, please order in multiples of five. For Canadian and foreign orders, add postage and handling charges as above. Credit card (VISA, Master Card, American Express) orders are accepted. Charge card orders only may be phoned free ($15.00 minimum order) within the U.S.A. or Canada by dialing 1-800-THE-MOON. Customer service calls dial 1-612-291-1970. Mail Orders to:

LLEWELLYN PUBLICATIONS
P.O. Box 64383-Dept. 289 / St. Paul, MN 55164-0383, U.S.A.

Prices subject to change without notice.

THE NEW A TO Z HOROSCOPE MAKER AND DELINEATOR
by Llewellyn George

This is a new and totally revised edition of the text used by more American astrologers than any other—135,000 copies sold. Every detail of: How to Cast the Birth Chart—time changes, calculations, aspects & orbs, signs & planetary rulers, parts of fortune, etc.; The Progressed Chart—all the techniques and the major delineations; Transits—how to use them in prediction; also lunations and solar days. Rectification. Locality Charts, a comprehensive Astrological Dictionary and a complete index for easy use. It's an encyclopedia, a textbook, a self-study course and and a dictionary all-in-one!

0-87542-264-0,600 pages, 6 x 9, softcover.   **$12.95**

ASTROLOGY FOR THE MILLIONS
by Grant Lewi

First published in 1940, this practical, do-it-yourself textbook has become a classic guide to computing accurate horoscopes quickly. Throughout the years, it has been improved upon since Grant Lewi's death by his astrological proteges and Llewellyn's expert editors. Grant Lewi is astrology's forerunner to the computer, a man who literally brought astrology to everyone. This, the first new edition since 1979, presents updated transits and new, user-friendly tables to the year 2050, including a new sun ephemeris of revolutionary simplicity. It's actually easier to use than a computer! Also added is new information on Pluto and rising signs, and a new foreword by Carl Llewellyn Weschcke and introduction by J. Gordon Melton.

Of course, the original material is still here in Lewi's captivating writing style—all of his insights on transits as a tool for planning the future and making the right decisions. His historical analysis of U.S. presidents has been brought up to date to include George Bush. This new edition also features a special In Memoriam to Lewi that presents his birthchart.

One of the most remarkable astrology books available, *Astrology for the Millions* allows the reader to cast a personal horoscope in 15 minutes, interpret from the readings and project the horoscope into the future to forecast coming planetary influences and develop "a grand strategy for living."

0-87542-438-4, 464 pgs., 6 x 9, tables, charts, softcover   **$12.95**

ASTROLOGY FOR BEGINNERS
by William Hewitt

Anyone who is interested in astrology will enjoy *Astrology for Beginners*. This book makes astrology easy and exciting by presenting all of the basics in an orderly sequence while focusing on the natal chart. Llewellyn even includes a coupon for a free computerized natal chart so you can begin interpretations almost immediately without complicated mathematics.

Astrology for Beginners covers all of the basics. Learn exactly what astrology is and how it works. Explore signs, planets, houses and aspects. Learn how to interpret a birth chart. Discover the meaning of transits, predictive astrology and progressions. Determine your horoscope chart in minutes without using math.

Whether you want to practice astrology for a hobby or aspire to become a professional astrologer, *Astrology for Beginners* is the book you need to get started on the right track.

0-87542-307-8, 288 pgs., 5-1/4 x 8, softcover   **$7.95**

SIGNS OF LOVE
by Jeraldine Saunders, foreword by Sydney Omarr

Love Signs is an indispensable, fun-to-read guide that will give you all the basics for creating a better, more meaningful love life. With the aid of astrology, numerology, palmistry and other intimate and mystical knowledge, you will discover everything you need to know about your love prospects with a given individual. As you learn your unique purpose, you will be able to distinguish whether another person's desires are compatible with yours.

Noted author Jeraldine Saunders shows you how to look for love, how to find it, and how to be sure of it. Examine the characteristics of all twelve zodiacal signs. Find out how auric vibrations can affect your seductive charisma. Discover the secrets behind your lover's facial features. Use numbers to learn about that hidden intimate nature. With *Love Signs*, a more meaningful love life is possible for you!

0-87542-706-5, 320 pgs., 6 x 9, illus., softcover   **$9.95**

YOUR PLANETARY PERSONALITY
by Dennis Oakland

This book brings together everything you need to construct your birth chart, and then follows through with everything you need to interpret the the planetary positions, your houses, and the signs. Then author Dennis Oakland furnishes insightful analyses of the personalities that the melding of planets, houses, and signs produced.

Your Planetary Personality will help you rediscover yourself, unlocking those elements of character that may have been repressed and submerged in your unconscious mind in order to survive or adapt to your environment. The book will help you understand the significance of events in your life; their timing and purpose; your reactions; your place within your family and community; your talents, skills, and drives; and it will show you how to use this knowledge to improve your life in every way. The author's interpretations are the product of many years of study of psychology, various sciences, and Eastern philosophy. His insights will provide you with the tools you need to gain self-knowledge and self-awakening.

0-87542-594, 584 pgs., 7 x 10, softcover **$19.95**

PSYCHOLOGY, ASTROLOGY & WESTERN MAGIC
by Luis Alvarado

Now for the first time you can learn how the God-image is linked with such diverse sciences and disciplines as psychology, astrology, myths, and Western magic. This book examines this connection and its implications: psychological, historical and theoretical. Learn how the power of myths and images relates to human change and growth.

Based on 14 years' experience in the counseling field, as well as extensive study of magic in the western tradition, the author brings an intriguing perspective to this study of images and symbolism. Tarot and the Qabalah provide the structure within which he analyzes subjects and clients. Here are broader and fresher perspectives, developed for the challenging years ahead—yet nurtured and rooted in the accumulated wisdom of the past.

0-87542-006, 288 pgs., 6 x 9, illus., softcover **$12.95**

Prices subject to change without notice.

Llewellyn's Astrological Services

There are many types of charts and many different ways to use astrological information. Llewellyn offers a wide variety of services which can help you with specific needs. Read through the descriptions that follow to help you choose the right service. All of our readings are done by professional astrologers. The computer services are set up on Matrix programs and the interpretations are tailored to your needs. Remember, astrology points out potentials and possibilities; it will serve as your resource guide. Only you can decide what is right. Astrology should help you guide your life, not control it.

If you have never had a chart reading done before, we suggest that you order the Complete Natal or the Detailed Natal Service. We encourage informative letters with your request so that our astrologers can address your needs more specifically. All information is held strictly confidential. Be sure to give accurate and complete birth data: exact time, date, year, place, county and country of birth. Check your birth certificate. *Accuracy of birth data is important.* We will not be responsible for mistakes made by you! An order form follows the descriptions of Llewellyn Astrological Services.

Personalized Astrology Readings

These chart readings are done by professional astrologers and focus on your particular concerns. Include descriptive letter.

APS03-119 Simple Natal: Your chart calculated by computer in whatever house system stated. It has all of the trimmings, including aspects, midpoints, Chiron and a glossary of symbols, plus a free book! We use Tropical/Placidus unless you state otherwise. Include full birth data. . . . $5.00

APS03-101 Complete Natal: Our most thorough reading. It not only gives you the computer chart and detailed reading, but also interpretation of the trends shown in your chart for the coming year. It is activated by transits and focuses on any issue you specify. Include full birth data and a descriptive letter. $125.00

APS03-500 (3 months) **APS03-501** (6 months) **APS03-502** (1 year) **Transit Forecasts:** These reports keep you abreast of positive trends and challenging periods. Our reports can be an invaluable aid for timing your actions and decision making. Reports begin the first day of the month you specify. . . . . $15 (3 months), $30 (6 months), $50 (1 year).

APS03-105 Progressed Chart With Transits: Your birth chart is progressed by techniques to determine what it says about you now. Use this reading to understand the evolution of your personal power. Provides interpretation of present and future conditions for a year's time with a special focus as stated by you. Include descriptive letter. $85.00

Prices subject to change without notice.

APS03-102 Detailed Natal: Complete natal chart plus inter-pretation with the focus on one specific question as stated by you. Learn about aspects of your chart and what they mean to you. $65.00

APS03-110 Horary Chart: Gives the answer to any specific question. This is divination at its best, Should you marry? Will you get a new job soon? Give precise time of writing letter. $50.00

APS03-503 Personality Profile Horoscope: Our most popular reading! This ten-part reading gives you a complete look at how the planets affect you. It is an excellent way to become acquainted with astrology and to learn about yourself. Very reasonable price! $20.00

APS03-114 Compatibility Reading: Determines compatibility of two people in an existing relationship. Give birth data for both. $75.00

Prices subject to change without notice.